A History of

FILM MUSIC

. . . .

Mervyn Cooke

CAMBRIDGE
UNIVERSITY PRESS

CAMBRIDGE UNIVERSITY PRESS
Cambridge, New York, Melbourne, Madrid, Cape Town, Singapore, São Paulo, Delhi

Cambridge University Press
The Edinburgh Building, Cambridge CB2 8RU, UK

Published in the United States of America by Cambridge University Press, New York

www.cambridge.org
Information on this title: www.cambridge.org/9780521010481

First published 2008

Printed in the United Kingdom at the University Press, Cambridge

A catalogue record for this publication is available from the British Library

Library of Congress Cataloguing in Publication data
Cooke, Mervyn.
A history of film music / Mervyn Cooke.
  p.   cm.
Includes bibliographical references and index.
ISBN 978-0-521-81173-6 (hardback) – ISBN 978-0-521-01048-1 (pbk.)
1. Motion picture music – History and criticism.   I. Title.
ML2075.C68   2008
781.5'4209 – dc22   2008019383

ISBN 978-0-521-81173-6 hardback
ISBN 978-0-521-01048-1 paperback

For Sally

Contents

Illustrations

Preface and acknowledgements

As cinema moves into its second century, it is surprising that relatively few comprehensive historical accounts of film music have so far appeared in print. This is by no means to say that there is a dearth of perceptive and thought-provoking writing about film music: on the contrary, since the 1980s the field has become a rich growth area in both academic and popular circles, and an ever-growing understanding and appreciation of the filmic medium's often strikingly varied musical potentialities have helped rescue the film musician's craft from the stigma of hack commercialism which constantly blighted its reputation from the earliest years. At the same time, and equally late in the day, film scholars have begun to draw wider attention to the need not only to regard a film's soundtrack as an indivisible composite element, but also to consider it as at least equal to – and in some cases arguably more important than – the moving images which, as cinema's *raison d'être*, were traditionally viewed as its overridingly dominant parameter. Hopefully the days when it was possible to devote an entire volume to a discussion of the aesthetics of cinema without adequately addressing either its sound or music (for an example, see Arnaud *et al.* 1983) are long since gone.

Of the many varied histories of film music that could, and hopefully will, be written, the present enterprise aims to provide a straightforward introduction to the development of film-music techniques in a selection of Anglophone and non-Anglophone cinemas, with emphases placed on the practical roles of composers, musicians, music directors and supervisors, their changing working conditions, cultural contexts and creative aspirations, and the various ways in which their work has been received. At the risk of stating the obvious, this book is neither a history of film-music theory nor a history of film-music literature, though seminal observations from each are introduced liberally throughout the text where they are directly relevant to the practice and consumption of such music at various points in its history. Readers desiring coherent accounts of the film-music literature are recommended to consult the admirable critical summaries by Martin Miller Marks (1997, 3–25) and Robynn Stilwell (2002). Among the most readable and concise overviews of general trends in film-music theory is that offered by Annette Davison in the first three chapters of her recent book on contemporary film (2004).

For the era of silent film (Chapter 1) the principal sources for contemporaneous commentary are technical manuals on film accompaniment, the film industry's trade press, newspapers and other journals, which discuss matters relating to film music both practical and aesthetic – though rarely in significant depth. As Rick Altman and other modern scholars have shown, the early silent era demonstrated considerable diversity in its sonic provision before standardization took hold and subsequently shaped the often formulaic accompanying practices of the sound film. Aesthetic debate about the value and potential of film sound and music, on the part of both theorists and practitioners, grew markedly more heated with the introduction of synchronized soundtracks in the late 1920s (Chapter 2), and was at times related to a perceived conflict between the demands of stage-influenced theatricality and the more adventurous realms of filmic fantasy (Chapter 4). Some bold film-makers experimented with 'contrapuntal' uses of sound which jarred with the visual image (for examples from the early Soviet sound film, see Chapter 9). Others, notably in France (Chapters 2 and 8), refused to allow dialogue to achieve the overarching supremacy which was later to be one of the most obvious characteristics of mainstream narrative cinema in Hollywood (its typical practices considered in detail in Chapters 3 and 5) – and indeed ever since.

In the 1930s, many aspects of the film composer's craft were rationalized to fit with a range of standard musico-dramatic requirements, and intelligent manuals discussing both practical and aesthetic issues were published by Leonid Sabaneev (1935) and Kurt London (1936). Critical and analytical writings on film music significantly increased in the 1930s and 1940s, with perceptive commentary and analysis issuing from the pens of George Antheil, Hans Keller, Lawrence Morton, F. W. Sternfeld and others; a fairly substantial bibliographical survey was published at the start of the 1950s (Zuckerman 1950). Ongoing debates at this time included the relative usefulness of music that either supported or contradicted the implications of the visual image; the extent to which film music needed to be clearly audible rather than perceived subliminally; thorny issues of structure, principally the tension between autonomous musical form and its apparent irreconcilability with the mostly subservient role that music was constantly called upon to play in its filmic context; and the usefulness (or otherwise) of continuing to compare film-music techniques with those of nineteenth-century opera and the other well-established musico-dramatic genres from which it appeared to have derived many of its basic processes. These debates generally failed to address the views of film spectators, which were first systematically canvassed by an expansion in market research undertaken within the industry from the late 1960s onwards (though filmic formulae had already been influenced by the outcome of preview screenings, even as early as the silent era); viewers' reactions have more recently been analysed with the scientific scrutiny of the cognitive psychologist.

During the Hollywood Golden Age (*c.*1935–55) it became evident that film music was widely regarded by intellectual commentators as an impoverished cousin of worthwhile concert music, morally dubious in its overt commercialism and mass-production, and often of lamentable quality: this view was perpetuated by some concert composers who were seduced into film work solely for the generous remuneration it offered (for examples in the United Kingdom, see Chapter 6). A few – notably Copland and Vaughan Williams – warmly welcomed film scoring not only for its practical and aesthetic challenges, but also as a rare instance of a medium through which living composers were assured of regular airings of their latest music performed by top-class musicians. It was not until the 1980s that a thorough scholarly reassessment of the mainstream film industry's working practices and aesthetic aims rescued conventional film music and its composers from a wearying critical malaise that had at times in the interim led its staunch defenders to embark on somewhat misguided and unnecessary attempts to claim for it an intellectual status equivalent to that of concert music. This initiative seemed increasingly futile after the film industry's unpredictable course in the sometimes unstable 1960s and 1970s had potently demonstrated the viability of alternative scoring practices, chiefly those involving a foregrounding of popular music and electronics that synergistically exploited the considerable commercial potential of recorded-music sales.

The turning point in achieving a level-headed appreciation of traditional orchestral scoring came with a scholarly reappraisal of the so-called 'classical' cinema of the 1930s and 1940s, whose tenets to some extent continue to condition mainstream film scoring in the present age. Claudia Gorbman (1987), followed by Caryl Flinn and Kathryn Kalinak (both of whose influential monographs were published in 1992), all drew salient ideas from the burgeoning discipline of film studies in their willingness to view film music as largely inextricable from its immediate filmic and wider cultural contexts, and offered varying views of how nondiegetic scoring – no matter how formulaic and unoriginal – could (paradoxically) contribute to filmic 'realism' by manipulating a viewer's emotional responses or by graphically supporting or even mimicking the action, while also showing itself capable of suggesting visions of (at least partial) utopias fully in accord with the escapism purveyed by the Hollywood dream factory. The ideas of this groundbreaking school of film-music theorists inevitably inform not only the account of Golden Age Hollywood advanced in Chapter 3, but also certain key techniques of the so-called 'New Hollywood' blockbusters that were resurgent in the late 1970s and which continue to dominate film production and international distribution at the time of writing (Chapter 12).

In their temperature-check on the state of film-music literature in the mid-1990s, James Buhler and David Neumeyer (1994) noted the various healthy contributions to the modern study of film scoring of ideas borrowed and developed from semiotics, Marxism, feminism, psychoanalysis and cognitive science, and provided a concise overview of the neo-formalist 'historical poetics' which informed the influential attitude towards the history of mainstream narrative film advanced by David Bordwell, Janet Staiger and Kristin Thompson (1985; see also Bordwell 1985). To this list may be added the important fields of filmic genre studies and *auteur* theory, both of which have continued to shape the lively debates surrounding film music. It seems scarcely credible – and it is certainly no fault of theirs – that Buhler and Neumeyer in 1994 were not able to include in their summary any consideration of the alternative, pop-based scoring practices that long before had radically changed both intellectual and popular conceptions of what music in film could be expected to achieve. Only in the late 1990s was pop scoring tackled with the kind of sympathetic understanding and intellectual rigour Gorbman had devoted to the classical orchestral film score, notably in the work of Jeff Smith (1998) which set a new standard for combining aesthetic insights with telling commercial and industrial contextualization. Until the 1990s few general books on film music had tackled pop scoring or non-Hollywood films convincingly, Roy Prendergast's widely used textbook (1977, revised 1992) typical of its time in combining numerous practical insights based on personal experience of the US film industry with rather limited critical engagement. This situation changed significantly with Royal S. Brown's stimulating overview of a wide range of film-scoring practices (1994), his work notably strong on the films of Hitchcock, French cinema and the manifold aspects of postmodern film scoring, which allowed the diversity of film music to speak for itself without the need for any forced theoretical unification.

Since then, rigorous academic studies of film music – including several devoted to pop – have largely been conducted in the context of edited symposia that provide a convenient outlet for relatively specialized research projects. This has resulted in one of the unfortunate, if perfectly understandable, drawbacks of modern film-music scholarship: its tendency to examine only a handful of films (or even a single film) as evidence to support a particular theoretical premise, an approach particularly encouraged by the symposium format. Whilst as a result the rich diversity of film-scoring practices is often thrown into sharp and vivid relief, the wider relevance of theoretical approaches applied to sometimes unrepresentative examples of a multi-faceted commercial art form can often seem somewhat limited. Not surprisingly, perhaps, the commentators whose thinking appeared most helpful for citation in an introductory text such as the present book have tended to be those who, to varying degrees, combine practical knowledge of film with either common sense (for example, Jean Mitry) or provocative ideology (Theodor Adorno and Hanns Eisler), or whose scholarly work was so important and timely as to lay the foundations for much modern thinking about film music (Gorbman, Flinn, Kalinak, Brown, Smith and Michel Chion, amongst others). Alongside the academic literature exists a sizeable corpus of anecdotal material in secondary sources on (primarily Hollywood) film music and film composers' biographies and autobiographies, much of which is highly illuminating and frequently cited here. In general, for the present remit I have mostly prioritized factual information above theoretical abstraction and hope that my citations from a wide range of film-music commentators of differing temperaments will serve to stimulate readers to go on to explore, at their leisure, particular avenues of interpretative, commercial or technical interest in greater depth.

While Hollywood film-making is inevitably allocated a lion's share of the present text, given its longstanding global domination of film production and consumption both commercially and conceptually, film music from six other major film-producing countries is also examined in some detail. To cover all world cinema in equal depth in a volume of this size has not been feasible, and it is to be hoped that in due course international film-music developments will receive a truly comprehensive coverage to rival that of such impressively wide-ranging film histories as those by Kristin Thompson and David Bordwell (2003) and David Cook (2004). For the present book, in addition to its central focus on American cinema, I have elected to concentrate on film music in the United Kingdom (Chapter 6), France (Chapter 8), the early Soviet Union, India, Italy and Japan (Chapter 9): the first because of its close but not always easy relationship with Hollywood and linguistic common ground, the second as much for its international influence on film-making techniques in two seminal periods (1930s and 1960s) as for its own distinctive characteristics, and the remaining four because in their own different ways they have each managed to retain clear national identities while at the same time (in certain directors' hands) transcending the sometimes seemingly unbridgeable gaps between indigenous cultures and international appeal. Film music in certain other regions – for example Australasia, China, Germany, Greece and Scandinavia – is discussed more briefly at various points. Uses of pre-existing popular and classical music in film are for convenience of comparison given chapters to themselves (Chapters 10 and 11), as are the special generic cases of documentary and animation (Chapter 7). The main thrust of the book inevitably centres on the narrative fiction film which has long been the dominant international norm.

Dates given for individual films are, unless otherwise specified, those of the film's initial release in its country of origin. In checking much of this data I have frequently relied on two sterling reference resources: the phenomenal Internet Movie Database (http://uk.imdb.com) and wonderfully user-friendly and often trenchantly opinionated *Halliwell's Film, DVD and Video Guide* (Walker 2006). Titles originally in languages other than English are variously rendered in the original, in transliteration, in English translation, or in alternative English titles approved for export, as appropriate: readability and concision here seemed more helpful than a rigidly systematic approach which in some cases would have resulted in giving up to four different titles for a single film (the original sometimes unpronounceable except to specialists in the relevant language). Where a film was released with different English titles in the USA and UK, both are given. The identity of a film's director is usually given at its first mention, though (again in the interests of readability) I have sometimes omitted this information where films are occasionally listed in groups rather than discussed individually.

As terminology relating to film music is in a constant state of flux (in academic circles, if not in the film industry) I have generally avoided fashionable jargon as much as possible, and I have also been sparing with technical musical terms – apart from the most familiar, or those of which the meaning is hopefully clear enough from the context – in the hope that this book may have something to say of interest to the general reader as well as to the specialist. For the sake of clarity and consistency when dealing with a wide range of material it has seemed prudent to retain the well-established terms 'diegetic' and 'nondiegetic' (defined in Chapter 1) broadly to describe music that respectively exists within or entirely outside of the constructed world portrayed by narrative films. As many of the soundtracks discussed in the succeeding pages demonstrate, the most interesting musical effects in film often occur in the ambiguous imaginative region between these two simple poles, and much work remains to be done to establish precisely why this strategy can be so emotionally potent, and how such 'in-between' music specifically functions in certain types of film – principally the musical (Chapter 4) and animation (Chapter 7) – in which the lack of a clear distinction between diegetic and nondiegetic is the genres' defining sonic characteristic.

It is a pleasure to thank the many friends and colleagues whose input has informed the project, beginning with Penny Souster at Cambridge University Press, whose enthusiasm for it spurred it into being (and to whom I should apologize for not being able to see it into press before her retirement). Her successor Vicki Cooper and editor Becky Jones have both been tremendously supportive and helpful with practicalities at all stages of the book's production, and it is difficult to imagine working with more congenial and encouraging publishers. Special thanks are due to copy-editor Ann Lewis and production editor Jodie Barnes. For helpful input in the book's early planning stages I am indebted to Peter Franklin and Christopher Reynolds.

I owe a particular debt of gratitude to David Cooper for reading a draft of the book in typescript and for his helpful comments on the text. I am also grateful to Fiona Ford for her eagle-eyed reading of the text, and for pointing me in the direction of a number of sources and sharing her specialized knowledge of silent film, early sound cinema and Shostakovich's film music with me. Thanks are extended to Jan Butler for her advice on various aspects of popular music in film, and for many other pertinent comments on the text. George Fenton deserves thanks not only for agreeing to read the book before it went to press but also for the many insights into film music and related matters he has offered me – with characteristic modesty, thoughtfulness and good humour – over a number of years. As always, Philip Weller has constantly inspired me by his heart-warming blend of formidable intellect, humanity and common sense. Thanks are also extended to the following for their help with various matters: Jeremy Barham, Jonathan Burns, Kate Daubney, Annette Davison, John Deathridge, Katy Gow, Dan Grimley, Chris Grogan, Finn Gundersen, Sophie Hacker, Norman Hirschy, Stephen Horne, Edward Dudley Hughes, Nicole Jacob, Dimitri Kennaway, Jan Kopinski, Liz Long, Colin Matthews, Stuart Nicholson, the late Stanley Sadie, Lucinda Sanderson, Nigel Simeone and Peter Wright.

Finally, I must thank both the University of Nottingham's School of Humanities and the Arts and Humanities Research Council (AHRC) for granting me the periods of research leave necessary to complete the project. I am also grateful to the University of Nottingham for its contribution towards the cost of reproducing the illustrations.

 Arts & Humanities Research Council

The AHRC funds postgraduate training and research in the arts and humanities, from archaeology and English literature to design and dance. The quality and range of research supported not only provides social and cultural benefits but also contributes to the economic success of the UK. For further information on the AHRC, please visit www.ahrc.ac.uk.

1 The 'silent' cinema

As has often been remarked, the cinema has never been silent: the so-called silent films which represented the first flowering of the medium from the 1890s to the late 1920s often used sound as a vital part of the filmic experience. Accompanying music was only one of a diverse range of sonic options available to exhibitors in the early years of cinema; yet the familiarity of the fairly elaborate musical provision characterizing the later years of silent film (*c.*1914–27) has tended to result in the assumption that music was both constantly used and deemed aesthetically viable well before this period. As Rick Altman has argued, however, during the early development of the moving picture (*c.*1895–*c.*1913) it was not uncommon for films to be projected with no organized sound component at all (Altman 2004, 193–201). Yet, by the start of the 1920s, film-music pioneer George Beynon could declare without fear of contradiction: 'Allowing the picture to be screened in silence is an unforgivable offense that calls for the severest censure. No picture should begin in silence under any conditions' (Beynon 1921, 76).

Why sound?

Altman's careful research established that 'silent films were in fact sometimes silent, ... and what's more it did not appear to bother audiences a bit' (Altman 1996, 649), but audience noise and direct audience participation were more prominent at the turn of the twentieth century than they are in today's cinema in the West, so to this extent films were never truly experienced in silence. When Andy Warhol made his almost static silent films in the 1960s he assumed the audience would supply sounds, thereby participating in the artistic event (Weis and Belton 1985, 369); and audience noise, though reduced in modern times, has remained part and parcel of the cinematic experience, most prominently in India. The desirability of masking or discouraging audience noise is one of the many possible explanations – some practical and others aesthetic – that have been advanced to account for the provision of some kind of sound element to accompany screenings of silent films.

Another reason for the provision of sound in the early years of cinema may have been to mask intrusive noise both inside and outside the projection venue, including the sound of traffic passing by and the distracting whirring

[1]

of the projector itself. Conventional modern projectors still generate a fair degree of noise: the experimental film-maker Stan Brakhage, who attempted to make genuinely silent films in the 1950s, attested to his irritation at having neglected the fact that viewers would in effect never be able to watch his films in total silence because the sound of the projector would always be present. Mechanical quietness was used as a selling-point when some early projectors were marketed: around 1900, for example, publicity for the Optigraph noted that with rival projectors 'the noise is so great that, as a rule, it is necessary to keep a piano or other musical instrument going while the motion pictures are being shown, to prevent annoyance to the audience' (quoted in Altman 2004, 89). The issue of projector noise duly became a much-vaunted but not entirely convincing theory for the origins of film music: as film theorist Siegfried Kracauer pointed out, 'this explanation is untenable; . . . the noisy projector was soon removed from the auditorium proper [into a projection booth], whereas music stubbornly persisted' (Kracauer 1960, 133).

In those silent films that purported to represent reality, the absence of naturalistic sounds might have been considered a more serious impediment to plausibility than the absence of dialogue. Yet even when films are screened without any accompanying sound, the viewer will tend to imagine noises that correspond to the images depicted. It is difficult to watch the plate-smashing sequence in Sergei Eisenstein's silent classic *The Battleship Potemkin* (1925) or the images of spoons striking glass bottles in Dziga Vertov's *The Man with the Movie Camera* (1929) without 'hearing' the appropriate sound internally. (Vertov's sensory suggestiveness even extended to implying a smell: he directly juxtaposed images of nail-polishing and film editing, both of which use acetone.) Audiences responded appropriately to such visual stimuli from the earliest years of cinema: at an early screening of *The Great Train Robbery* (dir. Edwin S. Porter, 1903), silent images of gunshots reportedly caused spectators to put their fingers in their ears (Altman 1996, 648). MGM's trademark roaring lion was born in the silent era as a result of the studio's desire for an arresting image that would 'sound' loud. In 1929 French director René Clair, lamenting the use of gratuitous sound effects in the early sound film, declared that 'we do not need to *hear* the sound of clapping if we can *see* the clapping hands' (Weis and Belton 1985, 94). Such internalized sounds were believed by Brakhage to emanate from a 'silent sound sense' (Brakhage 1960). This phenomenon, referred to as subception or subliminal auditive perception by psychologists, was exploited by numerous makers of silent films, who peppered their products with visual simulations of sound ranging from simple knocks at the door to graphically realized explosions. Some silent films, such as Franz Hofer's *Kammermusik* (1914), placed a heavy emphasis on scenes of music-making and on the act of listening to music, which may have a powerful associative effect even if no music is heard by the audience (Abel and Altman 2001, 93,

96–7, 102–6). Furthermore, a direct correspondence between images representing the production of music and other sounds, and the act of listening to such sounds, became after *c.*1909 a useful device – unique to the cinema – not only for implying the existence of diegetic space beyond the confines of the screen, but also a simple (and at the time novel) form of narrative linkage in the montage; thus some silent films came to have what have aptly been termed a 'virtual sound track' (Altman 2004, 214–16).

In real life, movement is never viewed in strict silence; indeed, without special acoustic facilities, total silence is a physical impossibility even when viewing static objects. In modern sound films, room tone (i.e. ambient sound appropriate to the location depicted on screen) is specially recorded so that it can be dubbed onto ostensibly silent scenes and thereby prevent the audience from simply assuming that the sound system has failed (Weis and Belton 1985, 395); it can also be used to replace ambient background noise lost during the process of dubbing dialogue. Actual silence on the soundtrack would be unrealistic in both cases, and unacceptable except in contexts where it is used deliberately as a means of disconcerting the viewer, as in the work of French director Jean-Luc Godard. When Alfred Hitchcock wanted to create a threatening silence in *The Birds* (1960), he preferred the use of a subliminal electronic humming noise rather than a complete absence of sound (Truffaut 1967, 225). As film theorist Béla Balázs observed, the silent film was a paradox: it could not of itself reproduce silence as an artistic effect, since silence is relative and can only be appreciated within a context of sounds (Balázs 1953, 205); thus, when a car is driven away in complete silence at the end of *The Birds*, the same vehicle having demonstrated its noisy engine in a previous scene, the effect is unsettling. In short, as French director Robert Bresson pointed out, 'the sound track invented silence' (quoted in Weis and Belton 1985, 323) – or at least gave it a value that it did not possess in the silent film.

Silence in a musical context, however, has since the earliest years been an important stock-in-trade of accompanists of silent films and film composers, who have appreciated the fact that the sudden cessation of music when the latter is expected to be continuous can have an enormous dramatic impact on an audience. The phenomenon was debated in the motion-picture trade press during the heyday of the silent film, with some commentators approving of a strategic use of silence and others advocating continuity at all costs: in 1912, *Moving Picture World* advised musicians that a maximum silence of ten seconds was a useful rule-of-thumb (Kalinak 1992, 49). Organist Dennis James related how, when his instrument malfunctioned during a live accompaniment to a modern screening of a silent Harold Lloyd comedy, one member of the audience afterwards praised him for interpolating so dramatic and unexpected a silence (McCarty 1989, 66–7). Even well after the advent of the sound film, Leonid Sabaneev anxiously warned film composers against recoursing to abrupt silence on the grounds that the device 'gives rise to a feeling of aesthetic perplexity' (Sabaneev 1935, 21), though a few years earlier the trenchant critic Harry Alan Potamkin – in the context of his general lambasting of the excessive use of music in the exhibition of silent films – praised a Paris showing of Abel Gance's *J'Accuse* (1918) for the orchestra's 'terrific' silence when the war dead come to life: 'What vaudeville "fan" does not know the effectiveness of silence during an acrobatic feat? This is the point: since music is inevitable, we can make the best use of silence by selecting the intervals carefully at which the music will be hushed' (Potamkin 1929, 295).

In silent comedies dependent upon slapstick, and to enhance the excitement of major sound events in serious silent films, real sound effects were supplied by special machines such as the Kinematophone or Allefex, which might be located behind the screen to enhance spatial verisimilitude, or by performers using the kind of sound-generating paraphernalia still familiar in modern radio drama. In France, these sound-effects performers were known as *bruitistes*, and some commentators believed that, if handled creatively, an imaginative use of sound might correspond to the *bruit musical* developed by Italian futurist artists during the First World War (Lacombe and Porcile 1995, 24–5). Unfortunately, no such high artistic aims prevailed in movie theatres, where the mindless use of sound effects was roundly criticized by many contemporaneous critics on account of its essential crudity and often excessive volume. This habit was in part responsible for the all-too-frequent recourse to unsubtle sound effects in modern commercial cinema, in which Foley artists (named after Jack Foley, who pioneered such techniques in his work on early sound films in Hollywood during the 1940s) habitually supply artificial and over-prominent sounds for virtually all noises in a film, no matter how trivial. Many are both redundant and somewhat condescending to audience intelligence, but sound-effect production had become so slick by the advent of the talkies that its retention in the sound film was inevitable. In the work of sound-sensitive modern film-makers, however, effects may be integrated with the musical score so that they work together in the sound-track, the latter (as has long been overlooked, even in film scholarship) now being increasingly treated as an indivisible composite greater than the sum of its parts (Altman *et al.* 2000, 341).

Why music?

Music may initially have been supplied at film screenings simply because it has always been an inevitable adjunct to almost all forms of popular entertainment. Early moving-picture shows in the mid-1890s were little more

than show-booth attractions: fairgrounds, vaudeville and travelling shows
have traditionally been noisy affairs, and for the latest novelty spectacle to
have been presented without some kind of aural stimulation would have
been inconceivable. In this regard, it is important to note that music was
not necessarily performed inside an exhibition venue, nor at the same time
as a film was being shown. Altman has drawn attention to the significance
of music as a ballyhoo device for attracting custom before patrons had even
set foot in the venue: live music might be played at the entrance, or recorded
music blared out into the street through a barker phonograph horn (Altman
1996, 664, 674), and even the musicians inside the projection room might
be instructed to play loudly so they could be heard in the street (Altman
2004, 131). As cinema music became more elaborate and of better quality,
the live performance of musical numbers – again not necessarily related to,
or played simultaneously with, the films being shown – could be as strong
an attraction to customers as the moving pictures on offer.

The author of one of the first serious texts on film music stated that
music had been specifically conceived as compensation for the absence of
naturalistic sound (London 1936, 34). One of its early exponents, Max
Winkler, opined categorically that music was added to film in order to fill
the void created by the absence of dialogue: 'music must take the place of
the spoken word' (quoted in Limbacher 1974, 16). But music was by no
means the only medium that might be used for these purposes. Apart from
sound effects, other techniques included live narration, which had been a
prominent feature of magic-lantern shows and fairground moving-picture
attractions when barkers had provided a simultaneous commentary on the
images. Sometimes reciters (also known as 'impersonators') delivered lines
in an attempt to synchronize with the lip movements of the film actors,
an activity in which the comedian Leopold Fregoli specialized in the late
1890s (Prendergast 1992, 4). As late as 1908, an American venue secreted
actors behind the screen and had them perform synchronized dialogue in an
attempt to trick the audience into believing that the 'talker' film they were
witnessing constituted a genuine technological miracle (Abel and Altman
2001, 156–66). The most celebrated live narrators were the Japanese *benshi*,
who were star attractions in the silent cinema and survived well into the
sound era (Dym 2003); elsewhere, however, verbal narration died out once
film-makers had evolved editorial techniques sophisticated enough for the
sequencing of the film's visual images to carry the necessary narrative information (Fairservice 2001, 11).

As silent cinema developed, and especially after *c.*1912, music came to
play a crucial role in shaping and conditioning the viewer's response to
moving pictures. Kathryn Kalinak has proposed that music, by its very
physical presence, created a sense of three-dimensionality singularly lacking

in the projected image: while the film was projected from the rear of the hall to the screen at the front, so music played at the front was projected backwards over the audience and 'through a kind of transference or slippage between sound and image, the depth created by the sound is transferred to the flat surface of the image' (Kalinak 1992, 44). The process of humanizing the silent moving image with music was regarded by some commentators, notably Theodor Adorno and Hanns Eisler, as a quasi-magical process in which the spectator's fear of the irrationality of the ghostly medium was exorcized:

> Music was introduced as a kind of antidote against the picture. The need was felt to spare the spectator the unpleasantness involved in seeing effigies of living, acting, and even speaking persons, who were at the same time silent . . . [M]usic was introduced not to supply them with the life they lacked – this became its aim only in the era of total ideological planning – but to exorcise fear or help the spectator absorb the shock.
>
> Motion-picture music corresponds to the whistling or singing child in the dark. (Adorno and Eisler 1994 [1947], 75)

This view was echoed by Kracauer, who found soundless moving pictures 'a frightening experience' and that film music had a beneficial effect on them: 'Ghostly shadows, as volatile as clouds, thus become trustworthy shapes' (Kracauer 1960, 134–5). More mundanely, the use of exciting or tear-jerking musical accompaniments of an increasingly elaborate nature became perhaps the most effective mechanism for persuading spectators willingly to suspend their disbelief. As Claudia Gorbman has pointed out, this process – as familiar in the modern sound film as it was in the silent cinema – conveniently involved an abrogation of critical faculties, rendering the viewer 'an untroublesome viewing subject': 'When we shed a tear during a pregnant moment in a film melodrama . . . instead of scoffing at its excess, music often is present, a catalyst in the suspension of judgment' (Gorbman 1987, 5–6). Thus film-makers from the early days used music as 'their panacea for encouraging audience empathy' (Bazelon 1975, 13). This concept was expressed as early as 1926 by Paul Ramain:

> all that is required of the orchestra in the cinema is to play harmonious background music with the idea not of being heard but of creating an atmosphere to sink us into our subconscious and make us forget the rustling paper, the shuffling feet, etc. in the auditorium . . . The role of music is therefore subsidiary, helping to put us in a trance with a vague background hum. (quoted in Mitry 1998, 248)

Cognitive psychologists have begun the daunting task of attempting to explain how the brain's functions enable this to happen (Cohen 2000, 365–8).

The birth of film music

The origins of film music are traditionally traced to Paris in the early 1890s, where Emile Reynaud's animated *Pantomimes lumineuses* were presented in November 1892 with piano music specially composed by Gaston Paulin, and a showing of short films by the Lumière brothers in December 1895 received a piano accompaniment from Emile Maraval, and a harmonium accompaniment when their show opened in London in the following year. At the launch of Vitascope in a New York music hall in April 1896, Dr Leo Sommer's Blue Hungarian Band performed. The experimental film-maker Georges Méliès played the piano himself for the Paris première of his *Le Voyage dans la lune* in 1902. These ventures continued the long-standing practice of accompanying other types of popular entertainment, such as magic-lantern shows, vaudeville and melodrama, with appropriate music.

Many nineteenth-century lantern shows were elaborate affairs carefully sequenced for dramatic effect, and bolstered by narration and (even in the case of some illustrated scientific lectures) appropriate musical accompaniment. 'Illustrated songs', in which popular tunes were accompanied by lantern slides while the audience sang along, were one form of entertainment that was carried over directly into early cinemas, which in the first part of the silent era continued to provide a varied bill of vaudeville-style fare; early projectors combined both motion-picture and lantern-slide technology (Altman 1996, 660–7). So popular were illustrated songs in the USA – and so essentially different from the frequently melodramatic tone of imported European films in the early days of silent movies – that Richard Abel has plausibly suggested they were responsible not only for the initial success of the nickelodeon industry (see below) but also as an early example of a distinctively American psychology that would come to be important in the later development of a national cinematic style (Abel and Altman 2001, 150–1). Illustrated songs gradually disappeared from nickelodeons in 1910–13, perhaps in response to a widespread desire for movies to be taken more seriously: this new-found aura of respectability required silent contemplation on the part of the audience, and an avoidance of popular culture.

Although it would be decades before synchronized pre-recorded sound established itself in the cinema, several leading inventors attempted to combine image and sound in this way as early as the 1890s. Thomas Edison's Kinetograph, on which work began in 1889, was developed specifically to provide a visual enhancement to music reproduced on his already successful phonograph – a reversal of the more common subordinance of music to visual image that soon came to dominate mainstream cinema. Both Edison's

Kinetograph (camera) and Kinetoscope (projector) were conceived with the aim of synchronizing image and sound, and it is now known that Edison took the credit for some technological marvels that had in fact been invented by others (Allen and Gomery 1985, 57–8); but, no matter who was responsible for it, the challenge of synchronization proved to be too ambitious for its time and the handful of Kinetophone sound films his team produced had unsynchronized accompaniments. After other devices for recording accompaniments on disc or cylinder were demonstrated at the Paris Exposition in 1900, some film-makers furthered the attempt to use pre-recorded sound; in Germany, Oskar Messter worked on his Kosmograph disc system from 1903 onwards and began to release *Tonbilder* films in 1908 with recorded music, and films of musical numbers accompanied by 'an incredible gramophone synchronized to the pictures and driven by compressed air' enjoyed popularity in Sweden in 1908–9 (Lack 1997, 14–15). These experiments were less than satisfactory on account of poor synchronization, lack of amplification and the need to change sound cylinders or discs every five minutes or so. The absence of a standardized system also meant that the initiatives were not commercially viable: apart from a short-lived revamping of Edison's Kinetophone productions in 1913–14, such ventures had already dwindled in importance around 1910.

As the craze for moving pictures spread, the nature of their musical accompaniment varied considerably according to the context in which they were shown. Mechanical instruments were popular initially, and these preserved an audible link with the fairground; even as late as 1913, three-quarters of projection venues surveyed in San Francisco still had nothing but mechanical music, and close on 90 per cent had provision for it (Altman 1996, 685). Nevertheless, live music was always common, especially in cases where touring motion-picture attractions were presented in vaudeville theatres or music halls to the accompaniment of the venues' resident ensembles. This appears to have been the case with tours of the Vitascope and Biograph shows and similar attractions in both the USA and Europe during the later 1890s; in Paris, café-concert and music-hall entertainments also came to include motion pictures, which formed part of the bill of fare at famous venues such as the Olympia and Folies-Bergère. The German entrepreneurs Max and Emil Skladanowsky toured Scandinavia with their Bioskop show in 1896, and the incomplete set of performing parts that survives reveals the musical accompaniment to have included both specially composed cues and an extract from Glinka for use with a sequence depicting a Russian dance. Another compilation, similar in function, was prepared by Leopold Wenzel for a royal cinematographic show at Windsor Castle in 1897 (Marks 1997, 30–50). The American touring exhibitor D. W. Robertson set out with a newly purchased Edison Kinetoscope in 1897 and by 1906 was advertising shows with 'descriptive musical accompaniment' (Abel and Altman 2001, 125).

The success of these and other itinerant motion-picture enterprises led to a major boom in the establishment of nickelodeons in the USA, which began to appear in *c.*1905 and numbered some 10,000 by 1910; after their humble beginnings, these establishments catered for increasingly discerning audiences who would pay more for luxuries such as comfortable seats and music. A parallel development in France, also beginning in 1905–6, saw Charles Pathé and Léon Gaumont establish *salles de cinéma* in numerous provincial towns. It was in venues such as these that the initial showbooth-style 'cinema of attractions' became gradually supplanted by more substantial films with a strong narrative orientation, and with these came more ambitious musical accompaniment. Comments published in the trade press seem to indicate that a perceived need for incidental music was growing stronger by *c.*1907 and that, by *c.*1911, music accompanying the picture was regarded as more useful than the independent musical numbers that had been performed previously; musical provision also became increasingly standardized as a result of the systematic attempts of production companies to promote a consistent manner of film accompaniment in preference to the widely contrasting types of aural stimulation on offer at various establishments, which had formerly been regarded by the latter as competitive selling-points (Altman 1996, 677–9, 690). The production companies did this partly through the medium of live demonstrations, either given by touring representatives or by invitation to exhibitors to attend presentations at major urban venues, especially in the period 1911–14 (Altman 2004, 272–3).

Categories of film music

At an early stage it was recognized that there were two fundamentally different types of film music. On the one hand, the music might be what modern film scholars describe as diegetic: in other words, it formed part of the film's narrative world (diegesis) and its purported source was often, though not exclusively, visible on the screen. On the other hand, the music might be nondiegetic, serving as appropriate background listening. Diegetic music-making in the visual image could easily be matched by a synchronized instrumental or vocal accompaniment – whether supplied live or on a gramophone recording – and this procedure became especially popular in *c.*1907–8 (Altman 1996, 682), being referred to specifically as 'cue music'. As greater attention was paid to the provision of nondiegetic music, such accompaniments drew increasingly on features of the well-established symbiosis between music and drama that had in the nineteenth century shaped the development of major theatrical genres such as opera, ballet and (above all) melodrama (Shapiro 1984). According to one early twentieth-century commentator, the basis of the musical component in melodrama ('which accompanies the dialogue and reflects the feeling and emotion of the spoken lines') is simplicity of construction and subservience to the words: 'It usually accompanies the most sentimental passages in the play . . . , following the hero and heroine most obstinately. But the villain too will have his little bit of *tremolo* to help him along his evil path' (O'Neill 1911, 88). Recapitulation is used 'to remind the audience of a previous situation', later a standard film-music technique; but on the whole 'both music and drama of this class have no great artistic value. The music is simply called in to bolster up the weakness of the drama. It is used to stimulate (by what I may call unfair means) the imagination of the audience, and to help the actor' (O'Neill 1911, 88).

Since many influential silent-film directors had been schooled in melodrama, the transferral of its characteristics to the silver screen was inevitable. Stagings of melodrama had utilized live organ or orchestral incidental music to enhance the audience's emotional response and to suggest character types or geographical locations, the choice of appropriate music being indicated in the scripts and aided by the existence of anthologies of specially selected musical extracts. These were all features of early film music, which directly inherited melodramatic clichés such as the use of string tremolo and delicate pizzicato for tension and furtiveness respectively, and loud stinger chords to emphasize physical action or rousing lines (Gorbman 1987, 33–5; Marks 1997, 28). These simple devices, combined with background music lulling the spectator into an uncritical state, remained useful in inferior melodramatic film drama because, as Yves Baudrier put it, 'if the music is taken away, there is a risk of losing the necessary minimum emotional warmth which must exist for us to believe (however temporarily) in the sentiments we are supposed to be feeling, attracting, through a sort of magic, the complicity of the audience' (quoted in Mitry 1998, 253).

The importance of music as a mood-enhancer in early cinema was reflected in the common practice of having live or recorded music played on film sets during shooting to inspire the actors, a procedure later occasionally used in the making of sound films by directors such as John Ford, Alfred Hitchcock (who, while shooting *The Birds*, used a drummer on set to terrify the actors in the absence of the film's sophisticated avian sound effects), Stanley Kubrick, Sergio Leone, David Lynch, Ken Russell and Peter Weir. Cecil B. DeMille, for example, used the slow movement of Dvořák's *New World* Symphony to establish the mood for his portrayal of

1.1 Live music-making was often employed to inspire actors during the shooting of silent films, as seen here in the making of *The Little French Girl*, directed by Herbert Brenon in 1925. (Museum of the Moving Image)

the Exodus in *The Ten Commandments* (1923). Geraldine Farrar, a silent-film star who combined careers as an opera singer and screen actress, recalled that after her first experiment with using an on-set pianist to inspire her performance, 'I always had a musician at my elbow whose soulful throbs did more to start my tears than all the glycerine drops or onions more frequently employed by less responsive orbs' (quoted in Karlin 1994, 162). The image of music as a substitute for glycerine was echoed by later observers of film-making practices, and contemporaneous commentators found some pathos-inducing music laughably self-indulgent, for example Alphons Czibulka's *Wintermärchen* (1891), its theme identical with the contemporaneous hit tune *Hearts and Flowers* by Theo Tobani. The most stereotyped and clichéd idioms used to accompany silent films survived into the sound era almost exclusively in a context of parody, figuring prominently in comedy and cartoon scores; but the tributes were often affectionate.

Improvised accompaniments to screenings of silent films might typically be provided by a pianist or harmonium player, sometimes resourceful enough simultaneously to play piano with one hand and harmonium with the other (Huntley [1947], 25). In its idealized but rarely attained form, a good keyboard accompaniment mediated between the image and the spectator, just as an effective pre-composed score would come to do in the sound cinema: as Bernard Herrmann later observed, film music may be considered as 'the communicating link between the screen and the audience, reaching out and enveloping all into one single experience' (Herrmann 1945, 17). One major advantage of improvised accompaniments was their ability, when skilfully executed, to lend a sense of continuity to the narrative; film music in the later silent era was sometimes continuous from start to finish, though pre-arranged compilation scores (see below) tended to be highly sectionalized; strategically placed gaps in the aural continuum were also sometimes necessary merely for practical reasons. The ability of all kinds of music to create continuity and enhance a sense of momentum became increasingly evident in the second decade of the century. Kurt London believed that the raison d'être for film's musical accompaniment was 'the rhythm of the film as an art of movement' (London 1936, 35). Kracauer described music as 'a meaningful continuity in time' and declared that music in film causes us to perceive 'structural patterns where there were none before. Confused shifts of positions reveal themselves to be comprehensible gestures; scattered visual data coalesce and follow a definite course. Music makes the silent images partake of its continuity' (Kracauer 1960, 135). Mitry concluded that the 'real time' component of music 'provides the visual impressions with the missing time content by giving them the powers of perceptible rhythm' (Mitry 1998, 265) and felt that musical continuity was necessary to compensate for what he felt was an inherent inadequacy of film editing:

> it is all too apparent that the editing of a series of fixed shots establishes *a feeling of continuity* but is unable, unlike moving shots, to create the *sensation* of the continuous, since this sensation is reconstructed intellectually and not perceived as such – which means that reality appears as though it were an idea or memory; or, to put it another way, it appears *restructured*.
>
> (Mitry 1998, 162)

The habitual use of intertitles to convey information or dialogue essential to the narrative was a major impediment to the continuity of silent films, though the ease with which they could be replaced by intertitles in different languages for export was one factor contributing to the rapid international dissemination of new releases.

Another of music's many functions was to play mild intellectual games with the film's spectators, who might be amused by appropriate references to certain popular songs they were already familiar with through participation in illustrated-song shows. This practice proliferated in the first decade of the century when the popular-song industry enjoyed its own boom, but as early as 1910 at least one commentator had noted that it was an entirely pointless procedure if members of the audience failed to recognize, or did not know, the song being quoted (Abel and Altman 2001, 238). These topical allusions were sometimes unaccountably light-hearted even during serious scenes: for example, at a British screening of *The Queen of Sheba* (dir. William Fox, 1921) the ensemble cheerfully trotted out 'Thanks for the Buggy Ride' during the spectacular chariot race (Karlin 1994, 156). One technical manual went so far as to lambast such musical puns as 'not only worthless, but offensive' (Beynon 1921, 2). Such literal-mindedness in thematic allusion persists in mainstream narrative cinema, which frequently draws on appropriate song tunes which the audience might be expected to recognize. Tin Pan Alley songs and jazz standards are today usually heard as diegetic performances, since these seem marginally less contrived than thematic allusions in the nondiegetic score; the tunes are often rendered by instruments alone in an attempt to make the allusion subtler by suppressing the relevant lyrics. Woody Allen's *Manhattan* (1979) and *Hannah and Her Sisters* (1981) provide good examples of the use of appropriately entitled instrumental standards in their nondiegetic music tracks, though these are spotted with structural as well as punning intent (Marshall and Stilwell 2000, 14). A far less subtle example occurs in *An American in Paris* (1951; see Chapter 4) when Gene Kelly dances with his love in a jazz café to the diegetic accompaniment of Gershwin's '(It's Very Clear) Our Love is Here to Stay' – and feels the need to point out the title to her in case it wasn't quite clear enough.

The popular classics were plundered for suitable extracts for use with silent films, while the style of freshly composed cues drew heavily on the idioms of romantic opera and operetta. The most influential by far was that of Wagner, whose name is invoked time and again in contemporaneous commentary on music in the silent cinema. A journal proclaimed in 1911 that all musical directors were disciples of Wagner (Flinn 1992, 15), and the influence was manifested both in specific compositional techniques such as the use of leitmotifs as both narrative and structural device – considered to be a cutting-edge technique in early film music and persisting to the present day, in spite of the attempts of later commentators to discredit it – and in an aspiration towards *unendliche Melodie* in the interests of musico-dramatic continuity. The Wagnerian ideal of the *Gesamtkunstwerk* became applied to the cinematic medium as a whole, and the connection emphasized the vital role played by music in shaping the impact of the drama (Paulin 2000).

Camille Saint-Saëns and *film d'art*

Original scores were rare in the early years of silent film. A singular example came into being when French cinema, which achieved international market dominance in 1906–10 largely through the phenomenal success of Charles Pathé's production company and the work of Léon Gaumont, attempted to reach a high artistic plateau with the launching of the intensely theatrical style of *film d'art*. Unlike other film companies, the Société Film d'Art employed renowned stage directors, screenplay writers, actors from the Comédie Française and established composers in its striving for a quality product. The best-known music by Camille Saint-Saëns, such as 'The Swan' from *The Carnival of the Animals*, was already familiar in French cinemas (R. S. Brown 1994, 53), so it was logical enough that he be invited to compose a score for Henri Lavédan's eighteen-minute *L'assassinat du Duc de Guise* (dir. André Calmettes and Charles Le Bargy), which launched *film d'art* on 17 November 1908 in a programme at the Salle Charras featuring two other films with original music by Fernand Le Borne and Gaston Berardi.

The ever-practical Saint-Saëns made his film-scoring task easier by reworking extracts from an unpublished work, his symphony *Urbs Roma* (B. Rees 1999, 382) – and, according to a review of *L'assassinat* published two weeks after its première screening, composed his film score 'in front of the screen as the film was being projected' (quoted in Abel and Altman 2001, 54). In contrast to the bittiness of much film music in this period, Saint-Saëns' music for *L'assassinat*, performed by classical instrumentalists drawn from the orchestras of the Concerts Colonne and Concerts Lamoureux, showed how structural coherence could articulate the drama across relatively broad time-spans, and it proved to be prophetic of the later mainstream film composer's art. Prophetic too was Saint-Saëns' decision to recycle his film music for concert use (as Op. 128, for the original ensemble scoring of wind, piano, harmonium and strings), a procedure later adopted by many composers who wished to rescue their film music from its ephemeral source; his publisher, Durand, also issued a version for solo piano intended for use in projection venues which could not afford the full ensemble.

Contemporaneous reviewers of *L'assassinat* declared that the promoters of such productions 'cannot imagine them without the help of a *powerful music* which from the point of view of the audience will replace the *human voice* in the minute details of its expressivity . . . [T]here is the great display, the whole kit and caboodle of *invisible* yet *present* music, the mystery appropriate for cinematographic evocations' (quoted in Abel and Altman 2001, 50–1). The film received critical acclaim in France, though some observers lamented its utter subservience to old-fashioned theatricality, and others later exhibited it with designedly ridiculous music (Sadoul

1948, 541). It exerted a powerful influence on global film production, which quickly turned to canonic works of literature – and even opera – as fodder for more ambitious silent-film treatments. In the UK, an early original score was written by operetta composer Edward German for the Ealing film *Henry VIII* in 1911 (Huntley 2002); in the USA, original scores did not begin to be produced in earnest until later in the decade.

Cue sheets and anthologies

Production companies had meanwhile begun to take a keen interest in the nature of the music that might accompany exhibitions of their products. In 1907, for example, Gaumont began publishing a weekly pamphlet entitled *Guide Musicale* for distribution to exhibitors in France. In 1909, Edison Pictures in the USA started publishing cue sheets in the pages of its *Edison Kinetogram* to encourage the selection of appropriate musical numbers from both classical and popular sources to accompany screenings of its films, and a range of similar suggestions began to appear in the trade press. A major motivation behind this initiative was the apparent ineptitude of many movie-theatre pianists, amongst whom the standard of proficiency was wildly variable. Few intelligent movie-goers seemed to agree with Jean Cocteau's opinion that 'one can only love this pianist who created *sound* cinema' (quoted in Lacombe and Porcile 1995, 27). London recounted a typical example of what was undoubtedly widespread audience dissatisfaction with shoddy accompaniments:

> a man in a cinema audience . . . had been sitting in long-suffering silence while a very bad pianist accompanied the film. When the heroine was about to seek an end of her troubles by plunging to a watery grave, he called out to her image on the screen, in a voice full of disgust: 'Take the pianist with you, while you're about it!' (London 1936, 41)

In France, mediocre pianists were so commonplace that they had their own name (*tapeurs*).

Cue sheets were supplemented by, and sometimes made specific reference to, more substantial published anthologies of motion-picture music that were organized by mood or dramatic type. In France, no fewer than 30 such anthologies were available by 1910, and some original pieces were specially commissioned for this purpose (Lacombe and Porcile 1995, 30–1) – a procedure that adumbrated the modern practice of setting up music libraries from which pre-existing cues can be sourced relatively cheaply. One of the first anthologies to appear in America was Gregg A. Frelinger's *Motion Picture Piano Music*, issued in 1909. Another

American pioneer of these publications was Max Winkler, who persuaded his employer, the New York publisher Carl Fischer, to back the issuing of cue sheets; Winkler claimed this occurred in 1912 but Altman has demonstrated this date to be erroneous, the relevant initiative having probably dated from as late as 1916 by which time many other rivals were involved in similar enterprises (Altman 2004, 346–7). In Winkler's own much-quoted words, 'extracts from great symphonies and operas were hacked down to emerge as "Sinister Misterioso" by Beethoven, or "Weird Moderato" by Tchaikovsky' (Max Winkler 1951, 10). A popular favourite was Rossini's *William Tell* overture, which proved ideal for chases or what were termed 'hurry' scenes, while Beethoven's *Coriolanus* overture was deemed 'suitable for tree-felling or lumber-rolling' (Irving 1943, 225).

In 1913 John S. Zamecnik, a former pupil of Dvořák's, published a collection of 23 original keyboard cues as the first volume of a series entitled *The Sam Fox Moving Picture Music*, his approach to the task showing a typical predilection for short repeated segments. Other American publishers who provided scores and parts for movie music were G. Schirmer and Morse Preeman. In 1916, Walter C. Simon conceived a novel 'Phototune' format in which eleven different eight- or sixteen-bar keyboard compositions were superimposed in a single-page chart, the principal barlines extending unbroken from the top to the foot of the page to show the alignment, and related keys used 'to enable the musician to instantly jump from place to place on the sheet as may be desired' (facsimile in Altman 2004, 264). Giuseppe Becce's *Kinothek* (its title a contraction of 'Kinobibliothek'), published in instalments in Berlin in 1919 and in the USA by Belwin, was a seminal anthology, and Becce later collaborated with Hans Erdmann and Ludwig Brav to produce the encyclopaedic *Allgemeines Handbuch der Filmmusik* in 1927. In 1924 Ernö Rapée, a Hungarian with wide experience of musical direction in cinemas both in Europe and the USA, issued in New York his *Motion Picture Moods for Pianists and Organists*, and followed this a year later with an *Encyclopaedia of Music for Pictures*. Rapée recognized a general paradox of film music, to which attention is still often drawn today:

> If you come out of the theatre almost unaware of the musical accompaniment to the picture you have just witnessed, the work of the musical director has been successful. Without music the present day audience would feel utterly lost. With it they should obtain an added satisfaction from the show, and still remain unconscious of the very thing which has produced that satisfaction.　　　　　(quoted in Lack 1997, 34)

Several of the themes and techniques popularized by cue sheets and anthologies such as Rapée's, many of which were directly inherited from melodrama, became clichés that remain firmly in the popular imagination:

for example, diminished-seventh chords for villains, 'weepie' love themes on solo violin and the bridal march from Wagner's *Lohengrin* for wedding scenes. The last was brutally dismissed by Adorno and Eisler: 'The person who around 1910 first conceived the repulsive idea of using the Bridal March from *Lohengrin* as an accompaniment is no more of a historical figure than any other second-hand dealer' (Adorno and Eisler 1994 [1947], 49). Diminished-seventh harmony was routinely used for scenes of evil and villainy, as shown by a typical cue entitled 'Treacherous Knave (Villain Theme, Ruffians, Smugglers, Conspiracy)' composed by Zamecnik for *The Sam Fox Moving Picture Music* in 1927 (facsimile in Kalinak 1992, 62). The importance of this simple chord, already long outdated in concert music, as a melodramatic device was outlined by a pianist in Anthony Burgess's novel *The Pianoplayers* (1986) recalling the basic instructions he had received from his mentor as he embarked on the art of silent-film accompaniment:

> Here's a chord you can't do without, he said, if you're a picture palace pianoplayer. You use it for fights, burst dams, thunderstorms, the voice of the Lord God, a wife telling her old man to bugger off out of the house and not come back never no more. And he showed me . . . Always the same like dangerous sound, he said, as if something terrible's going to happen or is happening (soft for going to happen, loud for happening) . . . and you can arpeggio them to make them like very mysterious.
>
> (quoted in Kershaw 1995, 125)

'Soft for going to happen, loud for happening' was to remain an absolutely fundamental approach to dynamics in much later film music.

So-called 'special music', expressly designed to accompany specific films, became more common after *c.*1910. The idea originated in the use of musical extracts to accompany highly compressed silent films of popular operas, which may be one reason why the subsequent development of film music was so indebted to operatic prototypes. In 1911, for example, the commercially successful Italian film *Dante's Inferno* appropriated music from Boito's *Mefistofele* (Marks 1997, 73–4). In the same year, the Kalem Company in the USA commissioned the first sustained series of special piano scores, featuring the work of Walter C. Simon, an experienced theatre musician who also published a *Progress Course of Music* for budding cinema pianists. Simon's highly sectionalized scores, which included one for the three-reel *Arrah-Na-Pogue* (dir. Sidney Olcott, 1911), juxtaposed arrangements and original compositions, consolidating existing performance practices. Many of the items were structured on the principle that short segments could be repeated *ad lib.* until a visual cue (e.g. an intertitle card) prompted a shift to a new musical idea. Kalem's venture was followed in 1913 by a similar series of piano scores issued by Vitagraph. From *c.*1916 onwards there was a

proliferation of 'photoplay' library music arranged for flexible instrumentation (ranging from large orchestras down to a violin-and-piano duo or
solo piano as a bare minimum), taking the form of both classical extracts
and original cues based on compositional principles similar to those in the
early keyboard anthologies. Prominent composers and arrangers of such
library music were Ernst Luz (Photoplay Music Co.), Zamecnik (Sam Fox
Photoplay Edition), J. C. Breil (Schirmer) and Otto Langey (Chappell).

Although such music was offered at competitive prices, and some of it was
evidently geared towards players of limited abilities (the difficulty of sight-
reading more elaborate 'special' scores in advanced keys having been one
factor which inhibited the widespread adoption of accompaniments based
on complex classical repertoire), interest in the idea was not as widespread
as might have been predicted, since many projection venues continued to
arrange their own music to cut costs. Similarly, as film music developed
during the sound era so studios came to realize that commissioning original
music was often cheaper than having to pay to use copyright material or
meet reproduction fees on existing recordings.

Venues and ensembles

The often modestly appointed nickelodeons were very different from the
luxurious picture palaces that became prominent in the second decade of
the twentieth century. The first venue of this kind, the Omnia-Pathé, opened
in Paris in December 1906; nearly five years later, the former hippodrome at
Place Clichy was transformed into the 3,400-seat Gaumont-Palace, featuring
a Cavaillé-Coll organ and, at the venue's inauguration on 11 October 1911,
an orchestra of 60 conducted by Henri Fosse. A description of a Gaumont-
Palace programme from January 1913 reveals that an orchestral overture
was followed by the screening of short *actualités* (including a colorized
documentary about butterflies) and a comedy film, followed by an orchestral
entr'acte, after which came more documentaries and a two-part film about
Napoleon (Lacombe and Porcile 1995, 22, 27). The first of the gargantuan
American picture palaces was the Strand on Broadway, New York, which
opened in 1914 and could also seat in excess of 3,000 spectators; its music
was provided by a 30-piece orchestra and enormous Wurlitzer organ.

In keeping with the grandeur of the viewing facilities, serious narrative films had grown considerably longer in duration and more sumptuous in their production values. Most early movies were only one reel in
length, a single reel holding up to 1,000 feet of film stock and running for
approximately fifteen minutes at the projection speed of sixteen frames per
second often used in silent films (though shooting and projection speeds

could vary considerably: see Brownlow 1980). As multi-reel 'feature' films became popular, so narrative continuity became even more important and the more lavish production values seemingly cried out for correspondingly elaborate musical accompaniment. It was not uncommon to exploit the performance space by using antiphonal effects, such as the locating of trumpets at the rear of the hall to provide an echo device in a Belfast tour of *The Four Horsemen of the Apocalypse* (dir. Rex Ingram, 1921), screenings of which also featured special sound effects to suggest the hooves of the galloping horses (Huntley [1947], 27–8). Prestigious screenings were sometimes mounted in revered theatrical venues. For example, Eugene Goossens conducted the London Symphony Orchestra in the Royal Opera House for the screening of a silent version of *The Three Musketeers* (dir. Fred Niblo), starring Douglas Fairbanks and shown in the USA with a score by Louis Gottschalk. For the London show, part of a season of silent epics mounted at the opera house by United Artists in 1921–2, Goossens based his compilation score heavily on the work of August Enna, an obscure composer whose music 'fitted anything, and also conveyed a spurious impression of great emotional depth, making it very suitable for my purpose' (quoted in Kershaw 1995, 128; see also Morrison 2004, 176). In 1926, a silent film of Richard Strauss's opera *Der Rosenkavalier* was shown in the Dresden Opera House, not in a popular projection venue – as Adorno and Eisler, who were disturbed by the cultural implications of the venture, might well have preferred it to have been (see Chapter 4). In 1925, the Paris Opéra hosted the première of Pierre Marodon's film *Salammbô*, featuring music by Florent Schmitt, and two years later the same venue screened Abel Gance's *Napoléon* (see below), with a lavish accompaniment featuring live actors and full chorus. In New York, the finest film-related musical performances were those masterminded by respected music director Hugo Riesenfeld at picture palaces that rivalled opera houses in their opulence; his classical credentials as a former leader of the Vienna Opera and the Metropolitan Opera orchestras were impeccable.

Instrumental ensembles resident in movie theatres of varying sizes ranged from duos (e.g. violin and piano, or piano and drums), through small groups of five or six players up to (by the 1920s) large orchestras with 40 players or more – the formation of the latter in major cities in both the USA and Europe sometimes resulting in a dwindling of the ranks of leading symphony orchestras. A lone pianist might be employed to accompany films during the week, with an ensemble brought in for better-attended weekend shows or to launch a high-profile new picture. Some featured soloists, especially violinists and 'funners' who specialized in witty musical commentaries, commanded considerable popular followings in their own right (Berg 1976, 244–5). The small ensembles were often versatile. Cinema organist Gaylord Carter recalled:

> The first thing you had to have, if you had any kind of a combo, was the
> drummer. So you could get the punches and rifle shots and cataclysmic
> things like an earthquake. You'd need a trumpet for bugle calls. And it would
> be nice to have a clarinet . . . You had to have usually one violin and a second
> violin. You wouldn't have a viola, but you'd have a cello and maybe a bass.
>
> (interviewed in McCarty 1989, 49–50)

Violas were considered to be a dispensable luxury (London 1936, 46), and
they are still often omitted in the string arrangements of modern film
scores, which may feature just one rather than the two violin lines customary in classical orchestras. Percussion was absolutely vital in providing
onomatopoeic effects. According to a contemporaneous report, a resourceful percussionist at the Bijou Dream theatre in New York in 1909 made the
screen characters appear to 'talk, almost; they groan, they laugh, kiss, whisper
under his magic touch' (Marks 1997, 67). Comic drumming effects in particular were a direct holdover from vaudeville. Alberto Cavalcanti noticed
that percussive effects could produce a far greater impact than realistic
sounds:

> An airplane was flying towards us [on screen]. The music director 'cut' the
> orchestra, and a strange, frightsome sound began, and got louder and
> louder. It was nothing like an airplane, but very frightening. When I got
> home I was still wondering how this noise was done. Then I got it. It was a
> noise I had known all my life – an open cymbal beaten with two soft-headed
> drumsticks. How familiar! Yet it had lost its identity, and retained only its
> dramatic quality, used in conjunction with the picture. Pictures are clear and
> specific, noises are vague. The picture had changed a cymbal noise into an
> air-noise. That is why noise is so useful. It speaks directly to the emotions.
>
> (Weis and Belton 1985, 109)

As Altman has shown (1996, 698–9), production of musical sound effects
was by no means restricted to the drummer, and the piano proved to be
equally versatile in capable hands: such diegetic effects appear to have dominated accompanying music in *c.*1908–12.

Resident music directors were variously referred to as music illustra-
tors, fitters or synchronizers – the last term then used differently from its
modern application, in that synchronization was more a matter of finding
music of exactly the right length for a particular scene rather than attempting to tie its details to specific on-screen events (Kalinak 1992, 58). Music
directors were responsible for arranging and conducting appropriate repertoire drawn either from the classical extracts or short original pieces published in anthologies, from cue sheets, or preparing freshly selected passages;
such pre-existing material might be linked by specially composed or improvised transitions. The fact that music was often accorded a high degree of

importance is shown by the working practice of Riesenfeld, who habitually edited segments of film himself or had the projector run at variable speeds so that the images would fit better with the musical extracts he had selected (Buhrman 1920).

Photoplayers and cinema organs

Silent-film pianists had frequently struggled with inferior instruments and limited technique, one journal's editorial making a plea that nickelodeon pianos should either be tuned or burnt – and preferably replaced by instrumental groups (*Moving Picture World*, 3 July 1909). The piano and humble harmonium were supplanted in grander venues by mechanical keyboard instruments (photoplayers) which exploited up-to-date pneumatic and electric technology to include integrated sound-effect mechanisms, and then by specialized and highly versatile cinema organs, of which noted manufacturers included Compton, Marr and Colton, Robert Morton, Estey, Barton and Moller. The most imposing organs were made by Kimball and Wurlitzer, both regarded as status symbols for any venue prosperous enough to be able to afford them. Wurlitzer became involved in the motion-picture industry in 1909 when they found an application for their mechanical instruments as vehicles for nickelodeon ballyhoo, but from 1910 onwards they devoted attention to the cinema organ and by 1916 organ sales had begun to overtake the dwindling demand for photoplayers (Altman 2004, 335). At the grand end of the spectrum was the Kimball organ at the Roxy Theatre, New York, originally planned to have been played by no fewer than five organists seated at five independent consoles – an ambitious scheme later reduced to three performers, who nevertheless still had at their disposal a total of eleven manuals and three pedal boards operating in excess of 300 stops.

Most theatre organs had at least two manuals, and the console could often be raised and lowered on a special elevator for added visual impact; translucent panels were designed to reveal patterns of coloured lights within the instrument's casing, and this enhanced the sense of virtuosic showmanship. Capacity for mechanical sound effects was considerable and could include the sounds of surf, hail, aeroplanes, birds, various whistles (e.g. police, train and steamboat), horses' hooves, fire gong, klaxon horn, electric bell and a crockery-smashing effect comprising 'a cleverly devised electro-pneumatic crane which literally drops metal plates onto a metal surface below' (Whitworth 1954, 308). Cavalcanti scathingly observed that the provision of such novelties 'will give you some idea of the absurdity of referring to "the great days of the silent cinema"'

(Weis and Belton 1985, 101). Genuine untuned percussion instruments (traps) were operated by thumb and toe pistons, with tuned percussion (various metallophones, chimes and xylophones) played via the keyboards. Ranks of pipes might be disposed antiphonally on opposing sides of the projection screen, and the enormous Christie instrument at London's Marble Arch Odeon even included full-length 32′ reeds.

In many venues both organist and orchestra would be involved in performances, with the organist playing a reduction of the orchestral music for matinées and participating with the orchestra in the evening shows; it was common practice for the organist gradually to start playing after the orchestra had been in action for 30–45 minutes, allowing the instrumentalists to drop out one by one and take a break before reassembling for a grand finale (McCarty 1989, 24). The organist might also be called upon to provide improvised transitional passages between orchestral items. Organists were primarily required to imitate orchestral effects, and those who sounded as if they were playing in church were unpopular. Among the most respected American organists during the 1920s were Gaylord Carter, Milton Charles, Jesse Crawford, Lloyd Del Castillo, Ann Leaf, John Muri, Henry B. Murtagh, Albert Malotte and Alexander Schreiner, and their art was taken sufficiently seriously for the Eastman School of Music in Rochester to be founded specifically to provide instruction in it (McCarty 1989, 45), with similar training provided by special schools in other American cities. Reginald Foort made history by giving a radio broadcast from the organ of the New Gallery Cinema in London's Regent Street in 1926 and, along with artists such as Quentin Maclean and Firmen Swinnen, helped establish the cinema organ as a concert instrument in its own right.

The many composers and musicians who benefited from apprenticeships as silent-film accompanists on piano and/or organ included composers such as Jacques Ibert in France; Dmitri Kabalevsky, Dmitri Shostakovich and Dimitri Tiomkin in the Soviet Union; and, in America, jazz musicians Count Basie and Fats Waller. The cinema organ survived well into the sound era, but playing standards continued to vary wildly. As late as the early 1950s, one commentator lamented (in terms equally applicable to commercial film music in general) that

> the music demanded from the cinema organist by managements is only too
> often cheap and tawdry. Frequently it is associated with songs of a sickly
> sentimentality that has fostered an abuse of the tremulant and a paucity of
> registration . . . Managers have a habit of insisting that this is the kind of
> thing the public demands, forgetting or choosing to overlook that
> picture-going audiences do not know what they want, but accept what they
> are given and imagine it must be good if it is played to so large a public.
>
> (Whitworth 1954, 309)

Music for silent epics

Among the most ambitious films distributed on the eve of the First World War were the Italian historical epics that took the movie-going world by storm in 1913–14. *Quo vadis?* (dir. Enrico Guazzoni, 1913) occupied nine reels and for its New York screenings in 1914 was furnished with a score compiled from music by composers such as Gounod, Puccini and Wagner by exhibitor Samuel L. Rothapfel. Though musically uneducated, 'Roxy' Rothapfel was a sensitive businessman who felt that clichéd and over-familiar music should be avoided, as should novelty trap drumming and gratuitous sound effects; his quest for musical quality seems to have been successful, since one reviewer remarked that the admission price for *Quo vadis?* was justified by the music alone (Marks 1997, 97). The Punic War epic *Cabiria* (dir. Giovanni Pastrone, 1914) was even more lavish, occupying twelve reels and shot to a massive budget with thousands of extras. It was furnished in Italy with a score compiled by Manlio Mazza from popular classics linked by modulatory passages. For American showings of the film, Mazza's score was adapted by Joseph Carl Breil, a composer of incidental music for stage plays who had compiled scores for various *films d'art* in 1911–13, among them the famous Sarah Bernhardt vehicle *Queen Elizabeth* (dir. Louis Mercanton, 1912), for which Breil claimed his score was entirely original apart from its (anachronistic) use of the British national anthem to accompany the defeat of the Spanish Armada (Marks 1997, 102). Breil's adapted score for *Cabiria* – which, like his music for *Queen Elizabeth*, fea-tured leitmotivic construction – was an extravagant affair scored for large orchestra and unseen chorus. It undoubtedly served as a useful preparation for his subsequent and influential collaboration with the ground-breaking director D. W. Griffith, whose refinement of narrative editing techniques and encouragement of a naturalistic style of acting established him as the most important film-maker of the era.

Griffith's Civil War epic *The Birth of a Nation* (1915), costing in excess of $100,000 and the longest film so far made in the USA, met with phenom-enal success and considerable controversy arising from its racist content – which led to its being banned in numerous states and censored in others. The film was first screened (under the title *The Clansman*) in Los Angeles in February 1915 with a score compiled by Carli Elinor, who believed that 'there was no need for original music since so many good tunes had already been written' (Darby and Du Bois 1990, 3). The theatre's publicity proudly proclaimed: 'The arrangement and selection of the music for "The Clans-man" was accomplished after a diligent search of the music libraries of Los Angeles, San Francisco and New York. To select and cue the scenes it was necessary to run the twelve reels comprising the story eighty-four times;

and also to render a perfect score six complete full orchestral rehearsals were necessary' (facsimile in Marks 1997, 134). Composers whose work was featured in Elinor's compilation included Beethoven, Bizet, Flotow, Mozart, Offenbach, Rossini, Schubert, Suppé, Verdi and Wagner. A sextet of vocal soloists joined the orchestra for certain items.

Breil's hybrid score for this three-hour epic, partly original and partly compiled, contained well over 200 individual musical cues and was first used when the film was screened in New York in March 1915. The score appears to have been prepared under the close supervision of Griffith himself, and included metronome markings as an aid to synchronization (Karlin 1994, 161). The director evidently regarded the New York opening as more impor- tant than the West Coast première, as suggested by reporter Grace Kingsley in the *Los Angeles Times* (8 February 1915), who noted that Breil and Griffith were collaborating on the score for the upcoming New York screenings and commented that the music was to be

> no less than the adapting of grand-opera methods to motion pictures! Each character playing has a distinct type of music, a distinct theme as in opera. A more difficult matter in pictures than in opera, however, inasmuch as any one character seldom holds the screen long at a time. In cases where there are many characters, the music is adapted to the dominant note or character in the scene.
>
> From now on special music is to be written in this manner for all the big Griffith productions.

Breil's original cues included a theme for 'The Bringing of the African to America' which took its lead from Dvořák in its use of syncopation and hints of pentatonicism, several numbers in popular dance forms (with a clear penchant for waltz rhythm), an attempt to represent the diegetic music sung by the character of Elsie Stoneman as she strums her banjo, and an *amoroso* love theme. Civil War songs appeared alongside extracts from the classics, the most memorable of which was the use of Wagner's 'Ride of the Valkyries' to accompany the equestrian riders of the Ku Klux Klan. According to actress Lillian Gish, director and composer argued intensely over the 'Valkyrie' material: Griffith wanted some of the notes to be altered but Breil refused to 'tamper' with Wagner, whereupon the director remarked that the music was not '*primarily* music' but rather 'music for motion pictures'; he clinched his argument by noting that 'Even Giulio Gatti-Casazza, General Director of the Metropolitan Opera, agreed that the change was fine' (Gish and Pinchot 1969, 152). Jane Gaines and Neil Lerner have demonstrated how Breil's syncopated 'African' theme (which acquired the label 'Motif of Barbarism' when published in a piano album in 1916) was used throughout the film to promote the image of black men as primitives (Abel and Altman 2001, 252–68). A simple repeated falling semitone in the bass was used to punctuate and create tension in the scene in which Gus preys on Flora, this technique looking ahead to modern economical scoring methods.

Breil's love theme from *The Birth of Nation* met with success of its own when it was entitled 'The Perfect Song' and furnished with lyrics for publication; other selections from the score were issued in arrangements for piano and for ensemble. These were amongst the earliest commercial spin-offs in the history of film music, and later silent-film scores began to include a 'big theme' in an attempt to cash in on the marketability of such material. By 1927, the abuse of 'theme scores' had become so acute that one commentator lamented the film composer's tendency towards '*theme-ing* an audience to death' (quoted in Altman 2004, 376). In an early example of using film tie-ins to sell independent popular songs, the faces of Charlie Chaplin and other movie stars began to be featured on the covers of sheet music, no matter how tenuous the connection between music and film (Barrios 1995, 106). Major hit songs from film scores began with the theme song to *Mickey* (dir. F. Richard Jones and James Young, 1918; music by Neil Moret), and towards the end of the silent era million-copy sales were achieved by Rapée's songs 'Charmaine' and 'Diane', from *What Price Glory?* (dir. Raoul Walsh, 1926) and *Seventh Heaven* (dir. Frank Borzage, 1927) respectively: the trend continued with hit songs from the Jolson vehicle *The Singing Fool* during the transition to pre-recorded soundtracks (see Chapter 2).

Breil's and Griffith's collaboration on *Intolerance* (1916) failed to equal either the artistic or commercial success of *The Birth of a Nation* in spite of a grossly excessive budget of nearly $2 million. Other joint projects included *The White Rose* (1923) and *America* (1924), Breil also contributed original music to films by other directors, including *The Birth of a Race* (dir. John W. Noble, 1918). In 1930, after the introduction of the sound film, a compressed version of *The Birth of a Nation* was released with a synchronized orchestral score adapted from Breil's by Louis Gottschalk, who had been responsible for the music for several of Griffith's later silent films (including *The Fall of Babylon*, 1919). The familiarity of Breil's score for *The Birth of a Nation* on both sides of the Atlantic led to an increased interest in the composition of original film music, no doubt prompted by the realization that the more sophisticated narrative structuring pioneered by Griffith seemed to demand more sophisticated accompaniment. Breil had shown how the character of individual Wagnerian leitmotifs could be transformed to serve dramatic developments: as he himself put it in 1921, 'the motif must in its further presentations be varied to suit the new situations. And the greatest development of the theme must not appear in the early part of the score, but towards the end where is the climax of the whole action' (quoted in Marks 1997, 156).

An entirely original score was composed for *The Fall of a Nation* (dir. Thomas Dixon, 1916) by Victor Herbert who, like some later commentators, objected to the use of pre-existing classical music on account of the potential distraction it offered to an audience already familiar with the material. (However, as Mitry pointed out (1998, 31), visual images of familiar objects can just as easily conjure up distracting personal reactions in a viewer.) According to a review in *Musical America*, 'Mr. Herbert's stimulating score clearly indicates the marked advance that music is making in the domain of the photoplay and should prove encouraging to composers who have not yet tried their hand at this type of work' (quoted in Karlin 1994, 161). *The Fall of a Nation* proved to be Herbert's sole venture into film scoring, but others were more prolific: among the notable composers of original scores in the USA were William Axt, Gottschalk, Henry Hadley, Leo Kempinski, Ernst Luz, David Mendoza, Joseph Nurnberger (who supplied an overture to Elinor's score for Griffith's *The Clansman*), William F. Peters, Rapée, Riesenfeld, Victor Schertzinger (including a score for Thomas Ince's *Civilization*, 1916), Louis Silvers, Mortimer Wilson and Zamecnik. Several of these had started their careers in film as cue-sheet compilers, and some collaborated with others in joint arrangements. A well-known pairing was Axt and Mendoza, who provided music for *Ben-Hur* (dir. Fred Niblo, 1925) and many other Metro-Goldwyn-Mayer productions; such team efforts continued as a familiar working pattern in Hollywood music departments during the early sound era. It remained common for individual films to be screened with different scores in different locations: *The Four Horsemen of the Apocalypse*, for example, was scored independently by Axt, Gottschalk, Luz and Riesenfeld (McCarty 2000, 119). High-profile original scores composed on the eve of the advent of sound films were Wilson's *The Thief of Bagdad* (dir. Raoul Walsh, 1924), and Riesenfeld's *The Covered Wagon* (dir. James Cruze, 1923), *Beau Geste* (dir. Herbert Brenon, 1926) and *Sunrise* (dir. F. W. Murnau, 1927) – the last reissued with synchronized recorded music in the same year as the phenomenal success of *The Jazz Singer* marked the demise of the silent film.

Although original scores were generally favourably received, Wilson's landmark contribution to *The Thief of Bagdad* was harshly criticized in one review for its harmonic boldness that incorporated 'bizarre extensions, augmentations, depleted sixteenths, vigorous minor forte passages and other incongruous music idioms under the guise of oriental music', the complainant picking up on the press agent's infelicitous hyperbole to ask: 'When the music of the world is at the disposal of an arranger and the libraries are rich in beautiful numbers, written by renowned composers, suitable for accompanying such a delightfully fantastic picture, why worry any one man to write a new "note for every gesture"?' (quoted in Anderson 1987, 288–9).

Charlie Chaplin and music for comedies

One successful director and star of silent films who took music especially seriously was Chaplin, who began his acting career as a protégé of the silent-comedy director Mack Sennett in 1913. In the following year Chaplin starred in Sennett's feature-length *Tillie's Punctured Romance* (1914), which includes a scene inside a typical nickelodeon of the day, complete with pianist located to one side of the projection screen. Chaplin directed all his own films from 1915 onwards and the popularity of his baggy-trousered tramp character earned him a million-dollar contract with First National in 1917. Chaplin liked to control all parameters of his films and as such can be regarded as an early *auteur* director. A self-taught amateur musician, he 'composed' the music for many of his films, believing (like many of the more didactically inclined film commentators of the time) that filmed entertainment could expose to good music audiences who might not otherwise be minded to listen to it. In reality, Chaplin depended heavily on the skills of various orchestrators and arrangers in order to realize his sometimes primitive musical raw material. On the evidence of the music by Eric James and Eric Rogers accompanying the 1971 re-release of Chaplin's directorial feature debut, *The Kid* (1921), a characteristic mixture of physical comedy and melodrama, the main ingredients were a sentimental lyricism, mock-sinister music for villains, circus slapstick for comic capers, a light operetta style enlivened by occasional ragtime syncopations, folksy jauntiness, stentorian pomposity and banal Edwardian waltzes. Use might also be made of familiar song melodies appropriate to the plot: examples are to be found in Arthur Kay's score to *The Circus* (1928), prepared under Chaplin's supervision at the time and reconstructed by Gillian Anderson in 1993. Wilfrid Mellers, commenting on Chaplin's recourse to banality as a source of pathos, described his music as a paradoxical 'apotheosis of the trivial' (Irving *et al.* 1954, 104).

After the advent of sound, Chaplin resisted dialogue but showed himself keen to use synchronized music and sound effects in his films; he claimed the credit for the music of all seven of his sound features for United Artists, including *City Lights* (1931), *The Great Dictator* (1940) and *Limelight* (1952), which won the Academy Award for Best Score when re-released in 1972. He confessed that a major advantage bestowed on his work by the sound film was the fact that he could now exert absolute control over the constitution of the soundtrack and not be at the mercy of the exigencies of differing projection venues, as was the case in the silent era. Among the composers who assisted him were Arthur Johnston (*City Lights*), Meredith Willson (*The Great Dictator*), Raymond Rasch and Larry Russell (*Limelight*). Carl Davis later paid tribute to the consistency of Chaplin's ideas: 'how is it that the Chaplin style maintains itself through widely differentiating and widely changing arrangers? There is a line that goes through, no matter who is working with him. He's saying, "I like it like this," he's humming the tunes, he's making the decisions about the harmonies and orchestrations. There are important lessons in melody and economy to be learned from Chaplin's music' (quoted in E. James 2000, xv).

In *Modern Times* (1936), silent segments featuring typical Chaplin clowning were juxtaposed with sometimes satirical sound elements; the

1.2 Charlie Chaplin (left) and David Raksin (right), reminiscing about their collaboration on *Modern Times* (1936) after seeing a final print of *Limelight* in 1952.

elaborate score was conducted by Alfred Newman and arranged by Edward Powell and newcomer David Raksin, who updated the silent-era idiom with a greater use of ostinato and dissonance. Raksin recalled the collaboration:

> Charlie would come in with these musical ideas and we would work on them together, because he didn't read or write music. It's a total mistake for people to assume that he did nothing. He had ideas. He would say, 'No, I think we should go up here, or we should go down there' . . . But he had fired me after a week and a half because he was not used to having anybody oppose him. And I was just saying, 'Listen, Charlie, I think we can do better than this.' Eventually, he hired me back on my own terms.
>
> (interviewed in R. S. Brown 1994, 285)

Raksin recalled the friction coming to a head when he dared to suggest Chaplin's old-time music-hall idiom was vulgar; after his reinstatement on the project he spent hours with Chaplin developing musical sketches while running the film repeatedly in the projection room (Raksin 1985, 162). During the subsequent recordings sessions, Newman snapped his baton and refused to work with Chaplin when the latter accused his exceptionally fine orchestra of complacency: the sessions had to be completed by orchestrator Eddie Powell, Raksin having sided with Newman in the dispute (Raksin 1985, 170).

Newman's and Raksin's Chaplin-based score in places included examples of a technique popularly known as 'mickey-mousing': illustrative musical effects synchronized with specific events in a film's physical action. The term was derived from Walt Disney's famous cartoon character (who first appeared on screen in 1928), but the procedure had also been common in music for live action. animation had borrowed some of its musical techniques from the circus, vaudeville and silent live-action comedies such as those starring Buster Keaton and Harold Lloyd. Gaylord Carter provided organ music for many of Lloyd's films in the later 1920s, and recalled how the comedian instructed him to make effects with musical devices, such as stinger chords, rather than resorting to realistic sound effects, and well understood the power of music to bolster weaker moments in his films: on one occasion Lloyd told the organist, 'when they're laughing, play soft. It's when they're *not* laughing that I need you' (McCarty 1989, 53–7). After its initial popularity in serious sound films of the Hollywood Golden Era, mickey-mousing became discredited for its essential redundancy and frequent crudity, and even as early as 1911 some commentators had expressed the opinion that comedies were best played without musical accompaniment to maximize their effectiveness (Altman 1996, 681).

Chaplin himself disliked mickey-mousing and strove to avoid it altogether when adding synchronized music to his silent films after his relocation to Europe in 1952. Between 1958 and 1976 he worked in Switzerland on new but old-fashioned scores to his classic comedies with his 'music associate', Eric James, who was legally bound not to claim authorship of any of the films' music – even when on their final project he had to suggest virtually all the material to the ailing Chaplin (E. James 2000, 66, 111–12). Like Raksin's, James's account of their collaboration reveals that Chaplin could not read music, nor play the piano with any more than three fingers, and would messily thump out tunes on the keyboard or sing them, using a tape recorder to preserve his ideas if his music associate were not present at the time, so that they could be polished, harmonized and subsequently scored: the process often took an inordinate length of time, with great attention paid to detail and much irascibility on Chaplin's part. An unusual form of shorthand, which demonstrated how unoriginal his thematic style could be, was to jot down verbal *aides-mémoire* indicating, for example, 'first two notes of Grieg's "Morning", next four notes, those in the opening bars of Liszt's "Liebesträume"' and so on (E. James 2000, 71). His obsessive desire to control all aspects of the soundtrack extended to personal interventions at recording sessions, on matters concerning both recording levels and aspects of scoring – James learning that if he cued principal melodies into various alternative instruments' performing parts in advance it would save considerable time when Chaplin changed his mind.

Early film music in Europe and the Soviet Union

The early market dominance of French and Italian film productions was checked by the First World War, which effectively allowed Hollywood to take the lead, though for a time film-making continued to flourish in those Scandinavian countries that took no part in the conflict. During the early war years, a major Hollywood studio could easily release several feature films per week, going on to make massive profits through distribution practices such as enforced block-booking and the monopolization of theatre ownership. At the end of the First World War, 90 per cent of all films shown in Europe were of American origin (D. Cook 2004, 41). As European cinema regained its strength during post-war reconstruction, it was not uncommon for established composers of concert music to compose film scores for major silent productions, this situation contrasting sharply with that prevailing in the USA. As Bernard Herrmann once remarked of later Hollywood practice, 'America is the only country in the world with so-called "film composers" – every other country has composers who sometimes do films' (quoted in Thomas 1997, 189).

In France, several prestigious scores accompanied bold films made by young avant-garde directors associated with the film theorist Louis Delluc. One of the most memorable of these so-called 'impressionist' films was Marcel L'Herbier's *L'inhumaine* (1924), featuring a score by Darius Milhaud and described by David Cook as 'an essay in visual abstraction thinly disguised as science-fiction; it ends with an apocalyptic montage sequence designed to synthesize movement, music, sound, and color [tinting]' (D. Cook 2004, 305). Swiss composer Arthur Honegger was asked to provide scores for Abel Gance's *La Roue* (1922), which Cocteau deemed to be as important to the development of cinema as Picasso had been to the development of painting, and *Napoléon* (1927), a film which Gance himself described as 'music of light which, gradually, will transform the great cinemas into cathedrals' (Ballard 1990, xxi). According to Henri Colpi, Gance drew his cinematic inspiration from musical structures: he used musical notation to help him edit part of *La Roue*, this notation then being passed on to Honegger so that he could match the filmic rhythm with appropriate music (R. S. Brown 1994, 20); but Honegger testified to Mitry that he in fact 'ran out of time and did not compose a single note for *La Roue*. He merely assembled an arrangement with special sound effects' (Mitry 1998, 384). Famously, the breathless editing in the film's depiction of the rapid motion of a train inspired Honegger's mechanistic symphonic poem *Pacific 231* (1924), a score which later formed the basis for filmic interpretations by Mikhail Tzekhanovsky (1933) and by Mitry himself (1949). Before his collaboration with Honegger, Gance had already conducted notable experiments with the music for his films, using it as a potent structural tool: for example, in *La Dixième symphonie* (1917; music by Michel-Maurice Levy), the continuity of the score compensated for, and complemented, the designedly bitty nature of the film's treatment of the process of assembling a symphony worthy to succeed Beethoven's Ninth (Lack 1997, 36–7).

Gance had been strongly influenced by Griffith's *Intolerance*, both in specific shooting and editing techniques and in a tendency towards megalomania. *Napoléon* originally ran to 28 reels in length, itself merely the first part of a planned six-film cycle, and was designed to have images shown on three screens simultaneously using the Polyvision process; Gance claimed that he developed this triple-screen presentation in order to realize his ambition that the 'visual harmony' and complexity of cinematic images should become directly analogous to a musical symphony (Lacombe and Porcile 1995, 34). Similar parallels were drawn by other French film-makers and theorists such as Emile Vuillermoz ('composition in the cinema is without a doubt subject to the confined laws of musical composition. A film is written and orchestrated like a symphony'), Léon Moussinac ('cinegraphic rhythm . . . has an obvious counterpart in musical rhythm . . . the images being to the eye what the musical sounds are to the ear'), Germaine Dulac ('only music is capable of stimulating the same sort of impression as the cinema . . . the visual idea . . . is inspired by musical technique far more than any other technique or ideal') and Léopold Survage ('The basis of my dynamic art is *colored visual form* (serving a similar function to that of sound in music)': quotations from Mitry 1998, 111–13). Survage declared the structural functions of musical and cinematic rhythm to be similar, though such parallels were felt to be specious by Mitry and many others (Mitry 1998, 118). Nevertheless, an overriding concern to achieve audio-visual 'rhythm' was an explicit preoccupation in Gance's screenplay for *Napoléon* and its visual realization. While shooting, Gance had music played on set by a trio of violin, cello and organ, claiming (somewhat more prosaically) that it was necessary 'not only to give the mood, but to keep everyone quiet. You can capture their attention more easily by the use of music. In the scene where the young Napoleon lies on the cannon . . . he had to cry in that scene. He couldn't, until the musicians played Beethoven's *Moonlight Sonata*' (quoted in Anderson 1988, xlii). During editing, some elaborate montage sequences were cut to fit music that had already been composed. The screenplay called for the *Marseillaise* and *Dies irae* to take starring roles: in a deleted scene, the organist playing the latter 'looks up with strange, terrible eyes . . . stops playing momentarily, and says in solemn, terrifying tones: "I am burying the Monarchy!"' (Ballard 1990, 40). Later versions of the film with synchronized sound featured a form of stereophonic reproduction for Honegger's score (D. Cook 2004, 308) and alternative music by Henry Verdun, a former silent-film pianist who hailed from the music halls and did not possess an academic background (Lacombe and Porcile 1995, 48).

Erik Satie composed an idiosyncratic score for *Entr'acte* (dir. René Clair, 1924), a short avant-garde film, designed to be screened between the two acts of Francis Picabia's Dadaist ballet *Relâche*, which (like many provocative artistic events in Paris at the time) came close to provoking riots amongst its first audiences. Satie not only composed the music: he also appeared in the film (as Milhaud was later to do in *La P'tite Lilie*), clutching his umbrella and appearing to jump off the terrace of the Théâtre des Champs-Elysées. Surrealist and witty, the essentially non-narrative *Entr'acte* was matched by fragmentary music which, while referring ironically to contemporaneous popular styles in places and wryly distorting Chopin's Funeral March to accompany shots of a camel-drawn cortège, remained as detached and dispassionate as its composer's concert works (Marks 1997, 167–85). As Stravinsky later commented of Satie's importance to twentieth-century music in general, he opposed to 'the vagueness of a decrepit impressionism a precise and firm language stripped of all pictorial embellishments' (Stravinsky 1936, 93). Satie's music, which was revived in a synchronized re-release of *Entr'acte* in 1967, was considerably ahead of its time in its use of obsessive repetition (easier to synchronize than fully blown themes, as later film composers were to discover) and fragmentary, unrelated ideas in a kaleidoscopic aural montage ideally suited to the creative dissolves, superimpositions and trick photography of Clair's cinematography. At times Satie chose to draw out the black humour in the images: for example, popular dance-hall clichés are heard when we see, in slow motion, the mourners cavorting behind the cortège. When they begin to run after the out-of-control hearse, however, the music turns surprisingly sombre and eventually builds up an extraordinary momentum for the frenetic and dizzying rollercoaster ride with which the film concludes. Some sense of autonomous structure is created by Satie's use of a spiky and insistent ritornello figure for the full ensemble, serving as an obvious musical punctuation mark whenever it recurs.

Less adventurous composers active in the French silent cinema were Marius François Gaillard (*El Dorado*, dir. L'Herbier, 1921), Roger Desormière (*A quoi rêvent les jeunes films?*, dir. Henri Chomette, 1924), Henri Rabaud (*Le Miracle des loups*, dir. Raymond Bernand, 1924; *Le Joueur d'échecs*, dir. Bernand, 1925) and Yves de La Casinière, who collaborated with Cavalcanti (*Rien que les heures*, 1927; *En Rade*, 1928). Concert composer Jacques Ibert provided music for Clair's *Un Chapeau de paille d'Italie* (1927), while *Le Mensonge de Nina Petrovna* (dir. Hanns Schwarz, 1929) launched the career of Maurice Jaubert, celebrated in the 1930s as the doyen of French film composers (see Chapter 8).

Cinema in Germany before the First World War featured substantial compilation and hybrid scores, such as those by Joseph Weiss for *Der Student von Prag* (dir. Stellan Rye, 1913), its Faustian scenario treated in a refreshingly non-theatrical manner, and by Becce for *Richard Wagner* (dir. Carl Froelich and William Wauer, 1913). Expressionism and *Angst* took their hold on post-war German cinema after the impact of *Das Cabinet des Dr Caligari* (dir. Robert Wiene, 1919), which was screened in New York in 1921 with an unorthodox selection of modern music by Debussy, Mussorgsky, Richard Strauss, Prokofiev, Ornstein, Schoenberg and Stravinsky (Altman 2004, 315), all arranged by Rothapfel and Rapée. Traditional compilation scores continued to be prepared in Germany by Becce, Erdmann and Friedrich Holländer for the films of F. W. Murnau (including *Nosferatu*, 1922) and other seminal directors. Gottfried Huppertz prepared the score for Fritz Lang's *Siegfried* (1923), which retold the Wagnerian myth without the accompaniment of Wagner's music. Lang detested Wagner, and resented the addition of Wagnerian cues to the film when it was shown outside Germany (D. Cook 2004, 98): in the USA, for example, *Siegfried* was screened in 1925 with a compilation score by Riesenfeld. Huppertz provided lush music for Lang's futuristic *Metropolis* (1927), couched in an expansive idiom clearly influenced by Strauss and Zemlinsky but in places hinting at the harmonic adventurousness of early Schoenberg. Rooted in leitmotivic procedures, including use of pre-existing themes such as the *Dies irae* and the *Marseillaise* (which is subjected to distortion when the underground workers turn rebellious), Huppertz's music includes mechanistic writing for machinery, dark-hued textures for the subterranean setting, an opulent Viennese waltz for flirtation in the gardens, pulsating and struggling music for the building of the Tower of Babel, delicate love music, and atmospheric impressionism for special effects such as the creation of the robot.

The Viennese composer Edmund Meisel achieved international fame with his music for German screenings of Soviet director Sergei Eisenstein's controversial *The Battleship Potemkin* (1925). One of at least three independent scores composed for the film at the time, Meisel's music remains the best known on account of the scandal it created: its hard-hitting idiom was deemed sufficiently disturbing as to warrant suppression of the score in some countries, including Germany. Eisenstein believed that *Potemkin*'s spectators should be 'lashed into a fury' by the music, and Meisel achieved this by composing aggressively percussive and militaristic cues that use repetitive material to powerful cumulative effect. As Alan Kriegsman commented of the combined impact of Eisenstein's vivid imagery and Meisel's score, 'For sheer visceral agitation, there is nothing in all film history to rival it' (quoted in Prendergast 1992, 14). In the words of an early American reviewer,

> The score is as powerful, as vital, as galvanic and electrifying as the film. It is written in the extreme modern vein, cacophonies run riot, harmonies grate, crackle, jar; there are abrupt changes and shifts in the rhythm; tremendous chords crashing down, dizzy flights of runs, snatches of half-forgotten melodies, fragments, a short interpolation of jazz on a piano.
>
> (*New York Herald Tribune*, 29 April 1928)

The writer noted, however, that the score was not bombastic throughout, and he was particularly moved by a melody Meisel introduced to represent the people of Odessa: 'It soars and endears itself to the heart. It is full of gratitude and the love of man for man. It's one of the warmest, tenderest passages that has found its way into the cinema-music repertoire.' Especially impressive was the manner in which the combination of Eisenstein's montage techniques and Meisel's obsessive music manipulated the spectator's temporal perceptions, as when a few seconds of real-time tension on the Quarterdeck are stretched out to form an utterly compelling extended climax in the final reel.

As evidenced by his later collaboration with Prokofiev (see Chapter 9), whose services he initially wished to acquire for *Potemkin*, Eisenstein believed in the necessity to establish a genre of 'sound-film' in which the music and images were governed by an interdependent audio-visual structure far more sophisticated than the formulaic approach to scoring already prevalent in the popular film industry. But not all commentators were lavish with their praise for the music of *The Battleship Potemkin*. The English composer Constant Lambert declared that Meisel's score was 'a great improvement on the ordinary cinema music of the time, but it would be idle to pretend that it was a worthy counterpart of the film itself' (Lambert 1934, 223). While recognizing that Meisel was only a 'modest composer' and that his score was 'certainly not a masterpiece', the ever-elitist Adorno and Eisler nevertheless praised him for avoiding a commercially viable idiom and noted that the music's modernistic aggressiveness impacted powerfully on the film's spectators (Adorno and Eisler 1994 [1947], 123–4).

Meisel also wrote music for Eisenstein's *October* and Walter Ruttmann's experimental documentary *Berlin: Symphony of a Great City* (both 1927; for the latter, see Chapter 7). Eisenstein drew attention to the audio-visual structural parallel by which Meisel's cue for the toppling of the statue of Alexander III in *October* was played in retrograde when the statue subsequently 'flew back together' (Taylor 1998, 181). In his music for Ilya Trauberg's *The Blue Express* (1929), Meisel used a jazz band, though the film was in some countries accompanied by Honegger's *Pacific 231* (Lambert 1934, 209). Meisel was fascinated by the possibilities of sound montage, undertaking experimental work at Berlin's German Film Research Institute and in 1927 issuing (on the Deutsche Grammophon label) recordings of onomatopoeic instrumental sound effects for filmic use; in 1930, shortly before his untimely death, he recorded his music for both *Battleship Potemkin* and *Blue Express* for the purposes of sound-on-disc synchronization when the films were re-released.

The development of cinema in the Soviet Union had been personally encouraged by Lenin, who (for its propaganda value) regarded it as the most important of all art forms: film production came under the control of the People's Commissariat of Education in 1919, two years after all those who worked in film – including pianists – were organized into a trade union. As in other countries, Soviet silent films could be accompanied by anything from a lone pianist up to a full orchestra of 60 players, as was to be found in Kiev's Shander cinema, where complete Tchaikovsky symphonies might be performed as part of the programme. Original but pastiche scores – one dating from as early as 1908 – were composed by Alexander Arkhangelsky, Dmitri Astradantsev, Yuri Bakaleinikov, Igor Belza, Mikhail Ippolitov-Ivanov and Georgii Kazachenko (Robinson 1990, 46–9; Egorova 1997, 5–7). Musical cue sheets proliferated in the early 1920s, the Soviet film industry having accelerated production in the wake of the enormously successful importation of Griffith's *Intolerance*.

Shostakovich, the most famous musician who worked in the Soviet silent cinema, initially gained valuable experience as a pianist at the Bright Reel, Splendid Palace and Piccadilly theatres in Leningrad, where he worked in the mid-1920s in order to support his family. Later he composed a flamboyant orchestral score for *The New Babylon*, directed by Grigori Kozintsev and Leonid Trauberg in 1929; as was the case with Saint-Saëns' score for *L'assassinat du Duc de Guise*, the music was made available in a version for solo piano for use in small venues. According to Kozintsev, 'we at once came to an agreement with the composer that the music was to be connected, not with the exterior action but with its purport, and develop in spite of the events, regardless of the mood of the scene' (quoted in Egorova 1997, 8). For this reason, Shostakovich in places supplied what might on the surface have appeared to be anempathetic accompaniment: in an article bemoaning the impoverished state of much film music, the composer drew attention to a scene in an empty restaurant at the end of the second reel which is overlaid with music depicting the imminent onslaught of the Prussian cavalry, and to a moment in the seventh reel in which the music depicts the melancholy and anxiety of a soldier, not the merry-making by which he is surrounded (Shostakovich 1981, 23; Pytel 1999, 26). Synchronization between image and music is notable during a seminal scene in the sixth reel in which piano music by Tchaikovsky is supplied for a diegetic keyboard meditation; however, as Fiona Ford has noted in her unpublished study of the film's musical sources, by building repeated material and pauses into the score at appropriate places Shostakovich afforded the conductor several 'recovery opportunities' so that image and music would not come to diverge too uncontrollably in live performance (Ford 2003, 39). Typical of its composer's early style and replete with sardonic parodies of popular idioms, including several slick waltzes to characterize the bourgeoisie and circus-like galops reminding the listener that Soviet film in the silent era remained deeply rooted in the cinema of attractions, Shostakovich's score made effective use of famous melodies such as Offenbach's can-can (from *Orpheus in the Underworld*) and the *Marseillaise*, these being appropriate to the film's French setting; no fewer than three songs from the French Revolution are used to support the Soviet ideology underlying the film's action. The *Marseillaise* had previously been used by Meisel (for a similar reason) in *Potemkin*.

In spite – or perhaps because – of its visual and musical interest, *The New Babylon* was not a success. Audiences found the film and its music incomprehensible, and some alleged that Shostakovich had been drunk when he composed the score. Like *Potemkin*, international paranoia resulted in the banning of the film in various countries. In the Soviet Union, Shostakovich's overly challenging music was quickly ditched, and thus one of the most intriguing and original scores of the silent era lay forgotten until its revival in the 1970s (see below).

The strong tradition of artistic independence from international styles that characterized the German and Soviet silent cinemas was the exception rather than the rule. Elsewhere the global market was dominated by films imported from the USA, and (to a lesser extent) influential European countries such as France, Germany, Italy and the UK; in less powerful countries, indigenous cinema and its associated film music inevitably struggled to come into existence during the silent era. A typical example was the situation in Greece. Film music in the silent era was here considered not for its aesthetic value, but principally as a means of luring audiences into cinemas; lavish orchestral accompaniments were reserved almost exclusively for American films featuring famous stars, with native Greek films usually having to make do with a pianist, sometimes with the addition of two to three instruments and perhaps a singer (Mylonás 2001, 22, 197). The high-profile nature of music for imported films was perpetuated by the fact that these films made the most money, thus readily permitting cinemas to finance the often costly orchestras required: one of the most popular ensembles serving this function in c.1914–15 was that directed by Iánnis Krassás at the Kyvélis cinema in Athens. By the end of the silent era, Krassás was music director at the capital's Pántheon cinema, where his contribution still mainly consisted of conducting popular classical pieces (such as overtures by Adam, Suppé and Rossini) as simple introductions and interludes to each film screened; there was no direct link between the subject-matter of the music and the subject matter of the picture. Original Greek film music first emerged in 1917 when Theófrastos Sakellarídis wrote a score for the Italian film operetta *The Nine Stars* and, in the following year, Dionýsios Lavrázas composed original music for voices and a fourteen-piece ensemble to accompany the imported film *Pierrot's Ring*. Sakellarídis went on to compose music for two more foreign films, *Daughter of the Waves* and *Barbara, Daughter of the Desert* – the latter featuring an original song entitled 'Kamómata' ('Antics'), which became a popular attraction and was featured by Krassás at the Pántheon in 1928–9. The first original score for a Greek silent film was that by Manólis Skouloúdis for *Daphnis and Chloë* (dir. Oréstes Láskos, 1931), partly based on 'archaic motifs'; but by this time the sound cinema had already made its way to Greece (Mylonás 2001, 18–23).

Postlude: the silent-film revival

The flexibility of sound provision in the silent cinema made the medium unpredictable, with films never shown in precisely the same way on more than one occasion. This spontaneity was immediately lost once synchro-nized soundtracks were permanently fixed onto film stock in the 1930s; but, although it may have seemed so to pessimists at the time, the loss was not irrevocable. Connoisseurs of silent cinema long lamented the sound era's inevitable neglect of film as an art enhanced by live sound, and various attempts were made to reinstate something of this abandoned dimension: the experimental film-maker Ken Jacobs, for example, mixed pre-recorded and live sound in screenings of his work (Weis and Belton 1985, 370), while Warhol, in *The Chelsea Girls* (1966), used two screens, one silent and the other with sound. Film-music scholars soon afterwards began to resurrect the glories of the silent era by embarking on a systematic preservation of historic scores, and this initiative was subsequently enhanced by the creative work of numerous composers – many of whom were born long after the demise of the silent cinema – commissioned to provide classic silent films with new music that at once tapped into the strengths of the old tradition and made the works seem more relevant to the modern age.

Landmark authentic scores for silent films were reconstructed, by schol-ars and performers such as Gillian Anderson and Dennis James, not merely to languish in historical archives but more importantly for resurrection in live performance in conjunction with screenings of the images for which they were originally prepared. Anderson's first such project was a recreation in 1979 of Victor Alix's and Léo Pouget's score to one of the last great classics of the silent era, *The Passion of Joan of Arc* (dir. Carl-Theodor Dreyer, 1928); her later reconstructions included Breil's score for *Intolerance* and Wilson's for *The Thief of Bagdad*. James resurrected the art of the cinema organist in a series of screenings at Indiana University, the Ohio Theatre and elsewhere from 1969 onwards, and in 1971 reconstructed the score to Griffith's *Broken Blossoms* (1919); he worked on many other reconstructions and live organ accompaniments, including music for Gance's *Napoléon* (McCarty 1989, 61–79). Many historic scores were systematically catalogued and preserved at national and university archives in the USA, with some institutions (notably New York's Museum of Modern Art) committed to mounting live perfor-mances of them to accompany showings of the relevant films. High-profile tours that married screenings and live orchestral accompaniment became relatively common, an important example being the exposure accorded to Shostakovich's music for *The New Babylon*: commercially recorded for the first time (in the form of a suite) by Soviet conductor Gennadi Rozhdestven-sky in 1976, Shostakovich's complete score was relaunched with the film at that year's Paris Film Festival and was widely performed live to accompany screenings in both Europe and the USA in 1982–3. At around the same time, the performing parts for Meisel's *Battleship Potemkin* music were dis-covered, permitting this seminal score to be reconstructed (Kalinak 1983).

Silent films were revived earlier than this within the Soviet Union, sometimes with memorable results: a new score to *Potemkin* was composed by
Nikolai Kryukov in 1950, and in 1967 a surprisingly effective score compiled
(by others) from pre-existing orchestral works by Shostakovich accompanied a re-release of *October* on the occasion of the fiftieth anniversary of
the Revolution, the composer's propulsive ostinato textures fitting well with
images such as the rapid jump cuts conveying the stuttering of machine-
gun fire and here proving just as agitational as Meisel's *Potemkin*. Similarly, a new score for *Potemkin* was fashioned from parts of Shostakovich's
symphonies when the film was restored to mark its fiftieth anniversary in
1975.

New scores were widely commissioned in the 1980s to accompany re-
releases of silent films in theatrical, televisual and video formats. Carl Davis
scored *Napoléon* (1980) for Thames Television and the British Film Institute, including some of Honegger's original music, and received a standing
ovation at the London première (Ballard 1990, xiii); Davis also scored *The
Thief of Bagdad* (1984), *Intolerance* (1986) and the 1925 *Ben-Hur* (1987),
his music for the last taking inspiration from Bruckner to achieve reverence
in biblical scenes. Other Davis projects included Griffith's *Broken Blossoms*
(1919) and Eric von Stroheim's *Greed* (1923), and a British tour of his new
music to *The Phantom of the Opera* (dir. Rupert Julian, 1925) with the Hallé
Orchestra in 2002 continued his popular successes in the field. In 1986,
Griffith's *Intolerance* celebrated its seventieth birthday and was furnished
with a new score by Antoine Duhamel and Pierre Jansen at the Avignon
Film Festival. In sharp contrast to traditional scoring techniques, Giorgio
Moroder supplied an up-to-date (and therefore almost instantly dated) synthesized music track to a shortened and colour-tinted restoration of Lang's
Metropolis in 1983; the inclusion of modern pop songs provided, according
to Claudia Gorbman, 'a choruslike commentary on what is seen, sometimes with brilliant irony. Some listeners, their primary attention divided
between the lyrics and the [newly subtitled] "dialogue," find this difficult
to assimilate' (Gorbman 1987, 20). *Metropolis* has inspired many modern
musicians to endow it with new music, including the Alloy Orchestra, Club
Foot Orchestra, Peter Osborne, Bernd Schultheis and Wetfish. Huppertz's
original orchestral score was reconstructed by Berndt Heller for video release
in 2002. Two years later the Pet Shop Boys' Neil Tennant wrote a new score
for *Potemkin*.

Other composers, arrangers, keyboard players and ensembles who contributed to the silent-film revival included James Bernard, Neil Brand (of
London's National Film Theatre), Carmine Coppola (who provided a conventional hybrid score for the American release of *Napoléon* in 1980), The
Curt Collective, Alan Fearon, Edward Dudley Hughes, Robert Israel, Adrian

Johnston, Benedict Mason, Richard McLaughlin, David Newman, Michael Nyman, Paul Robinson, Geoff Smith (applying his hammered dulcimers to classics of German silent expressionism), Joby Talbot, Jo Van den Booren and Wolfgang Thiele (who reworked Erdmann's music to *Nosferatu*). Veteran cinema organists such as Gaylord Carter came out of retirement to contribute their own reminiscences of the silent era: Carter had remained active as a silent-film accompanist in the 1960s and in 1986–7 recorded historically authentic accompaniments for the video release of Paramount silents. These included Lang's *The Golden Lake* (1919) and *The Diamond Ship* (1920), and DeMille's *The Ten Commandments* (1923), the original compilation score for which had helped to popularize Dvořák's *New World* Symphony and Tchaikovsky's Piano Concerto No. 1 (Huntley [1947], 27). At the other end of the stylistic spectrum, British saxophonist Jan Kopinski's slowly evolving modal jazz found an unlikely application in his 2004 score to Alexander Dovzhenko's *Earth* (1930), where it was nevertheless perfectly in tune with the leisurely pace and haunting visual beauty of the Russian director's bold images.

Adrian Johnston's music for Harold Lloyd's *Hot Water* (1924; Thames TV, 1994) is a model example of a silent-film score conceived for a modern

1.3 George Fenton conducts a live performance of his orchestral music from the BBC television series *The Blue Planet* at Manchester in 2006, sustaining the venerable tradition of touring exhibitions of silent film.

television audience. It uses a mere six instruments with resourcefulness and imagination in an idiom sufficiently sophisticated to satisfy contemporary tastes but deeply rooted in traditional scoring techniques, even down to the prominent use of the *Dies irae* in a ghostly sequence. Carter recalled how he used this melody in his organ accompaniment to the unmasking scene of *The Phantom of the Opera*: as seen above, the plainchant was used in Huppertz's score for *Metropolis* and thereafter remained one of the most frequently quoted melodies in later film music. Prominent later appearances in films of widely differing styles and genres include *Foreign Correspondent* (dir. Alfred Hitchcock, 1940; music by Alfred Newman), in which it is sung diegetically by an unseen choir in London's Westminster Cathedral before an attempt is made to push the film's hero off the tower; in Erik Nordgren's score to Ingmar Bergman's *The Seventh Seal* (1957), where it is several times suggested merely by its first four notes, in addition to receiving a full-blown arrangement sung diegetically by a procession of monks in the context of the Black Death; in three of Bernard Herrmann's scores: his music for the death of Hydra in *Jason and the Argonauts* (dir. Don Chaffey, 1963), in *The Bride Wore Black* (dir. François Truffaut, 1967), and delicately on a harp for a graveyard scene in *Obsession* (dir. Brian De Palma, 1975); in *The Shining* (dir. Stanley Kubrick, 1980; music by Walter Carlos), where an electronic version alluding to its arrangement by Berlioz creates a sense of foreboding in the main-title sequence; in *Sleeping with the Enemy* (dir. Joseph Ruben, 1990; music by Jerry Goldsmith), where its famous incarnation in Berlioz's *Symphonie fantastique* appears diegetically on a hi-fi system as a symbol for the male protagonist's depravity; and in the fantasy animated musical *The Nightmare Before Christmas* (dir. Tim Burton, 1993; music by Danny Elfman).

Such is the renewed popularity of silent-film screenings with live musical accompaniment that other media, such as television documentary, have in recent years been adapted for this purpose. Extracts from British composer George Fenton's substantial orchestral score to the monumental BBC TV series about the oceans, *The Blue Planet*, have been performed live in several countries, commencing with a show in London's Hyde Park in 2002 in which Fenton conducted a live accompaniment to a large-screen projection of the stunning wildlife photography from the series. The venture led to a release of a documentary film for theatrical exhibition, *Deep Blue* (dir. Andy Byatt and Alastair Fothergill, 2004).

2 Sound on track

With our modern obsession with technology, and related tendency to equate technological advancement with improved quality, the introduction of synchronized sound to the motion picture in the late 1920s seems, with hindsight, to have been not only inevitable but downright essential – a *sine qua non* of the development of a meaningful cinematic art. In spite of this widely held view, film soundtracks were until the last quarter of the twentieth century almost entirely ignored by film scholars and theorists, who continued to devote exclusive attention to the visual image. Rick Altman has argued that this situation arose as a result of two deeply ingrained fallacies: one historical, in which the introduction of sound to the cinema may be regarded as an afterthought, and the other ontological, in which it is believed that sound must by its very nature always be regarded as subservient to the primacy of the image as the chief vehicle of meaning and expression (Weis and Belton 1985, 50). Theorist Rudolf Arnheim went so far as to consider the introduction of sound as directly violating the motion picture's ontological status (Flinn 1992, 41). At the opposite extreme was Walter Ruttmann's experimental documentary *Week-End*, which in 1930 took the bold step of dispensing with an image track altogether and simply running through the projector a suggestive soundtrack made up from dialogue, noise and music (Winter 1941, 154).

It is a curious paradox that the most famous of early film pioneers, Thomas Edison, had established recorded sound first and then sought to add moving images to it – a reversal of most film-makers' subsequent priorities. Tom Gunning has drawn attention to the enormous and lasting psychological impact of Edison's innovations, noting that 'the phonograph had in effect separated the human senses, divorcing ear from eye, and . . . Edison's original intention in pursuing motion pictures was to bring them back together'. This ideal was not motivated by a 'need for perfect representation or a bourgeois desire for coherence', but sprang from 'a deep anxiety aware of the manner in which technology, while doubling the human, also seems to be splitting it up, transforming the nature of human subjectivity' (Abel and Altman 2001, 16, 29).

A sound debate

Naturalistic sound in a motion picture may be deemed necessary only in the interests of cinematic realism. Even from the earliest days, however, directors had shown markedly differing attitudes towards the latter concept, and their work had tended to polarize in one of two directions. On the one hand, the Lumières and their followers devoted their efforts to a naturalistic, quasi-documentary style of reportage, their films termed *actualités*. On the other, the illusionist Méliès had developed a style of fantasy narrative laced with symbolism which was important not only for breaking away from realism, but for developing a whole host of technical devices (including time-lapse photography, superimposition and dissolves) in order to achieve freshness and originality of presentation: in short, Méliès 'broke from the photographic impulses of the primitives to show that the movie camera could lie' (Parkinson 1995, 18). As with painting and photography, it was quickly shown that, even if such a thing were attainable, a realistic presentation of events was not necessarily desirable.

The introduction of synchronized sound, on the simple realist level a natural extension of the filmic medium, necessitated a marked shift of emphasis in terms of the medium's visual syntax. As the French film composer Maurice Jaubert commented of the soon-to-be-outmoded silent film:

> Driven by the absence of speech to a lengthy method of visual paraphrase in order to make the story clear, the silent film built up for itself, little by little, a special idiom designed chiefly to compensate for the silence of the actors. This convention became familiar to all habitués of the cinema, who believed, legitimately in those days, that it gave occasion for a special art of the screen – an art which in its finest development would be essentially allusive, and so poetic. But as soon as speech came to destroy this early convention, the cinema – although hardly anyone recognised it at first changed its character. It became, it is, and it remains *realistic*. (Davy 1937, 106)

The relationship of the new sound component to the cinema's musical provision, and the artistic possibilities opened up by the sound element itself, proved to be more complex than might have been the case without this fundamental shift in aesthetic emphasis.

Many influential film-makers and theorists in the 1920s were deeply sceptical about the value of synchronized sound, and it is instructive to examine the principal arguments generated by consideration of whether the sound film represented a significant advance on the potentialities of the silent medium. Documentary maker Paul Rotha complained in 1930 that 'The attempted combination of speech and pictures is the direct opposition of two separate mediums, which appeal in two utterly different ways', and feared that an obsession with sound would now take precedence over the visual image (D. Cook 2004, 225). Others continued to draw attention to the redundancy of sounds which merely duplicated or reinforced the actions portrayed on screen. (Considering so much effort had been expended on finding mechanisms by which sound and image could be accurately synchronized, as detailed below, this was somewhat ironic.) Béla Balázs predicted that the sound film would 'destroy the already highly developed culture of the silent film', going so far as to deem it 'a catastrophe, the like of which had never occurred before in the history of any other art'. As late as the early 1950s he found little cause to revise this bleak prophecy, lamenting the preponderance of 'speaking photographed theatre' and still expressing the hope that, as the silent film had before it, the sound film would finally reveal 'new spheres of human experience . . . based on new principles' (Balázs 1953, 194–5).

In 1928, the Soviet film-makers Sergei Eisenstein, Vsevolod Pudovkin and Grigori Alexandrov published their *Statement on Sound* in which they stressed the importance of continuing the suggestive montage techniques already developed in the Soviet silent cinema, now threatened by the new technology. If sound were to be used merely realistically, they argued, it

> will destroy the culture of montage, because every mere *addition* of sound to montage fragments increases their inertia as such and their independent significance; this is undoubtedly detrimental to montage which operates above all not with fragments [*per se*] but through the *juxtaposition* of fragments.
>
> *Only the contrapuntal use* of sound vis-à-vis the visual fragment of montage will open up new possibilities for the development and perfection of montage.
>
> *The first experiments in sound must aim at a sharp discord with the visual images.* (Braudy and Cohen 1999, 361; emphases in original)

The writers predicted that such tension would result in an 'orchestral counterpoint' of vision and sound, and claimed that their 'contrapuntal method' of structuring would have the benefit of becoming a truly international cinematic language. (This last concern was, in their case, the result of artistic idealism: in contrast Hollywood moguls at this time were, for more commercial reasons, concerned that the sound film, with its heavy dependency on dialogue, would not prove to be as exportable as had been the case with silent films, which readily permitted the insertion of intertitles in the language of countries to which they were sold.) In a book on film technique published in 1929, Pudovkin asserted that 'the first function of sound is to *augment the potential expressiveness of the film's content*' (Pudovkin 1958, 184) and advocated the imaginative use of asynchronous sound to this end. Examples of varying degrees of audio-visual counterpoint in Soviet films made in *c.*1930–34 have been closely analysed by Kristin Thompson (1980).

The term 'counterpoint' has persisted in theoretical writings on film music, not without controversy. Jean Mitry felt that only through the use of multiple screens, as in Gance's *Napoléon*, could visual images meaningfully reflect the independent simultaneous strands of true musical counterpoint (Mitry 1998, 142), and condemned fashionable and ill-considered uses of the term to describe the combination of music and image: 'Counterpoint is precisely the sort of impressive word which looks very good in magazine articles; however, that does not mean that it is any the less irritating, since it is generally misused . . . [T]o refer to counterpoint with reference to the opposition of feelings expressed by music and film is utter nonsense. Would it be an oversimplification to use the only really appropriate word to describe the effect, namely *contrast*?' (Mitry 1998, 250). The influential French film theorist Michel Chion also drew attention to the inappropriate way in which the term has often been used when divorced from its strictly musical meaning, noting that 'dissonant harmony' might be a more accurate musical parallel for 'momentary discord between the image's and sound's figural natures' (Chion 1994, 37). Kathryn Kalinak asserts that the concepts of 'parallel' and 'contrapuntal' music in film reinforce a regrettable tendency for music always to seem subservient to the visual image (Kalinak 1992, 24–6), though overstates the case somewhat, since the theorists she cites – Rudolf Arnheim, Balázs and Kracauer – all stress that music can be free to pursue its own course in film in addition to reinforcing what is latent in the image. As far as the early makers of sound films were concerned, the relationship between music and image centred far more on the difference between 'realistic' diegetic music, for which the source was immediately obvious, and more ambiguous applications of music and sound in which their possibly diegetic source was not explicit. The two approaches were later dubbed 'synchronous' and 'asynchronous' respectively (Kracauer 1960, Chapter 7). Although opinion was sharply divided between these two options in the early years of the sound film, as with many other technical innovations in art of all kinds the most fruitful way forwards proved to be various hybrid accommodations between the two approaches. In modern cinema, carefully manipulated contrasts between diegetic and nondiegetic music and sound, and the blurring of the distinction between the two categories, remain powerful tools for creating tension or ambiguity.

One obvious drawback of a fixed soundtrack was its inevitable exclusion of any possibility that a film's sound provision might differ from one screening to the next. (This rigidity in film exhibition of course applies equally to the fixed visual images, and Polish director Krzysztof Kieślowski dreamt of releasing his *La Double vie de Véronique* (1991) in numerous slightly different versions so that movie-going would retain an element of chance, the spectator not knowing in advance which of them would be screened at a particular venue: see Stok 1993, 188.) Few musicians would argue against the notion that, in many ways, live performance is preferable to recorded music – for reasons such as spontaneity, immediacy of impact, richness of sound, spatial awareness and so on; another important factor is that live performances of the same piece, as in different performances of the same play, can vary significantly. The importance of these performative variables disappeared from sight as a result of the general misconception that silent-film music was – like the silent cinema in general – essentially 'primitive'. It was only with the renascent interest in live music for films towards the end of the twentieth century that this vital dimension of the art was recaptured. The principal negative factors in the special case of live cinema music are the difficulties of synchronization with the visual image and effective balance of volume with other elements of the total sound component, though the latter is no more challenging than the task facing the conductor of opera or concerti.

Whatever the artistic merits and demerits of the use of recorded music in the cinema, a direct practical consequence of the introduction of pre-recorded soundtracks in the late 1920s was the catastrophic downturn in the employment opportunities available to musicians who had made careers for themselves in movie-theatre bands. A formerly flourishing livelihood disappeared almost overnight, in spite of vociferous protests by several musicians' unions, most prominently the American Federation of Musicians. The problem was by no means restricted to the USA: in the UK, for example, as much as 80 per cent of all professional music-making in *c.*1928 came as a direct consequence of the silent film (Ehrlich 1985, 199). In Germany, musicians were in early 1929 dismissed without notice as movie theatres were adapted for sound: the 200 players who had in 1928 been working for the theatres of Berlin's powerful conglomerate, UFA (Universum Film Aktiengesellschaft), had dwindled to around 50 by 1930, these having been retained because silent films had not yet fully died out. In late 1930, some 8,000 German musicians had been sacked as a direct consequence of the advent of the sound film, this figure nearly doubling in the following three years (Kater 1992, 26). In France, an article in *Ciné-Journal* published on 7 December 1928 drew attention to what the editors regarded as 'perhaps the greatest danger since professional musicians first came into existence':

> Mechanical music is substituting immediate, human performance.
> Everyone is threatened: already some cinema orchestras are being abolished and replaced with soundtrack equipment. Others will follow. No musician,

no conductor should be indifferent to such a threat. If strenuous measures
are not taken, an army of unemployed will be created, who will threaten
colleagues still in employment . . . But aren't the musicians, in the
circumstances, the architects of their own misfortune? . . . [A soundtrack]
repertoire is being created that will one day supplant orchestral
performance almost completely . . . Faced with such a danger, and while
awaiting new regulations appropriate to the new situation, the union
committee [of the Fédération Française de la Musique] has decided to
forbid, until further notice, all soundtrack recordings.

(Lacombe and Porcile 1995, 44)

As might have been predicted, in the face of industrial action French producers simply set about recording their soundtracks abroad, an act provoking
further hostility from the trade press – in which cultural chauvinism reared
its ugly head. On 3 January 1930, *Ciné-Journal* deplored the glut of foreign
films with foreign music and declared that 'a significant part of the musical
accompaniment of synchronized films shown in France must be given over
to French music . . . the cinema should not become in France the instrument
of the infiltration of foreign views into the national culture' (Lacombe and
Procile 1995, 45).

New technology

Towards the end of the silent era, various devices had been introduced to
aid musicians in their attempts to synchronize their performances with
the action on screen. In Berlin, for example, Carl Robert Blum invented a
rhythmonome, which he exhibited in 1926. This recorded sound in the form
of a rhythmogram, which charted the exact rhythmic course of the music in
a diagrammatic form that was played back in accurate synchronization with
the image projector so the conductor could match the tempo to the moving
diagram; the device found an application in live theatre, being used for the
first production of Ernst Křenek's opera *Jonny spielt auf* in 1927. Milhaud,
who used the device at Hindemith's suggestion at Baden-Baden in 1929 (see
Chapter 7), recalled that Blum's apparatus made it possible

to run off the film at the same time as a reel of similar size bearing two
staves on which the music was written, so that the music could follow the
slightest movement of the picture. During the performance, the musical
score was thrown on the conductor's desk at the same time as the images
were projected on to the screen. In this way the conductor was able to
synchronize his playing exactly with the film.   (Milhaud 1952, 174)

A similar invention, named *cinépupitre*, had been developed in Paris by Pierre de la Commune and used by Honegger when conducting his music for Gance's *La Roue* in 1922 (London 1936, 66–8). At the Paris Opéra première of Gance's *Napoléon* in 1927, the unusual priority accorded to the music saw the conductor equipped with a device for altering the speed of the projection to suit the pacing of the score (Abel 1996, 40).

The next important step, which sounded the death knell for live music in the cinema, was the use of phonograph recordings of music linked to the projector and played back with some degree of synchronization – an idea with which inventors had been toying since the first attempts around 1900 by Messter in Germany and Gaumont in France. Use of recorded music was relatively common in early movie theatres, being especially popular in France where Pathé, like Edison, had a vested interest in promoting his phonographs as much as his moving pictures; but, because they were not yet synchronized, phonographic accompaniments to film screenings were generally considered to be inferior to those provided by live ensembles. In the 1920s, appropriate recordings could be sourced from sound libraries that supplemented printed cue sheets for live music, and synchronized playback equipment became more widespread. The sound operators, who controlled the turntables while watching the screen, were sometimes musical directors from the silent era whose jobs were now in peril. According to London,

> The individual turn-tables had a sound-overlapping plant, that is, the music on one record could be made to fade into the next . . . If a third turn-table was available, one could venture at certain junctures on an attempt to set some noise, perhaps even words, in counterpoint against the running music . . . These 'acoustic overlaps' . . . were at that time necessary to preserve the illusion of continuous line in the musical accompaniment to some extent . . . Individual volume controls, one fitted to each turn-table, which enabled the dynamics to be graded at will, completed this system.
>
> (London 1936, 86–7)

Cinematic disc-jockeys were aided by the availability of 'illustrative scores' for specific pictures, which gave correspondences between the duration of each segment of film and the recorded music intended to accompany it. Films which had live sound recorded on disc at the time of shooting, or which had orchestral music specially recorded in synchronization with the image, were screened using automated playback devices:

> The projecting machine for the sound-on-disc film consisted of a normal projector, from which a flexible coupling proceeded to revolve the appropriate gramophone record . . . The difficulties of the transition from one record to the next were overcome as follows. Shortly before one record had finished playing, an electromagnetic coupling was switched on through a small metal cell attached at a suitable point in the perforation holes of the

film strip running through the projector. This coupling in turn set the
second record in motion by means of the flexible driving shaft mentioned
above. When the latter had reached the proper speed, the first record
stopped, and the operator could then change the records at his leisure and
arrange their 'entrance' at the exact point indicated.   (London 1936, 106)

An example of a silent film which was intended to be screened with a portion
of disc-recorded music was Griffith's *Dream Street* (1921), the first American
film to include a mechanically synchronized song; in the event, the synchronized sequence was quickly abandoned on account of poor synchronization
and inferior sound reproduction (Barrios 1995, 15). Prophetically, the large
discs used in many movie theatres played at a speed of $33\frac{1}{3}$ revolutions per
minute, many years in advance of the recording industry's adoption of this
as the standard speed for the long-playing record.

The most successful method for supplying sound-on-disc was the Vitaphone system developed by the Western Electric Company and purchased
by Warner Bros. in 1925. At first sceptical about its potential, both artistically
and commercially, Warners restricted the new technology to the recording
of musical accompaniments in standard silent-film idioms, not daring to
attempt to record and synchronize dialogue; they nevertheless marketed
the technology aggressively, both in the USA and Europe, by drawing attention to the fact that even small movie theatres could now, in effect, house
their own large (if pre-recorded) orchestras with none of the expense or
inconvenience such accompaniment had formerly entailed. The system was
launched at a lavish presentation in New York in August 1926, at which
several short sound films showcasing the work of prominent musicians
were followed by the screening of a major new feature, *Don Juan* (dir. Alan
Crosland), with a special Vitaphone score composed by William Axt and
David Mendoza and recorded by the New York Philharmonic. In a specially
filmed address, Will H. Hays (the leading light of Motion Picture Producers
and Distributors of America Inc., a regulatory body popularly known as the
Hays Office) informed the audience:

> In the presentation of these pictures, music plays an invaluable part. The
> motion picture too is the most potent factor in the national appreciation of
> good music. That service will now be extended as the Vitaphone will carry
> symphony orchestrations to the town halls of the hamlets. It has been said
> the art of vocalists and instrumentalists is ephemeral, that he [*sic*] creates
> but for the moment. Now neither the artist nor his art will ever wholly die.
>   (quoted in Barrios 1995, 22)

The Vitaphone shorts essentially perpetuated the vaudeville-like bill of
fare at typical movie theatres: they could be shown as part of a variety
programme, only now the minor live performers of the provinces were

2.1 Poster for *The Jazz Singer* (Warner Bros., 1927), depicting one of the sensational scenes in which Al Jolson's voice was recorded live and synchronized with the marvel of Vitaphone technology.

replaced by the finest and most famous singing and acting stars of the day in recorded form.

Eager to capitalize on the success of Vitaphone, which had impressed far more in the shorts than in the highly conventional *Don Juan*, Warner Bros. quickly released the first 'talkie', *The Jazz Singer* (dir. Crosland, 1927), starring Al Jolson, which was accompanied by a Vitaphone score conducted by Louis Silvers. Jolson had already appeared in Vitaphone shorts, but *The Jazz Singer* now made his a household name. The film's main attractions, which had materialized almost by accident, were the brief sequences of dialogue which Jolson reportedly improvised on set as the recording apparatus was running: unlike the stiff and stilted formal presentations of speech and music in the shorts, 'here was Jolson not only singing and dancing but speaking informally and spontaneously to other persons in the film as someone might do in reality. The effect was not so much of *hearing* Jolson speak as of *over-hearing* him speak, and it thrilled audiences bored with the [melodramatic] conventions of silent cinema' (D. Cook 2004, 210). Jolson's featured songs were diegetic, and recorded on set live. In all other respects, *The Jazz Singer* was a thoroughly conventional silent film, with intertitles used to render other dialogue and essential information, to which a disc-recorded synchronized score had been added in an equally conventional silent-film idiom. An old warhorse of the compilation score, the love theme from Tchaikovsky's fantasy overture *Romeo and Juliet*, featured prominently – not because it had the remotest relevance to the film's plot, but simply because it was a popular tune of the day; it appeared alongside the equally well-known Jewish melody *Kol Nidre*, used to establish the cultural milieu for the plot.

In 1928, Warner Bros. issued *Tenderloin* (dir. Michael Curtiz) and *Glorious Betsy* (dir. Crosland), both hybrids that united silent-film procedures with sporadic Vitaphone inserts carrying synchronized dialogue and song; in *Glorious Betsy*, the *Marseillaise* was sung by a star of the Metropolitan Opera, André de Segurola. The first film to do away with silent sequences altogether was Warners' *Lights of New York* (dir. Bryan Foy), released in the summer of 1928 and significant not only for its use of synchronized dialogue throughout, but also for its uncredited but competent musical score. Warners' preferred Vitaphone composer remained Silvers, who for their second 'all-talkie', *The Terror* (dir. Roy Del Ruth), supplied an 'elaborate wraparound musical score' that threatened to swamp the actors' voices (Barrios 1995, 48). In September of this same momentous year, Warners issued a second Jolson vehicle, *The Singing Fool* (dir. Lloyd Bacon), another uncomfortable hybrid of stilted silent-film presentation and live Vitaphone inserts for which Silvers provided more overblown and omnipresent orchestral music; the film contained two spectacularly successful songs, one of which (Buddy DeSylva's 'Sonny Boy') not only sold over a million copies as sheet music but also a million sound recordings (Sanjek 1988, vol. 3, 106–7). Both *The Jazz Singer* and *The Singing Fool*, which owed their appeal far more to their star's charisma and sheer novelty value rather than to any inherent artistic merit, were widely exported – in both Vitaphone and silent versions – and Warner Bros. saw its profits increase six-fold within a year. After the advent of sound-on-film, the company doggedly persisted with outmoded Vitaphone technology and only began to employ soundtracks recorded on celluloid in January 1931; even then, it continued to release films in both formats until the middle of the decade (Barrios 1995, 117).

In an attempt to rival Warners' initial success with Vitaphone, the Fox Corporation released *Sunrise* (dir. F. W. Murnau) with a synchronized score by Hugo Riesenfeld in 1927, and re-released in New York the silent films *Seventh Heaven* (dir. Frank Borzage) and *What Price Glory?* (dir. Raoul Walsh) with synchronized music by Ernö Rapée replacing the compilation scores prepared by R. H. Bassett for the Los Angeles premières of both films (McCarty 2000, 36, 237). More important was Fox's development of a sound-on-film system called Movietone, launched in a series of newsreels also commencing in 1927. The Fox newsreels were shot with a single sound-and-image camera, which permitted a rapid development of the film (no editorial synchronization being required) ideal for the prompt reporting of newsworthy events; Movietone's first film, of the West Point parade, demonstrated how diegetic sound could provide its own spatial perspective, since the music of the marching band inevitably crescendoed as it came towards the camera (Barrios 1995, 30). Western Electric was also developing a sound-on-film system at the same time as it was promoting Vitaphone; another rival optical soundtrack system, Photophone, was under development at Radio Corporation of America (RCA). In 1927, a Big Five agreement was signed by five leading studios, in which they undertook to adopt whichever sound-on-film system proved best suited to their needs; this was considered to be the Western Electric system, though RCA's Photophone remained an important competitor, and was showcased by the company's newly merged studio interest, Radio-Keith-Orpheum (RKO), which began producing sound films in 1929.

Hundreds of silent films in production at the time of these momentous innovations had optical soundtracks added to them so that the work and investment would not be wasted, while the rewiring of cinemas to accommodate the new technology proceeded at a phenomenal rate. The operation was horrendously expensive – even the Vitaphone system cost some $23,000 per installation (Barrios 1995, 26) – and required substantial backing from investors. Consequently it was the introduction of sound that was in large part responsible for the domination of film production by wealthy businessmen-turned-producers who subsequently came, quite literally, to call the shots in Hollywood.

Photographing sound

Sound-on-disc was both cumbersome and limited in its applications, and for many years before its advent inventors had been vying to perfect and patent various methods of recording synchronized sound directly onto film stock. In 1904, Eugène A. Lauste carried out the first successful attempt to record sound as an optical pattern using a photo-electric process. Similar experiments, in France, Germany and the USA, explored ways of recording sound on a film strip in the form of surface indentations, swollen thicknesses, roughened surfaces and differences of electrical resistance in the material itself (London 1936, 101); there had also been some experimentation with magnetic tape, though this was not to be generally adopted for sound recording until the 1950s. The leading sound-on-film system was developed by Tri-Ergon from *c.*1918, and their films were screened in Germany in 1922. Developments proceeded apace once important innovations in the field of radio and telephone technology were adapted for use in experimental sound-on-film systems. The American inventor Lee De Forest exhibited his sound-on-film movies in New York from 1923, including some with pre-recorded musical scores composed by Riesenfeld. De Forest made his name primarily as a pioneer of the electrical amplifier; he had attempted to persuade the Hollywood studios to adopt his sound-on-film system, without success, but briefly enjoyed fame in London in 1925–6 when his films – which featured recorded dialogue, sound effects and musical scores – were screened to some acclaim (Huntley [1947], 30). Only in 1935 was De Forest's innovative film work legally recognized in the USA, when he received substantial compensation for the widespread efforts of his unscrupulous competitors to infringe upon his patent.

Optical-soundtrack technology was, in conception if not execution, very simple. During the recording process, electrical impulses from a microphone were fed via an amplifier to a light source which illuminated the film stock as it ran past a small slit. The resulting soundtrack ran down the extreme edge of the same strip of celluloid that carried the visual images, and was blanked off when run through the projector so that it did not appear on the screen. The projector housed a photo-electric cell that contained selenium, a substance of which the electrical conductivity varies according to the intensity of the light striking it; the cell converted the optical soundtrack patterns back into electrical impulses which were fed to an amplifier and loudspeaker. Although sound and image were directly synchronized by this method, the soundtrack patterns for each photographic frame were recorded nineteen frames in advance of the relevant image, for two reasons: this physical separation was required by the distance between the image projection gate and the audio photo-electric cell (which could not be housed in the same part of the projector), and the gap also meant that a transport mechanism could be devised whereby the film could be made to pass smoothly across the photo-electric cell in contrast to its designedly jerky frame-by-frame motion through the visual projection gate, which would have seriously distorted audio output. Tri-Ergon had invented and patented a mechanism for precisely this purpose, and their monopoly on the device earned them a considerable income from projector manufacturers before William Fox acquired the rights to their invention in 1927 (D. Cook 2004, 207). The nineteen-frame separation was ideal for sound synchronization in large cinemas but the distance was later increased, first to 20 frames and then 21 frames, in order to reflect the demands of differing projection conditions. When films appear to have poor sound synchronization in the modern cinema, this is usually because the operator has threaded the film incorrectly through the projector (Weis and Belton 1985, 417).

There were two ways of recording the soundtrack, according to whether the recording mechanism involved a lamp or a mirror. A variable-density (or variable-intensity) soundtrack took the form of a pattern of parallel lines, not unlike a modern computer barcode, their differing thicknesses reflecting the strength of the emissions from a lamp flashing through the recording slit. A variable-area soundtrack was a zigzag pattern of varying width, cre-ated by linking a galvanometer to a small mirror which was deflected by different extents according to the strength of the current it received and cast correspondingly varied patterns of light on the film (London 1936, 108–11; Sabaneev 1935, 4–9). The variable-density method, developed by Western Electric, proved better for dialogue than music, while the opposite was true of the variable-area method, used in RCA's Photophone system; the latter was therefore modified in 1936 to remove dialogue distortion and the opti-cal variable-area soundtrack – to give it its full name – became the industry standard.

Regardless of whether a single sound-on-film camera or two separate cameras (one recording images, the other sound) were used, it was at first only possible for the soundtrack to be recorded simultaneously with the shooting of the visual image. Severe restrictions were caused by inadequate microphones hidden on set and the need for the cameras – which had become noisy since they were motorized to operate at a new speed of 24 frames per second in order to improve the quality of the soundtrack – to be housed in sound-proof booths; this in turn made the camera apparatus exceptionally unwieldy and limited the range of camera movements at a director's disposal. It was virtually impossible to ensure silence on set, where the hiss of the arc lights was a constant distraction. Exactly as Eisenstein and his colleagues predicted, imaginative montage was abandoned in favour of static, theatrical blocking of the action in which everything was dependent on the location of the fixed microphones.

Control over the quality of the soundtrack was primitive. Where multi-ple microphones were used, the signals were mixed on set before entering

2.2 A Vitaphone sound camera in the late 1920s.

the sound camera, which ran in synchronization with the image camera. In the single-camera system, the soundtrack was already at nineteen frames' remove from the image track, as was the combined release print of the film stock from the two-camera system, and this meant that cut-and-paste editing was virtually impossible until the introduction of the sound Moviola (see below). Everything in these early years was therefore filmed and recorded live in single takes. As with the sound-on-disc recordings in *The Jazz Singer*, a variety of camera shots within a single scene could only be achieved by the expensive business of running multiple cameras simultaneously in different locations – as is done with video cameras in modern television studios – so that the resulting images could be intercut without sacrificing sound synchronization (Fairservice 2001, 229). Background music would either have to be recorded live on set at the time of shooting, or else recorded in advance and mechanically reproduced on set so it could be re-recorded simultaneously with the dialogue. Both methods yielded lamentably poor sound quality, partly because the low-contrast film stock ideal for image photography failed to provide the level of contrast needed for the sound-track patterns.

Disappointing recording fidelity was only one of several reasons that contributed towards the general avoidance of nondiegetic music in films from the period *c.*1928–33. The novelty of synchronized diegetic sound temporarily put background scores out of fashion: music that appeared to emanate from the motion picture itself could, in the interests of realism, be better justified if it were strictly diegetic in origin. In Hollywood, many early sound films included music only for opening and closing credits in addition to diegetic needs; as Max Steiner related, a violinist might be gra-tuitously included in the background of a love scene solely to justify the use of what would otherwise be invisible romantic underscoring (Naum-berg 1937, 219). Some theorists and film-makers were dubious of the very nature of nondiegetic music, Paul Rotha commenting that 'Music in the form of accompaniment to realist story-films – no matter how well com-posed and written – is an anachronism, a hangover from the silent cinema which few film-makers are brave enough [even in the 1950s] to discard . . . All non-source music is an artificial aid to stimulate the emotions of the audience and not an integral and valid part of the film aesthetic' (Rotha 1958, 22–3, n.1). When nondiegetic music was reintroduced after *c.*1933, its function had subtly changed, a shift summarized by Kalinak: 'the basis of the silent film score, the principle of continuous playing and selective reproduction of diegetic sound, was rejected in the sound era in favor of a model based on the principles of intermittent music and faithful repro-duction of diegetic sound' (Kalinak 1992, 40). Along with intermittency came a reduced need for coherent structuring, as Mitry observed: 'Good film music can do without musical structure provided that its intrusion *into the film* at a specific moment should have a precise signification . . . from which it gains all its power once associated with the other elements: images, words, and sounds'; he cited Roland-Manuel's dictum that 'music must deny its own structure if it is to be an ally of the image' (Mitry 1998, 249).

In 1929–30, King Vidor and Lewis Milestone experimented with sound dubbing in their respective films *Hallelujah!* and *All Quiet on the Western Front*, shooting certain sequences with fluid camera movements (as had been possible in silent films) and adding the soundtrack afterwards. In the same period, Ernst Lubitsch made creative use of dubbing in several features, notably *Monte Carlo* (1930; music by W. Franke Harling *et al.*), in which the rhythmic clatter of a train's wheels merges into the film's theme song. Such postsynchronization had obvious technical and artistic advantages, and by the mid-1930s several independent tracks were used for the separate recording of dialogue, music and sound effects. Sound quality significantly improved from the poor fidelity apparent in, for example, the nondiegetic music mixed into the soundtracks of Laurel and Hardy films of 1931–2 (Weis and Belton 1985, 42). With the development of lighter and more mobile sound-proofed (blimped) cameras, the portable boom microphone and relatively silent incandescent lighting, sound recording on set also became much more versatile.

The Moviola, an editing device introduced in 1924 which allowed footage to be stopped on an individual frame without the risk of setting fire to the extremely flammable film stock (as would invariably happen in a conventional projector at this time), was in 1930 adapted for sound. It could run image and sound film stock in parallel, with the playback heads either locked together or independent; only for the final release print was the soundtrack pulled down to run in advance of the relevant images, enormously simplifying the editor's task. (The Moviola remained the principal editorial tool until it gradually yielded to video monitors and computer software in the 1980s.) The seamless editing of soundtracks was enabled by the invention of blooping, which was the superimposition of a black triangular sticker – later a diamond-shaped blob of black paint – above the thick ridge of film where two pieces of film stock were spliced together, this bump having formerly produced a loud bang when played back through the projector: the black bloops obviated the abrupt changes in electrical signal that had caused the obtrusive noise (Fairservice 2001, 234–5). This technique allowed the editorial process to appear as transparent (i.e. invisible) in the soundtrack as it became in image editing, such transparency becoming a dominant feature of mainstream cinema until the 1950s.

The acoustic limitations of primitive sound-recording technology remained a source of irritation to composers throughout the 1930s. Stringed instruments sounded poor in reproduction so, in Paris, Eric Sarnette and Hanns Eisler took the radical step of trying to do away with them altogether in favour of more 'microgenic' instrumental timbres – not entirely for practical reasons, as Sarnette, like Stravinsky in his 1920s concert works, was suspicious of the emotive power of string clichés and felt the instruments represented a regrettable 'feminist' dimension in modern music (London 1936, 193). Recording fidelity of other instruments was variable, though the comments of contemporaneous musicians are fairly subjective on this point with, for example, one judging the bassoon a poor instrument for recording purposes (Sabaneev 1935, 60) and another praising its qualities (London 1936, 171). In conjunction with Adolphe Sax, Jr, Sarnette developed special 'microphone instruments', such as the saxotromba with its movable bell, the saxotrombone and a bass trumpet with a bell shaped like a saucepan lid (London 1936, 191). These instruments had little impact and now seem quaint, but their use should not be divorced from Sarnette's devotion to 'a clean and plastic method of composition'. London declared that '[Sarnette's] orchestra conceals nothing; the almost pitiless clarity of sound-production requires of composers that their every note should have sense and meaning. The days of romantic sound-painting with chords and sound-mixtures of indefinite nature are over' (London 1936, 194). Similarly, Saba-neev recommended that aspiring film composers should avoid complex har-monies, more than two contrapuntal lines, extremes of register and cluster chords low in the texture (Sabaneev 1935, 37). These strictures were not just the result of limitations in recording fidelity, but part of a growing European feeling that the increasingly overblown romantic idiom of Hollywood film music was inappropriate for the modern age.

Animated sound

An even more radical method for bypassing poor sound reproduction was so-called 'animated sound', experiments with which began almost as soon as optical soundtrack technology became widely available. These involved the use of graphic patterns drawn, printed or photographed directly onto the soundtrack in order to generate synthetic sounds without the need for audio recording.

In Germany during the early 1930s, Rudolph Pfenninger and Oskar Fischinger created synthetic musical tones with soundtrack patterns writ-ten by hand that gave 'the impression of a remarkable abstraction of tone, reminiscent of certain electrical instruments, which can be traced to the absence of overtones' (London 1936, 198). Similar procedures were sub-sequently developed by director Rouben Mamoulian (see below), and also by the Bauhaus artist László Moholy-Nagy (who believed that composers could henceforth 'create music from a counterpoint of unheard of or even non-existent sound values'), by Evelyn Lambert in Canada, Jack Ellit in Lon-don, John and Jack Whitney in the USA, and by Arseni Avraamov and N. V. Voinov at the Scientific Experimental Film Institute in Leningrad. Avraamov achieved microtonal effects and won recognition for them as early as 1931, while Voinov developed graphic representations of the notes of a seven-octave chromatic scale and used these to prepare animated soundtracks real-izing pre-existing pieces of classical music, as did Pfenninger independently using a similar method (Prendergast 1992, 198–200; R. James 1986, 81–4).

Following on from Pfenninger's pioneering work, Canadian artist Norman McLaren's system of animated sound employed a 'small library of several dozen cards, each containing black and white areas repre-senting sound waves, [which] replaced traditional musical instruments and noisemaking devices' (McLaren 1953). When Francis Poulenc saw

McLaren's *Blinkity Blank* at Cannes in 1955, he singled it out as the most musically revelatory film of that year's festival and hailed the director's demonstration of the ongoing need for film-makers to continue striving to find new techniques uniquely suited to the medium of film (Lacombe and Porcile 1995, 121: see Chapter 7 of the present volume for further discussion of McLaren's work).

Outside the limited realm of experimental visual art, however, it was virtually impossible to secure sustained financial backing for commercial applications of these ventures: when David Fleischer patented an animated-sound system in 1931, it was bought by Paramount but apparently never used (R. James 1986, 86). Occasional experiments with graphic sound were made in narrative features such as *Dr Jekyll and Mr Hyde* (see below) and *The Devil and Daniel Webster* (see Chapter 5), but such novel procedures would soon lose out to the ever-more frequent use of far more conveniently achieved and increasingly versatile electronic sonorities prominent in film scores from the 1940s onwards.

Creative possibilities

Most early commercial sound films seem crude by any standards, and do not stand comparison with the artistic successes achieved by the best examples of the final flowering of the silent film in the late 1920s. Because synchronized and realistic sounds were initially a gimmick, they often drew attention to themselves in a manner that today seems both obsessive and naïve. French director Jean Renoir, annoyed by the trend, revealed of his first sound film, *On purge bébé* (1931):

> to register my bad mood, I decided to record the sound of a toilet flushing. This was a kind of revolution that did more for my reputation than the shooting of a dozen worthwhile scenes. The most noteworthy artists and scientists of the great sound communities declared that this was an 'audacious innovation'.   (Lacombe and Porcile 1995, 233)

Imaginative directors, however, boldly experimented with the illusory and emotional possibilities offered by both sound effects and music in the new synchronized medium.

Former theatrical director Rouben Mamoulian enthusiastically threw himself at the challenge, strongly believing that film sound 'should not be constantly shackled by naturalism. The magic of sound recording enabled one to achieve effects that would be impossible and unnatural on the stage or in real life, yet meaningful and eloquent on the screen' (quoted in Lack 1997, 84). It is worth noting that by no means all creative American film-making in this era was monopolized by Hollywood: Mamoulian's first film *Applause* (1929) was shot in Paramount's studios in Astoria, New York. He used experimental techniques such as double-track mixing of pre-recorded whispering and singing, and included many examples of his belief that the source of a diegetic sound need not be visible on screen. (Asynchronicity of this kind was later investigated by Chion, who coined the term 'acousmatic' to describe it and 'acousmêtre' for specific instances where it involves the powerful effect of a disembodied voice, which he felt to be deeply rooted in traditional notions of the unseen voice of a deity: see Chion 1994, 128–31, and Chion 1999, 17–57.) *Applause* is also notable for its use of a sound dissolve – the noise of bottles and a glass at the end of one scene merging into diegetic cymbal playing in a restaurant band at the start of the next – and a yearning convent girl's dream sequence accompanied by an appropriate collage of popular tunes and the 'Ave Maria' (Weis and Belton 1985, 241–2); its mobile camera work – and mobile microphones – became a reality only after fierce confrontations between the director and his crew, whose mentality was deeply rooted in static theatrical blocking. Mamoulian's *City Streets* (1931; music by Karl Hajos) contains the first example of a voiced-over flashback repeating dialogue heard earlier in the film. In *Dr Jekyll and Mr Hyde* (1932) Mamoulian used a mélange of avant-garde sonic expressionism, which became dubbed 'Mamoulian's stew', to accompany the transformation from urbane Jekyll to monstrous Hyde: the astonishing sonic collage was created by using a mixture of animated sound, reversed recordings of gong strokes, amplified heartbeats and reverberat-ing bells. With commendable restraint, Mamoulian used this extraordinary effect only once in the film, thereby immeasurably intensifying its emotional impact. Its outlandish and deeply disturbing quality is strikingly prophetic of alien soundscapes that did not become commonplace in film soundtracks until decades later.

Among the first important sound films in Europe were Alfred Hitch-cock's *Blackmail* (1929), which was initially shot as a silent then partly remade to include a synchronized score, and René Clair's *Sous les toits de Paris* (1929), both of which transferred the major conventions of silent-film music to the sound screen but also made significant creative use of diegetic song. Both Hitchcock and Clair were, in different ways, keenly aware of the creative possibilities offered by the soundtrack. On a basic level, both – like Mamoulian – used diegetic sound to promote a sense of three-dimensional space. And the necessity of adding sound to films that had been conceived as silents in the event proved to be more of a liberation than a hindrance, given that large parts of their transitional soundtracks had to be prepared using flexible postproduction techniques.

At this stage in his career Hitchcock, like most other directors in this period, tended to avoid nondiegetic music. In *Blackmail* the sporadic nondiegetic scoring (by Hubert Bath *et al.*) is sometimes crude, notably in the cue that accompanies the opening and closing police chases, which is rooted in melodramatic clichés and stolidly sequential in construction. But the score also incorporates impressionistic reworkings of a motif borrowed from a song first heard diegetically and then used to comment on aspects of the drama as it unfolds, a technique anticipating the similar procedure used many years later by Steiner and others. As Royal S. Brown comments: 'it is not, of course, the whole song that has left the diegesis and made its way to the nondiegetic music track but rather small fragments of it: in essence, the entire song ['Miss Up-to-Date', by Billy Mayerl] and its ironies are expressed in the isolation of its first four notes' (R. S. Brown 1994, 43). Hitchcock's *Murder* (1930) is more typical of its time: after conflating the opening of Beethoven's Fifth Symphony and the rhythmically similar scherzo theme from the same symphony to serve as 'fate knocking on the door' main-title music, the film's music is restricted to diegetic cues – including a long segment from the opening of Wagner's *Tristan und Isolde*. Although the introduction of the latter and its justification both seem crudely executed by today's standards – the music is evidently present solely to provide an atmospheric background accompaniment but Hitchcock over-emphasizes the fact that its source is diegetic, making us listen to a stilted radio announcer telling us precisely what we are about to hear – this does not lessen the originality of the scene in question, which is the first use of stream-of-consciousness voice-over in cinematic history. At the film's climax, diegetic music is again contrived to serve as suitable dramatic accompaniment: as a trapeze artist sets about hanging himself in full view of the horrified public, the diegetic circus music (implausibly) grows more tense and melodramatic, stopping altogether so that the grisly act is carried out in disturbing silence. At the end of the film, we see hero and heroine united in a fond embrace and assume that the lush accompanying music is nondiegetic – until the camera dollies backwards revealing them to be actors framed by a proscenium arch, and the love music is therefore now presumed to be issuing from the theatre's orchestral pit. *Murder* affords further examples of asynchronous sound: the source of the scream at the opening is not seen, court-room dialogue at the moment of pronouncing the verdict is dubbed over shots of the empty room that the jury has just left, and a dialogue flashback gives insight into the accused's thoughts as she sits alone in her police cell.

In the opening commuter sequence from Hitchcock's *Rich and Strange* (1931), Hal Dolphe's nondiegetic score catches every action – including pointing out successive entries in a ledger, a book slamming shut and

umbrellas snapping open – to create a cartoon-like sequence of almost balletic mickey-mousing. Later in his career, however, Hitchcock remained concerned that nondiegetic music might detract from filmic realism, famously
requiring none in *Lifeboat* (1944) on the grounds that one would not expect
to encounter an orchestra playing in the middle of the ocean. To this suggestion, David Raksin equally famously replied, 'ask him where the camera
comes from and I'll tell him where the music comes from!' (quoted in
Kalinak 1992, xiii). Nonetheless, Hitchcock's extended collaboration with
Bernard Herrmann in the 1950s and 1960s elicited some of the most celebrated film scores is cinema history, even if the critical acclaim accorded to
Herrmann's music placed some strain on their relationship (see Chapter 5).

Clair's use of music in the early sound era was more adventurous than
Hitchcock's, and formed part of the French director's vision for developing a
type of intellectual yet popular sound film in which dialogue was avoided in
favour of a sustained application of sound effects and music. In this regard
he directly influenced Mamoulian, by whom dialogue was similarly considered as only one of the sonic possibilities available to the director – a view
also shared by Jean Renoir. At a conference on the sound film held in Brus-
sels in 1926, Clair's fear that dialogue would come to dominate all aspects
of film production led him to condemn the new technology as a 'terrible
monster, a creation against nature, courtesy of which the screen will become
an impoverished theatre – the poor man's theatre' (Lacombe and Porcile
1995, 225). *Sous les toits de Paris*, featuring music by Armand Bernard and
a popular song by Raoul Moretti, owes its success in large part to Clair's
fine sense of integration between visual dynamics and aural momentum; as
Arthur Knight has pointed out, the relationship between music and movement in Clair's films often resembles a ballet (Weis and Belton 1985, 217),
a comparison useful to an understanding of the function of nondiegetic
music in many sound films of the succeeding generation. Clair's fluid camera work and asynchronous use of sound may have been partly inspired by
Harry Beaumont's seminal musical *The Broadway Melody*, which he saw in
London in May 1929 (Barrios 1995, 68–9). As Gorbman notes in her analysis of *Sous les toits* (Gorbman 1987, 140–50), Clair avoids naturalistic sound
until the climactic street fight, which suddenly restores it and then displaces
the tension by overdubbing the noise of an unseen train in an example
of what she terms 'auditory masking'. Music is not present in this scene, its
absence adding to the stark effect, but is elsewhere pervasive and prominent.
It too serves as auditory masking when it directly replaces dialogue, and it
can stimulate a new sense of spatio-temporal perception when it appears
to bind together disparate characters and locations through the agency of
pseudo-communal singing – as when the camera pans slowly from one tenement window to another and every character it encounters along the way

is singing or playing (in real-time continuity) successive phrases from the title song, first introduced diegetically by a plugger trying to sell the sheet music to the neighbourhood crowd at the beginning of the film. The wit here lies in their irritation that they cannot now rid their minds of the tune: 'Ça va, ça va! On la connait!', snaps one character in a bar before the theme is again taken up by others in the succeeding interior shots. Towards the end of the film a recording of Rossini's *William Tell* overture, played diegetically on a gramophone in the bar (where it conveniently accompanies a brawl), is the mechanism for more wit characteristic of Clair: the needle sticks in the groove and, as the music jerkily repeats the same bar over and over again, an old punter watching the fight thinks he must surely be drunk.

While working on *A nous la liberté* (1931), Clair demonstrated the importance of music to his overall conception of the film by involving the composer, Georges Auric, in all aspects of the production from the writing of the script onwards. Before working with Clair, Auric had already begun his collaboration with Jean Cocteau, historically significant for its experimentation with random associations between image and ostensibly unrelated music (see Chapter 8). In *A nous*, Auric supplied a sparkling comedic score, very much in the brittle manner of Les Six and featuring prominent saxophone, cor anglais and percussion, in its moments of comic capering directly anticipating his later work for Ealing Studios (discussed in Chapter 6). Auric's music is constantly foregrounded because Clair's direction remains rooted in the purely visual humour of the silent cinema and for large stretches is not reliant on dialogue. The music track sometimes sharply manipulates moods in a rather basic fashion, as when cheerful music for toys seen in close-up turns sombre when the camera reveals them being manufactured by convicts. Literal-minded mickey-mousing occurs when rays of sunshine strike each of a prison cell's window bars in turn to the individual notes of an arpeggiated vibraphone chord, an idea wittily recapped when the prisoner attempts to hang himself from the same bars, which buckle under the strain and allow him to escape through the window instead. Immediately after this illustrative cue, Clair disconcerts his viewers by playing with their expectations of film sound: a woman's singing has been issuing enticingly from a window, but the music deteriorates, stops and restarts incongruously once she has emerged into the street, revealing the source of the singing to have been a recording played from another apartment. This trick, exposing the essential artificiality of all film music, later became an endearing cliché of comedy soundtracks. Other felicitous touches include Auric's delicate accompaniment while convicts eat in diegetic silence, a cue that later returns to accompany a scene of an industrial conveyor-belt production line – thereby underscoring the film's suggestion that, for some, life outside prison bars is not much more inspiring than life behind them.

In contrast, two parallel scenes of workers clocking in at their factory are given different musical accompaniment even though the images are virtually identical: the first receives mechanistic industrial music typical of many concert composers' experiments in the 1920s, while the second cue is surprisingly dreamy. Diegetic music is used creatively in the passage-of-time montage during which another escaped convict progresses from lowly gramophone salesman to become a magnate of the hi-fi industry (featuring a series of overlapping recordings played on increasingly sophisticated gramophone equipment), and the title song creeps in and out of the diegesis, the two lead characters chipping vocal lines into the nondiegetic score when least expected.

Germany was another centre for musical experimentation in the early years of the sound film. Wolfgang Zeller contributed a substantial through-composed score to Carl Dreyer's *Vampyr* in 1932, the year before Steiner put nondiegetic film music firmly on the map with *King Kong* (see Chapter 3). A creative use of original diegetic music was made by Karol Rathaus, who scored *Der Mörder Dimitri Karamasoff* (*The Brothers Karamazov*, dir. Erich Engels and Fyodor Otsep, 1931) in conjunction with Kurt Schröder. Rathaus' score was much admired by Herrmann, who commented in a lecture in 1973:

> This, to me, was the first great realization of the dream of melodrama . . . [Rathaus] treated for the first time the music of a film as an integral part of the whole, not as decoration. Because the film deals with one of the Karamazovs falling in love with a prominent harlot and visiting her in her establishment wherein a gypsy orchestra plays, the music of the picture begins with a gypsy orchestra simply playing Russian gypsy music. But as the picture progresses and the brother becomes more and more involved with the harlot, the music stops being ornamental and becomes an emotional mirror of him. It becomes more and more tragic and more and more hysterical. It reaches its greatest moment, I think, when the brother hysterically drives a troika through a raging blizzard accompanied musically by a great battery of percussion instruments.   (S. Smith 1991, 359–60)

Director Josef von Sternberg, like Mamoulian, was an early exponent of the art of using asynchronous diegetic sound to suggest the existence of space outside the limits of the screen. Working in America, he first included an ironic use of diegetic song in his Paramount film *Thunderbolt* (1929), for which main-title music was composed by Hajos. Like Hitchcock's, however, Sternberg's attempts to include atmospheric accompanimental music by using strictly diegetic pretexts were somewhat contrived, as shown by the implausibility of the appearance of music-making prisoners on death row (Kalinak 1992, 69). Made in Germany in 1930 and catapulting Marlene

Dietrich to international stardom, his *The Blue Angel* (*Der blaue Engel*) – which was shot in parallel German, English and French versions – significantly furthered both techniques. The stark manner in which the closing door of the dressing room used by the vamp Lola-Lola (Dietrich) frequently cuts off the sound of the band in the eponymous night-club may today seem unduly crude and overly repetitive – it was clearly a novelty at the time – but the film is shot through with other sound events crucial both to the furthering of the narrative (e.g. the chiming of a clock) and characterization, especially that of the protagonist, Professor Immanuel Rath, with his trombone-like nose blowing, whistling and cockerel imitations. As Sternberg commented, 'the sound film affords me the opportunity to orchestrate an action in such a way that the instrumentation becomes a necessary organic constituent of the entire work' (quoted in Sudendorf 2001).

Friedrich Holländer's music for *The Blue Angel* is almost exclusively diegetic, apart from a brief medley overture that immediately introduces the sound of a tolling bell that becomes so important later in the film, and an evocative orchestral epilogue accompanying Rath's death in a haze of shimmering Wagnerian harp arpeggios harmonizing the asynchronous tolling of his death knell; this last cue was a memorable afterthought added eleven days after the film's première at Berlin's Gloria Palast. Dietrich's interpretations of Holländer's songs are accompanied by the most famous German dance band of the time, Stefan Weintraub's strongly American-influenced Syncopators (with whom Holländer had provided music for Berlin revues since 1927), and these numbers retain their power both to tease and promote dramatic irony: 'the images were startling, irrevocable, the most overtly sexual yet connected with musical performance' (Barrios 1995, 320). Recordings of songs from the film sold widely on their tie-in release in 1930, but their independent commercial success obscured the songs' real power in the film, which lay in throwing the progress of the pathetic and deranged Rath's downfall into sharp relief. Throughout the film, ironic use is also made of pre-existing melodies: Holländer's overture pointedly quotes a theme sung by Papageno in Mozart's *Magic Flute*, the ever-present clock chimes a song-tune concerned with loyalty and fidelity, and the African musical doll examined by the Papageno-like Rath in Lola-Lola's bedroom plays him a theme from Schubert's *Die schöne Müllerin*.

The Blue Angel grossed a record $60,000 in just one week after it opened at New York's Rialto in December 1930 and this success significantly boosted the American careers of both Sternberg and Dietrich, who collaborated there on *Morocco* (1930) and *Dishonored* (1931), both with music by Hajos, and *Shanghai Express* (1932) and *Blonde Venus* (1932), both with music by W. Franke Harling. In 1933, *The Blue Angel* was proscribed in Germany by the Nazis, Joseph Goebbels considering it to be '"offal," spewed out by the fetid city'; the Jewish Holländer's music for the film *Jungle Princess* was also banned (Kater 1992, 23, 45). The Weintraub Syncopators wisely failed to return to Germany after an international recital tour in 1933, most choosing to remain in Australia apart from their pianists Holländer and Franz Wachsmann who, like Dietrich, emigrated to the USA and later became well known in Hollywood under the Anglicized names of Frederick Hollander and Franz Waxman. Other members of the band were less fortunate: trumpeter Adolf Rosner was exiled to Siberia by Stalin and pianist Martin Roman was murdered in Auschwitz.

Undoubtedly, the film musical was the most important genre to emerge during the earliest years of the sound film: it had inspired experimentation in continental Europe, including G. W. Pabst's version of Brecht's and Weill's *The Threepenny Opera* (see Chapter 4), and a sometimes stunning but more commercially oriented sense of adventure in its Hollywood incarnation. The widespread popularity of featured songs in this period inevitably led to their inclusion in otherwise non-musical dramatic films on both sides of the Atlantic, often as a means of promoting sales of sheet music. Typical American examples from 1930, cited by Richard Barrios (1995, 309–10), are the domestic drama *Young Man of Manhattan* (dir. Monta Bell) and the Joan Crawford vehicle *Our Blushing Brides* (dir. Harry Beaumont). In France, the 1931 crime drama *Tumultes* (dir. Robert Siodmak) similarly contained three gratuitous songs. Partly responsible for this situation was the fact that many early sound-film actors in both countries were seasoned stage-show singers, and were capitalizing on their existing reputations. As film genres steadily became more formulaic in the later 1930s, so the tendency to break into song was rigorously channelled into the unique domain of the film musical, the growth of which in America was partly influenced by the success of Clair's films stateside. The ground-rules for a style of nondiegetic instrumental music suitable for dramatic features and utterly subservient to the narrative were established in Hollywood; and in the meantime Clair's imaginative ideal of the 'musical film' – in which music would be more important than dialogue in articulating the drama – was consigned to history.

3 Hollywood's Golden Age: narrative cinema and the classical film score

With millions of dollars having been invested in the technological revolution that endowed the silent film with synchronized sound, cinema in the 1930s had to be made to pay its way. As the novelty value of soundtracks wore off, the wider economical effects of the Depression helped contribute to a substantial decline in movie attendance in the USA: approximately one-third of the nation's movie-theatres were forced to shut down in 1933, by which time audiences had dwindled to two-thirds of their former size over a period of just two years. The industry survived the crisis largely on account of its aggressive promotion of a formulaic product designed to appeal to a mass spectatorship. The conveyor-belt production line responsible for establishing this *lingua franca* of narrative film-making – represented by what is customarily termed the 'classical' film, in which music was destined to become (for the most part) as stereotypical as other parameters of film production – was squarely located in the studios of Hollywood.

Small production companies had first installed themselves in Hollywood around 1908, when it was just a village, and when American film-making still had to compete with European output. California held attractive possibilities for convenient location shooting in generally fine weather; its scenery was varied, and could be made to pass for a wide range of geographical regions, from pseudo-Mediterranean and tropical seascapes to the deserts of the Wild West, from lush vegetation to spectacular mountainous regions. The West Coast was also attractive in offering a less fiercely regulated and litigious environment than that prevailing on the East Coast. Thanks to its burgeoning film output, Hollywood prospered and was annexed by neighbouring Los Angeles in 1919, by which time the ravages of the First World War had seriously impaired the formerly flourishing European film industry. The leading Hollywood studios were all established during the 1920s, in a surge of lucrative creative activity that saw their products exported across the globe; this boom was made possible by heavy investment from Wall Street, not only occasioned by the investors' clear eye to profits but also fed by cinema's perceived suitability for a mass propaganda rooted in the nationalist and anti-Communist sentiments born of the years of paranoia immediately after the end of the catastrophic war (D. Cook 2004, 236). In 1927, the Academy of Motion Picture Arts and Sciences (AMPAS) was founded, a body which attempted to hold the industry's growing trade-unionism in check until it withdrew from such concerns a decade later; its annual awards ceremonies (instituted in 1929) honoured both technical accomplishment and artistic achievement, and still remain today – for better or worse – a source of enormous international prestige and commercial influence.

Following the introduction of the talkies, a major influx of literary talent, classically trained actors and composers arrived in Hollywood from both the East Coast and Europe, boosting the quality of script-writing, acting and musical provision demanded by the new sound film. When in top form, their complex collaborative efforts produced such fine and enduring work that Erwin Panofsky could, as part of a spirited defence of commercial art written in 1934, legitimately compare Hollywood personnel with those responsible for the building of a medieval cathedral:

> The comparison may seem sacrilegious . . . because the movies are commercial. However, if commercial art be defined as all art not primarily produced in order to gratify the creative urge of its maker but primarily intended to meet the requirements of a patron or a buying public, it must be said that noncommercial art is the exception rather than the rule, and a fairly recent and not always felicitous exception at that. While it is true that commercial art is always in danger of ending up as a prostitute, it is equally true that noncommercial art is always in danger of ending up as an old maid . . .
>
> It is [the] requirement of communicability that makes commercial art more vital than noncommercial, and therefore potentially much more effective for better or for worse. The commercial producer can both educate and pervert the general public, and can allow the general public – or rather his idea of the general public – both to educate and to pervert himself.
>
> (Braudy and Cohen 1999, 290–1)

Thomas Schatz goes further, describing the classical Hollywood era as

> a period when various social, industrial, technological, economic, and aesthetic forces struck a delicate balance. That balance was conflicted and ever shifting but stable enough through four decades to provide a consistent system of production and consumption, a set of formalized creative practices and constraints, and thus a body of work with a uniform style – a standard way of telling stories, from camera work and cutting to plot structure and thematics. It was the studio system at large that held these various forces in equilibrium; indeed, the 'studio era' and the classical Hollywood describe the same industrial and historical phenomenon.
>
> (Braudy and Cohen 1999, 605)

However, the demands of star-driven casting, a heavy reliance on a limited range of dramatic genres, formulaic production values, constant prioritizing of quantity and speed of production over quality (well over 7,000 features were produced by Hollywood between 1930 and the end of the Second World War), plus a general avoidance of commercially risky artistic and technical experimentation, all conspired to make many Hollywood films of this era less than impressive or durable.

Both artistically and in terms of its social relevance, Hollywood cinema was after its heady early days further stilted by self-imposed censorship of what would today be termed adult issues – principally those concerned with violence, sex, crime and immorality – and a firm belief in the apparently overwhelming and increasingly predictable necessity for good always to triumph over evil. These tendencies were enforced by the draconian Production Code, agreed by the industry in 1934 (under pressure from the powerful Catholic Church), which wielded its repressive influence until it was openly flouted by film-makers in the 1950s. In some ways, mainstream Hollywood films until this time existed in a disconcerting vacuum, cut off from many of the concerns of the real world; and, as Caryl Flinn (1992) has persuasively argued, the outmoded and highly romantic style of musical accompaniment with which the majority of features were provided gave the diverting products of the Hollywood dream-factory an appropriately utopian aural dimension.

The studio system

In order to understand the role played by both music and its composers in Hollywood cinema from the early 1930s to the mid-1950s – its so called 'Golden Age' – it is necessary to situate them in the context of a filmic production line driven above all by commercial interests, and in which the financial investors had an absolute power of veto over the work of the creative artists in their employ. One of the most egregious outcomes of this scenario, the ability of producers to reject and replace completed film scores on a whim, is still very much in evidence today. And the mythology of Hollywood is replete with tales of musical ignorance on the part of producers, witty enough to recount but enormously frustrating and dispiriting for those who have to deal with them in a pressurized working environment. Many have passed into the realms of legend: Hugo Friedhofer's having been told to use French horns for a film set in France; a producer requesting a solo flute play full chords; another proposing to fly Brahms out to Hollywood; yet another demanding music for clarinet and then, when duly given it, complaining that the composer had made a mistake – only to discover that by 'clarinet' he had really meant 'oboe'; and David Raksin's delight when asked to write a score in the atonal idiom of Berg's *Wozzeck* having been somewhat dented by the producer in question later dismissing the opera as 'crap' when hearing it unannounced on a gramophone recording (Flinn 1992, 19; Kalinak 1992, 76–8).

From the early 1930s onwards, five major and three minor Hollywood studios dominated film output, categorized thus according to their relative wealth and influence. The majors, benefitting from vertical integration by possessing their own theatre chains and therefore directly controlling the exhibition of their products, were Metro-Goldwyn-Mayer (MGM), Paramount, Warner Bros., Twentieth Century-Fox (formed by the merger of two studios in 1935) and Radio-Keith-Orpheum (RKO); the minors were Universal, Columbia and United Artists, who owned no theatre circuits and were dependent upon the majors for their screen time. In the mid-1930s many new smaller studios, such as Republic Pictures and Monogram Productions, were also established, primarily to produce the low-budget 'B' films that formed part of the double-bills designed to lure reluctant audiences back into movie theatres following the decline in ticket sales during the Depression.

The leading studios' generic specialisms were already well defined in the 1930s. Most at some point cashed into the early craze for musicals (see Chapter 4); amongst other genres, MGM produced comedies, Paramount epics and comedies, Warner Bros. gangster movies and swashbuckling period adventures, Twentieth Century-Fox westerns and period drama, and RKO both musicals and (later) *film noir*. Of the minors' achievements, one of the most important was Universal's ground-breaking work in horror films. While a romantic and melodramatic style of film scoring, inherited from the silent and early sound cinema, was often deemed equally suitable for all genres, at the hands of the most adventurous directors and composers specific changes in musical style could help to define the character of certain genres as they developed: this was particularly noticeable, for example, in the case of *film noir*, the western and the horror film, and the innovative music for these would in time come to have an impact across numerous other genres. Much research remains to be carried out into the fascinating musical cross-fertilizations between the various genres of narrative film, such inter-generic relationships having been long ignored in hermetically sealed generic studies of film history (Altman 1987, 114).

Each of the major studios housed a permanent music department, with contracted composers, arrangers, orchestrators, copyists, librarians and music editors, plus a resident orchestra, all working under a senior music director. The latter was a vital intermediary between those toiling at the musical workface and the upper echelons of the studio moguls. Composer Elmer Bernstein recalled that for his first film assignments in the early 1950s he was responsible only to the music director and not to the producers or directors:

> and that was good, because the music directors took responsibility for the spotting of the picture [see below] and were right there to the end of the dub. If there was something wrong with the score, it was the music director who took the flak and stood between the composer and the producer. The composer was therefore in a much more comfortable position because he was dealing with a colleague, someone who could read music.
>
> (quoted in Thomas 1997, 12)

The organization of a typical department fell into three sub-departments, all of which were answerable to the music director. One dealt with research and preparation, including negotiating clearance for the use of pre-existing music, apportioning the relevant budgets, and maintaining libraries of sheet music and disc recordings; a second was responsible for production, i.e. the scheduling of recordings and the employment of all staff and performers participating in them, including not just conductors and orchestral players but also those required for rehearsal purposes, such as voice coaches and keyboard répétiteurs; a third dealt with postproduction and general scoring matters, including the preparation of the cue sheets that listed music required in individual films (Prendergast 1992, 37). Both production and postproduction dealt with the studio's sound department, which was responsible for all aspects of recording, dubbing and soundtrack mixing.

Given the tendency towards hack production that affected many Hollywood films in the 1930s and 1940s, it is all too easy to assume that studios in general, and their music departments in particular, were somewhat complacent. Nothing could be further from the truth. Studio staff and musicians worked astonishingly hard, took much pride in their tasks and endured unrelentingly punishing schedules. The orchestral players gave 'a daily exhibition of the highest technical proficiency, and no one who witnessed it will ever forget it or disclaim it' (Previn 1992, 154). Max Steiner's orchestrator, Hugo Friedhofer, remembered having to prepare a score nearly 1,000 pages in length for Michael Curtiz's *The Charge of the Light Brigade* in 1936 (Palmer 1990, 46), and labour of this order was not uncommon. Steiner recalled that he was given only six days in which to write 70 minutes of music for *We Are Not Alone* (dir. Edmund Goulding, 1939), commenting that the lack of sleep this necessitated 'is a terrific strain on the eyes and the heart, so I would not advise anyone who is not in good physical condition to undertake this vocation, especially as this pressure occurs almost constantly' (quoted in Daubney 2000, 10). Although four to six weeks, not six days, was the normal time allotted for the composition and recording of a film's score, the fact that the music was in the vast majority of cases the last ingredient to be added to the film meant that its creation was (and still remains) at the whim of various vicissitudes in other aspects of the production which were considered to be more important. Steiner recalled:

Many times I have to work two days and two nights in succession without an hour's sleep. The reason for this is that pictures are sold in advance and if thru any fault of the studio, delays occur, such as changes in the script, illness of the players [i.e. actors], and numerable unforeseen 'accidents,' the picture still has to be completed and ready to start on its engagement on the day scheduled, so the only thing to do in this case is to work day and night to get it out.

(Daubney 2000, 10)

As the work of individual film composers became more respected, these problems still refused to go away. John Green, who became Head of the Music Department at MGM in 1949, recounted an incident which shows that the conveyor-belt mentality persisted well into the 1950s:

E. J. Mannix and J. J. Cohen were the architects of those ridiculous schedules . . . and they'd put four or five guys on to finish a picture. I'll never forget the first time that I became involved in that. It was one of Miklós Rózsa's pictures and Mickey [Rózsa] couldn't possibly finish writing [his score] by the tax date when the film had to be shipped out of the state . . . I was in a meeting with Mannix and Cohen and I said, 'You cannot have this picture ready for the tax date. You just can't have it!' I thought Eddie Mannix was going to have a stroke – he grew purple. 'What do you mean "we can't?"' I said, 'You can't have it because you can't have it. You are not dealing with a sausage machine, you're dealing with a tremendously gifted artist, Miklós Rózsa.' 'Well, give him some help, put four or five guys on it.'

(E. Bernstein 2004 [1977], 352)

Not surprisingly, perhaps, from the late 1940s onwards various industrial disputes over musicians' working conditions, copyright issues and royalty payments were to accelerate the demise of the permanent studio establishments (see Chapter 5).

In its heyday, however, the studio system fostered a formidable sense of team-work, and this was graphically reflected in the early 1930s when the provision of music for films was mostly undertaken as a collaborative effort involving several composers, arrangers and orchestrators rather than any one named individual: scores were considered as team efforts and those responsible for them were not given screen credit (see Raksin in McCarty 1989, 167–81). Indeed, when AMPAS instituted its annual Music Award for Scoring in 1934, it was until 1938 awarded not to individual composers but to studio music departments *en masse*, with only the relevant music director being named; its assignment to the 'Technical' category of awards inevitably signified the industry's view of composing as a functional craft subservient to other parameters of film production. (Film music had routinely been discussed under the 'technical' section of the film industry's trade press in the 1920s.) Well after the work of individual film composers began to dominate Hollywood soundtracks, collaborative composition continued in the rapid-turnaround environment of the B-movie studios. This collaborative spirit was only possible because the heavy emphasis on commercially viable narrative films, and intense pressures on production staff to maintain a prolific output, inevitably led to a stereotyped manner of scoring in which the work of one composer was readily interchangeable with another's; many low-budget movies were 'tracked' with music from previous productions until this practice was prohibited in 1944. Nevertheless, film composers have (both before and since) repeatedly borrowed from their own music – and some have occasionally committed blatant plagiarisms – in the interests of both meeting tight production deadlines and giving directors the specific musical idioms they requested.

Practicalities

The vast majority of film scores for Hollywood narrative features were composed and recorded after shooting of the image track was completed, with composers working to a rough cut of the film. While in one sense this was an ideal practice, since composers could easily imagine themselves in the position of a viewer of the finished product and score the film according to their own perceptions of its particular postproduction requirements, in other ways it was far less beneficial. First, as we have seen, it put enormous pressure on composers and musicians to complete their work with often undue haste. Second, it inevitably led to a feeling that the composer could be responsible for rescuing a film by supplying music to bolster weaknesses of pacing or communication that did not emerge until the editing stage, and this effectively prevented any more meaningful symbiosis of image and music that might have been nurtured had director and composer worked fruitfully together from the outset of a production. (Several composers and commentators likened the film composer's task to that of a mortician improving the appearance of a corpse: for examples, see Flinn 1992, 45.) Third, the composer often faced the enormous practical difficulty of composing music to a rough cut only to find that the director and/or editor subsequently imposed significant changes on the editing that necessitated corresponding – and often instant – alterations to the music. Heavyweight independent producer David O. Selznick and Steiner clashed bitterly over musical problems caused by the former's editorial tinkering with *Gone With the Wind*, for example (Daubney 2000, 17). Sabaneev recommended that film composers should develop an ability to write 'extensile music' that might readily be expanded if necessary, which he deemed easier than having to compress a cue that turned out to be over-long; this procedure might involve (as in some silent-film music) the careful deployment of pauses, rests, sequences and short phrases that could easily be lengthened, repeated or otherwise manipulated on demand and, in extreme cases where pragmatism overrode all other considerations, he declared that composers might well be advised to write some emotionally neutral cues that a music editor could repeat over and over again in order to fill unforeseen gaps (Sabaneev 1935, 43–7). Such neutral music, which most obviously exemplifies Claudia Gorbman's belief that film music can often be regarded as easy-listening music designed to allay the spectator's anxieties and promote suspension of disbelief, was identified by Aaron Copland (1949) as being well established in the 1940s and perhaps the ultimate example of what was at the time widely considered to be film music's inherent necessity not to draw attention to itself (Sabaneev 1935, 22).

Normal initial procedure was for director, music editor and composer to meet for a 'spotting' session in which they agreed the quantity, location and type of musical cues for a film on the basis of a screening of its rough cut, these cues subsequently being detailed on a typed cue sheet which gave precise footage counts and timings (calculated on a Moviola), together with detailed verbal descriptions of the appropriate on-screen action. Cues were denoted by their position in each ten-minute reel of film – the duration of a reel had decreased by around five minutes since the silent era owing to the increase in film speed to a standardized 24 frames per second in the sound film – and composers generally wrote and recorded music on a reel-by-reel basis. Pressure of time compelled most composers to use one or more orchestrators to prepare performing parts on the basis of short-score sketches; sometimes no full score was prepared, with appropriate instrumental parts being copied out directly from the short score. Fair copies of the latter were often used by the conductor in the recording session – a common-enough procedure in the musical theatre, from which many early Hollywood composers and music directors hailed. When full scores were required, this work was paid at a standard rate per four-bar page. As MGM employee Leo Arnaud recalled, an unscrupulous orchestrator might be tempted to rewrite triplet passages in 4/4 as single bars of 3/8 as a way of getting one over on musically illiterate producers by increasing the fee fourfold (Previn 1992, 34). Similar ruses were perpetrated in England, where canny London musicians conspired to have orchestrators make gratuitous use of ancillary wind instruments (e.g. piccolo, cor anglais, bass clarinet, double bassoon) so that the woodwind players could claim a 'doubling fee', and a musical director might prolong recording sessions to lengths unwarranted by the difficulty of the music in order that players might be paid for their additional hours in the studio (Morrison 2004, 177).

During the process of composition, the precise length of individual cues had to be monitored by the use of a simple stopwatch. At the recording session, during which the film was projected onto a screen at the back of the orchestra, two useful devices helped the conductor (who was often, but by no means invariably, the composer) to synchronize the music with the images. A click-track, championed by Steiner but first introduced in early Disney sound cartoons (Barrier 1999, 582), consisted of a series of holes punched by the music editor in film stock so that they would produce a metronomic clicking sound when played back through a Moviola's or projector's sound head, these clicks being audible only via headphones and arranged to proceed at the speed or varying speeds that best suited the musical requirements of a particular segment of film. To save time, music editors might have at their disposal complete sets of pre-prepared click loops which produced continuous pulses of anything between 48 and 240 beats per minute (Thomas 1997, 18). From the musicians' point of view, click tracks and loops were hardly conducive to interpretative leeway or spontaneity of expression; as one witness said of the podium deportment of Leo Forbstein, who became music director at Warner Bros. in 1929: 'It was the most mechanical thing you ever saw. He was just waving the stick to the tempo clicks' (LoBrutto 1994, 14). For moments when a specific musical gesture had to be exactly synchronized with the images, such as a sudden stinger chord coinciding with a physical act or emotional shock registered on screen, streamers and punches might be used. The streamer was a diagonal line scratched across a segment of image frames which, when projected, appeared as a vertical line moving across the screen from left to right as a warning of the impending event; a hole was punched in the image frame at the precise moment of intended synchronization, immediately after the streamer line met the far right-hand edge of the screen, so that a bright flash of light signalled the relevant event to the conductor (Weis and Belton 1985, 110–11).

Although the orchestra's performance might be recorded by between four and eight microphones in the interests of adapting the balance between groups of instruments, in the early days their signals were mixed directly onto the optical soundtrack and the quality of the recording could not be evaluated until after the film had been developed. It was therefore common practice for a wax or glass (later aluminium) disc to be cut simultaneously so that the instant playback it offered would assist those involved in evaluating each take before it was too late to correct it (LoBrutto 1994, 14). In the 1930s, the dialogue mixer was also responsible for the mixing of the film's music as part of the composite soundtrack. Although these functions later came to be separated, with the soundtrack being prepared by three mixers (one each for dialogue, sound effects and music), all working under a supervising sound editor, the old procedure undoubtedly helped perpetuate another major problem affecting the film composer's task: the fact that the music was almost always seen as the least important element in any situation when it came into apparent competition with dialogue and/or sound effects, both of which were deemed to be of superior narrative usefulness. Composer Ernest Gold commented of dubbing sessions:

> It is at this point that the composer frequently feels that his fee is not so much in the nature of monies earned for services rendered but rather a reparation paid by the studio in view of the occupational injuries sustained. What fiendish tortures await the composer at those sessions! That tender cello solo, his favourite part of the entire score, lies completely obliterated by a siren which the director decided was necessary at that exact spot in order properly to motivate the reaction on the hero's face! Or that splendid orchestral climax, the ONE place in the entire score which the composer decided to orchestrate himself, held down to a soft *pp* because of a line of narration that had to be added at the last moment in order to clarify an important story point.
> (Thomas 1973, 30)

Underscoring – a term often misapplied to nondiegetic film music in general, though it more correctly refers to music written specifically to accompany speech – was thus one of the most thankless tasks facing the composer of music for commercial sound films. Ducking systems for summarily lowering the volume of music beneath dialogue were commonplace. Arthur Piantadosi, who worked as a recording mixer at Warner Bros. in the late 1930s, recalled:

> The sound department punched in a down arrow for the music to go down when the actors spoke and an up arrow for the music to go up when the actors didn't speak. The arrow was punched in twenty frames [i.e. just under one second] before the cue, so you had time to go up and down. That was unsatisfactory because the music had been designed dynamically on the music stage and didn't take well to automatic dumps up and down.
> (LoBrutto 1994, 15)

In addition to the arrow system, ducking could in some sound departments be accomplished by an 'up-and-downer' machine that responded to dialogue input by automatically and instantly lowering the music's volume. In 1935, sound engineer Edward Kellogg attempted to justify the device by likening its results to the cocktail-party effect whereby listeners (or, in this case, the sound mixer) can choose which of several simultaneous aural elements warrant their primary attention (Gorbman 1987, 77).

The punched-arrow ducking system was still in use in 1954 when Piantadosi joined the staff at Twentieth Century-Fox. He attempted to ignore the often ineptly placed arrow punches, and strenuously persuaded his colleagues to make the music dynamically suitable for synchronization through careful prior planning and rehearsal rather than summary manipulation at the mixing stage. This unconsciously echoed the sage advice given to film composers some two decades earlier by Sabaneev, who recommended they should ideally compose their underscoring of dialogue

> on the assumption that, in such cases, it will be barely audible.
> Inexperienced musicians very frequently write lyrical, passionate, and strongly dynamic music, with the result that it has to be relegated to the background and the whole purpose of the composition comes to naught.
>
> (Sabaneev 1935, 40–1)

When Rózsa wrote an elaborate cue to accompany dialogue in *Thunder in the City* (dir. Marion Gering, 1937), the director explained to him that 'in order to allow the dialogue to be heard the music would need to be dubbed at such a low level that all we would hear would be a vague irritation of upper frequencies, principally the piccolo. So far from enhancing the scene the music would merely distract the audience' (Rózsa 1982, 66). The practical lesson Rózsa learned from this experience was heeded in many of his later film scores, which often demonstrate an economical and sensitive under-scoring of dialogue, but it proved impossible for hard-pressed composers to avoid this pitfall altogether. In Steiner's score to *Now, Voyager* (dir. Irving Rapper, 1942), a ludicrous effect is created when the volume of a cue is abruptly lowered even though the music is self-evidently embarking on a crescendo. In some cases, not just directors but even producers might spell out precisely how they wished the volume of music to be accommo-dated to other elements of the soundtrack. One such example was Hal B. Wallis at Warner Bros., whose written production notes were formidably detailed (see facsimile in Kalinak 1992, 77). While working on *Quo vadis?* (dir. Mervyn LeRoy, 1951), Rózsa was greatly put out by overhearing his producer shout to the sound editor: 'Louder, the noises! I can still hear the music!' (Lacombe and Porcile 1995, 260); as the composer wryly recalled in his memoirs, 'When Korngold was asked if he was going to nominate the music [for an Academy Award], he replied that he couldn't nominate what he hadn't heard' (Rózsa 1982, 154). And in *El Cid* (dir. Anthony Mann, 1961), Rózsa composed a carefully structured ceremonial cue that cunningly inte-grates diegetic trumpet fanfares with a rousing nondiegetic march – only to have the latter abruptly lowered in volume by the sound mixer when-ever the actors speak their lines; he was so angry with the sound-effects person for having repeatedly 'tried to persuade the director to take out the music that interfered with her precious clicks and booms' that he can-celled a publicity tour when he discovered on seeing the finished film at the première that whole sections of his music had been abandoned (Rózsa 1982, 183).

Style

The orchestral music for narrative features written by Hollywood film composers in the 1930s and 1940s was steeped in a late nineteenth-century romanticism that was several decades out of date in the concert hall. Only in the special case of scores for musicals did a more up-to-date symphonic jazziness assert itself, and this occasionally intruded into other genres to depict urban sophistication. Indeed, a 'symphonic' and indestructibly tonal romanticism was so deeply ingrained in the consciousness of movie-goers and film composers that any dash of colour such as jazz, extreme chromaticism or atmospheric harmonies and suggestive instrumentation borrowed from more modern French impressionist composers such as Debussy and Ravel was instantly perceived as exotic and 'other' to the prevailing heart-on-sleeve melody-based norm.

Several explanations for this phenomenon have been advanced. First, many of the leading first-generation Hollywood composers were European émigrés who might naturally have been expected to have brought a thorough knowledge of the styles of Wagner, Puccini, Strauss and Verdi with them across the Atlantic. However, those who hailed from Austria and Germany – such as Steiner, Erich Wolfgang Korngold and Franz Waxman – might equally well have proved to be staunch adherents of the more dissonant idiom of Schoenberg and the Second Viennese School (which they were not), so this proposition is not especially convincing. Second, and more plausibly, a good number of both the European and American film composers who congregated in Hollywood in the early 1930s had already pursued careers in the commercial musical theatre, both in Europe and on Broadway, and were therefore thoroughly schooled in an idiom in which a musical conservatism rooted in melodiousness and straightforward tonal harmony has always been a prerequisite for popular success. Third, from its inception film music has frequently been deemed to be, in its very essence, a close cousin of opera – hence the reliance of its early composers, so the argument goes, on the musical language and tried-and-tested compositional techniques of the great operatic masters of the late nineteenth century. Whilst this argument has often been overstressed (see, for example, Prendergast 1992, 39–40), and the term 'operatic' is itself susceptible to many different interpretations (Citron 2004, 424), it is undeniable that certain techniques from opera composition, principally the leitmotif and recitative-style underscoring of dialogue, have remained prominent in film scoring to the present day: Robynn Stilwell (1997a) provides a thought-provoking analysis of an example of quasi-recitative in an action blockbuster from the late 1980s. Korngold famously described film music as opera without the singing (see below), and opera provides a plausible model of a genre in which musical details are specifically tailored to the dramatic needs of a pre-existing narrative.

One simple explanation for the persistence of outdated musical romanticism in the cinema is that it perpetuated the manner of accompaniment firmly established in the silent cinema over the previous three decades. Another proposes that, because film music's primary purpose is to communicate something to the spectators, its 'meaning' must be instantly recognizable and therefore dependent far more on stereotype than innovation: 'As something not very consciously perceived, it inflects the narrative with emotive values via cultural musical codes . . . [T]he core musical lexicon has tended to remain conservatively rooted in Romantic tonality, since its purpose is quick and efficient signification to a mass audience' (Gorbman 1987, 4). Yet another is that people generally like memorable melody, and a leitmotif-oriented tonal language is a good medium in which to give it to them.

If one agrees with Bernard Herrmann that the primary justification for music in films is that 'a piece of film, by its nature, lacks a certain ability to convey emotional overtones' (quoted in Manvell and Huntley 1975, 244), then a reliance on unequivocal romantic rhetoric seems logical enough. But one might go further, as Christopher Palmer does, and assert that such rhetoric functions as a kind of musical escapism fully in accord with the film-makers' wider objectives:

> This musical isolationism was wholly typical: the 'real' world would have decried the music of Korngold, [Alfred] Newman and Steiner as anachronistic and refused it a place, whereas the 'fantasy-world' of Hollywood not only wanted it but encouraged its procreation in vast quantities. 'Romantic' music, music of romance, of fantasy, dream, illusion: what more logical than that it should find a final refuge in the real world's dream-factory? (Palmer 1990, 23)

Flinn has rationalized the apparently deep-seated need for such musical nostalgia in Hollywood cinema by arguing that it stems from a desire for the 'restoration of plenitude' (Flinn 1992, 40); in other words, it supplies something fundamental that would otherwise be absent from the filmic end-product. This plenitude is created by romantic music's characteristic 'utopian dimension – its excess' (Flinn 1992, 90). Borrowing the thoughts of Richard Dyer on the film musical, she argues that classic Hollywood film music gives an impression of 'what utopia would *feel* like, rather than how it would be organized', and demonstrates that in some cases 'it seems appropriate to describe Hollywood utopias in terms of their being partial utopias, for [some] films do not promote a full escape so much as the promise or suggestion of one' (Flinn 1992, 101). Gorbman is more specific, compiling lists of binary oppositions in which those in the right-hand column, she argues, were those most often subjected to emotional enhancement from film music:

Logic	The Irrational
Everyday Reality	Dream
Control	Loss of Control . . .
Man	Woman
Objectivity	Subjectivity
Work	Leisure
Reason	Emotion
Realism	Romantic Fantasy . . .
The Particular	The Universal
The Prosaic	The Poetic
The Present	Mythic Time
The Literal	The Symbolic
	(Gorbman 1987, 80–2)

Wagner and the filmic leitmotif

The spirit of Wagner remained a crucial presence in music for the sound film. According to Steiner, 'If Wagner had lived in this century, he would have been the Number One film composer' (quoted in Thomas 1997, 157). As contemporaneous commentators began to justify the sound cinema as arguably the only new art form in the twentieth century, so its unique sym-biosis of visual, literary and auditory elements inevitably raised parallels with Wagner's concept of the *Gesamtkunstwerk*. In terms of compositional tech-nique, the film composer's contribution continued to be heavily indebted to Wagner's example, most notably in a tendency towards *unendliche Melodie*, through-composition, and a widespread use of leitmotifs: 'For both Wagner and Hollywood, the leitmotiv was primarily motivated by dramatic and not musical necessities, a fact that hints at the subservient relationship music ultimately serves to narrative' (Flinn 1992, 26). Flinn notes that leitmotifs in the classic Hollywood score are mostly associated with specific on-screen characters, and Kate Daubney explains this by suggesting that such identifi-cations may have been rooted in the demands of the star-system (Daubney 2000, 18). (This tendency to equate musical themes with specific actors survives today: few movie-goers would be able to hear John Williams's *Indiana Jones* march without conjuring up a vivid image of Harrison Ford, for example.) Gorbman, whose approach to film music is largely based on its semiotic value, goes further in seeing some leitmotifs as examples of film music's 'connotative values so strongly codified that it can bear a similar relation to the images as a caption to a news photograph'; she goes on to draw attention to the signification of such cultural encoding, and borrows Roland Barthes's term 'ancrage' to describe the process: 'Music, like the caption, anchors the image in meaning, throws a net around the floating visual signifier, assures the viewer of a safely channeled signified' (Gorbman 1987, 58). She cites Jack M. Stein's description of Wagner's own leitmotivic practices to show how thematic repetition can accrue additional emotional significance on each occurrence (Gorbman 1987, 28). James Buhler notes that film music has 'secularized the leitmotif, demythologizing it precisely by emphasizing its linguistic quality, the process of signification' (Buhler 2000, 42).

Codified scoring practices based on the economic variation of recognizable themes according to dramatic context had been clearly laid out for film composers and arrangers as early as Edith Lang's and George West's *Musical Accompaniment of Moving Pictures*, which gives a demonstration of straightforward thematic transformations ideally suited to the rapidly changing dramatic moods of a typical filmic narrative (Lang and West 1920, 8–11). Some commentators, however, strongly objected to film composers' apparent obsession with leitmotifs because it departed from a (widely misunderstood) Wagnerian model, few apparently realizing that Wagner's own deployment of them had been remarkably flexible and undogmatic, and that he himself never used the term. The tendency in film-music commentaries to look uncritically for assumed Wagnerisms also blighted analyses of post-Wagnerian opera, in which context John Deathridge has lamented what he calls 'the Great Leitmotif Hunt or the chase for the proverbial *Gesamtkunstwerk* in which all the arts are supposed to find themselves miraculously on an equal footing', which 'inevitably spilt over with disconcerting regularity into accounts of operas by other composers where they were used – and often still are – like Rorschach tests to diagnose "Wagnerian" tendencies' (Deathridge 2005, 16). Wilfrid Mellers, echoing the opinions of Adorno and Eisler, criticized the use of leitmotifs outside large-scale musical forms and drew attention to their alleged inappropriateness for the episodic structure of film (Irving *et al.* 1954, 104), while Copland lamented the essentially formulaic quality of the technique (Kalinak 1992, 104–5).

Adorno's and Eisler's comments on applications of the leitmotif in film music are provocative enough to warrant quotation at some length:

> Cinema music is still patched together by means of leitmotifs. The ease with which they are recalled provides definite clues for the listener, and they also are a practical help to the composer in his task of composition under pressure. He can quote where he otherwise would have to invent.

... They function as trademarks, so to speak, by which persons, emotions, and symbols can instantly be identified. They have always been the most elementary means of elucidation, the thread by which the musically inexperienced find their way about. They were drummed into the listener's ear by persistent repetition, often with scarcely any variation, very much as a new song is plugged or as a motion-picture actress is popularized by her hair-do. It was natural to assume that this device, because it is so easy to grasp, would be particularly suitable to motion pictures, which are based on the premise that they must be easily understood. However, the truth of this assumption is only illusory.

The reasons for this are first of all technical. The fundamental character of the leitmotif – its salience and brevity – was related to the gigantic dimensions of the Wagnerian and post-Wagnerian music dramas. Just because the leitmotif as such is musically rudimentary, it requires a large musical canvas if it is to take on a structural meaning beyond that of a signpost. The atomization of the musical element is paralleled by the heroic dimensions of the composition as a whole. This relation is entirely absent in the motion picture, which requires continual interruption of one element by another rather than continuity. The constantly changing scenes are characteristic of the structure of the motion picture. Musically, also, shorter forms prevail, and the leitmotif is unsuitable here because of this brevity of forms which must be complete in themselves. Cinema music is so easily understood that it has no need of leitmotifs to serve as signposts, and its limited dimension does not permit of adequate expansion of the leitmotif.

Similar considerations apply with regard to the aesthetic problem. The Wagnerian leitmotif is inseparably connected with the symbolic nature of the music drama ... Wagner conceived its purpose as the endowment of the dramatic events with metaphysical significance ... There is no place for it in the motion picture, which seeks to depict reality ... At the same time, since it cannot be developed to its full musical significance in the motion picture, its use leads to extreme poverty of composition.

(Adorno and Eisler 1994 [1947], 4–6)

Here the authors, by no means for the only time in their trenchant but prejudicial tract, make the error of judging film music using artistic criteria more appropriate to the opera house than the movie theatre, merely because of a superficial similarity between operatic and filmic scoring practices. Their comments reveal strikingly basic misapprehensions about the function of music in narrative cinema, which can scarcely be said to depict 'reality'. These misapprehensions are tainted by an elitist dogma which views functional film music as a poor cousin to art music. There is nothing inherently wrong about providing a 'thread by which the musically inexperienced find their way about' if it is recognized that commercially successful narrative films have to be 'based on the premise that they must be easily understood'; there is of course a subtext at work here, shown by the authors' comment that

'Cinema music is so easily understood that it has no need of leitmotifs', which stems from their rigid belief that such music should aspire towards a state of modernist originality that is inherently more difficult for the average movie-goer to comprehend.

Structure

Adorno's and Eisler's comments on the leitmotif raise important issues concerning the structure of film music that are germane to understanding how music functions in the classical Hollywood film. They demonstrate two basic misunderstandings. First, the use of self-contained short musical structures in narrative film scores is rare, and certainly not conditioned by any perceived need for 'brevity of forms which must be complete in themselves'. Instead, film music depends heavily for its illusion of through-composition on a deliberate lack of closure, and as a result it often has an open-ended quality that a composer sensitive to this attribute may choose to exploit right up until a film's end titles: indeed, it is a cliché for individual cues to end with some kind of interrupted cadence (another Wagnerian mannerism), a particularly common method of rounding off main-title music by extending it into the opening shots of the first scene and leaving the harmony unresolved in order to create a sense of expectancy. By the time of Herrmann's widely admired film scores of the 1950s, such lack of tonal resolution could be constant and unremitting – and it remains a powerful emotional tool, even when consciously manipulative and formulaically overworked. This phenomenon is directly relevant to the second of Adorno's and Eisler's misapprehensions, namely that film scores lack 'heroic dimensions' because of 'continual interruption of one element by another rather than continuity'. Their mistake here is to divorce the score from the film and judge it as a piece of would-be autonomous music. Even laying aside the obvious objection that epic film scores of the Hollywood Golden Age, such as Steiner's for *Gone With the Wind*, routinely exceeded the length of many late-romantic operas in playing time, it should be noted that the duration and pacing of a film in themselves play a vital role with relation to the cumulative impact of the musical cues and timing of leitmotivic reminiscences, whether or not the music plays continuously throughout.

These arguments and counter-arguments raise another fundamental question about the nature of the Hollywood film score, which has repeatedly been labelled 'symphonic' – far more frequently than it has been called 'operatic', presumably because of the general absence of nondiegetic singing. Beyond the bare facts that most film music in the Golden Age was scored for a full orchestra and employed a tonal harmonic language and prominent thematic developments, it is difficult to see how the epithet 'symphonic' is justified on structural grounds. Gerard Carbonara, a prolific composer of film scores in Hollywood during the 1930s and 1940s, drew a clear distinction between film music and symphonic music: unlike Adorno and Eisler, he viewed leitmotivic techniques as an absolute necessity in film scoring precisely because only in symphonic (i.e. concert-hall) music can a composer's themes 'be worked out in their original entirety without being subjected to forced cutting' (quoted in Kalinak 1992, 105). Specious comparisons between symphonic and film music, in which successful scores are those deemed to be 'unified' in some satisfyingly coherent and autonomous sense, have only recently been subjected to critical scrutiny; the splintering of film-music styles and practices since the 1960s has shown how stream-of-consciousness fragmentation – and even the juxtaposition of wildly contrasting musical styles within a single film – can often be just as dramatically effective as the kind of cogent musical argument to which composers versed in the classical tradition felt film music ought ideally to aspire.

Those, like Carbonara, who had first-hand experience of forging workable narrative film scores under pressure knew only too well that production practices dictated an altogether more pragmatic approach to the task. The classic and much-cited exposition of Hollywood's overriding compositional principles was formulated by Gorbman, and deserves quotation in full:

I. *'Invisibility'*: the technical apparatus of nondiegetic music must not be visible.

II. *'Inaudibility'*: Music is not meant to be heard consciously. As such it should subordinate itself to dialogue, to visuals – i.e., to the primary vehicles of the narrative.

III. *Signifier of emotion*: Soundtrack music may set specific moods and emphasize particular emotions suggested in the narrative (cf. ♯ IV), but first and foremost, it is a signifier of emotion itself.

IV. *Narrative cueing*:
   • *referential/narrative*: music gives referential and narrative cues, e.g., indicating point of view, supplying formal demarcations, and establishing setting and characters.
   • *connotative*: music 'interprets' and 'illustrates' narrative events.

V. *Continuity*: music provides formal and rhythmic continuity – between shots, in transitions between scenes, by filling 'gaps'.

VI. *Unity*: via repetition and variation of musical material and instrumentation, music aids in the construction of formal and narrative unity.

VII. A given film score may violate any of the principles above, providing the violation is at the service of the other principles.   (Gorbman 1987, 73)

It is interesting to note here that unity – or perhaps we might better refer to an illusion of unity – is created by 'repetition and variation of musical material and instrumentation', hinting at pervasive leitmotivic practices and the even simpler device of using instantly recognizable instrumental colour (e.g. a cliché such as a seductive-sounding saxophone for a female character of easy virtue) to convey a narrative point. Another type of unity might be thought to reside in a composer's careful tonal planning – especially important in cases, as outlined above, where lack of tonal resolution is a dynamic feature of the music. Yet the vast majority of analyses of Hollywood film scores give absolute priority to thematic and leitmotivic transformations and recurrences (see, for example, the exhaustive thematic analysis of a single Steiner score in Daubney 2000, 58–91), either because these are the most obvious features of the music, or perhaps also because detecting more esoteric compositional principles requires the demonstration of the kind of technical expertise possessed only by analysts who allegedly approach film scores as if they were – or should be – concert works. (According to Flinn (1992, 4), for example, film-music scholarship is beset by the problem of 'an aesthetic and formalist tendency that treats film music as a discrete, autonomous artefact'.) Even in the realm of tonal procedures, however, the omnipotence of the producer could sometimes assert itself. Irving Thalberg of MGM once instructed his studio's composers to desist from using minor chords in their main-title music: his framed dictat on this subject remained bolted to the wall of the studio's music department for decades, and ominously resisted a spirited attempt to remove it (Previn 1992, 152). And the vast majority of Golden Age Hollywood features end with an upbeat major-key surge as 'The End' appears on screen.

Whatever one's view on the issue of unity, it is abundantly clear from Gorbman's summary that the type and quantity of musical cues in the classic Hollywood score was overwhelmingly dependent on practical considerations of narrative clarity and strength. Since it was felt that music should not normally draw attention to itself, its entrances and exits were carefully planned in spotting sessions in order to coincide with dramatic events that naturally seemed to require reinforcement, such as the opening or closing of a door, or producing a weapon; a cue might be terminated by the intrusion of a diegetic sound or dialogue (Sabaneev 1935, 40). Where no such events provided a pretext for musical stops and starts, the music might be 'sneaked in' almost inaudibly so that an audience would not be consciously aware of its entrance; it might also be 'sneaked out' by being made to fade away to nothing. These devices strengthened the sense of open-endedness common in music cues.

Apart from so-called 'saturation' scores in which nondiegetic music played almost continually throughout the film (an overreaction to the stark avoidance of nondiegetic music in the early years of the sound film), the much-vaunted property of continuity attributed to film music since the silent era generally remained as partial and localized as the notion of unity was elusive. As Kalinak observed: 'composers of the classical score gravitated toward moments when continuity is most tenuous, to points of structural linkages on which the narrative chain depends: transitions between sequences, flash-forwards and flashbacks, parallel editing, dream sequences, and montage' (Kalinak 1992, 80); a specific reason for the signalling of flashbacks by musical means was the fact that in essence cinematic images can only exist in the present tense (Mitry 1998, 52). Musical continuity across temporal disjunctures was more effectively accomplished when scoring highlighted mood, emotion or atmosphere rather than specific diegetic details at a local level.

Such mood music was generally recognized as one of two principal types of nondiegetic scoring in the Golden Age, the other being the graphically illustrative music popularly known as mickey-mousing, or 'catching the action'. Franz Waxman's (uncredited) score for *To Have and Have Not* (dir. Howard Hawks, 1945) provides representative examples of this procedure in both comedic and serious contexts. When Humphrey Bogart prepares to empty a bucket of water over his dozing buddy, the prank is prepared by an expectantly sustained tritone before the music proceeds to illustrate not only the water's splash in general terms but even a tiny specific detail: a piccolo flourish coincides with the moment when the rudely awoken partner spits out some of the water he has ingested. In a contrastingly serious scene, in which the two men cruise in their boat at night, the question-and-answer flashes of signalling lamps are dutifully and atmospherically 'caught' by synchronized and subdued chordal stabs from the orchestra. As Kalinak points out (1992, 86), techniques such as these can foster the illusion of music's invisibility by giving a precise narrative justification for the presence of its gestures, and this may account for the popularity of the device in the early Hollywood sound film. The paradox has been aptly summarized by James Buhler and David Neumeyer, who note that nondiegetic music 'endangers illusion: it poses the constant threat of calling attention to the constructed nature of the filmic illusion. The synchronization of music to image reduces precisely this tension and so permits nondiegetic music to exist within the aesthetic of the realist film' (Buhler and Neumeyer 1994, 378). But the detailed mickey-mousing of serious action was, even in those early days, dismissed as 'ludicrous' by one commentator (Sabaneev 1935, 50) and 'ridiculous' by Selznick, who in 1937 had a major disagreement with Steiner about the latter's apparent obsession with it (quoted in Karlin 1994, 80). Apart from its essential redundancy, catching the action at every available opportunity presents a serious impediment to continuity: it requires a particular kind of musical genius to bind together detailed musical illustration in a cogent and meaningful nondiegetic manner, and such expertise is most often encountered in the field of animation (see Chapter 7).

Max Steiner

Generally considered to have laid the indestructible foundations for the style of narrative film scoring outlined in the preceding pages, Steiner's legendary achievements in Hollywood were made possible by his extensive prior experience of theatrical music, tremendous hard graft – and, not least of all, being fortunate enough to be in the right place at the right time. That place was, of course, Hollywood, where he arrived in 1929 to join the music staff of RKO. Before his move west, he had been a conductor and composer of musicals on Broadway since emigrating to the USA in 1914. And before that he had worked in musical theatre across Europe, principally in his native Vienna – where his family were influential producers of operetta, his grandfather having commissioned works from the likes of Franz von Suppé and Johann Strauss II – but also in London (1907–11). This theatrical experience meant that when Steiner moved to Hollywood, he was already a competent composer in the styles of late romanticism, operetta and Broadway's jazz-inflected musical comedies, and a highly efficient orchestrator and musical director.

Steiner had been in demand for film work during the silent era, when he did some scoring for Fox films at the instigation of Roxy Rothapfel, for whom he composed and conducted an original score for *The Bondsman* in 1915 at the age of only seventeen (Altman 2004, 291). Louis Silvers unsuccessfully attempted to lure Steiner to Hollywood in the early 1920s, and his eventual decision to work for RKO was occasioned by the slump in theatrical activity in New York attendant upon the Wall Street Crash; his first assignments at the studio were as an orchestrator, working under Roy Webb. It was an inauspicious time to embark on a career in film music, which in 1930 seemed almost on the verge of extinction as producers continued to avoid nondiegetic accompaniments; and the future even looked bleak for the one genre in which music took a leading role, the musical, examples of which had recently suffered at the box office. That nondiegetic music limped back into dramatic features in 1931 was the result of improved post-production techniques, and RKO's bold decision to let Steiner loose on a limited amount of scoring for the western *Cimarron* (dir. Wesley Ruggles, 1930) and *Symphony of Six Million* (dir. Gregory La Cava, 1932). For the latter, Steiner was authorized by executive producer Selznick to score the entire reel in which the protagonist's father dies – which he does to the accompaniment of Steiner's arrangement of the same Jewish melody, *Kol Nidre*, that had captured the melancholy side of *The Jazz Singer*'s cultural milieu a few years before. RKO evidently deemed their experiment a success and commissioned much larger quantities of background music from Steiner for *Bird of Paradise* (dir. King Vidor) and *The Most Dangerous*

Game (dir. Ernest B. Schoedsack and Irving Pichel), both released in 1932.

Steiner's ambitious score for *King Kong* (dir. Merian C. Cooper and Schoedsack, 1933) is universally acknowledged as his most important achievement, one that almost single-handedly marked the coming-of-age of nondiegetic film music: it established a style and technique of scoring that was not only much imitated during the Golden Age, but continues to be reflected in mainstream narrative scoring practices to the present day. In many ways its turbulent and dissonant idiom was, in its filmic context, so outrageous for its time that many later scores – including Steiner's own – seem tame by comparison. Such modernism (the term is relative, since in many respects Steiner's score was still no more advanced than the most adventurous music Richard Strauss composed decades before) was justified, and indeed encouraged, by the producers' concern that their animated gorilla puppet would provoke laughter rather than terror amongst the film's spectators: the nondiegetic music is therefore a *locus classicus* of the promotion of suspension of disbelief. The film's sound effects were equally effective in this regard, the monster's roar in particular having been created by considerable experimentation in the sound department. Thus the first landmark nondiegetic music track must be viewed as only part of a greater composite soundtrack that broke considerable new ground both technically and aesthetically. Strikingly, the climactic aeroplane attack launched on Kong as he sits astride the Empire State Building takes place without music, the deafening sound of the biplanes' machine guns dominating the montage so that when music eventually returns it is all the more effective.

Kong illustrates all the features that were to remain typical both of Steiner's dramatic scoring in particular and Golden Age narrative music in general. The main-title music presents two contrasting idioms, one aggressive (the monster) and the other romantic (the object of his affection); the binary opposition between disruptive chromaticism and stable tonality exemplified here was especially characteristic of Steiner's simple musico-dramatic language. Kong's chromatic leitmotif recurs throughout the film at appropriate moments, Steiner's decision to restrict it to just three notes allowing him to bring it in almost anywhere with ease; at one point it invades a diegetic cue, and at the climax it merges with the love theme as Kong is forced to part from his amour: 'Here the music is required, perhaps for the first time in an American film, to explain to the audience what is actually happening on the screen, since the camera is unable to articulate Kong's instinctive feelings of tenderness towards his helpless victim' (Palmer 1990, 28–9). Some of the music is superbly effective, in particular that accompanying the fog-bound approach of the explorers' ship towards Skull Island, which is impressionistically scored on the basis, not of themes, but of tensely subdued ostinati through which diegetic tribal drumming (a sonic element deployed pervasively) can faintly be heard: this remarkable cue would not sound out of place in a modern film. Steiner's score seems dated only in its slavishly graphic mickey-mousing of such moments as the deliberate plod of the tribal leader's feet as he descends a flight of steps to meet the explorers – one can even hear the conductor's attempts to decelerate and accelerate in exact synchronization with the actor's somewhat erratic tread – and the literal-mindedness with which romantic underscoring on deck is twice interrupted and then resumed in accordance with abrupt shot changes to and from the interior of the ship's bridge. Some of the musical stereotyping, such as the use of parallel fourths and fifths for the 'primitive' natives, may also make modern audiences cringe – even though this seemed a useful and economical formula at the time and later appeared ubiquitously in Holly-wood scores for 'other' peoples as diverse as Native Americans and ancient Romans. *Kong*'s heady mixture of exotic monster and ripely expressionistic music immediately fell prey to its inherent self-parody: a sequel, *Son of Kong*, released later the same year and replete with more slavish mickey-mousing and a reworking of the diegetic drums and chromatic motif from Steiner, was such a flop that it had to be remarketed as a comedy.

The musical depiction of a character's inner feelings was also promi-nent in Steiner's score for *Of Human Bondage* (dir. John Cromwell, 1934) in which he showed how an individual theme can become 'an index of strongly subjective point-of-view' (Gorbman 1987, 84). For his score to John Ford's *The Informer* in 1935, Steiner won RKO one of the film's four Academy Awards. The main-title music epitomized his 'ability to crystal-lize the essence of a film in a single theme' (Palmer 1990, 29): this passage economically combines a sense of oppression with suggestions of Irish tra-ditional music appropriate to the film's setting. Motivic techniques are in places as epigrammatic as those in *Kong*, a good example being a pregnant four-note motif used to represent money. Unusually, Steiner had began work on his score to *The Informer* in advance of the film's shooting, with Ford filming certain scenes in synchronization to pre-recorded cues; thus, for example, the distinctive walk of protagonist Gypo Nolan was rehearsed to reflect illustrative music Steiner had already written for him rather than the music having been inspired by the acting (Kalinak 1992, 115). Even a moment of graphic mickey-mousing was set up in advance: for a sequence involving dripping water, Steiner recalled that 'The property man and I worked for days trying to regulate the water tank so it dripped in tempo and so I could accompany it. This took a great deal of time and thought because a dripping faucet doesn't always drip in the same rhythm' (quoted in Thomas 1979, 78). Steiner declared that he felt this piece of ingenuity had been partly responsible for his Academy Award, but even in the 1930s many criticized the obviousness and inbuilt redundancy of such synchronization. Maurice Jaubert curtly dismissed it as childishness and felt it demonstrated a lack of comprehension of the essential function of film music (see Chapter 8), though a more positive view of it was later taken by Chion (1994, 51–4; 1995, 123–4).

As literal-minded as his use of leitmotifs was Steiner's habitual quotation of pre-existing melodies appropriate to the plot. In *The Gay Divorcee* (1934), a sea voyage from France to England begins with a quotation of the *Marseillaise* and ends with 'Rule, Britannia'. In *The Informer*, 'Yankee Doodle' is heard when Gypo sees an advert for a transatlantic passage, and a dark minor-key variation of 'Rule, Britannia' captures his resentment towards the British. Minor-key variations on familiar themes were a favourite device of Steiner's, and had indeed been a stock-in-trade of music for silent films (see, for example, Breil's dramatically motivated transformations of the tune 'Wild Irish Rose' in his score to Griffith's *Intolerance*). In his epic score to *Gone With the Wind* (dir. Victor Fleming *et al.*, 1939), the burning of Atlanta is accompanied by brass interjections based on the Civil War song 'Dixie', the idea that they be in the minor apparently having emanated from Selznick who, presumably in addition to the obvious dramatic appropriateness of such a dark variant, may have intended to 'steer film auditors away from "improper" (i.e., southern) political allegiances, even in their listening habits' (Flinn 1992, 109). In *Casablanca* (dir. Michael Curtiz, 1942), mention of the arrival of the Germans in Paris is accompanied by a slow and sombre minor-key version of the German national anthem. The effect of Steiner's jaunty inclusion of the *Marseillaise* to set the action of this film firmly in French North Africa has been analysed by Brown:

> even the briefest recognizable snippet of such a piece . . . can evoke in the listener an entire political mythology. For the tune or fragment is not simply a motif incorporated into a larger musical or musico-dramatic fiber, but rather stands as the kind of second-degree sign that Roland Barthes defines as myth . . . All Max Steiner needed to do at the beginning of his overture for *Gone With the Wind* was to briefly allude to 'Dixie' and to set one motif to a banjo to immediately evoke what Barthes might have called 'old-southicity' – this via two different types of (second-degree) musical signifiers, one thematic, the other instrumental.   (R. S. Brown 1994, 52)

One category of such cues became known as 'locational' music, designed to establish a geographical region aurally: the main-title sequence of *Casablanca*, for example, also includes appropriately 'primitive' music for the Moroccan setting. Sometimes Steiner's literal-mindedness in this regard

3.1 Ready to play it again: Dooley Wilson at the piano (as Sam, left) with Humphrey Bogart (as Rick, centre) and Ingrid Bergman (as Ilsa, right) in *Casablanca* (1942). Wilson memorably performed Herman Hupfeld's 'As Time Goes By' (1931) on screen, much to the frustration of the film's composer Max Steiner, who wanted to write his own song.

sets a dramatically inappropriate mood, as when Gary Cooper arrives at a Swiss airport in *Cloak and Dagger* (dir. Fritz Lang, 1946) to the sounds of a jolly nondiegetic Alpine dance strangely at odds with the sinister context.

Perhaps the most notable feature of Steiner's *Casablanca* score is its use of Herman Hupfeld's song 'As Time Goes By' (1931), first heard diegetically when Sam famously plays it on his piano in Rick's bar and subsequently taken up in the nondiegetic score as a signifier of Rick's and Ilsa's romantic involvement, in the classic leitmotivic manner of gradually accumulating emotional significance. (Steiner apparently disliked the song and wished to replace it at a rather late stage with one of his own: since this would have involved reshooting several of Ilsa's scenes, the displeased studio executives prevented his doing so on the pretext that Ingrid Bergman had already changed her hair style for her next film.) The film furnishes a classic instance of what became a stock technique: a later diegetic performance of the song ushers in a lengthy flashback sequence scored with elaborate nondiegetic music. Flinn sees the procedure as typical of film music's being 'compulsively used to signal temporal disphasures' (Flinn 1992, 109) and thereby providing nostalgic release from the present to the past. More telling still was Steiner's treatment of a diegetic song in *Key Largo* (dir. John Huston, 1948): a bright and jazzy nondiegetic saxophone solo represents a lush (brilliantly portrayed by Claire Trevor, who won an Academy Award for her performance), but after she has sung a tragically pathetic song the saxophone returns, now playing in a much bleaker manner that makes clear reference to her diegetic melody.

Each scholar of film music has her or his own favourite Steiner scores: Gorbman (1987, 91–8) offers a case-study of *Mildred Pierce* (dir. Michael Curtiz, 1945); Palmer (1990, 32) singles out *The Letter* (dir. William Wyler, 1940), *The Big Sleep* (dir. Howard Hawks, 1946) and *The Glass Menagerie* (dir. Irving Rapper, 1950); Daubney (2000) devotes a whole book to *Now, Voyager* (dir. Rapper, 1942), a film score also subjected to thematic and tonal analysis by Charles Leinberger (2002). *Now, Voyager*, for which Steiner received his second Academy Award, again featured signposting quotations ('Yankee Doodle' for a ship's reaching New York) and graphic mickey-mousing (coins dropping into a public telephone, footsteps going down stairs). It was one of no fewer than eighteen dramas and 'women's films' scored by him that featured actress Bette Davis; this was his preferred genre, and Davis paid tribute to the insight into the stories his music demonstrated (Thomas 1997, 149). But no commentator has been able to claim that Steiner's mass-produced music – in 1947–8, for example, he scored no fewer than 22 features and by the time of his retirement in 1965 he had composed in excess of 300 film scores – was unerringly even in quality. Palmer is more explicit and specific in his criticisms than most, singling out the music for *The Treasure of the Sierra Madre* (dir. Huston, 1948) for its failure to capture the ruggedness of the director's vision and its complacent use in the main title of 'routine Spanishry which may superficially suggest a Mexican location but fails to give any intimation of the mood of the film or the true role of the natural background, which is anything but colourful or picturesque' (Palmer 1990, 35), and blaming Steiner's prolific output of scores for often sentimental melodramas for having led him firmly into a stylistic rut (Palmer 1990, 38). Certainly his work contains many crudities and clichés, such as the saccharine modulations to the major when a sick child recovers in *Sierra Madre* and after the villain dies at the climax of *Key Largo* – a film replete with predictable stingers and melodramatic orchestral flourishes.

At the same time, however, Steiner's phenomenal ability to meet deadlines and his sheer pragmatism set a formidable standard of working practice amongst studio composers. Although his unorthodox collaboration with Ford on *The Informer* produced impressive results, Steiner later avoided studying film scripts in advance because they bore so little resemblance to the eventual rough cuts on the basis of which he preferred to compose. His work generally followed the same pattern: at the drawing up of the cue sheet, he sketched out themes for the principal characters and narrative topics, declaring in a newspaper article that 'every character should have a theme' (Steiner 1935). Next he paid special consideration to those scenes where music might serve a useful function in quickening or slowing the dramatic pace; then he reviewed each reel in turn and composed specific cues with the aid of a stopwatch. His detailed short-score sketches were passed on to trusted orchestrators, principally Bernhard Kaun at RKO and Friedhofer at Warner Bros. (for whom Steiner worked from 1936 onwards, composing their trademark fanfare in the following year); the nearly four-hour score for *Gone With the Wind*, composed in just twelve weeks with the aid of copious quantities of Benzedrine, was realized by a team of no fewer than five orchestrators (Thomas 1997, 150–1). The problem of dialogue underscoring was generally negotiated by supplying low-pitched music for a high-pitched speaking voice, and vice versa (Daubney 2000, 27). To save labour, passages from one film score might occasionally be recycled in another, as with the self-borrowing in *They Died With Their Boots On* (dir. Raoul Walsh, 1941) of battle music previously composed for *Santa Fe Trail* (dir. Michael Curtiz, 1940; Daubney 2000, 29).

Steiner commented of his work: 'I've always tried to subordinate myself to the picture. A lot of composers make the mistake of thinking that the film is a platform for showing how clever they are. This is not the place for it' (quoted in Thomas 1979, 81). By ensuring that every musical gesture did exactly what the narrative dictated it should do, Steiner established the formulaic principles that dictated the idiom of a whole generation of Hollywood films, and in doing so became the first individual studio composer to win renown for his achievements.

Erich Wolfgang Korngold

Another Viennese composer who achieved fame in Hollywood during the 1930s was Korngold who, unlike Steiner, had already enjoyed a formidable international reputation as first a child prodigy and then as a front-rank opera composer in Europe before he accepted an invitation to arrange Mendelssohn's music for a Shakespeare film in 1934 (see Chapter 4), after which he worked increasingly for the movies. Numerically, Korngold's achievements as a film composer pale into insignificance alongside the colossal output of his compatriot: Korngold composed only nineteen original film scores (all but one of which were principally orchestrated by Friedhofer)

between 1935 and his retirement in 1947, a period during which the prolific Steiner produced 101. Yet Korngold's stylistic influence on other film
composers was enormous: obvious examples are encountered in the work
of figures as diverse as Friedhofer (*The Bandit of Sherwood Forest*, 1946) and
John Addison (*The Black Knight*, 1954) when working in the swashbuckling genre in which Korngold to some extent specialized, and the influence
has persisted to the present day thanks to the contemporary reworking of
certain aspects of his spirited idiom by John Williams and others.

One factor that contributed to Korngold's success was the prestige he
enjoyed as a widely acknowledged musical genius from the classical arena,
which immediately put him in an entirely different perceptual category from
Steiner and lesser studio hacks. It is one thing to talk about the widespread
influence of Richard Strauss on film music at this time, but quite another for
a composer to possess a personal testimonial from Strauss himself declaring
that the boy Korngold's 'assurance of style, this mastery of form, this characteristic expressiveness, this bold harmony, are truly astonishing!' (Carroll
2000, 823). Warner Bros., with whom Korngold signed an exclusive contract, basked in the kudos of their association with the composer, who was
thereby enabled to issue all kinds of demands normally impossible even for
musicians of the stature of Steiner (who worked for the same studio at the
same time, and had already won his first Academy Award). Korngold thus
limited himself to scoring just two films per year, was guaranteed working
time way in excess of the normal studio turnaround period, reserved the
right to decline any film he disliked, and was assured of prominent accred-
itation (Karlin 1994, 181–2). Last, but by no means least, he did not assign
the copyright in his music over to the studio, which greatly facilitated his
incorporation of material from his film scores into concert works (see Leck
1994). A well-known example relates to his final film score, *Deception* (dir.
Rapper, 1947), for which he composed a diegetic Cello Concerto – mimed by
actor Paul Henreid with the assistance of the arms of two cellists handling his
instrument through false sleeves – that was simultaneously recycled as the
composer's *bona fide* Cello Concerto in C major, Op. 37. These exceptional
prerogatives may be contrasted with RKO's earlier treatment of Steiner, who
had left the studio under a cloud when he dared to ask for a pay rise and
was summarily replaced as music director by Nathaniel Shilkret.

Like Steiner's, Korngold's film music followed what were already becoming well-established conventions: it cultivated a leitmotif-based romanticism ('symphonic' was the term used by Korngold himself to describe it),
with fundamental narrative orientation, the music almost always subordinate to the primacy of the visual image and dialogue. He became celebrated
for his flamboyant scores to Warners' series of Errol Flynn costume dramas including *Captain Blood* (1935), *The Adventures of Robin Hood* (1938;

analysed in detail in Winters 2007), *The Private Lives of Elizabeth and Essex* (1939) and *The Sea Hawk* (1940), all directed by Curtiz. Korngold believed that film music was essentially operatic music without the singing, quipping that Puccini's *Tosca* was 'the best film score ever written' (quoted in Thomas 1997, 175), and he brought his experience of operatic composition to bear in his work for the silver screen. Although his music was as much indebted to the examples of Wagner, Strauss and Puccini as that of any other Hollywood composer in the 1930s, it demonstrated a lush self-confidence that was ideally suited to the Flynn swashbucklers, and at the same time achieved the kind of structural sophistication only to be expected of someone from Korngold's background. As Palmer noted, Korngold's talents had 'enough inbuilt vitality to stop short of the kind of maggoty over-ripeness into which the idiom degenerated in the hands of less-accomplished practitioners . . . The scores he wrote for pictures whose other component parts accorded perfectly with the inherent character of his music have survived the test of time to emerge as models of their kind' (Palmer 1990, 52–3).

In working practices, too, Korngold differed markedly from Steiner. Korngold preferred to read a film's script in advance of setting to work on it, since he felt the script corresponded to the opera libretti of which he had considerable experience. His initial sketches were sometimes conceived on the basis of keyboard improvisations carried out while viewing rough cuts, preserving a link with the silent cinema (in which his wife Luzi had acted) and suggesting that continuity was all-important – especially at Warners, where Jack Warner was infamous for his fondness for saturation scores. While recording, Korngold scrupulously avoided click-tracks and stopwatches, preferring to rely on his innate musicality to aid the process of synchronization; he sometimes wrote carefully notated rubato effects into his melodies so that the illusion of spontaneity would be created without sacrificing the regular beat necessary for reliable co-ordination with the images (R. S. Brown 1994, 100).

Similar in ilk to the Curtiz swashbucklers was *The Prince and the Pauper* (dir. William Keighley, 1937), also starring Flynn and providing a clear illustration of the simple means by which Korngold's music achieved structural cogency. His score contains just enough surprises to prevent any single idea, even the most hackneyed, from overstaying its welcome: thus the robust scoring of the routine main-title theme is delightfully dissipated into a delicate variation as the 'Foreword' title card appears before the first scene. This Lydian-inflected theme – a good example of a specific modal colouring later adopted by Williams in his Korngold-inspired music – occurs throughout the score, which at times verges on the monothematic. Since it serves as a general-purpose melody associated with various different activities and situations, its use never seems mechanical or over-literal; and the recurrence of the delicate variation on several occasions imparts a broader sense of structural articulation. Similarly, a furtive pizzicato idea is rescued from cliché by being punctuated with surprising splashes of colour on the vibraphone, and this cue is also given a formal recapitulation later in the film, with modified scoring. After Korngold mickey-mouses the Prince's leaping onto the King's bed with a blunt cadence that brings the preceding cue neatly to a close, the idea becomes familiar in two later recurrences that seem in retrospect to justify what might in lesser hands have seemed a redundant illustrative gesture. Although there is plenty of easy listening and sometimes sentimental string underscoring for intimate dialogue scenes, the political machinations at court are left devoid of music and therefore thrown into stark, clinical relief. Occasional dashes of tonal and textural adventurousness, notably the use of parallel major seconds for nocturnal atmosphere and dark false-relation dissonances for the most ominous moments in the plot, enliven the basically outdated idiom. Yet Korngold, great musician or not, suffers the same indignities as the hack composers: his bustling music for the opening street scene is rendered virtually inaudible beneath a welter of cannon shots, shouted lines and crowd noise.

That Korngold was wary of falling into the trap of writing superficially descriptive music to order is shown by his reluctance to score *The Adventures of Robin Hood*, which he claimed would leave him 'artistically completely dissatisfied' because 'I have no relation to it and therefore cannot produce any music for it. I am a musician of the heart, of passions and psychology; I am not a musical illustrator for a ninety-percent-action picture' (quoted in Behlmer 1989, 84). The project, which Korngold eventually accepted owing to the worsening political climate in Vienna which threatened his future livelihood in Europe, resulted in another fine score that won him his second Academy Award. (The first had been for Mervyn Le Roy's *Anthony Adverse* in 1936.) Partly based on material from a concert work, *Sursum Corda*, that had flopped nearly two decades before (Duchen 1996, 86), the music is thoroughly Austro-Germanic, with suggestions of Mahler and Reger audible through the Straussian norm. In common with other film scores before Rózsa revolutionized the scoring of period films (see Chapter 5), there is no attempt to capture the spirit of the times: the musical style is thoroughly anachronistic to the plot (though no more so, it might be argued, than Wagner's is in *Die Meistersinger*) and it may disconcert modern audiences to hear a lush *fin-de-siècle* Viennese waltz accompanying a medieval banqueting scene. The final climax, which involves little dialogue, allows Korngold to do what he arguably did best: compose a miniature and solidly crafted Straussian symphonic poem that deftly supports the action without losing continuity (and at the same time manages to incorporate diegetic fanfares).

Both *Captain Blood* and *The Sea Hawk* are essentially similar in style. In *Captain Blood*, the seventeenth-century pirates at one point launch into an incongruously Viennese winching song; the score is articulated by well-placed climaxes, the most impressive being the first example of Korngold's cogently developed swordfight cues, but the music is frequently drowned out by the noise of the battle sequences. The ubiquitous ducking of dialogue underscoring was meticulously planned by producer Hal B. Wallis on his editorial notes, for example: 'Hold the music down under the dialogue in the bunk house . . . Hold the music way down under the dialogue' (from facsimile in Kalinak 1992, 77). Pressure of time forced Korngold to use pre-existing music by Liszt to flesh out what was otherwise his first original film score, with the result that he was – on his own insistence – merely credited as arranger rather than composer (McCarty 2000, 9). In *The Sea Hawk*, Korngold showed his awareness that music could create physical sensations not necessarily visible on screen, such as the force of the wind and the motion of a ship's oars, and used a battery of exotic percussion for the film's segments set in Panama; his use of leitmotifs is more character-specific than in *The Prince and the Pauper*, and he sometimes trots them obligingly out in accordance with whoever happens to be on screen at any one moment.

Korngold's score for *King's Row* (dir. Sam Wood, 1941) was so popular that the studio received numerous letters asking if a recording of it were available. (It was only in the 1970s that an RCA anthology of Korngold's film music achieved wide circulation and was partly responsible for the renewed interest in his manner of scoring: see Palmer 1990, 65–6.) But in 1946, after seeing the delayed release of *Devotion* (dir. Curtis Bernhardt, 1943), critic Celeste Hautbois – while praising certain aspects of Korngold's score, chiefly its sense of atmosphere, continuity and unobtrusive mickey-mousing took him to task for weaknesses in his music she alleged were caused by an unfortunate triumph of style over content:

> *what* he says is much inferior to *how* he says it. There are too many points
> when the apparently deep and mature emotions being portrayed on the
> screen are accompanied by music suggesting adolescent sentimentality and
> superficiality, in utter contrast to the story contents . . . From the orchestral
> viewpoint, the almost continuous use of harp glissandi [prominent in many
> of Friedhofer's orchestrations] gave a cheap and slick tinge to the score
> which might have been more convincing if clothed in more sensitive and
> lean orchestration.   (quoted in Karlin 1994, 149)

Alternatively, Korngold's music might seem overly rich and prominent for its meagre dramatic context, as in *Of Human Bondage* (Edmund Goulding's 1946 remake for Warners of the RKO film originally scored by Steiner in 1934; it was remade again in 1964 with a score by Ron Goodwin), which

Tony Thomas likens to 'an expensive suit hanging on a scarecrow' (Thomas 1997, 180).

An unavoidable consideration, though increasingly hard to contemplate in an age when the notion of quality in music is viewed with deep suspicion, is the question of whether Korngold's film music – because of his compositional credentials – was so much better than Steiner's (or anyone else's) that it should have warranted such favourable working conditions and publicity; and whether the criticisms of his later work quoted above suggest that its quality and appropriateness declined. Two well-known anecdotes, both containing a significant grain of truth, may provide a partial answer. According to Korngold's son, when the composer was asked by his wife why Steiner's music apparently got better but Korngold's declined during their employment at Warners, her husband replied: 'Simple. I'm copying him and he's copying me!' (quoted in Karlin 1994, 197). And at the very end of his career in films, when asked to explain why his music seemed less vibrant than it used to be, he commented: 'When I first came here, I couldn't understand the dialogue – now I can' (quoted in Thomas 1997, 181).

Franz Waxman: horror and sophistication

Alongside Steiner's score to *King Kong*, Waxman's to *The Bride of Frankenstein* (dir. James Whale, 1935) may be regarded as one of the most important of the Golden Age in demonstrating just how effective original film music could be as an instrument of both terror and suspension of disbelief. Waxman's career in films had begun six years earlier in Berlin, where he served as arranger and musical director for *Der blaue Engel* (see Chapter 2), and it was the decision of the film's UFA producer, Erich Pommer, to seek work in Hollywood that lured the composer to the USA: in 1934, Waxman (having already moved to Paris to escape anti-Semitism in his native Germany) settled in Los Angeles and collaborated with fellow-expatriate scriptwriter Billy Wilder and actress Gloria Swanson on Pommer's Fox production of the operetta *Music in the Air*. Soon after, Waxman briefly served as music director at Universal, which had already begun to make its name with innovative work in the horror genre (Rosar 1983).

Prior to Waxman's music for *The Bride of Frankenstein*, Universal's horror pictures had been musically tame and predictable. Both *Dracula* (dir. Tod Browning, 1931) and *The Mummy* (dir. Karl Freund, 1932), for example, made strictly limited use of music and relied on the time-honoured melodramatic idiom inherited from silent cinema: the famous oboe melody from Tchaikovsky's *Swan Lake* makes a prominent appearance in both, intensifying the dream-like melancholic atmosphere of these films rather than scaring the audience. Just as Steiner had terrified his spectators in *Kong*, so Waxman took them squarely by the scruff of the neck with his music for *The Bride of Frankenstein*. Its high dissonance level was rare at the time, though perfectly in accord with the darkly disturbing visuals inspired – as in the case of so many early horror films and, a little later, *films noirs* – by the lighting and camera angles of German expressionist cinema. Waxman follows convention in penning a two-theme main-title overture, but even his lyrical love theme is enriched by sensual dissonances. Much of the score is rooted in familiar leitmotivic procedures: the pithy rhythmic cell representing the monster is as economical and easily recognizable as that for Kong in the earlier Steiner score. But in its sophisticated impressionism for the forest and use of effective tension-building devices such as string tremolo and *sul ponticello* effects, and in the use of an insistent timpani pulse to represent both the monster's heartbeat and the mounting dramatic tension (a device later much imitated), Waxman's score broke significant new ground. Wise to his achievement, Universal later repeatedly recycled Waxman's music from *The Bride of Frankenstein* in its other productions.

Waxman worked for MGM from 1937 and Warner Bros. from 1943, undertaking freelance film scoring for various studios from 1948 until his death in 1967; in 1954 he resigned from AMPAS when Alfred Newman's music for *The Robe* was not nominated for an Oscar and the snub seemed symbolic of the Academy's insufficient acknowledgement of the importance of film music. Like Herrmann (who also resigned from AMPAS late in his career), Waxman was an active concert-hall composer who attempted to pursue dual careers with some success; amongst his most notable achievements outside the cinema was his foundation of the Los Angeles International Music Festival in 1948, with which (as conductor) he showcased works by leading contemporary composers. Not surprisingly, as with other film composers with cultural affiliations to classical music, Waxman's esoteric compositional preoccupations occasionally found apt applications in his film music. Particularly noteworthy was his resourceful use of fugue and passacaglia forms, both autonomous musical structures that in the hands of various composers had been used to parallel dramatic events on both stage and screen. In twentieth-century opera, for example, the repetitive thematic basis of the passacaglia was adopted by composers as diverse as Berg (*Wozzeck*, 1925) and Britten (*Peter Grimes*, 1945) as a highly effective musical device for portraying obsessive behaviour. Waxman scored the climaxes of both *Sorry, Wrong Number* (dir. Anatole Litvak, 1948) and *Dark City* (dir. William Dieterle, 1950) as tense passacaglias, and also exploited repetitive Stravinskyan bass lines in *Night and the City* (dir. Jules Dassin, 1950). In *Sorry, Wrong Number*, actress Barbara Stanwyck helplessly awaits the arrival of her would-be killer: 'The final climax, as the passacaglia theme riding the full orchestra coincides with the footsteps approaching the door, and everything, including Stanwyck's demented scream, is lost in the roar of the overhead railway, is one of the most frightening in film music' (Palmer 1990, 101). In *Objective Burma!* (dir. Raoul Walsh, 1945), Waxman uses fugal counterpoint to accompany the climbing of a hill, and the sudden dissipation of this firm and purposeful texture as the summit is reached is especially effective in context; fugal cues also occur in his scores to *The Bride of Frankenstein, A Place in the Sun, Sayonara* and *Taras Bulba*.

Similar structural ideas have been used by other film composers. Rózsa reinforced the tension at the climax of *The Secret Beyond the Door* (dir. Fritz Lang, 1948) with the aid of a passacaglia based on a simple five-note motif, and passacaglia technique was extensively deployed in David Raksin's score to *Forever Amber* (dir. Otto Preminger, 1947). Jerry Goldsmith included a grimly determined passacaglia for First World War German pilots struggling to stem their army's retreat in *The Blue Max* (dir. John Guillermin, 1966). Busy fugal textures were exploited by, amongst others, Walton in *The First of the Few* (see Chapter 6), Alex North in *The Misfits* (dir. John Huston, 1961) and Williams in *Jaws* (Chapter 12), generally in contexts of industrious productivity, athleticism or relentless pursuit; the idea extends back to a wide range of classical music from the baroque to the romantic era, where fugues might be used to suggest conflict, as in a battle sequence from Verdi's *Macbeth* cited by Eisenstein (1948, 128). Rózsa admitted that he often scored chase scenes in a fugal manner, noting that the Latin word *fuga* means flight (Rózsa 1982, 24). Another pre-existing form occasionally pressed into cinematic service was theme and variations, used by Herrmann in *Citizen Kane* (see Chapter 5), and also appearing prominently in the balletic vignettes that present the many contradictory sides of Leslie Caron's character in the 1951 musical *An American in Paris* (see Chapter 4).

Waxman's classical training also allowed him to compose effective diegetic cues, such as the 'classical' piano music in Hitchcock's *The Paradine Case* (1947), and to distort pre-existing music for dramatic effect. In *Possessed* (dir. Curtis Bernhardt, 1947), he ingeniously modified Schumann's *Carnaval* by removing all the accidentals so that it would sound disconcertingly ugly and the spectators would therefore identify with the disturbed emotions of actress Joan Crawford, whose character suffers from unrequited love for the man with whom Schumann's piece is associated throughout the film. Although subjective point-of-view camera work became relatively common in later narrative cinema, subjective point-of-hearing effects such as this are much rarer, except in cases where simple spatial realism is the motivation behind them.

Waxman's association with Hitchcock elicited a memorable score for *Rebecca* (1940), in which the eerie atmosphere was created partly by the use of an electronic keyboard instrument (novachord) at a time when such outlandish sonorities were beginning to assert themselves in contexts of the supernatural or paranoid (see below). Not for the only time in his career, Waxman's music was too adventurous for some tastes and Selznick employed Steiner to make the score more overtly romantic in places (Thomas 1997, 97); too much may be read into this decision, however, since the anxious Selznick had also kept Waxman waiting in the wings to provide a score to replace Steiner's for *Gone With the Wind* in the previous year, should it have failed to meet with his approval (Flinn 1992, 18–19). *Rebecca* is also notable for the effectiveness of its overall sound design, heard most clearly when the second Mrs de Winter sits at Rebecca's desk and the music works together with stark sound events (a telephone ring, the breaking of an ornament) and sound non-events (the silent footfall of the unsettling Mrs Danvers) to create a satisfying composite soundtrack. Later Hitchcock–Waxman collaborations included *Suspicion* (1941), for which the composer again used electric sonorities (an amplified violin), and *Rear Window* (1954), for which he composed the song 'Lisa' which tellingly moves from the diegetic to the nondiegetic.

More fruitful still was Waxman's ongoing collaboration with Billy Wilder, which brought the composer his first Academy Award, for *Sunset Boulevard* (1950). Waxman brilliantly caught the dark neurotic atmosphere of this compelling drama about the manic delusions of fading Hollywood star Norma Desmond (Gloria Swanson), instantly setting an edgy tone at the outset by combining brooding features of *film noir* underscoring with a jazzy brittleness characteristic of the movies' habitual musical portrayal of cityscapes. The obsessiveness at the heart of the film is captured by certain techniques familiar from earlier Waxman scores (e.g. pedal points and repeated timpani pulsations), but a major new feature is the use throughout of graphically neurotic instrumental trills inspired by the ghoulish music for Salome's thirsting for the severed head of John the Baptist in Strauss's opera; the 'Dance of the Seven Veils' from *Salome* provided Waxman with a model for Norma's final demented performance in front of the news cameras, for which he composed a climactic distortion of a sultry habañera previously associated with her hedonism. While the trill motif recurs obsessively throughout the score, other cues are self-contained set-pieces, such as the (nondiegetic) wrong-note vaudeville music with prominent honkytonk piano accompanying Norma's parody of Chaplin's tramp, and the delicate reworking of musical clichés from westerns as two would-be lovers stroll at night through a Wild West studio set. What at first appears to be a supernatural throbbing sound is revealed to be the wailing of the wind through the previously unseen pipes of an organ in Norma's mansion; later, a skilful manipulation of (nondiegetic) orchestration causes her butler's white-gloved (diegetic) performance of Bach's Toccata in D minor to emerge as if from a sonic dream (Palmer 1990, 106). In 1953, Waxman provided a terse score for Wilder's seminal prisoner-of-war drama, *Stalag 17*, in which the prophetic blend of black comedy and grim realism – strikingly anticipatory of 1970s black comedies such as *M*A*S*H* – was adroitly captured by a spirited use of 'When Johnny Comes Marching Home Again' and simple but tense cues scored for percussion alone.

In a few of its cues, *Sunset Boulevard* saw Waxman experimenting with the sound of the saxophone for symbolic effect, most prominently when its wailing accompanies Norma's handing cash over to her kept man. Identifications between the saxophone and dramatic topics such as venality, sensuality, sleaze and corruption became commonplace and consistent in the later 1950s (see Chapter 5), and Waxman exploited this connection in his next score, *A Place in the Sun* (dir. George Stevens, 1951), for his work on which he became the first composer to win two Academy Awards in consecutive years. The discomfiting use of the saxophone in this score so perplexed the director that he engaged Victor Young and Daniele Amfitheatrof to rewrite over a third of the film's music – an interesting instance of a composer having interpreted a film in a more ironic manner than the director had himself envisaged (Palmer 1990, 111). The culmination of Waxman's interest in jazz came in his music for *Crime in the Streets* (dir. Donald Siegel, 1956), with its screaming big-band-style riffs, sultry saxophone solos and walking bass-lines showing him to be perfectly *au fait* with changing Hollywood styles.

Waxman's film output in the 1950s continued to demonstrate a much higher degree of imagination and flexibility than the work of many studio composers. He tackled the genre of the western without recourse to clichéd Americana, his atmospheric music for *The Indian Fighter* (dir. André de Toth, 1955) being rooted in two of his most prominent stylistic characteristics: a rich and suggestive harmonic language and expressive writing for ancillary wind instruments, here the moody sound of the alto flute. His score for *Sayonara* (dir. Joshua Logan, 1957) was one of the first to draw on non-Western music for dramatic ends. At the same time, however, his work perpetuated the strong tradition of narrative orientation and clear thematic developments on which the Golden Age film score had been founded, and carried these seminal elements forward into the 1960s. *Taras Bulba* (dir. J. Lee Thompson, 1962), his penultimate score, was a compelling blend of the traditional and the innovative: true to the film's epic and exotic quality there is plenty of well-researched music (both diegetic and nondiegetic) with a rousingly Slavonic flavour, and the whole is given a sense of cogency by strategically deployed variations on a prominent love theme cast in the manner of an East European melancholic waltz. As usual, the score features colourful harmony and resourceful orchestration, ranging from a pastoral cor anglais solo to glittering percussion for the allure of Kiev. Waxman's consummate command of traditional techniques is shown by the continuity his music provides for a transition from a nocturnal carol-singing scene to a daytime sleigh ride: the diegetic singing merges into scherzo-like music that combines the (mickey-moused) tobogganing antics of the Cossacks with the approach of the sleigh bearing the Polish Governor's daughter who, when recognized, is unobtrusively supplied with a slow variant of the love theme in deft contrapuntal combination with a continuation of the scherzo.

Although adept at illustrative techniques such as these, Waxman's music was distinguished by its sometimes aggressive modernism, up-to-date references to popular idioms, novel sonorities and structural resourcefulness. His work fits far less comfortably into the romantic stereotype which most commentators have considered to be the prevailing studio norm and, perhaps as a result, he is only mentioned in passing in influential but selective critical texts (e.g. Gorbman 1987, Flinn 1992, Kalinak 1992) that prefer to concentrate instead on the dated idiom of Steiner and Korngold; Flinn even goes so far as to describe Waxman's score to *Rear Window*, misleadingly, as 'an uncharacteristically discordant, jazz-influenced work' (Flinn 1992, 114). Waxman was one of a select group of Hollywood composers interested in contemporary concert music who helped inject new life into an idiom that had already grown stale by the 1940s.

Alfred Newman

Arguably the most influential music director in Hollywood, both in terms of his prolific output and in his continuing legacy as a shrewd talent-spotter who promoted the work of younger film composers (some of whom remain active at the time of writing), Connecticut-born Alfred Newman made his name in film music at a time when in America it was dominated by European composers. Like Steiner's, Newman's early career conducting musicals on Broadway came to an abrupt end after the Wall Street Crash. In 1930, he likewise moved West to gain employment in the film industry in response to an invitation from Irving Berlin, who wanted him to be musical director for a film version of *Reaching for the Moon* (dir. Edmund Goulding, 1931). Until 1938 Newman was employed by United Artists, which handled films by independent producers and had no studio facilities of its own.

Newman's first significant break came with *Street Scene* (dir. King Vidor, 1931), the music from which was recycled in later productions with an urban theme extending right up to the early 1950s; some of the later projects were scored by other composers, but his own score to *Cry of the City* (dir. Robert Siodmak, 1948) showed how the 'cool, Gershwinesque sophistication of the music' had in the intervening years come to be 'at variance with the sombre poetry of the city as captured in this film and others like it' (Palmer 1990, 93). Symphonic jazz for bustling metropolitan scenes had seemed viable enough in the 1930s; but attitudes towards city locations changed markedly after the 1940s and Newman's conservatism had not kept pace with the trend. Some composers, such as Waxman in *Sunset Boulevard*, managed to preserve the link with Gershwin while suggesting something altogether darker, while others – notably Rózsa and Copland – created entirely different city soundscapes. In his music for *Panic in the Streets* (dir. Elia Kazan, 1950), however, Newman showed himself aware of the growing trend to equate a more up-to-date jazz style with urban decay.

Newman worked at Twentieth Century from 1933; he became General Music Director at Twentieth Century-Fox in 1939, serving in this capacity until 1959 when he was succeeded by his brother Lionel. The rousing fanfare which Alfred composed for Fox's trademark in 1933, two years before the studio's merger with Twentieth Century, remains in use today and is perhaps the single most recognized piece of film music in the history of the industry: for generations of movie-goers, its buoyant optimism has encapsulated in just a few seconds the feel-good factor at the heart of mainstream commercial cinema. His output was almost as prodigious as Steiner's: by the time of his death in 1970, Newman had provided music for no fewer than 250 films. He was the most honoured of Hollywood composers, winning nine Academy Awards – although only one was for an entirely original score, the others being awarded for collaborative musicals – and having received an astonishing 45 nominations.

It is surprising, therefore, to note that Newman was what David Raksin termed a 'reluctant composer'. Newman dismissed himself as a 'hack' (Thomas 1997, 66–7), and was under no illusions about the quality of his creative work: 'If I want to write great music, I've no right to be working in a film studio' (Thomas 1997, 73). He seems to have regarded film composition as an occupational hazard that went with the job of studio musical director, and there is no doubt that his principal passion was for conducting. Gregarious by nature, he delighted in working with musicians and they paid him enormous respect; he was exceptionally thorough in rehearsals, and tolerated no slackness or unprofessionalism. John Williams, who early in his career was a keyboard player in the Fox orchestra, paid generous tribute to Newman's consummate musicianship, likening his technique to that of the British conductor Sir John Barbirolli and noting that Newman's ability to shape phrases musically in accordance with dramatic requirements was an especially valuable asset in recording sessions (Palmer

1990, 70). Instead of slavishly relying on audible click tracks, Newman utilized a more flexible system developed for him by music editor Charlie Dunworth: strategically placed on-screen flashes were created by multiple punches (each set of punches producing an illumination lasting a little under one second), which Newman could see in his peripheral vision without taking his eye off the conducting score. This 'Newman System' was only intended as a rough guide to synchronization, the flashes giving him a clear sense of how his performance was shaping up to the running time of a film segment and allowing him to adapt his pacing accordingly. As far as the music mixers were concerned, however, Newman's infamous perfectionism could be a source of some irritation, as amusingly recounted by Arthur Piantadosi:

> Once I was being so bothered by Alfred Newman, I finally asked him if he would just handle the dial for a trumpet solo so I could take care of the rest of the orchestra. I had him on a dummy [meter]. Here's a guy who owns the industry, and he's sitting there playing with this trumpet dial, barely moving it just a speck, and I've really got the trumpet dial doing what I think I need to do with it – but it got him off my back. (LoBrutto 1994, 19)

Newman's compositional style was thoroughly European in idiom, and in essence little different from that of Steiner and Korngold. He tended to avoid complex contrapuntal textures and leitmotivic procedures, often favouring contrasted blocks of instrumental colour and an exhaustive use of a single theme within an individual film, as in *All About Eve* (dir. Joseph Mankiewicz, 1950); this monothematic tendency would have far-reaching consequences when wholeheartedly adopted by his protégé Raksin in the mid-1940s (see below). Stylistic parallels with the lush Straussian idiom of Korngold are most prominent in Newman's scores for adventures, such as *The Prisoner of Zenda* (dir. John Cromwell, 1937; music reused for 1952 remake, dir. Richard Thorpe) and *Captain from Castile* (dir. Henry King, 1947), the latter featuring a flamboyant march for the Conquistadors; references to the Korngold style are still to be found in Newman's music as late as *Camelot* (dir. Joshua Logan, 1967). The conventional Hispanic locational music in *Captain from Castile* suggests that, like its efficient and economical command of melodramatic clichés, Newman's approach was in essence more directly aligned with that of Steiner: the innate musico-dramatic instincts of both ex-Broadway composers were combined with a studio-rooted practicality, with substantial creative tasks delegated to orchestrators and assistants (though Newman always ensured they received due credit) and judiciously reworking material in more than one score. Like Steiner, Newman tended to lapse into an easy-going Viennese dance idiom as a fallback style, which he evidently felt equally suitable for settings as diverse as the streets of medieval

Paris (*The Hunchback of Notre Dame*), a ball in nineteenth-century York-shire (*Wuthering Heights*) and a political meeting in 1930s England (*Foreign Correspondent*). From the 1940s onwards he occasionally produced a more American sound – see, for example, the presidential epic *Wilson* (dir. Henry King, 1944) and *How the West Was Won* (dir. John Ford *et al.*, 1962) – though this never achieved the prominence and pervasiveness it did in the work of younger American composers. His music for 1950s epics (dis-cussed in Chapter 5) cultivated a sensitive balance between opulence and restraint.

Newman, as Steiner had before him, used music to illuminate a charac-ter's personal point of view – a technique to be seen in his Oscar-winning score to *The Song of Bernadette* (dir. Henry King, 1943), parts of which were released by Decca on four 78rpm gramophone discs. The story's author, Franz Werfel, had already attempted to secure the commission for Stravin-sky, who had begun to compose music for the scene featuring the apparition of the Virgin to Bernadette – a cue that, when Stravinsky's projected involve-ment in the film failed to materialize, was recycled as the second movement of his Symphony in Three Movements, completed in 1945 (White 1979, 429). When Newman came to score the same scene, he resisted the temptation to accompany Bernadette's vision with stereotypical religious music. Having tried and rejected an idiom reminiscent of Wagner's *Parsifal*, Newman

> now wrote music I thought would describe this extraordinary experience of
> a young girl who was neither sophisticated enough nor knowledgeable
> enough to evaluate it as anything more than a lovely vision. With this in
> mind, I thought the music should not be pious or austere or even mystical,
> or suggest that the girl was on the first step to sainthood. She was at that
> point simply an innocent, pure-minded peasant girl, and I took my musical
> cues from the little gusts of wind and the rustling bushes that accompanied
> the vision, letting it all grow into a swelling harmony that would express the
> girl's emotional reaction. And it was important that it express *her* reaction,
> not *ours*.   (quoted in Thomas 1997, 70)

A later film in which Newman took considerable pains to interpret events from the point of view of the protagonist was *The Diary of Anne Frank* (dir. George Stevens, 1959), for which he accordingly injected much of his music with a sense of youthful innocence rather than impending tragedy.

Newman's use of a wordless and distant chorus in the vision scene of *The Song of Bernadette* became a familiar element of his style. Such cho-ruses (mostly arranged by Ken Darby) occur throughout his oeuvre, and not just in religious contexts; they were especially effective when handled at a low dynamic level and sneaked in. At the end of *Wuthering Heights* (dir. Wyler, 1939), for example, singing voices enter almost imperceptibly as Cathy dies in Heathcliff's arms, intensifying an effect of transcendence already strong in a finely wrought passage where a stinger chord for the moment of death initiates a hauntingly lovely modulation to a remote key. Here, as often in Newman's work, the sheer beauty of the orchestral playing contributes greatly to the effect, his intense string sonorities in particular having met with widespread acclaim (though not from his colleague Herrmann, who reportedly liked to shout at the Fox orchestra 'Get that hysterical sound outta the strings!': see S. Smith 1991, 82). The vocal idea is first used near the beginning of the film when Cathy's ghostly voice is heard calling through the bedroom window as it flaps in the wind: the music here imparts a fairy-tale quality to a scene that could easily have been handled in a more predictably frightening manner, this restrained and affective treatment presumably having been inspired by a later comment in the script that hers is the voice of love not terror. In *How Green Was My Valley* (dir. John Ford, 1941), a wordless female chorus imbues the male-dominated coal-mining setting with a wholesome atmosphere of gentle domestication. It is only when Newman's voices swell in volume, as they do over the end credits of *Wuthering Heights*, that choral idioms such as these may seem excessive. Such 'heavenly choruses' were later wickedly parodied by Elmer Bernstein in his music for *Airplane!* (dir. Jim Abrahams *et al.*, 1980) – a spoof of *Airport* (dir. George Seaton, 1970), the final film assignment of Newman's career and one which achieved an excitingly American sound. During the course of *Airplane!* Bernstein makes his chorus ascend so stratospherically that they collapse under the physical strain. Whether or not a modern audience responds emotionally to Newman's most spiritually tinged music will be deeply rooted in subjective matters of taste: one commentator may choose to praise his work for its integrity, elegance and sincerity (Palmer 1990, 88) while another film composer feels justified in dismissing it as 'the nadir of vulgarity' (Benjamin Frankel, quoted in Palmer 1990, 83).

The occasional unevenness of Newman's work may be illustrated by a comparison of two scores composed in 1939–40. *The Hunchback of Notre Dame* (dir. William Dieterle, 1939) has its fair share of clichés: the crude segue from reverberant archaic choral music into warmly romantic string music for the scene-setting scrolling title at the opening; the stinger followed by melodramatic bustling as Quasimodo kidnaps Esmeralda, which turns into incongruously jolly music as he is pursued heroically by the cavalry; and, in places, sentimental underscoring of dialogue. But much of this substantial score is finely judged. The film's carnival music has a distinctive brashness with wrong-note humour; several cues are athematic, being based on cascading ostinato figurations capturing the eerie atmosphere surrounding Quasimodo; archaic musical gestures are transformed into majestic orchestral chorales; and the vertiginously swirling music at the climax, in which chromatic violins are later combined with firm major chords, seems prophetic of Herrmann's 1950s style. (A similar but subtler texture was used for the wailing wind at the opening of *Wuthering Heights*.) In contrast, *Foreign Correspondent* (dir. Hitchcock, 1940) is a much more pedestrian affair. The first three notes of its main theme are subjected to mechanical variation on numerous occasions, and a good deal of the dialogue is underscored with neutral easy-listening music; there are snatches of the atmospheric Quasimodo-type cue to build up dramatic tension (most extensively in the windmill scene), but spotting of cues seems haphazard and the tension is most effective when in several climactic scenes the music is absent altogether. Locational music is gratuitous, whether in the form of the quotation of 'Rule, Britannia' just before the equally gratuitous establishing shots of Big Ben in London, or the rustic dance introducing the Dutch sequences. The use of a Broadway syncopated idiom with prominent saxophone to represent the American reporter's links with his homeland lends an unfortunately superficial tone to the film at times: after it briefly accompanies his writing of a telegram to New York in a hotel bedroom, the music becoming obligingly sinister as two strangers posing as policemen enter the room. The triumphant appearance of the US national anthem at the conclusion was blatant propaganda, and part of the film's unsubtle attempt to influence American thinking towards participating in the escalating European war.

Miklós Rózsa, Roy Webb and David Raksin: *film noir* and the music of psychological drama

One of the last of the first-generation expatriate European composers to arrive in Hollywood was Miklós Rózsa, who had worked in the British film industry and crossed the Atlantic in order to finish *The Thief of Bagdad* for Alexander Korda in 1940 (see Chapter 6). The film's success provided Rózsa with further freelance scoring assignments, followed by a prominent staff position at MGM from 1948 until 1962. As a composer with a training in the conservatoire tradition, Rózsa pursued dual careers in film and the concert hall; his only regret about his film music was that it came to be typecast no fewer than four times. The first was attendant on the success of *The Thief of Bagdad*, which had shown his resourcefulness as a composer of vividly coloured orchestral impressionism for exotic fantasies. The fourth and last was his innovative work in scoring historical epics in the 1950s and early 1960s (discussed in Chapter 5). In between came his development of strongly characterized music for what he termed 'dark psychological subjects' and 'hard-hitting crime pictures' (Thomas 1997, 129), two genres for which he supplied scoring inspired by both the melancholic folk traditions and concert-hall modernism of his native Hungarian musical heritage. In the process he became one of the first Hollywood film composers to break partly away from the clichés of the 1930s – while at the same time retaining much that was conventional.

In Golden Age film scores, a limited modernism – principally mani-fested as a relatively high level of dissonance and an avoidance of fully blown melodic statements in favour of stream-of-consciousness fragmentation – had occasionally been permissible in contexts where the disturbing nature of the subject-matter warranted it. In this connection it is noteworthy that, much earlier in the twentieth century, ground-breaking modernist compo-sitions such as Schoenberg's *Erwartung* (1909) and Stravinsky's *The Rite of Spring* (1913) had appeared to justify their bold experimentation as a direct expression of extra-musical considerations such as barbarity, violence and emotional turmoil; in the concert hall, high levels of dissonance in abstract instrumental music came somewhat later, becoming in time a stylistic norm rather than a special event. Various attempts on the part of Hollywood producers to secure the services of modernist luminaries from the classical arena, such as Schoenberg and Stravinsky themselves (both of whom settled in Los Angeles), ended in failure – though more because of intransigent and unrealistic demands made by these self-important and surprisingly mer-cenary composers than by lack of interest from the moguls. For example, MGM's Irving Thalberg made a serious and sympathetic attempt to persuade Schoenberg to score *The Good Earth* (dir. Sidney Franklin, 1937), for which music eventually had to be provided by Herbert Stothart when Schoen-berg demanded a fee of $50,000 in addition to requiring total personal control over both the film's actors and soundtrack dubbing (see 'I Don't Write "Lovely" Music', in Silvester 1998, 186–8). Boris Morros, a forward thinking music director at Paramount, attempted to lure both Schoenberg and Stravinsky into the studio in the late 1930s, but resigned in disillu-sionment in 1939 after his ambitious plans had fallen through. (Morros later gained notoriety when in 1957 he revealed himself to have been a Soviet double agent: see Silvester 1998, 326.) Significantly, two composers who held strong views about the desirability of modernism in film music failed to live up to their own aesthetic standards when confronted with the harsh realities of studio work. Hanns Eisler's passion for modernism was evident from his theoretical writings but in rather short supply in his own modest output of narrative film music during his time working in Hol-lywood (1942–8), which included a lush romantic score for *The Spanish Main* (dir. Frank Borzage, 1945) that was seemingly 'a violation of all [his] rules' (Dümling 1998, 498); but his work in low-budget European docu-mentaries was consistently challenging (see Chapter 7), and he collaborated memorably with Brecht and Lang on the anti-Nazi film *Hangmen Also Die!* (1943), its score nominated for an Academy Award but losing out to New-man's *Song of Bernadette*. George Antheil, an outspoken film-music critic in the 1930s who did much to foster intelligent appreciation of the medium, showed himself capable of originality in his score to *The Plainsman* (dir. Cecil B. DeMille, 1936) but lapsed into dreary and repetitive banality even for such a potentially atmospheric *film noir* as *In a Lonely Place* (dir. Nicholas Ray, 1950).

Along with special cases such as Steiner's score for *King Kong* and Wax-man's for *The Bride of Frankenstein*, Rózsa's work in *film noir* and psycho-logical drama in the 1940s helped initiate a modest modernist trend in film music that only came fully to the fore in the more adventurous work of composers such as Bernard Herrmann and Leonard Rosenman in the following decade (see Chapter 5). Rózsa's style was dissonant enough to cause consternation with his employers on several occasions. The head of the music department at Paramount, Louis Lipstone, attempted in 1943 to persuade Rózsa to edit out a specific dissonance in his score to Wilder's *Five Graves to Cairo* ('Why don't you make it a G natural in the violas as well – just for *my* sake?'); he lost his temper when Rózsa refused, and Lipstone was curtly told by Wilder not to interfere (Rózsa 1982, 119–20). (In the light of this anecdote, one can readily understand Steiner's apparent need to write 'Dissonance on purpose' on his sketches as a warning to his orchestrator: see Kalinak 1992, 130.) Following a preview screening of *A Double Life* (dir. George Cukor, 1947), studio executives demanded the removal of the main-title music because it was 'too modernistic'; after bitter protests from composer and director, the offending music was retained and Rózsa's com-pact score earned him his second Academy Award. In his memoirs, Rózsa laid the blame for the inveterate conservatism of Hollywood film music squarely at the feet of the studio music directors, whom he described as 'men from jazz bands and theater pits who hadn't the faintest notion of music as an adjunct to drama, and always wanted to "play it safe" (liter-ally). They were the arbiters of musical taste in Hollywood, and since they employed hacks when real composers were available they caused the ruin of many potentially good films' (Rózsa 1982, 142).

Film noir (thus dubbed by French critics in 1946) is often interpreted as a direct reflection of a growing post-war cynicism in the USA that resulted in dark-hued narrative films steeped in a bleak and often violent nihilism. Predominant were gritty crime dramas, including filmed treatments of tough detective novels by Raymond Chandler and others, influenced by the moody visual style of German expressionist cinema (many were the work of expatriate German directors) and demonstrating elements of con-temporaneous Italian neo-realist cinema. The atmosphere of *film noir* came to permeate other genres, and this was also true of the appropriately hard-hitting musical style evolved by Rózsa and other composers who worked on *noir* assignments. For example, Rózsa's music for *Five Graves to Cairo*, which is set in North Africa, shares the grim determination of his *noir* music, though it harks back to an earlier age by quoting 'Rule, Britannia' to represent the British troops and their victory at El Alamein. Although the surface style and underlying philosophy of *film noir* were new, its devices – such as complex plots with flashbacks, and fantasy dream sequences – were extensions of existing techniques borrowed from other genres, and in essence it remained rooted in conventional Hollywood narrative procedures. The continuing prioritizing of narrative, even more important as plots now became convoluted to the point of incomprehension, doubtless accounts for the functional conservatism and leitmotivic orientation of even the boldest of *Angst*-ridden *noir* music.

The simplest way to appreciate Rózsa's stylistic freshness is to compare his seminal score for Wilder's *Double Indemnity* (1944) with Steiner's music for *The Big Sleep* (dir. Howard Hawks, 1946). Both films are typically hard-boiled *noir* detective thrillers that helped define the genre. Steiner's work in the 1940s rarely shows much interest in characterizing individual genres, however, and his music tends to colour a wide range of dramatic settings with the same melodramatic romanticism. In *The Big Sleep*, the sizzling sexual chemistry between Humphrey Bogart and Lauren Bacall and the labyrinthine plot (so complex that even the story's writers claimed not to understand it) are tempered and sanitized by a solid late-romantic idiom little different from that in *Gone With the Wind*. Rózsa's music for *Double Indemnity* (analysed in detail in R. S. Brown 1994, 120–33) is markedly different in its creation of a brooding, claustrophobic atmosphere perfectly attuned to both setting and plot, and its tendency to disturb rather than romanticize. Ostinati are used for the underscoring of dialogue and voice-overs (the latter a trademark of the genre), not conflicting with the audibility of the words but creating a feeling of underlying tension quite incommensurate with the simplicity of the means employed. In this regard, and in both Rózsa's characteristically sweeping and angular melodic style and his propulsive rhythmic patterns, the influence of his compatriots Bartók and Kodály is clearly discernible. Dissonance level in the score is generally high, but always within a fundamentally tonal context so that certain harmonizations can appear appropriately 'rancid' (Palmer 1990, 197); the brutality of the climax comes almost entirely from the music since the murder takes place just outside the camera's field of vision. While Rózsa was working on this project, Lipstone again hauled him over the coals for writing music that belonged in Carnegie Hall: 'I thanked him', recalled the composer, 'but he said he hadn't meant it as a compliment' (Rózsa 1982, 121).

Later projects which allowed Rózsa to develop his personal and refined brand of musical brutality included *The Killers* (dir. Robert Siodmak, 1946), *Brute Force* (dir. Jules Dassin, 1947), and *The Naked City* (dir. Dassin, 1948), a score particularly notable for its evocative metropolitan soundscape. The first two of these adopted a semi-documentary style that was to influence the starkly realist work of many 1950s social and crime dramas. *The Killers*, which features a striking cue during which manic diegetic piano playing in a bar is harmonized by nondiegetic orchestral underlay, is representative of those elements in Rózsa's style inspired by Bartók: pulsating ostinati, dissonant chords derived from octatonic scales, false relations between major and minor thirds, snappy dotted and lombard rhythms inspired by Hungarian folk music (particularly well suited in their jerkiness to scenes of a nervous or tense nature) and saturated chromaticism. This Hungarian flavour permeates Rózsa's concert music, including his Violin Concerto No. 2, written for Jascha Heifetz in 1953–6, which Wilder requested the composer rework for his witty period film *The Private Life of Sherlock Holmes* (1970). Conan Doyle's violin-playing sleuth dabbles with the concerto's solo part diegetically, and its three movements were adapted by Rózsa as nondiegetic cues designed to depict respectively Holmes's addiction to cocaine, the film's love interest and the Loch Ness monster. Given that Rózsa was heavily critical of composers who supplied music of a period or geographical style inappropriate to a film's setting, it is disconcerting to hear him making the Baker Street of 1880s London sound as if it were located in downtown Budapest in the 1920s.

The purported but in essence highly stylized 'realism' of 1940s crime thrillers (occasionally inspiring directors to avoid nondiegetic music altogether, as in John Huston's prototypical heist movie *The Asphalt Jungle* (1950), with its very slender score by Rózsa) was to some extent additionally reflected in pictures dealing with issues of social consciousness, for which Rózsa used essentially the same idiom since they dealt with their up-to-date subject-matter in a similarly stark way – and often with a substantial dose of *Angst*. *The Lost Weekend* (dir. Wilder), the first film to deal openly with the subject of alcoholism, was one of two he scored in 1945 that employed the eerily oscillating sound of the theremin. Invented in Russia and demonstrated by its inventor, Leon Theremin, in the USA in 1927–8, this electronic device had already been heard in Soviet film scores by Shostakovich (*Alone*, 1931) and Gavriel Popov (*Komsomol: The Patron of Electrification*, 1934) before its Hollywood debut in Robert E. Dolan's 1942 score to *Lady in the Dark* (dir. Mitchell Leisen; released 1944). The instrument's mass-production by RCA was a commercial failure; too difficult for amateurs to play, it also failed to establish itself as a serious instrument in spite of being showcased in virtuosic recitals at prestigious concert venues during the 1940s. One leading practitioner, Clara Rockmore, declined to perform in Rózsa's film scores because she felt Hollywood's appropriation of the instrument, almost without exception exploiting its irrational sound in order to scare audiences, would seal its populist fate (Glinsky 2000, 253). This indeed proved to be the case, as the success of Samuel Hoffman's playing on Rózsa's and numerous other film scores from the mid-1940s onwards – stimulated by a best-selling gramophone recording of music from *Spellbound* – allowed Hoffman to enjoy a lucrative career as a popular recording artist.

Rózsa's prominent use of a theremin in *The Lost Weekend* came not without renewed opposition from Lipstone and the film's producers, who for a preview screening had used a temporary music track in a standard symphonic-jazz idiom that misled the audience into expecting a comedy and as a result had them walking out when the picture suddenly turned serious on them (Rózsa 1982, 128–9). Waxman had already exploited the electronic sonorities of a novachord and amplified violin in *Rebecca* (1940) to suggest a quasi-supernatural atmosphere, and Rózsa's contribution to this trend helped create an indelible association between electronics and the other-worldly or irrational that persists in film music to this day – and was one of the very few ways in which film music in the 1940s anticipated developments in concert music rather than following them, often at several decades' remove. Rózsa treated the theremin more as a simple extension of the conventional orchestral palette than as a novel timbre with its own possibilities, constantly doubling its melodies with the violins (as did Messiaen when using the ondes martenot in his orchestral works: see Ashby 2004, 370). In *The Lost Weekend*, its timbre represents not the act of consuming alcohol, but the inexorable craving that leads an alcoholic to search out the next drink. It is first heard, briefly, as Don Birnham (Ray Milland) realizes he has to pack something crucial in his suitcase, then returns as he searches for a bottle of liquor that he finally discovers dangling on a string outside his window (this was the point at which the preview audience had inappropriately laughed); significantly, the theremin falls silent at the moment when he first downs a comforting shot. Once inebriated, Birnham talks floridly to the accompaniment of standard orchestral scoring, and the theremin returns only when we see a shot of his empty glass. Later psychological dramas of this kind included *A Double Life*, for which Rózsa's modernistic music for the protagonist's mental breakdown contrasted with restrained pastiche for the segments featuring Shakespeare's *Othello*, and the socially conscious *The Snake Pit* (dir. Litvak, 1948), controversial in its time as the first movie to be set in a mental institution and furnished with an uncharacteristically astringent score by Newman, his music clearly influenced in places by Rózsa's melodic style.

Hitchcock's psychological melodrama *Spellbound* (1945) deals with paranoia, and Rózsa's score relates the electronic timbre to irrational behaviour, being exclusively associated with the various images of parallel lines that trigger mental instability in the protagonist. The basic scoring techniques used by Rózsa in this film, for which he won his first Academy Award, are identical to those in his crime thrillers, with ostinati to the fore and Salvador Dali's dream sequence (like the disturbing hallucination scene in *The Lost Weekend*) providing an effective set-piece. A strong vein of conservatism is nevertheless apparent, and Hautbois lamented the over-use of divided violin parts which gave 'certain moments a tinge of cheapness' and the fact that the colour of the wind instruments 'was almost invariably suffocated in a mist of strings and harp glissandis' (quoted in Karlin 1994, 147). Among Rózsa's later psychological dramas was *The Red House* (dir. Delmer Daves, 1947), after which he deliberately abandoned the theremin in order to prevent his music from becoming stereotyped. For Lang's *The Secret Beyond the Door* (1948), he experimented with having a cue played backwards so that the recording could be reversed to produce a disquieting effect as the heroine flees from the room in which she believes her husband will soon murder her. (Retrograde playback was also used by Amfitheatrof in *The Lost Moment* (dir. Martin Gabel, 1947), in which a reversed choral effect sounds like the gulps of a person drowning: see Palmer 1990, 230.) Rózsa's score is also notable for the transformation of a verbal rhythm ('Why had he gone? Why had he lied?') into a naggingly insistent orchestral ostinato – appropriately enough, a free inversion of the love theme – underscoring the wife's voiced-over anxieties.

Another leading exponent of *film noir* scoring was Roy Webb, a prolific composer who worked almost exclusively for RKO until 1952. Like Steiner, he had joined the studio in 1929 after gaining experience as a conductor of Broadway musicals, and his versatility allowed him to compose for filmic genres as diverse as screwball comedy, orientalist fantasy and horror. His breezy easy-listening scores for the Cary Grant comedies *Bringing Up Baby* (dir. Hawks, 1938) and *My Favorite Wife* (dir. Garson Kanin, 1940) typically combine Gershwinesque symphonic jazz with gentle mickey-mousing, the orchestra participating in the humour with stock devices such as descending timpani glissandi and swanee-whistle swoops to reflect shock reactions, and deft touches such as the orchestral imitation of a page-boy's verbal calls in *My Favorite Wife*. Webb's fantasy music, exemplified by that for *Sinbad the Sailor* (dir. Richard Wallace, 1947), comes from the same exotic and luxuriant mould as Rózsa's *The Thief of Bagdad*. Webb ventured onto *noir* territory somewhat earlier than Rózsa, scoring Boris Ingster's influential B-movie *Stranger on the Third Floor* in 1940. This powerful study of guilt demonstrated a prototypical use of such seminal *noir* features as stream-of-consciousness voice-overs, paranoid moods, expressionistic lighting and the prominent flashbacks that seem to give many later *films noirs* their fatalistic sense that the action has somehow been pre-ordained (Blandford *et al.* 2001, 98). Webb begins and ends his score with brief symphonic-jazz cues, serving as a framing device to establish and re-establish urban everyday life as the state of normality from which the viewer is temporarily isolated during the central action – a stylistic identification similar to that used by Newman in his score to *Foreign Correspondent*, made in the same year. But as guilty feelings overtake the protagonist, Webb supplies insidiously evocative music similar to Rózsa's in some regards but distinctively his own in manner. This idiom recurs consistently in many of his later scores, such as *Journey into Fear* (dir. Norman Foster and Orson Welles, 1942), a shipboard thriller in which such music is reserved almost entirely for interior cabin and corridor scenes to promote the sense of claustrophobia, with potentially evocative exterior seascapes left consistently unscored.

The essential ingredients of Webb's understated expressionism are an avoidance of extended themes in favour of ostinati and simple repetitions of pairs of chords; static harmony, which draws heavily on the non-functional octatonic and whole-tone scales; melodic fragments supplied by solo winds, or paired winds moving in parallel thirds, above pedal notes or prolonged chords; colouristic dissonances such as those built on perfect and augmented fourths (reminiscent at times of Scriabin and Berg); and tremolando strings floating chromatically above slowly moving bass lines. The music achieves its disturbing effects subtly and subliminally, never conflicting with the dialogue or monologues it is frequently called upon to accompany. Webb's score for Edward Dmytryk's *Farewell My Lovely* (1944) foregrounds the theremin during a drug-induced dream sequence, and demonstrates how a sophisticated harmonic language can permit an unobtrusive use of the stinger chords so gratuitously blatant in the hands of others. Because Webb's stingers tend to be of medium volume and cast as dissonances that are a natural component of his harmonic style, they support the action discretely and are sometimes used structurally, providing musical and dramatic punctuation; in *Farewell My Lovely*, for example, two different stingers in rapid succession illustrate a struggle with a door and at the same time create an inconclusive cadence that rounds off the preceding cue with a musical question mark.

As with Rózsa's, Webb's *noir* style spilled over into related genres. Somewhat typecast for his scores for a series of RKO horror films with 'Cat' in their title, subtler Gothic horrors with a period setting – such as two films from 1945, *The Body Snatcher* (dir. Robert Wise) and *The Spiral Staircase* (dir. Siodmak) – provided him with an opportunity to pit his darkly atmospheric music against a sunnier diatonicism more reminiscent of Newman's idiom. In *The Body Snatcher* Webb made use of Scottish folksong, locationally appropriate to a story set in 1830s Edinburgh, one example of which is sung diegetically by a beggar woman who, to judge from her vocal skills, appears to have had professional singing lessons; she is murdered off-screen in mid-song, while ascending a tonic triad, and her theme is immediately taken up by the orchestra. The score provides further examples of understated whole-tone and octatonic impressionism, and of stinger dissonances deftly integrated into the ongoing musical flow, and disappoints only in the stock response to the portrayal of elegant women (richly romantic music for strings, even though there is no corresponding dramatic emotion), and a sudden optimistic lurch into a triumphant *tierce de picardie* at the end of the concluding minor-key folksong setting. *The Spiral Staircase*, a prototype for the modern serial-killer thriller, inspired one of Webb's finest scores. As in *Farewell My Lovely*, stingers unobtrusively bolster the action without sacrificing musical coherence, notably in support of the climactic gunshots; sometimes they anticipate the modern device of 'red herring' stingers which make the audience jump at a moment of apparent threat (e.g. a shadow suddenly darkening a character's face) which is immediately revealed to have an innocent explanation. Webb demonstrates how just one or two notes on a theremin, here associated with the killer and becoming searingly intense as the camera dives deep into a close-up of his manic eye, could be far more suggestive than Rózsa's sometimes overblown treatment of the instrument; the theremin was on this occasion recorded on its own track to permit maximum reverberation (Palmer 1990, 173–4). The sonority is so distinctive that it can instantly and economically point towards the true identity of the murderer at the denouement. As Rózsa had in *Double Indemnity*, so Webb uses graphically dissonant music to suggest violence taking place outside the camera's field of vision. In the brief cue where Helen wanders alone in the wood, he moves from luxuriant romanticism into unsettling modernism in order to catch her changing mood as the wind begins to howl and her anxiety increases. A distorted point of view typical of afflicted *noir* characters, for whom 'imaginings and hallucinations . . . appear as stark realities' (Erwin Panofsky in Weis and Belton 1985, 282), is given appropriate musical treatment by Webb in *Notorious* (dir. Hitchcock, 1946) when we experience a poisoning at first hand. In *The Window* (dir. Ted Tetzlaff, 1949), the point of view is that of a child who unwittingly becomes the witness to a murder, and Webb contrasts dark scoring with music of a childlike innocence; the crucial killing scene is left unscored and as a result seems horrifically matter-of-fact.

In 1944, a little-known composer working under Newman at Twentieth Century-Fox was thrust into the limelight for his boldly original score for Otto Preminger's *Laura* (1944), an unorthodox assignment which had been turned down by both Newman and Herrmann, and which has in recent years excited much debate amongst film scholars fascinated by issues of gender and sexuality in *film noir*. What at the time would have been simply interpreted as a detective's romantic yearning for the image of a supposedly murdered woman he has never met, an image embodied in a portrait which dominates her apartment and is shown throughout the film's main-title sequence, is now regarded as unhealthily fetishistic. As Kalinak comments, this is 'a film in which structural ambiguity and ideological confusion impede a consistent reading. Criticism, most notably by feminist film critics, has exposed this structural ambiguity and posited its ideological consequences. *Laura* has become an archetypal example of the ways in which female sexuality threatens classical narrative and of the processes by which classical stratagems both contain and fail to contain that threat' (Kalinak 1992, 161). Kalinak applies such an interpretation to the film and, intriguingly, considers that Raksin's music is sometimes 'at odds' with the implications of the image track (see, for example, Kalinak 1992, 168–9) – or at least their implications for a modern spectator, if not the original audience. Nevertheless, there can be little doubt that Raksin's music is the prime agent in creating the hauntingly elusive character of the deceased Laura, by whom the detective McPherson becomes increasingly obsessed, and the music's powerful commentating presence directly overrides any putative visual or verbal encoding in the images or dialogue.

A similarly absent and alluring woman had been given memorable musical characterization by Waxman in *Rebecca* a few years earlier, but Raksin went further by saturating the first half of the film with a single theme which the dialogue tells us at the outset was one of Laura's favourite tunes: it is frequently heard diegetically (in recorded form on a gramophone, played live in a restaurant, turned into jazz at a party), and developments of it come to dominate the nondiegetic score as the detective grapples with his growing feelings. A clear distinction between diegetic and nondiegetic music is therefore deliberately blurred, as Steiner had done in *Casablanca* – a model also recalled when Raksin uses a diegetic performance of the theme to initiate a flashback in which it becomes nondiegetic. (The effectiveness of Laura's pervasive musical aura can be gauged by comparing the film to *Gilda* (dir. Charles Vidor, 1946), in which Friedhofer's slender score does nothing to characterize the eponymous character played by Rita Hayworth, whose diegetic songs and clichéd lines are inadequate to the task.) Raksin harmonized his shapely *Laura* melody (which had been created as a replacement for Preminger's first choice, Duke Ellington's 'Sophisticated Lady') with roving harmonies that designedly never come to rest: this lack of resolution creates a sense of incompleteness which, as proposed earlier, can allow even brief cues to exert an influence on the listener beyond their audible limits. At first reluctant to overwork the theme, it was at Newman's insightful insistence that Raksin made it dominate the first part of the film's action (Prendergast 1992, 64). Significantly, however, at the moment when Laura is revealed to be very much alive – and very ordinary – her plot-twisting entrance is left unscored, and in context seems utterly mundane: from this point on, her theme almost entirely disappears now that the detective's fantasy has come abruptly to an end. This crucial moment occurs at the end of a brilliant musical sequence in which his emotional confusion and dream-like state are reflected in substantial nondiegetic developments of Laura's theme, concluding with the unearthly sonority of electronically modified piano chords as he falls asleep in her empty apartment. To create this effect Raksin had the chords recorded without their initial percussive attack and then mixed them using bumpy playback heads to create a wavering effect (Prendergast 1992, 65–7). In spite of its harmonic sophistication, Laura's theme became a hit when lyrics were added by Johnny Mercer after the film's release and, popularized by Dinah Shore, Raksin's song quickly became a standard – in the process ensuring that the concept of monothematic film scoring based on a potentially lucrative song would in the future became a staple and sometimes abused procedure.

Influenced variously by Schoenberg (with whom he studied), Berg and Stravinsky, Raksin went on to compose highly chromatic music for *Force of Evil* (dir. Abraham Polonsky, 1948), a film which treated the subject of the numbers racket in New York as an allegory for diseased capitalism. Typically, he made telling use in certain cues of reduced scoring rather than full-blown orchestral textures, an economical approach also seen in his score to *Man With a Cloak* (dir. Fletcher Markle, 1951). At the end of *Force of Evil*, Raksin broke with tradition by supplying slow music for a running character in order to indicate the latter's new-found resolve, subtly underlining the ensuing climax by recourse to functional tonality rather than sheer volume (R. S. Brown 1994, 286; Prendergast 1992, 79–84). The distorted jazz influence on this score, with its prominent and sometimes atonal saxophone solos, directly adumbrates later scoring trends; his other projects to utilize jazz elements were the violent thriller *The Big Combo* (dir. Joseph H. Lewis, 1955) and *Too Late Blues* (dir. John Cassavetes, 1961).

Film noir survived into the 1950s, in musical terms either retaining links with earlier decades, as in Waxman's *Sunset Boulevard*, or updating the idiom with an injection of greater dissonance and brasher scoring, as in Frank de Vol's music for *Kiss Me Deadly* (dir. Robert Aldrich, 1955); the genre also laid the foundations for the hard-hitting and socially aware realism explored by directors such as Preminger and Elia Kazan (see Chapter 5). Following the success of Roman Polanski's *Chinatown* (1974; music by Jerry Goldsmith), a sense of neo-*noir* coloured many Hollywood thrillers and its stylistic influence remains strong to the present day. Rózsa himself contributed a score to *The Last Embrace* (dir. Jonathan Demme, 1979), in which his now old-fashioned brand of moodiness seems like a fish out of water when divorced from the production characteristics that had defined the original genre back in the 1940s: the bland daylight cinematography of modern New York makes his music seem inappropriately nostalgic where once it had been genuinely threatening. More successful, though only on account of self-parody, was Rózsa's score for Carl Reiner's spoof *film noir*, *Dead Men Don't Wear Plaid* (1982): never a comfortable scorer of comedy, Rózsa was instead encouraged to supply music identical to his 1940s *noir* scores, even down to the inclusion of a theremin, and with this undignified final project of his distinguished career he – perhaps unwittingly – came to participate in the new manner of dead-pan comedic scoring initiated by Elmer Bernstein's devastating parody of Newman's style in *Airplane!* two years before.

Dimitri Tiomkin and others

Tiomkin's prodigious output typifies the best and the worst of Hollywood compositional practice in the Golden Age. At its finest, Tiomkin's music demonstrates a high level of creativity and its impact is impressive; at its most mediocre, it coasts its clichéd way amiably enough through a film and subsequently proves to be instantly forgettable. His studio work from 1931 to 1968 was, along with the music of Newman, Rózsa and Waxman, largely responsible for the survival of the typical Golden Age style through the unsettled post-war decades. In some respects, however, Tiomkin's approach and style differed from those of his contemporaries. Although his harmonic idiom was often rich and subtle, it tended to colour the music at a local level rather than establishing longer-term structural trajectories, and a similar lack of interest in esoteric compositional procedures is revealed by his pri-oritizing of the simple emotion of the moment over complex leitmotivic or contrapuntal developments. His initial career had been as a concert pianist (he had also accompanied silent films in St Petersburg with characteristic showmanship): many other Hollywood composers were also fine keyboard players, but in Tiomkin's case he showed little aptitude for the refinements of orchestral scoring and his multiple orchestrators had to convert the pianistic manner of his sketches into idiomatic instrumental textures.

Tiomkin's love for the Russian ballet stemmed not only from his early musical studies in St Petersburg but also from his later marriage to chore-ographer Albertina Rasch, with whom he first moved to Hollywood in 1929 (as part of the post-Crash migration westwards) so that she could devise

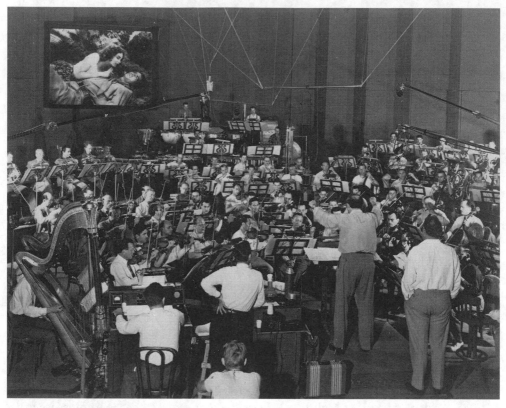

3.2 Dimitri Tiomkin conducting his score to the 1947 western *Duel in the Sun*.

danced sequences for MGM, for which he composed the music. There is a strong balletic feel to Tiomkin's later scoring of both action scenes and light-hearted comedic routines in narrative features; a balletic flavour also imparted a strong dynamism to tension-building scenes in thrillers such as *Strangers on a Train* (dir. Hitchcock, 1951). The influence of ballet, as the supreme example of music-as-movement, on the art of film scoring has long been neglected by scholars on account of the emphasis traditionally placed on sometimes unconvincing parallels with the classical genres of opera and symphony. Yet elements of ballet in general, and the attractively coloured instrumentation of Russian ballet music from Tchaikovsky to Prokofiev in particular, are ubiquitous in mainstream Hollywood scoring – a stylistic debt obvious not only in Tiomkin's music, but also in the work of other Hollywood composers from the 1950s who had active connections with the ballet. One such was Alex North, who also hailed from Russian stock and was married to an accomplished dancer, Anna Sokolow; North likened the strictures of his film work to the challenge of writing dances to pre-set metrical patterns (Henderson 2003, 14–15, 21). Audible links with Russian ballet traditions prevail to the present day in the music of John Williams and others (see Chapter 12).

Tiomkin's talents first came to prominence with his music for *Lost Horizon* (dir. Frank Capra, 1937), for which he was aided by no fewer than seven orchestrators, and which allowed him (or them) to exploit the musical exoticism that was such a strong feature of Russian music at the turn of the twentieth century (Palmer 1990, 128). After extensive work on wartime documentaries, he soon became typecast as a composer for westerns. His score for *The Westerner* (dir. Wyler, 1940), co-composed by an uncredited Newman, had already given him a command of certain stock musical devices associated with the genre: not just bustling music for chases and dramatic stingers, but a type of Americana featuring simple cowboy songs and strummed mandolins, guitars and banjos for a rustic flavour. These elements reappeared in the higher-profile series of westerns he later scored, beginning with *Duel in the Sun* (dir. King Vidor *et al.*, 1947), in which his task was helped by producer Selznick's old-fashioned and stereotypical instructions about which music should suggest 'Sentimental love', 'Jealousy', 'Conflict' and so on (Karlin 1994, 15). Undoubtedly Tiomkin's best-known western assignment was *High Noon* (dir. Fred Zinnemann, 1952), for which he received Academy Awards for both his orchestral score and the song 'Do Not Forsake Me, Oh My Darlin''. The success of the latter, sung in the film by Tex Ritter to lyrics by Ned Washington, spectacularly demonstrated – along with Raksin's earlier *Laura* – the commercial potential of a score based largely on a single memorable melody. A major difference from the circumstances in which the *Laura* theme subsequently became famous was the aggressive pre-release exposure of the *High Noon* song by United Artists, who intended it to be a popular hit from the outset. No fewer than six interpretations were recorded as singles by different vocalists, and in Europe the song was played in cinema foyers in the run-up to the film's release; in both sheet-music sales and radio airtime it had thus become universally familiar, even before the film was screened. Such innovative and efficacious saturation marketing has been summarized by Jeff Smith as 'a kind of shotgun style of promotion; like the spreading pellets of a shotgun blast, the proliferation of single and album versions of a film theme increased the probability that it would hit its target audience' (J. Smith 1998, 60). Songs carrying titles identical to those of the films to which they were attached were at the same time beginning to exploit the attractive proposition that the films would inevitably be mentioned every time the songs were broadcast; not surprisingly, producers were quick to seize on a phenomenon that neatly combined the generation of additional royalties with free airtime advertising.

The success of the song in *High Noon* meant that little attention was paid to more interesting features of Tiomkin's score, such as its abandonment of violin parts and the brilliantly edited climax in which the (pre-composed) metronomic music, inspired by the ticking of the clock as the noontime showdown inexorably approaches, is made to rationalize the rapid cross-cutting of various images – including a long succession of shot changes timed to occur once per quadruple-time bar of music in a powerful coincidence of visual and rhythmic emphases. Tiomkin reprised his monothematic approach even more inventively in *Gunfight at the OK Corral* (dir. John Sturges, 1957), using the device of a commentating ballad-singer with supporting male chorus, a technique distantly reminiscent of ancient Greek drama and arguably making the film 'not a mere Western but a myth of the West and touched with the objective inevitability of classical tragedy' (Palmer 1990, 144). For the rambling Texan soap-opera *Giant* (dir. George Stevens, 1956), Tiomkin's old-time western style continued to sit happily alongside Tchaikovskyan ballet music for outdoor equestrian action. Many of the cues are old-fashioned, including the love music (though the idiom is nicely refreshed by unexpected support from close-harmony saxophones) and the use of easily recognizable pre-existing tunes such as 'Dixie' and 'Auld Lang Syne'; but in a sequence such as the honeymooners' first train journey to Texas, in which the love music is combined with swirling sandstorm impressionism in a magical but non-threatening way, Tiomkin shows his solid grasp of the dramatic requirements of individual moments. The more modern style of western music that came to supplant his nostalgic brand of Americana by the end of the decade (see below) seems largely to have passed him by.

Tiomkin worked in a wide variety of genres: his music for epics is discussed elsewhere, as are those scores based on adaptations of pre-existing classical music. Space precludes detailed consideration of the many other Hollywood composers of the Golden Age who helped score an average output of over 400 movies per year when the system was at its height, and who for the most part worked within the strict stylistic limits defined by the leading figures investigated in this chapter. Among those who hailed from Europe were Daniele Amfitheatrof, Adolph Deutsch, Ernest Gold, Werner Heymann, Frederick Hollander, Bronislau Kaper, Cyril Mockridge and Hans J. Salter; their American contemporaries included George Antheil, David Buttolph, Hugo Friedhofer, John Green, Ray Heindorf, Herbert Stothart and Victor Young. Deutsch, Heindorf, Green and Stothart specialized in musicals, a genre discussed in Chapter 4, though their versatility was reflected in work for many other genres too.

Kaper, a native of Poland who worked for MGM (1940–68), had a gift for melody that spawned several popular hit themes (*Green Dolphin Street*, 1947; *Invitation*, 1952; *Lili*, 1953), and he developed a manner of scoring natural disasters such as earthquakes and floods so that the music would build up and then drop out to allow sound effects to take over at the climax: this trick was so successful that he received letters of praise for his skilful handling of noisy sequences which had in fact included no music (Thomas 1979, 122). Actors praised Kaper's music for persuading spectators that their acting was rather better than in fact it was: George Peppard noted of an extended scene in *Home from the Hill* (dir. Vincente Minnelli, 1960), in which he was required to walk to a cemetery, 'People are always saying what a fine piece of acting it was. Actually, I didn't do anything but walk and stare ahead. All the acting was done by Kaper' (quoted in Thomas 1997, 104).

Young, who was employed by Paramount (1935–56), typified the career pattern of many first-generation American film composers by starting out as concert violinist, vaudeville conductor and silent-film composer, and later proving as adept at writing hit songs (e.g. 'Stella by Starlight', from *The Uninvited*, 1944) as he was at efficiently reproducing a watered-down version of the Newman style in dramatic features. *For Whom the Bell Tolls* (dir. Sam Wood, 1943) is a well-known example: the music is competent rather than individual, and contains a predictably clichéd Spanish flavour that does little to establish the atmosphere of Hemingway's narrative. There are moments where Young's formulaic approach jars with the suggestions of the visuals, most notably when an uncharacteristically androgynous Ingrid Bergman, hair close cropped (immediately post-*Casablanca*) and dressed as a man, makes her first appearance on screen in a rocky outcrop – to the accompaniment of the saccharine string music which many Hollywood composers automatically provided for leading ladies without apparently sparing a moment's thought to the dramatic context.

Aaron Copland and the sounds of America

Although he scored only eight films, Copland exerted an enormous influence on American film composers and helped shape a distinctively nationalistic style that broke finally away from the overblown Eurocentric romanticism which dominated Hollywood scoring in the 1930s and 1940s. Copland was the first established classical composer in the USA to engage seriously with the medium of film, and his involvement lent a new prestige to film music which – though such respect was relatively common in Europe, where leading composers tried their hand at film scoring – had formerly been widely condemned as the second-rate work of talentless hacks. But Copland's impact on film scoring went far deeper. Long before his first film assignment, his music for theatrical and concert-hall genres had taken major steps towards defining a new American nationalism in music, at first rooted in elements of jazz and subsequently drawing on the simplicity of folksong. Copland's combination of folk-style melody and gentle diatonic dissonances, heard paradigmatically in his ballet *Appalachian Spring* (1944), offered film composers a distinctively American sound which increasingly permeated Hollywood films with domestic settings and provided a sharp and timely contrast to the turgid and stereotypical gestures of the conventional romantic-melodramatic score – and this in spite of the often overlooked irony that Copland's 'American' style was in fact heavily indebted to the neo-classicizing tendencies of that prominent expatriate composer from Europe, Stravinsky. The rhythmic excitement and acerbic dissonances of Stravinsky's early Russian ballets in time came to have their own direct influence on younger film composers (notably Jerry Goldsmith); but it was the filtering of Stravinsky's neo-classicism through Copland's music that produced a refined, pure sound which film composers found they could apply to images of domestic contentment or rustic simplicity, or merely use as straightforward background music with rather neutral emotional connotations. When this idiom acquired an overtly patriotic flavour, as it had in Copland's *Lincoln Portrait* (1942) and *Fanfare for the Common Man* (1943), it provided a direct model for the dignified music still heard in modern American films: the war-film cliché of the noble diatonic trumpet sounding its lone heroic voice, often in the distance, is inconceivable without this precedent. And when the idiom acquired a rustic, cowboy flavour, as it did in Copland's much-imitated ballet *Billy the Kid* (1938), it spawned a fresh style of scoring westerns that also persists to the present day.

The new Americana first emerged in film music in documentaries scored by Copland and Virgil Thomson in the late 1930s, discussed in Chapter 7. Copland's first feature assignments followed in 1939–40, when he provided music for cinematic treatments of John Steinbeck's *Of Mice and Men* (dir. Lewis Milestone) and Thornton Wilder's *Our Town* (dir. Sam Wood), the association with distinguished American literature of itself helping to lend his music an aura of nationalistic classicism. According to Copland, Hollywood producers had previously felt his concert idiom to be inappropriate for film scoring and had only been moved to invite him to work there once they had heard the effectiveness of his score to the documentary *The City* in 1939. Copland was called in to score *Of Mice and Men* only after the picture was otherwise finished. As he recalled:

> Here was an American theme, by a great American writer, demanding appropriate music . . . [Milestone] was willing to let me do as I saw fit and gave me none of the usual 'advice.' (He actually added four seconds to the film for the sake of the musical score when I told him it was needed for a particular scene.) Milestone sensed that there were scenes where music

> should take over to express the emotions of the characters, and others
> involved with the production wanted a composer who would not follow the
> formulae for movie music. Not even the music director got in my way . . .
> [Milestone and the film's producer, Hal Roach] knew my objection to the
> lush sort of Hollywood music that often had little relationship to the action,
> emotions, or ideas in a movie. Full-blown symphonic music throughout a
> film might be fine for a nineteenth-century theme like that of *Wuthering
> Heights*, but it was not appropriate to the California wheat ranch in *Of Mice
> and Men*. I discovered that piano music was not suitable either for outdoor
> scenes, so I tried more natural-sounding instruments – solo flute, flutes
> together, and a guitar for a campfire scene. I insisted on doing the
> orchestration myself.
>
> (Copland and Perlis 1984, 297–8. According to McCarty 2000, 72, orchestrations
> were in fact prepared by George Bassman)

Copland deliberately eschewed leitmotivic procedures and mickey-
mousing, and resisted quoting from folksongs. He found it easy to score
overtly dramatic moments such as the crushing of a hand (which takes
place to the accompaniment of a dissonant chord prolonged to an uncomfortable length), 'But the background music was difficult for me. It seemed a
strange assignment to write music that is actually meant to be uninteresting.
Yet this kind of "neutral" sound is often needed to "warm" the screen or to
connect one piece of action to another' (Copland and Perlis 1984, 299). In
spite of clashes with the sound engineer when Copland resented the constant ducking of his music under dialogue, he found his first experience of
film work generally positive, and revelled in an environment that – in spite
of its many drawbacks – at least promoted the work of living composers on
a daily basis.

When Copland returned to Hollywood to score *Our Town*, he was confronted with a project 'which looked back at an America of simple, home-
spun values that seemed [in 1940] to have been lost' (Copland and Perlis
1984, 302). Inspired by the quasi-documentary style of Wilder's play, and
sketching some of the score's themes before he had even seen the film, Copland again avoided quoting pre-existing tunes, which he felt would detract
from the universality of the story, but instead exploited hymn-like harmonies
associated with New England communities. Like many other classical composers who worked in film, Copland extracted music from his film scores
for concert use and in 1943 dedicated the suite *Music for Movies* to Milhaud
in recognition of the latter's own contribution to film scoring. Also in 1943,
Copland scored Milestone's *The North Star*, a big-budget propagandist feature aimed at promoting admiration for the people of the US's wartime
ally, Russia. Drawing on Russian folksong, Copland 'developed fragments
of a few carefully chosen tunes until they became very much my own, while

still retaining a sense of their Russian derivation' (Copland and Perlis 1992, 15), and also supplied diegetic song-and-dance routines to lyrics by Ira Gershwin.

Admiration for Copland's film work was not universal, and a possible explanation was advanced by Marian Hannah Winter in her article 'The Function of Music in Sound Film' (1941), in which she commented that the critical malaise surrounding the success of the score to *Of Mice and Men* stemmed

> from Copland's apparent conviction that films have no sustained and constant rhythm of their own, and need an evangelical saviour in the guise of composer. Oddly, Copland mentions Honegger with approval in his article (*New York Times*, 10 March 1940), for no composer of our time has understood more thoroughly than Honegger the function of film music and the importance of *non-musical* sounds to his scores, to say nothing of the occasional striking use of silence. Honegger scrupulously respects film continuity and rhythm, which Copland seems to regard as factors to be supplied by the composer.   (Winter 1941, 164)

Winter perceives the classical composer's desire for what she herself terms a 'symphonic' approach as 'a concept that continues to account for some of the most exasperating and persistent atrocities in film music', citing Newman's score to *Wuthering Heights* as a typical example of 'what is essentially a cheat, musically and cinematically'.

Copland's last significant film scores were written in 1949, when he worked on adaptations of two more American literary classics: Steinbeck's *The Red Pony* (dir. Milestone) and a stage version of Henry James's *Washington Square*, filmed under the title *The Heiress* (dir. Wyler). *The Red Pony* was an uncharacteristically prestigious production by a B-studio, Republic Pictures, from which Copland received $15,000 for ten weeks' work: 'I had to come up with fifty-two minutes of orchestrated music in eight weeks and be ready to record it during the last two weeks of my contract', claimed the composer in his memoirs (Copland and Perlis 1992, 89–90). Once again he neglected to mention that he was ably assisted by two professional orchestrators; when questioned about why he had felt able to delegate this task, he reportedly replied 'If I dictate a letter and it is typed for me, who actually wrote the letter, me or my secretary?' (Previn 1992, 157). The film attracted Copland by the manner in which it dealt with 'the unexpressed feelings of daily living', and it seemed to demand a combination of the rustic simplicity of his earlier film scores and 'some of the inevitable steady rhythmic accompaniment to simulate cowboys on horseback' (Copland and Perlis 1992, 88). Drawing on the idiom of *Billy the Kid*, suggestive in places of the awesome nature of the wide open plains, and including passages in quintuple metre for an uneven, lolloping effect, Copland here laid the foundations for a style that was to dominate the future scoring of westerns. The influence of Stravinsky remains prominent, especially in the final cue with its bustling diatonic folksiness strongly reminiscent of *Petrushka* (the score of which had been reissued in a revised orchestration in 1947). Again the project spawned a spin-off concert suite, and when Copland unsuccessfully attempted to persuade Steinbeck to write a verbal commentary for it, intended for children, the writer praised him for letting 'the sombre come into your music to balance the gaiety and to give it proportion and significance' (Copland and Perlis 1992, 91).

The spiky, buoyant diatonicism of Copland's brand of Stravinskyan neo-classicism proved ideally suited to *The Heiress*, which seemed to demand (as the composer expressed it in preliminary correspondence with the director) 'music of a certain discretion and refinement in the expression of sentiments'. Perhaps because of the film's period setting, Copland finally felt comfortable about having recourse to leitmotivic techniques as a structural principle, citing their usefulness for underlining character development as a prime motivation; he also exploited passacaglia form to 'generate a feeling of continuity and inevitability, as well as provide the necessary dissonance when combined with other music', and reworked musical idioms based on dance forms from the 1850s. (Once more he relied on an orchestrator, this time the experienced Nathan Van Cleave, in order to meet the studio's deadline.) After the audience laughed at a crucially serious dramatic moment during a preview screening, Copland wrote a new and highly dissonant cue (based on a discarded sketch from his Piano Variations of 1929) and the problem did not recur; he also used the procedure known as 'sweetening', whereby the orchestral string section is recorded twice and the takes combined to create a richer sonority. Economical chamber textures are nevertheless a far more characteristic feature of the score. Copland received an Academy Award for his music, which was competing with nominated scores by Steiner and Tiomkin in 1950, in spite of the fact that his main-title music had been excised at a late stage and replaced by a populist arrangement of the song 'Plaisir d'Amour'. Copland later wondered if his outspoken letter to the press disassociating himself from the replacement title music had been a factor contributing towards the paucity of invitations he received from Hollywood thereafter (Copland and Perlis 1992, 98–107). (For an analysis of representative segments of *The Heiress*, with music examples, see Prendergast 1992, 88–95, an account based on Sternfeld 1951.)

One of the first film scores by another composer to betray the influence of Copland's fresh-sounding idiom was Friedhofer's to *The Best Years of Our Lives*, directed in 1946 by Wyler, who treated the affecting story of three war veterans returning home to middle America with the same marked lack of sentimentality that had characterized his wartime documentaries (discussed in Chapter 7). Friedhofer's score won him an Academy Award, and he commented that Copland's influence 'helped me weed out the run-of-the-mine schmaltz and aim to do more straightforward and simple, even folklike scoring' (Thomas 1991, 213), and this idiom accompanies scenes of domestic simplicity and homely values. Nevertheless, the music remained indebted to conventional leitmotivic procedures, in places drew on standard comedic devices (with a skilful use of parody) and included Webb-like expressionism for a nightmare sequence: dissonance level is high when justified, as in the climax when Captain Derry sits in a derelict B17 bomber in the boneyard to the accompaniment of grim music, replete with dissonant stingers, as he spots the missing engines from the bomb-aimer's nose glazing. Just a year after the film's release, Friedhofer's eclectic score was subjected to intelligent analysis by Frederick Sternfeld in an early example of technical film-music commentary in a musicological journal (Sternfeld 1947, a source quoted at length in Prendergast 1992, 77–9). Four years later, Sternfeld went on to publish a perceptive appreciation of Copland's film music in the same journal (Sternfeld 1951).

More than anywhere else, it was in the musical development of the western in the 1950s that Copland's example helped crystallize in sonic terms the outgoing and optimistic American spirit so characteristic of this genre and others to have come under its influence. This phenomenon is not so surprising when one considers that the western is arguably the only Hollywood genre to show virtually no debt to dramatic traditions outside the USA: its conception is truly American, and the provision of unashamedly nationalistic music for it was entirely fitting. In 1954, Robert Warshow offered a penetrating account of the genre's evolution (reprinted in Braudy and Cohen 1999, 654–67) in which he unravelled the various layers of meaning it had accumulated, including what he saw as the ill-advised stratum of self-conscious social realism added to the basic yarn in *High Noon* alongside such crudities as the use of the ticking clock (with Tiomkin's synchronized music) to build up suspense. The musical evolution of the western progressed from old-time and sometimes sentimental Americana to extrovert reworkings of Copland's basic cowboy idiom. John Ford's *Stagecoach* had already injected new life into the genre in 1939, but Warshow pointed out that Ford's 'unhappy preoccupation with style' led him to

> yield entirely to its static quality as legend and to the 'cinematic' temptations of its landscape, the horses, the quiet men . . . [T]he same director's *My Darling Clementine* (1946), a soft and beautiful movie about Wyatt Earp [with music by Mockridge], goes further along the same path, offering indeed a superficial accuracy of historical reconstruction, but so

> loving in execution as to destroy the outlines of the Western legend,
> assimilating it to the more sentimental legend of rural America.
>
> (Brandy and Cohen 1999, 664)

Stagecoach was supplied with music by a team of arrangers, including Richard Hageman (who specialized in the genre), and was partly based on folksong. Although the pentatonic flavour of the folk melodies naturally affected the music's harmonic style somewhat, it was still solidly anchored in the Steiner norm, with a concomitant sense of nostalgia at times, and perpetuated such stereotypes as organum fourths for the natives. Steiner himself scored westerns, such as *The Searchers* (dir. Ford, 1956), his music for which makes little attempt to escape from outmoded melodramatic clichés – although the film does include a title song in deference to the success of Tiomkin's *High Noon* a few years earlier.

Musically the most prophetic parts of *Stagecoach* were the outgoing cues accompanying passage-of-time shots of the eponymous vehicle in motion. Mitry was impressed by the film's deployment of its main theme, which 'translates the movement of the coach, giving the film the dynamic lift it needs. By overlapping the story-telling, the music first of all signifies through its relation with the images, and then, through a kind of symbolic transference, it assumes the descriptive role originally assigned to them' (Mitry 1998, 252). The apogee of such hard-driving optimism was Jerome Moross's thrilling music to *The Big Country* (dir. Wyler, 1958), where the 'big theme' now typical of the genre accompanies a dynamic title sequence designed by Saul Bass. A friend of Copland's, Moross had orchestrated parts of *Our Town* and *The Best Years of Our Lives* and had for years remained relegated to this ancillary studio role: his big break as a composer came when he stepped in to score *The Big Country* after Copland had declined the invitation from Wyler to score it himself. Moross's famous and much-imitated theme, in which cowboy melodic brashness meets the swirling ostinati of Widor's equally famous organ Toccata, ultimately provided the prototype for such similar evocations of Texan expansiveness as the theme tune to the television drama series *Dallas*, composed by Jerrold Immel in 1978.

Moross used a distinctive harmonic shift: the major triad on the flattened seventh of the scale is followed by the dominant triad, in which the major third (i.e. leading note of the scale) immediately cancels out the flat seventh in a optimism-inducing moment of false relation. This simple but colourful device, probably inspired by the flatwards inflections in such Copland cues as 'The Walk to the Bunkhouse' from *The Red Pony*, became a staple of western themes, for example being found in Elmer Bernstein's score to *The Magnificent Seven* (dir. John Sturges, 1960). Bernstein, who studied with

Copland, recalled in a television interview that he had long wished to tap Copland's particular brand of folksy Americana in a filmic context, and for this assignment he also emulated the Mexicanisms of Copland's *El Salón México* (1936). In later westerns scored by Bernstein, such as *True Grit* (dir. Henry Hathaway, 1969), elements from the old-fashioned and post-Copland western comfortably co-exist: a main-title pop song (with lyrics by Don Black) updates the formula initiated by *High Noon*, while an expansive prairie theme for the story's picaresque elements draws as much from the style of *Billy the Kid* as Bernstein's more reflective and intimate moments for chamber ensemble are indebted to *Appalachian Spring*. The idiom was adopted by Jerry Goldsmith in *Lonely Are the Brave* (dir. David Miller, 1962) and *Rio Lobo* (dir. Howard Hawks, 1970), though in *Bandolero!* (dir. Andrew V. McLaglen, 1968) and *Take a Hard Ride* (dir. Antonio Margheriti, 1975) Goldsmith also tapped the then fashionable sound of Morricone's spaghetti-western scores from Europe (considered in Chapter 9). The US western as a whole provides an admirable case-study of a genre of which the surface flavour has been changed by musical innovation, itself in turn being enshrined as a new set of compositional formulae, while the dramatic elements have remained remarkably constant over several decades. As Milton Berle quipped of the modern 'adult' western, 'the hero still kisses his horse at the end, only now he worries about it' (quoted in J. Walker 1995, 628).

4 Stage and screen

In his short but provocative discussion of the pros and cons of filming opera, Béla Balázs drew a clear distinction between the straightforward filmic preservation of theatrical opera productions (which he viewed as 'very useful in improving the musical taste of the public') and the exciting possibility of a film opera 'intended and directed and composed for the film from the start, [being] a new musical form of art with new problems and new tasks' (Balázs 1953, 275). Echoing the opinions of commentators in the 1930s, he dismissed the notion of filming pre-existing stage works in a realistic cinematic style as completely incompatible with the highly stylized idiom of operatic acting and singing. Balázs nevertheless advocated a degree of flexibility of direction and, above all, mobile camerawork in order 'to loosen up the old-fashioned rigidity which is scarcely tolerable even on the stage to-day', and praised René Clair for his ability to parody in effective cinematic terms the 'grotesquely unnatural character of stage style' by such fluidity of directorial technique (Balázs 1953, 276). Balázs's mention in this context of Clair, whose bold and imaginative ideal of the 'musical film' was examined in Chapter 2, suggests that certain fundamental aesthetic considerations inform an understanding of the pleasures and pitfalls of reworking both highbrow and middlebrow music-oriented dramatic forms on celluloid. Although Clair's 'musical film' quickly gave way to the more commercially minded 'film musical', these parallels persisted, especially when film musicals were based directly on stage works.

This chapter will briefly summarize trends in opera films from the silent era to modern times, and the role of operatic music and settings in other types of film, before tracing the development of the far more populist, prodigious and lucrative film musical in Hollywood and elsewhere. (For discussion of the musical in Indian cinema, see Chapter 9.) Issues of elitism and prestige at the heart of filmed opera, very different from the sheer entertainment and vernacular energy of the best film musicals, also feed into a discussion of the role of film music in the significant body of sound films based on Shakespeare's plays, which deserve a focused examination not only because they have frequently involved the skills of front-rank composers specifically hired to lend the products a prestige similar to that of opera, but also represent encouragingly varied and often genuinely creative responses to similar problems of musico-dramatic style and structure – and sometimes also spring from a desire to bring high culture to the masses.

Opera on film

Cinematic interpretations of scenes from popular operas were widespread in the era of the silent film. By as early as 1904, extracts from Wagner's *Parsifal*, Rossini's *Barber of Seville* and Gounod's *Faust* had been recorded on film and projected with live music. The sumptuous Gounod film, *Faust et Marguerite*, was directed by pioneering film-maker Georges Méliès, who himself appeared as Méphistophélès. In 1908, two developments contributed towards a boom in such ventures: first, the founding of the influential *film d'art* movement in France (see Chapter 1), which intensified interest in cinema as an art form; second, the introduction of more stringent copyright legislation which henceforth compelled film-makers to plunder non-copyright classics of literature and the operatic stage in the interests of economy. A further consideration in the issuing of operatic extracts on film was the desire to promote gramophone recordings of the singers featured, a commercial concern that sat uncomfortably alongside the growing feeling that operatic source material could lend the medium of film a prestige that had formerly eluded it.

'Canned theatre' (in the parlance of the day) thus came to include 'canned opera', with both Pathé and Edison releasing new versions of Gounod's *Faust*, in 1909 and 1911 respectively; Pathé also made a film based on Verdi's *Il trovatore* in 1910. Other operas subjected to film treatment included Thomas's *Mignon*, Auber's *Fra Diavolo* and Wagner's *Siegfried* (all 1912). Appropriate musical extracts from the operas were suggested by the distributors to guide projection venues in fitting live performances to the images, and these performances generally lacked the vocal parts (Marks 1997, 72); venues were at liberty to use any other music of their choice, and often did. In the case of a film based on Mozart's *Le nozze di Figaro* (1914), the distributor declared in its trade advertisement that 'Music adapted from the famous Opera will be supplied gratis' (Marks 1997, 193). Biopics based on the lives of Wagner and Verdi appeared in Europe in 1913 and 1914 respectively, and operatic films continued to be produced in large numbers in France, Germany and Italy. Bizet's ever-popular *Carmen*, already given a filmed treatment by Edison in 1910, formed the basis for a silent film starring operatic soprano Geraldine Farrar in 1915 – and wickedly parodied a year later by Chaplin in his *Burlesque on Carmen*. Produced by Cecil B. DeMille for Paramount, the Farrar film was launched in the USA to the accompaniment of arrangements from Bizet's score prepared by Riesenfeld and Rothapfel. In 1917, Puccini refused to allow his music to be used for a film version of *La Bohème*, his gesture reinforcing the problem of tackling works still in copyright; but production of non-copyright opera films continued apace. By the 1920s silent films had grown longer in duration and relatively sophisticated in technique, and later operatic ventures were accordingly more satisfying. Among them, several films based on *La Bohème* finally appeared (in 1921, 1922 and 1926).

A silent film of Strauss's *Der Rosenkavalier* was made in 1925, and this is occasionally screened today – as it was at Aldeburgh in 2002 – with live piano accompaniment. The film's production credentials were impressive, with direction by Robert Wiene (responsible for the legendary expressionist film *The Cabinet of Dr Caligari* in 1919), design by Alfred Roller (designer of Max Reinhardt's original staging of the opera) and the direct participation of both librettist and composer. Strauss originally intended to have little to do with the project, which was scheduled to be screened at the Dresden Opera House in January 1926; he agreed to compose a new march, but left the task of adaptation to Otto Singer and Karl Alwin. In December 1925 the librettist Hofmannsthal wrote to the composer to say: 'I must admit that your refusal to conduct the film in Dresden came quite unexpected and is a grave blow to me . . . I cling to the hope that it may perhaps be tempered with "blessed revocability", but if it were irrevocable, I foresee for you (and consequently also for me) . . . the loss of very considerable financial expectations' (Hammelmann and Osers 1961, 411). Hofmannsthal was impecunious at the time and clearly had a vested interest in generating revenue from the project: his awareness of its commercial potential is telling. In a later letter Hofmannsthal passionately argued that the film would provide 'a positive fillip and new impetus to the opera's success in the theatre' (quoted in Jefferson 1985, 123). Strauss duly relented, and conducted the shambolic first screening in which it rapidly became apparent that he possessed neither the technical expertise nor sympathy with the medium necessary to ensure accurate synchronization with the projected images: he suffered the humiliation of being forced to yield his baton to an experienced film conductor (London 1936, 69). In April 1926 Strauss was in London to conduct the first English screening, on which occasion he also recorded orchestral excerpts with the Tivoli Orchestra. Released by His Master's Voice, these recordings were an early example of a film 'tie-in'.

Reflecting on the tension between populist film music and modernist music 'driven into the esoteric' because of its minority appeal, Eisler and Adorno took a hearty swipe at both *Der Rosenkavalier* and its composer:

> at the time when motion-picture music was in its rudimentary stage, the breach between middle-class audiences and the really serious music which expressed the situation of the middle classes had become unbridgeable. This breach can be traced back as far as *Tristan*, a work that has probably never been understood and liked as much as *Aïda, Carmen*, or even the *Meistersinger*. The operatic theater became finally estranged from its audience between 1900 and 1910, with the production of *Salome* and

Electra, the two advanced operas of Richard Strauss. The fact that after 1910, with the *Rosenkavalier* – it is no accident that this opera has been made into a moving picture – he turned to a retrospective stylized way of writing reflects his awareness of that breach. Strauss was one of the first to attempt to bridge the gap between culture and audience, by selling out culture.

(Adorno and Eisler 1994 [1947], 57)

It is worth reiterating, however, that the first screening of the *Rosenkavalier* film took place in a prestigious opera house, not a picture palace, and that (as we saw in Chapter 1) more elaborate presentations of silent feature films were often mounted in similar venues. The boundaries between art and popular entertainment were becoming blurred even at this early stage, and Adorno's and Eisler's 'breach' between the allegedly self-contained audiences for both is clearly an over-simplification.

Various attempts were made in the 1920s to improve synchronization between sound and image in operatic films, notably in Germany, and these included Blum's rhythmonome (see Chapter 2). In 1922 the first opera specifically intended for the silver screen, Ferdinand Hummel's *Jenseits des Stromes*, included musical notation as part of the projected image as a guide to the conductor, but the film has not survived (Evidon 1992, 196; Fawkes 2000, 27). At the Vitaphone launch in New York in 1926 the feature film *Don Juan* was prefaced by a series of short films of musical and vaudeville performances: several star singers from the Metropolitan Opera had been signed up by Vitaphone specifically to make synchronized shorts of popular operatic excerpts. As sound-on-film technology developed rapidly after 1927, Hollywood's penchant for musical comedy resulted in the production of many filmed operettas in the USA, while films of 'serious' operas appeared mostly in Europe. An early highlight, which trod a middle ground between the popular and the esoteric, was G. W. Pabst's interpretation of Weill's *The Threepenny Opera*, shot in 1930 in both German and French versions using two different casts (Hinton 1990, 42–3). Pabst was a pioneer of cinematic *neue Sachlichkeit*, his innovative montage techniques developing methods of continuity editing still prevalent today. As with Max Ophüls's film of Smetana's *Bartered Bride* (1932), Pabst showed how a front-rank director could significantly enhance the impact of a stage work by skilfully adapting it to the new medium. The script for *The Threepenny Opera* was partly the work of Balázs, librettist of Bartók's *Duke Bluebeard's Castle* in addition to being a noted film theorist, and the cinematography revelled in the restless, searching camera movements, high-contrast lighting and shady settings typical of Weimar cinema. Although the musical content was drastically pruned, it was treated inventively throughout: creative use was made of diegetic cues, as when 'Mack the Knife' is accompanied by a barrel organ

4.1 G. W. Pabst's film of Kurt Weill's and Bertolt Brecht's *The Threepenny Opera* (1931) stimulated sheet-music sales, the work's publisher (Universal Edition) issuing this tie-in edition of four of the film's songs.

in a street scene (with the recording level manipulated to suggest distance in a long shot), and songs used in instrumental versions played in a tavern and brothel. A débâcle surrounding the film's contractual arrangements drew attention to the ongoing dangers in tackling copyright material: both Brecht and Weill were legally entitled to have exclusive control over alterations to the screenplay and music respectively, and both independently took the production company to court when their entitlement was openly flouted. Brecht lost his case, but Weill won his – securing in the process a hefty cash settlement and potentially lucrative options to score further films by the same company. On the film's release in 1931, Universal Edition issued a tie-in album containing four of the score's most popular songs (Hinton 1990, 44–6).

In the UK, the 1930s saw the production of two expensive opera films in colour, one based on Leoncavallo's *Pagliacci* (destroyed by the distributor, Trafalgar Films, after its completion in 1937 owing to the lack of revenue generated by its release) and the other of Gilbert's and Sullivan's *The Mikado* (dir. Victor Schertzinger, 1939). The latter was intended as the launch vehicle for an ambitious series of G&S films featuring the D'Oyly Carte company and London Symphony Orchestra, but the series was halted by the outbreak of the Second World War. *The Mikado* met with mixed reviews, one critic declaring that 'the mechanical nature of the screen-photograph (added to its self-complete realism in its own sphere) precludes any direct inter-action between audience and performers' (quoted in Huntley [1947], 48). The most celebrated post-war British opera film was Michael Powell's and Emeric Pressburger's interpretation of Offenbach's *The Tales of Hoffmann* (1951), in which dancing and powerful special effects combined to create a new kind of cinematographic theatricality that appeared to be located in a fruitful middle ground between fantasy and reality, described by film theorist André Bazin as 'an entirely faked universe . . . a sort of stage without wings where everything is possible' (quoted in Joe and Theresa 2002, 51). The film was a major influence on director Martin Scorsese, its techniques directly affecting his production methods in films as varied as *Raging Bull, Taxi Driver* and *New York, New York* (Thompson and Christie 1989, 6). Also in 1951, a film of Menotti's *The Medium* received critical acclaim and subsequently won an award at the 1952 Cannes Film Festival; this was an appropriate accolade for Italian filmed opera in general, the country having remained at the forefront of cinematic treatments of grand opera throughout the previous two decades. Like Weill's, Menotti's musico-dramatic instincts were located somewhere between the popular and the sophisticated, and for a brief time in 1947 he had found himself under contract to MGM during the heyday of that studio's production of musicals, but left when his script entitled *The Happy Ending* was not adopted – this scarcely coming as a surprise since the happy ending concerned involved a group of children leaving their horrible grandmother to freeze outside at Christmas (Fordin 1996, 222). A few years later Menotti would strike a more universal chord with the success of his warm-hearted Yuletide opera, *Amahl and the Night Visitors* (NBC, 1951), the first opera written specifically for television.

Debate had in the 1930s begun to rage on the apparently fundamental tension between filmic realism and stage theatricality which concerned Balázs. Because of the conceived incompatibility of the two approaches, several early commentators on film music bluntly predicted no future for filmed opera. Sabaneev identified the principal stumbling block as 'the fact that the art of the cinema . . . is a photographic art, and is therefore obliged to be naturalistic and anti-theatrical' (Sabaneev 1935, 26). London declared filmed opera to be 'impossible and intolerable', and continued:

> Those elements for which on the operatic stage even to-day allowance is made, under the influence of the personalities of live artists, must on the screen have an insipid, ridiculous, and anachronistic effect. The camera brings the singer's pathos much too close to the spectator; a close-up of a photographed high C, on which the distorted face of the tenor, with wide-open mouth, is to be seen, at once destroys the effect of even the most beautiful melody and resolves it into laughter or even disgust.
>
> (London 1936, 139–40)

In his account of the problematic nature of filmed opera, London concluded: 'The unreal world of opera and the naturalistic film have nothing whatever in common'. This view was elaborated by Kracauer in the early 1950s, when he declared 'The world of opera is built upon premises which radically defy those of the cinematic approach . . . Opera on the screen is a collision of two worlds detrimental to either' (quoted in Joe and Theresa 2002, ix). London's assertions that 'opera is static, film dynamic' and that 'well-known works of operatic literature have become rigid conceptions which may not be touched by the film' (1936, 140, 142) will amuse contemporary opera audiences, accustomed as they are not only to a spectacular diversity of production styles beyond the wildest dreams of both film and opera audiences in the 1930s but also to the expectation that opera singers must be able to act convincingly as well as to stand still and sing.

As early as 1913, Schoenberg had explored the possibility of filmed opera in an unnaturalistic style when contemplating a hand-tinted silent film of *Die glückliche Hand*. Writing to his publisher, he characteristically stipulated that he should retain total control over all aspects of the live musical performance, and showed himself to be in sympathy with the exigencies of movie distribution by being prepared to consider the use of a cinema organ instead of an orchestra if dictated by the size of the projection venue. Schoenberg's comments on the style of the visual images were far-sighted in their experimental nature and awareness of the unlimited potential for illusion inherent in the medium of film:

> the basic unreality of the events, which is inherent in the words, is something that they should be able to bring out even better in the filming (nasty idea that it is!). For me this is one of the main reasons for considering it. For instance, in the film, if the goblet suddenly vanishes as if it had never been there, just as if it had simply been forgotten, that is quite different

from the way it is on the stage, where it has to be removed by some device.
And there are a thousand things besides that be easily done in this medium,
whereas the stage's resources are very limited.

My foremost wish is therefore for something the opposite of what the
cinema generally aspires to. I want:

The utmost unreality!   (Hahl-Koch 1984, 100)

Significantly, Schoenberg was considering Roller as one of three possible
designers (he was in good company: the other options were the expressionist
painters Kokoschka and Kandinsky), having been impressed by the anti-
realist tendencies he had shown in his production of *Tristan* for Mahler at
the Vienna Opera in 1903. Roller's positive attitude towards cinema early in
the century was shown by a striking statement he made six years later in an
essay bemoaning what he perceived as a general lack of interest in theatrical
experimentation on the part of opera directors: 'So why do we stick to a kind
of theatrical activity which seems no longer to be viable? Granted, new and
contemporary forms are continually arising, but in their lack of tradition
they are naturally not exalted enough to meet with serious encouragement
or to win favour with the cultivated! Isn't a good film to be preferred to a
bad performance of Schiller?' (Roller 1909).

A prolific output of filmed opera was produced by the Soviet Union from
the 1950s onwards, in tandem with a series of films of well-known Russian
ballets. Following the stage-bound film versions of Rachmaninov's *Aleko*
(dir. N. Sidelev, 1953) and Mussorgsky's *Boris Godunov* (dir. Vera Stroyeva,
1955), more creative cinematography was demonstrated in Tchaikovsky's
Eugene Onegin (dir. Roman Tikhomirov, 1958). Tikhomirov later directed
films of Tchaikovsky's *Queen of Spades* (1960) and Borodin's *Prince Igor*
(1971). Other treatments of standard repertoire items included two films
by Vladimir Gorikker, of Tchaikovsky's *Iolanta* (1963) and Rimsky's *Tsar's
Bride* (1964). The most notable Soviet opera film was based on a twentieth-
century score: Shostakovich's *Katerina Izmailova* (the revised version of
Lady Macbeth of Mtsensk, withdrawn in 1936 after the composer's infamous
lambasting in *Pravda*). The opera was filmed in 1966 by director Mikhael
Shapiro, working in close collaboration with the composer, and Galina Vishnevskaya took the title role as she had in the revised opera's first staging in
1963. Shapiro combined sophisticated montage techniques with two features common in later Soviet opera films: realistic settings and a double
cast (one of actors, the other of dubbed singers; the only exception was
Vishnevskaya, who fulfilled both functions). According to Tatiana Egorova,
the film's only 'serious mistake' was the exclusion of naturalistic sound and
sound effects from the final soundtrack, with the result that 'the visual element of the film resembled an animated illustration, a pantomime of the
recorded opera' (Egorova 1997, 190).

Outside the Soviet Union, the output of filmed opera had dwindled somewhat, being largely confined to straightforward filmings of staged productions, such as Paul Czinner's films of the Salzburg productions of *Don Giovanni* (1955) and *Der Rosenkavalier* (1961), or films designed for the greater intimacy afforded by the medium of television, such as Ingmar Bergman's *Die Zauberflöte* (1975) and Jean-Pierre Ponnelle's *Le nozze di Figaro* (1976). Also dating from 1976 was a more ambitious project in which Jean-Marie Straub and Danièle Huillet directed an austere outdoor version of Schoenberg's *Moses und Aron* that 'represented the zenith of the Brechtian anti-aesthetic trend in cinema' (Joe and Theresa 2002, 215). This film was too esoteric in both its choice of opera and style of presentation to be widely influential, and interest instead began to focus on the commercial viability of straightforward treatments of popular operas in lavish period settings.

The 1980s vogue for full-scale grand opera in the cinema was initiated by Joseph Losey's film of *Don Giovanni* (1979), performed on the soundtrack by the Paris Opéra under Lorin Maazel. The project was conceived by Rolf Liebermann, who considered Patrice Chéreau and Franco Zeffirelli as possible directors before deciding on Losey – who had never seen the opera. The action was shot entirely on location amongst the impressive Palladian architecture of Vicenza and in the Venetian islands, and viewers who merely revelled in the visual splendour of the cinematography may have been surprised to learn that the stunning locations were used 'to erect a Marxist critique of class relations' (Citron 2000, 11–12). Critical responses ranged from Julian Rushton's curt dismissal of the project as an 'elegant imbecility' (Rushton 1981, 80) – a remark which might also be applied to a good deal of the operatic repertoire itself, even in its unfilmed state – to David Caute's attempt to prove that this 'masterpiece ravishing to both ear and eye' is dramatically superior to a stage interpretation:

> Losey met the challenge by flooding the picture with sunlight and water,
> paintings and sculpture, his camera movements boldly responsive to
> Mozart's music, a dazzling fusion of the fine and performing arts.
> Confronted by the visual stasis of operatic convention, Losey eased apart the
> orchestral and the dramatic, reuniting them in the cutting-room on his own
> terms. (Caute 1994, 431)

At the time of the film's release, the critical response in the UK and USA was almost unremittingly negative. Only in France did massive publicity on the part of the producers (Gaumont) help the film to score an enormous success at the box office and receive the critical adulation that eluded it elsewhere. This was in spite of a major rift between Liebermann and Losey when the former objected to the latter's inattention to matters of dynamics in the score, and his tendency (in marked contrast to Shapiro's in *Katerina Izmailova*) to allow sound effects to dominate the singing; as Liebermann put it, unconsciously echoing Breil's defence of Wagner, 'Mozart did not compose film music' (Caute 1994, 430–1).

Zeffirelli brought his considerable stage experience, as both director and designer, to bear in a film version of Verdi's *La traviata* (1982), with a music track performed by the Metropolitan Opera under James Levine. Characteristic of its director were the opulent costumes and sumptuous interiors with warm lighting, and the simple use of stock cinematic devices such as flashbacks (to illustrate a character's thoughts), slow zooms in and out, and the occasional use of voice-over in soliloquies – the last a neat way of avoiding the intrusiveness of close-up photography of singing mouths. In the opening sequence, a flash forwards to the dying Violetta's dustsheet-clad apartment, and again during the Prelude to Act III, the combined effect of the mute visual images and Verdi's heart-on-sleeve music was remarkably similar to that of silent-film melodrama of the 1910s. A follow-up film of Verdi's *Otello* (1986), conducted by Maazel, took significant liberties with the score in the interests of serving the visual images, to the extent that the defensive director prevented music critics from attending the New York première (Citron 2000, 74). *Otello* failed to repeat the success of *La traviata*, even though (like the same director's *Romeo and Juliet* of 1968) it predictably netted the Academy Award for best costumes. In a television interview in 1997, Zeffirelli claimed that he felt opera to be the most complete artistic form, combining 'dance, drama, poetry, music and the visual arts' (R. Jackson 2000, 212); yet, in spite of their surface gloss, his filmed operas were deeply conservative in their production values and offered little to stimulate either the intellect or the emotion, treading a careful middle-ground between restraint and excess.

More successful was Francesco Rosi's version of Bizet's *Carmen* (1984), which also used traditional costumes and appropriate exterior locations. Produced by Gaumont and again featuring a music track conducted by Maazel, this flamboyant and colourful interpretation was distinguished by effective crowd scenes, several of which used voice-overs instead of mimed singing to achieve greater visual realism and freedom of movement. The main titles appear over a slow-motion bullfight to the accompaniment of crowd noise and distant snatches of music; the overture crashes into life at the precise moment when Escamillo's sword enters the bull's neck and the animal drops lifeless to the ground. An effective sequence in its own right, this prologue forms a symmetrical counterpart to the bull-fighting climax with which the film concludes. Bizet's score proved to be admirable for cinematic adaptation in those instances where purely instrumental passages could be treated by Rosi as straight underscoring to the action on screen. As H. Marshall Leicester has shown, Rosi's refined cinematography – which at times purports to be as realistic as Zeffirelli's – subtly underlines the contrast in the score between vernacular musical idioms and conventional operatic gestures: 'Rosi converts "realism" into a textual element, making use of the rich reference to actuality in a way Zeffirelli, the exemplar he emulates and parodies, never dreamed of. He exploits the oddness of people singing in what looks so much like real life to specify and reinforce the psycho-social implications of a difference in musical style' (Leicester 1994, 273).

The diversification of opera films in the 1980s resulted in several contrasting ventures entirely different from the heady energy of Rosi's *Carmen*. Hans Jürgen Syberberg's interpretation of Wagner's *Parsifal* (1982), played out on a massive set modelled on the composer's death mask, combined boredom and pretension in equal measure; singer Robert Lloyd (who played Gurnemanz) recalled that 'none of the cast really understood what Syberberg was on about, they simply did what he asked' (Fawkes 2000, 182). The portmanteau film *Aria* (1988) was a hotchpotch compilation of operatic excerpts interpreted by no fewer than ten different directors with varying degrees of flair and success; according to Derek Jarman, 'not one of the directors opened the music up; in nearly every case they used it as a backdrop for a series of rather arbitrary fantasies, none of which had the depth or complexity of the original work' (Jarman 1989, xi). (For a detailed audio-visual analysis of the segment based on Lully's *Armide*, directed with characteristic idiosyncrasy by French New Wave director Jean-Luc Godard, see N. Cook 1998, 215–60.) Losey had been planning a film of *Tosca* before his death in 1984; Puccini's opera received an over-ambitious live-on-location filming in 1992, and an accomplished interpretation by director Benoît Jacquot in 2001 in which full-colour costumed scenes in luminous Zeffirellian settings were disconcertingly intercut with monochrome footage of the singers recording the soundtrack in modern dress – a rather gratuitous reminder that the singing in the film is, as usual, entirely pre-recorded.

Film in opera; opera in film

Berg's *Lulu* (1935) was one of several stage operas that imported a filmic element into their dramaturgy. Based on plays by Wedekind filmed by Pabst in 1929, *Lulu* features at its mid-point a palindromically scored film interlude depicting Lulu's incarceration and subsequent release from jail: this device serves both as a convenient compression of stage time and as a graphic illustration of the turning point in the drama before various elements in the second half start to run in reverse. Filmed segments also featured in Satie's ballet *Relâche* (1924), in Hindemith's *Hin und zurück: eine Zeitoper* (1927) and in a production of Wagner's *Ring* in Berlin (1928). In Milhaud's *Christophe Colomb* (1930), according to the composer's wife, 'for the first time in an opera one could see moving films showing scenes a little different from what was happening simultaneously on stage' (Nichols 1996, 39). In 1994, Glass conceived his *La Belle et la bête* as a simultaneous (silent) projection of Cocteau's 1946 (sound) film of the same title with a new musical accompaniment provided by live but static singers (Joe and Theresa 2002, 59–73). Glass's novel venture was a follow-up to his *Orfée* (1993), an operatic version of another film by Cocteau, and caused considerable critical controversy in France (Walsh 1996).

Conversely, a steady succession of narrative films featured operatic excerpts in their screenplays. An opera-house setting was memorably used in the silent film of *The Phantom of the Opera* (dir. Rupert Julian, 1925), starring Lon Chaney, and remade with sound in 1943. The Marx Brothers incorporated an extended segment of *Il trovatore* in their riotous comedy *A Night at the Opera* (1935), but later cinematic appropriations of opera were generally serious in intent. The diegetic opera in *Citizen Kane* (see Chapter 5) was a rare example of specially composed operatic music: more typical has been the use of pre-existing operas from the popular repertoire. In the film version of Peter Shaffer's play *Amadeus* (dir. Milos Forman, 1984), numerous lavishly staged extracts from Mozart's operas provided spectacular punctuation to the drama but somewhat impaired the narrative flow. Elmer Bernstein's score to Scorsese's *The Age of Innocence* (1993) evocatively superimposed haunting original music onto a diegetic performance of Gounod's *Faust* in order to suggest the romantic enchantment of the two protagonists as they meet in a box at the theatre. In *The Godfather Part III* (dir. Coppola, 1990) a diegetic performance of Mascagni's *Cavalleria rusticana* forms an ironic and cohesive backdrop to a climactic series of killings. Nino Rota's music for the two previous films in the *Godfather* trilogy (1972 and 1974) drew heavily on the *bel canto* idiom of Italian opera, and Verdi's music in particular remained a popular choice for film-makers outside a specifically Italianate setting (see Chapter 9).

Several idiosyncratic uses of operatic subject-matter are to be found in non-Anglophone films. Krzysztof Kieślowski's *Personnel* (1975), in which a young man for whom opera represents a pinnacle of fantasy has his illusions cruelly shattered by the mundanity of working behind the scenes at an opera house, plays out a political metaphor of repression in Poland: according to the director, 'our dreams and ideas about some ideal reality always clash somewhere along the line with something that's incomparably shallower and more wretched' (Stok 1993, 96). In Jean-Jacques Beineix's *Diva* (1981), a fictional opera star is idolized by a young lad who records her singing illicitly (see Chapter 8), and much play is made on the artificiality of nondiegetic music in film. (Diegetic and nondiegetic music in film are broadly comparable to Carolyn Abbate's conception of the 'phenomenal' and 'noumenal' in opera: see Abbate 1991.) In Werner Herzog's *Fitzcarraldo* (1982), the building of an opera house in the middle of a Peruvian jungle is 'paradigmatic of the desire for an opera and for an art generally to be situated outside the commercial pressures that have previously constituted the arts' (Tambling 1987, 18; see also Rogers 2004). Federico Fellini's *E la nave va* (*And The Ship Sails On*, 1982) is a delicious parody of operatic decadence on board an ocean liner heading out to sea to scatter the ashes of a deceased diva in 1914: the music of Verdi is poised fantastically between the diegetic and the nondiegetic in the manner of a film musical, and the production celebrates the operatic medium's inherent theatricality not only in the two-dimensionality of its principal characters but by using patently flimsy cardboard cutouts and crude models of ships set in a heaving sea of plastic sheeting. The not inconsiderable poetry created by the sumptuous cinematography and music – artificial sets and stereotypical characters notwithstanding – is utterly negated at the close by the camera's eye turning (in typical New Wave fashion) away from the shipboard set to reveal the mechanics of the modern film studio in which the illusion has been mounted. Particularly iconoclastic was Alexander Kluge's deconstruction of both operatic music and its institutionalization in *The Power of Emotion* (1983), in which the imposing architecture of the opera house, like both factories and power stations, itself represents a bastion of authority generating dubious emotional outpourings (Flinn 2004, 151).

Disembodied recordings of operatic performances also figure prominently in narrative films. In *The Shawshank Redemption* (dir. Frank Darabont, 1994), a recording of Mozart's *Figaro* is relayed through prison loudspeakers to symbolize freedom – and this universal message is instantly comprehended by all classes of inmate. An identical device appears in *Life is Beautiful* (dir. Roberto Benigni, 1997), where recorded Offenbach similarly lifts the spirits of those incarcerated in a Nazi concentration camp. A recording of an aria from Giordano's *Andrea Chénier* illuminates various aspects of character and cultural context in *Philadelphia* (dir. Jonathan Demme, 1993). All these instances use an outdated musical idiom to suggest a sense of timelessness or nostalgic yearning, much in the fashion of the aural utopia conjured up by old-fashioned Hollywood film music. But, as Marc A. Wiener points out, operatic music can be used in films for diametrically opposed purposes according to context: 'When it represents particularity, opera signifies entrapment, and when it functions as a sign of the universal, it represents freedom' (Joe and Theresa 2002, 83).

The ongoing links between cinema and opera have been fostered not only by composers working in both genres, but also by a clutch of influential directors and designers whose work straddles both media. Directors of both staged opera and feature films include Baz Luhrmann, Chéreau, Eisenstein,

Herzog, Nicholas Hytner, Losey, Rouben Mamoulian, Ken Russell, Luchino Visconti and Zeffirelli. Film designer Georges Wakhevich worked on Peter Brook's 1948 Covent Garden production of Mussorgsky's *Boris Godunov* – a staging which Ernest Newman explicitly condemned for its filmic qualities (Sutcliffe 1996, 20–1). Some opera singers have made a significant impact as screen actors, including Maria Callas in a magnificent interpretation of the title role in *Medea* (dir. Pier Paolo Pasolini, 1970) – described by one critic as 'an opera without music' (J. Walker 2006, 750) – and Teresa Stratas in a powerful performance as a self-absorbed singer who neglects her autistic-savant daughter in the Canadian production *Under the Piano* (dir. Stefan Scaini, 1995). Stratas had previously received critical acclaim for her inter-pretation of the title role in Götz Friedrich's film of Strauss's *Salome* (1974).

The first and virtually the only opera specifically conceived as a sound film was *The Robber Symphony* by Friedrich Feher (1936), and in those heady days of the early sound film it seemed to bode well for the genre's future. An anonymous contemporaneous critic commented: 'The intimate alliance of music and fantasy is in principle wholly commendable . . . Here, perhaps, may even be opera's legitimate successor – the transmutation of that hitherto over-synthetic medium into something more complex and closely-knit' (quoted in Huntley [1947], 45). Ernst Toch went further, predicting that

> The focus of film music to come is the original film opera. This cannot be
> done by adapting old operas for the screen, for the conception of
> stage-opera music is bound to be different from what film-opera must be.
> To adapt existing operas . . . means to mutilate either screen action or the
> music itself. Music of film-opera has to create and develop its own forms
> out of typical screen action, combining its different laws of space, time and
> motion with constant music laws. The first film-opera, once written and
> produced, will evoke a host of others.   (Toch 1937)

Two years after these lines were written, Shostakovich was 'contemplating writing a film-opera, exploiting the principles of realism to the full', con-fessing himself to be 'very attracted to the limitless possibilities opened up by the cinema screen' and citing Prokofiev's *Alexander Nevsky* music as an inspiration (see Chapter 9), but lamenting that all his attempts to secure the necessary collaborators had come to naught (Shostakovich 1981, 78–9). As we have seen, later filmed operas were invariably based on existing repertoire, and the kind of creative vision demonstrated by Schoenberg's unachieved plans for *Die glückliche Hand* was reflected only in the Powell–Pressburger *Tales of Hoffmann* in 1951. That same year marked the birth of opera conceived for television, which bypassed some of the perceived problems inherent in filming opera for the big screen, while presenting new challenges of its own. Since the brief burgeoning of interest in tele-vision opera in the 1950s and 1960s, when the dramatic style was steeped in multi-camera studio techniques, more recent productions aimed at the small screen have returned to an on-location realism and widescreen glossi-ness influenced by cinematic techniques and shot on film rather than video. The striking difference between the two may be examined by a comparison between the BBC's and Margaret Williams's productions of Britten's *Owen Wingrave*, made in 1971 and 2001 respectively (see Cooke 2005, 285–9). As recently as 2003 a television film of John Adams's *The Death of Klinghoffer* (dir. Penny Woolcock) for the most part cultivated a detailed cinematic real-ism consistently at odds with the extreme stylization in the music. Adams's score cries out for a corresponding degree of visual stylization, and the unnecessary realism in this film version paradoxically makes suspension of disbelief well-nigh impossible. Realistic terrorists with realistic guns on a realistic ship in a realistic ocean seem a viable cinematic proposition right up to the moment when the characters open their mouths and break into apparently diegetic song, and this problem seems far more acute in works with a topical modern setting than in the case of, say, Losey's period-dress *Don Giovanni* where the stylization is a natural extension of setting and ambience. The difficulties of negotiating the conflicting demands of cin-ematic realism and operatic theatricality remain as strangely problematic today as they did at the birth of the sound film.

The film musical

Operas specially written for film have always been exceptionally rare and, although rather more have been commissioned for television, the combined total is still small. This select repertoire has been notable for its surprisingly low level of dramatic and visual experimentation – possibly a consequence of understandable attempts on the part of those composers involved to write works which would transfer relatively easily to the live operatic stage and thereby stand a chance of securing a living future in the theatre. Clearly the commercial non-viability of filming modern opera for exhibition in cinemas has been a major factor contributing towards the paucity of original film operas. But the roots of the problem of filming opera go right back to the 1930s when the film medium was generally perceived as too lowbrow to be applied to the interpretation of great works of art. The debate that raged in the 1940s on the subject of the relative merits of realism and theatricality in filmed opera productions singularly ignored the fact that the stunningly entertaining Hollywood musicals of the 1930s had already shown what could be achieved when music and image were creatively combined and fantasy allowed free rein, and it is a considerable irony that this degree of artistic experimentation seemed acceptable only in the context of a popular and commercially viable genre.

As we saw in Chapter 2, the success of the Jolson vehicles *The Jazz Singer* and *The Singing Fool* derived from a combination of two of the least permanent attributes of popular entertainment: technical novelty and star quality. Both films were to some extent rooted in silent-film techniques, and inspired an immediate glut of similarly plotted 'mammy' pictures starring Jolson, Eddie Dowling and French crooner Maurice Chevalier – the last negotiating his transfer from the Parisian stage to Hollywood celluloid with ease. Next came a glut of backstage scenarios which began to demonstrate the extraordinary potential of the sound film for the production of more flamboyant musical dramas, while to a large extent continuing the traditions of vaudeville and the titillating Gallic dance spectacles typified by the annual Ziegfeld Follies (1907–31). The backstage genre not only represented a departure from the standard fare of the silents: it thrived on a combination of spectacle, music, dance, romance, star attractions and sheer virtuosity that put all rival media in the shade. A perceived need for both songs and dance to be justified by the diegesis and the initial necessity of recording music and sound live on set were two reasons why the revue format was initially popular, and this blossomed into a widespread craze for comic backstage plots which served to justify the inclusion of stage routines. Critic Alexander Bakshy discussed what he viewed as an essential incompatibility between theatrical comedy and these screen antics, opining that on stage a musical 'disregards the absurdities of the plot or the antics of the characters, because it never associates them with real life' and lamenting the fact that makers of film equivalents 'place their characters in perfectly natural surroundings, and introduce them as perfectly normal people, and then make them behave as if they were escaped lunatics' (Bakshy 1930a). He also noted that the mass-production of backstage films was not driven by public desire but because 'Hollywood finds in stage life the easiest formula for making a song and dance show realistically plausible', and went on to demand more cinematic imagination instead of merely 'aping the stage' (Bakshy 1930b). For all their surface sophistication and candid voyeurism, the early backstage releases 'were simply glossy repackagings of the Protestant work ethic, preachments of virtue and talent rewarded, and proved to be the easiest, most elementary foundation for musicals' (Barrios 1995, 190). They nevertheless soon cross-fertilized with other genres, notably the gangster and underworld movies for which Warners became notorious.

The prototypical backstage musical was *The Broadway Melody* (dir. Harry Beaumont, 1929), made by MGM and featuring songs with music by Nacio

Herb Brown and lyrics by Arthur Freed, dressed up with jazzy orchestration akin to the style of popular bandleaders Paul Whiteman and Jean Goldkette. Originally conceived in a part-talking format like the Jolson films but transformed into the very first 'all talking, all singing, all dancing' spectacular during production, the film won an Academy Award and (thanks to the use of subtitles in export prints) fame abroad, netting some $4 million in box-office takings. Shot mostly with four simultaneously running cameras to facilitate soundtrack editing, the film departed from this procedure in its Technicolor sequence, 'The Wedding of the Painted Doll', which embodied a retake in which the music had not been re-recorded live: the Movietone soundtrack from the first take had instead been played back on set and then postsynchronized to the new image track. This major breakthrough in editing techniques had arisen from the studio's desire to cut costs by not recalling the musicians for the new take (Barrios 1995, 65). Although the camera work at times offered a far more intimate experience to the spectator than would have been possible in live theatre, *The Broadway Melody* nevertheless suffered from a static and essentially theatrical approach to stage blocking and a proscenium-like framing of its images. The film was at its creative best when a diegetic pretext in the opening scene generated an exhilarating mélange of Dixieland, stride and popular-song styles, all rehearsed simultaneously by different performers in the adjoining offices of a music-publishing company. Rehearsal scenes were to remain a staple ingredient of backstage musicals precisely because they permitted this kind of informality, and served as a useful halfway point between everyday realism and performative stylization. Later, dream sequences became a stock method for introducing elements more fantastic than diegetic realism might otherwise have permitted, intensifying the feeling that the act of performance – whether realistically stage-bound or surreal – constitutes a cathartic release from the humdrum cares and responsibilities of both the cast's and audience's everyday lives (Altman 1987, 61).

    The Broadway Melody spawned a series of sequels in the 1930s and a direct remake with new songs (*Two Girls on Broadway*, 1940), plus a bizarre MGM short called *The Dogway Melody* (1930) which satirized the studio's own product in the shape of a miniature backstage musical performed entirely by anthropomorphic dogs, including a parody of 'Mammy' sung by a black dog named Al J. Olsen and a fully dogeographed finale on Freed's and Brown's song 'Singin' in the Rain' – a recent hit from MGM's *The Hollywood Revue of 1929*. Direct competition to MGM immediately came from RKO (*Syncopation*, dir. Bert Glennon), Paramount (*Close Harmony*, dir. John Cromwell and Edward Sutherland), Universal (*Broadway*, dir. Paul Fejos) and Warner (the all-colour *On With the Show!*, dir. Alan Crosland), all released in 1929. Fox's *Sunny Side Up* (dir. David Butler, 1929) was significant not only for its original screenplay but also for its attempt to integrate musical numbers into the narrative. Universal exploited the enormous popularity of the Whiteman band and showcased it in the big-budget *King of Jazz* (dir. John Murray Anderson, 1930), a lavishly entertaining film much vilified by jazz scholars on racial grounds but including bold innovations such as an animated sequence in colour.

Relative newcomer RKO typified the synergistic marketing of popular music enabled by its commercial interests in vaudeville and particularly radio, using the latter not only to plug its songs relentlessly but also to broadcast complete performances of the *Syncopation* soundtrack, recorded using the Photophone technology of its parent company RCA (Barrios 1995, 86–7). The major studios had significant commercial interests in popular music publishing, their acquisition or foundation of sheet-music businesses both freeing them from the need to pay punitive synchronization rights to others and opening up opportunities for generating additional revenue. The history of film musicals was thus indissolubly tied to a desire on the studios' part to minimize expenditure on musical copyright and maximize dissemination of their own hit songs in print, airwave and recorded forms. The revenue-generating power of the last had been spectacularly shown by million-mark sales of Jolson's recording of 'Sonny Boy', from *The Singing Fool*. Towards the end of 1929 no fewer than 90 per cent of the most popular songs in the USA were directly related to films. By 1939 approximately two-thirds of the royalty payments made by the American Society of Composers, Authors and Publishers (ASCAP) to publishing houses went to those with Hollywood affiliations, and the earning power of a film musical might typically expect to be augmented by around $1 million thanks to radio broadcasts, sheet music and record sales (J. Smith 1998, 31). When film musicals were based directly on stage shows, the original hit songs might be replaced by inferior songs produced in-house in the interests of economy, and more durable studio songs could be recycled in later productions by the studio which owned the rights (Barrios 1995, 108–11). A studio might also acquire the entire song catalogue of a popular tunesmith, showcasing the material in biopic musicals loosely based on the composer's life story or a fictionalized equivalent. Wilful distortion of the biographies of these famous musicians in many films in this category (for jazz examples, see Chapter 5) served to deflect attention from the commercial basis of much of their creative activities. As Rick Altman puts it, 'biographical events are ignored in order to make the semantic givens of the biopic conform to the syntax of the show musical. Music must never be seen as something one does solely to make a living. To make music is to make love; to make love is to inspire art' (Altman 1987, 238).

4.2 *Gold Diggers of 1933*: Busby Berkeley's chorines dance with electrified violins to 'The Shadow Waltz'.

The backstage musical acquired stunning visual interest and choreographic flair at the hands of Busby Berkeley, who cut his teeth on Samuel Goldwyn's production of *Whoopee!* in 1930 and secured his reputation with a series of spectacular dance routines for Warner Bros., including those in *42nd Street* (dir. Lloyd Bacon, 1933), *Gold Diggers of 1933* (dir. Mervyn Le Roy), *Footlight Parade* (dir. Bacon, 1933), *Gold Diggers of 1935* (dir. Berkeley), *Gold Diggers of 1937* (dir. Bacon) and *Gold Diggers in Paris* (dir. Ray Enright, 1938). The first item of the Gold Diggers series was a remake of *Gold Diggers of Broadway* (dir. Roy Del Ruth, 1929), a Vitaphone colour film that survives incomplete, which had featured the hit song 'Tiptoe Through the Tulips' and netted Warners some $4 million. Warners' ailing fortunes in the Depression years were comfortably revived by *42nd Street*, with its sassy scripting, superlative cast and impressive production values helping the project tie directly in with the upbeat optimism of the new Roosevelt administration. Virtuosic as much in their novel camerawork (involving elaborate tracking shots and birdseye crane views) and stylish editing as for their infamously fetishistic and elaborate chorine formations, Berkeley's choreography and visual flair in his interpretations of songs by Harry Warren and Al Dubin opened the backstage genre out into the realm of pure fantasy – though it is easy enough to dismiss his work for giving 'ingenuity and vigor . . . rampant precedence over taste' (Barrios 1995, 247). Highlights include the ubiquitous cash props in 'We're in The Money', the multiple neon-glowing electrified violins of 'The Shadow Waltz' in *Gold Diggers of 1933*, and the massed ranks of no fewer than 52 swirling white grand pianos in 'The Words Are in my Heart' sequence in *Gold Diggers of 1935*. Stephen Banfield has noted how the 'modulor' principle in popular-song composition permitted basic 32-bar AABA structures to be extended to considerable lengths in the process of instrumental arrangement for the purposes of choreographing set-pieces such as these (Banfield 1998, 333).

Arguably the finest of the earliest show films was Paramount's *Applause*, released in the boom year 1929, which embodied Mamoulian's experimentation with mobile cameras and novel sound combinations, and showed a reluctance to buy slavishly into the genre. Mamoulian approached even closer to Clair's ideal of the integrated musical film in *Love Me Tonight*, a Paramount vehicle for Jeanette MacDonald and Chevalier made in 1932, but his imaginative ideas for the genre were later submerged. When he subsequently worked for MGM and was asked in 1945 by Freed, now a powerful producer, to direct a musical version of Eugene O'Neill's play *Ah, Wilderness!*, Mamoulian demonstrated his awareness of the essential incompatibility between stage technique and cinematic drama: 'If you take something written for the stage and put it on the screen, you're going to lose certain values. Now, if you cannot compensate for these values, add to them, make them expand and flourish – then you shouldn't touch it' (quoted in Fordin 1996, 186). In a later memo he expanded on the theme:

> It is obvious that to turn a dramatic play into a musical you have to make drastic cuts in it in order to allow time for music, songs and dancing. It is equally obvious that you cannot drastically cut a good dramatic play without spoiling it, crippling its subject and emaciating its characters. A tenuous story filled out with elaborate and overblown 'musical numbers,' unrelated specialties of dance and song, comedy routines, etc. has for long been the standard stuff that musicals were made of . . . However, this is not the kind of musical we want to make . . .
>
> What we want to do is, for the lack of a better and newer definition, a 'musical play' – meaning by that a story which will be told through the medium of integrated dialogue, songs, dance and music, with each of these elements taking an organic and vital part in the telling of that story. What happens in this case is that the dialogue scenes, which have been cut out of a

> good play, are not thrown overboard, but are actually translated into their
> musical equivalent of song and dance. As a result the story has not suffered,
> nor has it changed, but the *manner* of telling it has changed, and it has
> been enriched by added emotional values which the right kind of music
> brings. (Fordin 1996, 188)

In this instance the resulting film (*Summer Holiday*, 1948; songs by Harry
Warren and Ralph Blane) was one of MGM's few flops, losing $1.5 million
at the box office. Although this failure might ostensibly have suggested a
doomed future for creative experimentation, Mamoulian's work had a significant influence on the later development of musico-narrative integration
in the genre.

In his critical analysis of the American film musical (1987), Altman identifies two principal subgenres in addition to the show category (which he
extends from backstage examples to embrace musical films concerned with
mounting many different kinds of performance): the fairy-tale musical and
the folk musical. The fairy-tale subgenre, to which Mamoulian's *Love Me
Tonight* belongs, was a natural development from popular operetta, with
its old-fashioned waltz-dominated style retained from its former European
stage incarnation, and first arrived on the silver screen in the shape of Warner
Bros.' *The Desert Song* (dir. Roy Del Ruth, 1929; remade in 1943 and 1953).
This 1926 stage show by Sigmund Romberg and Oscar Hammerstein II
transferred to film with the help of a Vitaphone score recorded on set under
the musical direction of Louis Silvers; like rival products, the film included a
Technicolor sequence. (Many of the colour segments of early films have not
been preserved, and survive only in far more durable monochrome prints
prepared for archival purposes. When sold to television companies in the
1950s, only monochrome prints were useful for broadcasting and colour
prints were mindlessly destroyed: see Barrios 1995, 435 n.1.) Even in 1929,
reviewers lamented the stage-bound nature of *The Desert Song* transfer and
yearned for a more cinematic treatment. RKO's contemporaneous hit transfer *Rio Rita* (dir. Luther Reed) was just as wooden in its theatricality, but
at least featured some location shooting. Stilted films of fairy-tale operettas
seemed poised to occupy a uniquely middlebrow niche at a time when modern popular styles were still tainted by their sometime insalubrious vernacular origins. The first written expressly for the screen was Paramount's *The
Love Parade* (1929), starring Chevalier and MacDonald with music by Victor
Schertzinger, which benefited from the lightness of touch and deft wit of
expatriate German director Ernst Lubitsch, among whose innovations was
the thorough organization of actors' movements according to regular rhythmic beats in order to facilitate synchronization with the music. Warner Bros.
squandered its massive profits from the early sound boom on miscalculated

operetta projects when the industry's Depression slump was imminent, the economic disaster occurring at the same time as the sound film lost its initial novelty value. After the fallow years 1931–4, creative experimentation dwindled and the musical's subgenres were destined to become even more rigidly defined and constantly regurgitated.

The Love Parade initiated a trend towards romantically pitting contrasting voice- and character-types against one another in the kind of binary opposition which, as Altman has argued (1987, 16–27), replaces linear narrative structure in many later musicals. The 'dual-focus' narrative structure he identifies can variously involve contrasts between the two sexes, two attitudes (e.g. work versus play, manifested specifically as business versus entertainment in *Silk Stockings* (1957), and seriousness versus fun in both *Funny Face* (1956) and *The Sound of Music* (1965)), or two classes – often shown by two different singing styles, an operatic aristocratic female and a rough down-to-earth male, or by two dancing styles, as with the contrast between Fred Astaire's tap-dancing and Ginger Rogers' classical elegance. Narratives of this kind achieve eventual union between the opposing poles not through the chronological and causal linear structures common in other genres, but through simultaneity and comparison, as in the parallel scenes and songs for the male and female leads in MGM's *Gigi* (1958). The dual-focus approach explains why the apparently intrusive set-piece routines are vital in developing and exploring the binary oppositions rather than interrupting a (non-existent) linear narrative to its detriment. Vocal duets and dancing couples not surprisingly become central to this discourse.

The folk musical began its screen life with Universal's patchwork production of *Show Boat*, which started out as a silent drama and was rejigged in 1929 with interpolated songs following the success of Jerome Kern's and Hammerstein's stage musical; remakes followed in 1936 (dir. James Whale) and 1951 (dir. George Sidney). The Kern–Hammerstein treatment was of incalculable importance in demonstrating how musical numbers could be justified by plot and character, and exerted a powerful influence on the development of the so-called 'integrated' musical (in contrast to the cumulative effect of the loosely episodic 'aggregate' show); their work also broke new ground in departing from operetta stereotypes in search of a more conversational musical style derived from vernacular idioms. According to Banfield, the stage show was 'more a foretaste of what the sound film might be expected to attempt with popular music than the theatrical breakthrough it is always taken to be . . . Its epic dimension . . . boils down musically to a superior silent-film technique of motivic underscoring' (Banfield 1998, 327). In this and other folk musicals, singing becomes natural expression rather than stylized performance, and is more often than not rooted in the everyday activities of an enclosed community. The new style was evident in Mamoulian's treatment of Kern's and Hammerstein's songs in his own venture onto folk territory, *High, Wide and Handsome* (Paramount, 1937). With the addition of a chorus of ordinary folk indulging in joyous dance routines, the folk subgenre became indestructible, and it owed this element largely to the 1943 Broadway production of Richard Rodgers' and Hammerstein's *Oklahoma!*, which had been directed for the stage by Mamoulian.

A unique contribution to the early film musical was King Vidor's *Hallelujah!* (MGM, 1929; musical direction by Eva Jessye), a folk project considerably ahead of its time in its creative semi-documentary portrayal of the everyday lives of black workers. In the course of Vidor's provocative and thoughtful dramatic intertwining of sexual and religious fervour, musical expression in a variety of ethnic genres (including spirituals, the blues and jazz) likewise seemed a direct extension of both character and circumstance. The protagonist Zekeil becomes a preacher and sermonizes in a melodious *Sprechstimme* that can easily blossom into fully blown song, while community dance and song seem an entirely natural means of expression; the intensity of the singing in the spiritual numbers and the almost minimalist riffs of the diegetic banjo song accompanying dancing children are unforgettable. MGM returned to the all-black musical with *Cabin in the Sky* (1943), the first film directed unaided by Vincente Minnelli, soon to become the artistic lynchpin of MGM's musicals production unit headed by Freed. Pitting rural simplicity against the corrupting power of urban sophistication, *Cabin in the Sky* in the process showed how racial stereotyping had if anything deteriorated since Vidor's generally sympathetic film. Now the focus of interest was on a kind of commercially successful jazz, represented in the film by the music of Duke Ellington and others, an attitude reflecting what James Naremore has described as 'a chic, upscale "Africanism," redolent of café society, Broadway theater and the European avant-garde' and which Krin Gabbard summarizes as 'uptown Negrophilia' (Gabbard 1996, 181–2). In the same year, Fox's *Stormy Weather* (dir. Andrew Stone) revisited both backstage and biopic formulae in the shape of an all-black revue featuring such stellar talents as Fats Waller, Cab Calloway and Lena Horne.

Plots in later white folk musicals were founded in a nostalgic regard for family values, usually in a small-town or rural setting, and tapped memories of familiar period tunes and iconography from the graphic arts and other cinematic genres (e.g. the western) as appropriate. The turning point was MGM's *Meet Me in St Louis* (dir. Minnelli, 1944), superbly inventive visually and with an integrated score including both original songs by Martin and Blane and arrangements of fondly remembered period tunes such as the lilting title song and 'Skip to My Lou'. The dynamic staging of the 'Trolley Song', a complex routine perfected by Judy Garland in a single take, set a new standard in rhythmicized vernacular song style directly inspired by physical motion. According to Flinn, it is dramatically significant because 'where non-representational signs work so strenuously to convey an advanced technological utopia, the representational component of the lyrics reassures listeners of a very simple, down-home quality since they convey, after all, the simple pangs of young love' (Flinn 1992, 122). The song was plugged in advance of the film's release, the writers refusing to truncate it when the publishers had baulked at its non-standard length, which would exceed the normal limits of a piece of sheet music (Fordin 1996, 118). As in so many Golden Age Hollywood products, the film's considerable artistry was made to appear effortless, an obvious example being the use of playback techniques, which permitted singers to lip-synch without need for the facial contortions necessary in real singing. Like Kurt London, Balázs lamented the facial contortions of singers, never intended to be viewed in the merciless close-up detail beloved of the movie and television camera, and noted that playback techniques had improved the situation (Balázs 1953, 277–8). Such apparently easily won perfection helped promote the utopian feeling at the heart of this quintessentially feel-good genre – a process particularly noticeable in Garland's two Christmas songs 'You and I' (Freed/Brown) and 'Have Yourself a Merry Little Christmas' (Martin/Blane).

A rash of period-set folk musicals followed in the wake of *Meet Me in St Louis*, including Fox's *State Fair* (dir. Walter Lang, 1945; songs by Rodgers and Hammerstein; remade 1962) and *Centennial Summer* (dir. Otto Preminger, 1946; songs by Kern and Hammerstein), MGM's *Summer Holiday* (see above) and Universal's *Meet Me at the Fair* (dir. Douglas Sirk, 1952; music from various sources). The *Oklahoma!* tradition continued in such musical westerns as MGM's *Annie Get Your Gun* (dir. George Sidney, 1950; songs by Berlin), *Seven Brides for Seven Brothers* (dir. Stanley Donen, 1954; songs by Johnny Mercer and Gene de Paul) and Paramount's *Paint Your Wagon* (dir. Joshua Logan, 1969).

A crippling generic complacency was vividly demonstrated by Rodgers' and Hammerstein's impoverished attempts to transfer their stage hits to the screen in a series of overblown and stiltedly theatrical widescreen productions for Fox: *Oklahoma!* (dir. Fred Zinnemann, 1955), *Carousel* (dir. Henry King, 1956), *The King and I* (dir. Walter Lang, 1956) and *South Pacific* (dir. Joshua Logan, 1958), with scores supervised variously by Alfred Newman, choral arranger Ken Darby and Adolph Deutsch. Gerald Mast characterizes these four films as 'the personal revenge of Broadway creators on a rival entertainment industry that had treated them shabbily two decades earlier. The industry's subtle retaliation was that these films barely lived on the screen and do not survive appreciatively in critical repute' (Block 2002, 101). Mast goes so far as to dismiss them as 'opera films' because they constitute 'reverential attempts, in a blockbuster era of Hollywood desperation, to hang decorative sights on important music. They reject one of the earliest discoveries of movie musicals – going back to 1929 – that space need not remain constant while characters sing.' He points out that in all but *Oklahoma!* the camera does not for a single instant depart from the singer, throwing emphasis on the song as song performance rather than plausible extension of character. The beach scenes in *South Pacific* remain sterile stage routines in spite of a sumptuously realistic setting. Wooden actors and characterless dubbed singing (the benefits of the then state-of-the-art six-track stereo technology notwithstanding) sounded the death knell on Fox's stagebound ventures, at a time when no studio attempting a Broadway transfer would dare risk alienating an audience familiar with a prior stage production and its bestselling cast recording by indulging in even modest creative experimentation.

The 1950s Fox extravaganzas, with their level of creativity in inverse proportion to their budgets, were particularly disappointing since almost two decades earlier MGM had shown just how magical and captivating a truly imaginative musical screenplay could be. *The Wizard of Oz* (dir. Victor Fleming, 1939), based on a fairy-tale story already treated on Broadway (in 1903) and in the medium of silent film (in 1910 and 1925), was the first out-and-out fantasy film musical, receiving Academy Awards for both its score and Harold Arlen's song 'Over the Rainbow' – the latter famously slated for jettisoning by studio moguls who considered it too dull. Musical director Herbert Stothart, who provided sophisticated scoring for narrative portions of the film including a memorably impressionistic soundscape for Dorothy's first tentative footsteps in Oz, commented two years later: 'We learned that a musical episode must be so presented as to motivate a detail of the plot, and must become so vital to the story that it cannot be dispensed with. The test today is – "If a song can be cut out of the musical, it doesn't belong in it"' (quoted in Flinn 1992, 35). Although its profits were modest on account of its huge budget, *Oz* secured MGM its position as the finest and most prolific purveyor of original musicals in all subgenres until the bottom dropped out of the market in the 1960s, and many of the studio's less ambitious projects in its heyday comfortably grossed four times their budgets at the box office.

Key members of the Freed Unit at MGM responsible for this string of successes were staff musicians who combined creative talent with administrative acumen, among them Roger Edens (both vocal arranger and associate producer), Kay Thompson and Lela Simone; arrangers, composers, orchestrators and musical directors including Georgie Stoll, Conrad Salinger and the teenage prodigy André Previn; and front-rank directors like Mamoulian (his last foray into the genre being the unremarkable *Silk Stockings* in 1957) and the ubiquitous Minnelli. The on-screen talent numbered Judy Garland (until her tantrums and absences from shooting grew to such unacceptable levels that her contracts were suspended in 1949–50), Mickey Rooney, Cyd Charisse and Gene Kelly, the last revolutionizing the role of solo dance in the genre (see below). Johnny Green assumed full executive powers as studio music head in 1949 and claimed only Alfred Newman and Ray Heindorf rivalled him in influence at their respective studios (Fox and Warners). Green's formidably controlling personality mistrusted the informal family atmosphere of the Freed Unit, which habitually rebelled against his weekly departmental administrative meetings at which musicians of the stature of Rózsa, Kaper, Raksin and Deutsch were compelled to sit at undersized school desks in order to listen to administrative minutiae (Fordin 1996, 301–2). Freed left MGM in 1970, by which time its fortunes had seriously diminished: when executive James T. Aubrey was appointed to overhaul the studio in 1969, he ordered the destruction of most of its music library, including huge amounts of irreplaceable material in both notated and recorded form. Four years later the studio ceased production and distribution of motion pictures, opting to make its money through television series and gaining further income from commercial ventures such as its own hotel in Las Vegas (Fordin 1996, 524).

Even more than in other Hollywood genres, and reflecting a trend that persists to the present day, much of the orchestration and other aspects of musical arrangements appeared needlessly overdone – even to some professionals in the thick of such work. The score for Fox's *Carousel* transfer was not atypical in involving the work of no fewer than six orchestrators, including Earle Hagen, Nelson Riddle and Herbert Spencer. At MGM, Deutsch attempted to make a stand on what he perceived as a pressing need for simple orchestration: 'At the first production meeting [in 1950] I said that I would only do *Show Boat* if I could approach Kern's music simply, as he intended it to be heard and played'. (Kern was notorious for his abhorrence of jazzed-up versions of his tunes.) Deutsch was obliquely referring to the efforts of his colleague Salinger, who had worked on the Kern biopic *Till the Clouds Roll By* (1947), about which Deutsch was 'a little uncomfortable because the arrangements, vocal as well as instrumental, were, I thought, a little overembellished and overranged for a man who was as simple as Jerome Kern' (Fordin 1996, 336–7). Revealingly, when Previn was first given sole responsibility for the scoring of an MGM musical in 1955 (*It's Always Fair Weather*, dir. Kelly and Donen) – which he recalled was the first time a single musician and not a team of composers and arrangers had been responsible for all aspects of the score from inception to recording – he still found the arranging instincts of his apprenticeship got the better of him, admitting 'I don't think that too many of the songs were very good and that's because I was too intent on having them sound clever or well arranged' (Fordin 1996, 435). Nevertheless, the process of arrangement could produce understated poetry when the art was at its finest: Salinger's orchestration in the lyrical moments of *Meet Me in St Louis*, for example, was economical and beautifully executed in performance by Stoll, who brought forth an extraordinary warmth of string tone and sensitive rubato from his players.

Elaborate dance routines had always been just as important in some musicals as song, not only dances performed by massed forces – whether stomping folk dancers in the old west or Berkeley's psychedelically swirling chorines – but those conceived as an expression of a character's individuality. In the mid-1930s Berkeley demonstrated how dance might spectacularly release the visual images from their primary need to serve the diegesis (Altman 1987, 70), but did not exploit the medium as an agent of character or narrative. Contemporaneously, Fred Astaire and Ginger Rogers showed in a series of virtuosic films for RKO how an integrated use of dance could articulate romantic plots in a dynamic and thoroughly modern manner: solo dance becomes self-expression, and the dancing couple dramatizes the shift towards inevitable romantic union. Astaire and Rogers first appeared together in *Flying Down to Rio* (dir. Thornton Freeland, 1933) and then made *The Gay Divorcee* (dir. Mark Sandrich, 1934), which received the first Academy Award for Best Song (Con Conrad's and Herb Magidson's 'The Continental', forming the basis for the film's danced climax). The pair went on to showcase the songs of Berlin in *Top Hat* (dir. Sandrich, 1935), of Kern in *Swing Time* (dir. George Stevens, 1936) and of the Gershwins in *Shall We Dance* (dir. Sandrich, 1937). The scores for Astaire's and Rogers' first three films were supervised by Max Steiner before his move to Warner Bros. and replacement by Nathaniel Shilkret.

On the one hand, Astaire's elegant and sophisticated dance routines continued to promote the aura of utopian romance central to the genre as a whole. As Altman puts it, 'Time and again we watch Astaire and his various partners fall in love only when they step into that privileged land of make-believe created by dance. If lovers' hearts beat in time to each other, then the dance provides an opportunity to rehearse that rhythm, to slide imperceptibly from indifference to passion' (Altman 1987, 85). This was only to be expected in the fairy-tale subgenre, which since Lehár's *The Merry Widow* of 1905 (filmed by Lubitsch for MGM in 1934), with its apotheosis of the waltz, had equated dance with love. In Astaire's partnership with Rogers, however, the romantic interest was sharpened with an innovative love–hate flavour, their dances sometimes beginning as bickering then moving towards union (Altman 1987, 161). Furthermore, Astaire's skills in tap-dancing were directly and symbolically pitted against Rogers' classical dancing, nowhere more so than in *Shall We Dance* where the entire plot revolves around his attempt to entice her into a vernacular mode of physical expression (Braudy and Cohen 1999, 621–5). The film's closing ballet parodies the impersonality of Berkeley's massed ranks of faceless chorines by making Astaire search out the true Rogers from a bevy of dancers masked with two-dimensional reproductions of her face, the parody all the more telling since Rogers had herself previously appeared in *42nd Street* and *Gold Diggers of 1933*. Berkeley's choreography was also parodied alongside spoof examples of the operetta style in the Marx Brothers' *Duck Soup* (dir. Leo McCarey, 1933), which muddles up idioms as diverse as spirituals, ragtime and hillbilly music in its performative 'orgy of chaos' (Marshall and Stilwell 2000, 48) when war is declared in the Ruritanian state of Freedonia – the name punning on Fredonia, NY, whence the brothers fled in disgrace after a disastrous performance at the local opera house in their early vaudeville career.

Gershwin's music for *Shall We Dance* came at the end of his ambivalent relationship with Hollywood, which began with *Delicious* (dir. David Butler, 1931) and intensified when he moved to the West Coast following the East Coast launch of *Porgy and Bess* in 1935, which had been directed by Mamoulian and featured Eva Jessye's choir. *Porgy*, renowned as an inventive and satisfying treatment of African American subject-matter (albeit filtered through the sophisticated uptown musical sensibilities identified by Gabbard in *Cabin in the Sky*) and filmed by Preminger for Columbia in 1959, had more than any other of his works reflected Gershwin's serious artistic aspirations; consequently, his reputation as a popular tunesmith seemed in danger of dipping, and when about to commit himself to Hollywood in 1936 he cabled his agent to say in his own defence: 'Am not highbrow. Have written hits before and expect to write them again' (Wyatt and Johnson 2004, 240). In the event, *Shall We Dance* elicited some of his most enduring standards ('They Can't Take That Away from Me', 'They All Laughed' and 'Let's Call the Whole Thing Off') and the composer benefited from the usual song-plugging in advance of the film's release, telling a correspondent in April 1937 that the finished product 'is practically ready for public gaze and if you turn on your radio you will hear the songs from it achieving a rather quick popularity' (Wyatt and Johnson 2004, 259). In spite of failing health, part of his therapy for which was playing tennis with Schoenberg in Beverly Hills, Gershwin also contributed music to RKO's *A Damsel in Distress* (dir. Stevens, 1937), starring Astaire but this time alongside Joan Fontaine, and including the songs 'A Foggy Day' and 'Nice Work if You Can Get It'. In a common move, MGM later bought the rights to several Gershwin titles (e.g. *Strike Up the Band* in 1940 and *Lady Be Good* in 1941), using them as crowd-pullers for their films though only utilizing a smattering of Gershwin's music in the course of the relevant picture. In 1943 the studio made a complete version of Gershwin's 1930 Broadway hit *Girl Crazy* (dir. Berkeley and Norman Taurog), throwing in 'Fascinating Rhythm' (from *Lady Be Good*) for good measure.

At MGM, Gene Kelly's blend of virtuosic exhibitionism in dance routines and childlike immaturity of screen persona was very different in effect from the polished sophistication of Astaire. Leo Braudy has summarized the contrast between the two in terms which again suggest the tension between theatricality and realism at the heart of so much cinema:

> Astaire is the consummate theatrical dancer, while Kelly is more interested in the life outside the proscenium. The energy that Astaire defines within a theatrical and socially formal framework Kelly takes outside, into a world somewhat more 'real' (that is, similar to the world of the audience) and therefore more recalcitrant . . .
>
> Astaire may mock social forms for their rigidity, but Kelly tries to explode them. Astaire purifies the relation between individual energy and stylized form, whereas Kelly tries to find a new form that will give his energy more play. Astaire dances onstage or in a room, expanding but still maintaining the idea of enclosure and theater; Kelly dances on streets, on the roofs of cars, on tables, in general bringing the power of dance to bear on a world that would ordinarily seem to exclude it.   (Braudy and Cohen 1999, 624)

Kelly's ascendency in song and dance coincided with the development of the interpolated ballet sequence in film musicals, a natural consequence of the dream sequences and Berkeley fantasy inserts in the 1930s. At the hands of Minnelli, these increasingly elaborate ballets often took the form of a basic psychoanalytical probing of the protagonists' diegetic preoccupations (Marshall and Stilwell 2000, 31). Among the choreographers influential on this trend was Agnes de Mille who, amongst her many other achievements, had choreographed the *Oklahoma!* première and was responsible for Louise's dream ballet in *Carousel*. Her comments on the need for a modern and vernacular dance style instead of outworn (and therefore inexpressive) classical movements in essence parallels the relationship between the up-to-date jazzy style of music that conflicted with doggedly persisting operetta modes of composition:

> Ballet gesture up to now had always been based on the classic technique and whatever deviated from this occurred only in comedy caricatures. The style throughout, the body stance, the walk, the run, the dynamic attack, the tension and controls, were balletic even when national folk dances were incorporated into the choreography.
>
> We were trying to diversify the root impulse and just as Gershwin impressed on the main line of musical development characteristics natural to his own unclassical environment, we were adding gestures and rhythms we had grown up with, using them seriously and without condescension for

> the first time. This is not a triviality; it is the seed and base of the whole
> choreographic organization. If dance gesture means anything, it means the
> life behind the movement.   (De Mille 1952, 307)

De Mille believed that each gesture should be a natural extension of the performer's assumed character, and that therefore the distinction between acting and dancing was being eroded.

At MGM substantial balletic set-pieces, from which dialogue and song absented themselves in order to foreground symbolic dance and elaborate orchestral music, became a house speciality; but their increasingly elaborate nature and length led to accusations of pretentiousness from critics who felt the genre was here over-reaching itself. Examples include the surreal ballet for Astaire and Lucille Bremer in *Yolanda and the Thief* (dir. Minnelli, 1945), choreographed by Eugene Loring; Kelly's choreography for *The Pirate* (dir. Minnelli, 1947), starring Garland and Kelly and featuring songs by Cole Porter; the 'Slaughter on Tenth Avenue' ballet in the Rodgers–Hart biopic *Words and Music* (dir. Norman Taurog, 1948); and the disconcerting juxtaposition of vivid location shooting and the stylized studio 'Turnstiles' and 'A Day in New York' ballets in the reworking of Leonard Bernstein's *On the Town* (dir. Kelly and Donen, 1949). The climaxes of Kelly's MGM dancing career came with *An American in Paris* (dir. Minnelli, 1951), *Invitation to the Dance* (dir. Kelly, 1952) and *Singin' in the Rain* (dir. Kelly and Donen, 1952). Reverentially regarded by cineastes as diverse as Truffaut and Resnais, and even by trenchant critic Pauline Kael, *Singin' in the Rain* celebrates the heady years of Hollywood's transition to sound, so it was appropriate to have Freed's 1929 hit song at its heart, now transformed by the memorable addition of Edens's 'chic, riff-like fill . . . constantly dancing rings around its harmonic progression' (Banfield 1998, 317). The plot also permitted the film to celebrate the backstage tradition from a sophisticated perspective that drew on the studio's long experience of various other generic subtypes, and a focal point is a fifteen-minute 'Broadway Ballet'.

The seventeen-minute ballet sequence in *An American in Paris*, which received its own main-title card, was a flamboyant interpretation of a man-gled version of Gershwin's symphonic poem in which a black-and-white-clad Kelly cavorts amidst the saturated colours of a theatricalized French capital, and is middlebrow fayre *par excellence*. More telling was Kelly's artistry in the film's intimate moments, whether joining local kids in a stichomythical interpretation of 'I Got Rhythm' or his wonderfully under-stated nocturnal courtship dance with Leslie Caron by the banks of the Seine, which rivals Astaire for its indissoluble link between technique and expression. Even the virtuosic tap routine performed by Kelly atop the piano in Oscar Levant's garret – the extrovert modern dancer throughout the film pointedly contrasted to the depressive and egotistical unemployed classical musician portrayed by Levant – seems to grow naturally from the diegesis. The film, which (like *On the Town*) hedged its aesthetic bets by juxtaposing naturalistic location shooting and highly stylized theatrical sets, won no fewer than six Academy Awards, including one for the arranging skills of Saul Chaplin and Johnny Green.

The 'Circus Ballet' in *Invitation to the Dance* ran for half an hour of screen time. Made at Elstree studios in the UK, the sequence had a score commissioned from Jacques Ibert and recorded by the Royal Philharmonic Orchestra in primitive circumstances and with inadequate equipment that shocked both musicians and producers, the project progressing even less auspiciously when Ibert had to interrupt work owing to the death of his daughter in mysterious circumstances (Fordin 1996, 379–6). To add to Kelly's headaches, English composer Malcolm Arnold's score for the 'Ring Around the Rosy' sequence was rejected, even though it had already been recorded, and was replaced by Previn (here undertaking his first composing assignment for the studio and being presented with the daunting task of having to write ballet music to a predetermined image track). Another composer working in the UK, Canadian-born Robert Farnon (later well known for his grimly defiant signature tunes to the BBC's 1970s wartime dramas *Colditz* and *Secret Army*) was asked to provide music for a further sequence destined for the cutting-room floor. The wary Lela Simone wrote to Freed from England: 'I am sticking with [Farnon] very closely so that we get an American song sequence and not polite, English jazz. I have played a lot of tracks from our pictures for him; this will give him an idea as to what we want to hear' (Fordin 1996, 387). A highlight of the film, demonstrating the close links between dance and the audio-visual rhythms of the cartoon, was the 22-minute 'Sinbad the Sailor' ballet with music by Rimsky-Korsakov orchestrated by Salinger and conducted by Green, and animation by the capable team of Hanna, Barbera and Quimby. This over-ambitious film was put on ice and not released until 1957, by which time its arty nature coincided with the general slump in the industry and it consequently made a loss. Greater contemporary resonance was achieved by the jazz-dance style of United Artists' *West Side Story* (dir. Robert Wise and Jerome Robbins, 1961), of which the stereo soundtrack album long retained a record-breaking place at the top of the *Billboard* album charts (Banfield 1993, 39), though the distinctively energetic choreography had already been a prominent element in the stage show and the theatrical conception of the work now clashed somewhat against the cinematographic realism of the film version.

As Heather Laing has argued, formal song types in the musical transcend their structural limitations and enhance the narrative even as they appear to interrupt it:

> While everything else is undergoing radical disruption, the music is at its most contained, formulaic and, by extension, familiar and safe. The use of song is bound to make the audience more aware of its presence as music, potentially reducing some of the unique extremes of its narrative power. Apart from the pleasure in the familiarity of the form, however, the presentation of the number actually counteracts this possibility of narrative weakening, by concentrating the credit for excessive intensity, immediacy, and emotional depth, away from the actual music, and onto the performing character.   (Marshall and Stilwell 2000, 10–11)

This musical emphasis on character is naturally most effective when the performer is blessed with both a powerful personality and a singing voice that is not (or at least does not obviously appear to be) dubbed. Not surprisingly, therefore, as the musical emerged from its decline in fortunes in the later 1950s its sporadic continuation depended heavily on the star quality of its performers. Some reinvented themselves. Astaire's later career, for example, replaced his pre-war image of modernity and youth into its precise opposite: in the 1950s he was often portrayed as the older mentor of younger women to whom he presented an image of conservative maturity (Cohan 2002, 95). Allied to phenomenal record sales and enormous sex appeal, Elvis Presley's charisma certainly accounts for the success of his films, dismissed by Altman as 'poorly made in every way' (Altman 1987, 194); other popular performers had discovered in the show subgenre a convenient way to disseminate their modern styles on screen, a process most spectacularly shown by the international success of Bill Haley and the Comets in *Rock Around the Clock* (dir. Fred F. Sears, 1956), and emulated by emerging pop stars in the UK (see Chapter 10).

A more chaste newcomer in the traditional fairy-tale genre was Julie Andrews, who gave brilliantly fresh and direct performances in Disney's *Mary Poppins* (dir. Robert Stevenson, 1964) and Fox's *The Sound of Music* (dir. Robert Wise, 1965), showing what Peter Kemp has identified as a refreshing commitment to the narrative importance of songs rather than merely treating them as vehicles for display (Marshall and Stilwell 2000, 60). *The Sound of Music*, dating from after Hammerstein's death, was far more compelling than the earlier Rodgers–Hammerstein screen transfers; unlike the lifeless ocean in *South Pacific*, the stunning Alpine scenery here almost becomes a character in the drama. Contemporaneous hit stage transfers featuring British talents were *My Fair Lady* (dir. George Cukor, 1964) and the multiple Oscar-winning *Oliver!* (dir. Carol Reed, 1968). Flamboyant charisma and powerful musical and creative talents were the hallmarks of Barbra Streisand, whose personality stamped its indelible presence on *Funny Girl* (dir. William Wyler, 1968) and its sequel *Funny Lady* (dir. Herbert Ross, 1975), and her idiosyncratically self-authored drama *Yentl* (dir. Streisand,

1983), the last with Oscar-winning music by Michel Legrand (whose Franco-phone film musicals are discussed in Chapter 8). When Streisand performed numbers live on set in *Funny Girl,* her accompaniment was fed to her via a small speaker which had to be kept from the camera's view, necessitating close-up photography (LoBrutto 1994, 7).

The fantasy musical had passed squarely to Disney, since animation not only aided suspension of disbelief in an increasingly cynical world but proved to be an ideal medium in which to perpetuate the genre's longstanding association with wholesome and uncontroversial family entertainment. Among Disney's roster of fairy-tale musical features after the groundbreaking *Snow White and the Seven Dwarfs* in 1937 (to which *The Wizard of Oz* had consciously set itself up as a live-action rival two years later) were *Cinderella* (1950), *The Lady and the Tramp* (1955), *The Sword in the Stone* (1963) and *The Jungle Book* (1967). The studio's commitment to the musical continued until the end of the century and beyond, with a canny use of up-to-date pop idioms aiding the success of more recent ventures such as *The Little Mermaid* (1989), *Beauty and the Beast* (1991), *Aladdin* (1992), *The Hunchback of Notre Dame* (1996) and *Hercules* (1997), all featuring the music of Alan Menken, and *The Lion King* (1994), including the voice of Elton John. Banfield notes that in several places the music for *Beauty and the Beast* pays direct homage to the operetta tradition, and this may in part account for the successful reverse-transfer process which put the film musical on the Broadway stage in 1994 (Banfield 1998, 333). A stage version of *The Lion King,* premièred in Minneapolis in 1997 and directed by Julie Taymor, also met with critical acclaim and popular success. That these transfers from screen to stage could equally prove to be commercially disastrous, however, was shown by the Broadway staging of *Gigi* which bombed in 1973 (Fordin 1996, 495), even though MGM's original 1958 film had broken all previous records for the genre by receiving nine Academy Awards, including Best Picture, Best Song, Best Director (Minnelli) and Best Scoring (Previn). A 1989 Broadway production of *Meet Me in St Louis* similarly flopped (Steyn 1997, 264).

In contrast to unthreatening familial conservatism, the later film musical found a particular niche as an expression of camp. Amongst the stars who were reincarnated after their early success, Garland was transformed from the girl next door into a camp icon after her androgynous 'Couple of Swells' routine in Irving Berlin's *Easter Parade* (dir. Charles Walters, 1948). Later film musicals turned camp to very different ends, whether as an expression of a regional gay culture such as that in Spain (see José Arroyo in Marshall and Stilwell 2000, 70–9) or as a darker dramatic agent in adult reworkings of the backstage subgenre. Most flamboyant of all was Tim Curry's extraordinary performance in the travesty role around which the screen transfer of

Richard O'Brien's *The Rocky Horror Picture Show* (dir. Jim Sharman, 1975) revolves. This musical was significant not only for its cross-generic borrowings from science-fiction and horror, but also for the way in which its filmic version only achieved belated cult status through late-night showings involving a direct audience participation that added a further voyeuristic level to that of the on-screen onlookers who formed an essential part of the diegesis. Subtler and more disturbing was the role of the MC in *Cabaret* (dir. Bob Fosse, 1972; songs by John Kander and Fred Ebb). Another stage transfer, but effected with a keen eye for idiomatic cinematography and sometimes powerfully symbolic montage (with parallel editing, for example, used to link a diegetic Tyrolean slapping dance with the brutality of Nazi brownshirts in order to suggest a link between hedonism and sadism), the film recounts its central bisexual love triangle in a period backstage setting inevitably tapping memories of that finest of all early German film musicals, *The Blue Angel* (see Chapter 2), aided by the dynastic star quality of Liza Minnelli, charismatic daughter of Garland and Minnelli. As Mark Steyn notes, Fosse 'shrewdly eliminated all the "book numbers" ... and kept only the "real" songs, performed in the Kit Kat Klub; Fosse understood that young moviegoers no longer accepted the musical's defining convention – that a guy could walk down the street and burst into song with full orchestral accompaniment' (Steyn 1997, 214–15). A few years later Liza Minnelli joined Robert De Niro in Scorsese's *New York, New York* (1977), an attempt to update the musical through the medium of jazz: influenced by the work of John Cassavetes (see Chapter 5), Scorsese included scenes improvised by the actors in a structural debt to the aesthetic of jazz extemporization. Following the example of Vincente Minnelli, he developed a method of editing camera shots in accordance with the lengths of musical phrases, such carefully rhythmicized montage also retained in his later non-musical films (Thompson and Christie 1989, 69).

Also in the 1970s, two trends emerged that gave the film musical a new lease of life without significant impact on its general conventions. First, flamboyant and energetic rock operas transferred from stage to screen with some success, notably Andrew Lloyd Webber's *Jesus Christ Superstar* (dir. Norman Jewison, 1973) and The Who's *Tommy* (dir. Ken Russell, 1975). Second, a new pretext for featured song and dance was launched with the dance musical, in which romantic, social and even period settings were all geared squarely towards a youth audience, and dance re-emerged as a vehicle for self-expression. This movement was spearheaded by the disco milieu of *Saturday Night Fever* (dir. John Badham, 1977), the phenomenal soundtrack sales of which are examined in Chapter 10; its star John Travolta went on to appear in the commercially successful screen transfer of the more amiable *Grease* (dir. Randal Kleiser, 1978), and later examples of the dance-oriented genre included *Fame* (dir. Alan Parker, 1980), *Flashdance* (dir. Adrian Lyne, 1983) and *Dirty Dancing* (dir. Emile Ardolino, 1987), the formula persisting into the new century with *Save the Last Dance* (dir. Thomas Carter, 2001). Disco and dance scenes featuring dialogue were generally shot with the aid of a subsonic 'thumper' beat, sounding below the lowest pitch range of dialogue and not therefore interfering with its recording: 'You play the music with the thumper', commented production sound mixer Les Lazarowitz, 'drop out the music, and you just leave the thumper going – it gets the crowd going'; to minimize noise further, dancers sometimes performed in bare feet or on carpets (both kept carefully out of the camera's field of vision), and principal actors received the music on earphones to aid synchronization while the remaining dancers performed without it (LoBrutto 1994, 122–3).

In the late 1980s Altman was pessimistic about the film musical's future: 'Down one path lies the death of the musical by subservience first to Broadway and then to the recording industry; down the other lies the death of the musical by self-inflicted wounds. Today we retain only a limited production of children's musicals (usually cartoons), adolescent musicals (usually dance fad or concert-oriented), and old folk musicals (nostalgia compilations or throwbacks)'; he lamented that visionary maverick directors like Fosse remained few and far between (Altman 1987, 121). The situation had not changed two decades later, with the sporadic appearance of stage transfers such as *Evita* (dir. Alan Parker, 1996), *Chicago* (dir. Rob Marshall, 2002) and *Rent* (dir. Chris Columbus, 2005), a steady trickle of (now mostly CGI) animated musicals in the Disney tradition, and the very occasional burst of originality from a bold director. Two entirely different examples of the latter are the by turns realistic and surreal irruptions of song in the narrative of the Homeric jailbreak comedy *Oh Brother, Where Art Thou?* (dir. Joel and Ethan Coen, 2000) and the kaleidoscopic audio-visual exuberance of Baz Luhrmann's *Moulin Rouge!* (2001) – the latter a heady MTV-style updating of various generic formulae with wildly anachronistic music capitalizing on contemporary pop hits. This triumph of fashionable style over banal content retained a strong debt to its forebears, including backstage elements in its musical-within-a-musical, the gesture now acknowledging the global village in its inclusion of a Bollywood routine. The main strength of *Moulin Rouge!* lies in its vivid sense of fantasy and sometimes lurid stylization, its original screenplay light-years away from problematic modern stage transfers with their tendency to abandon theatricality in favour of detailed realism (*Evita*) or package dramatic stylization into specific numbers rather than the whole (*Chicago*). A further and significant glimmer of hope for the genre came in 2007 with Tim Burton's stunningly imaginative (and hideously gory) interpretation of Stephen Sondheim's *Sweeney Todd: The Demon Barber of Fleet*

Street, a film distinguished not only by its perfect wedding of nightmarish Gothic fantasy with stylized theatricality but also by its bold initiative in using only the actors' natural singing voices on its soundtrack; Sondheim's characteristic skill in moving seamlessly from speech to arioso and thence to fully blown song was a major factor in the venture's success.

Perhaps the most important aspect of the musical in terms of the general history of film music is the genre's bold breaking down of the distinction between the diegetic and nondiegetic, which 'blurs the borders between the real and the ideal' (Altman 1987, 63). Crucially, the idealized music tends to predominate, being pre-recorded and frequently dictating the course of the narrative, with ambient and other diegetic sounds suppressed to create what Altman terms a 'supra-diegetic' music: in this context strictly diegetic music functions as a bridge between a music-less reality and the superabundance of music in the idealized realm, permitting an 'audio dissolve' between the constituent sonic planes. Rhythmicized bodily motion can also effect this transition, for example Astaire's metrical walking allowing him to move seamlessly from conversation to song and dance, the rhythmic organization of quotidian physical activities in *Oklahoma!* such that 'The rhythm of life already constitutes a dance' (Altman 1987, 307), the rhythmicized dialogue matching train noises and the paralleling of gossips with clucking hens in *The Music Man* (dir. Morton Da Costa, 1962), and the numerous examples where characters hum tunes to themselves as a seemingly natural mechanism for the implausible calling forth of an invisible orchestra (Altman 1987, 67–8).

Scoring Shakespeare

In an age increasingly suspicious of the concept of literary and musical canons, and the cultural elitism inevitably engendered by them, film versions of William Shakespeare's plays no longer need to be defended from accusations of populism. At their time of writing, in any case, Shakespeare's plays were a prime example of commercial art, and depended entirely upon popular success for their survival in the playhouse repertoire; and there has been no more commercial an art than cinema, which has been responsible for disseminating the bard's work to a much wider audience than would have been possible through the medium of live theatrical performance. Nevertheless, some might choose to agree with Erwin Panofsky that Shakespeare in the cinema will still receive its highest accolades from those 'not quite in sympathy with either the movies *au naturel* or Shakespeare *au naturel*' (Braudy and Cohen 1999, 284), even if the international power of cinema is such as to have entirely altered our collective awareness of how certain of Shakespeare's filmed plays might otherwise be interpreted (Hammond 1981, 71).

In addition to illustrating various approaches to the task of making modern adaptations of 'classic' texts, and providing representative and contrasting examples of the achievements of some of the foremost composers who have worked for the cinema, filmed Shakespeare (as do filmed opera and filmed musicals) generates discussion of the general problems inherent in creating screenplays from theatrical works: for example, the essential difference between the framing device of the theatre's proscenium arch and the implied continuation of diegetic space beyond the borders of the cinema screen; the fact that the camera watches the action on behalf of the spectator, picking and choosing points of view that in the live theatre the spectator can amend according to personal curiosity; the challenge of finding a workable balance between realism and theatrical stylization; and the need to make both individual visual images and narrative method cinematically viable, often involving techniques such as the use of flashback to illustrate a narrated event (e.g. the drowning of Ophelia in *Hamlet*). This last device has been widespread, resulting from a 'modern tendency to add substance to what Shakespeare leaves shadowy' (Craik 1995, 91), though it may be noted that, as early as Colley Cibber's production of *Richard III* in 1700, the young princes were murdered on stage in order to increase the element of violence in the play, this being contrary to Shakespeare's evidently deliberate strategy of keeping all murders unseen until the death of the title character himself (Hammond 1981, 69, 98).

As far as production styles are concerned, film directors are given generous leeway on account of the paucity of specific stage directions in Shakespeare's texts. This freedom has been fully explored in modern Shakespeare stagings in the theatre, and the fact that productions of the plays were anachronistic even in Elizabethan times has been a justification for attempts to modernize settings in some film treatments. Music for Shakespearean films has tended to follow conventions well established in other genres, with mixed results, and Michael Hattaway has noted that 'poetical or lyric passages are deemed to need music to signal their "abnormality"' (R. Jackson 2000, 90), giving as an example the treatment of 'She Never Told Her Love' from Trevor Nunn's *Twelfth Night* (1995; music by Shaun Davey), intercut with images of crashing waves.

Shakespearean plots were a popular subject for magic-lantern presentations in the nineteenth century, and silent film continued the tradition by constructing animated tableaux based on the bard's plays. One of the first silent Shakespeare films was a five-minute *Hamlet* shown at the 1900 Paris Exposition and starring Sarah Bernhardt in the title role (R. Jackson 2000, 117). As we have seen, a tightening of copyright legislation in 1908 led to a rash of film productions based on non-copyright literature and opera, and Shakespeare's plays thus became a favourite source for single-reel silent films. These pocket-sized productions – a representative selection of which was released on DVD by the British Film Institute in 2004, with new music commissioned from Laura Rossi – were originally screened with the same stereotyped music as other silent films, and featured the exaggerated acting (designed to be effective when viewed from a distance in a live theatrical production but inappropriate to the intimacy of the screen) typical of the *film d'art* movement. Among the more enterprising early attempts to unite the silent image with an element of sound was actor Frederick Warde's textual recitations accompanying a 1913 silent film of *Richard III*, the earliest extant full-length American feature film (R. Jackson 2000, 47). In the UK, a silent version of *A Midsummer Night's Dream* featured music compiled by prolific film arranger Hans May (Huntley [1947], 28).

With the advent of the sound film and its capability for recording Shakespeare's words, fundamental critical issues concerning the propriety of screen adaptations began to come into play. At the same time, productions of Shakespeare had moved increasingly away from nineteenth-century romantic values. For example, as early as 1901 a seminally minimalist production of *Henry V* at the Shakespeare Memorial Theatre, Stratford-upon-Avon, demonstrated the usefulness of continuous action, an innovation later adopted as an essential feature of filmed Shakespeare (Craik 1995, 84). In the 1930s, many commentators were disappointed by what they perceived as the sound cinema's reversion to the dated mannerisms and procedures of the old actor-manager's theatrical spectacle, involving not merely melodramatic styles of acting and pictorial set design, but a return to such perceived inauthenticities as cavalier cutting of the text. In addition, cinematic realism seemed at odds with the tendency towards austerity and stylization in modern theatrical productions. A reliance on incidental music in a heavily romantic style seemed distinctly old-fashioned – and, even worse to modern theatrical sensibilities, background music might typically be used to bolster dialogue.

These problems were aired after the appearance of the first treatment of a Shakespeare play as a sound film: the opulent version of *A Midsummer Night's Dream* directed for Warner Bros. in 1935 by veteran Austrian stage director Max Reinhardt, who had staged the play on Broadway. According to one anonymous reviewer, it demonstrated 'all the faults that grandiose stage productions of Shakespeare once committed but have now happily outgrown' (*The Times*, 17 October 1935), while Mitry condemned its stage-bound theatricality as an 'absurd cardboard fairyland totally out of place in the cinema' (Mitry 1998, 323). The film, which utilized Mendelssohn's incidental music arranged by Korngold and featured fairies choreographed in a manner recalling the great Berkeley musical routines, was dismissed by Panofsky as 'probably the most unfortunate major film ever produced' (Braudy and Cohen 1999, 284). Kracauer took Allardyce Nicoll to task for suggesting that the film aimed to rekindle the audience's interest in Shakespeare's words through the use of sensuous visual stimuli, and criticized it for failing to achieve the necessary balance between text and image (Weis and Belton 1985, 129). Alberto Cavalcanti, lamenting in 1939 the fact that film music in general still persisted in using outdated romantic styles, criticized MGM's rival treatment of *Romeo and Juliet* (dir. George Cukor, 1936; mus. dir. Stothart) for both its highly romanticized production and reliance on Tchaikovsky's over-used melody. Cavalcanti noted that Tchaikovsky's music

> fitted the production perfectly – that is to say, it was music of the indoors, heavy with scent, unventilated, introverted, consorting well with the glorified seraglio that was the set designer's picture of ancient Verona . . . This is the musical accompaniment, if you please, of a play by Shakespeare which presents one of the purest love-stories of all time – full of stark, sharp terrifying beauty . . . [I]n another production, I should certainly like to entrust the music to a good modern composer. Shakespeare's strangely universal genius needs to be interpreted anew in every age – by the most modern means. The recent film *Romeo and Juliet* was thirty years out of date all the way through.
>
> Not for the dignities of Shakespeare only, but also for all other dramatic presentations, I plead for modern music, mood-music, because I am sure that it has a great deal to contribute.   (Weis and Belton 1985, 107)

One 'good modern composer' who soon made an international reputation for himself as a composer of fine Shakespearean film scores was William Walton. His music for *As You Like It* (dir. Paul Czinner, 1936) was not entirely successful in negotiating the usual problems attending the composition of comedic scores, and has been criticized by Hattaway for 'perfunctory and incongruent set-pieces' suggesting 'that tone in a comedy of wit is probably best modulated primarily through verbal delivery' (R. Jackson 2000, 93). The young Benjamin Britten wrote a review of Walton's score for the journal *World Film News* in April 1936 in which he described 'the Grand Introduction over the credit titles – pompous and heraldic in the traditional manner', the use of Elizabethan songs, some effective dovetailing and restrained use of a leitmotif – all of which would remain features of Walton's later film scores. At the same time, Britten felt that Walton had not always troubled to adapt his scoring to the demands of recording technology: 'One cannot feel that the microphone has entered very deeply into Walton's scoring soul. A large orchestra in which strings are very prominent has been used, and in the accompanying pastoral music one is conscious of the energetic ranks of the London Philharmonic sweating away behind the three-ply trees' (Kildea 2003, 21).

As You Like It starred Laurence Olivier as Orlando, and it was under Olivier's direction that Walton went on to achieve his most accomplished Shakespearean scores. In 1944 they collaborated on *Henry V*, its vision of the English victory at Agincourt carrying a clear wartime propaganda message: in the main titles the film is dedicated 'to the Commandos and Airborne Troops of Great Britain, the spirit of whose ancestors it has been humbly attempted to recapture', and the project was partly conceived as a morale-booster in the year of the Allied D-Day landings in Normandy. Its climactic battle sequence drew heavily on both the visual imagery and musical style of the Battle on the Ice from Eisenstein's and Prokofiev's equally propagandist *Alexander Nevsky* (1938); the influence of D. W. Griffith's epics and Errol Flynn's swashbucklers has also been noted (Craik 1995, 94). As befitted such a prestigious production, the music budget was not abstemious and the total cost of preparing the music track was in excess of £25,000 (Huntley [1947], 76). Olivier's direction was fresh and original, with the film combining both overtly theatrical presentation and exterior realism. Walton's music enables a smooth transition from the opening panoramic view of Elizabethan London (accompanied by rousing music for chorus and orchestra in a modal style redolent of Vaughan Williams) to the interior of the Globe Playhouse, featuring pseudo-Elizabethan diegetic music, from where the scene is 'transported' to exterior locations in France via impressionistic underscoring as the chorus/narrator describes the channel crossing by Henry's army. The substantial orchestral cues accompanying the Agincourt charge and battle, which include reworkings of fanfares first heard diegetically in the Globe Playhouse scene (where the diegetic music features tabor and harpsichord to create a dash of authentic period colour), at times betray the clear influence of Sibelius in their use of driving rhythmic patterns animating a fundamentally slow harmonic rhythm. The thrilling battle sequence (analysed in detail, with photographic stills, in Manvell and Huntley 1957, 79–91) was singled out by many as the high point of the score. Olivier himself pointed out that Walton's music was the only thing that made the charging French knights seem plausible; in reality, they were Irish farmers riding their own horses (Walton 1988, 94–5). It had originally been intended to pre-record the music for this scene as a 'guide track' so that the live action could be filmed in synchronization with it, and a piano reduction was recorded for this purpose but, in the event, not used (Kennedy 1989, 123); as a result, Walton declared the film 'more of a bloody nuisance than it is possible to believe . . . I seem to get no chance of settling down to the music & of course there is going to be the usual hell of a rush' (Hayes 2002, 147). With higher spirits the composer had previously written to his assistant Roy Douglas to ask 'How does one distinguish between a crossbow & a long bow musically speaking?' (Hayes 2002, 145). In the event the archers were not furnished with music, and praise was subsequently lavished on the editorial decision not to underscore the sound of the first volley of English arrows, which occurs immediately after a climax in the music. Other passages in Walton's score demonstrated an understated poignancy, notably the haunting passacaglia accompanying the death of Falstaff; the sombre ground bass is, in an appealingly ironic gesture, derived from a traditional drinking song heard in earlier comedic moments at the Boar's Head inn. In the gently lyrical cues for scenes featuring Katherine of Valois and the Duke of Burgundy, Walton captures the fairy-tale quality of Olivier's vision of the French landscape with music reminiscent of Delius (and incorporating a French folksong). As Anthony Davies has pointed out, the French are here not only seen as an enemy: 'the poised elegance of the frankly one-dimensional and stylised castles and the landscape of France accompanied on the sound track by Walton's wistful music . . . and finally Burgundy's portrait of "this best garden of the world" spoken again over Walton's evocative music, all suggest qualities of civilised life which the English need and for which they unconsciously yearn' (R. Jackson 2000, 169). Extracts from Walton's score became popular concert items after they were performed at the 1945 Promenade Concerts, and the two movements for strings alone issued on a gramophone recording under the composer's baton in the same year.

The high point of the Olivier–Walton collaboration was *Hamlet*, released in 1948 and shot in monochrome, which distinguished itself internationally as the first non-American film to receive the Academy Award for Best Picture. Although the costumes and settings were traditional enough, both production design and cinematography were heavily steeped in the expressionistic mannerisms of *film noir* (high-contrast lighting, low-level upward camera shots, point-of-view camera roving restlessly down long corridors, beckoning spiral staircases, and voice-overs in soliloquies); in this respect, and in Walton's avoidance of pomp-and-circumstance musical style in favour of more atmospheric writing, the film offered a contemporary feeling to its first viewers as a Shakespearean thriller (a whodunit, in fact, since Hamlet sets out to expose the uncle who has murdered his father). Among the score's felicitous moments are the disconcerting harmonization of a diegetic tolling bell with chords variously dissonant and concordant with it; an intense chromatic fugato first representing 'Something . . . rotten in the state of Denmark' and then, like the labyrinthine castle interiors, used to portray Hamlet's tortured psyche; irrational, non-functional harmony for both the apparition of the ghost of Hamlet's father and Ophelia's descent into madness; and the blurring of diegetic and nondiegetic music during the play-within-the-play. In places, the orchestration is decidedly unorthodox, as when the voice-over describing Ophelia's suicide is backed by a recitative for unaccompanied violins, and when the concluding funeral march (its style appropriately reminiscent of Rózsa's *film noir* scores) seems to fizzle out on a high and greatly prolonged violin note before the final statement of the tonic in the bass.

After this extraordinary achievement, the Olivier–Walton *Richard III* (1955) came as a disappointment. In its way as patriotic in outlook as *Henry V*, the film's preoccupation with 'The Crown of England' (the final stark caption of the main titles) was stimulated by undimmed national memories of the Coronation of Queen Elizabeth II two years before; not surprisingly, Walton drew heavily on the idiom of his own coronation marches to create stirring music that now seems dated. Walton, who wrote the score in haste, clearly responded with tongue in cheek to the director's request for ceremonial music, and added to the score of the Prelude the facetious marking 'Con prosciuto, agnello e confitura di fragiole' ('with ham, lamb and strawberry jam': see Kennedy 1989, 194). Olivier's film was a transfer of an existing stage production, shot at speed with little understanding of the technical difficulties of Paramount's widescreen VistaVision; the film succeeded mostly on account of Olivier's extraordinary acting, which included addresses direct to camera. Walton's music reuses some gestures from his earlier scores (e.g. lyrical solo oboe and strings for both Hamlet's Ophelia and Richard's Anne), is in places cloyingly sentimental (e.g. Clarence's prayer in the Tower), and frequently resorts to mickey-mousing more appropriate in a *Carry On* comedy (e.g. Anne's collapse on the stairs beneath Richard's throne, Richard's prodding Buckingham in the chest and – most graphic of all – Richard's dying spasms and final collapse). Given the effectiveness of the extraordinarily dissonant outburst as the deformed Richard stares with cold menace at young York after the latter's taunt ('you should bear me on your shoulders!'), it is regrettable that the score as a whole seems consistently reluctant to engage with the powerful psychological undercurrents of Shakespeare's play.

Walton and Olivier were to have collaborated on a fourth Shakespeare film – a version of *Macbeth* – but this project folded in 1958 owing to a lack of financial backing. By this time Orson Welles had also applied his directorial talents to Shakespeare, filming two plays, both with music by European composers. His *Macbeth* (1948), like Olivier's *Hamlet* (to which it was unfavourably compared at the time), revealed both expressionistic and theatrical influences, and was furnished with an eerie score by Jacques Ibert (standing in for Herrmann, who had left the project) that included choral breathing effects and impressionistic string harmonics for the supernatural elements. When the film was restored to its original form in 1980, having previously been dubbed with American accents and cut by Republic Pictures,

Ibert's substantial overture was included (D. Cook 2004, 349). Between 1948 and 1952, Welles worked on *Othello* in Europe and this film, with music by Francesco Lavagnino and Alberto Barberis, won the Grand Prix at the 1952 Cannes Film Festival; it was restored, with the orchestration reconstructed by Michael Pendowski, in 1981 and re-released in 1992 to celebrate its fortieth birthday, on which occasion the music track was digitally re-recorded. Welles returned to Shakespearean subject-matter with *Chimes at Midnight* (1966), a Spanish–Swiss co-production based on *Henry IV* and once again scored by Lavagnino, whose tense modernism had contributed immeasurably to the impact of *Othello*.

At the time when Miklós Rózsa's attentions were increasingly engaged by epic topics (see Chapter 5), he provided a score to Shakespeare's *Julius Caesar* (dir. Joseph Mankiewicz, 1953). As with his other epic scores, Rózsa employed quartal harmony and organum passages to create an archaic effect, especially in ceremonial fanfares, and – like Walton – had recourse to the church modes, especially the Mixolydian, with its major tonality and flattened seventh always making it a favourite for pseudo-archaic ceremonial music. Perceptively, Rózsa refrained from providing music for Caesar's assassination since the event is portrayed as banal, and the perpetrators are unable to grasp the enormity of their actions. From this point on, there is no music for approximately half an hour: underscoring returns only when Mark Antony incites the crowd to revenge. Drawing on Elizabethan raw materials, Rózsa reworks John Dowland's lute song 'Now oh now I needs must part', which is first heard diegetically when performed by a young boy accompanying himself on a lyre; it is immediately taken up in the underscore and is much later developed in a sombre orchestral fantasia (as often in this composer's work, clearly influenced by the style of his compatriot Bartók) when the shattered lyre is discovered by a centurion amongst post-battle debris. Among the simple but effective stock devices used elsewhere in the score are non-functional harmonies scored for string harmonics for the appearance of Caesar's ghost, and ritualistic drum ostinati lending excitement to the climactic Battle of Philippi.

Zeffirelli made his first foray into filmed Shakespeare with *The Taming of the Shrew* in 1966, casting Richard Burton and Elizabeth Taylor in the leading roles for obvious commercial reasons. The score was composed by Nino Rota, who balanced lyrical scoring with an archaic mood well suited to the period décor; Hattaway has noted how the romantic theme at the opening was given 'an Elizabethan flavour' when the scene moved to within the walls of Padua (R. Jackson 2000, 93), a scheme recalling the similar balance between Walton's diegetic 'Elizabethan' music in the Globe Theatre scenes of *Henry V* and more flamboyant orchestral accompaniment for exterior scenes. It was the follow-up film of *Romeo and Juliet* in 1968, also with music by Rota, that did most to establish Zeffirelli's international reputation, being spectacularly more successful than Renato Castellani's 1954 film of the same play (with music by Roman Vlad). Having taken the risk of casting two unknown youngsters in the title roles, and against all predictions to the contrary, Zeffirelli's *Romeo and Juliet* netted two Academy Awards (for costumes and cinematography) and grossed $50 million, injecting much-needed funding into the then-ailing Paramount.

Rota's score for *Romeo and Juliet* centred on a simple romantic love theme, utterly Italianate in character with its hints of Verdi and Puccini and clearly a strong influence on the melodic style of other Italian film composers such as Ennio Morricone (see Chapter 9). Such was the popularity of this theme that Capitol Records were persuaded to issue a soundtrack album when none had originally been planned (M. Walker 1998, 172). The theme first appears as a diegetic song, accompanied by flute and harp, then grows increasingly intense in the underscore as an accompaniment to the protagonists' first kiss, when later they part company, as a prominent companion to the preparations for Juliet's feigned death, and at the climax of the denouement in the mausoleum. Far from being a simple 'theme' score, however, Rota's music is elsewhere finely judged for dramatic effect. As in *The Taming of the Shrew*, pseudo-Elizabethan style is employed under the Prologue (spoken by Olivier as a voice-over to the opening shots of Verona), and simple diegetic music with a period flavour is predominant – and carefully matched to the prevailing dramatic mood – until the love theme begins to assert itself. Rota's fine sense of pacing is evident in the first balcony scene: simple lyricism underscores the intercut soliloquies of the lovers, ceasing abruptly when they first address each other to allow the sharpness of the dialogue full projection; music then returns as they exchange passionate vows, thus framing the scene. A simple restatement of the love theme leads into shots of Romeo rushing deliriously away, accompanied by frisky dance music first heard diegetically earlier in the film. Following this sequence, music is used sparingly, with the lovers' kiss in Friar Laurence's cell enacted in silence, and virtually no music provided for the prolonged sword-fight sequences apart from a simple contrapuntal lament for the death of Mercutio and a brief burst of activity as Romeo pursues Tybalt.

By the time Zeffirelli tackled *Hamlet* in 1990, Rota (who had continued to collaborate with the director on theatrical Shakespeare projects, including in the 1970s an aborted plan to write a musical on *Much Ado About Nothing*) was long dead and, as with the third film of the *Godfather* trilogy, another composer had to be found. Morricone supplied a darkly coloured and economical score, far removed from the Italianate lyricism of the director's earlier Shakespeare projects. The pulsating ostinati of the main titles suggested the pagan mood of Carl Orff, with the use of organ for Elsinore carrying a hint of the Gothic and the underscoring of the opening internment of Hamlet's father an echo of the solemnity of Wagner's *Parsifal*. The music was predominantly minor in key, with luminous major triads reserved for the apparition of the ghost of Hamlet's father and his son's swearing of revenge; elsewhere the tonality was designedly ambiguous, even in the more expansive music underscoring dialogue between Hamlet and Ophelia. As in Walton's treatment of the same scene, the play-within-the-play benefited from the blurring of diegetic and nondiegetic music in which subtle use of percussion instruments played an important part. At no point was there any attempt to sentimentalize or ennoble Shakespeare's action (for a contrasting treatment, see below), and only for the end credits did Morricone compose a mournful oboe theme, bringing the drama to a conclusion marked by dignified yet expressive restraint.

No box-office success remotely comparable to that of Zeffirelli's *Romeo and Juliet* attended Roman Polanski's film of *Macbeth* (1971), the commercial failure of which may well have contributed to the paucity of film adaptations of Shakespeare in the 1970s and 1980s. (A further factor was the saturation of the international television market by the ambitious series of studio Shakespeare productions undertaken by the BBC at this time.) Controversial at the time for its nudity and graphic violence – the climactic demise of Macbeth at the hands of Macduff remains one of the grisliest decapitation scenes in the history of cinema – the film featured idiosyncratic music by The Third Ear Band. Their intimate quasi-theatrical score deployed restrained avant-garde twitterings and scratchings for the irrational elements of Shakespeare's play – witches, apparitions, ghosts and paranoid dreams (Macbeth's 'sorriest fancies', as Lady Macbeth puts it) – and simple lyricism (oboe and guitar in unison melody) for moments of tenderness between Lady Macbeth and her husband. A remote Celtic atmosphere was created by using folk-like drumming, bagpipe sonorities with dissonant drones and designedly out-of-tune wind instruments. Very rarely was background music called upon to create additional tension in the drama, this being generally achieved through an absence of music altogether or, in one memorable instance, agitated diegetic dance music underpinning Lady Macbeth's taunting of her husband with an accusation of cowardice. As in Rózsa's otherwise very different score for *Julius Caesar*, Polanski's *Macbeth* featured simple ritualistic drumming to intensify the preparations for impending battle.

Non-Anglophone cinema has – with the exception of the Italian films discussed above – made relatively sparing use of Shakespeare's plays in recognizable form. The foreign director who engaged most thoroughly with Shakespearean scenarios was Akira Kurosawa, whose *Throne of Blood* (1957) was based on *Macbeth*, and *Ran* (1985) was a Samurai reinterpretation of *King Lear*. (For discussion of the music in Kurosawa's films, see Chapter 9.) Film-makers in the Soviet Union made several notable films of Shakespeare in Russian translation, beginning with Sergei Yutkevich's *Othello* in 1956, with music by Aram Khachaturian that (in a time-honoured gesture) quoted the *Dies irae* chant for the murder of Desdemona. Director Grigori Kozintsev commissioned Shostakovich, who had worked with him many decades before, to provide scores for his film versions of *Hamlet* (1964) and *King Lear* (1970), both films using the Russian translations by Boris Pasternak. Shostakovich had already composed music for theatrical productions of the two plays, and enjoyed a close working relationship with Kozintsev, who often gave the composer unusually precise instructions about the nature of specific musical cues.

In Shostakovich's music for the film *Hamlet*, parallels with the style of the composer's later symphonies are discernible, and Egorova has gone so far as to call the score a 'programme symphony' for which she proposes a sonata-form archetype for the organization of the themes for Hamlet, the ghost of his father, and Ophelia (Egorova 1997, 172–3). While this interpretation may be regarded as somewhat forced, it is nevertheless notable that the style of Shostakovich's film music is generally consistent with that of his concert works and makes no concession to commercial considerations. Three of the composer's trademark idioms are prominent in *Hamlet*: acerbic scherzo writing (for the strolling players), austere music of grim defiance, and a brittle militarism. In addition, the composer includes naïvely stylized harpsichord music for Ophelia's dancing lesson and a lilting melody in compound time, also for Ophelia, inhabiting a soundworld of archaic lyricism; that Shostakovich intended to tap Old English associations is indicated by his reuse of the same melodies for Ophelia's songs as those in the Walton–Olivier film, which had originated in productions of Shakespeare's play at London's Theatre Royal, Drury Lane, in the eighteenth century and were published in 1816 (Ford 2007, 24). A marvellously agitated climax accompanies Claudius as he stumbles from the players' dumb show in Kozintsev's film, aware that they are portraying his heinous crime, and much of Shostakovich's score is saturated by variants of Hamlet's theme. (The realization that the latter bears a generic similarity with Shostakovich's own musical monogram, as used in the Tenth Symphony and Eighth String Quartet, will intrigue those keen to trace autobiographical elements in the composer's work.) Kozintsev's interpretation of the play reflects Soviet ideology in his view of a fundamentally heroic Hamlet, and this is mirrored in Shostakovich's music: here the man of action overcomes his vacillations, and his heroism is celebrated at the film's end in forthright funeral music, 'not an epitaph to a hero who perished in vain, but a baton handed over to future fighters' (Efim Dobin, quoted in Egorova 1997, 184).

Shostakovich's score to *King Lear* again exemplifies three of the composer's most characteristic moods: bleakness, restrained wit and stark militarism. In several places the music makes a contribution to increasing dramatic tension, especially when Lear storms out (rather like Claudius in *Hamlet*) after pairing off his rejected daughter Cordelia with the King of France, and when the militaristic music for images of wild horses builds to a climax – although the effect here is weakened by the abrupt lowering of the music's volume when it threatens to compete with dialogue. The most memorable musical gesture in the film is the simplest: the gloomy melody for an unaccompanied and thinly toned E flat clarinet that accompanies the opening titles, strikingly economical and suggestive of music for a live stage production, is later revealed to be the Fool's theme when he performs it diegetically on his pipe as Cordelia and Lear are reconciled. This takes an effective liberty with the original text, in which the Doctor's line 'Louder the music there!' is not addressed to the Fool, who takes no part in the action at this point. In the words of Egorova, the melody combines 'sorrow with a lucidity which leaves hope for purification through suffering' (Egorova 1997, 221).

The most prominent purveyor of filmed Shakespeare in the last decade of the twentieth century was British actor/director Kenneth Branagh, whose Renaissance Films company drew on the success of stage productions by the Renaissance Theatre Company. Composer Patrick Doyle joined Branagh's troupe in 1987, and went on to compose the music for all the director's Shakespeare films to date. Their cinematic collaboration began with *Henry V* (1989), widely regarded as a conscious critique of Olivier's interpretation of the play. Although a period setting was retained, the cinematography was more up-to-date and the Agincourt scenes in particular strove to achieve a mud-and-gore realism more appropriate to the post-Vietnam era. Much of Doyle's music was concise and eloquent, with traces of the contrasting influences of (spiky) Shostakovich and (noble) Elgar, and some boldly rhetorical orchestral gestures contrasting with laconic simplicity (as when the King of France is introduced by unaccompanied bass clarinet). Full string textures based on ostinati were the perfect accompaniment to images of the English doggedly marching through the mud, and the choral setting of *Non nobis* (initiated diegetically by Doyle himself, playing the role of Court) was, in spite of its rather naïve optimism, a rousing conclusion to the battle sequence – so much so that, at a screening in New York, the audience mistakenly assumed that the hymn indicated the end of the film and began to leave the theatre (Rosenthal 2000, 41). In several places, however, Doyle and Branagh included music cues without compelling reason, and Doyle's tendency to indulge in his neo-Elgarian *nobilmente* idiom as a means of dignifying a scene – a technique which becomes increasingly prominent in the second half of the film – at times seemed overdone. In places, the uncomfortable disparity between image and music seems to have resulted from a lack of insight rather than deliberate anempathy. As Samuel Crowl has commented of Doyle's scores in general, they are 'emblematic of Branagh's desire to employ an extravagant film vocabulary', and in *Henry V* the music 'romanticises the English victory in a way that the battle's images do not, opening the door for Branagh's detractors to accuse such moments in his films of being ideologically unstable and politically pernicious' (R. Jackson 2000, 228). One particular scene in the battle sequence combined slow-motion photography of brutal fighting with incongruously expressive music, an anempathy directly echoed in Ridley Scott's Roman epic *Gladiator* and other modern Hollywood epics (see Chapter 12).

The tendency to include musical cues at every obvious opportunity grew more acute in Branagh's *Much Ado About Nothing* (1993). The film's undiscriminating spotting has been criticized by one Shakespeare scholar for using almost continuous music 'to smoothe over the prickliness of the text. By inflating the play's brittle epitaph scene (Act 5 scene 3) with orchestra and full chorus accompanying a procession of penitents, Branagh made the sequence operatic and compounded the film's leaning towards melodrama' (Hattaway in R. Jackson 2000, 93). In the musing soliloquies spoken by both Beatrice and Benedick as they overhear scheming gossip, Doyle's music fluctuates between superficial comedic gestures and a gratuitous sentimentality that weakens the liveliness of Benedick's soliloquy in particular. Such accusations hark directly back to the earliest critical anxieties about the application of easy-listening background music to Shakespeare's sophisticated and often disquieting poetry. As in *Henry V*, the score featured songs performed diegetically by Doyle himself, that sung at Hero's tomb descending into cloying sentimentality. The main-title music, however, was both epic and colourful, building in bustle and excitement to end on a well-timed ceremonial flourish as the two opposing groups of men and women finally came face to face.

Branagh's *Hamlet* (1996) set the complete text of Shakespeare's play in a film lasting some four hours. The production, which located the action in the nineteenth century, was distinguished in its acting and cinematography, while Doyle's score included felicitous moments such as the ceremonial march taking us into the highly stylized interior of Elsinore, and the disquieting string music for Ophelia's flashbacks to her lovemaking with Hamlet. Yet in three fundamental regards, all adumbrated in his earlier work, Doyle's score was disappointing. In the first place, music cues were so numerous (and often unnecessarily prolonged) that they often failed to have much impact – a problem made more acute by the extreme length of the film as a whole. Second, neutral music with fussy detail frequently competed directly with dialogue while adding nothing to the prevailing mood. Third, Doyle's quasi-Elgarian 'ennobling' music seemed directly at odds with the dramatic

4.3 Shakespeare meets the Hollywood musical headlong in Kenneth Branagh's flamboyant *Love's Labour's Lost* (1999). The director is second from right.

action in a number of important places, for example when Hamlet snarls 'O most pernicious woman!' (of his mother) and spits out a tirade against his environment ('the earth seems to me a sterile promontory, this most excellent canopy the air . . . appeareth nothing to me but a foul and pestilent congregation of vapours'), and when – in the most supremely undignified moment of the entire play – he wrestles on the ground with Ophelia's brother at her funeral. The use of such music to provide 'depth' to a scene had, not for the first time in the history of film music, evidently become a stock and clichéd response applied without due consideration being paid to the relevant dramatic context.

In the late 1990s, both traditional and updated settings for filmed Shakespeare remained equally viable. A new version of *Othello* (1995, dir. Oliver Parker) with a sumptuously realistic period setting received a sombre and economical score by Charlie Mole. Far more flamboyant was Baz Luhrmann's *William Shakespeare's Romeo + Juliet* (1996; music by Nellee Hooper, Craig Armstrong and Marius de Vries), which was squarely aimed at the youth market and followed the contemporary fashion for including the name of the author of 'classic' texts in the film's title – presumably so that no unsuspecting cinema-goers could reasonably ask for their money back afterwards. (Lest this comment should seem unduly cynical, it might be noted that when a British national newspaper ran a multiple-choice general-knowledge test for young people in the late 1980s, the majority of participants stated that *The Tempest* was written by pop star Kylie Minogue.) Luhrmann's contemporary West Coast setting is infused with images of the media, and the film's visual style dominated by the dynamism and restlessness of MTV pop videos; the music track veers with equal unpredictability from a sombre choral-orchestral style inhabiting territory somewhere between Orff and Mozart's Requiem (used for long-shot cityscapes), to heavy rock beats and pop songs (both diegetic and nondiegetic). This was not the first Shakespeare film rooted in contemporary popular culture – Derek Jarman's interpretation of *The Tempest* (1979) had a punk ambience, with electronic music by Wavemaker and a deliciously camp wedding scene bringing together sailors dancing to the panpipes of Gheorge Zamfir and a bluesy rendering of 'Stormy Weather' by diva Elisabeth Welch – but it was certainly the most exhilarating. In a quite unexpected shift of cultural emphasis, Luhrmann imposed the high romanticism of the 'Liebestod' from Wagner's *Tristan und Isolde* on the denouement of the tragedy. Classical music also features earlier in the film, when the pompous bustle of the preparations for the ball at the Capulets' mansion is accompanied by Mozart. Shot through with self-parody and occasional parodies of other genres (e.g. the initial confrontation between Montagues and Capulets at the gas station, in which both visuals and music ape the conventions of the spaghetti western), the film is sensitively spotted, and often makes its musical points economically. Some techniques are conventional, such as the use of diegetic music followed by the suppression of ambient sound when Romeo and Juliet first meet; here, as in the sudden outburst of lively music at the end of the first balcony scene, there are clear parallels with Zeffirelli's treatment of the same play.

Richard Loncraine's film of *Richard III* (1996; music by Trevor Jones) sets the violent action in a fictional 1930s civil war and charts the increasing fascist domination perpetrated by Richard's faction, with obvious parallels to the rise of the Nazi party. The dark scoring, with its sultry saxophone theme, fits comfortably into a modern thriller style, but more memorable is the handling of popular music appropriate to the period setting. A poem by Shakespeare's contemporary Christopher Marlowe, 'Come live with me and be my love', is given a full-blooded diegetic setting in the style of big-band swing at the opening of the film, and this infectiously lively music returns in the underscore when Richard coldly decides to take a wife, neatly reflecting the capricious amorality of his Machiavellian manipulations. Richard's coronation is seen from Anne's drugged perspective, with Charpentier's *Te Deum* distorted before the scene turns monochrome and the recording quality of the soundtrack is suitably downgraded as we then flash forwards to see Richard viewing the ceremony as a movie projection. Novel use of a film-within-a-film also distinguished Michael Almereyda's updating of *Hamlet* (2000; music by Carter Burwell), in which the dumb show is played out as a silent film accompanied by a medley of traditional scoring styles.

Branagh's flamboyant interpretation of *Love's Labour's Lost* (1999) drew on sparkling arrangements of 1930s hit songs that form the basis for brief but compelling dance numbers paying homage to the Hollywood musicals contemporaneous with the updated action, set in Oxford around the time of the Second World War; the narrative is clarified by newsreel-style interludes throughout. Branagh's comic conception works brilliantly, and the film is a satisfying celebration of Hollywood classicism, canonic popular song and timeless poetry. In Michael Hoffmann's lacklustre version of *William Shakespeare's A Midsummer Night's Dream* (1999; music by Simon Boswell), the updating of the action to a bicycle-infested nineteenth-century Italy did not mask the fact that the soundtrack was deeply conventional, and in some respects harked directly back to the earliest Shakespeare sound films. Like Reinhardt's 1935 treatment of the same play, Mendelssohn's incidental music was prominently featured: in the main-title sequence, Mendelssohn's Overture (at first crudely edited and then recomposed in pastiche style) accompanied an animation of flitting fairy lights which would not have been out of place in Disney's *Fantasia*, while the Nocturne and Wedding March appeared at relevant points in the plot. Predictably, the most colourful scoring was reserved for the supernatural elements of the play, and mickey mousing employed for comedic moments, while the drinking song from Verdi's *La traviata* and other Italianate material served as locational music.

In addition to the many films directly based on Shakespeare's plays, numerous others have taken the bard's work as a starting point. Discussion of the music for some of these films will be found elsewhere in the present volume: see, for example, *Forbidden Planet* (a sci-fi reworking of *The Tempest*), *West Side Story* (a musical based on *Romeo and Juliet*) and the Greenaway–Nyman collaboration, *Prospero's Books* (also inspired by *The Tempest*). Perhaps the starkest illustration of the wide range of musical styles acceptable when dealing with Shakespearean themes, even in Elizabethan costume, are Tom Stoppard's two comedy screenplays, *Rosencrantz and Guildenstern are Dead* (dir. Stoppard, 1980; music by Stanley Myers) and *Shakespeare in Love* (co-writer Marc Norman, dir. John Madden, 1998; music by Stephen Warbeck). *Rosencrantz*, which was itself originally a stage play, is a devastatingly witty gloss on *Hamlet* seen through the eyes of two of Shakespeare's shadowy minor characters, and the surrealism of the text is perfectly captured in the incongruous down-to-earth blues that accompanies the front and end titles, while the dark undercurrents of the film are hinted at by atmospheric electronics. In contrast, the Oscar-winning music for *Shakespeare in Love*, like that film's much less intellectually demanding screenplay, is an easy-listening romantic score in keeping with the commercial bias of the enterprise.

The last major Shakespeare film of the twentieth century was one of the finest. Julie Taymor's *Titus* (1999) was a visually stunning adaptation of the bard's grisly revenge tragedy, *Titus Andronicus*, its production design a surreal mixture of ancient, 1930s and modern elements and its score consistently resourceful. As a representative compendium of the manifold scoring techniques available to the film composer at the turn of the century, Elliot Goldenthal's music for *Titus* is exemplary. The initial and highly stylized approach of Titus's army is accompanied by a thumping march for percussion, which yields to austere choral incantations with orchestral accompaniment in a style reminiscent (like Morricone's *Hamlet* music) of Orff's *Carmina Burana*, here tinged with the swirling paganism of Mussorgsky's *Night on Bald Mountain* and setting a Latin translation of part of Shakespeare's text. For the first daylight exterior shot of a perplexingly futuristic ancient Rome, the idiom switches abruptly into a 'boogie-cool jazz amalgam' (Taymor 2000, 182) to accompany the entrance of Saturninus's motorized cavalcade. Thereafter the soundtrack presents a myriad of stylistic allusions, including Stravinskyan fanfares, shades of John Adams's dynamic minimalism, a Mahlerian 'fate' motif (juxtaposing a high major third with a low minor triad), an up-dated swing-band idiom with electric guitars for the first orgy scene, an atonal walking bass line in free-jazz style for the brawl between Tamora's sons, manically pulsating hunting music, a bizarre scherzo leading up to the lopping off of Titus's hand, head-banging electronics (produced by Richard Martinez) for the arcade games in the den of Tamora's murderous sons, and Carlo Buti's sentimental old song 'Vivere' to accompany the serving up of the sons' flesh in meat pies for unwitting consumption by their mother. The jazz and popular elements reinforce the black comedy of the play's more grotesque scenes, as when Titus's hand is dropped neatly into a polythene bag for delivery to the Emperor, and kaleidoscopic carnival music (of a kind Goldenthal previously explored with Taymor in the theatre) accompanies the shocking moment when the hand is returned to Titus along with the severed heads of his own sons. In spite of such manifold eclecticism, the film's strong visual style and first-rate acting both lend a compelling sense of coherence to the whole, and Goldenthal's extraordinary musical journey culminates in a cathartic end-title fantasy of considerable beauty.

5 The mainstream divides: post-war horizons in Hollywood

The diversification of musical styles and techniques in narrative cinema from the 1950s onwards was partly caused by momentous changes in the film industry during that watershed decade, although these musical developments coincided with what in any case seemed set to have been a period of enhanced experimentation on the part of both directors and composers. Several trends from the 1950s were to have a lasting impact: the consolidation and expansion of existing orchestral scoring associated with the burgeoning of big-budget genres such as ancient and biblical epics; the growth of newer genres such as science-fiction and fantasy, both of which by their very nature demanded imaginative music that was out of the ordinary; a marked increase in relatively modern compositional techniques such as atonality, athematicism and non-functional harmony; and an enhanced public awareness of exactly how much a composer's individuality could add to the overall success of a film – a realization most strikingly to be seen in the critical appreciation of arguably the decade's most respected film composer, Bernard Herrmann. This was also the decade in which title- and theme-song sales were increasingly seen as an important source of additional revenue for studios, and in which up-to-date popular music began to feature in movies; with the advent of rock'n'roll, an emerging youth culture started to shape the tastes and preoccupations not only of American cinema, but of film-making across the globe (see Chapter 10). Many of these developments and shifts in emphasis were occasioned by the breakdown of the Hollywood studio system as it tried to come to terms with various technological, political and social changes taking place in the immediately post-war period.

In 1949, 90 million movie tickets were sold in the USA each week, but by 1956 this figure had fallen to 45 million; in roughly the same period some 5,000 movie theatres closed (Denisoff and Romanowski 1991, 4). By 1969 weekly domestic ticket sales had further slumped to 15 million – a mere sixth of the 1940s peak. The movie industry's biggest competitor had in the meantime become television. Viewing figures for the new broadcasting medium in the USA rose from one million in 1949 to a staggering 20 million just four years later, by when 45 per cent of households had acquired their own TV sets (Silvester 1998, xiv–xix). In 1948 the Hollywood studios lost a lucrative source of revenue when they were finally deprived of their right to own movie theatres: prior to this they had controlled 70 per cent of all theatrical outlets in 92 major American cities. Big-budget epics, shot in sumptuous widescreen format with stereophonic sound and full colour, and exploiting lavish production values of which television companies could only dream, were one obvious attempt to lure audiences back into the movie theatre in the 1950s; but the initiative was self-defeating as the huge inflation in acting fees commanded by star performers and generally excessive budgets meant that, once the initial novelty had worn off, few epics could break even at the box office – let alone make a profit. Less expensive but equally mercenary in intent was the introduction of drive-in movie outlets aimed at the new youth market, which numbered nearly 5,000 by the middle of the decade. Gimmicks such as 3-D projection, vaunted in *House of Wax* (dir. André de Toth, 1953; music by David Buttolph) and *The Creature from the Black Lagoon* (dir. Jack Arnold, 1954; music by Herman Stein and Hans Salter), rapidly came and went. The death knell of the studio system had been clearly sounded and, as the power of individual studios dwindled, so independent productions burgeoned and directorial styles changed and became more distinctly personal.

As far as the livelihood of studio musicians was concerned, industrial action and litigation on various contractual issues did little to make their post-war employment prospects either stable or lucrative. When in 1947 ASCAP attempted to raise its already substantial licensing fees for the use of copyrighted music in motion pictures, such fees at that time being paid by both producers and theatrical outlets, the result was a court case that three years later ruled against the Society and seriously diminished composers' income from royalties (Prendergast 1992, 57–8). Spurred on by the foundation of the Screen Composers' Association in 1945, composers meanwhile continued to campaign vociferously for the intellectual rights they felt they should enjoy over their creative output – a sentiment entirely alien to the mentality of producers, who regarded film music as their own property just as were a studio's scenery and costumes. Without the backing of strong and coherent union representation, however, the composers' agitation ultimately 'helped cripple their own case in the struggle for copyright control by adhering to an anachronistic conception of authorship . . . By representing themselves as artists who transcended the usual relations of production and consumption, studio composers undermined their efforts to better these very relations' (Flinn 1992, 33). These issues again came to the fore in 1971–2 when the Composers and Lyricists Guild of America went on strike, and the copyright cause continued to be passionately championed by Elmer Bernstein throughout his career. Performers, too, had become more belligerent about working conditions, not always to their advantage. In 1958 strikes by several musicians' unions crippled recordings of film scores: one casualty was Herrmann's score to *Vertigo*, the recording of which had to be shifted from Los Angeles to London (where it was conducted by Muir Mathieson); when the English orchestral players also took industrial action, the project was completed in Vienna, and for contractual reasons the cues recorded in Austria did not appear on the soundtrack album (Cooper 2001, 50–1). Herrmann's score to *The Seventh Voyage of Sinbad* was recorded in Germany as a result of the same dispute. Such industrial action was sufficiently serious in its wider impact that it effectively finished off the concept of permanent studio orchestras, ensuring that most scoring work from the 1960s onwards was to be accomplished on an essentially freelance basis.

Political machinations were another factor contributing to Hollywood's post-war crisis. In 1947 the witch-hunt against Communists spearheaded by the House Un-American Activities Committee (HUAC) focused on the film industry and made high-profile targets of the scapegoat 'Hollywood Ten', who (unlike Walt Disney, Gary Cooper and Ronald Reagan) refused to inform on their colleagues: the ensuing blacklist drove many talents underground and made Hollywood 'a wasteland of vapidity, complacency, and cowardice for well over a decade' (D. Cook 2004, 382). At MGM, musicians with questionable political views were fired so promptly they were not allowed to return to the studio to collect their belongings, and when André Previn – then at the start of his film-composing career – was questioned by Sam Goldwyn about the sympathies of the orchestral players under his direction, he was threatened with immediate dismissal if his assurances that they were 'too busy playing music to pass out pamphlets' turned out to be misplaced (Previn 1992, 63). During the Los Angeles 'Hearings of the US Congressional Committee Regarding the Communists' Infiltration of the Motion Picture Industry', Bertolt Brecht was questioned about his dealings with Hanns Eisler's brother Gerhart, a known Communist. Brecht bluntly denied being a Communist but pointedly left for East Berlin shortly afterwards. The Eislers' unpleasant sister stirred up public disaffection against her brothers; arrested but swiftly jumping bail, Gerhart managed to leave the country and was accordingly accused of being a spy. In spite of the public support of a number of high-profile creative artists, Hanns (whose telephone had been tapped by the FBI) fled to Europe in March 1948 and was subsequently prevented from ever re-entering the USA; at the time of his departure he was at work on a score for Chaplin's *The Circus* (1928), and he continued to write film music in East Germany. Eisler's friendship with director Joseph Losey, who stayed regularly with him when working for MGM, resulted in Losey's also coming under FBI surveillance (Caute 1994, 99) and helped precipitate the director's move to Europe in 1952.

5.1 Survival of a genre: Alfred Newman conducts a percussion ensemble for the ballet 'The Small House of Uncle Thomas' in the film of the Rodgers and Hammerstein musical *The King and I* in 1956. The recording took place on Stage One at the studios of Twentieth Century-Fox.

A second set of hearings in 1951 was televized, the broadcasts vastly increasing public awareness of the issues involved. By 1952 over 300 film personnel had been fired and prevented from working in the industry, and between 1956 and 1958 known Communists and those who had not co-operated with government enquiries were banned from being nominated for Academy Awards: 'Thus, vitiated, frightened, and drained of creative vitality, Hollywood experienced in miniature what the whole of American society was to experience during the McCarthy-era witch-hunts – intellectual stagnation and moral paralysis' (D. Cook 2004, 384). The rapidly developing genre of the science-fiction film was appropriated as a vehicle for thinly veiled anti-Communist propaganda, with aliens from outer space attempting to infiltrate the American way of life and rob citizens of their individuality; at the same time the genre confirmed the excitement and political potency of the 'space race' between the USA and the USSR, and in its fondness for mutant life-forms found new creative outlets for the horror impulse. Other genres such as the western and musical flourished for different reasons, chiefly because of their safely uncontroversial and uplifting subject-matter, and in the process both acquired some of the overblown mannerisms of the epic.

The epic and the intimate

The lavish and hugely expensive Hollywood epics of the 1950s and 1960s have been described by Vivian Sobchack as belonging to a genre that 'defines history as occurring to music – persuasive symphonic music underscoring every moment by overscoring it' (Grant 1995, 281). Perhaps the most significant aspect of music for historical epics in the 1950s was not its scale, which was in essence no different from that of earlier extravaganzas such as *Gone With the Wind*, but a new 'authenticity' that required nondiegetic music to reflect to some degree the musical characteristics of the historical period in which a film was set. The pioneer of this approach was Miklós Rózsa, whose musicological research was a deliberate stand against the ineptitude of musical anachronisms in historical movies prior to his own first project in the new manner, *Quo Vadis?* (dir. Mervyn LeRoy, 1951). Rózsa's prime intention was that authentic music should support filmic realism and – although his innovations in this regard were influential and persist to the present day – his historicized idioms continued to draw not only on the romantic mannerisms of earlier soundtracks, but also on clichéd gestural associations. Thus, for example, the ubiquitous use of parallel perfect fourths and fifths in organum-style chants, and fanfares of a designedly archaic flavour, while continuing (as with his quartal harmony) to reveal Rózsa's debt to the music of his compatriots Bartók and Kodály – and to Stravinsky, too, who quipped that the fanfares in his own opera-oratorio *Oedipus Rex* (1928) seemed in retrospect like the 'badly tarnished trumpets' of Twentieth Century-Fox (Stravinsky and Craft 1968, 30) – also reinforced Hollywood's inveterate equation of the ancient with the primitive: grandly imperial Romans are at times characterized in musical terms essentially similar to those portraying Apache warriors in stereotyped westerns. Rózsa had previously used organum fourths to create an austere African setting (*Five Graves to Cairo*, 1943), and found an inventive application for diegetic fanfares in *The Thief of Bagdad* (1940) where they neatly frame and merge into nondiegetic skirmish music during the sack of the Basra marketplace.

For the diegetic cues in *Quo Vadis?*, Rózsa supervised the preparation of replica instruments modelled on surviving Roman artefacts; not knowing what these would have sounded like, he represented plucked stringed instruments by employing a Scottish harp (clarsach), defamiliarizing the sound of his brass section by including cornets and creating the sound of the venerable aulos by blending alto flute and cor anglais. In the absence of Roman musical sources, he drew on the evidence attesting to the nature of the ancient Greek music which he presumed to have influenced the later Roman tradition, but constantly kept an eye on the needs of what he termed the 'lay public' by avoiding 'musicological oddities' such as monody, which he felt would not be sufficiently entertaining or emotionally appealing (Thomas 1997, 127–9). In addition to organum, modal harmonizations partly replaced the romantic chromaticism of standard Hollywood scoring; these were archaic in effect but in their own way just as anachronistic. As Rózsa admitted of his music to the later Roman project, *King of Kings* (dir. Nicholas Ray, 1961): 'From the musicological point of view, it might not be perfectly authentic, but by using Greco-Roman modes and a spare and primitive harmonization, it tries to evoke in the listener the feeling and impression of antiquity' (Thomas 1997, 135). The groundwork established by *Quo Vadis?* bore further fruit in the phenomenally successful *Ben-Hur* (dir. William Wyler, 1959), Rózsa's score for which – including a magnificent seven-minute pre-main-title overture, marking the apogee of what was essentially a holdover from silent-film and operatic practices – received one of the film's record-breaking clutch of eleven Academy Awards. Here the ceremonial ancient march style was intensified and contrasted with ethereal music for Christ, scored for pipe organ and string harmonics instead of the theremin the producers had wished Rózsa to employ ('you can't use electronics for the first century', he retorted); Rózsa's passionate crusade against blatant musical anachronism was so intense that he threatened to quit when requested to use the medieval Christmas hymn *Adeste Fideles* for the nativity scene (Thomas 1997, 125, 134). Elsewhere in the score, however, the Mixolydian and Lydian modality and parallel triads suggest the influences of Vaughan Williams and Kodály rather more than that of classical antiquity.

Rózsa's other historical projects covered a wide range of periods. For *Ivanhoe* (dir. Richard Thorpe, 1952) he reconstructed twelfth-century idioms from the Norman sources that antedate the relevant Saxon culture; *Plymouth Adventure* (dir. Clarence Brown, 1952), about the Pilgrim Fathers' voyage on the *Mayflower*, featured music from a seventeenth-century psalter and the idiom of contemporaneous lutenists; *Young Bess* (dir. George Sidney, 1953) received music appropriate to its Elizabethan setting; for the Van Gogh biopic *Lust for Life* (dir. Vincente Minnelli, 1956), Rózsa drew on French impressionism; and the medieval Spanish atmosphere of *El Cid* (dir. Anthony Mann, 1961) was enhanced by music he composed in Spain while searching for appropriate thematic material in monasterial libraries. Joseph Mankiewicz's 1953 film of Shakespeare's *Julius Caesar* (discussed in Chapter 4) could have been treated musically in either a Roman or Elizabethan manner, but Rózsa decided on this occasion to abandon putative authenticity

5.2 Miklós Rózsa conducting his influential score to the historical epic *Ben-Hur* in 1959.

and compose in his own idiom. In his extended and detailed discussion of the manifold riches of Rózsa's incident-laden epic scores, Christopher Palmer asserts that, like Stravinsky, Rózsa's principal achievement was the absorption of a wide range of historical mannerisms into his own coherent personal style, so that the speciousness of the music's purported authenticity (which Rózsa clearly overstated) is not at issue: he tries 'merely to be himself, musically speaking, at a variety of points in times past' (Palmer 1990, 208). As a result, and somewhat ironically, it was not his quest for authenticity but his own synthetic style that was to exert a potent influence on other film composers. As Jon Solomon puts it, this style established 'a newly recreated aesthetics of "ancient" cultural norms' and the composer's innovations 'led not to renewed interest in [ancient] music but to a musical stereotype heard today in any films or film segments set in antiquity, not least in parodies of ancient films' (Martin Winkler 2001, 336). Nevertheless, most subsequent composers made obvious attempts to relate the idiom of their scores to considerations of historical period and geographical locale. In a series of lectures on the craft of film composition at the University of California at Los Angeles in the early 1960s, Leith Stevens advocated a period-specific approach in all situations apart from films containing 'a dramatic problem of such universality that it is greater than the time and the place', in which eventuality he considered a contemporary or even serial idiom to be justified regardless of the apparent expressive dictates of the diegetic milieu (Brill 2006, 347–8).

The technological advances and spectacular thrills offered by widescreen picture format showcased the opulence and sheer scale of these big-budget epics. The CinemaScope process, for example, used anamorphic lenses that produced a picture format of 2.35:1 rather than the previous Academy standard of 1.33:1, the image track of which had been shrunk to accommodate the additional space required to carry the soundtrack (and on which television screens had initially been modelled, hence the suitability of pre-1990s TV sets for the broadcast of movies shot in the old Academy format). Along with sheer visual impact came stereophonic sound, a four-track system being introduced in the first CinemaScope production, *The Robe* (dir. Henry Koster, 1953), with a score by Alfred Newman. The increase in audio quality was significant, and the widely separated stereo speakers permitted more spatially realistic sonic illusions than ever before: the soundtrack to *Julius Caesar* provides good examples. The adoption of soundtrack recording on 35 mm magnetic tape in 1950 now permitted far more flexible editing techniques, although sound recordings continued to be converted into optical soundtracks for theatrical release prints until the end of the century. (In 1958, the launch of the lightweight Nagra III transistorized tape recorder, which could be synchronized with a movie camera, revolutionized location sound work, both in terms of its operational convenience and superb recording fidelity. In the same year the Academy Award for Sound Recording was renamed as simply Sound in acknowledgement of the wider effort involved in putting together a creative soundtrack.) *The Robe*, although rather mediocre in some respects, proved to be the third most commercially successful feature film after *The Birth of a Nation* and *Gone With the Wind*, but Fox subsequently found it difficult to sell their expensive stereo system along with the new optical technology and many purchasers of CinemaScope opted to retain monophonic sound in order to cut costs. After 1960, CinemaScope was supplanted by the better-quality and more efficient Panavision system (2.25:1), which was to remain the industry standard.

Less reliant on historical research than Rózsa's, Newman's music for *The Robe* used non-functional triadic juxtapositions to create a sense of what Palmer – who also notes the appearance of this essentially Debussyan technique in the music of Rózsa and Herrmann – terms 'archetypal solidity and strength' (Palmer 1990, 84), but which are more explicitly associated with appearances of Christ and his garment. (This harmonic technique has persisted to the present day as a stock-in-trade: see, for example, James Horner's music for *Titanic* (1997), discussed in Chapter 12.) Newman's triadic idea is first heard in the main-title music along with a characteristic wordless chorus, and the chords are later transformed into a grimly effective funeral march for the procession to Calvary; parallel triadic patterns featuring false relations and Mixolydian flattened sevenths are also prominent in Newman's militaristic and fanfare cues, which generally avoid the quartal harmony so typical of Rózsa. Newman efficiently combines his militaristic music with both an exotic Middle Eastern idiom (augmented seconds and monody, to introduce Jerusalem) and with more lyrical, understated scoring at various points. Some of the music from *The Robe* was recycled by Waxman in a sequel, *Demetrius and the Gladiators* (dir. Delmer Daves, 1954), and in the earlier film Newman had already judiciously recycled some swashbuckling Straussian music from *The Hunchback of Notre Dame* for Demetrius's heroic rescue from captivity; the transfiguration at the end of *The Robe* recycled a 'Hallelujah Chorus' Newman had previously used in both *The Hunchback* and *The Song of Bernadette*, though the director of *The Greatest Story Ever Told* (George Stevens) evidently thought enough was enough and ditched Newman's fourth attempt to use this cue in 1964, replacing it with the famous example from Handel's *Messiah*. Other epics scored by Newman included *The Egyptian* (dir. Michael Curtiz, 1954), another Fox Cinema-Scope offering in which he became involved when it emerged that Herrmann would not be able to meet the deadline to complete his own music for the film; the two composers traded sketches and ideas about modes but, far from producing the 'homogeneous' score described by Tony Thomas (1997, 72), the disparity between their styles remained acute, with each conducting his own cues in the recording studio and Newman's mixture of exoticisms (reminiscent of Rimsky-Korsakov) and pseudo-archaic harmony contrasting sharply with the brooding melancholy of Herrmann's strings and deep-pitched reed instruments. Here the manner which later became so celebrated in Herrmann's scores for Hitchcock (see below) is overly ponderous and does little to remedy the slack pacing of a generally wooden and soporific production.

Other well-established composers tackled epic assignments with suitable expansiveness and continued to draw on both traditional Golden Age scoring methods and period research. George Antheil's score to the Napoleonic yarn *The Pride and the Passion* (dir. Stanley Kramer, 1957) vividly demonstrates a would-be modernist composer (who once dismissed formulaic film music as 'unmitigated tripe': see Marks 1997, 17) apparently frustrated by the dictates of the genre: rare moments of inventive scoring are overwhelmed by a heavy reliance on well-worn classical models – Mahler's First Symphony for distant fanfares over a dissonant pedal point, Mussorgsky's *Boris Godunov* for a cathedral scene and Ravel's *Bolero* for what Palmer would term routine (and in this case irritatingly pervasive) 'Spanishry'; there is even recourse to a Newmanesque wordless chorus and an overlong and flippant treatment of 'The British Grenadiers' to signpost the arrival of the British officer (a woefully miscast Cary Grant). More accomplished examples include Waxman's score to *Taras Bulba* (1962), discussed in Chapter 3, and Tiomkin's to *The Fall of the Roman Empire* (dir. Mann, 1964). Tiomkin's approach to the task differed from Rózsa's in avoiding period research altogether: the main-title overture is an extraordinary mixture of pastiche Bach-like organ music and full-blooded Russian romanticism, the strong sense of melancholy continuing subtly throughout the first scene, in contrastingly intimate chamber scoring. Shades of Rachmaninov's late style are heard in both the passionate string writing and harmonically rich material for brass, whose spirited fanfares hail more from Rachmaninov's Symphonic Dances (1940) than from the Hungarian roots of Rózsa's much-imitated ceremonial manner. Uncharacteristically, autonomous musical forms are developed by Tiomkin at some length: these include a theme and variations for the succession of tribal tributes paid to Marcus Aurelius (the integrity of the cue impaired by compulsive ducking to make way for sporadic dialogue) and a grimly determined fugue for strings as his troops muster. In both its stirringly epic sweep and certain details of instrumentation (notably the use of etiolated artificial violin harmonics), Tiomkin's score demonstrates that the best bravura Golden Age film music was in some respects remarkably similar to its modern incarnation in the Spielberg–Williams blockbusters of the late twentieth century; and much of the credit for this longstanding consistency is due to the sterling work of orchestrators, no fewer than six of whom converted Tiomkin's sketches into scoring of often dazzling inventiveness.

Alex North, whose importance as the originator of a symphonic-jazz style of film music in the 1950s is considered below, scored two major productions with ancient settings: *Spartacus* (dir. Stanley Kubrick, 1960) and *Cleopatra* (dir. Mankiewicz, 1963), which commanded budgets of $12 million and $40 million respectively. *Spartacus*, shot in the Super-Technirama 70 mm format, was the least typical of Kubrick's films, since he was brought in to replace director Anthony Mann and compelled to use North by the studio. Most unusually, North had been given over a year in which to compose his score by the film's producer and star, Kirk Douglas: this afforded the composer the opportunity to spend several months researching Roman music after the example of Rózsa, though in the event he preferred to 'write music that would interpret the past in terms of the present' (quoted in Henderson 2003, 131). His approach is similar to Rózsa's in terms of its militaristic brashness, use of modes (including pentatonicism) and quartal harmony, and keen sense of orchestral colour, but is generally more dissonant and avoids lapsing into cliché. Some battle sequences were edited to temporary music tracks for two pianos and percussion which were later orchestrated; Kubrick recommended North study Eisenstein's *Alexander Nevsky* as an illustration of how effective a music-driven battle montage could be (Henderson 2003, 133), though some of this temp-track was later replaced (LoBrutto 1998, 187). *Cleopatra*, shot in 70 mm Todd-AO format and featuring six-track stereo sound, required a score amounting to over three hours of music – and conceived for a colossal orchestra including a vast array of percussion, large saxophone ensemble (including the rare contrabass variety) and a quartet of alto flutes – which was, for all its boldness, still rooted in leitmotivic procedures. The film's director drew attention to the thematic tautness of the assassination scene: 'Utilizing the three basic themes of Caesar, Cleopatra and Caesar–Cleopatra [North] brings all three to a finish as fateful and terrifying as that of Caesar himself' (quoted in Henderson 2003, 65). North undertook research into renaissance music when scoring the Michelangelo epic *The Agony and the Ecstasy* (dir. Carol Reed, 1965), and made a final contribution to the genre with the acclaimed fantasy-epic *Dragonslayer* (dir. Matthew Robbins, 1981).

The widescreen sound remake of *The Ten Commandments* (dir. Cecil B. DeMille, 1956) was scored by Elmer Bernstein who, like North, had embarked on his film career at the start of the decade and played his own part in the development of jazz-based scoring (see below). *The Ten Commandments* showed his solid grasp of the basic musical elements of 1950s historical epics: expansive overture and entr'actre, regal fanfares, delicate writing for flute and harp serving as 'ancient' diegetic music, mystic triads (first heard as the final main-title card proclaims the film's source to be 'Holy Scripture'), exotically colourful dance music, and a heroic and exuberant manner of march-like brass writing that – like Tiomkin's *Fall of the Roman Empire* – looks ahead to the swagger of later adventure scores. Although Bernstein later became associated with similarly exuberant scoring – as, for example, in two films by John Sturges: *The Magnificent Seven* (1960), discussed in Chapter 3, and *The Great Escape* (1963) – both he and North accomplished some of their most telling work with far more economical resources. Even in their epic scores, both composers made strategic use of restrained writing for reduced ensembles. North commented that he found it difficult to empathize with the more grandiose aspects of his epic assignments, preferring to concentrate on aspects of character and relationships which were better portrayed by intimate scoring (Henderson 2003, 63–4). This may partly have been because not all directors knew how to handle close-up photography in widescreen format, which was one reason why techniques such as composition-in-depth and extended single takes became more prominent throughout the 1950s and ultimately formed the basis for much New Wave cinematography in the 1960s.

Chamber scoring was evident from the very start of North's film career, when he reworked an alto-flute melody from his 1949 incidental music for Arthur Miller's *Death of a Salesman* in the 1951 film version, and had already been a feature of David Raksin's scores from the late 1940s. Bernstein's early score to the melodrama *Sudden Fear* (dir. David Miller, 1952) similarly demonstrated a tendency to restrict resources by including passages for a small number of instruments, or solo instruments. Lean, uncluttered chamber textures became a regular feature of both composers' later scores. The apogee of Bernstein's chamber scoring came in his music for *To Kill a Mockingbird* (dir. Robert Mulligan, 1962), in which his childlike piano melody is first heard during the evocative main-title sequence; some of the robust music for the children later in the film harks back to the rural style of his Copland-influenced western scores. The pacing and economy of the extended music cue after the courtroom verdict is a model of refined textural control: a dignified chorale from the small string ensemble yields to a desolate clarinet solo, soon joined by a bassoon in two-part counterpoint before further wind pairings (clarinet/flute, clarinet/bassoon) are subsequently augmented by a harp accompaniment and violin line; then a solo cello is supported by the harp before strings and wind converge in a unison line, the strings emerging into full harmony as the piano reprises its modal melody from the film's beginning, the wind also finally adopting chords.

Such chamber scoring – which, whether intense or simple in effect, was invariably allied to economy of compositional technique – later came to be a defining feature of much television music in the 1970s and 1980s, where it brought the additional benefit of requiring a low budget. In the 1950s, although budgetary concerns became an important consideration after the demise of the permanent studio orchestras, leanness and clarity of scoring were as much the by-product of a stripping away of the tonal and colouristic indulgences of film music in the previous decades, and with the new economy came a renewed interest in modernism.

Modernism

As suggested in Chapter 3, 'modernism' in film music must be regarded as a relative term: even at its boldest, the scoring of narrative features during the 1940s lagged decades behind technical innovations in the field of concert music and, where limited dissonance, thematic angularity and textural fragmentation were present, they were invariably justified by the *Angst*-ridden atmosphere of such genres as *film noir*, intense psychological drama and the horror film. Although its influence showed rarely in their work, certain Hollywood composers nevertheless pursued active interests in contemporary music outside the film studio, and in the 1950s modern stylistic traits – atonality in particular – began to figure in certain narrative scores as a more orthodox musical language: one which assuredly remained primarily associated with expressionistic contexts, but now at times might be made to serve more neutral purposes. The apt term 'phantasmagoric modernism' was coined by Arved Ashby to describe this use of up-to-date techniques in order to create the kind of supernatural musical 'antidote to the picture' perceived by Adorno and Eisler; the tendency towards fragmentation in this approach contrasted with the opposing pole of 'formalist modernism' typified by the serial Schoenberg (Ashby 2004, 367, 372).

As with jazz influences, dissonant scoring was encouraged by a few musically sensitive directors in the 1950s, notably Elia Kazan, Otto Preminger and Nicholas Ray. When Kazan approached Leonard Bernstein to score *On the Waterfront* (1954), a film which appeared to endorse the act of informing, the composer was at first reluctant to be involved because Kazan had collaborated with the HUAC investigators, as had one of the film's actors and its scriptwriter. (For this reason, hostility towards Kazan persisted until the end of his life: when he accepted an honorary Academy Award in 1998, many in the audience hissed and refused to get to their feet.) But when confronted with the powerful acting and stark narrative in the film's rough cut, Bernstein changed his mind and not only provided a fine nondiegetic score but also played jazz piano in a bar scene, a service for which he received a standard fee of $39 in addition to his $15,000 for the project as a whole (Burton 1994, 237). Bernstein's score draws heavily from the idiom of Copland, especially in its opening horn theme and limpid two-part wind counterpoint, and in the restraint of its diatonic love theme; in his concert music Bernstein had already emulated Copland's early symphonic-jazz style, and its jazz-based harmonies and exciting additive rhythms (again ultimately deriving from Stravinsky) are heard in some of the film's scenes of struggle and conflict. As the beaten-up Terry – played by Marlon Brando, whose Method acting seems to have inspired music of compelling leanness from various composers at this time – staggers back to work at the end, the main-title theme is developed in a manner directly reminiscent of the statuesque prairie music in Copland's *Billy the Kid*.

Given Bernstein's wholesale indebtedness to Copland, it is perverse to find Hans Keller praising the *Waterfront* score for being more effective than film music penned by Copland himself (Burton 1994, 237), and Bernstein's one-off foray into film scoring met with harsh criticism from other commentators, principally Roy Prendergast (Prendergast 1992, 130–2). Kazan himself drew attention to the inappropriately bustling and menacing music at the start of the film when all the spectator sees is a group of anonymous men on a dockside, commenting 'I didn't like the opening piece of music. It says, "These are the heavies." It sets a tone of highfalutin melodrama that's more befitting *Aida* than *Waterfront*' – though he declared the rest of the score to be 'excellent' (Young 1999, 182–3). Kazan's principal cause for regret was that Bernstein's musical personality was too forceful and therefore drew undue attention to itself. Prendergast is more specific in criticizing what he terms the score's 'linear quality' which 'competes with the dramatic action', citing by way of example the relentless continuation of the love theme 'regardless of what is going on up on the screen' (Prendergast 1992, 132). Although Prendergast would evidently not be in favour of the kind of independent music tracks encountered in New Wave European cinema just a few years later (which his book does not discuss), his point nevertheless highlights the innate tendency of the classical composer to structure a film score in a more autonomous manner than might be required by the assignment. Significantly, Bernstein himself drew attention to the score's 'thematic integration' in a programme note to the first performance of the 'symphonic suite' he reworked from *On the Waterfront* in 1955. It seems, however, that Kazan was partly to blame for the uncertainty of aim in his soundtrack. Bernstein related that Kazan had agreed to let a substantial orchestral climax drown out the 'prosaic bits of dialogue' when Terry and Edie have a drink together:

> But then, Kazan decided he just couldn't give up that ineffable sacred grunt which Brando emits at the end: it was, he thought, perhaps the two most eloquent syllables the actor had delivered in the whole script. And what happens to the music? As it mounts to its greatest climax, as the theme goes higher and higher and brasses and percussion join in with the strings and woodwinds, the all-powerful control dials are turned, and the sound fades out in a slow diminuendo.   (quoted in Prendergast 1992, 131)

At around the same time, Leonard Rosenman eloquently demonstrated how flexible and versatile a partly atonal idiom could be when applied to film scoring. Rosenman's film music is heavily indebted to the soundworld of the composers of the Second Viennese School: Schoenberg (with whom he studied in Los Angeles), Webern and especially Berg, with the latter's rich harmonic language in particular providing him with a potent stylistic model for both astringent dissonance treatment and lush chromatic chords based on quartal patterns mixing both perfect and augmented fourths. The Viennese influence was not restricted to aspects of advanced harmonic language: equally important was the use of fluid counterpoint to articulate long cues which, as Schoenberg had first discovered, was one of the few ways of making atonal music comprehensible in the absence of structurally functional tonal harmony. Rosenman came to work for Kazan at the suggestion of iconic actor James Dean, who was the composer's piano pupil. With his Cinema-Scope production of John Steinbeck's novel *East of Eden* (1955), in which Dean starred, Kazan showed how widescreen technology could be applied to intense domestic drama as well as to bombastic epics. The film's brooding and sometimes claustrophobic character was enhanced by Rosenman's haunting music, conceived during close consultation with the director at all stages in the film-making process. An excellent illustration of the suggestive potency of a modern and tonally elusive orchestral idiom is the understated cue that accompanies the moody shot of Dean as he follows the woman, dressed in dark brown and mysteriously veiled, whom he believes to be his long-lost mother. Tortuous music for the isolation of Dean's character (Cal) and the violence which is its expression is generally contrasted with a more gently modal style not surprisingly – given the rural Steinbeck context – distantly reminiscent of Copland, the whole remaining based on pervasive character-associated leitmotifs in the traditional Hollywood manner. Rosenman's highly chromatic style jars tellingly with the diegetic ragtime music played on the piano in the bars and brothels of Monterey in 1917, where the action is set, further increasing the sense of Cal's isolation from his sometimes cheerful surroundings. As Palmer has shown, a more solid sense of tonality is made to assert itself in the final scene through an extended and thematically culminatory cue designed to reflect the new-found stability of the protagonists (Palmer 1990, 306–7).

Another Dean vehicle of the same year, *Rebel Without a Cause* (dir. Ray), was scored by Rosenman in a similarly adventurous manner, and again the topic of juvenile rebellion was to some extent a pretext for uncompromising musical expressionism, with roving and sometimes atonal chromaticism perfectly capturing the sense of youthful restlessness at the film's heart. (In part this roving chromaticism was directly inspired by Bartók's *Music for Strings, Percussion and Celesta*: see Ashby 2004, 369.) As in *East of Eden*, Rosenman used a tension-generating device that was destined to become a cliché of later dissonant scoring: the gradual stacking up of multiple pitches to form a complex dissonance crying out for a resolution that never comes (a device also used by Bernstein in *On the Waterfront*). Although in the first part of *Rebel* the atonal music seems neutral in mood, and is often mixed in the soundtrack at a low volume level, at a number of startling moments (e.g. the simulated celestial explosion in the planetarium and the climactic car race over the cliff edge) it comes to the fore in screamingly dissonant orchestral tuttis. In one instance, dissonant music was added to a scene expressly to prevent the audience from laughing at the unintentionally comic effect when Dean petulantly strikes a tabletop and hurts his hand in the process (Dalton 1975, 237–8). Jazz influences are occasionally prominent, partly serving the time-honoured tradition of portraying youthful drunkenness and swagger but also espousing a dissonant angularity that makes them sound a natural extension of more modernist elements of Rosenman's style. Given the uncompromising idiom of the score, it is interesting to note that in the main-title cue the lyrical love music (always used subtly and unobtrusively in the course of the narrative) is subjected to an uncharacteristically lush arrangement, conforming to prevailing industry stereotype and giving an entirely false impression of the musical experience to come.

Rosenman's atonal music for a third film from 1955, *The Cobweb* (dir. Minnelli), was suggested by the film's mental-institution setting. More abstract was his score for *The Savage Eye* (dir. Ben Maddow *et al.*, 1959): the film was edited to pre-existing autonomous chamber music specially written by Rosenman (Prendergast 1992, xvii), a rare approach more often encountered in New Wave French cinema, where atonality has also received numerous intelligent applications (see Chapter 8). In both *The Cobweb* and the sci-fi picture *Fantastic Voyage* (dir. Richard Fleischer, 1966) Rosenman made use of twelve-note techniques, as did Rózsa to portray the Satanic elements in *King of Kings*. The mechanics of strict serialism remain aurally unintelligible even to audiences steeped in classical music, and in the cinema perhaps the best such procedures can expect to do is guarantee the composer a certain degree of consistent atonality; in the case of *The Cobweb*, however, Rosenman declared that he wanted to depict something of the unseen neuroses affecting the minds of the characters, and felt certain that the predominantly athematic music – which was in part inspired by Schoenberg's Piano Concerto – would be summarily rejected by the producers as being far too avant-garde (Prendergast 1992, 119–24). As we have seen, Leith Stevens in the early 1960s considered serial techniques and *musique concrète* to be 'best related to very contemporary or psychological plays that deal with great tension' and that carried universal dramatic meanings transcending the time and place of the diegesis (Brill 2006, 348). Atonality was by then sufficiently common to surface even in low-budget projects such as Roger Corman's *Little Shop of Horrors* (1960), with its over-actively dissonant music by Fred Katz not especially well suited to the understated black humour of the scenario.

The career of another modernist film composer, Jerry Fielding, was blighted for a decade after he was blacklisted in 1953 by HUAC, but his work came to wider attention when he embarked on a series of collaborations with director Sam Peckinpah notorious for their explicit violence. For Peckinpah's western *The Wild Bunch* (1970), Fielding drew on elements of the Copland–Bernstein style such as rousing syncopations and additive rhythms reminiscent of *The Magnificent Seven*, and continued to tap folk associations by using guitar and harmonica, though in a fresh and often dissonant harmonic idiom that did not seem unduly derivative. His score for the same director's *Straw Dogs* (1971), however, borrowed so heavily from Stravinsky's *The Soldier's Tale* (1918) – with Fielding's cues in several places modelled bar-by-bar on the specific harmonic and textural details of the Stravinsky original – that one inevitably wonders if *The Soldier's Tale* was used as a temp track and then consciously imitated. As in his music for Peckinpah's *The Killer Elite* (1975), Fielding utilized twelve-note techniques in parts of the *Straw Dogs* score; by now, Hollywood had grown relatively accustomed to atonality in its soundtracks and the scores for both *The Wild Bunch* and *Straw Dogs* were nominated for Academy Awards. *The Wild Bunch* contained a striking example of a musical technique for promoting extreme tension that would become relatively common in later films: the use of dissonant nondiegetic scoring in direct conflict with simultaneously consonant diegetic music. In this case sustained string discords are pitted against old-time banjo and fiddle music during a flashback to a shooting in a brothel.

In 1974, David Shire composed a twelve-note score to Joseph Sargent's *The Taking of Pelham 123*, a thriller about the hijacking of a New York subway train. Although atonal, the instrumentation and idiom contained strong jazz and funk elements in a deliberate nod towards the metropolitan setting, and the music was anchored in catchy electric-bass riffs not derived from the otherwise ubiquitous note-row. The result was perhaps the ultimate expression of jazz as nationalistic modernism, a concept discussed later in this chapter. (For an exposition of Shire's row and its permutations, see Karlin and Wright 2004, 246–7; see also the analysis in Adams 1996.) Meanwhile, the potent influence of Stravinsky's dissonant and highly rhythmic early 'Russian' style received a fully digested manifestation in the work of Jerry Goldsmith (whose work is further considered in Chapter 12), in such scores as *The Planet of the Apes* (dir. Franklin Schaffner, 1968) – one of the more enduring science-fiction franchises of the era. As James Gilbert points out, it uses the distanciation provided by the genre 'to depict (and disguise) a contemporary social question' (Kolker 2006, 37), in this case racism. The sequel *Beneath the Planet of the Apes* (dir. Ted Post, 1969) was scored by Rosenman in similarly modernist vein, his music including a memorable diegetic parody of a church service. Goldsmith returned to the series to work on *Escape from the Planet of the Apes* (dir. Don Taylor, 1971), for which his main-title music fashionably combined Stravinskyan electric-bass riffs and octatonic harmony with a pulsatingly syncopated jazz-rock feel.

One of the most fascinating aspects of modernist film music is that most movie-goers are perfectly content to listen in the cinema to the kind of grittily dissonant, often athematic and seemingly randomly shaped avant-garde propositions that they would be unlikely to tolerate when divorced from the visual images by which they seem to be justified. Rosenman recalled his experience of 'hearing musically unenlightened people comment positively and glowingly on a "dissonant" score after seeing [a] film. I have played these same people records of the score without telling them that it came from the film they had previously seen. Their reaction ranged from luke-warm to positive rejection' (quoted in Prendergast 1992, 217). This observation suggests that such scoring is quickly forgotten when it does not feature a memorable melodic or rhythmic component.

In addition to high levels of dissonance, another obvious manifestation of modernist leanings in 1950s film music came in the shape of electronic timbres, a natural development of earlier experimentation with the ondes martenot and theremin. Interest in electronic sonorities was already so widespread in the previous decade that the noted pioneer of electronic and microtonal music, Ivor Darreg, prophetically declared: 'The day will come when a film without music from electronic orchestras will be as outdated as the silents' (Darreg 1946). After its initial deployment in *film noir* (see Chapter 3), the other-worldly sound of the theremin became inextricably associated with the burgeoning sci-fi genre (Glinsky 2000, 286). Its first sci-fi outing came with Ferd Grofé's score to *Rocketship X-M* (dir. Kurt Neumann, 1950), and the instrument's virtuosic exponent Samuel Hoffman subsequently played it on numerous soundtracks, including *The Thing* (UK title *The Thing from Another World*; dir. Christian Nyby, 1951; music by Tiomkin), *The Five Thousand Fingers of Dr. T* (dir. Roy Rowland, 1953; music by Hollander), *It Came from Outer Space* (dir. Jack Arnold, 1953; uncredited music by Irving Gertz, Herman Stein and Henry Mancini), the 3-D film *The Mad Magician* (dir. John Brahm, 1954; music by Emil Newman), *The Day the World Ended* (dir. Corman, 1955; music by Ronald Stein), and *Earth vs. the Spider* (dir. Bert I. Gordon, 1958; music by Albert Glasser) – the last also cashing into the then current craze for rock'n'roll. Herrmann made full use both of electronic sonorities and selective experimentation with animated sound and electronic sound processing as part of his general search for timbral novelty (see below), and served as Hitchcock's 'sound consultant' for *The Birds* (1963) in order to advise Remi Gassmann and Oskar Sala on their soundtrack made up entirely of electronically generated bird calls prepared in Germany by Gassmann's Studio Trautonium keyboard.

Leith Stevens provided music for many sci-fi scores. Like Herrmann, he had a background in radio music and was no stranger to the timbrally unorthodox, being equally at home in a jazz idiom or his teacher Joseph Schillinger's mathematical compositional strategies (Rosar 2006). While working on *War of the Worlds* (dir. Byron Haskin, 1953) Stevens explored the novachord and Stroh stringed instruments, his advanced quartal writing demonstrating that his modernist leanings were both timbral and harmonic, though at times he still resorted to the time-honoured *diabolus in musica* of the tritone for outlandish subject-matter (Rosar 2006, 402, 428–33). Other Stevens sci-fi projects included *Destination Moon* (dir. Irving Pichel, 1950), which used Sonovox technology for timbral manipulation, and *When Worlds Collide* (dir. Rudolph Maté, 1951), which won an Academy Award for its special effects. All three of these films featured the novachord but otherwise relied on conventional impressionistic instrumentation. Stevens described his music to *Destination Moon* as 'largely polytonal. It was considered by some at the time to be a very harsh and un-melodic kind of music, but since it has become quite accepted' (quoted in Rosar 2006, 349).

The era's boldest experiment in soundtrack design came in 1956 with *Forbidden Planet* (dir. Fred M. Wilcox), a sci-fi reworking of Shakespeare's *The Tempest* for which Louis and Bebe Barron provided an audio track formed exclusively from 'electronic tonalities', and in the process set a standard for the electrified alien soundscapes which came to dominate the genre until Alex North (*2001: A Space Odyssey*, 1968) and John Williams (*Star Wars*, 1977) redressed the balance in favour of the traditional orchestral score, North with disastrous personal consequences (see Chapter 11) and Williams with considerable success (see Chapter 12). The Barrons had previously been associated with such luminaries of the avant-garde as John Cage and Earle Brown, and were hired for *Forbidden Planet* to produce (in their New York studio) electronic effects – derived from the processing of cybernetic circuitry – that would provide supplementary atmosphere to what was planned to be a conventional orchestral score. When it was decided to make the music track exclusively electronic, the studio's concern that the innovation would elicit protests from the AFM influenced the adoption of the famous 'electronic tonalities' label rather than 'music' or 'score', against which the Barrons – who regarded themselves as composers not technicians – rebelled and initiated a lawsuit which destroyed their chances of further work in Hollywood (Wierzbicki 2005, 9–10, 14). At the same time the appellation unwittingly drew attention to the ambiguity between music and sound effect – and, in the context of spaceships and alien planets, an uncertainty as to what may be defined as nondiegetic background noise or as the sounds of advanced diegetic technology – central both to this groundbreaking film and its many imitators.

Bernard Herrmann: the composer as *auteur*

Herrmann has long been regarded as one of the finest and most influential film composers in the history of the medium. When an anthology of interviews with contemporary film composers was compiled at the turn of the twenty-first century (Russell and Young 2000), the editors were so

struck by the frequency with which Herrmann's name was cited as an ongoing influence that they decided to include an additional chapter (Cooke
2000) devoted to the work of the 'acknowledged master' – the only deceased
composer to be featured in the volume. Soon after, an entire double issue
of a scholarly journal was devoted to a detailed examination of his work
(Rosar 2003). Such singling out of an individual film artisan for sustained
attention has caused discomfort amongst scholars attempting to shift the
emphasis in film studies from romanticized aesthetics to other avenues of
interpretation and appreciation, and to resist canon-formation. Gorbman,
in a lucid general essay on film music, has drawn attention to 'an auterism
of the Romantic sort' surrounding celebrated film composers:

> Post-structuralism's dethronement of the individual artist has simply not
> occurred for film composers, since much academic discussion of film music
> occurs in contexts such as film music festivals of the Society for the
> Preservation of Film Music in Los Angeles, where there is a certain pressure
> to see and appreciate the music through the composer's eye and ear. The
> canon of film composers is a subject of lively debate. There has developed a
> virtual industry of Bernard Herrmann criticism, for example, in the form of
> a stream of books and articles, and passionate partisanship in Internet
> forums, fed by new CD releases of Herrmann scores, new concert editions
> and performances, and an hour-long documentary film about Herrmann
> (directed by Joshua Waletzky, 1994) shown on public television.
>
> (Gorbman 1998, 44)

This view echoes that of Flinn, who singled out Herrmann as an obvious
example of attempts to 'rescue' film music 'from its apperceived neglect
or undervaluation by championing the creative abilities of individual composers who, like the directors with whom they collaborated, are usually
approached as great auteurs' (Flinn 1992, 4–5). Herrmann was himself partly
if unwittingly responsible for promoting this image: like many composers
with dual careers in film and the concert hall, he conducted his film music
in concerts and had made new recordings of it (for Decca in the 1960s and
1970s) long before the glut of even newer Herrmann recordings appeared in
the 1990s. In several of his re-recordings Herrmann changed his tempi, often
slowing the music down now that the cues were freed from the exigencies
of synchronization.

As Mitry pointed out (1998, 6–11), the perceived *auteur* of a film need not
be the director when the writer of a cogent screenplay or striking dialogue
has a stronger personality to exert, and this comment has equal relevance
when films are endowed with highly charismatic production design, cinematography or music. (Mitry drew on parallels with classical music to
liken a purely functional director to the competent conductor whose task
is efficiently to realize a predetermined score planned by a greater creative

genius; where the director's personality comes to the fore, he compared this process to the way in which an inspired conductor draws exceptional contributions from orchestral players, whom he likened to the technicians and artisans of the film studio; in exceptional cases, he felt the director to be analogous to the opera composer stamping 'authorship' on a libretto.) The idea of the film composer as *auteur* was most likely to arise in the case of musicians who, like Herrmann, were highly trained and acclaimed for their work in the concert hall: indeed, some scholars continue to find it justifiable to analyse a Herrmann film score as if it were an 'autonomous piece of Western art music' (Cooper 2001, xiv).

Although Herrmann's early apprenticeship in experimental radio drama during the late 1930s undoubtedly honed his compositional resourceful-ness – particularly as far as unorthodox instrumentation and the ability to compose short cues to tight deadlines were concerned – and was also the means by which Orson Welles (with whom he collaborated on 'Mercury Theater on the Air' broadcasts) introduced him to film scoring, Herrmann's formidable armoury of compositional techniques and freshness of style came more from his classical background and wide knowledge of twentieth-century concert music. Like Korngold, Herrmann did not compromise the idiom of his concert music when working for films, and conversely his film experience was carried over into other works, which included a lengthy opera based on Emily Brontë's *Wuthering Heights* (1952). This project was directly suggested by the experience of having composed a score for a film version of Charlotte Brontë's *Jane Eyre* (dir. Robert Stevenson, 1943) which was partly based on thematic material from an earlier radio score; material from the film score was in turn reused in the opera. A substantial passage from the opera was reused wholesale as the main-title cue in Herrmann's score to *The Ghost and Mrs Muir* (dir. Mankiewicz, 1947), a film which has been the subject of a monograph by David Cooper (2005).

The libretto for *Wuthering Heights* was written by Herrmann's first wife, Lucille Fletcher, who also collaborated with him on the diegetic operatic music he composed as part of his famous score for Welles's *Citizen Kane* (1941), his first foray into film scoring. Here he was required to provide vocal music for Kane's second wife, Susan Alexander, an aspiring opera singer for whom Kane had an opera house specially built. Herrmann composed a pas-tiche segment from a fictional opera entitled *Salammbô*, designed to show how she was inadequate to the task of performing it: the music was wil-fully over-scored and then deliberately recorded by a weak-voiced soprano (Palmer 1990, 261). In a montage sequence depicting Susan's performances on tour, the music of *Salammbô* was brought into conflict with Herrmann's nondiegetic music representing Kane's selfish ambition, 'which after one statement is reduced to an obsessive rhythmic hammering on drums, as if beating poor incompetent but sensitive Susan to a mental pulp' (Palmer

1990, 259). Welles's respect for Herrmann's contribution to the film was demonstrated by the fact that other sequences were edited to pre-composed music, and that balance levels in the soundtrack dubbing were carefully planned. The music for the climactic final scene, for example, was written in advance and played back on set so that the camera operator could follow its rhythm. The composer felt his experience in radio drama had been inspirational in working on *Kane*, commenting how in radio

> every scene must be bridged by some sort of sound device, so that even five seconds of music becomes a vital instrument in telling the ear that the scene is shifting. I felt that in this film, where the photographic contrasts were often so sharp and sudden, a brief cue – even two or three chords – might heighten the effect immeasurably. (Herrmann 1941)

Memorable longer cues include the set of variations accompanying the montage depicting the breakdown of Kane's first marriage and the miniature dance movements underscoring events in the newspaper offices, in both of which Herrmann demonstrated how pre-existing musical forms could be adapted for the cinema without being accorded undue prominence: the structures complement the action on screen while retaining a certain degree of autonomy. Working even at this early stage in his film career with unorthodox instrumental forces (the score requiring no fewer than twelve members of the flute family), Herrmann nonetheless adhered to conventional leitmotivic techniques and took pride in the fact that the solution to the plot's famous 'Rosebud' mystery was spelled out by a telling motif at the outset of the film. This revelation was part and parcel of his strong belief that a film's musical 'overture' should precisely indicate the general nature and even the specific detail of the story ahead.

Both *Citizen Kane* and Herrmann's next Welles project, *The Magnificent Ambersons* (1942), used fairly conventional thematic transformations to highlight narrative events. (For an account of the music to *Ambersons*, including the notorious débâcle when RKO executives mutilated the film prior to its release and included new cues composed by Roy Webb, see Kalinak 1992, 135–58. Half of Herrmann's score was jettisoned without his prior knowledge, and he consequently insisted his name be removed from the film's credits.) When Herrmann began to devote more sustained attention to film work in the early 1950s, having initially found it difficult to establish himself in Hollywood as an outsider from the East Coast ('I was told by the heads of many music departments that there was no room for people like me there . . . They had a tight little corporation going': S. Smith 1991, 72), his style changed markedly. His music for *On Dangerous Ground* (dir. Nicholas Ray, 1951) contained certain elements – chiefly a tense and restrained manner of underscoring dialogue, and obsessive ostinati – that seemed to grow naturally from the idiom of *film noir*, while also exploring darkly unusual instrumental sonorities such as viola d'amore and bass clarinet. The score to *Five Fingers* (dir. Joseph L. Mankiewicz, 1952) relied on chordal ideas and edgy ostinato figures rather than fully blown melody, and also featured prominent low strings and winds (cor anglais and bass clarinet, and two bass clarinets moving in parallel fifths), the strings sometimes restricted to lean two-part counterpoint. As William H. Rosar has pointed out, Herrmann's preoccupation with low wind sonorities may have originated in the pragmatic 'microphone instrumentation' that in the early days of the sound film aimed to compensate for deficiencies in recording stringed instruments (Rosar 2003, 136); but, like Stravinsky and Sarnette, he was also suspicious of the ease with which their expressive timbre could conjure up romantic emotions.

Herrmann's penchant for imaginative instrumentation, strikingly shown in the gamelan-like sonorities serving as exotic local colour in *Anna and the King of Siam* (dir. John Cromwell, 1946), came fully to the fore in his responses to a succession of the fantasy and sci-fi screenplays that became increasingly popular throughout the 1950s. While a quirky sense of humour is evident in the often parodistic and brittle cues he wrote for the stop-frame animations of Ray Harryhausen in the fantasy adventures *The Seventh Voyage of Sinbad* (dir. Nathan Juran, 1958) and *Jason and the Argonauts* (dir. Don Chaffey, 1963), in more atmospheric contexts his sonorous experimentation became the perfect tool for creating other-worldly sonorities that were light years removed from standard orchestration. He felt there was little rationale (beyond the economic) in feeling bound to use a conventional symphony orchestra for film scores which, by their very nature, are only performed once – in the recording studio. Furthermore, he had as early as 1938 expressed the view that when a recognizable orchestra played in radio drama the listener's attention was more easily distracted than if the sonorities were unfamiliar: 'My idea is to disassociate in the minds of the audience from the thought of an orchestral accompaniment, so they can fix all their attention on the drama itself' (quoted in S. Smith 1991, 62), which was a further reason why he tended to avoid strings. This philosophy led to a succession of bizarre but always telling instrumental combinations in his later film scores, in which electronics and creative sound recording played important roles.

As early as *The Devil and Daniel Webster* (*All That Money Can Buy*; dir. William Dieterle, 1941), for which Herrmann received his only Academy Award, the Satanic elements were reinforced by experimental recording techniques in which the singing of telegraph wires was combined with animated sound painted directly onto the celluloid soundtrack, and multi-track recording of a solo violinist created a devilish effect in a hoe-down scene. In

The Day the Earth Stood Still (dir. Robert Wise, 1951), Herrmann employed two theremins, electric bass, electric guitar, electric violin, three organs, multiple brass, four harps, four pianos and percussion, using reversed recordings and an oscillator for special effects and linking the sound of the theremin with the robot Gort's laser-like ray to suggest 'the dangers of technology as threatening Other' (Ashby 2004, 372; see also Fiegel 2003). No fewer than nine harps were heard on the soundtrack to *Beneath the Twelve-Mile Reef* (dir. Robert D. Webb, 1953), Herrmann's first film score to be recorded in stereo, and multiple drummers dominated *King of the Khyber Rifles* (dir. Henry King, 1953). Five organs were featured in *Journey to the Center of the Earth* (dir. Henry Levin, 1959), a score from which the strings were boldly omitted altogether – as they were later to be in his music for *Twisted Nerve* (dir. Roy Boulting, 1968). At the climax of *The Day the Earth Stood Still*, when the earth literally grinds to a halt as global electricity supplies fail, the mind-numbingly dissonant chords show how inextricable sonority and harmony had already become in Herrmann's style; the same phenomenon is vividly illustrated in *Journey to the Center of the Earth*, where static chords are animated by shifting instrumentation in a kind of Schoenbergian *Klangfarbenharmonie*. Each Herrmann score had its own distinct sonorous identity, and the fact that he always orchestrated his own scores lent further credence to the concept of auteurism in the field of film music. As he put it, with characteristic bluntness, in an interview given shortly before his death in 1975:

> Color is very important. And this whole rubbish of orchestration [by others] is so wrong. You know, they make everything shit. I always tell them, 'Listen, boys. Don't give me this shit. I'll give a thousand dollars. I'll give you the first page of the *Lohengrin* prelude, with all the instruments marked. You write it out. I bet you won't come within 50 percent of Wagner.' To orchestrate is like a thumbprint. People have a style. I don't understand it, having someone orchestrate. It would be like someone putting color to your paintings.   (R. S. Brown 1994, 292)

After the introduction of stereo soundtracks, Herrmann's attention to timbral detail extended to the creative spatial separation of instrumental resources, which he indicated in his composition sketches.

Herrmann is best remembered for his ten-year collaboration with Hitchcock, for the greater part of which the director demonstrated enormous respect for his composer's input, for example including in his soundtrack notes for *Vertigo* comments such as 'we should let all traffic noises fade, because Mr. Herrmann may have something to say here' and 'All of this will naturally depend upon what music Mr. Herrmann puts over this sequence' (S. Smith 1991, 220). The collaboration commenced with a heavy-handed black comedy, *The Trouble with Harry* (1955), and first matured in *The Wrong Man* (1957). The latter's nondiegetic score prominently featured the jazz-playing protagonist's instrument, the double bass, and was the first of Herrmann's Hitchcock projects to showcase the composer's ability to create music of a coldly oppressive nature that had rarely been heard in previous film scores. The composer took pride in a perceptive review which described his 'gaunt sound-track music' as 'a series of plucked low notes from the musician's own double-bass, always in a rhythm to suggest foot-falls of a ghost – and this gives a weird feeling that ghastly intangibles are stalking the "hero" into a world of eerie bewilderment and horror' (quoted in S. Smith 1991, 211). Ghastly intangibles of various kinds subsequently informed Herrmann's most celebrated Hitchcock scores, composed for *Vertigo* (1958), *North by Northwest* (1959) and *Psycho* (1960). In all three, the starkly abstract graphics of the main-title sequences, designed by Saul Bass, allowed Herrmann free rein in setting the mood of the picture to come; in the case of *Psycho*, the music came first and the graphic animation was fitted to it. The compositional techniques employed in these opening sequences were idiosyncratic, though in some respects these 'overtures' were a thor-oughly conventional idea – and Herrmann famously reacted with horror when Brian De Palma dared to suggest that his film *Sisters* (see below) should commence without mood-setting music.

Most prominent in Herrmann's later Hitchcock scores was a heavy reliance on ostinato figurations, which stubbornly refuse to transform them-selves into conventional melodies: instead, the fragmentary repeating pat-terns are either formed into kaleidoscopic musical textures that tread a pre-carious middle ground between stability and instability (*Vertigo*) or reduced to an obsessive degree of insistent economy (*Psycho*). Herrmann's ability to extract the maximum interest from a tiny handful of pitches had been demonstrated in *Anna and the King of Siam*, where his resourceful manip-ulation of Balinese pentatonic scales foreshadowed Britten's later creative appropriation of Balinese music (which almost bore fruit in a late Britten film score: see Cooke 1998, 249). Fred Steiner coined the term 'module technique' to describe how Herrmann's ostinato-based textures tend to regenerate themselves in a block-like way (F. Steiner 1974a, 34), a formulaic and pragmatic approach to structure well suited to the production of what Sabaneev called 'extensile' music, and much appreciated by hard-pressed music editors forced to make unforeseen cuts and extensions to cues at short notice. As Fox's music editor Len Engel put it, 'Benny [Herrmann] was our idol because of the way he composed. He had a vertical form of four-bar phrases that was so easy to cut' (quoted in S. Smith 1991, 179). Leitmotifs with concrete dramatic associations are mostly avoided, though in a telling analysis of the score to *Vertigo* David Cooper has argued that on a local level Herrmann's development and recontextualization of short motifs in the service of the narrative has clear technical precedents in music of the romantic era (Cooper 2003), and specific Wagnerian influences on this particular score have been noted by others (e.g. Schroeder 2002, 237–43). Uneasy bitonality had been a seminal feature of Herrmann's style as early as *The Ghost and Mrs Muir*, and remained one of several harmonic devices used by Herrmann to promote a sense of instability or tension. Particularly characteristic was his obsessive use of major-seventh chords based on minor triads, one of which is so ubiquitous that Royal S. Brown dubbed it the 'Hitchcock chord' (1994, 160–2). Dissonances rarely resolve into familiar concords, even at the end of long cues (though Stilwell (2002, 34) contests their need to in the modern age): the title sequence of *North by Northwest*, for example, ends without resolution; the music of *Vertigo* is shot through with superimposed unrelated triads (an old idea of Stravinsky's now acquiring a new lease of life); and the closing seconds of *Psycho* are emphasized by an unresolved dissonance that can only leave the viewer feeling uncomfortable. In handling both ostinati and harmonic elements, Herrmann skilfully manipulated the audience's responses: the listener is encouraged to think that an extended melody or harmonic resolution is imminent, but it never (or rarely) comes. Without the visual images, a listener to Herrmann's music might feel constantly cheated, but in its cinematic context this inconclusive and ambiguous music precisely achieves the desired emotional effect, and has been aptly described by Brown as 'music of the irrational' (1994, 148–74).

Herrmann's score to *Psycho* is universally acknowledged to be one of the most original and influential in cinema history, and distinctly unorthodox in its exclusive use of strings. Considered (fancifully) as a monotimbral complement to the monochrome photography, the choice of strings was as much dictated by the film's unusually low budget, and they were treated in what the composer termed a 'very cold and very factual' manner, in deliberate contrast to the sweet string sound of Alfred Newman's scores (Cooper 2001, 31). Their use prevented any recourse to the time-honoured rhetorical clichés of horror-film scoring. *Psycho* brings the simple yet intense techniques of Herrmann's earlier work to saturation point. Most memorable of all is the famous shower scene, which Hitchcock originally intended to play without music; Herrmann persuaded him to think otherwise (the director later bluntly commenting that his proposal not to have music had been an 'improper suggestion'). So novel were the harshly recorded screeching and slithering string glissandi accompanying Janet Leigh's watery demise that some critics at the time thought they were electronically generated, while the sheer brutality of the music led others into thinking that the scene was far more gruesome visually than it really is. *Psycho*'s legendary shower scene has overshadowed subtler elements of Herrmann's score, such as the precise but unobtrusive synchronization of the doom-laden pulsating music to the action of the windscreen wipers of Leigh's car as she drives through the night. There is nothing inherently disturbing about the way in which this car journey is photographed: without Herrmann's disturbing music, as he himself observed, Leigh could just as well be on her way to a supermarket as fleeing from a crime scene.

Hitchcock and Herrmann parted company when the latter's score to *Torn Curtain* (1966), a film which came hard on the heels of their box-office flop *Marnie* (1964), was tetchily and publicly rejected by the director during a recording session. Herrmann's music had been conceived for a characteristically idiosyncratic orchestra featuring twelve flutes, sixteen horns and nine trombones. The reason for the score's rejection was ostensibly Hitchcock's and his producers' desire for a youth-oriented pop score, which Herrmann was unwilling and indeed unable to provide. (A partly easy-listening replacement score was provided by John Addison, who nevertheless aped Herrmann's style in several places, including the propulsive dance rhythm of the main-title theme.) This pretext masked other reasons for the rupture, which included Herrmann's increasingly outspoken antipathy towards what he saw as Hitchcock's sell-out to commercial interests, and Hitchcock's annoyance that Herrmann had been recycling musical ideas in his work for other directors. Herrmann's score to *Cape Fear* (dir. J. Lee-Thompson, 1961), for example, contains edgy string writing directly recalling *Psycho*, rhythmicized major-second dyads and ethereal upper strings moving in parallel thirds strongly reminiscent of *Vertigo*, and a simple falling semitone motif suggestive of both. (*Cape Fear* nevertheless contains characteristic touches of originality, notably the stark presentation of the four-note main-title motif in a simple but disturbing texture based on contrary chromatic motion, and the inspired use of thick chords for *divisi* double basses and the choked sound of hand-stopped horns to represent the threat of brutality.) Perhaps Hitchcock had come to the uncomfortable realization that Herrmann's music had, in the opinion of many, been the defining factor behind the success of his greatest films. Significantly, when Henry Mancini scored Hitchcock's *Frenzy* (1972) his music was rejected by the director because it sounded too much like Herrmann, and it was replaced with a new score by Ron Goodwin (S. Smith 1991, 293). In the opinion of Claude Chabrol, 'once Hitchcock got rid of Herrmann, Hitchcock's music was good only when it was imitating Herrmann' (Waletzky 1994).

Chabrol was one of a clutch of French directors on whom Hitchcock exerted a potent influence, and it was appropriate that Herrmann went on to compose two memorable scores for another of them: François Truffaut. *La Mariée était en noir* (*The Bride Wore Black*, 1967) was scored without violins and, appropriately enough, included distorted nondiegetic versions of Mendelssohn's Wedding March, in its unadulterated organ arrangement an audible punctuating device coinciding with the film's many flashbacks to the shooting of the bridegroom on the steps of the church. In the film's opening stages, Herrmann's busy scoring seemed overdone when set against the matter-of-fact visuals. His music for the futuristic Ray Bradbury story *Fahrenheit 451* (1966) returns to the quirkiness of his earlier fantasies to accompany shots of the futuristic fire engine as its crew heads off to burn books: instead of the anxious, exciting music we might expect with such an image, we hear instead the cold clarity of an almost childishly naïve xylophone melody. Truffaut had employed Herrmann on *Fahrenheit 451* because he wanted his futuristic vision to be accompanied by music of clarity and almost neo-classical simplicity, rather than an avant-garde complexity which he thought would tie the concept too firmly to the twentieth century rather than look ahead to the future. But this music is all the more effective for the contrast it creates when juxtaposed with the tender and lyrical love music that is finally allowed to dominate the score, and after the project was complete Truffaut wrote to Herrmann to say 'Thank you for humanizing my picture' (quoted in Thomas 1997, 194). Herrmann's respect for Truffaut was later eroded when the latter made alterations to the music track of *The Bride Wore Black*, parts of which the director felt to be too dark in mood – another reason why Hitchcock had rejected Mancini's Herrmann-tinged score to *Frenzy*.

Amongst Herrmann's final projects were his scores to De Palma's *Sisters* (UK title *Blood Sisters*, 1973) and *Obsession* (1975), the former receiving temporary tracks from the scores to *Psycho* and *Marnie*, and the latter temped with music from *Vertigo* specifically in order to influence the producers to hire Herrmann for the assignment. When Herrmann watched an initial screening of *Sisters* and heard the *Marnie* music issue from the temp track, he characteristically lost his temper: 'How can I think about anything new with that playing?' (quoted in S. Smith 1991, 321). *Obsession* proved to be so close in subject-matter and mood to *Vertigo* (and, since the plot commences in 1959, even in its historical setting) that it elicited music from Herrmann very similar in parts to his earlier Hitchcock score, with an admixture of the statuesque Gothic horror of *Cape Fear*. Most unusually for a mid-1970s thriller, much of the *Obsession* music is romantic and at times strongly redolent of the impressionism of Debussy: shimmering whole-tone harp music for a violent abduction might seem strangely old-fashioned, were it not for the director's desire to create a film directly imitating the lush visual style and obsessive love story of *Vertigo*, to which end both Herrmann's omnipresent score and the constantly diffused photography combine to create an almost fairy-tale sense of romantic nostalgia. De Palma so respected

Herrmann's opinion that he significantly shortened the screenplay at the composer's personal insistence in order that the film might have a more focused dramatic impact (De Palma 2002). While working on the Agatha Christie mystery *Endless Night* (dir. Sidney Gilliatt, 1971), Herrmann's long-standing interest in electronics led him to adopt the then cutting-edge Moog synthesizer at the suggestion of Howard Blake, who had assisted him with the jazz arrangements of *Twisted Nerve* (S. Smith 1991, 312). Herrmann later used the electronic instrument in *Sisters* and *It's Alive* (dir. Larry Cohen, 1974), though the perpetuation of traditional associations between electronic timbres and horror and psychological disturbance, and its use as a simple extension of acoustic timbres, were both somewhat conventional.

Herrmann's final score, for Martin Scorsese's *Taxi Driver* (1975), was imbued throughout with the claustrophobic expressionism the composer had sporadically exploited for De Palma. It also showcased a sultry blues theme (arranged by Christopher Palmer) that paid tribute to the longstanding cinematic tradition of using jazz to symbolize urban decay and corruption. Scorsese, who considered the project to be a 'dream-like . . . cross between a Gothic horror and the New York *Daily News*' (Thompson and Christie 1989, 54), praised Herrmann's success in establishing the fundamental psychological basis of the entire film, and the music's combination of jazz with sometimes violent modernistic elements seemed to presage a new direction in Herrmann's style – in part related to earlier experiments in fusing Latin dance rhythms with advanced harmonic and rhythmic techniques (as in the main-title music for *The Wrong Man*, the relentless fandango of the title sequence in *North by Northwest*, or the lilting but disquieting habañera that conjures up the aura of the deceased Carlotta in *Vertigo*). This fusion of the popular and avant-garde was another of Herrmann's enduring legacies to subsequent film composers. His health ailing at the *Taxi Driver* recording sessions, Herrmann nevertheless found the energy to suggest creative and innovative effects, such as the use of a reversed recording of a glockenspiel to soften the impact of a note played as a stinger (S. Smith 1991, 355).

Herrmann did not live long enough to score De Palma's *Carrie* (1976; music by Pino Donaggio), for which parts of the *Psycho* score were used as a temp track, but allusive snippets of the notorious shower-scene's violin screeches were retained in the finished film. The enduring power of his film music was later demonstrated by its retention in remakes of two of his films, *Cape Fear* (dir. Scorsese, 1991; music supervised by Elmer Bernstein) and the utterly pointless colour remake of *Psycho* (dir. Gus Van Sant, 1998; music supervised by Danny Elfman) – both representing an exceptionally rare phenomenon, since remakes usually aim to update the originals in all parameters. Contemporary allusions to, and plagiarisms of, his music are too numerous to list: amongst the wittiest are the knowing parodies of specific Herrmann exemplars in Alf Clausen's music to the long-running animated sitcom, *The Simpsons*, and music from *Psycho* occurs in Almodóvar's voyeuristic *Kika* (1993); one of the more recherché citations is Quentin Tarantino's use of the catchy whistled melody from *Twisted Nerve* in his *Kill Bill, Vol. 1* (2003). Herrmann's potent stylistic influence on Elfman and others is discussed in Chapter 12.

Perhaps even more important to younger composers than Herrmann's innovative compositional techniques was the realization that, with work of such consistent and uncompromising quality, film music had at last come of age. His commitments in the classical arena as both composer and conductor forced him to work on a strictly limited number of film projects, but he always approached his film commissions with undiminished artistic standards and refused to compromise those standards in the face of commercial pressure. His disgust at the motion-picture industry's refusal to accord film composers the respect and recognition he felt they deserved led to his resignation from AMPAS in 1967 in protest that film music continued to be categorized as a 'technical credit' and the giving of awards judged by mediocrities. Herrmann's influence thus persists both in terms of specific scoring techniques and in his almost mythical status as a composer with a stature sufficient to command the respect (not to say dread) of the directors with whom he worked. His cutting remarks on producers ('musical ignoramuses'), directors ('they really have no taste at all . . . I'd rather not do a film than have to take what a director says'), and even Hitchcock ('he only finishes a picture 60%: I have to finish it for him': quotations from Thomas 1997, 194, and R. S. Brown 1994, 148) may not have endeared him to the Hollywood moguls, but the steady stream of artistic successes produced by his stubbornness has ensured that he has remained a potent role model for a new generation of film composers. Herrmann felt music to be 'the communicating link between the screen and the audience, reaching out and enveloping all into one single experience' (1945), and in exploiting this link with such constant resourcefulness he showed how the composer, not the director, could sometimes be a film's true *auteur*.

Jazz and its influence

Jazz in the early sound cinema, and for several decades into the Hollywood Golden Era, was almost exclusively diegetic. Star performers made appearances on screen, as did Duke Ellington in *Black and Tan* and Bessie Smith in the all-black drama *St Louis Blues*, both directed by Dudley Murphy in 1929, but the tendency to restrict jazz to self-contained musical numbers in longer feature films facilitated the excision of any scenes featuring black performers when this was required by the sensibilities of white audiences in the USA. The boom in musicals brought with it an awareness that big names from the jazz world could provide a significant box-office attraction, and diegetic film work (including acting) was secured by many jazz performers from the 1930s onwards, with prominent appearances in feature films made by talents as diverse as Louis Armstrong, Hoagy Carmichael and Nat King Cole. Cartoons proved congenial to accompaniment by music in various jazz styles, especially in the 1940s – and the medium encouraged regrettable racial stereotyping – whilst easy-going symphonic jazz became explicitly associated with urban settings in live-action cinema. Genuine jazz performances were preserved as shorts, production of which flourished from as early as 1927: examples include *Rhapsody in Black and Blue* (dir. Aubrey Scotto, 1932), starring Armstrong, *Symphony in Black* (dir. Fred Waller, 1934), featuring Ellington and Billie Holiday, and the star-studded *Jammin' the Blues* (dir. Gjon Mili), produced by jazz entrepreneur Norman Granz and nominated for an Academy Award in 1944. In 1940–47, numerous three-minute 'soundies' were shot for reproduction on optical jukeboxes by the RCM Corporation in the USA.

Biopics devoted to celebrated white performers either featured the musicians themselves, as in the notoriously racist Paul Whiteman portrait *King of Jazz* (dir. John Murray Anderson, 1930) and *The Fabulous Dorseys* (dir. Alfred E. Green, 1947), or legendary players were impersonated by stars such as Robert Alda (as Gershwin in *Rhapsody in Blue*; dir. Irving Rapper, 1945), James Stewart (*The Glenn Miller Story*; dir. Anthony Mann, 1953), Steve Allen (*The Benny Goodman Story*; dir. Valentine Davies, 1955) and Sal Mineo (*The Gene Krupa Story*; dir. Don Weis, 1959). Biopics about black musicians came later, the best known being Cole's performance as W. C. Handy in *St Louis Blues* (dir. Allen Reisner, 1958) and Diana Ross's as Billie Holiday in *Lady Sings the Blues* (dir. Sidney J. Furie, 1972). The culmination of the jazz biopic was Clint Eastwood's labour of love, *Bird* (1988), starring Forest Whitaker as Charlie Parker, in which the largely diegetic music sometimes mixed the playing of modern sidemen with a solo saxophone track extracted from original recordings by Parker himself.

Meanwhile, jazz had continued to feature prominently as diegetic music in pictures narrating the exploits of fictional jazz musicians, such as *The Crimson Canary* (dir. John Hoffman, 1945) and *Young Man with a Horn* (dir. Michael Curtiz, 1950). The latter, starring Kirk Douglas and with trumpet playing dubbed by Harry James, was based on the life of Bix Beiderbecke and is seen by Krin Gabbard as emblematic of the many Hollywood jazz-inspired films that 'protect white subjectivity from the overwhelming black presence in the history of jazz' (Gabbard 1996, 67). More thoughtful in their treatment of racial and cultural issues were *A Man Called Adam* (dir. Leo Penn) and

Sweet Love Bitter (dir. Herbert Danska), both independent productions from 1966 that concerned black musicians and used jazz exclusively for their nondiegetic music tracks (Gabbard 1996, 89–93). Later fictional films set in and around jazz milieux include *New York, New York* (dir. Scorsese, 1977), *The Cotton Club* (dir. Francis Ford Coppola, 1984) and *Round Midnight* (dir. Bertrand Tavernier, 1986). The last featured Dexter Gordon as an anti-hero based on the characters of Bud Powell and Lester Young, together with Oscar-winning music by Herbie Hancock, partly performed live on set. The tradition of fictional jazz-set films continued with *The Fabulous Baker Boys* (dir. Steve Kloves, 1989), in which Dave Grusin's score included diegetic performances of standards by actress Michelle Pfeiffer, *Mo'Better Blues* (dir. Spike Lee, 1990) and *Kansas City* (dir. Robert Altman, 1995). In *Mo'Better Blues*, with music by Bill Lee and the Branford Marsalis Quintet, the choice of standards such as Ornette Coleman's 'Lonely Woman' and John Coltrane's 'A Love Supreme' to underscore appropriate dramatic moments (including a wedding), and Davis's 'All Blues' for a lovemaking scene, seemed scarcely an advancement on the gratuitous quotational signposting and equation of jazz with sex in much earlier narrative cinema.

A close identification between jazz and sordid low-life had been established during the silent era: a film entitled *Does the Jazz Lead to Destruction?* was made in Australia in 1919, for example, just two years after the first recordings of the Original Dixieland Jazz Band (B. Johnson 2002, 42). In black regions of American cities, movie theatres in this period had provided a valuable employment opportunity for African American musicians who could perform jazz within their own cultural milieu and without such associations: in her case-study of Chicago in this regard (Abel 1996, 234–62), Mary Carbine concluded that certain black artists nonetheless felt under considerable pressure to conform to musical practices that were considered 'proper', i.e. from the European classical tradition. From the 1940s onwards, the presence of jazz in film soundtracks habitually indicated alcoholism, drug addiction, crime, corruption, sleaze and sexual promiscuity, often in urban settings (see Butler 2002). W. C. Handy's 'St Louis Blues' had already been consistently applied as an emblem of female sexual transgression in a number of films starring Barbara Stanwyck in the 1930s (Stanfield 2005, 96). Eisenstein cited the French writer René Guilleré's view that the non-conventional structure of jazz directly accorded with the loss of familiar perspective in neon-lit modern nocturnal cityscapes, concluding that 'The modern urban scene, especially that of a large city at night, is clearly the plastic equivalent of jazz' (Eisenstein 1948, 82). This identification persisted well into the 1970s, as shown by Herrmann's jazz-tinged score for Scorsese's *Taxi Driver* – though David Butler has persuasively argued that the film's jazz references might also be viewed as a stylistic anachronism suggesting the alienation of the protagonist from his metropolitan surroundings (Butler 2002, 143).

But insalubrious or sexual associations, though they have been the most widely discussed, were by no means the only factor that propelled jazz into the movie limelight in the 1950s. Several composers viewed jazz as an ideal vehicle for American nationalism in music, and this sentiment resurfaced at a time when (as we have seen) modernism in film music was also on the increase. For film composers, jazz simultaneously satisfied both nationalistic and experimental creative urges. Although novel in the cinema, the potent conjunction of jazz, nationalism and modernism was far from new in American concert music. Back in the 1920s, Copland returned from his studies in Paris determined to build jazz elements into his compositions to create a new musical identity that other American composers could adopt, expressing in 1927 the hope that jazz would in time become 'the substance not only of the American composer's foxtrots and Charlestons, but of his lullabies and nocturnes' (quoted in Copland and Perlis 1984, 119). Copland's early symphonic jazz, best represented by *Music for the Theater* (1925) and the Piano Concerto (1926), was far bolder in conception than Gershwin's Broadway-rooted symphonic jazz, but in the 1930s Copland chose to abandon the marriage between jazz and concert music in favour of a more rarefied use of national folk materials, and it was the latter that informed his film scores. The development of symphonic jazz had meanwhile been spearheaded by Copland's protégé Leonard Bernstein, with works such as *Prelude, Fugue and Riffs* (written for Woody Herman) and the piano-and-percussion scherzo of his Second Symphony, *The Age of Anxiety*, both composed in 1949. As part of a spirited debate between Bernstein and Gene Krupa on the merits and demerits of symphonic jazz, published in the *Esquire Jazz Book* two years earlier, Bernstein declared that jazz had provided the 'serious composer' with a solution to 'the two problems of being original and of being American' (Gottlieb 1997, 781). As we have seen, however, when Bernstein made his solitary foray into film music with Elia Kazan's *On the Waterfront*, he followed Copland's example by avoiding nondiegetic jazz and cultivating an austere, and in his case more dissonant, orchestral idiom.

Kazan was also responsible for what is generally considered to be the first narrative feature to employ sustained and explicit jazz elements in its nondiegetic score: his adaptation of Tennessee Williams's play *A Streetcar Named Desire* (1951). The film's music was composed by Alex North, who demonstrated the insidious suggestiveness of jazz by creating a sultry musical idiom perfectly attuned to the drama's humid claustrophobia; the score was much admired by Miles Davis (Butler 2002, 103). The southern setting and proximity of the action to a diegetic jazz venue were obvious pretexts

for using jazz as a locational signifier, as had Alfred Newman in what Gabbard terms a 'culturally patronizing' scoring of Kazan's southern-set *Pinky*
two years earlier (Gabbard 1996, 134). But North's primary motivation
appears to have been nationalistic, for he declared that here was 'an opportunity to make music talk, and talk very much in the American musical
idiom of jazz, rather than to imitate the frequently overrated gods of music
in Europe, whose influence too frequently tends to dominate and stultify
American composers' (quoted in Henderson 2003, 98). Modernism was
clearly another germane impulse, North's score combining blues-tinged jazz
melodies and harmonies with increased dissonance levels, melodic angularity and economical chamber textures, thereby encapsulating four of the
most important film-scoring trends that increasingly asserted themselves
during the 1950s.

North's dissonant jazz idiom trod a designedly uncomfortable middle
ground between populism and modernism. His rawly expressionistic brand
of what he termed 'lowdown Basin Street blues' proved so potent in its sexual
suggestiveness that, where it coincided with close-ups of Stanley (Marlon
Brando) and Stella (Kim Hunter) in amorous mood, both visual images and
music had to be significantly toned down and re-edited in accordance with
the requirements of the Production Code; one music cue removed from this
scene had been conceived in the earthy, jungle style of Ellington (Henderson
2003, 113). Taking his hint from the play's stage directions, North attempted
on occasion to take the listener seamlessly from diegetic jazz played at the
local Four Deuces joint into the jazzy nondiegetic music that, along with
the surrealistic distortion of the naïvely simplistic 'Varsouviana' polka representing Blanche's delusions, are the most striking elements of the score.
The composer was conscious of the explicit link between jazziness and sensuality, annotating one passage in his manuscript with the label 'sexy, virile'
(Butler 2002, 98) and proceeding to associate a jazz motif with prostitutes
in his music for *The Rose Tattoo* (dir. Daniel Mann, 1955). The identification between jazz and the steaminess of Williams and the Deep South left
its mark on North's later scores for a trilogy of adaptations from William
Faulkner's novels: *The Long Hot Summer* (dir. Martin Ritt, 1958), *The Sound
and the Fury* (dir. Ritt, 1959) and *Sanctuary* (dir. Tony Richardson, 1961).
North later rejected a jazz idiom he had initially tried out for *Who's Afraid
of Virginia Woolf?* (dir. Mike Nichols, 1966), afraid that his film music was
becoming typecast; he also rejected an atonal idiom for the project before
alighting on a neo-baroque style. Meanwhile, the link between jazz and
alcohol-induced seduction was made most explicit of all in the film version
of Williams's *Cat on a Hot Tin Roof* (dir. Richard Brooks, 1958; uncredited
music by Charles Walcott), in which drinks trays and a glass seen in close-up
all reside on the gramophone/radio unit from which diegetic jazz emanates.

North's achievement in forging a stylistic hybrid with jazz at the forefront was paralleled in Otto Preminger's *The Man With the Golden Arm* (1955). Notorious for its frank treatment of the subject of heroin addiction, for which its Production Code Seal of Approval was withheld, its jazz-based score by Elmer Bernstein went further than North's by adopting a hotter big-band sound and utilizing the talents of West Coast jazzmen Shorty Rogers and Shelly Manne – both of whom appear in the film. Like North, Bernstein was motivated by a combination of nationalism, modernism and an awareness of the deep-seated emotive and associative power of jazz:

> The script had a Chicago slum street, heroin, hysteria, longing, frustration, despair and finally death. Whatever love one could feel in the script was the little, weak emotion left in a soul racked with heroin and guilt, a soul consuming its strength in the struggle for the good life and losing pitifully. There is something very American and contemporary about all the characters and their problems. I wanted an element that could speak readily of hysteria and despair, an element that would localize these emotions to our country, to a large city if possible. Ergo, – jazz.
>
> (quoted in Prendergast 1992, 109)

The film's main-title music – as in many seminal 1950s and 1960s features, set against stark graphic designs by Saul Bass – commences with a simple bass riff, swung cymbal rhythm and catchy head melody in hard-bop style; as the bass riffs mutate into a turbulently repetitive pattern, so the big-band brass superimpose their own frenetic riffs, both bass and upper strata of the texture repeatedly emphasizing the flattened blue fifth. This hot material is used throughout the film to represent the craving of the central character, would-be jazz drummer Frankie Machine (Frank Sinatra), for his next heroin fix; it climaxes in a number of screaming riff-based passages as each moment of injection approaches, after which the music relaxes. (The idea is essentially the same as Rózsa's in *The Lost Weekend*, where the theremin is exclusively associated with a craving for alcohol but not its actual consumption.) Bernstein also included cues composed in a non-jazz style for scenes between Frankie and his neurotic and emotionally dependent wife, using chamber-ensemble textures and, like his namesake, continuing to reveal the strong influence of Copland on this more classically oriented manner of scoring.

At a number of important points in the film, Bernstein deftly combines his jazz and non-jazz idioms. As the strings accompany an intimate domestic scene between Frankie and Zosh, the instruments subtly adopt jazz stylistic characteristics when Frankie talks about his addiction. Zosh, who is pretending to be wheelchair-bound, later grows frustrated with Frankie and is about to blow her emergency whistle after he has left her: because she is succumbing to her own craving (in her case, a pathological cry for attention), Bernstein reintroduces his jazz riffs but now in far darker tonal and instrumental garb, the stark sonic gesture lapsing as soon as she thinks better of it and – much to the spectator's surprise – gets up and walks to the window. Less striking but equally effective is the entirely natural way in which Bernstein picks up the rhythmic energy of Manne's diegetic drumming at the end of the disastrous audition scene, the trembling Frankie's precipitate exit from the rehearsal room being caught by nondiegetic music that seems to evolve naturally from the jazz idiom of Rogers' band. When Frankie's girlfriend Molly runs off, Bernstein combines nondiegetic drumming from Manne with poundingly dissonant solo-piano music and a frenetic pizzicato walking bass. It is at moments such as these that the film composer's appreciation of jazz as a quintessentially modern music is most obvious: it is not just a mindless response to stereotyped cultural and dramatic situations but a source of musical dynamism appropriate to the restlessness and *Angst* of the modern age. Central to the workability of the crossover styles created by North and Bernstein is the essential similarity between applications of the riff in jazz and of ostinato in much of the twentieth-century concert music in which their compositional styles were rooted, and common harmonic and rhythmic ground between the two idioms; again, the influence of Stravinsky (on both film composers and jazz musicians) was paramount. Bernstein returned to a jazz-inflected idiom for *Sweet Smell of Success* (dir. Alexander Mackendrick, 1957), featuring a diegetic appearance by the Chico Hamilton Quintet and highly unusual for its time in associating jazz with moral integrity in a story that was 'one of the American cinema's most unrelentingly negative portraits of US culture at the same time that it is one of the most flattering portraits ever of a [fictional] jazz musician' (Gabbard 1996, 128).

The Wild One (dir. Laslo Benedek, 1953), a Brando vehicle about untamed bikers which was banned in some regions because its thugs escape retribution, also demonstrated the close link between vernacular popular styles and modernism in its score by Leith Stevens. The film contains plentiful diegetic jazz played on jukeboxes whenever the Black Rebels Motorcycle Club descends: after they have finally left, there is a pointed shot of the jukebox now fallen silent. Diegetic music sometimes serves simultaneously as dramatic underscoring (one such cue, as Brando harasses a barmaid, even cadences at the last line of the scene), and similar up-to-date jazz is heard nondiegetically; when its source is not visible, it could be either diegetic or nondiegetic in origin. Significantly, Stevens's music track also includes aggressively dissonant material and an avant-garde nocturnal tone poem merging with the honking of the motorbikes' horns. Stevens's modernist

5.3 Left to right: director Otto Preminger and jazz musicians Billy Strayhorn and Duke Ellington at work on *Anatomy of a Murder* in 1959.

leanings were again evident in *Private Hell 36* (dir. Don Siegel, 1954), with its lean textures and near-atonal harmonic language allied to edgy, nervous riff-like interjections and prominent low-reed colourings – his style here well on the way to the distinctive type of urban big-band jazz developed by Henry Mancini and Lalo Schifrin (see below). The same director's *Crime in the Streets* (1956) saw Franz Waxman composing in his most modernistic vein, with explosive stingers and other dissonant rhetoric again allied to jazz elements such as violently energetic riffs, walking bass lines, stabbed percussive chords and sultry saxophone timbres. At one point, the predominant riff from the nondiegetic score disconcertingly migrates into the diegesis when sung by a youth as he listens to murderous plotting.

The category of 'anxiety jazz' identified by Butler is most strikingly to be heard in Johnny Mandel's score to *I Want to Live!* (dir. Robert Wise, 1958), a gritty anti-capital-punishment film relating the true story of an apparently innocent woman sent to the gas chamber, which opens with main-title riffs in the tradition of *The Man with the Golden Arm*. The condemned protagonist is an aficionada of modern jazz, which is the pretext for several diegetic jazz cues; but she is also associated with prostitution, sleaze and crime, and here jazz continues to fulfil its role as a signifier of the insalubrious. The director clashed with his producer about whether or not jazz was a 'decent' enough music to be used even in this context, though still had an eye to its commercial exploitation and was dissuaded from his plan to include a theme song (Butler 2002, 116–20, 129). West Coast performers such as Gerry Mulligan and Shelly Manne were prominent in both diegetic and nondiegetic cues, Mulligan's combo appearing on screen at the outset in a jazz-club setting filmed with angled cameras in the classic *film noir* manner. The music is strategically spotted so that once the protagonist is incarcerated she is no longer surrounded by the jazz sounds of her former milieu; and, in being forced to listen sporadically to them via the media of television, radio and gramophone, her isolation from the outside world is emphasized. Mulligan later appeared alongside other jazz talents in MGM's drama *The Subterraneans* (dir. Ranald MacDougall, 1960), a film for which Previn served as music director and later commented (with a surprisingly uncharacteristic vein of purism): 'Jazz, as an art form, was never designed to accompany anything, just as you can't expect visual action in a visual medium to be subservient to background music' (quoted in Fordin 1996, 502).

The first significant nondiegetic film music to be composed by African American musicians for a mainstream Hollywood feature was Duke Ellington's and Billy Strayhorn's score for Preminger's courtroom drama *Anatomy of a Murder* (1959). Although only a fraction of what they recorded made its way into the film's music track, their contribution is significant for generally avoiding the kind of cultural stereotyping formerly so prevalent in jazz scores, and for achieving an independence from slavish adherence to the visuals somewhat prophetic of musical developments in New Wave cinema of the 1960s (Cooke 2009). The night-time car drive immediately before the first court scene, for example, is underscored with an extended cue in which the band's cool-style parallel harmonies and fully rounded trumpet theme appear to pursue an autonomous and concentrated musical structure, as in any number of Ellington's earlier small-scale compositions; only when the mood darkens in conjunction with an optical fade-out at the end of the scene does the cue appear to have been conceived specifically to accompany the images.

Anatomy of a Murder also revealed Preminger's appreciation of the commercial potential of using a big-name jazz star. The soundtrack album from his *The Man With the Golden Arm* had been surprisingly successful, selling 100,000 copies – largely on the strength of its big-band music for the main titles, which is essentially similar in mood to the energetic blues, driven by the low reeds, in Ellington's main-title music to *Anatomy of a Murder*. By this time several Hollywood studios had begun to acquire subsidiary companies in the record business and independent record companies also routinely bid for the rights to issue soundtrack albums and spin-off singles. *The Man With the Golden Arm* spawned a successful song based on its score and performed by Sammy Davis Jr (Butler 2002, 146), while Ellington's main-title music for *Anatomy of a Murder* was released as both a stereo LP single and mono 45rpm single. That Preminger had a keen eye towards the profitability of record sales is shown by his receipt in 1960 of $250,000 from RCA Victor for the rights to the music for his film *Exodus*, the score for which (by Ernest Gold) won an Academy Award (J. Smith 1998, 46). There seems no convincing reason for Ellington to have made a personal appearance in *Anatomy* unless his visible presence on screen was intended to draw attention to his role in providing the film's music track. The pretext for jazz to figure prominently in the film's soundtrack is decidedly flimsy: the lawyer-protagonist has in the screenplay been turned into a jazz buff (which he is not in the novel by Robert Traver on which the film is based), this facet of his character explicitly referred to in the script to signify unorthodoxy in his character. We are told that his record collection spans 'from Dixieland to Brubeck'; and when he turns off a Dixieland record, asking his client's wife why lawyers aren't supposed to like music, she retorts, 'Well, not *that* kind of music!' His gratuitous reply is: 'Ah – I guess that settles it. I'm a funny kind of lawyer'. (This equation of jazz with unorthodoxy was somewhat behind the times: when confronted with pretentious jazz talk in *Jailhouse Rock* (dir. Richard Thorpe, 1957), Elvis Presley flees from the scene in a passionate rebellion against its exclusive elitism.) The lawyer plays solo jazz piano diegetically on two occasions, miming to pre-recorded Ellington tracks, the first neutral in tone and the second – in the recess before the verdict is pronounced – considerably more bluesy (on which occasion his sidekick moans 'Do you have to play that stuff?'). Ellington appears as jazz musician 'Pie-Eye', playing diegetically with his band as the locals dance to his music: the lawyer Biegler joins him in a brief snatch of piano duet, and the two characters engage in lame dialogue.

Later features scored by Ellington and Strayhorn included the jazz-milieu film *Paris Blues* (dir. Ritt, 1961), which featured source music recorded in advance so that the actors Paul Newman and Sidney Poitier could mime their performances to it, and nondiegetic cues geared towards conventional mood-enhancement and emotional intensification. The film included familiar Ellington standards in new arrangements, and a diegetic role for Armstrong. Ellington, who significantly received a credit in the film's theatrical trailer, had been attracted by the mixed-race romantic pairings of the film's draft scenario, though this aspect was eradicated in the final screenplay and a black saxophonist became a white trombonist, who is torn between his desire to be accepted as a jazz composer and his romantic involvement with a tourist. (For an imaginative but largely speculative interpretation of possible 'ambiguous messages' encoded in the score, which was nominated for an Academy Award, see Gabbard 1996, 202–3.) In the meantime, Charles Mingus had joined the growing ranks of African American film composers by supplying music for the far less conventional *Shadows* (dir. John Cassavetes, 1960) in which the spontaneous spirit of improvisation central to jazz became a clear metaphor for the improvisatory avant-garde filmmaking that was set to revolutionize cinema. Paradoxically, the attempt to provide spontaneous music for a movie featuring improvised dialogue made Mingus self-conscious and, according to his trombonist Jimmy Knepper, 'It came out very stiff 'cause it was written so precisely'; the music could as a result not be completed and recorded in a single studio date, as planned, so saxophonist Shafi Hadi was called in to improvise additional cues (Priestley 1982, 90–1).

By this time, French directors of the emerging *nouvelle vague* had taken a lead in foregrounding nondiegetic jazz in their soundtracks. Miles Davis, in his innovative but slender score to Louis Malle's film *Ascenseur pour l'échafaud* (1957), which was recorded in a single session (Carr 1998, 119), turned abstraction to his own creative advantage by exploring a modal manner of playing that would colour his tonal language for years to come. Although the apparently spontaneous improvisation in Davis's film score has been widely praised, it is intriguing to note the choice of wording in Davis's autobiographical account of the circumstances of the commission, in which he reports that Malle 'wanted me to write the musical score . . . I had never written a music score for a film before. I would look at the rushes of the film and get musical ideas to write down' (Davis and Troupe 1989, 207). This flatly contradicts Malle's recollection that the music was 'completely improvised; I don't think Miles Davis had had time to prepare anything' (French 1993, 19). Although the initial idea for using jazz in the film may have been because of its longstanding generic associations with crime thrillers and the *film policier*, Malle's intention to portray a cold and dehumanized world made the cool abstraction of Davis's modal playing singularly appropriate, and the music formed what the director termed an 'elegiac counterpoint' to the action. Referring to the separation of dramatic elements essential to the Brechtian concept of epic theatre, Brown notes that the music 'does not add substantially to our reading of *Ascenseur pour l'échafaud*, [and] it does tend to separate itself here and there, in a manner typical of French films of this period, as a parallel aesthetic component to the film's visual and narrative structures' (R. S. Brown 1994, 186). In a whole clutch of later French films, such as Jean-Luc Godard's *A bout de souffle* (*Breathless*, 1959), with its score by Martial Solal heavily based on a jazz lick reminiscent of Thelonious Monk, music came to be viewed as a more or less independent ingredient in the editorial mix – one that, in Godard's work in particular, might often be recorded in advance of the editing of the image track (and even composed without reference to the film's screenplay), then manipulated solely by directorial whim in the cutting room (see Chapter 8).

European cinema was quick to capitalize on the film-scoring potential of emotionally neutral small-ensemble jazz that tended towards abstraction, as shown by the collaboration in Poland between Roman Polanski and pianist Krzysztof Komeda, who also provided music for films by his compatriot Andrzej Wajda. In Polanski's *Knife in the Water* (1962), for example, Komeda's music is rarely used for dramatic pacing and tends to provide a sometimes incongruous distanciating effect. Davis's later film work, for example his contribution to the boxing film *Jack Johnson* (dir. William Cayton, 1970), lay firmly in the electronic realm of the innovative jazz-rock style he launched with his seminal Columbia fusion albums of 1968–9. An abstract manipulation of jazz cues more akin to Davis's work in *Ascenseur* is evident in scores as diverse as Ellingon's for *Anatomy of a Murder*, and of two films scored by John Lewis and the Modern Jazz Quartet. Lewis's coolly detached music for Roger Vadim's *Sait-on jamais* (*No Sun in Venice*), dating from the same year as *Ascenseur*, makes use of fugal techniques, regarded for centuries as among the most abstract of all structural strategies available to a composer. Lewis also scored *Odds Against Tomorrow* (dir. Robert Wise, 1959; see Butler 2009).

Other composers who exploited jazz elements include Neal Hefti, whose amiable Basie-derived style enlivened comedies such as *The Odd Couple* (dir. Gene Saks, 1967). The versatile Quincy Jones drew on jazz elements for crime films of both serious and comedic intent, including the sombre true-life Truman Capote story *In Cold Blood* (dir. Richard Brooks, 1967). Jones mixed pop and jazz elements in his score to *For Love of Ivy* (dir. Daniel Mann, 1968), and penned pulsating crime-caper scores with rock beats and electric instruments, for example in *Dollar$* (dir. Brooks) and *The Anderson Tapes* (dir. Sidney Lumet), both released in 1971, but soon afterwards left film scoring to work extensively in pop and television, partly from boredom with repetitive genre assignments but also frustration at the optical soundtrack's inability to record low-frequency sounds convincingly (Hasan 2001, 21): this had been a problem with the low-strings dominated score to *In Cold Blood*, a not altogether happy experience for Jones since the sound editor had responded to the director's dislike of a darkly descending cue by simply playing the recording backwards so it ascended (LoBrutto 1994, 17). Updated fusion and big-band idioms were to remain standard accompaniments to crime thrillers and TV detective series after they were first popularized by the work of Mancini and third-stream pioneer Schifrin.

Mancini's legendary themes for the TV series *Peter Gunn* (1958) and Blake Edwards's *Pink Panther* comedy movies (1963–93) have overshadowed his other more remarkable jazz-based scores, such as his music for the stylish updating of *film noir* conventions in Welles's *Touch of Evil* (1958), the soundtrack for which included evocative and sometimes nightmarish collages of different jazz styles emerging from nightclubs, heard in nocturnal street settings, rock'n'roll issuing from radios elsewhere, bass riffs in the nondiegetic score by turns threatening and violent, and Latin percussive elements (well suited to the Mexican setting) culminating in the murderous climax where supposedly diegetic big-band Latin jazz conveniently provides a dramatic stinger. In a later re-edited version, Mancini's main-title theme was excised by sound editor Walter Murch in accordance with Welles's original intention that there be no nondiegetic music in the film (Leeper 2001, 231; Mancini and Lees 1989, 78–9). In later scores, such as *Charade* (dir. Stanley Donen, 1963), Mancini showed unusual restraint in the scoring of action sequences, a telling use of solo vibraphone (a few notes on which, in a simple gesture later much imitated, can conjure up eerie, expectant or tense atmospheres), and the ability to move rapidly between jazz idioms and dissonant modernist gestures.

Schifrin is best known for his hard-driving signature tune to the TV series *Mission Impossible* (1966), in an urban-cool style with the same Latin jazz roots as Mancini's that also surfaced in Schifrin's music for the spirited TV detective series *Starsky and Hutch* (1975). For the big screen, Schifrin's cues to *Bullitt* (dir. Peter Yates, 1968) and *Dirty Harry* (dir. Don Siegel, 1971) and its sequels, though brief, covered similar ground, and their octatonicism – a scale shared both by twentieth-century classical composers and modern jazz musicians (who call it the 'diminished scale') – was a reminder of the composer's dual experiences as a composition pupil of Messiaen's at the Paris Conservatoire and as Dizzy Gillespie's regular pianist. (Schifrin later liked to recall that when Messiaen discovered his pupil was moonlighting in Paris jazz clubs, he immediately stopped talking to him.) Schifrin's modernist leanings, which included harsh dissonances and stabbing low-tessitura bass lines on piano for action sequences (also a feature of Goldsmith's action music), are well illustrated in the atonal jazz-rock of *Dirty Harry* – with its synthesized cluster chords, bubbling bass riffs, quartal harmony and effervescent drumming – and by his score to the Charles Bronson thriller *Love and Bullets* (dir. Stuart Rosenberg, 1978).

Only after the 1980s did jazz partly shed its longstanding aura of insalubrity. Respected as a viable art form, it could now be associated with images of refinement and good taste, as in *Indecent Proposal* (dir. Adrian Lyne, 1993), where a wealthy businessman hires Hancock to entertain his guests (Gabbard 1996, 102). More typically, it continued to be used as an agency for establishing period and cultural milieu, a straightforward example being the use of 1950s cool jazz in *L.A. Confidential* (dir. Curtis Hanson, 1997) where standards were selected both to suggest time and place and to mirror the emotions of the characters; cognoscenti would here enjoy the bit parts played by actors resembling cool icon Chet Baker and baritone saxophonist Gerry Mulligan. In many neo-*noir* thrillers, such as *Body Heat* (dir. Lawrence Kasdan, 1981) with its score by John Barry, a stereotyped saxophone-dominated jazz idiom is 'doubly anachronistic, for not only does it not appear in the noirs of the earlier period [1940s and 1950s] but its kind of smooth, sinuous and sultry "Midnight Jazz" is itself predominantly a product of the 1960s and later' (Dyer 2007, 124). For quasi-period ambience in *Quiz Show* (dir. Robert Redford, 1994), jazz trumpeter Mark Isham updated the 1950s big-band idiom by taking his inspiration from the more advanced post-Basie style of the Thad Jones–Mel Lewis orchestra, while for the neo-*noir* thriller *Romeo is Bleeding* (dir. Peter Medak, 1993) his music track incorporated a high degree of modern-jazz improvisation. A Davis-like muted trumpet and soprano saxophone were emblematic of loneliness and nostalgia respectively in Isham's jazz score for the Las Vegas comedy *The Cooler* (dir. Wayne Kramer, 2002), and at the turn of the century he remained one of the few Hollywood composers to engage creatively and consistently with a variety of jazz elements.

6 'Never let it be mediocre': film music in the United Kingdom

Although from the earliest days film music in Europe benefited from the close involvement of established composers of concert music, who often brought to their commissions a level of imagination and originality scarcely to be expected in the highly pressurized conveyor-belt production of film scores in Hollywood, this should not be taken to suggest that the European situation was particularly wholesome. In the UK, for example, the stigma attached to commercial composition blighted critical perceptions of a number of composers who worked regularly in film; those who simultaneously attempted to forge careers for themselves as symphonists, such as William Alwyn, Malcolm Arnold and Benjamin Frankel, inevitably suffered from an establishment view that they were somehow prostituting their art when they entered the film studio, or (even worse) that their concert works were merely pretentious film music. Although both Alwyn and Frankel wrote many fine symphonies, their concert music was destined to remain far less familiar than their film scores, and it was only posthumously in the 1990s that their serious compositions were widely recorded.

Before Benjamin Britten (whose early career in documentaries is examined in Chapter 7) quit film work and embarked wholeheartedly on his concert-music career, he wrote to his publisher in December 1937 about the inclusion of his music in a forthcoming radio series devoted to film scores to say 'I have about ten volumes of film music to my credit (if it be credit!) . . . I think this is worth bothering about because it is quite good publicity, & I'm always being told that I should bother about that kind of thing!' (Mitchell and Reed 1991, 535–6). In response to a questionnaire about his film work sent to him during his stay in New York in 1940–41, Britten went so far as to say 'I don't take film music seriously qua music' (Kildea 2003, 28). David Kershaw attributes attitudes such as these partly to 'British snobbery about the perceived lowly status of film composition, an attitude unfortunately shared by some composers who regarded such work as a well-paid chore necessary to buy time for "serious" music' (Kershaw 1995, 130). The harsh reality was that a career in film music was, and remains, one of the few genuinely lucrative options open to aspiring full-time composers, whether in Britain or elsewhere. Leading British composers, from Arthur Bliss and William Walton to Richard Rodney Bennett, confessed that the handsome fees paid for film work were the major incentive persuading them to embark upon it. Some British composers responded half-heartedly to the challenge of composing for films, but many made significant contributions to the art of film scoring – to the extent that the article on film music in the fifth edition of *Grove's Dictionary of Music and Musicians* (Irving *et al.* 1954) could, somewhat perversely and chauvinistically, ignore the work of all Hollywood composers with the exceptions of Herrmann and Copland, both of whose work conformed to the tenets of autonomous musical structuring that were clear desiderata of the article's authors.

Before the 1930s, cinemas in Britain were dominated by Hollywood movies, but the numerical balance between domestic productions and imported film entertainment became strictly regulated after the passing of the Cinematograph Film Act by Parliament in 1927; thereafter, domestic production doubled in just one year. Sound-on-film technology was embraced more quickly than anywhere else in the world outside America, with 63 per cent of cinemas in the UK wired for sound by the end of 1930 (Weis and Belton 1985, 27). Helped by the dip in Hollywood's fortunes during the Depression, the British film industry flourished in the early 1930s and, by 1937, the country was well established as the second-largest film producer in the world – some of its products standing up well internationally to American competition (D. Cook 2004, 291). This success was checked by the onset of the Second World War, by which time many British films – the so-called 'quota quickies' – had been produced specifically as B-movies designed both to accompany the screening of more lavish American imports in double bills and to keep the British film industry solvent in the face of the daunting transatlantic competition.

British cinema in the early 1930s achieved a seriousness of purpose through the hard work of Hungarian producer Alexander Korda (né Sándor Kellner), who founded London Films in 1932 and two years later hired Muir Mathieson as his youthfully energetic musical director. Film music in the UK was subsequently nurtured by the strenuous attempts of Mathieson to secure the services of front-rank composers who possessed an innate understanding of the filmic medium; according to film critic C. A. Lejeune, 'to him, the alliance of image and sound is something of a burning mission' (quoted in Huntley [1947], 34). Mathieson himself commented:

> Music is and always must be a vital part of film art . . . Music can help to humanise the subject and widen its appeal. Music can make a film less intellectual and more emotional. It can influence the reaction of the audience to any given sequence . . . It can develop rhythmic suggestions from words. It can carry ideas through dissolves and fade-outs. It can prepare the eye through the ear. It can merge unnoticeably from realistic

> sound into pure music. It can shock. It can startle. It can sympathise. It can
> sweeten. But for the love of mike, never let it be mediocre.
>
> (quoted in Huntley [1947], 163)

Similar zeal was shown by music directors at rival studios, principally Louis
Levy, a former silent-film conductor who worked at Gaumont–British, and
Ernest Irving, who moved from pit work in London's West End to Ealing,
where he became musical director in 1931. Producer Michael Balcon had
interests both at Gaumont and Ealing, where he became production chief in
1938, and was another important entrepreneur committed to quality film
production; later, in the 1940s, this mantle passed squarely to the business
interests of J. Arthur Rank. Rank's famous trademark image of two imposing
strokes on a huge dimpled gong (in reality made of cardboard, the strokes
overdubbed by percussionist James Blades on a comparatively tiny instrument) was incorporated into main-title music by several composers, most
ingeniously by Alwyn; the icon is lampooned in Rank's production *Carry
On Up the Khyber* (see below) when the Kasi (Kenneth Williams) is interrupted by a servant hitting a dinner gong and irritably declares: 'I do wish
he wouldn't keep doing that. Rank stupidity!'

The 1930s witnessed notable experiments in documentary film, in which
many distinguished composers were involved (see Chapter 7), and an accelerating production of feature films which, if rather stage-bound, were often
distinguished by fine acting. At first nondiegetic musical cues in feature films
were few and far between, as was the case in Hollywood at this time: Korda's
The Private Life of Henry VIII (1933; music by Kurt Schroeder), for example, has main- and end-title music but only one substantial nondiegetic cue,
poorly recorded and used to create continuity across several disparate shots
that culminate in a kiss underlined by a harp glissando. When the Australian
composer Arthur Benjamin scored the London Films production of *The
Scarlet Pimpernel* (dir. Harold Young, 1934), his music was almost entirely
restricted to the main and end titles and to pastiche period dance music
for diegetic use, some of it handled decidedly unrealistically – as when the
passage of time depicted by the library clock indicates that the band has
apparently been playing the same piece for at least 90 minutes. Hitchcock's
The 39 Steps (1935) contained minimal nondiegetic cues; the various composers involved were uncredited, but one was Hubert Bath, who had been
responsible for adding synchronized music to the same director's *Blackmail*
in 1929. Benjamin also scored the original version of Hitchcock's thriller *The
Man Who Knew Too Much* (1934) for Levy at Gaumont; this film featured no
nondiegetic music but used Benjamin's *Storm Clouds Cantata* prominently
for its assassination scene at a concert in the Royal Albert Hall. As might be
expected from Hitchcock, the film deployed other types of diegetic music

to dramatic effect, including the incongruous use of an organ to cover the din of what a local policeman terms 'disorderly behaviour in a sacred edifice' and the radio broadcast of the climactic concert underscoring a scene featuring the master criminal, who is listening in to learn the outcome of his fiendish scheme. The sound of the fatal gunshot was intended to have been drowned out by a cymbal crash in Benjamin's cantata: as the crook wryly puts it when briefing his hitman with the aid of a gramophone recording prior to the event, 'I think the composer would have appreciated that'. (When Hitchcock shot his generally inferior colour remake of the film in 1956, Benjamin's cantata – now reproduced with six-track stereo technology – was again used at the film's climax in a sequence affording a glimpse of Herrmann at work on the conductor's podium, directing the London Symphony Orchestra. As Brown notes, 'In both versions the villains control the music to such an extent that they even have a recording of it and are even able to miraculously put the tone-arm needle down at exactly the point of the four climactic notes' (R. S. Brown 1994, 78). For a comparison of the two versions, see Wierzbicki 2003.) Benjamin's later film work was praised for the clarity of its often chamber-like instrumentation, designed to gain maximum effect from the rather limited recording technology at his disposal: 'he considers it unnecessary to use an orchestra of more than about twenty players, and he is right: well-orchestrated music needs no mammoth body of players' (London 1936, 216).

The 1930s also saw debut film scores from Alwyn, Richard Addinsell (whose popular *Warsaw Concerto* is discussed in Chapter 11 in the context of British cinema's singular love-affair with the romantic piano concerto in the 1940s), Jack Beaver, Bliss, Britten and John Greenwood. Britten's work was mainly concentrated in documentary production, but in 1936 he scored his only feature film, *Love from a Stranger* (dir. Rowland V. Lee), an Agatha Christie mystery, afforded Britten few opportunities for imaginative cues, since most of his music was to be concentrated in the first half of the film in which little of interest occurs: this is a good illustration of a tendency, still prevalent in the industry, for music to be relied upon to bolster weaker scenes. Britten's most inventive cue, though very brief, occurs when scales played by a child on the piano are surrealistically distorted to portray her teacher's mounting shock when learning of a lottery win. Britten's score was conducted by Boyd Neel, who divided his time between film and concert work with the London Philharmonic Orchestra and was a significant champion of the young composer's work; other British conductors, including Hubert Clifford, would later juggle film careers with work in broadcasting.

An early high point in film scoring was reached with Bliss's score to H. G. Wells's science-fiction tale, *Things to Come* (dir. William Cameron

Menzies, 1935), recorded by members of the LSO conducted by the 24-year-old Mathieson in a marathon of fourteen studio sessions (Morrison 2004, 177). At Wells's insistence, music was recorded before shooting began and Bliss's score was therefore 'not intended to be tacked on; it is a part of the design' (Huntley [1947], 39). The opening medley on Christmas carols is disarmingly conventional, though anempathetic in the context of the scenes of war-scaremongering it accompanies. As tangible preparations are made for war, Bliss supplies an acerbic and modernistic march which reaches a terrifying climax as panic invades the streets, the music cutting off at its loudest point when anti-aircraft guns explode into life. Bleak scoring accompanies the ensuing passage-of-time montage, this and later cues largely athematic and based on ostinati. The futuristic scenes set in the 1960s in the aftermath of an apocalyptic global war, like the stop-time animation in *King Kong*, demanded strongly characterized music if the special effects were not to be felt risible, and Bliss's music may be considered largely responsible for the overall success of the film's impact. After extracts from *Things to Come* were performed at the 1935 Promenade Concerts, Bliss's music became popular both in the concert hall and through sales of a recording by the LSO, setting a trend for concert versions of British film scores from which Walton, Vaughan Williams and others later benefited. Interest in film music outside its original context was further stimulated by a series of six special radio broadcasts mounted by Mathieson in 1938, and in the meantime the players of the LSO and other leading orchestras had enjoyed a rise in session work, their involvement in film soundtracks having a palpable impact on performance standards.

Unscrupulous producers knew the value of a prestigious name such as the LSO's and used it without authorization even when only a handful of players in an ad hoc studio band hailed from the orchestra, a practice which resulted in sustained action from the LSO's management in 1935–7 (Morrison 2004, 177). The quality of British film music at this time did not go unremarked in the American press. The film critic of the *New York Herald Tribune* declared of Anthony Collins's score to *Victoria the Great* (dir. Herbert Wilcox, 1937), recorded by Mathieson and the LSO: 'the British take their film music seriously and despite the fact that American screen music has been improving at a rapid pace, no permanent symphonic ensemble in the US has yet the record in the screen world that the English group has' (quoted in Huntley [1947], 43). The LSO's film work again came to international prominence decades later when they recorded the music for *Star Wars* in 1977, their involvement a direct result of the personal connection between their then music director (André Previn) and the film's composer John Williams (see Chapter 12).

Visitors from abroad

As in Hollywood, early British film music was boosted by contributions from foreign visitors and expatriates. Examples included the Viennese composer Hans May; the Russians Nicholas Brodszky and Mischa Spoliansky, the latter renowned for his mickey-mousing; the Hungarians Matyás Seiber, who specialized in animation (see Chapter 7), and Miklós Rózsa; the German Walter Goehr, whose best-known score was for *Great Expectations* (dir. David Lean, 1946); and the Frenchman Georges Auric. The most influential of these internationally was Rózsa, who moved to the USA with Korda during the war and, after settling there in 1941, became one of the most important composers in Hollywood (see Chapter 3).

Rózsa's compositional technique was formidable, having been honed through studies at the Leipzig Conservatory in the 1920s, and he was already making a reputation for himself as a concert composer when he became interested in film music – and the income that came with it – as a result of a chance conversation with Honegger in Paris and hearing the French composer's score to *Les Misérables* the next day. Rózsa wrote his first film score for London Films' *Knight Without Armour* (dir. Jacques Feyder, 1937). Impressed by this debut, Korda gave his compatriot a formal contract with the production company and Rózsa quickly provided a new score, for *The Four Feathers* (1939; directed by Korda's younger brother, Zoltan), which featured a memorable cue depicting the onset of sunstroke in the desert with dissonances set against a hammered-out mid-texture pedal point, and which in places looked ahead to the darkly sweeping lyricism of the composer's *film noir* scores.

In *That Hamilton Woman* – one of Alexander Korda's trademark period dramas, released in 1941 and known in Britain at the time by the more genteel title *Lady Hamilton* – Rózsa showed himself to be a competent exponent of stock film-music techniques such as thematic allusion, including the almost obligatory 'Rule, Britannia' to accompany exterior shots of Nelson's warships, and two other stalwart quotations from the silent era: a triumphant variation on the *Dies irae* for the tolling victory bells and a suitably threatening version of the *Marseillaise* played by snarling muted brass as the French ships appear at Trafalgar. Rózsa also produced rousingly patriotic music, drawing on the idiom of Elgar and Walton, for the propagandist sections of the film, as when Hamilton makes his pro-commonwealth and anti-dictator speech (clearly suggesting parallels between Napoleon and Hitler), and when the Royal Navy famously runs up the flags spelling out the injunction 'England expects every man to do his duty'. But Rózsa also demonstrated rare ingenuity of a kind that would distinguish his later Hollywood work.

His manner of underscoring dialogue was both economical and unobtrusive, as at the beginning of the film when the downfallen Emma Hamilton is incarcerated in a French jail: her accompaniment is a simple tremolo pedal note from the strings, against which is set a pair of dissonant repeating dyads. (Such dialogue scoring became distilled in Rózsa's *film noir* work in the 1940s, when he was often called upon to write atmospheric music beneath the voice-overs that are such an essential part of the genre: see Chapter 3.) His melodic style, with its characteristic sweeping triplet figurations followed by plunging leaps downwards, was also readily recognizable at this stage of his career, as was his prominent use of a solo violin for intimate expressiveness.

The most elaborate of Rózsa's early scores was that to *The Thief of Bagdad* (dir. Michael Powell *et al.*, 1940), for which he received an Academy Award nomination; according to Christopher Palmer, it 'has a wonderful freshness and agelessness, a childlike spirit of enchantment and wonder . . . It glimmers in our consciousness like a fairy castle in the distance' (Palmer 1990, 190–1). As part of his lavish orchestral palette for this project, Rózsa had intended to include an early electric instrument, the ondes martenot; unfortunately its French inventor, Maurice Martenot, was caught up in the hostilities on the Continent and Rózsa recalled that he 'wrote back, from the Maginot Line, that he was very sorry he couldn't come but he was defending his country' (quoted in Prendergast 1992, 69). It was the necessity to complete the production of *The Thief of Bagdad* in Hollywood after the outbreak of the European war that compelled Rózsa's relocation to the USA, where he continued to work for the Kordas and reprised his exotic fantasy style in Zoltan's *The Jungle Book* (1942); Rózsa again received an Academy Award nomination, for a score that became popular in recorded and concert form (Rózsa 1982, 112). He found it difficult to adjust to the American practice – enforced by union regulations – of employing professional orchestrators, as in England only Richard Addinsell (whom he described as a 'dilettante') enjoyed that particular luxury; as a special concession, Rózsa was allowed to complete the orchestration of *The Thief of Bagdad* himself, but was forced to use an orchestrator for *That Hamilton Woman*: 'It was terrible. I had to redo the whole thing' (interviewed in R. S. Brown 1994, 278–9). Thereafter, all his Hollywood scores were orchestrated by others according to his short-score directions, following standard industry practice.

Although unfairly criticized by chauvinistic commentators for not being British by either birth or temperament, Auric nonetheless made a vital contribution to the growth of film music in the UK. His film apprenticeship had been served as a member of the Parisian avant-garde, during which time he composed several scores for cutting-edge directors such as Clair and Cocteau (see Chapters 2 and 8). His first British score was for the compendium chiller *Dead of Night* (dir. Cavalcanti *et al.*, 1945), for which the music had to be relayed to London from Paris as it was composed. He then scored Gabriel Pascal's lavish version of George Bernard Shaw's *Caesar and Cleopatra* (1945), which proved to be by far the most expensive British production of its time. In keeping with his megalomaniac ambitions, Pascal had longed to secure the services of a major composer to write the music for his epic, at first toying with the idea of inviting Prokofiev. Next he tried Walton, Bliss and Britten, all of whom declined. Britten had by this time decided not to return to film work for artistic reasons (he rejected all later overtures from producers, including one from Disney in 1956), his publisher noting that Britten disliked Shaw's script, but that his principal concern was that 'in doing it he would accomplish absolutely nothing towards the solution of his own problem[s] as a composer . . . He said that the money did not interest him' (quoted in Mitchell and Reed 1991, 1122). Britten wrote to his publisher in New York in December 1945: 'I expect you'll find Hollywood jubilant over the resounding flop of Caesar & Cleopatra! Something tells me I was wise to steer clear of that little picture. Anyhow that world is not for me' (Mitchell and Reed 1991, 1287). Britten had been partly responsible for bringing Auric to the attention of British musicians, and may have had a hand in securing him the Pascal commission. In any case, Pascal had previously employed Honegger to compose for his earlier Shaw project, *Pygmalion* (1938), and there were other Gallic connections in the British film industry at the time – Francis Chagrin had composed many film scores in Paris in 1934–7 before moving to Britain, Cavalcanti had collaborated in France with composers such as Jaubert, and so on – so the choice of Auric was natural enough. For *Caesar and Cleopatra*, Auric showed himself adept at three basic idioms (the sombrely epic, lushly exotic and downright romantic), and demonstrated considerable refinement in his beautiful diegetic harp music for the women's intimate scene in the royal palace. The style here was reminiscent of Satie who, as we saw in Chapter 1, composed experimental film music in the 1920s, but the air of modernistic detachment was not to all British tastes. Of the contrastingly grandiose moment when Caesar's galley departs, Shaw himself declared: 'Auric's music touches greatness. It is almost Handelian' (Huntley [1947], 81).

Auric's best-known British film scores are those he provided for the popular series of Ealing comedies, which were launched with *Hue and Cry* (dir. Charles Crichton, 1946). The witty bustle of the music for the graffiti-inspired title sequence was typical of a composer who was a member of Les Six, and proved to be ideal for the action sequences of the Ealing assignments. (For an opposing view, see Swynnoe 2002, xv, 170–2; a more balanced critical assessment of music in various Ealing comedies is offered in Daubney 2006.) An excellent example of Auric's ability to create contrasting musical characters with a minimum of fuss comes when we see two boys on the ground looking up at an apartment at the top of a high building: when sharing the point of view of the boys, the music is easy-going and elegant, but when the point of view shifts to the reverse shot (clearly representing the mysterious occupant of the apartment gazing down on the tiny figures below) the music darkens suggestively without drawing undue attention to itself. Such qualities are seen in Auric's other Ealing scores, including *Passport to Pimlico* (dir. Henry Cornelius, 1949) – the subject-matter of which cried out for a mixture of French and British elements – and *The Titfield Thunderbolt* (dir. Crichton, 1952). The latter, the first Ealing comedy to be shot in colour, is spotted with notable economy, and the music depicting the village folk pushing a railway carriage along by hand captures the effort involved with a minimum of notes. Other Ealing comedies were scored by Frankel, Tristram Cary and Irving himself. Irving adapted Scottish folksongs for use in *Whisky Galore* (US title *Tight Little Island*; dir. Mackendrick, 1948), and made a dark adaptation of a Mozartean idiom for *Kind Hearts and Coronets* (dir. Robert Hamer, 1949), after some resistance from the film's producers who felt the idea to be overly provocative (Huntley 2002). Cary's nondiegetic score for *The Ladykillers* (dir. Mackendrick, 1955) made ingenious use of the famous melody from a string quintet by Boccherini, played on a gramophone record diegetically to provide an alibi for a gang of crooks supposedly rehearsing the piece in their lodgings.

In the same year as he scored *The Titfield Thunderbolt*, Auric provided music for John Huston's *Moulin Rouge*, a project much more serious in tone, but still eliciting from the composer his characteristic balance between Satie-like naïvety and warm romanticism. Two notable cues were the harmonically elusive treatment of a pizzicato ostinato for the opening intertitles (an inventive response to the challenge of providing neutral background music), and the extended section in which Toulouse Lautrec attempts to gas himself, the music building from giddily revolving ostinato patterns to a triumphant climax as his inspiration suddenly returns and he emerges from his self-imposed isolation. Among Auric's later credits was a score to a suitably creepy film version of Henry James's *The Turn of the Screw*, directed by Jack Clayton under the title *The Innocents* (1961).

Ralph Vaughan Williams

Vaughan Williams, the doyen of English musical nationalism in the first half of the twentieth century, made a significant contribution to the art of film scoring. Like many of his younger contemporaries, this impulse was nurtured by a desire to contribute to British film propaganda during the Second World War, considered at the time as 'new developments in the cinema world, now geared to wartime needs of entertainment and factual reporting of the battle fronts' (Huntley [1947], 227). Propagandist films, known in the euphemism of the day as films 'of national importance', were given mandatory screenings at cinemas across the country. At the instigation of Mathieson, Vaughan Williams launched his film career with a score for *49th Parallel* (US title *The Invaders*; dir. Powell, 1941), a pseudo-documentary yarn about German submariners stranded in Canada which won an Academy Award for its original story by Emeric Pressburger. Vaughan Williams's score, which Mathieson recorded with the LSO, suggested a deep affinity with the medium. His music was at its expansive best in capturing the grandeur of the opening aerial shots of snow-capped mountains; most of the important cues were reserved for exterior shots in rural or maritime locations, in which the music could come to the fore without compromising other parameters of the production. The stark use of the Lutheran chorale melody *Ein' feste Burg* ('A Stronghold Sure') for the U-boat when it first surfaces, and subsequent developments of the chorale's simple head-motif, were the only parts of the score that made obvious deference to conventional leitmotivic techniques.

Vaughan Williams's second score, for the rousing documentary *Coastal Command* (dir. J. B. Holmes, 1942), made a strong impression on the staff of the Crown Film Unit who recorded it: 'we knew that here was something great, something, indeed finer and more alive than any music we had ever had before ... On the rare occasions when the music was slightly too long or too short to match the existing picture, then it was the visual material which suffered the mutilation' (Ken Cameron, quoted in Huntley [1947], 111). Other wartime documentaries with scores by Vaughan Williams included *The People's Land* and *The Story of a Flemish Farm* (dir. Jeffrey Dell; both 1943) and *Stricken Peninsula* (dir. Paul Fletcher, 1945). While writing the music for *Flemish Farm*, some of which was performed at the 1945 Promenade Concerts, Vaughan Williams's attention to detail led him to interpolate frequent bars of just one quaver's duration in order to compensate for the timings in fractions of seconds with which he was presented by the cue sheet. As Mathieson commented, 'It had the effect of "God Save Our (1/8) G-Gracious Queen"' (quoted in Kennedy 1980, 259). Two unused themes from this score later found their way into the composer's Sixth Symphony, completed in 1947. In the same year, he scored the film *The Loves of Joanna Godden* (dir. Charles Frend), for which he faced the challenge of composing music to accompany an outbreak of foot-and-mouth disease and the consequent burning of sheep.

Scott of the Antarctic (dir. Frend, 1948) proved to be Vaughan Williams's most famous film score, partly because it also became popular in a concert version – in this case the *Sinfonia Antartica*, first performed five years after the film's release. Irving, responsible for the final music editing, found the composer's responses to the imagery so consistent that he could relocate cues with ease: 'For instance, the music composed for the main titles . . . exactly fitted the climbing of the Glacier and stopped with a shuddering roll on the bass drum as the party reached the very edge of the fathomless crevasse – one more crotchet would have swallowed up the whole expedition!' (Irving 1959, 176). Similar wit is encountered in Irving's versified injunction that Vaughan Williams should not compose wordless vocal music to compete with dialogue:

> I very much regret to state
> your scheme for treating number 8
> has pulled us up with quite a jerk
> because we fear it will not work.
>
> Miss Mabel Ritchie's off-stage tune
> besides annoying Miss Lejeune,
> would cover, blur, confuse and fog
> our most expensive dialogue.
>
> (Vaughan Williams 1987, 258–9)

If Irving's attitude towards Vaughan Williams's music at times seems somewhat cavalier, it is important to note that the composer had a deep respect for his experience in the cinema, and pointedly dedicated the score of *Sinfonia Antartica* to him. As Vaughan Williams had advised would-be film composers in 1945:

> you must not be horrified if you find that a passage which you intended to portray the villain's mad revenge has been used by the musical director to illustrate the cats being driven out of the dairy. The truth is that within limits any music can be made to fit any situation. An ingenious and sympathetic musical director can skilfully manoeuvre a musical phrase so that it exactly synchronizes with a situation which was never in the composer's mind.
>
> (Vaughan Williams 1987, 162)

Irving and Vaughan Williams had nonetheless been careful, before setting to work on *Scott of the Antarctic*, to draw up a legal agreement to cover the use of the music in the film. Irving had suggested to the composer that the contract 'should include a stipulation that alterations must receive your consent or mine, and that no third person should be brought in to amplify or replace your work', later adding (via his solicitor) that he would respect Vaughan Williams's wishes 'down to the last tail on the last quaver and that this time I shall not arrange any carols for the penguins, but leave it to him' (quoted in Kennedy 1980, 297).

Vaughan Williams was one of the few major concert composers who felt that film music had an aesthetically significant future ahead of it, and this positive attitude must in part have been a response to the unusually high level of respect and deference shown towards him by those in the film industry with whom he worked, which permitted him (like Korngold) such luxuries as reading scripts well in advance of shooting. His optimistic thinking was expressed in an article entitled 'Composing for the Films' (containing the extract quoted above), in which he famously remarked that 'the film contains potentialities for the combination of all the arts such as Wagner never dreamt of' (Vaughan Williams 1987, 162). He identified two principal approaches to film scoring: the first was mickey-mousing, which 'requires great skill and orchestral knowledge and a vivid specialized imagination, but often leads to a mere scrappy succession of sounds of no musical value in itself'; the second 'is to ignore the details and to intensify the spirit of the whole situation by a continuous stream of music' (Vaughan Williams 1987, 161). The second approach was, on the composer's own admission, his preferred manner of working, although it could lay the composer open to the criticism levelled by Hans Keller against the score for *Scott*, which he felt 'tends to interpret monotony by monotony' (Irving *et al.* 1954, 99).

Several other British films with high-profile music tracks were released in 1948. David Lean's interpretation of Dickens's *Oliver Twist* featured a score by (as his screen credit put it) 'Sir Arnold Bax, D.Mus., Master of the King's Music'. Having previously only scored a single documentary, *Malta G.C.* (dir. Eugeniusz Cekalski and Derrick De Marney, 1942), Bax had scant film experience, and initially found himself disliking Dickens's subject-matter intensely, calling the Lean commission 'a very thankless task as there is no music in the subject. I cannot imagine any subject more unsuited to me' (quoted in Parlett 1999, 257). Lean was highly prescriptive about the music he required, and must take the credit for the dubious decision to portray Oliver's isolation by use of a solo piano (Swynnoe 2002, 65–7). Predictably competent, and often well characterized, Bax's score is solid enough but generally unimaginative in its deployment of stock devices such as stingers, mickey-mousing and over-stretched leitmotifs; the overly sensuous music heard as Oliver lies quietly in Mr Brownlow's bedroom tells us far more about Bax's stylistic preoccupations than anything of direct relevance to the dramatic situation.

Brian Easdale, William Alwyn and Benjamin Frankel

Also from 1948 dates Brian Easdale's extraordinary score to *The Red Shoes*, directed by Powell and Pressburger. One of the most important British directors of his generation, Powell had formerly taken a traditional view of music's supporting role in filmed drama, occasionally playing recorded music during filming to inspire his actors in the silent-film tradition, but wherever possible involving his composers at an early stage in production so that they had ample time to absorb the needs of a particular project. Some strain was placed on his creative relationship with Pressburger (who, like the Kordas, was Hungarian) when Powell declined to employ Rózsa to score *Contraband* in 1940 in the belief that insufficient English composers were entering film scoring, and opted to commission a score from Addinsell instead (Powell 1986, 341). (He seemed less concerned about this in 1956, when he and Pressburger commissioned a folk-tinged score from Greek composer Mikis Theodorakis for the wartime adventure *Ill Met by Moonlight*, though for that project a local Cretan flavour was of paramount importance; in 1964, Theodorakis went on to pen the archetypical Cretan film score, for Michael Cacoyannis's *Zorba the Greek*.) For a time Powell's favoured composer was Allan Gray, who scored the unusual black-comedy wartime romance *The Life and Death of Colonel Blimp* (1943) with a wide range of stock idioms and up-to-date swing, and to whose work on *A Canterbury Tale* (1944) and *A Matter of Life and Death* (1946) the director paid warm tribute – even taking the unusual step of including brief music examples from Gray's score to the latter in his autobiography (Powell 1986, 533). But Gray's preliminary work on *The Red Shoes* was rejected by Powell as inadequate, and Easdale was called in to provide a replacement score at short notice, having already scored Powell's highly acclaimed *Black Narcissus* (1947) because in that film the director had felt Gray's abilities were not up to Powell's confessed aim of creating an 'operatic' effect in which music and image would be indissolubly fused.

Seeking a highly skilled composer who also happened to be versed in Indian music, Powell was encouraged to contact Easdale on the recommendation of fellow director Carol Reed. Powell recalled his thinking at the time:

> Allan Gray . . . had a keen ear for a tune and wrote all his own orchestrations. His main gift was a dramatic one. He had the capacity to enter into the idea of a scene or a situation, but it was still film music in the traditional way, applied on, as it were, mixed into the sound-track and the dialogue of the actors, like the rich glazing on a ham. I wanted someone with a more creative approach. I wanted someone who was my superior in musical thought, a collaborator who would lead me out of my depth and whom I could tempt even further out of his. I wanted collaborators who were the best in Europe and I wanted a continuous argument with them. Nothing else seemed to me to justify the kind of work that went into making a film . . .

> In *Black Narcissus*, I started out almost as a documentary director and
> ended up as a producer of opera, even though the excerpt from the opera [a
> short sequence which Powell referred to as 'my first composed film'] was
> only about twelve minutes long. Never mind! It was opera in the sense that
> music, emotion, image and voices all blended together into a new and
> splendid whole . . .
> I insisted on rehearsing and shooting to a piano track and consulting
> Brian with a musical score in my hand over each set-up. But it worked! It
> worked! I have never enjoyed myself so much in my life. For the first time I
> felt I had control of the film with the authority of the music. It was
> astonishing to everyone, but particularly, of course, to the camera crew that
> we were able to compress or speed up the movement of the action just by
> saying: 'No, that wasn't fast enough. We've only got seven seconds [of
> music] for that bit of action.'
> (Powell 1986, 582–3)

Powell's desire to make an entire film in which music and fantasy were perfectly fused became a reality in his co-production (again with Pressburger)
of Offenbach's *Tales of Hoffman* (1951), widely regarded as one of the most
aesthetically successful of all opera films (see Chapter 4).

In the meantime, there had been the international success of *The Red
Shoes*, a ballet fantasy shot in sumptuous colour and requiring original
diegetic music for its elaborate danced routines. Easdale's replacement score
was a rich concoction of impressionistic harmony and sensual orchestral
textures, the obvious influences of Debussy, Ravel, Satie and Stravinsky
appropriate to the film's action, which takes place in a ballet company modelled on Diaghilev's Ballets Russes. (One of the real Ballets Russes' members,
Leighton Lucas, later went on to be a film composer who amongst other
projects scored *The Dam Busters* (dir. Michael Anderson, 1954), famous for
its rousing march by Eric Coates.) Easdale's music was recorded by the Royal
Philharmonic Orchestra under both Easdale and Sir Thomas Beecham,
the latter conducting the seventeen-minute self-contained ballet based on
'The Red Shoes' fairy-tale by Hans Christian Andersen; the suggestion to
approach Beecham had come from Easdale, who was anxious that the ballet sequence should be directed by a mature and experienced interpreter
of classical music (Powell 1986, 638–9). Among the felicitous moments in
the underscore is the sudden surge as the ballet's fictional composer, Julian
Craster, first hears the sounds of his new score in his head (an example of
what might be termed a 'metadiegetic' cue: see Gorbman 1987, 22–3).

Bliss once commented, of film music in general, that 'in the last resort
film music should be judged solely as music – that is to say, by the ear alone,
and the question of its value depends on whether it can stand up to this
test' (quoted in Huntley [1947], 40). While this view is no longer fashionable, it is nevertheless true that Easdale's ballet sequence in *The Red Shoes* is

that rare phenomenon in film music: a self-contained composition sophisticated enough to stand analytical comparison with music by established classical composers. This is especially important in the context of the film, since all too often films dealing with fictional composers are supplied with music supposedly written by them but of an execrable standard: Easdale's music by 'Julian Craster' is of such consistently imaginative quality that the character, who is portrayed as a wayward genius, is entirely plausible. Tellingly, once the musical argument of the film is complete the end credits play in a sombre silence unusual for its time. Easdale's music for *The Red Shoes* deservedly won the Academy Award for best score, and was the first British film score to be so honoured. (Another British first in 1948 was the bestowing of the Academy Award for best film to Olivier's *Hamlet*, with music by Walton: see Chapter 4.) Easdale's later scores included dissonant and partly octatonic music for *Peeping Tom* (dir. Powell, 1960), a controversial drama about voyeurism featuring idiomatic and versatile writing for solo piano, at times sounding like a modern accompaniment to a silent film – an appropriate identification given that home movies are the medium in which the voyeur preserves his lonely fantasies.

Alwyn's film scores also came to prominence in the momentous year 1948, which saw the release of three feature films with his music. His position was typical of several of the country's most prolific film composers: a solid craftsman with a wide range of dramatically useful stylistic idioms at his disposal, he honed his compositional technique in film scores at a time when he would far preferred to have been acknowledged as a composer of ambitious symphonies – of which he wrote five between 1948 and 1973. Looking back on his career in films, which began when he accompanied silent films as a professional flautist, he commented:

> I had many offers from Hollywood, but remembering those, once famous,
> composers who had responded to its lures only to have their talents dimmed
> and even obliterated by the demands of the film world, I resisted the
> temptation. In spite of my interest in film making, I was first and foremost a
> serious composer and each film score I had written was an opportunity for
> experiment and an exceptional chance, given the splendid orchestras who
> played my scores, to improve and polish my technique and widen my
> dramatic range.   (quoted in M. Alwyn 1993, 9)

Ironically, it was the challenge of film work that caused Alwyn to destroy many of his early concert works, which he felt were blighted by a 'woeful inadequacy' of technique. And it was certainly true that the standard of orchestral playing in British film studios was rarely less than superb: many of Alwyn's film scores were recorded by orchestras of the calibre of the RPO, Philharmonia and LSO, mostly under the capable and often inspiring direction of Mathieson. (The latter made an amusing cameo appearance as Sir Arthur Sullivan in *The Magic Box* (dir. John Boulting, 1951), conducting pastiche Sullivan composed by Alwyn.) Like Walton, Alwyn saw film work as a convenient source of income to subsidize concert projects, commenting that the commission to score *Safari* (dir. Terence Young, 1956) was necessary to fund the completion of his Third Symphony (I. Johnson 2005, 266).

Alwyn's substantial contribution to the fortunes of British cinema in its heyday, based on an output of some 86 feature-film scores, plus music for numerous documentaries, was recognized in 1958 by his election to a Fellowship of the British Film Academy. His common-sense lectures and writings on the art of film music included a spirited defence of stylistic flexibility ('Contemporary criticism is inclined to question the ability of a composer to be versatile'), a plea for the provision of cues to be governed by the interests of economy ('I do feel that far too much of my ingenuity is spent nowadays in persuading the filmmaker to keep music out of the film rather than to put it in') and an awareness that film music should not necessarily be obtrusive or memorable ('I am always a little worried if somebody says to me, "I liked your score for such and such a picture." It makes me wonder whether I have stepped outside my brief, which is to provide music which is as indigenous to the film as the camera angles and the film sets'; quotations from a lecture given in 1958, and published as W. Alwyn 1959). Alwyn felt that music could often do the actors' work for them, drawing attention to

> the remarkable faculty of music for portraying something which is happening in the actor's mind, and not what you see in his face or in his actions. In the old, silent film the actor had to rely on exaggerated gestures, the art of mime, to express his emotions: in the sound film he can behave naturally with the aid of words – the 'method' came into its own – but he can also remain silent and poker-faced while music expresses for him the emotion which is to be shared by his audience. (Incidentally I like to cherish the idea that many an actor's reputation I have made or marred by the surreptitious use of music.) (quoted in I. Johnson 2005, 175)

This final remark recalls actor George Peppard's tribute to the power of Bronislau Kaper's music to endow his acting with spurious depth (see Chapter 3).

Alwyn's film work became well known with his calypso-flavoured score to *The Rake's Progress* (US title *Notorious Gentleman*; dir. Sidney Gilliat, 1945), which was partly set in the Caribbean, and in two scores composed for films by Reed, and it might have become still better known had the composer not been abandoned by Reed when the latter opted to score *The Third Man* (1949) with what was to become spectacularly popular zither music by Anton Karas (I. Johnson 2005, 195). For Reed's *noir*-influenced

Odd Man Out (1946), a tale of a fugitive IRA leader, Alwyn's score studiously avoided traditional Irish music for political reasons, even though in several other films – for example, *Captain Boycott* (dir. Frank Launder, 1947), which was set less contentiously in rural Eire – he showed a fondness for the Celtic folk idiom. In *Odd Man Out*, as in the racing scene in *Boycott* (which eschews music until the horse stumbles), Alwyn elects to begin a cue on a specific moment of action for dramatic effect, director Karel Reisz commenting that Johnny's fall from a speeding car 'has significance beyond that of the culmination of an isolated exciting sequence: it is the motivating point of the whole film and as such its dramatic significance is conveyed by the sudden artificial entry of the music. Because the music has been used sparingly up to this point, its sudden entry makes a more precise and definite point than would have been possible with a continuous background score' (Reisz 1953, 267). Although much of Alwyn's score was written in advance during a period of close consultation with both director and sound editor, and one crucial part of the film was shot to pre-recorded music so that actor James Mason could respond to its funereal tread, economy had not yet become Alwyn's watch-word and the score has been criticized for being rather 'heavy-handed' (I. Johnson 2005, 157) in spite of its splendid main theme and exciting chase music. (For a full discussion of the music, see Manvell and Huntley 1957, 139–49.) Alwyn's score for Reed's *The Fallen Idol* (1948) also suffered from a superabundance in places but showed a sure grasp of both the heart-on-sleeve romanticism and effervescent comedic underscoring typical of film music at this time. The most imaginative and understated moment in this score is the delicately spiralling cadenza for solo violin as a child's paper dart, formed from an incriminating telegram, makes a leisurely descent of a staircase before coming to rest in the hands of a police officer. Unusually, a loud cue dubbed at an unnaturally low volume for a tense game of hide-and-seek was admired by the composer for adding 'a sense of strain to the sound-track – almost like trying to scream in a whisper' (M. Alwyn 1993, 8).

The comedy whodunit *Green for Danger* (dir. Gilliat, 1946) provided Alwyn with a rare opportunity to indulge in an elaborate autonomous structure, the flamboyantly bustling counterpoint of its main-title music having been unwittingly suggested by the director himself when, having warned the composer against doing a mickey-mouse score and 'Feeling that this was a bit negative, I added facetiously, "I mean, write a fugue, Bill." And that, when I got back [from America], I found was precisely what he had done' (quoted in I. Johnson 2005, 159). The crime melodrama *Take My Life* (dir. Ronald Neame, 1947) featured music heavily in its diegesis, both in the shape of a diegetic opera premièred at Covent Garden – and including an aria for the film's heroine with the same title as the film itself – and in a school song found as a manuscript sketch in the possession of the murder victim, which helps the killer to be tracked down and is taken up excitedly in the nondiegetic score as the heroine rushes by train to Edinburgh to find him (to a conjunction of music and images strongly reminiscent of the seminal documentary *Night Mail*). Alwyn's ability to tackle diverse genres was much in evidence at the end of the decade: he scored an adaptation of a stage play with disciplined and dignified romanticism (*The Winslow Boy*, dir. Anthony Asquith, 1948); indulged in vivid comedic scoring in *The History of Mr Polly* (dir. Anthony Pelissier, 1948), which included a Wagnerian climax culminating in a simultaneously diegetic and nondiegetic rendering of 'For He's a Jolly Good Fellow' over a pregnant dominant pedal point when Polly is unexpectedly propelled into the heroic limelight; and a harmonically advanced score, based largely on a simply four-note motif, which contributed immeasurably to the eeriness of *The Rocking-Horse Winner* (dir. Pelissier, 1949). Here the rocking horse's frenzied motion and other darker cues demonstrated Alwyn's ability – like Herrmann's, by whom he may have been influenced – to create disquieting effects by the simplest of ostinato dominated means. A notable feature of this score was the manner in which a verbal rhythm inspired by a line of voiced-over speech ('There must be more money!') was transformed into a naggingly insistent motif, rather in the manner of Rózsa's score to *The Secret Beyond the Door*, released in the previous year (see Chapter 3).

Alwyn's versatility became even more marked in the 1950s, ranging from the extreme economy of a few sustained notes in the highly theatrical submarine drama *Morning Departure* (US title *Operation Disaster*, dir. Roy Baker, 1950) to, at the other extreme, a Korngold-like opulence for the Burt Lancaster swashbuckler *The Crimson Pirate* (dir. Robert Siodmak, 1952). Formulaic stiff-upper-lip war films were much in vogue at this time. *Malta Story* (dir. Brian Desmond Hurst, 1953) featured laughable special effects and elicited from Alwyn the prototype of the boldly heroic idiom later popularized by Ron Goodwin (who more than anyone demonstrated that the long-lived British war film appealed as much to a boyish sense of adventure as to propagandist instincts); inspiration was clearly running dry on this project, as shown by the old-fashioned and gratuitous allusion to the US national anthem when we see a glimpse of the American aircraft carrier USS *Wasp*. (Dimitri Tiomkin repaid the compliment by quoting 'Rule, Britannia' for the appearance of the Royal Navy in *The Guns of Navarone* (dir. J. Lee-Thompson, 1961); the technique had become a thoroughly outdated and stock response even by the early 1950s.) *The Black Tent* (dir. Hurst, 1956) provided the opportunity to fuse Western and Arabian musical elements in the service of a desert drama about miscegenation, with the help of plenty of stereotypical augmented seconds for generic locational colour, while the by turns bustling and grimly determined action music of the nautical yarn *The Silent Enemy* (dir. William Fairchild, 1958) climaxed in a substantial dialogue-free cue which lent tension and momentum to a sustained knife battle between British and Italian divers attempting to retrieve secret documents from the underwater wreck of a crashed bomber. In *Carve Her Name with Pride* (dir. Lewis Gilbert, 1958), Alwyn's nondiegetic score reworked Chopin's D flat major Prelude – first played diegetically by a French soldier courting the film's heroine – for simple pathos, and neatly recomposed a flamboyant Straussian cue accompanying a daytime parachute jump so that it plays more dramatically for a nocturnal drop.

In his final years as a film composer, Alwyn continued to contribute music to a range of genres. The comedic scoring of *The Smallest Show on Earth* (dir. Basil Dearden, 1957), with its affectionate parodies of old-fashioned film music, and the conservative style of Disney adventures such as *In Search of the Castaways* (dir. Robert Stevenson, 1961) – in which Alwyn's sometimes quirky vaudeville-style music for implausible action scenes sat oddly alongside sugary songs showcasing the vocal talents of the film's star, Maurice Chevalier – were in marked contrast to the gritty modernism in the superior supernatural thriller *Night of the Eagle* (US title *Burn, Witch, Burn!*; dir. Sidney Hayers, 1961) and the partly twelve-note thematic material of *Life for Ruth* (dir. Basil Dearden, 1962). In visual terms, *Night of the Eagle* was influenced by the latest Hitchcock movies, and not surprisingly Alwyn's largely athematic score continued to pay veiled homage to Herrmann's dogged use of ostinato and obsessive rhythmic patterns, while at the same time adhering to stock devices such as an unsubtle use of the *Dies irae* to signify the devil – this theme at one point transformed into a yet more obvious *diabolus in musica* when performed by a xylophone in brittle parallel tritones.

Perhaps because of his artistic aspirations in other genres, Alwyn's functional film music was sometimes unfairly panned, as when Keller dismissed the score for *The Cure for Love* (dir. Robert Donat, 1950) as 'reeking Kitsch' and expressed his amazement that a Professor of Composition at the Royal Academy of Music should be capable of such 'indifferent' music (Keller 1950, 145) – though the same critic a few years later praised Alwyn's score to *The Rocking-Horse Winner* for its 'revolutionary musico-dramatic build' and concluded that the composer was at once the most 'retrospective' and 'expert' of all film composers in the UK (Irving *et al.* 1954, 102). For his own part, Alwyn had remained ever-practical but somewhat ambivalent about a kind of composing which he considered as 'musical journalism' (I. Johnson 2005, 304), and gave a spirited retort to the impertinence of his critics: 'One cannot label [film] music as mere "background" music in a derogatory sense merely because film music in the minds of uninformed music critics has always tended to be associated with the lush outpourings of third-rate hacks' (W. Alwyn 1967, 40). Chief among the reasons for his decision to leave the film industry in 1963 was the constant difficulty he had experienced in attempting to persuade producers to use economic scoring methods that did not involve a full symphony orchestra, which he felt 'is like the all-star cast, it provides a sort of Hollywood gloss and a pseudo-prestige value to the films . . . important sounding music makes the picture sound important', and the tendency to use twice as much music in the late 1950s than was customary a decade earlier, which meant that 'without silence the composer loses his most effective weapon' (1958 lecture, quoted in Swynnoe 2002, 189, 191).

Alwyn spent his retirement in the company of his second wife, Doreen Mary Carwithen, who was one of the very few female film composers to have made a name for herself in the 1950s. After an apprenticeship as a copyist and creditless ghost-writer aiding more established composers at Denham Studios, Carwithen scored a clutch of films in her own right between 1948 and 1956, including a novel balletic interpretation of 'The Twelve Days of Christmas' (*On the Twelfth Day*, 1956) directed by and starring Wendy Toye, with production design by Ronald Searle. Carwithen later commented that, like Alwyn, sophisticated composer Elisabeth Lutyens had no qualms about adapting her compositional style for films (Swynnoe 2002, 225), Lutyens's output in this medium including several features and documentaries released between 1946 and 1975. Among them were several mediocre horror films (see below), a genre which has traditionally admitted unusually high levels of dissonance and avant-garde techniques. Lutyens had been the first woman composer to score a feature film in the UK when she undertook *Penny and the Pownall Case* in that seminal year, 1948. In the following year, Grace Williams (a student friend of Britten's who served as the latter's amanuensis when he worked on *Love From a Stranger*) was commissioned to score director Jill Craigie's feature *Blue Scar*, her music for the project partly based on folksong material from Williams's native Wales. Unfortunately, most of the films on which these women composers worked in a thoroughly male-dominated industry have long since sunk into obscurity.

A notably robust and distinctive harmonic idiom is the principal characteristic of film scores by Alan Rawsthorne. Irving commented of Rawsthorne's music to *The Captive Heart* (dir. Basil Dearden, 1946) that the piquant harmony made '"sloppy" love scenes . . . bearable' (Irving *et al.* 1954, 102), elsewhere praising his lack of superficiality and refusal to pander to lowbrow tastes, citing a dramatically appropriate use of counterpoint to depict the weary march of debilitated prisoners at Dunkirk (Huntley [1947], 83). The leaden Ava Gardner vehicle *Pandora and the Flying Dutchman* (dir. Albert Lewin, 1950), an Anglo-American co-production, was enhanced by Rawsthorne's evocative and tonally elusive harmony: his score is freely evolving, without recurring motifs, and dislocated bass lines lend a sense of dynamic progression. In *The Cruel Sea* (dir. Frend, 1953) the composer avoided both sentimentality and the banal heroic style of many British maritime features through similarly elusive and sometimes acerbic advanced tonality. In Rawsthorne's robust idiom, unpredictable but logical harmonies are often a by-product of imaginative contrapuntal voice-leading – a central characteristic of his style in the concert hall (Dunwell 1960, 186).

Along with Alwyn, Benjamin Frankel was one of the most successful, highly paid and prolific British film composers of the 1940s and 1950s. His versatility was such that he began his career as a dance-band violinist and arranger, and director of West End musicals, and ended it as a composer of respected concert music (including eight symphonies), much of which embodied tonally rooted serial techniques. His first major film success was the score to *The Seventh Veil* (dir. Compton Bennett, 1946), one of many British films of the era exploiting classical repertoire (see Chapter 11) and hailed as 'an outstanding success in bringing music to a wider audience in an artistically satisfying, technically pleasing (even box office gratifying) manner' (Huntley [1947], 78). This stylish melodrama about a concert pianist's psychological and romantic problems fared unexpectedly well in America. The composer's theatrical experience made him an obvious choice to score film transfers from stage comedies such as the period pieces *Trottie True* (US title *The Gay Lady*; dir. Hurst, 1949) and *The Importance of Being Earnest* (dir. Asquith, 1952), both of which feature music-hall galops and gently parodic takes on parlour music. In 1951, Frankel scored one of the finest Ealing comedies, *The Man in the White Suit* (dir. Mackendrick). His music for Jules Dassin's *Night and the City* (1950), a London-set *film noir*, was for contractual reasons not used in the USA where an alternative score was provided by Franz Waxman; it seems likely that Frankel's economical music for the British Territories release was considered too dispassionate in effect for American tastes by the film's producers, and Waxman's replacement score (used in all other parts of the world, and later completely eclipsing the Frankel version when the film was released for broadcast on television) was certainly more firmly anchored in the well-established *noir* vein in its clear-cut expressionism (Husted 2003).

Frankel's film work fluctuated between a popular melodicism hailing from his light-music background and far more sophisticated compositional preoccupations. *So Long at the Fair* (dir. Terence Fisher and Anthony Darnborough, 1950) and *Footsteps in the Fog* (dir. Arthur Lubin, 1955) spawned the hits 'Carriage and Pair' and 'Lily Watkin's Theme' respectively (the latter popular with the British dance bands of the day), yet in the same year as he scored *Footsteps* Frankel experimented with serial technique in his music to Peter Grenville's *The Prisoner*, alongside lush non-functional triadic progressions for strings suggestive of Debussy at his most luminous. As other film composers discovered at around this time, the convoluted technical processes of dodecaphonic serialism proved most apposite in dramas concerned with *Angst* and terror, and Frankel's fullest serial essay in a film score came with his contribution to the Hammer production *The Curse of the Werewolf* (dir. Fisher, 1961) – though in spite of the self-imposed technical challenge he also found room for a bucolic cue imbued with Mahlerian diatonicism and the sounds of nature, and his serial conceptions were always characterized by melodic accessibility and affective lyricism, sometimes underpinned at climaxes by statuesque Stravinskyan ostinati in the bass. *The Night of the Iguana* (dir. John Huston, 1964) has tender modal writing for chamber textures, well suited to a tragi-comic stage transfer; that the music works well away from the film is due to a thematic unity that can bind short cues satisfyingly together (Kennaway 2002, 25).

Frankel's final film score, to Ken Annakin's all-star war epic *Battle of the Bulge* (1965), proved to be his magnum opus. A finely executed new recording of the full music track (see Kennaway 2000) revealed this to be one of the most inventive, substantial and vivid scores ever conceived for a genre that mostly elicited bombastic triumphalism and clichéd battle music from even the best composers who served it. Frankel's reworking of familiar militaristic and patriotic rhetoric is distinguished by appealing eccentricities helping to capture aspects of the participants' characters, for example an angular and jazzy hoe-down tune for a maverick US tank commander that perfectly complements (and can serve as a bustling counterpoint to) Adolf Hoffmann's banal *Panzerlied* anthem beloved of the German tank crews, this authentic song heard both diegetically and in the nondiegetic score. Although the music is structured according to traditional leitmotivic principles, Frankel's ever-resourceful harmonies, rhythmic propulsion and textural imagination constantly maintain freshness. Prominent stylistic fingerprints include polytonality, melodic chains of thirds and harmonies sustained from successive melodic notes (both suggesting the influence of Britten), expansive but restrained string lines layered with nervously fragmented brass and percussion, use of ostinati driving in layers over simply pounding bass lines, deftly balletic moments (e.g. to accompany an aerial pursuit), and contrasting sections of delicate lyricism. By way of contrast, John Addison's meagre score to the comparable all-star Second World War epic *A Bridge Too Far* (dir. Richard Attenborough, 1977), although in places achieving a delicate and restrained lyricism, for the most part utilized four-square and optimistically patriotic marches to punctuate the drama, their cheerfulness sitting oddly alongside the often graphic depictions of the devastating carnage of one of the worst defeats in British military history. So inappropriate did Addison's naïvely optimistic style seem, even to the film-makers, that only after a prolonged silence could the jolly main-title march be faded back in to accompany the latter stages of the end credits.

William Walton and Malcolm Arnold

By the time he composed his score to *Hamlet*, Walton had long enjoyed a reputation as a leading film composer, and freely confessed to having embarked on film work largely for the 'filthy lucre'. Walton's most celebrated film scores are those he composed for Olivier's trilogy of Shakespeare films, which are discussed in Chapter 4. He also provided music for eleven other films, including four early projects directed by Paul Czinner: *Escape Me Never* (1935), *As You Like It* (1936), *Dreaming Lips* (1937) and *Stolen Life* (1939). The commission for *Escape Me Never*, which was the first British feature for which an established composer with an international reputation had been engaged, 'helped to pay the mortgage during the composition of the First Symphony' (Kennedy 1989, 76; Walton 1988, 87). That money was the initial impetus for Walton's decision to move into film scoring is shown by a revealing letter to his publisher, written in March 1936 following a rumour that Clair wanted to hire him for his next film, when the composer wished to acquire a hard-hitting agent: 'I am coming more & more to the view that it is absolutely necessary to have someone who really lives in, & understands the film world inside out. Only they can get the highest prices and know how to haggle & bully this gang of would-be tricksters'; commenting on the then current negotiations of his contract for *As You Like It*, he confessed he felt like a babe in the wood 'wandering in a strange & predatory land' (Hayes 2002, 107–8). In May 1938 Walton was weighing the financial pros and cons of accepting either an American commission for a Violin Concerto for Jascha Heifetz or lucrative film projects, telling his publisher 'it all boils down to this, whether I'm to become a film composer or a real composer . . . In fact I think I can safely wipe out films, which have served their purpose in enabling me to get my house etc.' (Hayes 2002, 115).

In 1941 Walton scored a film version of Shaw's *Major Barbara* (dir. Pascal *et al.*), during work on which the playwright deigned to offer the composer detailed advice on how to reflect his words with suitable music, declaring 'If I were a musician I should not presume to suggest an alteration; but an amateur's comments should always be listened to' (quoted in Kennedy 1989, 110). Walton was exempted from military service in the Second World War on condition that he provide music for propaganda films. In addition to scoring three such projects for Ealing Studios in 1941–2, he composed a score for Leslie Howard's Ministry of Information production, *The First of the Few* (1942). A superior fictionalized account of the life of legendary Spitfire designer Reginald Mitchell, the film was provided with suitably rousing music, and Walton confessed that for this project it 'will have to be good & one can't rely on a quick film extemporisation technique for it, so it will need more time trouble & care' (Hayes 2002, 138). Extracts from the score quickly became popular in the concert hall under the title *Spitfire Prelude and Fugue*. The patriotic tone of the Prelude inhabits the same post-Elgarian soundworld as Walton's coronation marches, while the boisterous Fugue originally accompanied shots of the assembly line working intensely to produce the prototype aircraft. Elsewhere Walton employed the standard device of musical quotation at appropriate moments, including a leitmotif from Wagner's *Ring* for the Nazi domination of Europe and the US national anthem for the music accompanying that country's victory of the Schneider floatplane racing trophy. In a letter written in the spring of 1942, shortly before he embarked on the score, Walton commented that he felt film music to be

> entirely occasional, & is of no use other than what it is meant for & one won't be able to get a suite out of it.
>
> Which is just as it should be, otherwise it would probably not fulfil it's [*sic*] purpose. That is why I'm against my film music being played by Mr [Stanford] Robinson [a conductor of light music at the BBC] or anyone else. Film music is not good film music if it can be used for any other purpose . . . So I don't care where [the score of] Major Barbara is or any other of my films. The music should never be heard without the film.
>
> (Hayes 2002, 140)

At the time, Walton could hardly have been expected to predict how successful some of his film-music suites were to become in the concert hall, and the popularity of the *Spitfire Prelude and Fugue* was soon matched by that of various extracts from *Henry V*. Money remained a prime objective, and to his publisher he expressed concern that Vaughan Williams (who shared the same publisher) might in these war years under-sell himself to film producers: 'it is not a help for the rest of the composers if someone of his calibre & reputation is asking half what most of us get' (Hayes 2002, 128). By the early 1960s, Walton's need to earn had become less pressing, and he commented of his decision not to score David Lean's *Lawrence of Arabia* in 1962: '2 ½ hours [of music] for £5000 – not on my life'. He was still earning handsomely from royalties payable on his earlier film scores: in 1963, for example, he received £479 for Olivier's *Hamlet*, now fifteen years old, so the Lean offer must have seemed a poor deal indeed (Hayes 2002, 327, 330).

6.1 Malcolm Arnold conducting music for the British war film *Battle of Britain* (1969), with actress Susannah York (as Section Officer Maggie Harvey) on screen. All but a short segment of William Walton's score was rejected by the film's producers.

Walton's distinguished film career came to an ignominious end in 1969 when he was engaged to provide the music for another patriotic war film, *Battle of Britain* (dir. Guy Hamilton). By this stage Walton's compositional powers were declining, and he felt compelled to employ Malcolm Arnold as a creative assistant; Walton's lack of understanding of the technicalities of film-making was strikingly revealed when he naïvely commented to Arnold that some passages of the music would need to be 'fairly loud (I've put in no expression marks) as I imagine there [are] a lot of background airplane noises to overcome' (Hayes 2002, 385). The film's American producers disliked the music track when they heard it and, using the pretext that there was insufficient material to fill a soundtrack album, rejected it. John Barry was invited to supply a new score, but declined, and the commission was instead taken over by Ron Goodwin, who had written rousing action scores for war movies such as *633 Squadron* (dir. Walter Grauman, 1964) and *Where Eagles Dare* (dir. Brian G. Hutton, 1969), the former celebrated for its thrillingly memorable and much-imitated main-title theme. Only when Olivier (who played Sir Hugh Dowding) threatened to have his name removed from the credits of *Battle of Britain* did the producers agree to retain one small segment of Walton's original music. This 'Battle in the Air' sequence occurs towards the end of the film, and was clearly patched together with linking passages supplied by Arnold. In an attempt to make amends for this transatlantic insult to a nationally revered figure, the British Prime Minister Edward Heath successfully retrieved Walton's manuscript from United Artists in 1972 and presented it to the composer at his 70th birthday party, held at 10 Downing Street. With the release of *Battle of Britain* on DVD in 2004, Walton's slender score (the original recording of which was unearthed from the sound mixer's garage in 1990) was made available as an alternative music track; but its coronation-style march theme and flippant variation on Siegfried's heroic horn motif from Wagner's *Ring*, duly trotted out for appearances of the Luftwaffe (and, in one ineptly spotted cue on the DVD, when an RAF Spitfire attempts to land with its wheels up), are likely to come as a severe disappointment for those expecting to encounter a long-lost masterpiece of film scoring.

Arnold was in his own right one of the leading British film composers of the 1950s and 1960s. Like Britten and many others, he served an apprenticeship in documentary film, beginning in 1947 and scoring over ten films per year from 1948 until 1951, when he began to undertake more commissions for feature films. By the time he abandoned film work in 1969, he had contributed music to well over 100 projects, including collaborations with directors Huston, Mankiewicz and Reed. Among Arnold's strengths were a belief that composers should accept only those film commissions for which they entertained a genuine empathy, a compositional integrity which (like Herrmann's) drew no stylistic distinction between film and concert work, and a keen sense of economy and restraint. The latter was strikingly demonstrated when he refused to write anything except main-title music for Henry Koster's *No Highway* (1951), on the grounds that in this case background scoring would 'ruin a good script and a good film' (quoted in Burton-Page 1994, 53). Certain films involved research to find appropriate exotic raw material, as in his appropriation of Caribbean music for *Island in the Sun* (dir. Robert Rossen, 1957) and Indian music for *Nine Hours to Rama* (dir. Mark Robson, 1962), while in British-based features he occasionally resorted to regional folksongs to create a local flavour. *The Inn of the Sixth Happiness* (dir. Robson, 1958), which included stereotyped musical orientalism, somewhat overworked its main theme but cunningly combined it at the conclusion with the evacuee children's diegetic nursery song 'This Old Man'. In *Whistle Down the Wind* (dir. Bryan Forbes, 1961) Arnold again captured the innocence of a group of children, who on this occasion discover a murderer hiding in a barn and take him to be Jesus, with delicate scoring that includes an inventive arrangement of the Christmas carol 'We Three Kings'. With his witty scoring for the four films in the popular 'St Trinian's' series (1954–66), set amongst the badly behaved pupils in a notorious fictional girls' public school and inspired by the drawings of Ronald Searle, Arnold joined the ranks of composers not ashamed to have their names associated with the amiable crudities of British comedy.

Arnold's film music is perhaps best represented by the three very different scores he composed in the 1950s for critically acclaimed features directed by Lean. *The Sound Barrier* (1952), concerned with aviation pioneers of the early jet age, was in some respects a topical sequel to *The First of the Few*, and not surprisingly Arnold's music was imbued in places with a distinctly patriotic flavour strongly redolent of Walton. As in Arnold's concert music, multiple piccolos are used imaginatively, here suggesting both ethereal skyscapes and the mysterious allure of the unknown. A glittering waltz accompanies some of the aerial sequences, but tension in action sequences is more commonly generated not by music but by carefully sequenced sound effects, with the concluding sonic boom constituting the real climax of the soundtrack. In places Arnold's music appears to emerge from the sound effects, as when the roar of a Comet's jet engines spooling up merges imperceptibly into a gradual crescendo on a sustained orchestral chord. Music is absent from the sequence in which a biplane crashes and kills its novice pilot: only as the smoke spirals upwards from the wreckage does Arnold's cue begin, piccolo spiralling isomorphically upwards and initiating a solemn orchestral dirge which is prolonged well into the next scene in order to cast a shadow over the dead pilot's father as he studies the model of his elegant new jet aircraft design.

The second Arnold–Lean collaboration, *Hobson's Choice* (1953), received a fine comedic score in which Arnold avoided the pitfalls of mickey-mousing by ensuring that almost all directly illustrative gestures in the music occur in the context of a consistent rhythmic accompaniment with its own ongoing momentum, often based on repetitive dance-like patterns. Elements of music-hall burlesque, a sometimes disconcerting feature of Arnold's concert music, here find full-blooded expression, and although the instrumental stereotyping (e.g. lurching tuba and bassoons for drunkenness, and trombone glissandi for vulgarity) verges on caricature, such designedly banal musical material is refreshed by subtle twists. In the opening scene the camera pans across the ranks of different footwear in the cobbler's shop to the accompaniment of a sequence of balletic musical ideas (analysed in detail in Manvell and Huntley 1957, 138–42), and shy Willie Mossop's unduly protracted undressing on his wedding night is celebrated with a miniature nondiegetic violin concerto. Hyperbole is rife, with deliciously exaggerated love and triumph themes punctuating the score at crucial moments, and a brilliant touch of bathos occurs when an expansive climax on the love theme is brutally truncated as Willie is slapped on the face by the mother of the ex-girlfriend his new love has just forced him to jilt.

Lean declared of Arnold's Oscar-winning score to *The Bridge on the River Kwai* (1957) that it possessed size, sensitivity and guts, and showed that the composer was blessed with the instincts of a fine story-teller (Burton-Page 1994, 55). The widespread popularity of the score was in no small measure due to Arnold's ingenious treatment of the jaunty First World War march *Colonel Bogey* (composed by Kenneth Alford in 1916), which proved to be a hit when released in a film spin-off recording by Mitch Miller and his band in 1958. In the film, Alford's theme first appears when whistled diegetically by the marching British soldiers, with Arnold's buoyant nondiegetic countermelody creeping in inexorably beneath it and elsewhere appearing independently. In the prisoner-of-war genre the impact of these cheerful marching melodies was considerable, strong echoes in later films including *The Great Escape* (dir. John Sturges, 1963; music by Elmer Bernstein), in turn parodied in the British animated comedy *Chicken Run* (dir. Peter Lord and Nick Park, 2000; music by John Powell and Harry Gregson-Williams). Lean was impressed by those moments in *The Bridge on the River Kwai* when the composer allowed his music to 'spill over' and dominate the action, but the score is mostly restrained and, as in *The Sound Barrier*, sound effects and ambient sound often create the necessary tension. The starkest example of this occurs in the tense final segment of the film, when no music is heard for over twenty minutes of running time as the bridge is covertly wired with explosives by commandos and then destroyed.

Generic (re)takes: horror and comedy

Founded in 1947, Hammer Productions ventured into science-fiction in the 1950s and launched the film-music career of house composer James Bernard with *The Quatermass Xperiment* (US title *The Creeping Unknown*; dir. Val Guest, 1955), *Quatermass II* (US title *Enemy from Space*; dir. Guest, 1956) – both direct spin-offs from a successful BBC television series – and *X the Unknown* (dir. Leslie Norman, 1956), all three of which made the most of a low-budget ensemble of strings and percussion. Hammer's lucrative move into horror came with reworkings of Universal's favourite subjects from the 1930s: *The Curse of Frankenstein* (1957) and *Dracula* (US title *Horror of Dracula*, 1958), both directed by Terence Fisher and scored by Bernard; the first set a new standard of goriness influential on the genre as a whole, while the second aspired to intelligent production values that were sometimes sorely lacking in later Hammer films. Trademarks of Bernard's idiom already present in these soundtracks were obsessive three-note motifs derived from the syllables of both title characters' names, and 'a slow and dominant, often descending progression of notes over a rapid flurry of orchestral dissonance, growing and building in volume and register, advancing a relentless terror in coordination with the horrors on-screen, climaxing in a dynamic frenzy of wild orchestration' (Larson 1996, 21). These characteristics persisted in scores for sequels such as *Dracula, Prince of Darkness* (dir. Fisher, 1966), *Scars of Dracula* (dir. Roy Ward Baker, 1970) and *Frankenstein and the Monster from Hell* (dir. Fisher, 1973), which exploited direct clashes between leitmotifs representing either abstract good and evil or characters polarized in other binary oppositions.

Bernard had begun his career by acting as copyist on the manuscript full score of Britten's opera *Billy Budd* (1951). Britten, having long since abandoned film work himself, wrote to his former protégé about his film music in 1958: 'I think you have done splendidly – a real example to other composers who are often too grand (or too incompetent) to accept commissions of the sort that you have always done' (quoted in Bridcut 2006, 255). Bernard's Hammer music can be heard at its most typical in *The Devil Rides Out* (dir. Fisher, 1968), where the most effective rhetorical gestures are the simplest: an ascending rolled timpani glissando against tense string trills for the appearance of the goat-devil and a luminous oscillation of two chords for a hypnosis induced by reflections in a mirror, for example. Elsewhere the music relies heavily on prolonged sequential crescendos for its intensity, as in a scene of self-strangulation, and in embryonic form this technique also provides small building blocks of related material for short cues that can easily accommodate sporadic interruption by individual lines of dialogue. Much of the tutti scoring seems overdone for modern tastes, relying heavily on stingers and stereotypical instrumentation (e.g. snarling muted brass and string tremolos), and the pagan orgy scene is choreographed to primitive ritualistic music hardly representing a significant advance over Steiner's tribal music in *King Kong* written some 35 years earlier; bizarrely the sound levels are here manipulated to suggest that the music is diegetic by ducking the volume when the orgy is seen from a distance, even though the elaborate scoring (for orchestra with African drums) unwittingly makes a mockery of such attempted realism on the part of the dubbing mixers.

Hammer Productions were anxious to retain high-quality orchestral music to compensate for sometimes dubious production values, and to maintain a consistency of musical style to promote a coherent house identity. The studio's music directors, first classical conductor John Hollingsworth then Philip Martell from 1964 onwards, were perceptive talent-spotters fully committed to maintaining consistently high levels of composition and performance; unusually for its time, the music department was run on the old Hollywood model. Notable composers who scored Hammer films were

Don Banks, Tristram Cary, Christopher Gunning, Elisabeth Lutyens, John McCabe, Mario Nascimbene (see Chapter 9), Harry Robinson (né Robertson), David Whitaker and Malcolm Williamson. In a rare inversion of orthodox compositional priorities, Banks viewed his Hammer scores – which included *The Reptile* (dir. John Gilling, 1966) – as an opportunity to experiment with modernist devices he found too avant-garde for his concert work, seizing the opportunity to hone his twelve-note techniques (Larson 1996, 57–8). By contrast, Lutyens was well known as a serial advocate in her concert works but chose to modify her style significantly when working in film; in addition to scores for Hammer such as *Paranoiac* (dir. Freddie Francis, 1963) she also worked on a number of productions by the studio's rival in the genre, Amicus Films. Her music for the latter's *The Skull* (dir. Francis, 1965), scored for an unorthodox orchestra featuring cimbalom and two bass clarinets but no violins, shows her ability to mould modernistic rhetorical gestures into memorable patterns (Doran 2004). Williamson found his wings clipped when he wanted to score *The Horror of Frankenstein* (dir. Jimmy Sangster, 1970), a black comedy and the final member of Hammer's Frankenstein series, with a Herrmann-like ensemble of eight members of the clarinet family plus strings and percussion, only to be told that he had to include flutes and oboes for nature-effects and love-interest respectively (Larson 1996, 79). Fashionable electronics were generally avoided, though Bernard employed a novachord (in unison with a soprano) in his suitably complex score for *The Gorgon* in 1964 (dir. Fisher), Robinson used a Moog synthesizer to suggest psychological disturbance in *Demons of the Mind* (dir. Peter Sykes, 1972), and Cary was unusually commissioned to write complete alternative scores, one for electronics and the other for full orchestra, for *Quatermass and the Pit* (dir. Baker) in 1967. The electronics were true to their typecasting as agents of the irrational, and parts of both scores were used in the final dub (Larson 1996, 31, 93), but the music had an impossible task trying to rescue what was (apart from the film's hysterical climax) uniformly unatmospheric imagery, and the beautiful dirge accompanying the end titles was perversely not used at any point in the preceding narrative. In the same year Cary founded a pioneering electronic studio at London's Royal College of Music and went on to write prolifically for television.

In the 1970s, when Hammer music was dominated by the work of Whitaker and Robinson, some tension occurred when the studio bosses tried to plug pop songs for commercial gain, Robinson recalling that one such in *Lust for a Vampire* (dir. Jimmy Sangster, 1970) 'drew hoots and jeers from every audience that heard it' (quoted in Larson 1996, 109). When a contemporary rock score was commissioned from Michael Vickers for *Dracula A.D. 1972* (dir. Alan Gibson, 1972) the results were felt so lamentable that an uncredited Banks was brought in to rescore half of the film, which was further modified with additional library cues (Larson 1996, 131). Robinson's pop background was reflected in his use of AABA song form in main-title themes, including that to *Twins of Evil* (dir. John Hough, 1971), the score of which has been analysed in detail by David Huckvale (1990). Such updatings in idiom were partly the result of pressure from the American co-producers who, as with other British film ventures at the time, became heavily involved in financing them. One of Hammer's last films, *To the Devil a Daughter* (dir. Sykes, 1976), had a score by US composer Paul Glass in which the disjointed colouristic rhetoric showed that the ultra-dissonant horror score had run out of steam just as much as the studio's earlier neo-romantic Gothic scores. Hammer's final feature appeared in 1978, and two years later they entered television production with the series *Hammer House of Horror*.

Even more successful than Hammer in its heyday was the seemingly never-ending series of unsubtle but surprisingly enduring *Carry On* comedies, featuring a roster of well-know comic actors and deriving much of its inspiration from the unsophisticated humour and innuendo of the old-time music hall. Early titles in this series were scored in 1958–62 by Bruce Montgomery, who pursued a parallel career as an author of intelligent crime fiction under the pseudonym Edmund Crispin and who had previously written music for the 'Doctor' series of comedies in the 1950s (see Whittle 2007). Montgomery's early score for *The Kidnappers* (dir. Philip Leacock, 1953) had shown his work to be finely crafted but sometimes indulging in needlessly elaborate orchestral textures and occasionally incoherent mickey-mousing alongside melodramatic stingers, a pastoral Englishness reminiscent of Warlock and Delius, folk-music elements and a willingness to increase the level of dissonance where justified by the drama. The *Carry On* series found its winning and indestructible formula after Montgomery parted company with it, with unpretentious and tuneful music for the numerous productions from 1963 until its demise in 1978 provided by Eric Rogers to scripts by Talbot Rothwell and spirited direction by Gerald Thomas, all working under the aegis of Rank producer Peter Rogers.

Eric Rogers' musical responses to the widely variable quality of comedy with which he was confronted were resourceful, embracing a host of cinematic musical idioms appropriate to the generic parodies at the heart of the *Carry On* concept. These affectionate stylistic homages were generally more satisfying than the overly literal mickey-mousing effects he often used to underscore physical comedy, most obviously to be seen in *Carry on Doctor* (1967) in which the graphic musical isomorphism of events (for example, an ascending swoop up to a dissonant stinger as a doctor accidentally trips and injects a patient unceremoniously in the posterior) comes straight out of the cartoon-composer's stock repertoire. (For a transcribed example of similar catching the action from *Carry on Henry* (1971), see Kershaw 1995, 135.) Also old-fashioned and predictable is distinctive instrumentation appropriate to character-type (bassoon or bass clarinet for almost anyone above an average bodily weight, for example) and crudely mocking devices ('laughing' muted brass, trombones blowing raspberries). Allusions to well-known songs remain a direct holdover from the silent era, as when a boy with his head stuck in a chamber pot arrives at Accident & Emergency to a nondiegetic strain from 'Boys and Girls Come Out to Play'.

As a foil to the essential bittiness of mickey-moused local details, Rogers often punctuated his scores with amiably lumbering general-purpose ritornello themes. His generic stylizations were otherwise mostly played straight and without undue exaggeration, presumably in order not to detract from the comic immediacy of the acting; in this regard he adumbrated the mock seriousness of 1980s comedy scoring by many years. The technique is heard to good advantage in *Carry on Cleo* (1964), which paid straightforward tribute to the epic Roman idiom of Rózsa – whose martial trumpets could conveniently collapse into jazz-muted laughter at appropriate moments. (It is to be hoped that Rózsa would have appreciated the funny side of the parody more than did Twentieth Century-Fox, who obtained a court injunction to prevent the film's *Cleopatra*-spoofing poster from being displayed.) In *Carry on Screaming* (1966), a snappy main-title pop song in Elvis Presley style leads to eerie underscoring for an affectionate lampoon on the Hammer horror films; mickey-mousing is limited, and the thematic allusions are insular, the signature tune from the 1960s BBC TV police soap-opera *Z Cars* making a suitably silly (and, to a non-British audience, meaningless) appearance as inept Victorian coppers arrive at the crime scene. Perhaps the finest film in the series, the sharply scripted *Carry On Up the Khyber* (1968) allows the essential naïvety of authentic military band music to make itself sound daft without the need for additional help, and the film is full of audio-visual musical jokes strongly reminiscent of Golden Age cartoons: the rotating magazine of a sabotaged Gatling machine-gun plays a mechanical fairground tune, and during the film's climactic parody of upper-class Englishness, in which the white-tie-clad aristocrats attempt to maintain dignity at a dinner party in spite of the fact that their residency is being shelled by revolting natives, the palm-court piano quartet continues playing unfazed as the bombs burst around them. ('Terrible noise!' moans a frightened guest, to which the host replies: 'Yes, shocking isn't it? It's not a first-class orchestra. But mind you, they're doing their best.') Even after receiving a direct hit, the ensemble gets shakily to its feet and resumes playing a hesitant version of *The Blue Danube* to a honky-tonk accompaniment on their bombed-out piano.

End of an era

As in France, so in the UK film-making styles underwent a sea-change in the early 1960s as social realism, the lower-class way of life, political conscious-ness, sharp satire, a sometimes raunchy sexuality and the glossy fashions of the Swinging Sixties all variously left their mark on the British equivalent to the *nouvelle vague*: Free Cinema, born out of low-budget documentary-making in the late 1950s and spearheaded by the outspoken director Lindsay Anderson. Influential on the downbeat realism arising from the emerging social consciousness was the uncompromising dramatic style of a new gen-eration of playwrights including John Osborne, whose seminal *Look Back in Anger* was filmed by Tony Richardson in 1959, with music by jazz trombon-ist Chris Barber. For *Room at the Top* (1958; music by Mario Nascimbene) and *The Pumpkin Eater* (1965; music by Georges Delerue) director Jack Clayton turned to continental composers to break away from English musi-cal stereotypes. The first British feature film influenced by Free Cinema thinking to find commercial success was Karel Reisz's *Saturday Night and Sunday Morning* (1960), with a jazz score by John Dankworth. Set in Not-tingham, the film's anti-authoritarian stance and sexually liberated working-class subject-matter proved attractive at the box office – so much so that producer Harry Saltzman was as a direct result of its success empowered to embark on the internationally successful James Bond series (Cowie 2004, 94). Dankworth also scored Joseph Losey's *The Servant* in 1963, the year in which Anderson's uncompromising *This Sporting Life* somewhat bizarrely featured highly intellectual and dissonant music by Schoenberg's former pupil Roberto Gerhard for the story of a rugby-playing coal miner. Ander-son's anarchic and bitterly anti-Establishment public-school fantasy *If . . .* (1968; music by Marc Wilkinson) later became emblematic of the narrative daring of the British New Wave.

Saturday Night's co-producer Richardson directed his own northern-set comedy, *A Taste of Honey* (1961), and the young-offender story *The Lone-liness of the Long Distance Runner* (1962), both with music by his favoured collaborator John Addison. Addison also scored Richardson's lively inter-pretation of Henry Fielding's robustly comic novel *Tom Jones* (1963), based on a screenplay by Osborne; this multi-Oscar-winning venture imagina-tively combined authentic period detail with modern cinematographic tech-niques, Addison supplying a quirky harpsichord-dominated score drawing on aspects of baroque recitative in the accompaniment of voiced-over narra-tion, parodies of silent-film music and stock comedic devices similar to those in the *Carry On* series. Another director interested in lower-class scenarios, social realism and sexual liberation at this time was John Schlesinger, whose creative partnership with Richard Rodney Bennett is discussed below; music for Schlesinger's *Darling* (1965) came from Dankworth, the scenario's urban amorality typical of the age. Beginning in 1967 with *Poor Cow* (with music by Donovan), independent director Ken Loach embarked on a long series of documentary-style dramas that from the 1990s onwards benefited from the sustained involvement of experienced film composer George Fenton (see below).

Perhaps as a result of the steady influx of jazz and pop scoring that affected both British and international cinema in the 1960s, few concert composers embarked on film careers until Michael Nyman collaborated with director Peter Greenaway in the 1980s (see Chapter 12). A notable exception was Peter Maxwell Davies, who provided music for Ken Russell's productions of *The Devils* (1970) and *The Boy Friend* (1971). Music for the former, an outrageously lurid baroque horror film which made some of the musicians participating in the recording feel physically nauseated, was provided by Davies's celebrated avant-garde ensemble The Fires of London, with diegetic early music by the equally renowned period-instrument specialist David Munrow. Davies's score balances a lyrical but disturbing expressionism (rotting corpses) with avant-garde twitterings (plague victims) and queasy timpani glissandi (burning at the stake), with snatches of grotesque parody including an impressive conjunction of a diegetic *Dies irae* procession with extreme nondiegetic modernism – the latter throughout exceptionally well suited to such strong visual imagery. Far more conventional was his tuneful and impressionistic scoring of *The Boy Friend*, which included spirited pastiches of the Charleston and foxtrot for Polly's dream sequence.

Until the late 1970s, when his increasing dissatisfaction with the commercial bias of film music influenced his decision to work largely for television, Richard Rodney Bennett was perhaps the ultimate example of a front-rank composer equally comfortable with film and concert work. His youthful studies with Lennox Berkeley (1953–6) and Pierre Boulez (1957–9) left him well versed in both tonal and avant-garde idioms, and with a particular affinity for the English pastoral tradition, French neo-classicism and Schoenbergian serialism. He was also a gifted jazz pianist and cabaret performer, who (like the similarly versatile Schifrin) moonlighted at Paris jazz clubs during his formative years. These experiences left Bennett with an unusually wide range of stylistic possibilities at his creative disposal when he immersed himself in film work, which commenced when he was still only nineteen and found himself encouraged to embark on documentaries and thrillers by Hollingsworth. Bennett's output of film music thereafter co-existed alongside a steady stream of well-received concert works, the technical sophistication of which inevitably rubbed off at times on the often advanced harmonic language of his film scores.

Diversity was much in evidence in his early assignments, which included a lush easy-listening backdrop for the star-studded *Indiscreet* (dir. Stanley Donen, 1958), a cool-jazz score (conducted by Arnold) for Losey's *Blind Date* (US title *Chance Meeting*, 1959), and modernistic and often hyperbolic rhetoric in a number of Hammer thrillers: *The Man Who Could Cheat Death* (dir. Fisher, 1959), on which the music track featured electronic organ, reverbed percussion and a high level of dissonance; the dark Bette Davis vehicle *The Nanny* (dir. Seth Holt, 1965), with its prominent harpsichord and psychological insights underlined by music illuminating different points of view and, at the end, delusions; and *The Witches* (US title *The Devil's Own*; dir. Cyril Frankel, 1966), its score again dominated by percussion, including marimba to conjure up an aura of African black magic (Larson 1996, 72–6). Ken Russell's film of Len Deighton's thriller *Billion Dollar Brain* (1967), a more overtly commercial venture financed by the same team responsible for the contemporaneous James Bond series (United Artists and Saltzman), commenced with main-title music for the unorthodox forces of three pianos and orchestra, couched in a Poulenc-like idiom of Gallic suavity which Bennett confessed was directly inspired by Legrand's score for *La Baie des anges* (dir. Jacques Demy, 1962); French details in Bennett's response extended to the melodic use of an ondes martenot throughout the score (Phillips 2002, 25), which also included the then fashionable sonority of the harpsichord and a brilliant set-piece for an assassination on the steps of a Russian church in Finland featuring ritualistic Kremlin-like bell effects filtered through the clear influence of Stravinsky's *Les Noces*. Some years later it was in favour of a fashionable score by Legrand that Losey parted company with Bennett when the latter's score to *The Go-Between* (1971) was rejected by the director because he felt it to be 'too dramatic and climactic' (Caute 1994, 263), Legrand in turn incurring Losey's wrath because his replacement music too closely resembled the French composer's earlier score to *The Thomas Crown Affair*. But in the shape of two other musically sensitive directors, Schlesinger and Sidney Lumet, Bennett found lasting creative partnerships that inspired his most substantial and memorable film music.

The collaboration with Schlesinger began with the comedy *Billy Liar* in 1963, a witty tale of the surreal daydreaming of a restless undertaker's assistant furnished with economical music both gently parodistic and fashionably jazzy, and peaked with the Thomas Hardy adaptation *Far From the Madding Crowd* (1967). During work on the Hardy project Bennett's conviction that attending the filming process was of no benefit to a composer was confirmed by the fact that at the Dorset location shoot he merely 'sat there and sneezed and had no musical ideas at all' (quoted in Daniel 2000, 153). The Hardy score is a model of sensitive spotting and the kind of organic structural control at which the best conservatory-trained composers excel, as shown by the extended sequence in which the passage of Bathsheba's and Troy's initial courtship is persuasively underscored by gradual musical developments, each appropriate to the changing setting: beginning with their first nocturnal encounter, the music imparts continuity across the passage-of-time montage, shifting up a semitone into the beekeeping scene and introducing an appropriately onomatopoeic buzzing motif (related to the main theme), remaining designedly subservient under dialogue (where the theme is delicately hinted at by celeste); then, as the camera sweeps with Bathsheba into the open countryside, thematic developments become far more expansive yet harmonically unstable, permitting the incorporation of spirited mickey-mousing for Troy's flamboyant sword-play, and satisfyingly reserving the fully fledged form of what is now a love theme until the sequence's concluding kiss, this climactic theme having been alluded to all along by motivic patterns similar to both the intervallic shape and rhythm of its distinctive anacrusis. Bennett's score to Schlesinger's *Yanks* (1979) juxtaposed an English pastoralism, including delicate romantic underscoring with sufficient harmonic interest to safeguard against banality, with a tenser style best exemplified by the main-title cue which emerges from a Sousa-style opening to prolong the march rhythm with a dissonant bass line and searching, lyrical string theme (layered much in the manner of Frankel's distinctive texture in *Battle of the Bulge*), both helping to promote a sense of expectancy among American troops arriving in the north of England via a truck convoy.

For Lumet, Bennett scored the all-star Agatha Christie whodunit *Murder on the Orient Express* (1974), in which the motion of the elegant train was characterized by an energetic waltz tapping both popular-song associations and, in the melody's more atmospheric incarnations, the impressionistic sophistication of Ravel's *La Valse* (1928). (According to Elmer Bernstein (Waletzky 1994), the literal-minded Herrmann singularly failed to grasp why Bennett had composed a flippant tune for a 'train of death', Bernstein using this as an example of Herrmann's inability to understand light-heartedness.) Alongside the waltz, Bennett included snatches of the 1930s dance-band style which the director had originally planned to dominate the project, and drew attention to the inherently superficial nature of such glossy movie entertainment with a lushly romantic main-title overture in hyperbolic piano-concerto style. His technical sophistication came to the fore in the partly aleatoric music for the eerie kidnap montage that serves as the film's prologue, this and the subsequent octatonic stingers for the stark newspaper headlines later receiving a satisfying structural reworking as the same music returns for the flashback of the murder, each stinger recapitulated against the individual knife-stabs of the multiple killers who are wreaking their collective revenge. Bennett's music for Lumet's *Equus* (1977) is discussed in Chapter 11 for its dark allusions to the idiom of Bach's Passions. As in much of Bennett's film music, his advanced harmonic style here allows him to bring cues to an end with subtle unresolved dissonances in order to promote a sense of expectancy – a natural development of the somewhat more intrusive interrupted cadences that served this purpose in the Golden Age *lingua franca* of tonal film scoring.

Bennett became associated with historical costume dramas in the early 1970s through his Russian-tinged music for the stolid epic *Nicholas and Alexandra* (dir. Franklin Schaffner, 1971), and a lyrical score to *Lady Caroline Lamb* (dir. Robert Bolt, 1972) drawing heavily on the idioms of Finzi and Walton, especially the harmonic language of the latter's Viola Concerto (1929). Unlike some film composers, Bennett did not regard his later TV work as a poor cousin to music for the silver screen, and in 1999 he gave up a Royal Opera House commission in order to score the BBC's big-budget serialization of Mervyn Peake's *Gormenghast* novels (Daniel 2000, 152), commenting that working on his full-orchestral score for this project – his first to be orchestrated by another's hand – was 'like doing a film in the good old days' (quoted in Phillips 2002, 27). His occasional forays back into cinema had in the meantime included a collaboration with director Mike Newell, for whom he provided a dreamily romantic score for *Enchanted April* (1991) showcasing solo strings and ondes martenot, and delicately reharmonizing Elgar's *Chanson de matin* (first played diegetically by a solo oboe), and a score for the smash hit *Four Weddings and a Funeral* (1994), which at the end of the century remained the most commercially successful British film of all time, having netted £130 million at the global box office (J. Walker 2006, 422). Bennett dismissed this best-known of his film projects as 'a disaster musically because they changed the whole score' (quoted in Phillips 2002, 24), referring to the jettisoning of much of his carefully spotted love-affair music in favour of exploitative pop songs aimed at a youth audience.

The other British film composer to emerge with an international reputation in the 1960s, for very different reasons, was John Barry, who won Academy Awards for *Born Free* (dir. James Hill, 1965; awards for both score and song), *The Lion in Winter* (dir. Anthony Harvey, 1968), *Out of Africa* (dir. Sydney Pollack, 1985) and *Dances with Wolves* (dir. Kevin Costner, 1990). Apart from the historical epic *The Lion in Winter*, with its fine dramatic score featuring impressive choral writing, Barry's most memorable film music was inspired by the successful Bond franchise, on which he worked intermittently between 1962 and 1987, and his music for which is discussed in Chapter 10 in the context of the exploitation of pop styles in British film scoring of the time. His Oscars were awarded to tuneful scores well suited to natural or expansive imagery, and *Out of Africa* in particular established an immediately recognizable soundworld based on lyrical violin melody and slowly moving triadic harmony which the composer later reworked on numerous occasions.

Extremely prolific, Barry rarely recaptured the freshness of the best of his 1960s output and after the mid-1980s repeatedly resorted to formulaic applications of the same clutch of basic root-position triads, often scored in close position for trombones; he rarely adapted his style to generic requirements, with the result that expansive landscapes (*Out of Africa*), Sioux Indians (*Dances with Wolves*) and seventeenth-century puritans (*The Scarlet Letter*, dir. Roland Joffé, 1995) all ended up sounding much the same. Kevin Mulhall mildly expresses the sense of disappointment and missed opportunity often engendered by Barry's compositional recyclings, with particular reference to *Swept from the Sea* (dir. Beeban Kidron, 1997): 'The usual Barryisms are all here, including a headlining main theme, long-line monophonic melodies in song structures, . . . tonal harmonies, accessible chord progressions, the doubling of parts and the repetition of phrases . . . Other than an Eastern European composition ("Yanko's Dance"), there is no period or ethnic material . . . A solid if somewhat familiar effort from Barry' (M. Walker 1998, 38). Other commentators have been disappointed by the 'certain ad hoc quality' of Barry's compositional technique (Darby and Du Bois 1990, 391).

More versatile was the work of George Fenton, who entered film scoring in the 1980s with considerable experience of writing music for theatre and television behind him. His simplest film scores were those which discretely punctuated and supported the low-budget social dramas of independent British director Ken Loach (*Ladybird Ladybird*, 1994; *Land of Freedom*, 1995; *Carla's Song*, 1996; *My Name is Joe*, 1998; *Bread and Roses*, 2000; *Sweet Sixteen*, 2002; *Ae Fond Kiss*, 2004), for whom he continued to work loyally in spite of numerous freelance commissions from Hollywood which earned him no fewer than five Academy Award nominations in the period 1982–91. This international exposure began with *Gandhi* (1982), the first of Fenton's many collaborations with British director Richard Attenborough; the soundtracks of this and their later *Cry Freedom* (1987) were important for a sensitive use of ethnic musical elements (see Chapter 12). Fenton's music for Neil Jordan's *The Company of Wolves* (1984) demonstrated a sure command of both electronic and acoustic resources, and in period costume dramas he excelled at adapting pre-existing baroque music alongside freshly composed neo-classical cues (*Dangerous Liaisons*, 1988; *The Madness of King George*, 1994). The dark side of Victorian London was evoked by his broodingly modal string writing for *Mary Reilly* (dir. Stephen Frears, 1996) and a more wistful folk-like mood permeated the Hardy adaptation *The Woodlanders* (dir. Phil Agland, 1997).

For Hollywood, Fenton provided both easy-going pop scores for routine romantic comedies (e.g. *The Object of My Affection* and *You've Got Mail*, both 1998; *Sweet Home Alabama*, 2002; *Hitch*, 2005), and more imaginative – and at times appropriately surreal – music for offbeat projects such as *The Fisher King* (dir. Terry Gilliam, 1991) and Harold Ramis's unorthodox comedies *Groundhog Day* (1993) and *Multiplicity* (1996). Fenton's firm grasp of generic formulae was demonstrated by the Rózsa-like expressionism of his score to the neo-*noir* thriller *Final Analysis* (dir. Phil Joanou, 1992), the dignified patriotic and heroic music for the endearingly old-fashioned British war film *Memphis Belle* (dir. Michael Caton-Jones, 1990) and the virtuosity of his music for the animated feature *Valiant* (see Chapter 7). His most satisfying work was inspired by intelligent adaptations of thought-provoking literary sources such as the C. S. Lewis drama *Shadowlands* (dir. Attenborough, 1993) and Arthur Miller's play *The Crucible* (dir. Nicholas Hytner, 1996). In *Shadowlands*, a specially composed Anglican anthem performed diegetically at the outset by the choir of Lewis's college in Oxford provides the thematic basis for a tautly organized nondiegetic orchestral score that climaxes in a profoundly moving end-title cue (played with searing intensity by the LSO under Fenton's direction), its style alluding to Elgar's *nobilmente* idiom but the flow of the music subtly affected by unpredictable metrical changes. Even in less challenging genre assignments like *Final Analysis*, Fenton often clinched his musical arguments in freshly composed end-title music (rarely providing the lazy rehash of earlier cues and song themes typically used as padding for this part of a film): the final music in *The Crucible*, for example, provides a much-needed note of dignified human resilience as a release from the gloom of the tragic final scene. Admittedly, most spectators quit the cinema as soon as the end-title music begins; but Fenton composes these epilogues as much with his fine orchestral players in mind, giving them the cathartic opportunity to perform something more substantial and satisfying than the fragmentary cues which are their normal filmic fodder.

7 Defectors to television

Documentary and animation were two specialized genres of film conceived for theatrical release that flourished in this context only in the heyday of movie-going, when audiences still expected to see more than one attraction in a programme and something by way of contrast to the feature-length and mostly fictional narratives that formed the core of the presentation. The documentary film in the pre-television era fulfilled both didactic and entertaining functions – and, in times of war, totalitarianism or national crisis, often served as powerful propaganda aimed at a captive spectatorship. In both Europe and the USA in the 1930s and 1940s some documentary films acquired artistic prestige on account of an audio-visual experimentalism that was often sorely lacking in narrative films. By contrast, the animated short was generally comedic in nature and predominantly anthropomorphic in conception, but occasionally abstract or didactic in intent. The fortunes of both genres in the cinema seriously and permanently dipped towards the end of the 1950s when television established itself as the ideal medium for disseminating factual and current-affairs programmes, at the same time as a growing demand for uncontroversial family and children's viewing secured cartoons a firm (and, to the production companies, still lucrative) niche in the living room. This development occurred as theatrical features continued to become more adult-oriented in the wake of the long-awaited collapse of the moral strictures of Hollywood's Production Code. The firm foothold enjoyed by documentaries and animation in television schedules has more recently been further cemented by the success of satellite and cable channels dedicated to each: since the late 1980s it has taken the technological marvel of IMAX to lure spectators back into theatrical venues to see factual films, an initiative recalling the combination of up-to-date technology and sheer spectacle previously exploited by Hollywood to compete with the television boom in the 1950s.

The present chapter surveys the musical highlights of documentary films and the specialized musical provision for both commercial animation in Hollywood and experimental animated projects elsewhere up to the 1950s; in addition, it considers the sporadic attempts to revitalize the genres in more recent times. Also examined is the feature-length animated film, which in the hands of Walt Disney's groundbreaking production team has remained commercially successful in a theatrical context until the present day. As we shall see, Disney's studio was also an important player in the later history of the populist documentary.

THE DOCUMENTARY FILM

Documentaries in the early years of the sound film were an extension of the simple newsreel productions that had helped accelerate the development of sound-film technology in the late 1920s, such newsreels thereafter continuing to provide audiences with topical information alongside lengthier and more elaborate fact-based films. The first regular newsreel service was the Pathé Gazette, launched in 1910 and followed by similar weekly bulletins issued by Gaumont and Fox. Their early obsession with public spectacle and patriotism helped to create an indelible association between newsworthy images and military music – both marches and fanfares – and the films generally received appropriate locational music, all of which was supplied by the movie theatres' resident musicians in the normal manner (Altman 2004, 382). One of the more unusual musical ventures inspired by newsreels came as a result of Hindemith's persuading Milhaud to experiment with Blum's *Musikchronometer* at Baden-Baden in 1929 (see Chapter 2), which stimulated the French composer to write a suite of *Actualités* for concert use, carefully timed to newsreel images, because at the time he had 'nothing better to do' (Milhaud 1952, 174; Nichols 1996, 48).

In the sound era, pressures to issue newsreels to tight schedules meant that commissioning new music was impracticable, and editors relied heavily on stock library music instead. In the UK, much music of this kind – pre-recorded and archived in the medium of celluloid soundtrack, ready for rapid use – was prepared by Louis Levy for Gaumont British News, and in 1943 the London music publisher Boosey & Hawkes set up a similar enterprise (Huntley [1947], 133). Naïvely jolly march melodies remained common, with music of epic struggle customary for war footage, rousing title music for feel-good national events, easy-listening background music for domestic scenes, symphonic jazz for chic high-street fashions, and plentiful recourse to classical staples from the silent era, no matter how inappropriate: in a Pathé newsreel from 1937, for example, radium mining in Czechoslovakia is accompanied by Mendelssohn's *Hebrides* Overture. In propaganda newsreels, footage from enemy countries might be parodied by the use of distorted image editing and bitingly satirical music, as when Nazi goose-stepping was doctored to go both forwards and backwards in cartoon style to the accompaniment of the popular song 'The Lambeth Walk' in the 1940 Movietone newsreel *Panzer Ballet* (Huntley [1947], 135). Pathé ceased its newsreel production in 1956, having become part of the

Warner empire; Paramount's rival operation stopped a year later, with Fox Movietone following suit in 1963.

From the earliest newsreel years, sceptical observers questioned the legitimacy of borrowing manipulative narrative techniques from the fiction film in a context of (pseudo)objective photographic reportage (Hill and Gibson 2000, 43). This concern proved even more troubling when emotively suggestive music was also present, the modern manifestation of this trend being the use of crudely exploitative 'thriller'-type music behind TV news reports of real-life tragedies. The question of whether music for documentaries should be neutral or suggestive in mood has had to be confronted by all modern composers of new scores for the great factual films of the silent era, whether they emulate keyboard techniques appropriate to the period in which the film was made (as, for example, in Neil Brand's music to Shackleton's Antarctic epic *South* (dir. Frank Hurley, 1919), restored by the British Film Institute in 2002) or reflect changing fashions (as in the various scores to Robert Flaherty's seminal *Nanook of the North* by William Axt (1922), Rudolf Schramm (1947 sound reissue) and Stanley Silverman (1976)). Late highlights of the silent documentary received standard compilation scores on their initial release: Flaherty's South Seas project *Moana* was scored in 1926 by James C. Bradford, and the human-migration saga *Grass* (1925) and Siam-set *Chang* (1927), both made by the *King Kong* team of Cooper and Schoedsack early in their careers, were premièred with music by Hugo Riesenfeld.

The problem of emotional music with objective reportage was bypassed somewhat in experimental documentaries in the Soviet Union and Europe that took artistic risks not only in their visual images and editing but also their sonic provision. Mechanical music for a factual film was the subject of an experiment by director Jean Grémillon in his *Un Tour au large* (1926), which attempted to synchronize a Pleyela piano with the projector's mechanism (Lacombe and Porcile 1995, 222–3). Dziga Vertov's *The Man with the Movie Camera* (1929) offered a vivid and symbolic portrayal of everyday life in Soviet cities through virtuosic relational editing, and the director left detailed notes on his desired sound provision to guide the three composers from Sovkino's Music Council responsible for preparing its cue sheets. In the event, the composers in question merely stitched together gobbets of classical repertoire and it was not until 1995 that the synthesizer-and-junk-metal trio, The Alloy Orchestra, attempted to capture the witty and at times avant-garde nature of Vertov's imaginative soundscapes. The latter were summarized by Yuri Tsivian as

> his permanent tendency to start a sequence with conventional music
> steadily growing into the pandemonium of noises, his desire to 'freeze'

music, reverse it or make it sound 'slow-motion' in the same manner as film shots do, his bias towards 'found music' (comic chases, gramophones, song inserts, puppet theatre music, Chinese music, pub music, etc.) which makes the film 'sound' almost as documentary as it looks . . .

(Tsivian 1995, 95)

The Alloy Orchestra's virtuosic score – partly pre-composed, partly improvised and incorporating live sound effects, and likened by one critic to 'Rachmaninoff playing ambient music with experimental industrial band Einsturzende Neubauten' (Follett 1997, 15), was subsequently released on DVD by the British Film Institute together with a repetitive electronic score by In the Nursery as a less challenging alternative. The film was reissued in 2002 with a new music track by the Michael Nyman Band featuring their characteristic funky quirkiness and moments of haunting poetry – relatively little of which was directly allied to the specific suggestions of the visual images. Vertov himself went on to make both synchronous and asynchronous use of sound in his *Enthusiasm: Symphony of the Don Basin* (1931), much praised by Chaplin for the quasi-musical applications of mechanical noise in its soundtrack, and relied on music by Yuri Shaporin as a cohesive device in *Three Songs of Lenin* (1934).

The music-inspired subtitle of *Enthusiasm* was typical of experimental film-makers' equation of moving pictures with abstract musical structure in this period, and *The Man with the Movie Camera* belongs to a documentary subgenre generally referred to as 'city symphonies'. A celebrated example was Walter Ruttmann's *Berlin: Symphony of a Great City* (1927), its montage influenced by the work of Eisenstein and its close relationship between visual and musical rhythms not only explicit in the wording of the title but also reflected in the fact that the film was cut to suit the rhythms of the music by Meisel with which it was accompanied at major screenings in Germany (Barnouw 1993, 73–4). The 'symphony' label even occurred in an industrial context, as shown by *The Oil Symphony* (dir. Boris Pumpyanski, 1932), a semi-documentary about the heroic efforts of Azerbaidzhani labourers drilling for oil, with its motoric scoring by S. Paniev typical of Soviet musical experimentation before Stalin's clamp-down on decadent modernism soon afterwards (Winter 1941, 158).

Hanns Eisler

Another experimental city symphony was Dutch director Joris Ivens's short film *Rain* (1929), made up of shots of rainy Amsterdam and furnished with a chamber score by Hanns Eisler in 1941 as part of his film-music research project funded by the Rockefeller Foundation. The Eisler version was screened in Los Angeles in 1947 and New York in 1948 (Dümling 1998, 547). Very much in the Schoenbergian atonal mould (the published score begins with an anagram on Schoenberg's surname and the instrumentation is the same as *Pierrot lunaire*), Eisler's music attempted to achieve a balance between illustrative effects and autonomous structure, and is also known in the form of a concert work entitled *Fourteen Ways of Describing Rain* – the title referring to the sectionalized format (analysed in an appendix to Adorno and Eisler 1994 [1947], 135–65) in which the short musical structures at which he believed modernism to excel form the starting point for the scheme of cues. Ivens's evocative film received a new score by Edward Dudley Hughes (*Light Cuts Through Dark Skies*) at the Bath International Festival in 2001, in which Hughes's own sectionalization did not prevent a pleasing sense of linear continuity.

Earlier in his career Eisler had collaborated closely with Ivens on the documentaries *Komsomols* (1932), *New Earth* (1934) and *400 Million* (1938). The first of these was an account of growth in the Soviet steel industry for which Ivens insisted his composer acquire personal experience of the milieu, telling him: 'you cannot write this music if you do not see and hear the entire sound and work environment and the revolutionary spirit' (Dümling 1998, 504). In *400 Million* Eisler achieved a Brechtian distanciation in his music for the Japanese attack on China, and Ivens was content not to hear the score until it was a *fait accompli*. The much better-known *New Earth* combined an account of the draining of the Zuider Zee with protest at the artificial manipulation of wheat prices and achieved much of its impact from its uncompromising music, the third part of the film having been constructed according to the composer's creative input. Ivens accorded another composer similar editorial respect when, years later, he worked with Shostakovich on *The Song of the Rivers* (1954), commissioned by the World Federation of Trade Unions, and asked his advice on the editing: 'Although it may seem heresy in the music departments of Hollywood for me to say so, I believe that the composer can be a great help with suggestions for the cutting and timing of the visuals' (quoted in Riley 2005, 77).

Eisler's contributions to documentary and semi-documentary genres included *Kuhle Wampe* (dir. Slatan Dudow, 1932), a docu-drama about the youth activities of the Communist Party written by Brecht, in which Eisler's approach is comparable to the asynchronicity of Pudovkin's and Shaporin's contemporaneous *Deserter* (see Chapter 9). The film was produced by Prometheus (who in 1926 had been responsible for the German exhibition of Eisenstein's *Battleship Potemkin*); the company went out of business in the process, and the film was promptly banned by the Social Democrats because of its frank portrayal of the Depression in the Weimar Republic and allegedly subversive nature. Eisler commented of the film's depiction of the homes of the poor: 'These very quiet pictures were counterpointed with extremely energetic and stimulating music, which not only suggested pity with the poor, but at the same time provoked protest against such a state of affairs' (quoted in Winter 1941, 158). Anempathy is also encountered in the accompaniment of idyllic pastoral scenes by bleakly austere chamber music. Elsewhere Eisler's score is static in effect rather than developmental, virtuosic at the start in its neo-classical bustling ostinati, and with some muscular underscoring of scenes of heavy industry; the soundtrack also featured ballads sung by Helene Weigel (Brecht's partner) and Ernst Busch.

White Flood (1940) was an information film about glaciers made by a creative team at Frontier Films and scored by Eisler as part of his Rockefeller project. The composer's response was to write a sixteen-minute serial work that would also stand apart from the images, and the music was indeed subsequently heard notatim in concert performance as the Chamber Symphony, Op. 69 (1950). Eisler himself was thoroughly satisfied with his attempt to build specific illustrative details into his music without sacrificing its autonomous structural cogency or serial idiom, having opted to use the latter so as to avoid deeply ingrained associations between tonality and emotion, even though he felt that introducing dodecaphony to film music 'at first blush seems as absurd as using Hegelian terminology in a gossip column' (Eisler 1941). Wilfrid Mellers observed that the composer exploited illustrative motifs for water and ice as the basis for a passacaglia, chorale variations, scherzo, etude and finale in sonata form, with patterned ostinati suggestive of the 'eternal, timeless quality of icebergs' ensuring that the visual imagery was *'translated into terms that work through the language of music'* (Irving *et al.* 1954, 106; emphasis in original). Eisler's score to *The Forgotten Village* (dir. Herbert Kline and Alexander Hammid, 1941), shot to a script by Steinbeck about cultural change in Mexico, employed an economical serial technique alongside Mexican folk music, and was similarly episodic in construction.

Other notable directors who employed Eisler on documentary projects were Joseph Losey and Alain Resnais. Eisler scored Losey's short Technicolor puppet animation *Pete Roleum and His Cousins* for the Petroleum Industries Exhibition at the 1939 New York World's Fair (in collaboration with Oscar Levant) and the Nursery Educators' documentary *A Child Went Forth* (1940) as part of his Rockefeller enterprise. Eisler's most enduring filmic achievement was his highly regarded score to Resnais's *Nuit et brouillard* (*Night and Fog*, 1955), a meditation on the horrors of the Holocaust for which the economical music, sometimes changing texture without direct reference to the image sequence, juxtaposed rare moments of brutality and foreboding with a predominant sense of emotional neutrality emphasized by transparent chamber scoring. Neutrality extended into anempathy with the appearance of a perplexingly pleasant diatonic cue for flute and strings to accompany shots of the gas chambers at Auschwitz. Royal S. Brown has described Eisler's music as 'a perfect example of a nonnarrativizing, non-mythifying film score' which 'does not even attempt to join with the visuals and the voice-over narration to create a closed-off universe of consummated affect', its abstract quality reflecting 'the brutal irony of the indifferent ordinariness that can mask unspeakable horrors' (R. S. Brown 1994, 31). Like Ivens, Resnais paid warm tribute to Eisler's contribution to the shaping of the film as a whole and recalled that he 'showed me how to apply music to create something akin to a "second level of perception," something additional, contrariwise' (quoted in Dümling 1998, 578).

Documentaries in the United States

Eisler's experiments, though aesthetically notable, stood well away from the mainstream of documentary soundtracks. Far more influential on the course of film music in general were memorable scores to US documentaries composed by Virgil Thomson, Aaron Copland and others which helped to forge a distinctively American sound that left outmoded European romantic models far behind. Copland also worked selectively on Hollywood feature films in the 1940s (see Chapter 3), but Thomson scored no Hollywood films and made a modest name for himself as a film composer only in the field of independent but seminally important documentaries.

Thomson's simple nationalistic style of film music was launched in his score to the Depression documentary *The Plow that Broke the Plains,* directed by Pare Lorentz for the Roosevelt Government's Farm Services Administration in 1936. Both Lorentz and Thomson were newcomers to the medium of film. Shot to a budget of only $6,000, *The Plow* evocatively depicted the rural calamity of the dust bowl in the Great Plains States, suggesting in a short and prosaic epilogue (later cut by the director) that the government was working hard to remedy the situation. Thomson was sufficiently moved by Lorentz's efforts that he agreed to compose the music for the film for whatever fee the director was able to secure (Barnouw 1993, 115). Thomson composed as the film was shot, with some scenes edited to pre-existing music and others scored after editing; the music, recorded by members of the New York Philharmonic, directly matched the film's mood of betrayed innocence by discarding 'post-Wagnerian hyperbole and egomania in favour of what Wilfrid Mellers calls "the surrealistically childlike unsentimentality" of Satie and his own grass roots, first and foremost Baptist hymnody' (Palmer 1992, 4). Telling use was made of instrumental variants on the Old 100th, a tune instantly recognizable to Americans as the Doxology 'Praise God, from Whom All Blessings Flow'. The most important, and lastingly influential, of the score's stylistic innovations were its cultivation of a pure harmonic language, sometimes diatonic and sometimes modal, and the simple use of pre-existing folk melodies such as cowboy songs and a US Army marching song from the First World War. To accompany the plains' fertile wheat production, Thomson included a 'blues' cue, its dissonantly jazzy style reminiscent of Copland's symphonic-jazz concert works from the 1920s, in a remarkable montage that culminated in shots of a frenetic black jazz musician rapidly intercut with a tickertape machine communicating wheat prices.

The Plow struck an unpredicted chord with the film-going public, and was shown in 3,000 movie theatres in the USA in spite of growing opposition from Hollywood to what it saw as government-backed competition in the field of commercial cinema (Barnouw 1993, 118). Its success inspired Lorentz and Thomson to make a second documentary in 1937, a vivid treatment of flooding, social problems and New Deal model agricultural communities on the Mississippi entitled *The River*, which ended in an optimistic account of the building of the new Tennessee Valley dams. As in *The Plow*, Thomson's simply textured and often folk-inspired music played almost continuously, sometimes beneath lyrically inflected narration from baritone Thomas Chalmers: the overall result was described by Lorentz as 'operatic' (Barnouw 1993, 120). Shot to a much larger budget of $50,000, the film was distributed by Paramount and marked the high-point of government-backed documentaries before funding was withdrawn from such projects in 1940. Hollywood was at this time enabled to capitalize on the style of the Lorentz–Thomson collaboration with its own treatments of fictional rural tales, including several based on novels by Steinbeck such as *The Grapes of Wrath* (1940; dir. John Ford, music by Alfred Newman) and two directed by Lewis Milestone and scored by Copland, *Of Mice and Men* (1939) and *The Red Pony* (1949). As we saw in Chapter 3, Copland's music for the latter in particular exerted a powerful influence on the future course of the musical scoring of westerns.

Copland had come to Milestone's attention as a result of his music for the documentary *The City* (dir. Ralph Steiner and Willard Van Dyke, 1939). This utopian but inventive and witty vision of metropolitan design was funded by the American Institute of City Planners and, like Losey's *Pete Roleum*, made for exhibition at New York's World's Fair. Copland's music, clearly influenced by Thomson's example, offset rustic simplicity for the opening setting in a New England village with propulsively mechanical ostinato patterns accompanying city life – in the case of a sequence showing a traffic jam, somewhat ironically (Thompson and Bordwell 2003, 310). Erik Barnouw (1993, 122) sees a link between the film's 'choral voice montages' and trends in British documentaries at the time. Copland's score, which was much admired by Stravinsky, helped the film avoid what Copland himself described as 'two major pitfalls of documentaries, preachiness and symbolism, and the result was a human intimacy that appealed to all kinds of audiences' (Copland and Perlis 1984, 290). Van Dyke gave industrialization a similar treatment in a follow-up documentary, *Valley Town* (1940), with music by Marc Blitzstein, who also scored *Native Land* (dir. Paul Strand and Leo Hurwitz, 1942), and had previously collaborated with Thomson in selecting Spanish folksong for use in Ivens' US debut, *The Spanish Earth* (1937), a hard-hitting documentary about the Spanish Civil War scripted and narrated by Ernest Hemingway.

In later years Thomson scored important documentaries by directors Robert Flaherty and Thorold Dickinson. Flaherty's final film *Louisiana Story* (1948), sponsored anonymously by New Jersey's Standard Oil, told the tale of a young boy whose idyllic rural life is threatened by oil prospectors. Since the film focused on a simple Cajun community descended from eighteenth-century immigrants from Acadia, Thomson utilized Cajun folk and dance melodies in his score, which was recorded by the Philadelphia Orchestra; but he also reworked autonomous classical structures where dramatically justified, including a sombre passacaglia (for the robbing of an alligator's nest) and vigorously dissonant fugue (for the boy's fight with the alligator). The film's score, which therefore trod a middle ground between popular simplicity and esoteric sophistication (reflected in Thomson's decision to publish two separate orchestral suites from it, one devoted to the 'classical' cues and the other to the appealing 'Acadian Songs and Dances'), went on to win a Pulitzer Prize. Thomson's preoccupation with erudite counterpoint was later reflected in the inclusion of several fugues in his majestic score to Dickinson's documentary *Power Among Men* (1958).

Information films in the United Kingdom

Amongst the most celebrated documentaries of all time are some of the many films made in Britain during the 1930s by the General Post Office (GPO) Film Unit. As in other countries at this time, left-wing political beliefs here bore creative fruit under the influence of techniques pioneered by Soviet film-makers (whose work was frequently subjected to domestic censorship when exported). Even short films such as Paul Rotha's temporarily banned pacifist statement *Peace of Britain* (1936; music by Britten) could create a storm of controversy quite incommensurate with their technical and artistic substance. Rotha's earlier *Rising Tide* (1933), with a score by Clarence Raybould, initiated a long series of GPO projects in which advertising and marketing goals were combined with audio-visual experimentation. The key figure in the movement was producer-director John Grierson, who had coined the term 'documentary' in 1926. Grierson regarded cinema as a pulpit, telling his staff to avoid being 'aestheticky' and declaring that art should be a hammer for propaganda and not a mirror of life (Barnouw 1993, 85, 89); his 'factual' films took the form of a 'creative treatment of actuality' (Hill and Gibson 2000, 43). Grierson had been closely associated with Flaherty in the USA and Cavalcanti in France, for both of whom he secured work at the UK's Empire Marketing Board Film Unit (EMBFU) in 1933. While in Britain, Flaherty filmed his *Man of Aran* (1934) for Gaumont British, to mixed critical reaction: its score by John Greenwood created what François Porcile described as 'a calamitous marriage of the descriptive and the imitative' (Lacombe and Porcile 1995, 234).

Grierson had laid the foundations for the EMBFU in 1929 at around the time *Battleship Potemkin* – then banned in the UK – was screened at the private London Film Society. The Society also screened city documentaries, and in this context the almost newsreel-like appearance of *Potemkin*'s images would not have escaped attention: certainly Grierson's own work was significantly influenced by Eisenstein's montage techniques. The EMBFU became the GPO Film Unit during the production of Basil Wright's *The Song of Ceylon* (1934), made under the auspices of the Ceylon Tea Propaganda Board, with a widely admired score by Walter Leigh written and recorded in advance on multiple audio channels, the images edited to the recording (Mathieson 1948, 323). Leigh also composed music for *Pett and Pott: A Fairy Story of the Suburbs* (dir. Cavalcanti, 1934), and the GPO's spoof musical *The Fairy of the Phone* (dir. Wright, 1936), in which telephone operators double as singing chorines with appropriate balletic and comedic danceband-style scoring, all to a script culled from the wording of the London Telephone Directory. Leigh's promising career was cut short when he was killed on active service in 1942.

The GPO's film output vacillated between mundanity and memorability, its unevenness the result of two differing target audiences: those attending cinemas, for whom the Unit offered prestige productions, and those seeing films in their local youth clubs, village halls and schools, for whom lower-key productions shot in the economical and increasingly popular 16mm format were standard fare (Barnouw 1993, 95–7). The Unit's musical provision was rarely less than impressive, however, its soundtracks including music by Jaubert (*We Live in Two Worlds*; dir. Cavalcanti, 1937) and Milhaud, who scored *The Islanders* (dir. Maurice Harvey, 1939) with a Gallic style, voiced by an ensemble including saxophone, more appropriate for the sequences shot in the Channel Islands than those in the remote Scottish Isles. Early in what would prove to be a distinguished film-music career (see Chapter 6), Brian Easdale scored *A Job in a Million* (dir. Evelyn Spice, 1937), its music including dry and sometimes dissonant abstraction, jazz-influenced riffs (for traffic shots) and neo-classical diatonicism (suggesting the innocence of a young messenger boy). Alan Rawsthorne enlivened *The City* (dir. Ralph Elton, 1939) with his characteristically rich harmonic idiom, including brittle xylophone and nervous woodwind scoring for a pool of typists and modern quartal harmony for an underground mail train. Less adventurous but versatile nonetheless, Ernst Meyer demonstrated his ability to compose in both pastiche classical and romantic styles (*The North Sea*; dir. Harry Watt, 1938) and more up-to-date idioms (*Roadways*; dir. Stuart Legg and William Coldstream, 1937), his differing responses reflecting the strong contrast between natural beauty and mechanized society at the heart of much of the Unit's work.

Undoubtedly the most enduring GPO films proved to be those with soundtracks on which the poet W. H. Auden collaborated with Benjamin Britten during a short but intensely productive period in 1935–6. (It was this collaboration Michael Powell had in mind when he cuttingly dismissed the documentary genre as fit only for 'disappointed feature film-makers or out-of-work poets': see Powell 1986, 241.) Britten had joined the Unit fresh from college, launching his film career with an original but self-consciously elaborate score for *The King's Stamp* (dir. Coldstream, 1935), which exemplifies his dry and dissonant chamber scoring, and showed ingenuity in its effervescent mickey-mousing for the motions of the stamp factory's gumming and perforating machines. Auden joined the team to work on *Negroes* in the autumn of 1935, a Coldstream project about the abolition of slavery and subsequent evolution of the modern Caribbean which was not released until three years later, by which time it had been reworked under the title *God's Chillun*; its music by Britten was a characteristic mélange of West Indian melody, plainsong and sea shanties (Reed 2007, 12). Their final joint film project was *The Way to the Sea* (dir. Rotha, 1936), made by the GPO's spin-off company Strand Films (which produced the notorious *Peace of Britain* in the same year), a treatment of the subject of electrification of the railways with parodic music used to create 'a satirical subversive commentary in which, during the historical sequence, conventional period attitudes are attacked' (Reed 2007, 13). In between came the GPO documentaries *Coal Face* (dir. Cavalcanti, 1935) and *Night Mail* (dir. Watt and Wright, 1936).

Cavalcanti's longstanding interest in, and flair for, creative sound design peaked in *Coal Face*, an account of the British coal-mining industry which, while fulfilling its ostensible remit of demonstrating the industry's vital importance to the national economy, also drew attention to the plight of those working in an extremely dangerous and grossly underpaid job. The latter consideration may also have influenced the disturbingly expressionistic nature of much of the film's striking conjunction of image, music and text: according to a contemporaneous commentator, 'the general atmosphere of the film is dark, and its music neither makes it brighter nor does it underline the shadows superfluously. In a word, the power-ratio between picture and music is always most ideally balanced' (London 1936, 222). Assembled from a jumble of pre-existing footage, the film was made coherent by a continuous soundtrack boldly combining narration, text chanted rhythmically by multiple voices, choral singing and instrumental music, these elements sometimes superimposed or overlapping. In the absence of realistic recorded sounds, Britten's extended percussion section supplied ingenious sound effects in an avant-garde mixture of Foley techniques and *musique concrète* that would have stunned audiences of the time if divorced from the images and played in a concert hall. Alongside sandpaper, chains, drills and conventional percussion instruments, a reversed cymbal recording captured the sound of a train entering a tunnel – an effect probably inspired by Leigh's 'swinging microphone' technique (in which a microphone was swung past a vibrating gong: see Low 1979, 75), this composer's music for *Six-Thirty Collection* (dir. Watt and Edgar Anstey, 1933) also influential on Britten's score (Reed 1999, 68, 76). As in the otherwise utterly different coal-mining feature *How Green Was My Valley*, scored by Alfred Newman in Hollywood eight years later, female voices (here singing Auden's lyric 'O lurcher-loving collier') represent the sunlit domestic stability into which the miners ascend at the end of the film, their emergence from the ground accompanied by appropriately isomorphic music.

Night Mail similarly climaxes in a potent conjunction of poetry and music as the postal train speeds from London to Glasgow, a famous sequence in which the images were edited to a pre-prepared soundtrack. Auden's text 'This is the night mail crossing the border, / Bringing the cheque and the postal order' is declaimed by the commentator in train-like rhythms, supported by a side drum as part of motoric ensemble music that begins with soft dissonant semitones and minor ninths on a cello (*sul ponticello*) and an atmospheric underlay from sandpaper and wind machine. Again the extended percussion section creates the sound of machinery in motion, this time with the aid of compressed air, sandpaper rubbed on slate, clanking booms, a small trolley, hammer, siren and even some coal falling down a shaft (Evans *et al.*, 1987, 138). (Britten's interest in the sound of real trains extended to his personal involvement in location sound-recording, which was typical of the creative team spirit prevailing in the GPO Unit at the time.) As the train rushes headlong towards its destination, so the combination of music and poetry builds to a satisfyingly lyrical and expansive climax. Britten confided to his diary at the start of 1936, while still at work on *Night*

7.1 The manuscript of Benjamin Britten's setting of rhythmicized text by W. H. Auden at the conclusion of the celebrated British documentary film *Night Mail* (GPO Film Unit, 1936), scored for an unorthodox chamber ensemble including sandpaper and wind machine.

Mail, that his GPO commissions had provided a comfortable income of £5 per week 'but owing to the fact I can claim no performing rights (it being Crown property) with the possibility of it being increased to £10 per week or £2 per day'; however, he felt that working in the company of brains such as those of Auden, Wright and Coldstream had left him with 'a bad inferiority complex' (Mitchell and Reed 1991, 400).

Another significant collaboration of Britten's at the GPO Film Unit was with experimental animator Lotte Reiniger, for whom (at Cavalcanti's suggestion) he adapted the music of Rossini for *The Tocher* (1935), a 'film ballet' of animated silhouettes promoting the Post Office's Savings Bank in fairy-tale style. (Britten later dedicated the first of his two concert suites of these Rossini arrangements, *Soirées musicales* (1936) and *Matinées musicales* (1941), to Cavalcanti.) Reiniger's animated advert for greetings telegrams, *The HPO – Heavenly Post Office* (1938), was scored in light-music style by Easdale. The most daring animated experiments to emerge from the Unit were those made by Len Lye and his associate Norman McLaren, the latter joining the team in 1937 and later establishing himself as the most important innovator in the field of animation and graphically animated soundtracks (see below): designs were drawn directly onto film stock and no camera was therefore required. Lye's four-minute *A Colour Box* (1935) presented abstract colour patterns accompanied by a jolly beguine, the film's ending adapted by Grierson to turn it into an explicit advert for cheaper parcel-post rates (Low 1979, 104) and its novel combination of music and abstract animation reportedly influencing Disney's *Fantasia* (Thompson and Bordwell 2003, 321). In *Rainbow Dance* (1936), Lye mixed processed live-action choreography (performed by Rupert Doone) with colour animation and jazzy dance music to create an advert for the Savings Bank, while *Trade Tattoo* (1937) urged customers to post their letters in good time with a similar amalgam of live action, animation and the dance music of the Lecuona Band. McLaren was responsible for *Love on the Wing* (1939), a fantastic animated realization of Ibert's pre-existing Divertissement that achieved a delightful match between bubbly music and dynamic graphics: images of a letter literally winging its way overseas find themselves mixed up with a melodramatic love story in a witty yet lyrical advert for the Empire Air Mail service.

The movies at war: reportage and propaganda

In both the USA and UK during the Second World War, many prominent composers contributed to the war effort by providing music for government-funded propaganda films. Although much output of this kind was of inferior quality, in the hands of a few thoughtful directors and composers the end results were compelling. The foundations for the best of wartime documentary cinema in the USA were laid by director Frank Capra in his work on the 'Why We Fight' series (several of its films shown widely in other countries), which featured mostly anonymous contributions from Hollywood composers Friedhofer, Harline, Lava, Newman, Steiner,

Tiomkin and Webb. Another rising Hollywood star, Alex North, composed around 80 documentary scores for the Office of War Information while serving as a Captain in the US Army. Although such films made basic attempts to address significant social issues – for example in *The Negro Soldier* (1944), scored by Tiomkin – they were more important for reasons outlined by Barnouw:

> For the first time in history, the army was undertaking the political
> education of millions of Americans – who were, for the time being, a captive
> audience. It was called a 'morale' service, but the crystallization of attitudes
> on a wide range of issues – national and international – was very much a
> political matter . . . Civil libertarians who might have objected did not do
> so, perhaps because they were surprised and pleased by the films.
>
> (Barnouw 1993, 162)

A memorable collaboration that built on the work of Capra's influential documentary unit was that between director William Wyler and composer Gail Kubik. Like Herrmann and Britten, Kubik was an experienced composer of incidental music for radio who firmly believed that a composer should not sacrifice individuality of style in the interests of commerce. In 1945 he commented in a lecture on the subject of music for radio: 'More than anything else remember: write your own style . . . If you alter it stylistically to conform to someone else's taste, you are no better than the [hack] men you are trying to replace, and your composer prerogatives will dwindle with every score' (quoted in Donnelly 2001a, 118). His first documentary film scores were for *Men and Ships* (dir. George Gercke, 1940) and *The World at War* (dir. Sam Spewak, 1942); Kubik was furious about the summary treatment accorded to his music during the editing of the latter and entered on unsuccessful litigation in an attempt to buy back his rights to the score. It was his work for the Special Photo Signal Detachment of the US Army Air Force's First Motion Picture Unit that encouraged Kubik to move away from the tendency towards overscoring noticeable in his early film work, cultivating instead a flexible idiom – modern but never gimmicky – influenced by the fresh-sounding styles of Copland and Thomson. Kubik learned how to be selective in the spotting process, providing cues at strategic points rather than lapsing into wall-to-wall background music. In 1943 he identified the principal problem facing the composer of music for documentaries: 'can he discover the form which the film itself takes, and . . . can he then translate his reactions to the film's structure into terms that are both musically satisfying and convincing and yet which also supplement the dramatic impact of the film itself?' (quoted in Donnelly 2001a, 123). In an article published two years later, he went further: 'Music in the documentary film aids democracy to the extent that it is *creatively composed* music . . . it reflects the feelings of a free and unrestricted personality. I cannot believe that the democratic, the American concept of living is furthered by the writing of music dominated by any aesthetic values other than the composer's' (quoted in Flinn 1992, 30).

After working with director Jerry Chodorov (*Earthquakers*, 1943), Kubik scored in 1944–5 two films with Wyler that are widely regarded as perhaps the finest American war documentaries of this period: *The Memphis Belle* (1943) and *Thunderbolt* (made in 1944 but not released until 1947). Both celebrate the achievements of the USAAF in Europe in decidedly unsentimental terms, and the films' soundtracks are in large part responsible for their success. In both films musical cues are almost entirely restricted to scenes of activities on the ground and the stunning aerial sequences are left to speak for themselves, relying on gripping editing of genuine air-battle footage and powerful engine and machine-gun sound effects, all voiced-over with laconic stream-of-consciousness narrations. For the terra-firma scenes, Kubik's style draws on well-known folksongs and popular tunes in a manner reminiscent of Copland, using chamber scoring and often emotionally neutral harmonies, but making occasional excursions into dissonant territory that Copland's music at this time rarely allowed. At no time does Kubik indulge in the kind of cheerfully heroic or militaristic music that so often marred wartime propaganda films across the globe. Kubik's score for *The Memphis Belle*, which was orchestrated by Raksin (who had also orchestrated for Capra's unit), recycled the main-title music from *Earthquakers*, with its nicely judged harmonic twists and angularities. The soundtrack is articulated by an unusual structural parallel between music and narration: in the first part of the film, Kubik provides a series of stinger chords that catch the jump-cut editing in a montage of shots of B17 bombers seen from different angles as they lie at rest on the airfield, and when the music ceases once the cameras and planes are airborne the same audio-visual conjunction returns, but now with disjointed voiced-over phrases replacing the musical stingers on the jump cuts. In *Thunderbolt*, Kubik continued his practice of partly basing his score on appropriate pre-existing themes: Eduardo Di Capua's famous Neapolitan song 'O sole mio' is reworked alongside shots of Italian ruins, and spiky versions of 'Yankee Doodle' and 'The Camptown Races' accompany American airmen at leisure. Kubik uses dissonant bass lines and pedal notes under otherwise fairly conventional harmonies and rhythms, these devices (as in later scores to fictional war films by harmonically ingenious composers such as Frankel and Bennett) preventing the music from sounding banal – especially when combined with militaristic trumpet fanfares and straightforward march rhythms that in lesser hands might have sounded clichéd and bombastic.

In the UK, the GPO Film Unit became the Ministry of Information's Crown Film Unit at the start of the Second World War; along with the Army Film Unit and Royal Naval Film Unit, it continued to commission scores from (amongst others) Addinsell, Alwyn, Bax, Easdale, Greenwood, Jacob, Lambert, Leigh, Rawsthorne and Vaughan Williams (Huntley [1947], 106–23). Among the Crown Film Unit's directors was the inventive Humphrey Jennings, who in his GPO film *Spare Time* (1939) had extended the diegetic cues performed by workers' bands and an amateur choral society in order to serve as nondiegetic backdrop to imaginatively edited scenes of various leisure activities pursued by workers from the key industries of coal, steel and cotton. A similar music-led montage characterized his *Listen to Britain* (1942), which featured one of pianist Myra Hess's famed National Gallery recitals alongside popular songs, the film's scenes of everyday life accompanied solely with music and sound effects rather than narration. In stark contrast Jennings's *Fires Were Started* (1943), like many semi-documentaries of the time (including Copland's *The North Star* and Vaughan Williams's *49th Parallel*), was completely staged.

Fires Were Started was scored by Alwyn, who first made his name as a film composer largely in the medium of these wartime 'films of national importance'. Alwyn found himself called upon at short notice to compose a replacement score for *The Future's in the Air* (dir. Alexander Shaw, 1937), which interweaved its commentary about the journey of a flying boat from Britain to Australia with music that was 'lyrical, soaring, lifting and rippling' (Low 1979, 125); the soundtrack included quasi-gamelan sonorities for a sequence shot in Bali (I. Johnson 2005, 26). Clearly influenced by Britten's documentary work, Alwyn included a reversed cymbal crash in his music for the gas industry's *New Worlds for Old* (dir. Frank Sainsbury, 1938) and emulated the famous closing sequence from *Night Mail* in one of his later feature films (see Chapter 6). The highlight of Alwyn's wartime career was his involvement in the Army Film and Photographic Unit's critically acclaimed *Desert Victory* (dir. Roy Boulting, 1943), in which he included patriotic march music and a simple use of sequence in order to increase the tension before the climactic Battle of El Alamein: 'Alwyn uses a single persistent note which rises octave by octave until it feels like the stretched nerves of the waiting men and snaps when the barrage breaks loose in the wild crescendo of a great storm' (Manvell and Huntley 1975, 135). The march enjoyed commercial success in both sheet-music and recorded form, and the film won an Academy Award. Its sequel, *Africa Freed*, was suppressed owing to US political objections, and segments from it were redeployed in Capra's *Tunisian Victory* (1944) where Alwyn's music was supplemented by additional cues composed by Tiomkin and extracts from Rachmaninov's

Second Piano Concerto – some time before the latter was catapulted to popular fame in *Brief Encounter* (I. Johnson 2005, 76–80).

For director Carol Reed, Alwyn scored the semi-documentary feature *The Way Ahead* (US title *The Immortal Battalion*, 1944), which critic C. A. Lejeune declared to be the best wedding of sound and image since Lorentz's *The River* (*Observer*, 11 June 1944), and the end-of-war celebration *The True Glory* (1945). Alwyn was also involved in propaganda films perpetuating the British 'rural myth', such as *Spring on the Farm* (dir. Ralph Keene, 1943), in which 'the music is romantically dressing often naked facts. The MoI [Ministry of Information] could claim, "we are telling you how it is", but the pictures and particularly the music undercut the raw truths with delicious half-truths' (I. Johnson 2005, 63), and *Our Country* (dir. John Eldridge, 1945), which featured voiced-over poetry by Dylan Thomas and included in its rich tapestry of image and music treatments of urban and industrial subject-matter. Alwyn himself conducted several such scores with the London Symphony Orchestra.

The documentary film sometimes achieved audio-visual poetry in totalitarian regimes where attempted brainwashing generally prevailed. In Nazi Germany, for example, former 'mountain film' star and director Leni Riefenstahl made the frighteningly memorable epics *Triumph of the Will* (1935) and *Olympia* (1938), both with music by Herbert Windt, a pupil of Franz Schreker's and already an experienced opera composer (Mera and Burnand 2006, 17–18). Hitler passed over Ruttmann in order to secure the services of Riefenstahl to film his Nuremberg Rally in September 1934, and she agreed on condition there be no interference from the National Socialist Party. Made by UFA as *Triumph des Willens*, the film had no commentary and its striking images were shot by no fewer than 74 cameramen who took over 60 hours of footage. Windt's music was appropriately Wagnerian, occasionally updated with Straussian harmonic twists: as Hitler lands in his Junkers 52 aircraft, the mood is that of the heroic Siegfried, while idyllic shots of the city asleep are accompanied by music reminiscent of *Tannhäuser*. The score grows more impressionistic as the tent city for soldiers and workers is revealed, and here (as elsewhere) diegetic drumming and rustic music are used to link scenes. Given the enormous size of the crowd at the rally, the very soft slow chorale accompanying Hitler and Himmler as they pay their respects to the war memorial is especially effective. Riefenstahl, like many film-makers, likened her editing of the material to glorify the event as a 'symphonic climax' (Gladstone 2001, 12) and expressed the view that Germany was responsible for the belief that 'a true and genuinely powerful national experience can be kindled through the medium of film' (quoted in Barnouw 1993, 103).

Riefenstahl's substantial diptych *Olympia* commemorated the 1936 Berlin Olympic Games, and was two years in postproduction; like its predecessor, it featured stunning photographic techniques, and its power of suggestion was such that it was banned in the UK. The main-title sequence to Part I was scored by Windt with some resourcefulness, the music emerging from its syncopated, quartal-harmony beginning into a Wagnerian chorale as hazy images depict the emergence of ancient Greek ruins and slow-motion choreography of stylized athleticism. The concept is dark, decadent and undeniably powerful, and the orchestral playing (by the Berlin Philharmonic) first rate. Solidly crafted music redolent of Reger at his most extrovert accompanies the Olympic torch carried aloft, and the exciting fanfares for the flag-raising would not sound out of place in *Star Wars*. The sporting events themselves are mostly presented without music, though tension-inducing cues enhance the slow-motion climax of the triple jump, and a harp flourish and dissonant stinger underline the javelin throws, with rousingly heroic music celebrating the Germany victory in this event. A Wagnerian march accompanies the pole vault, and the marathon is underscored with music of repressed energy before the quartal material from the opening finally returns. Part II ('Festival of Beauty') again opens impressionistically, with scenes of nature scored by Windt in a lush Korngold-like idiom. A basketball sequence including black athletes receives jazzy music in ragtime style, and the diving competition is mickey-moused with descending glissandi; there is no music for the stadium events, but a dissonant ostinato-based cue adds a modern feel to the bicycle racing.

Theatrical documentaries for the modern age

Between the end of the Second World War and the genre's decline in the 1950s, the documentary film continued to flourish. In the UK, Britten's final contribution was his magnificent score for the Crown Film Unit's *The Instruments of the Orchestra* (dir. Muir Mathieson, 1946), a virtuosic set of variations on a theme by Purcell that became a popular concert work under the title *The Young Person's Guide to the Orchestra*. Alwyn continued to write prolifically for documentaries, to such an extent that in 1973 Rotha proposed the issuing of a retrospective 'Music for Documentary' recording of the best of Alwyn's 1940s scores (I. Johnson 2004, 56). Newcomers such as Malcolm Arnold and Richard Rodney Bennett entered film scoring through documentary work, Arnold's mechanistic score for *Report on Steel* (1948) spawning a symphonic study entitled *Machines* (1951). The Crown Film

Unit was dissolved in 1952, but the influence of wartime documentaries and newsreels (with their vivid footage and rousing scores) continued to be felt in the generic development of the fictional war film.

In the USA, future front-rank directors such as Stanley Kubrick cut their teeth in the documentary medium: his first collaboration with composer Gerald Fried, on *Day of the Fight* (1951), saw them researching various types and functions of film music together and taking a conscious decision not to score the film's climactic boxing match (LoBrutto 1998, 67). Fried's music was modern in idiom, atonal and bitonal in places and featuring sometimes aggressive quartal harmony, with the brooding ostinati that (since *film noir*) have always worked well under voice-over narration; the score's uncompromising nature was very different from the old-fashioned wall-to-wall easy-listening background to another Kubrick documentary from the same year, *Flying Padre*, written by veteran composer Nathaniel Shilkret, who wrote scores for numerous short factual films produced by RKO-Pathé.

In creative hands the documentary film had always lent itself to both personal and political expression, and throughout the 1950s it became increasingly associated with *auteur* directors determined to make their mark with low-budget factual projects, often at the start of their careers. The tendency is shown not only by Kubrick's entrée into film-making (from a background in photo-journalism), but also by Free Cinema directors in the UK, by East European directors such as Kieślowski, and most obviously of all by the leading lights of the French *nouvelle vague*. Not surprisingly, given their artistic preoccupations, New Wave directors appreciated that documentaries could be even more manipulative than fictional features, and that the traditional transparency of their methods of production was equally susceptible to destruction.

In France, Agnès Varda, Alain Resnais and Louis Malle all began their careers in documentaries. The musical consequences of this activity were sometimes of seminal importance: for example, Michel Legrand found his own 'passport to the Nouvelle Vague' by being invited to score François Reichenbach's *L'Amérique insolite* (1959), a foreigner's view of the USA with no commentary or dialogue in which 'the music became a substitute for a traditional commentary' (Lerouge 2005, 28). Resnais collaborated memorably with Eisler on *Nuit et brouillard* (see above). In the same director's *Toute la mémoire du monde* (1956), by turns moody and quirky in its depiction of Paris's Bibliothèque Nationale as a giant organism, a continuous score by Maurice Jarre combined neo-classical melodic fragments with pulsating percussion, sharp discords and obsessive ostinati recalling the spiky styles of both Stravinsky and Les Six. The tongue-in-cheek nature of some of the imagery justified the use of graphic mickey-mousing, such as an ascending xylophone glissando coinciding with a rapid panning shot across nearly 200 volumes of the library's catalogue, and the score included stinger devices such as discords synchronized with starkly juxtaposed static shots of the library's various departmental signs, and clapperboard slaps similarly reinforcing a succession of shots of striking prints. Jarre had previously provided music for Georges Franju's anti-militarist documentary *Hôtel des Invalides* (1952), his first film score. *Auteur* debuts by 'film poets' were prominent in other countries at this time: the Swedish pioneer of the nature film, Arne Sucksdorff, shot the evocative semi-documentary *The Great Adventure* in 1953 (with a score by Lars-Erik Larsson); the Dutch director Bert Haanstra won an Academy Award for *Glass* (1958), in which 'action is so synchronized with music that the viewer can hardly escape the feeling that the glass blower is producing the music'; the Polish director Kazimierz Karabasz's *Musicians* (1960) opened with a factory's cacophony, followed by the workers' evening music rehearsal, their music-making continuing over shots of the noisy machines fallen silent; and the Yugoslav director Vladimir Basara's *Hands and Threads* (1964) appeared to suggest that the activity of weaving conjured forth harp music (Barnouw 1993, 194–6).

This European artistry came in part as a conscious reaction to commercial documentaries purporting to depict real life. Popular natural-history films in particular were rendered cosily anthropomorphic with the aid of music that, as Royal S. Brown notes (1994, 15–16), was chock-full of stock rhetoric borrowed from the vocabulary of dramatic films. Rózsa's music for the live-action wildlife footage in *The Jungle Book* (1942) is a good early example. In their clear-cut moods, these family entertainments left the listener in little doubt as to the emotional effect intended by the film-makers, and laid the firm foundations for today's enduringly popular wildlife programmes on television. The studio pioneering this approach was Disney; their 'True Life Adventures' in the 1950s were scored by Paul J. Smith, who worked both on shorts such as *Water Birds* and *Bear Country* (both 1952), and the feature-length *The Living Desert* (1953), *The Vanishing Prairie* (1954), *The African Lion* (1955) and *Secrets of Life* (1956), all directed by James Algar.

In France, maritime explorer Jacques Cousteau pursued similar aims, to the point that his apprentice Malle (yet to make his name as a director in his own right) told the explorer in no uncertain terms: 'What you're trying to do, this is not documentary, this is show business. It is not what it should be, it is becoming like Walt Disney' (French 1993, 8). Prior to his television series *The Undersea World of Jacques Cousteau*, which was launched in 1966 and mostly scored by Walter Scharf, Cousteau's early films *The Silent World* (1956; co-directed by Malle, with music by Yves Baudrier) and *World Without Sun* (1964; music by Serge Baudo), both of which won Academy Awards, had evocative titles that seemingly made the provision of atmospheric music *de rigueur*. An ongoing and heavy debt to traditional French impressionism was later demonstrated by Baudo's compilation score for Cousteau's *Voyage to the End of the World* (dir. Philippe Cousteau, 1976), patched together from various dismembered works by Ravel and decried by Porcile as 'the limit of musical vandalism' (Lacombe and Porcile 1995, 293). At the other extreme, idiosyncratic electronic music previously commissioned from François De Roubaix to accompany Cousteau's footage of the Antarctic was rejected by the oceanographer as too modern. The unfortunate De Roubaix, son of a producer of industrial and educational films, was ironically killed in a diving accident in 1975.

Television documentaries on other subjects since the 1950s have enjoyed a sense of naturalism that resulted from technological advancements permitting sound to be tape-recorded on location in synchronization with the camera, this innovation encouraging a greater reliance on interviews and dialogue, and less on the creative montage and bolstering music that some critics of the genre's theatrical progenitor had viewed as direct attempts to combat its former absence of realistic sound. The new realism, intensified by the austerity of some of the *auteur* directors who began their careers in the genre (notably ethnographer Jean Rouch in the early 1960s), seemed to corroborate Powell's view that 'Documentary films started with poetry and finished as prose' (Powell 1986, 532). The *cinéma-vérité* trend was intensified by the rise of video technology in the 1970s, at a time when a synthetic format in which interviews and footage were 'glued together' by commentary and music was established – this unimaginative structure still prevalent in factual programmes today (Thompson and Bordwell 2003, 583). Apart from occasional pop-concert movies (discussed in Chapter 10), memorable documentaries for theatrical release remained few and far between at the turn of the next century.

An outstandingly original contribution to the genre was nevertheless made by director Godfrey Reggio and composer Philip Glass in their non-narrative trilogy comprising *Koyaanisqatsi* (1983), *Powaqqatsi* (1988) and *Naqoyqatsi* (2002), the first a contemplative and wordless impression of the USA, the second applying similar techniques to the Third World, and the third to digital media. *Koyaanisqatsi*'s novel audio-visual montage included certain visual techniques – for example, slow-motion (a space rocket blasting off) and time-elapse photography (clouds rolling over desert and canyon) – that were well suited to Glass's hypnotic minimalism, his ostinato-driven style also proving appropriate for shots of machinery, vehicles and industry. The music was at its most dissonant for the detonation of an atomic bomb and resultant mushroom cloud, while human interest was achieved by the use of a choir (entering as people appear in the film for the first time), and what amounts to a choral ballet for slowly manoeuvring Boeing 747s in a heat haze; an instrumental ballet-effect also accompanies footage of traffic on freeways. Gloomy strings threaten to emotionalize shots of desolate urban housing. Perhaps the film's most effective conjunction of sound and image is when the absolutely constant activity of factory machinery can appear to fluctuate in an uncanny illusion caused by the phasing of the music accompanying it. At the opposite end of the spectrum, and demonstrating the influence of manifold televisual techniques, was Michael Moore's controversial *Fahrenheit 9/11* (2004), which conveyed its partisan but powerful anti-government message partly through a wide range of musical references: a satirical use of pop songs with lyrics both appropriate and incongruous; sentimental 1930s newsreel-style orchestral cues to underline suggestions of brainwashing and naïvety; bluegrass for southern ineptitude; insidious sombre strings for the US Senate and thriller-type tension-inducing music (by Jeff Gibbs) for slow-motion shots of politicians preening themselves before the screen blacks out and the terrorist attacks on the World Trade Centre are reported solely by stark sound recordings. Here, as in the Reggio–Glass collaboration, are occasional glimpses of the audio-visual impact achieved by the documentary in its heyday.

ANIMATION

The Hollywood cartoon's heavy reliance on music was obvious enough from the titles of popular series of shorts such as Disney's 'Silly Symphonies' and Warner Bros.' 'Merrie Melodies' and 'Looney Tunes', and the on-screen pun pairing the names of the producers 'Harman-Ising' (i.e. harmonizing). The genre's debt to music as both a dynamic and illustrative device went far deeper than these high-spirited allusions would suggest. In addition to exploiting music's ability to create continuity and momentum, and its emotional suggestiveness (the latter especially necessary in order to humanize the artificially created imagery), the animated cartoon demonstrated a significant debt to musical techniques popularized in ballet and the circus, the former first identified as an influence in an article by Ingolf Dahl (1949). Cartoons were often distinguished by a satisfying symbiosis of music and image as mutually supportive dynamic entities, each contributing equally to a compelling choreography of sound and movement. In its tendency to be hyperbolically descriptive, cartoon music was well suited to the often ludicrous visual images: 'Since cartoons can, by definition, do things that we can't (or shouldn't) do, the music exaggerates and celebrates that difference. Cartoon music does more than simply add life to cartoons – it makes cartoons *bigger* than life' (Goldmark and Taylor 2002, xiv).

Cartoon music in the silent era

Silent animations became popular in the 1910s with the development of methods for drawing images on transparent 'cels' (celluloid sheets), and were conceived as shorts designed to fit into the mixed bill of fare already well established in movie theatres. Like live-action silent film, the silent cartoon originated in earlier forms of entertainment, some updating the illustrated song-slide tradition: one animated venture of this type donated its name ('Cartunes') to the new medium. Two early heroes of narrative cartoons in the later silent era were both cats: Felix (launched in 1922) and Krazy Kat (relaunched in 1925, but born much earlier in a newspaper comic strip). Musical imagery – some of it surreal – played an important part in these feline romps, such as Felix's attempt in *Oceantics* (*c*.1925) to get a picture of a pianola to play a strip of Swiss cheese as if it were a piano roll. Visual gags featuring musical instruments remained common in later sound cartoons, for example in the booby-trapped piano on which Bugs Bunny plays a naïve melody with a single finger, neatly avoiding the one key that we know has been wired to the explosive (*Ballot-Box Bunny*, 1950). Similar audio-visual humour came to be applied to other inanimate objects, such as Elmer Fudd's car backfiring its way along in a spirited conga rhythm (*Wabbit Twouble*, 1941). A fine later example of surreal humour involving a musical instrument is Daffy Duck's plucking a silent guitar then, when tetchily holding up a sign to the animators saying 'Sound Please!', producing machine-gun fire when he resumes his twanging (*Duck Amuck*, 1951)

In 1927, Hindemith made an enterprising attempt to provide his own music for a screening of *Felix at the Circus*, the venture proving problematic in rehearsal on account of an unreliable mechanism designed to run a mechanical keyboard in synchronization with the projector. The screening took place as part of Hindemith's festival at Baden-Baden which (like its immediate predecessor at Donaueschingen) set out to feature, amongst other artistic initiatives, contemporaneous film scoring and mechanical music – and devices designed to synchronize the two, such as those developed by inventor Robert Blum. For the 1928 festival, Hindemith composed a mechanical-piano score for the short surrealist film *Vormittagsspuk* (*Morning Phantoms*), directed by one of Europe's leading lights in experimental graphic animation, Hans Richter. Milhaud, who was present at the festival, recalled how Hindemith was 'scribbling furiously and passing each page [of music] as he finished it to two of his students who immediately transcribed it onto a pianola roll' (Milhaud 1952, 174). Film music for the Pleyela mechanical piano had already been tried in France by George Antheil in his notorious score for Fernand Léger's abstract experimental film *Ballet mécanique* (1924), and by Jean Grémillon (see above); the difficulties of synchronization had been amply demonstrated long before, when Louis Janssens launched his unsuccessful Synchronisation-Musico-Cinématographique player-piano rolls in 1912 (Winter 1941, 149).

Musical effects sheets for cartoons based on Æsop's fables were issued by Pathé in 1923 (Barrier 1999, 51), at a time when animated films were generally accompanied by improvised music provided by a keyboard player who attempted to follow the on-screen antics in some detail. In their manual on motion-picture accompaniment (1920), Edith Lang and George West declared it essential for a cartoon accompanist to be blessed with a genuine sense of humour, drawing attention both to the inherent unreality of the genre and its commercial context:

> Nothing is more calamitous than to see 'Mutt and Jeff' [popular comic-strip characters launched in animated form by Bud Fisher in 1913] disport themselves in their inimitable antics and to have a 'Brother Gloom' at the organ who gives vent to his perennial grouch in sadly sentimental or funereal strains . . . In the cartoons and in the comedies all sorts of other emotions, besides that of plain hilarity, may come into play; there may be sorrow, doubt, horror and even death; only all these emotions lack the quality of truth, and they must be expressed as 'mock' sorrow and grief, 'mock' doubt and death. This is very different from reality and should therefore be treated differently in the music . . .
>
> . . . The player should keep in touch with the publications of popular music houses, since it will repay him to establish a reputation which will make the public say: 'Let's go to the Star Theatre – you always hear the latest tune there.' This will prove a never-failing drawing card for the younger generation of movie-fans, and it will react most decidedly to the advantage of the organist in his relation to the box-office and his own earning power.
>
> (reproduced in Goldmark and Taylor 2002, 17–19)

These strategies continued to flourish after the advent of the sound cartoon, the music of which relied heavily on archaic melodramatic clichés in order to achieve strong but 'mock' emotions, and often featured allusions to old and new popular songs. A deeply ingrained belief in a need for 'catching the action' (mickey-mousing) persisted in later sound cartoons; and, while aficionados of the genre continue to defend slavish applications of the technique as a valuable source of otherwise absent vitality in animation (see, for example, the editors' introduction in Goldmark and Taylor 2002, xiv), there is no doubt that it resulted in a marked tendency towards the perpetuation of the loosely controlled episodic musical structures that were noticeable in the very first scores specially composed for the genre. Crude sound effects underlining slapstick action, provided either by realistic noise sources or onomatopoeic percussion, were also identified by Lang and West as an essential adjunct to the silent cartoon ('It may be stated candidly that these effects, and the best among them, are not always purely musical'); these remained an essential feature of sound cartoons, either interfering with or working together with the music, according to the sensibilities of different production teams. When Warner Bros. released its classic cartoon shorts on DVD in the early 2000s, the 'music-only' playback feature retained sound effects as an integral part of the non-dialogue track.

Walt Disney and the animated musical

The rise of Disney as a world-famous entrepreneur of animation was in part occasioned by his enthusiastic embracing of sound technology as soon as it became available. Launching his character Mickey Mouse in silent form in 1928, five years after founding his own studio, Disney immediately added synchronized sound to Mickey's adventures in *Steamboat Willie*, a film replete with visual musical imagery of a kind that could readily be exploited in an inventive soundtrack: for example, a cow swallowing the sheet music of 'Turkey in the Straw' and playing the tune back like a barrel organ when its tail is cranked, and Mickey playing the cow's teeth like a xylophone. Synchronization was achieved with the assistance of Wilfred Jackson, who prepared a 'bar sheet' for the film in advance: 'in the places where we had definite pieces of music in mind, the name of the music was there, and the melody was crudely indicated, not with a staff, but just with a little note that would go higher and lower' (quoted in Barrier 1999, 51). Jackson then supplied metronome markings for the benefit of Disney, who prepared exposure sheets for the animators that included detailed indications for the exact conjunctions of image frames and musical beats. The musical arrangements were recorded in New York using the Powers Cinephone system: music director Carl Edouarde's conducting followed the tempi of a bouncing ball that appeared on screen in the space to the side of the images where the final soundtrack would be located, an idea borrowed from animated illustrated songs such as *Oh Mabel* (1924). For other Mickey Mouse films then in production, Disney commissioned original music from Carl Stalling, a cinema organist from Kansas City with considerable experience of improvising accompaniments to silent cartoons. During the time he worked with Disney before quitting in 1930 after increasing personality clashes, Stalling provided music for 21 of the studio's animated shorts. And it was at Stalling's insistence that Disney embarked on imaginative projects such as *The Skeleton Dance* (1929), featuring a pre-composed score fitted to the images with the benefit of a prototypical click track; as Disney warned his animators in a continuity script, 'every frame of this is timed to music' (Barrier 1999, 61). It became explicit studio policy for the scores of these

'Silly Symphonies' to be more prominent and satisfying than those for the Mickey Mouse shorts, where the music remained strictly subservient to action and dialogue.

Following Stalling's departure, three other composers worked for Disney as his products became more ambitious in the early 1930s: Bert Lewis, who also hailed from the world of silent-film accompaniment; Frank Churchill, who had experience of providing on-set music during the shooting of live-action silent films; and Leigh Harline, whose previous work in radio allowed him to escape some of the episodic bittiness of quasi-improvised scores, attempting instead to shape his cartoon music with a greater degree of autonomous structuring (Barrier 1999, 101). Among Harline's more intriguing efforts were *The Goddess of Spring* (1934), with its parodies of grand opera and the jazz routines then popular at Harlem's Cotton Club, and *Music Land* (1935), in which the Isle of Jazz and the Land of Symphony are represented by an appropriate contrast of musical styles. However, it was the less capable Churchill's music that came to international prominence on account of two of Disney's greatest successes: *The Three Little Pigs* (1933) and *Snow White and the Seven Dwarfs* (1937, composed in collaboration with Harline), both made in colour. *The Three Little Pigs*, Disney's first venture into the realm of fairy-tales and his first animation to feature drawings based closely on the fluid movements of live action, not only had its protagonists play instruments (like many early cartoon heroes), but they also sang: elements from Churchill's original song 'Who's Afraid of the Big Bad Wolf' were creatively deployed throughout the film, and the song became a hit.

By the time of *Snow White*, Disney's first animated feature, his closely knit production team had achieved a formidable blend of comedy, fantasy, sentimentality and astute characterization that would serve as an inspiration to generations of animators to come. Piano temp tracks were used to accompany test reels of pencil sketches, and again the film was designed around what would become a hit song ('Someday My Prince Will Come'); as a full-scale animated musical, its score contained other catchy original songs that would soon have a commercial life of their own ('Whistle While You Work' and 'Heigh Ho'), even though they seemed inextricably linked to the endearing images they were designed to accompany. Music from the film was released by RCA Victor on a commercially successful 78rpm disc, generally considered to be the first soundtrack recording in cinema history.

Also in 1937, Disney expressed his desire that the years ahead would bring 'more Silly Symphonies in which sheer fantasy unfolds to a musical pattern . . . In the future, we will make a larger number of dance-pattern symphonies. Action controlled by a musical pattern has great charm in the realm of unreality' (quoted in Barrier 1999, 242). With the enthusiastic collaboration of conductor Leopold Stokowski, who proposed Stravinsky's *Rite of Spring* as a suitable modern piece on which to base an animation, Disney set about compiling a 'package feature' (i.e. a full-length film made up of self-contained segments, some of which could also be released as shorts) based exclusively on well-known pieces of classical music. The resulting *Fantasia* was released in 1940 in an ambitious and costly stereophonic format (Fantasound) that was soon abandoned because wartime strictures discouraged the rewiring of projection venues for multiple audio speakers (and using the live music mixer required to adjust the levels of constituent tracks according to the acoustical needs of individual venues). The venture met with a mixed critical reception and little commercial success at the time, failing to live up to Disney's grandiose conception ('this thing will make Beethoven', he is reported to have declared to Stokowski, though at other times he confessed that the film was nothing more than an attempt to be entertaining and make dull and stuffy music interesting). Among *Fantasia*'s unorthodox sequences was the opening interpretation of J. S. Bach's Toccata and Fugue in D minor, in an orchestral arrangement by Stokowski, animated partly to abstract designs begun by Oskar Fischinger that were directly inspired by the music's contrapuntal textures – an idea reportedly suggested by images that came to Disney when he fell asleep in a concert hall. But for most viewers the enduring highlights will remain the delightfully quirky mushrooms and thistles cavorting to the Chinese and Russian dances from Tchaikovsky's ballet *The Nutcracker*, and Mickey Mouse's hilarious antics as the title character in Dukas's symphonic poem *The Sorcerer's Apprentice*. The debt of cartoon choreography to classical ballet was in this film made more obvious than ever; yet some sequences were deemed pretentious enough – or in sufficiently poor taste – for critics such as Mitry to declare that the venture was mostly 'A travesty! . . . In fact, *Fantasia* was not only misguided but had the effect of discrediting the whole area of experimentation in audiovisual association, letting the public (even those who should have known better) believe that the purpose of these experiments was "to put pictures to music"' (Mitry 1998, 263–4). For his part, Stravinsky curtly dismissed the *Rite of Spring* sequence as 'an unresisting imbecility' (Stravinsky and Craft 1962, 146) and later used it as a stick with which to beat Herbert von Karajan, whose recording of the ballet he damned as 'duller than Disney's dying dinosaurs' (Stravinsky and Craft 1968, 88).

Disney's second animated feature was *Pinocchio* (1940), which won Academy Awards for Harline for both his orchestral score and the song 'When You Wish Upon a Star' (later to become the Disney Studio's signature tune), closely followed by *Dumbo* (1941) and *Bambi* (1942), both of which – though undeniably brilliantly executed and able to manipulate a tear from even the most cynical of spectators – preferred sentimentality to innovation, and still managed to do less than spectacularly well at the box office. Like *Pinocchio*, however, they fared well at the Academy Awards, with both films nominated for their music and *Dumbo* winning. *Dumbo* and *Bambi* were both scored by Churchill, whose music for the latter was not greatly liked by Disney: 'I hate to see us taking the risk of being subtle', he informed his production team. 'The music is inclined to be a little too different and new. We've got to take this thing out and make it appeal to a very broad audience' (quoted in Barrier 1999, 274). In one sequence Disney felt that lyrics should be added to an instrumental cue, and delayed the production schedule so that this insertion could be accommodated (Barrier 1999, 314). In 1941, two months of industrial action at the Disney studio and the subsequent entry of the USA into the Second World War both conspired to check the output of costly animated features; in the same year, Harline left to embark on a freelance career. A further blow came in 1942 with the suicide of Churchill, whose incomplete music for *Bambi* had to be realized by a team of composers and arrangers. Ambitious plans such as Disney's dream of releasing modified and updated versions of *Fantasia* annually were quickly shelved.

A major hit for the studio was the catchy song 'Zip-A-Dee-Doo-Dah', launched in the 1946 live-action/animation hybrid, *Song of the South*. Soon after, the feature-length animated musical made a steady comeback, beginning with *Cinderella* (1950), which – in a move dictated by both artistic conservatism and economics – was stolidly animated on the basis of live-action footage and the music (with the exception of the songs) composed to a rough cut and post-synchronized in a manner more akin to live-action features. With this release Oliver Wallace became Disney's approved feature composer: already experienced from providing music for numerous shorts starring Donald Duck, Mickey Mouse and Pluto since 1937, his feature credits came to include *Alice in Wonderland* (1951), *Peter Pan* (1953) and *Lady and the Tramp* (1955), projects which included song themes provided by several other composers, and in which Wallace developed a recitative-like approach towards underscoring dialogue (Goldmark and Taylor 2002, 34). Disney's productions continued to orient themselves towards old-fashioned sentimentality, and his studio's scores reflected this conservatism in their general avoidance of a modernism of which he was deeply suspicious. Yet Eisenstein admired Disney's work for its close integration of image and music, and declared in 1947 (with obvious reference to his own aesthetic theories of audio-visual montage and colour–sound correspondences) that 'Nobody else has managed to make the movement of a drawing's outline conform to the melody. In this Disney is inimitable. But, when he made the transition to colour, it seemed he could not make it "work" musically . . . [H]e failed to make a "colour melody" to ensure that there was not only an emotional correspondence between the colour and the music, but a precisely formulated musical correspondence' (Taylor 1998, 171).

Animated and part-animated musicals from the house of Disney were given a new lease of life by songwriting team Richard and Robert Sherman in the 1960s (*Mary Poppins*, 1962; *The Sword in the Stone*, 1963; *The Jungle Book*, 1967), and by the team of Alan Menken and Howard Ashman towards the end of the century (*The Little Mermaid*, 1989; *Beauty and the Beast*, 1991). The style of these last projects was closely allied to Broadway models, and both *Beauty and the Beast* and *The Lion King* (1994; songs by Elton John, other music by Hans Zimmer) gained further commercial shelf-life as live stage transfers. (For further on Disney's later animated musicals, see Chapter 4.) The *Fantasia* concept was belatedly updated with the making of a 60-years-on sequel, *Fantasia 2000*, the original sleeper having steadily begun to make a profit when re-released in 1963, 1969, 1977 (stereo remix), 1984 (newly recorded soundtrack) and 1991 (original soundtrack restored with re-creation of Fantasound concept).

Warner Bros. and MGM: comic shorts

More adventurous combinations of music and animation are to be seen in the shorts (usually around seven minutes in length) produced in the 1940s by other studios, notably Warner Bros. and MGM. Often furnished with continuous scores, stretches of music for these films would occasionally be composed before the animation commenced and the images synchronized to the music (a procedure naturally favoured by the composers involved), and this was essential in the case of featured song or dance numbers, such self-contained segments clearly reflecting the ongoing influences on the genre of vaudeville and the musical (Curtis 1992, 196). But normal procedure was for synchronization to be pre-planned beat-by-beat on 'detail sheets' and for composers to work directly from these rigid graphs, sometimes aided by a monochrome rough cut of the animation. During the 1930s the stilted operetta-style dialogue of the early sound cartoons had yielded to sassier script-writing – and, most importantly, to new levels of characterization in which anthropomorphic creations such as Donald Duck (launched by Disney in 1934) and Daffy Duck and Bugs Bunny (debuted by Warners in 1937 and 1939) became inconceivable without their distinctive speaking and singing tones. At Warners, the 'Looney Tunes' and 'Merrie Melodies' series (commencing in 1930–31), at first scored by Frank Marsales, drew more heavily on contemporary popular song than the Disney shorts: the contrast arose not only because Disney was notoriously reluctant to pay fees for the use of copyrighted musical material, but also because Warners owned several music-publishing interests and could freely plunder their own catalogues of up-to-date tunes. Thus cartoons which enjoyed widespread distribution became an effective and lucrative method of song-plugging, and for a time Warner composers were compelled (somewhat against their will) to use a Warner song in each of their assignments; the 'Merrie Melodies' and 'Looney Tunes' series both took instrumental versions of such songs as their main-title themes, each preceded by an attention-grabbing upwards glissando on electric slide-guitar synchronized with a rapid zoom in on the studio's logo.

In 1936, Stalling joined the staff at Warners and wholeheartedly embraced this new opportunity to tap a rich repertoire of modern tunes. Before his arrival, scores for Warners' animations had often featured variations on a single theme and technological limitations in the early 1930s had necessitated a stop–start approach to juxtaposing music, dialogue and sound effects – the last usually generated by instruments in the silent-film manner (Curtis 1992, 198–9). With better recording and mixing technology at his disposal, Stalling opted to catch the action in greater detail and drew on his experience as an improvising accompanist to string together a satisfying medley of fragments from popular songs as he did so: 'I just imagined myself playing for a cartoon in the theater, improvising, and it came easier' (quoted in Barrier 1999, 339). The music was recorded by the studio's resident orchestra, at its largest over five times bigger than the small ensembles with which he had worked at Disney, and a typical score for a short could be recorded in approximately three hours. Synchronization was achieved at first by the use of pulsating streamers on screen and, later, by click tracks piped to all individual players on earphones – thus making the conductor all but redundant. The task was made easier by Stalling's habit of composing in tempi that were multiples of 24 (the number of image frames per second of projection time), which enabled literally split-second timing (Goldmark and Taylor 2002, 52, 145); this procedure had been widely followed in early sound cartoons, which favoured 'twelve tempo' (i.e. a click track in which one click occurred every twelve frames, thereby producing a pulse of 120 beats per minute: see Prendergast 1992, 183). In conjunction with the work of sound editor Treg Brown and the vivid vocal characterizations of actor Mel Blanc, and working under the guidance of luminary director Chuck Jones, Stalling's music gave the best of the Warner shorts a heady dynamism and allusive wit rarely encountered before on screen.

Stalling's prolific output – he composed the music for more than 600 Warner cartoons before his retirement in 1958, completing each in a little over a week – featured an endearing mix of old-fashioned melodramatic clichés and a more up-to-date novelty idiom partly inspired by the screwball music of bandleader Raymond Scott. The latter, whose whacky idiom was also admired by Disney, sold the rights in his music to one of Warners' publishing interests in 1943, and his tunes could therefore be freely plundered by the studio's composers. (The most frequently quoted, 'Powerhouse', would later land Disney's modern studio in legal hot water when James Horner paid homage to it in his score for *Honey, I Shrunk the Kids* (dir. Joe Johnston, 1989): see Schelle 1999, 106.) Operetta style is often prominent, as in *Rabbit Seasoning* (1951) and *Bully for Bugs* (1952), and classical influences include the ubiquitous shaping of fragmentary mickey-mousing in the kind of irregular pacing typical of operatic recitative. No matter which genre was being parodied by an individual cartoon, Stalling's idiom (like Steiner's in live-action films) remained remarkably impervious to the character of the assignment, so a visually modern production such as the science-fiction spoof *Duck Dodgers in the 24½th Century* (1952) received the usual comedic and melodramatic clichés. Yet at its best his music was almost solely responsible for a cartoon's atmosphere and dramatic pacing, perhaps the best example of all occurring in *Duck Amuck* (1951) where Daffy is shunted from one contrasting location to another by the unseen animators, much to his annoyance, and changes of musical style coincide not with changes of scenic background but with Daffy's belated recognition that he has been plunged yet again into an alien environment (skiing from a snowscape directly into the Hawaiian tropics, for example). Similar to Stalling but sometimes more adventurous was fellow Warner composer Eugene Poddany, who first worked for the studio in 1950 and composed cartoon scores for MGM in the 1960s, and the prolific Milt Franklyn, who after Stalling's retirement in 1958 emerged as the studio's leading animation composer at the time when the genre was making its transition from cinema to television.

MGM's importance as a cartoon factory became apparent in the late 1930s, when producer Fred Quimby and director Friz Freleng benefited from the musical expertise of junior director William Hanna who (after Freleng's departure in 1939) teamed up with Joe Barbera to form one of the most celebrated animation teams of all. Given their own unit by Quimby, Hanna and Barbera launched the characters of Tom and Jerry in 1941, and the much-loved series featuring the graphically violent escapades of this cat-and-mouse duo netted five Academy Awards during the 1940s. The cartoons' slick comic timing and breakneck slapstick inspired composer Scott Bradley, who had formerly worked for Harman–Ising and joined them full-time at MGM in 1937, to create strikingly sophisticated and coherent supporting music. Working on detail sheets, his music was sketched on a short score of three staves beneath horizontal lines summarizing camera shots, action and sound effects. (For a facsimile of the detail sheet to *Heavenly Puss* (1949), see Prendergast 1992, 192–3.) Synchronization was so perfectly preordained by these documents that when it came to the recording session there was no need for the animation to be screened, and the musicians relied solely on click tracks (Goldmark and Taylor 2002, 117). Most impressive was Bradley's ability to catch the action in sometimes inordinate detail yet still bind his illustrative effects together in music that made autonomous structural sense – an achievement undoubtedly aided by the fact that, unlike their wise-cracking rivals from the Warner stable, the classic Tom and Jerry shorts were mostly free of dialogue, at least until the later 1950s, by which time the series had already run out of steam. This musical 'binding' was sometimes achieved by the simple device of tying the music in with rhythmicized actions in the images: examples include two cats bashing themselves into brick walls in *Trap Happy* (1946), metrical wood-chopping in *Little Quacker* (1949) and the pulling of a fishing line in *Life with Tom* (1953). But most of all the coherency was achieved by maintaining an often dance-like momentum in the music and, in more fragmentary recitative-like slapstick segments, by illustrating diverse gestures (e.g. nodding, staring, picking something up) with sequential statements of simple harmonic progressions – often just two chords, repeated and varied in different contexts.

Bradley, who was also a composer of music for the concert hall, wrote his cartoon scores in an idiom both jazzier and more modernistic than that of other cartoon composers of the time, taking a Gershwinesque symphonic jazz as its basis but sometimes venturing into atonal and even serial territory in order to reflect the unpredictable action on screen. Like Stalling he affectionately parodied melodramatic clichés and 'mock' emotional cues (Jerry tied to toy railway tracks in *Life with Tom*, for example), and obvious thematic allusions ('Old MacDonald Had a Farm' in *Little Quacker*, and a particular fondness for 'Rock-a-bye Baby'). Yet the chance to experiment with more adventurous techniques was clearly of paramount importance to him, and he explained how the particular demands of the genre made this possible:

> With animated cartoons . . . the action is lusty and uninhibited, and music has a fighting chance to be heard above the sound effects. I stoutly maintain that any progress in creative contemporary film music will be made in this medium because endless experiments in modern harmony and orchestration are acceptable. Since it deals in pure (sometimes, alas, not too pure) fantasy, more freedom in composition is allowed. Established rules of orchestration are blandly ignored, since beauty in cartoons is rarely even skin deep, and we must employ 'shock chords' which sometimes reach the outer limits of harmonic analysis.   (Bradley 1947)

Mildly dissonant, athematic music was Bradley's stock response to 'hurry' and chase scenes, and at times this manner of writing became decidedly bold. In his score to *The Cat that Hated People* (1947), for example, he used a twelve-note row (for Jerry) sounded simultaneously with its retrograde (for Tom), achieving through parody a sense of comedy that had been beyond the capabilities of Schoenberg himself, who had singularly failed to raise even a smile with his comic opera, *Von heute auf morgen* (1930). Bradley commented: 'I hope Dr Schoenberg will forgive me for using *his system* to produce funny music, but even the boys in the orchestra laughed when we recorded it' (quoted in Goldmark and Taylor 2002, 118). A few years earlier, Bradley had used freer twelve-note writing in his score to *Puttin' on the Dog* (1943), where an atonal theme accompanies the surreal wanderings of a disembodied dog's head (Goldmark 2005, 71). A witty example of Bradley's atonality is to be heard in *Designs on Jerry* (1955), in which draughtsman Tom's drawing-board representations of cat and mouse come to life at night to appropriately outlandish music. Also adventurous was the brittle tritone-based harmony of *Push-Button Kitty* (1952), representing a robotic cat, though in this instance (as often) the music is – in spite of Bradley's comments quoted above – drowned out by the overmixed sound effects. It is a considerable irony of film-music history that the kind of modernism so passionately advocated by Adorno and Eisler found one of its very few outlets in perhaps the most unpretentious and quintessentially entertaining of all motion-picture genres. In the case of twelve-note writing, Bradley's use of the technique came a decade earlier than its first appearances in live-action cinema.

Classical music

Popular classical music was a prominent element in many of the Hollywood animated shorts. Old chestnuts from the silent era doggedly persisted in Stalling's scores: Rossini's *William Tell* Overture, for example, appears in an accelerating form for a bear-chasing Elmer Fudd in *Wabbit Twouble* (1941), in a speeded-up version for ants scavenging at a picnic in *Ballot-Box Bunny* (1950), and in the western spoof *Drip-Along Daffy* (1950) – the last in an obvious allusion to the popular TV series *The Lone Ranger*, which had been launched in the previous year and originated in a 1930s radio show with the Rossini as its signature tune. Sometimes just the merest hint of a few bars of the *William Tell* theme suffices to tap its ingrained associations, as in *Big Top Bunny* (1950), while in *Yankee Doodle Daffy* (1943) the eponymous duck sings a song based on the Rossini theme but culminating in a jazzy ending. Another old favourite, Mendelssohn's *A Midsummer Night's Dream* Overture, initiates a sequence of classical tunes in *Rabbit's Kin* (1951) that also includes Chopin's Etude in E major and Brahms's Lullaby for Bugs

Bunny asleep underwater, and Chopin's statuesque Prelude in C minor for a Frankenstein-like horror setting. Many of the most celebrated of the shorts went far beyond these quotations and took extended pieces of classical music as their *raison d'être*. The most frequently used, by far, was Liszt's Hungarian Rhapsody No. 2, its contrastingly sombre and frisky sections perfectly suited to the genre's inveterate melodrama and slapstick. Two of the best-known examples are Freleng's *Rhapsody in Rivets* (Warner, 1941), in which its themes are cunningly reworked to illustrate the building of a skyscraper, and *The Cat Concerto* (MGM, 1947), in which with brilliantly inventive slapstick Jerry cruelly disrupts Tom's (solo) attempt to perform the piece, recorded in advance in a two-piano arrangement by Bradley containing disruptively jazzy interludes. Liszt's Rhapsody featured in many other cartoons of the era, and even saw commercial exposure when Daffy Duck released it as a single on the Capitol label in 1950.

Three Warner shorts have achieved legendary status as exceptionally creative responses to classical music. *Long-haired Hare* (1949; music arranged by Stalling), which announces its basic dramatic tension at the outset by starkly juxtaposing Italianate operatic pastiche for the main title with an inane banjo song immediately afterwards, begins with Bugs Bunny playing a variety of popular instruments (the banjo is followed by harp, then sousaphone), much to the annoyance of neighbouring opera singer Giovanni Jones, who brutally destroys all of them so that he can practise in peace. According to Philip Brophy, 'Bugs' singing generates a musicological discourse which *infects* the refined lineage of the operatic arias of the tenor. This clash is in effect a metaphor for the "infectious" quality of simple pop/folk melodies and how they are regarded as disease by a musical establishment which takes pride in its sanitary measures' (Brophy 1991, 97). Bugs takes his revenge on Giovanni at a climactic concert in the Hollywood Bowl, in which the sassy rabbit dons a white wig in a caricature of Stokowski (one of many caricatures of this maestro in 1940s Hollywood cartoons) and wreaks havoc with both the orchestra – from which he commands erratic musical gestures with equally erratic hand movements in a kind of reverse mickey-mousing – and Giovanni. In order to create the latter's vibrating voice when Bugs hits the roof of the Bowl prior to mounting the rostrum, the singer dubbing the vocal parts was hit in the throat while recording the soundtrack. (The same venue featured in a rival Tom and Jerry short, *Hollywood Bowl*, in the following year: Jerry sabotages Tom's conducting of a medley of popular classics, and the frantic feline is forced to play multiple instruments as his players successively crash through holes in the stage.) *Rabbit of Seville* (also 1949; music arranged by Stalling) saw Bugs seeking refuge from Elmer Fudd's bullets on the operatic stage, and the ensuing barber-shop antics choreographed to Rossini, with all dialogue sung. Figaro's 'Largo al

7.2 Poster for MGM's Tom and Jerry escapade *The Cat Concerto* (1947), in which Tom's attempt to perform virtuosic music by Franz Liszt is hilariously sabotaged by Jerry.

factotum' had already established itself as one of the most frequently used operatic arias in 1940s cartoons, also appearing in Woody Woodpecker's *Barber of Seville* (Universal, 1944; music by Darrell Calker), and in *One Froggy Evening* (Warner, 1955; music by Franklyn). Most famously of all, *What's Opera Doc?* (Warner, 1957; musical direction by Franklyn and Jones) featured a Wagner music track recorded in advance and affectionately parodied both grand-opera and cartoon conventions simultaneously, hilariously setting Fudd's catch-phrase 'Kill the wabbit!' to the Valkyries' motif from

The Ring. Other cartoons based on classical music were released by independent producer Walter Lantz in 1946–8 under the generic title 'Musical Miniatures'; his studio had also issued jazz-based cartoons in a series called 'Swing Symphonies'.

Migration to the small screen

The gradual decline in the fortunes of silver-screen animation in the 1950s coincided with a change of visual style influenced by a more modern sense of graphic design pioneered by United Productions of America (UPA), which went to some trouble to secure the services of established film composers such as former documentary specialist Kubik (whose music launched the Gerald McBoing Boing series in 1951) and Raksin (*The Unicorn in the Garden*, 1953). UPA's design influence was perceptible in Disney's *One Hundred and One Dalmatians* (1961), which employed new xerox technology to reproduce images and was scored by former UPA employee George Bruns (also responsible for the Oscar-nominated music, adapted from Tchaikovsky, for Disney's *Sleeping Beauty* two years before). The influence was also evident in later Tom and Jerry cartoons and Warner shorts such as *Deduce, You Say!* (1956). The Warner example nevertheless retained old-fashioned Stalling-style music by Franklyn, who was succeeded on his death in 1962 by William Lava, the latter's music particularly associated with the Road Runner series. At MGM, the new visual style and an increase in the amount of dialogue, combined with uninventive visual gags, led to some disappointing music from Bradley at the end of his career (e.g. *Blue Cat Blues*, 1956). MGM newcomer Steven Konichek found a way forwards by avoiding old-style chase music and concentrating on atmospheric underscoring, using a recording of a theremin for a ghostly diegetic effect in *Buddies Thicker Than Water* (1957) and dissonantly jazzy cues in *Calypso Cat* (1956), but his scores lacked the exuberant vitality of the best of Bradley's work. By the 1960s a sell-out to popular styles had resulted in the inclusion of easy-going pop themes supplied by Eugene Poddany and Dean Elliott (examples of their work for TV cartoons in the Tom and Jerry series from 1966 are *Brothers Carry-Mouse-Off* and *A-Tom-inable Snowman* respectively), though both managed to continue the tradition of deftly synchronized choreography, and Elliott in particular continued to pay aural tribute to the fingerprints of Bradley's style.

Production of animated shorts for theatrical exhibition did not survive the economic ravages affecting Hollywood in the 1950s, and the genre's future lay in the industry's newest and most dangerous competitor:

television. Even the seemingly indestructible Disney felt a need to become involved in TV work in the mid-1950s, where animated commercials provided a relatively lucrative niche for the studio's expertise. The last Mickey Mouse shorts were released in 1953, and the formerly flourishing output from MGM and Warner Bros. ceased soon after. At MGM, Quimby retired in 1956 and was succeeded by Hanna and Barbera, the studio's final Tom and Jerry being released in 1957 just as its cartoon department closed down; during its last three years it had been employing Bradley only on a freelance basis (Goldmark 2005, 47). Hanna and Barbera quickly found a new outlet for their talents in such successful TV animated series as *Huckleberry Hound*, *The Flintstones* and *Top Cat*, many with music by Hoyt Curtin, whose limited budgets often forced him to use synthesizers (Goldmark and Taylor 2002, 10–11). Warner closed its cartoon studio in 1962 after Bugs Bunny had defected to a primetime TV slot (1960–62), with Depatie and Freleng establishing themselves in the new medium in 1963. At this stage, TV shows allowed existing theatrical shorts to be broadcast with minimal expense in neatly packaged anthologies; later, newly made cartoons, often with inferior production values and cheap library music, came to dominate the airwaves and bombard a new and predominantly youthful audience to a point of saturation that has never abated; inevitably, rock and pop styles came to dominate the new style of scoring. With Alf Clausen's stylistic resourcefulness in the perennially popular animated sit-com *The Simpsons* in the 1990s, cartoon scoring recaptured something of its old-time virtuosity, but more through subtle allusions to a wide range of filmic genres and their associated musical idioms than by traditional techniques. The latter nevertheless appeared prominently in the programme's blackly parodic 'Itchy and Scratchy' cat-and-mouse tales. At around the same time, awareness of Stalling's achievements revived with the appearance of two CD recordings of his cartoon music under the title *The Carl Stalling Project* (Warner, 1990/1995).

In the meantime, animated features for theatrical release had become isolated curiosities, though sometimes involving sophisticated music. An example was Leonard Rosenman's score to a stodgy version of Tolkein's *The Lord of the Rings* (dir. Ralph Bakshi, 1978), in which the composer's characteristic tendency towards esotericism led him to include a climactic fugal passage in which voices intone the composer's name in retrograde and which, for its release as a soundtrack album, was resequenced to highlight the music's 'carefully designed structure' (M. Walker 1998, 170). Animated main-title sequences remained popular for musicals and comedies: accomplished examples include those for Blake Edwards's *Pink Panther* franchise (scored by Henry Mancini, 1963–93), *Grease* (dir. Randal Kleiser, 1978) and Marc Shaiman's slick stylistic allusions and mickey-mousing in *City Slickers* (dir. Ron Underwood, 1991) which drew wittily on traditional cartoon scoring's love of 'rapid-fire changes and unpredictable extremes' (Schelle 1999, 295). Rare but entertaining were the occasional hybrids of animation and live action, of which groundbreaking examples were the interpolated Bugs Bunny dream sequence in *Two Guys from Texas* (1949) and the dream sequence in *My Dream's Yours* (1949), the second based on Liszt's stalwart Hungarian Rhapsody; the most accomplished example of this technique was the feature-length hybrid *Who Framed Roger Rabbit* (dir. Robert Zemeckis, 1988; music by Alan Silvestri), its soundtrack praised by Chion as an example of his concept of sonic 'rendering' in which careful sound design gave 'material solidity to a graphic being' (Chion 1994, 117–18).

Full-length animation for the cinema revived with the computer-generated imagery (CGI) championed by Pixar Animation Studios, founded in 1986 and responsible (with the help of Disney's distributing power) for the hit films *Toy Story* and *Toy Story 2* (1995 and 1999), *A Bug's Life* (1998) and *Monsters, Inc.* (2001) – all with song-based scores by Randy Newman – followed by *Finding Nemo* (2003; music by Thomas Newman) and *The Incredibles* (2004; music by Michael Giacchino). The visual style of CGI features drew far more heavily from the photography and editing of live-action cinema rather than from traditional cartoon graphic design, and as a result these movies' underscoring demonstrated a clear debt to the various atmospheric and emotional formulae common in live-action genres. Occasionally a successful TV cartoon enjoyed a feature-length theatrical outing, as with *The Rugrats Movie* (1998) and *Rugrats in Paris* (2000), both scored by Mark Mothersbaugh with hip-hop and electronics, and the long-awaited *Simpsons* movie (2007). Mothersbaugh had long served as composer on the Rugrats TV series; inexplicably, wonderfully resourceful *Simpsons* composer Clausen was passed over in favour of Zimmer for the movie project.

Experimental animation

Outside the USA, animators showed an equally heavy reliance on music in order to bolster their imagery, but some of their work was too conceptually esoteric to have any perceptible impact in the commercial arena. Several graphic artists demonstrated their belief that the dynamism of abstract imagery paralleled aspects of musical form, and accordingly gave even their silent works titles directly influenced by classical music: examples include *Symphonie diagonale* (1922) by the Swedish artist Vicking Eggeling, *Rhythmus 21* (1924) by Hans Richter, and the *Opus* series (1923–5) by Walter Ruttmann, one of which was scored by Eisler in 1927 for a screening at Baden-Baden (Dümling 1998, 541–4). Richter and Ruttmann in particular regarded music as a direct analogue for abstract design (Hill and Gibson

2000, 54). Influenced by Ruttmann, Oskar Fischinger added music to the abstract animations he called *cinérythmes* (1932–5); as Mitry observed, Ruttmann's 'empty form and gratuitous cadence' in Fischinger's work now 'became rhythm through the musical content with which the forms were associated' (Mitry 1998, 256) but, like the work of McLaren after him (see below), the animation appeared somewhat haphazard when shown without the intended music track. As so often in the field of animation, parallels with the world of dance were obvious, Mitry drawing attention to the vital importance of music in this context by citing Henri-Louis Bergson's comment that 'we have only to stop up our ears against the sound of the music in a dance hall for the dancers to appear utterly ridiculous' (Mitry 1998, 385).

Lotte Reiniger, whose work with the GPO Film Unit was described above, collaborated with Ruttmann and Czech artist Bertold Bartosch on the feature-length animated fantasy *The Adventures of Prince Achmed* (1926), important as the only experimental film of its time to achieve a wide international audience: it was especially successful in Paris, where Reiniger's artistry was championed by the likes of Clair and Renoir. Reiniger's unique brand of silhouette animation was significantly enhanced by richly inventive original music composed by Wolfgang Zeller, in places lushly exotic and one of the most ambitious orchestral scores of the later silent era; Zeller worked closely with the animator, who cut the film to suit the proportions of his music. The film's original negative did not survive the ravages of wartime Berlin, but a full restoration by the Deutsches Filmmuseum, Frankfurt, in 1999 was based on a nitrate positive surviving in London and included a new recording of Zeller's score, materials for which were housed in the Library of Congress (Kemp 2001).

Another notable experimental project reflecting a conception of animation as plastic art rather than entertainment was the extraordinary 30-minute film *L'Idée*, animated by Bartosch in Paris in 1932 using the simplest of materials – principally plates of glass smeared with soap and illuminated with a lightbulb to create an eerily luminescent effect. A sound version prepared in 1934 received a substantial score by Honegger showcasing the ondes martenot, the instrument given a special on-screen credit and used both to project intense melodies and to provide graphically illustrative swooping glissandi. Based on woodcuts by the left-wing Belgian artist Frans Masereel, the film personifies a philosophical 'Idea' as a naked female form which variously represents liberty, equality and fraternity, and refuses to be crushed by oppression, ignorance or commercial greed: not surprisingly, it was banned in Germany by the Nazis. Since the film was made as a silent, and no sound effects were subsequently added, Honegger's continuous music reigned supreme in its atmospheric enhancements and structural bolstering via the use of recurrent themes. By turns austere, beautiful and tongue-in-cheek, the score embraced an unusually wide range of techniques and styles, including ambiguous and elusive tonality, revolving ostinato patterns based on static harmony (notably for the rotating ball of light from which the Idea is born, to an intense outburst from the ondes), parodic marches for political and military activism, jazzy music reminiscent of Les Six for scenes of city night-life, a highly dissonant climax as the Idea and her followers are attacked by troops, and a luminously diatonic apotheosis at the conclusion. In this period, sardonic parody was also an important element in the style of Shostakovich, who in the USSR composed music for two animated films by Mikhail Tzekhanovsky: *The Tale of the Priest and His Worker Balda* (unfinished, 1933–5) and *The Story of the Silly Little Mouse* (1940), both of which were scored in advance of the animation.

Canadian experimental film-maker Norman McLaren's unique body of work reflected an astonishing diversity of both animation techniques and sonic idioms, and often a perfect marriage of avant-garde novelty and sophisticated wit. His early abstract films *Boogie Doodle* (1940) and *Begone Dull Care* (1949) were both energetic visual interpretations of jazz recordings, the former by Albert Ammons and the latter by Oscar Peterson, at a time when the creative potential of jazz in film had yet to be realized, and in a decade in which jazz in Hollywood cartoons continued to be associated with racial stereotyping. McLaren later drew on an unusually wide range of musical styles to complement his technical explorations. He commissioned Ravi Shankar to provide an accompaniment for *A Chairy Tale* (1957), for example, in which the restless quality of the music and 'otherness' of its Indian timbres perfectly complement eccentric mime; a country-inflected diatonic score by Pete Seeger articulated the changing moods of the abstract animation *Lines-Horizontal* (1961); and a recording of Romanian panpipes and a folk orchestra was manipulated by his long-time musical collaborator Maurice Blackburn to create a hypnotic and static aura in *Pas de Deux* (1967). Blackburn composed music in various styles for a number of McLaren projects, including the hilarious *Le Merle* (1958), in which a traditional Canadian nonsense song is represented with cut-outs animated by stop-frame techniques, and McLaren's haunting *Narcissus* (1983), the final film of his career, in which a slow-motion balletic interpretation of the Greek myth is enhanced by a sensitive and substantial tonal score for voice, flute, harp, piano and strings.

Blackburn's music for *Blinkity Blank* (1955) was singled out for praise by Poulenc in the pages of *Cahiers du cinéma*, after he had seen the film at Cannes: 'for me, this was the musical revelation of the Festival. Music drawn, to a great extent directly onto the film, proves that we must search for a new technique in the mechanical domain of the cinema' (Lacombe and

Porcile 1995, 121). This was one of several McLaren soundtracks in which recordings of composed acoustic music merged with, or came into deliberate conflict with, experimental methods of animated sound, in this case patterns etched onto the soundtrack portion of the film stock to provide percussive thumps. In *A Phantasy* (1952), music by Blackburn for two saxophones was combined with synthetic tones generated by waveforms photographed onto the soundtrack that mickey-moused the gently dancing motions of spheres in a surreal landscape. In other films, McLaren was solely responsible for his soundtracks and sometimes gave himself a music credit in the main titles. *Neighbours* (1952), which used stop-frame live-action photography, synthesized its quirky sounds through the medium of undulating stripes photographed onto the film stock; *Mosaic* (1965) had an etched soundtrack creating gentle *musique concrète* to fit with abstract patterns of moving dots; and, most impressive of all, *Synchromy* (1971) used squared-off waveform patterns photographed onto the soundtrack strip that produced a musically satisfying composition reflecting strong jazz and boogie-woogie influences, the image track taking the form of a dynamically animated version of the graphic soundtrack patterns. In this last example, McLaren's almost unique status as an artist capable of exerting total control over all aspects of both image and music in his films was satisfyingly exerted.

Animation in Europe

The first animated feature film in the UK was a version of George Orwell's allegorical novel *Animal Farm*, made in 1954 and featuring music by expatriate Hungarian composer Mátyás Seiber, who had previously worked on cartoon shorts for Soho's Halas-Batchelor Unit. By strategic statements of a revolutionary song first alluded to (obliquely) in the main-title sequence and then appearing both as diegetic renditions by the rebellious animals and in instrumental variations – most substantially during a lengthy orchestral cue when messenger birds spread news of the revolution to the wider animal kingdom – Seiber gave the film a cogent structure, drawing on a range of styles including dark-hued *film noir* gestures with prominent bass clarinet (reminiscent of music by both his compatriot Rózsa and by Herrmann), snappy dance-band material, unpredictable harmonizations of popular-style melodies, traditional thematic allusions (the *Dies irae* chant underpinning a search for traitors), highly dissonant expressionism for violent scenes, and a subtle approach to mickey-mousing which ensured that illustrative gestures made autonomous musical sense. A later example of British feature-length animation based on another fine anthropomorphic novel, ostensibly similar to *Animal Farm* in its combination of superficially cuddly animals with behaviour reflecting disturbingly adult preoccupations, was a lacklustre interpretation of Richard Adams's *Watership Down* (dir. Martin Rosen, 1978), featuring Art Garfunkel's song 'Bright Eyes', in which neither the drab visuals nor the workaday music by Angela Morley and Malcolm Williamson – by turns jaunty and impressionistic – did as much justice to its literary source as the impressive Orwell project had done.

Apart from the one-off Beatles fantasy, *Yellow Submarine* (dir. George Duning, 1968), comprising pictorializations of the group's songs coloured by the psychedelic popular culture prevailing at the time and described by the group's producer George Martin as scraping 'the bottom of the Beatle musical barrel' (quoted in Denisoff and Romanowski 1991, 148), few British animated enterprises caught the popular imagination until the revival of stop-time techniques in the 1990s. The half-hour award-winning comic adventures of plasticine animations Wallace and Gromit (*A Grand Day Out*, 1989; *The Wrong Trousers*, 1993; *A Close Shave*, 1995) were produced by Nick Park's Aardman Films in Bristol, which went on to release the more ambitious anthropomorphic stop-time feature *Chicken Run* in 2000 and showcased Wallace and Gromit in the feature-length *The Curse of the Were-Rabbit* (2005). In the shift from half-hour short to full-length feature, the series' theme tune by Julian Nott lost some of its characteristically British understated charm as it was reworked for larger instrumental forces. In all these projects the vividly cinematic studio lighting and tongue-in-cheek humour sat well alongside music (in the case of *Chicken Run*, by John Powell and Harry Gregson-Williams, who scored the Hollywood CGI features *Antz* in 1998 and *Shrek* in 2001) that again drew more from the Elmer Bernstein method of 'serious' comedy scoring pioneered in *Airplane!* (see Chapter 12) rather than traditional cartoon techniques. As *Simpsons* composer Clausen pointed out of his own similar work for TV, 'you play the music straight, and you play the sincerity of the moment, and the absurdity of the actions are [*sic*] what make the scene funny' (Goldmark and Taylor 2002, 245). *Chicken Run*'s spoofing of wartime heroics was emulated in the first British CGI feature, *Valiant* (2005), in which music by George Fenton contained elements of military marches, Elgarian patriotism and an updated swing idiom enlivened by unexpected snatches of quintuple metre.

Elsewhere in Europe animation continued to veer between the avant-garde and the commercial, though projects rarely aspired to feature length. Eastern Europe's rich tradition of experimental and folktale-rooted animation began in the late 1940s with the Czech director–composer team of Václav Trojan and Jiří Trnka, who specialized in puppet animation. European animation festivals, such as that held in Norway's Fredrikstad Kino in 2004, continue to demonstrate an extraordinary range of audio-visual possibilities involving all genres of music. The Norwegian festival originated as the Oslo Animation Festival in 1994, initially specializing in rock soundtracks and quickly expanding to embrace trends in contemporary animation in neighbouring Scandinavian and Baltic countries; the 2004 anniversary showcased animated realizations of pre-existing music from the jazz, popular and classical repertoires alongside projects involving original soundtracks. Around the same time, the quirkily original French animated feature *Belleville Rendez-vous* (dir. Sylvain Chomet, 2003; music by Benoît Charest) deftly combined eccentric comedy and vivid atmosphere, eschewing dialogue and drawing on various jazzy idioms (from 1930s swing to 1960s urban cool) alongside typically Gallic accordion material, inventively reworking pre-existing classical gobbets (Bach and Mozart) and taking a simple delight in diegetic musical jokes reminiscent of 1930s films by Clair and Vigo.

That animated features could still occasionally enjoy commercial success had previously been demonstrated in France by the series of adventures brought to life from the Goscinny and Uderzo comicbooks starring Astérix and Obélix, the plucky ancient Gauls, which exported well when dubbed into other languages by local celebrity actors, and fared better internationally than corresponding animated treatments of Hergé's Tintin adventures, scored by François Rauber in the early 1970s. Gérard Calvi's scores to *Asterix the Gaul* (1967), *Asterix and Cleopatra* (1968) and *The Twelve Tasks of Asterix* (1976) were rooted in old-fashioned and often naïve circus-like scoring, predictable mickey-mousing and rhythmicized slapstick, with a silly main-title march akin to the idiom of the British *Carry On* films in its quirky theme, wrong-note humour and trombone glissandi. Vladimir Cosma supplied music for *Asterix versus Caesar* (1985) and *Asterix in Britain* (1986) which avoided mickey-mousing and espoused a sometimes confusing mélange of mainstream atmospheric scoring styles current in live-action cinema, sitting uncomfortably alongside tacky Eurovision-style pop tunes. More satisfying was experienced TV composer Michel Colombier's score to *Asterix and the Big Fight* (1989), recorded by the Budapest State Orchestra, which achieved greater atmosphere and intensity with sometimes complex harmonies, exploited Bradley-style atonal scurrying for violent scenes and included a well-judged funky disco-song with electric guitar for the bard Cacophonix set against a fantasy village scene with chorus and choreography. In 1999, *Asterix and Obelix* went live-action (with music by Jean-Jacques Goldman and Roland Romanelli), starring box-office attraction Gérard Depardieu; the 2002 sequel *Astérix et Obélix: Mission Cléopâtre* (dir. Alain Chabat; music by Philippe Chany) commanded one of the largest budgets in French cinema history. In a similar fashion, American comic-book heroes such as Batman, Superman and Spiderman gained a new lease of life in live-action fantasies in the 1980s and 1990s (see Chapter 12).

8 Film music in France

After its theatricality in the early silent era, French cinema was overhauled by the thinking of the influential theorist Louis Delluc, who became the figurehead of the first avant-garde school of directors including L'Herbier and Gance (the music for whose silent films was examined in Chapter 1). Experiments with elements of symbolism and impressionism on the part of these and other directors meant that Henri Langlois could aptly describe Jean Epstein's *La Chute de la maison Usher* (1928) as 'the cinematic equivalent of Debussy' (quoted in D. Cook 2004, 305). At the same time, the emerging surrealism of film-makers such as Germaine Dulac was destined to remain a seminal feature of much later French cinema. Delluc's foundation of *ciné-clubs* (the antecedents of modern arts cinemas) and promotion of lively intellectual debate on film ultimately led to its widespread acceptance in France as a valid art form. The foundation in 1936 of the Cinémathèque Française as a centre for the study and appreciation of this 'seventh art' symbolized the intellectual respectability that the medium had acquired. Surrealist tendencies were intensified by the work of the second avant-garde school, represented by the Dada-inspired films of directors Luis Buñuel and René Clair. (Clair's *Entr'acte* (1924) is discussed in Chapter 1; on the provocative use of classical music in Buñuel's *L'Age d'or* (1930), see Chapter 11.) With the introduction of sound and concomitant increase in production costs, surrealist experimentation began to dwindle and films of a documentary or quasi-documentary nature became popular – a contrasting tendency that was also to leave an enduring mark on modern French cinema, which has always fluctuated between the complementary approaches of its legendary founders, the realist brothers Lumière and the illusionist Méliès. An equally fruitful bipolarity existed between avant-gardism and elements of the popular culture it often press-ganged into service in order to shock audiences. Murray Smith's comment that French cinema in the 1920s embodies 'a dialectic . . . of avant-garde and popular culture: the avant-garde may oppose what it takes to be bourgeois taste, but in doing so it frequently embraces and transforms aspects of popular culture' (Hill and Gibson 2000, 17) was to remain equally true of certain *nouvelle vague* directors four decades later.

Symphony and song

Several of the established concert composers who had written music for silent films continued to work sporadically in the Francophone sound cinema. Swiss-born Arthur Honegger provided substantial orchestral scores for commercial features and showed greater daring in lower-profile projects such as experimental animation (see Chapter 7). His best-known film scores are those for grand literary adaptations such as *Les Misérables* (dir. Raymond Bernard, 1934), a trilogy of features later edited by the director into a single shorter film with consequent loss of some of the scoring, and *Crime et châtiment* (dir. Pierre Chenal, 1935), which featured the ondes martenot. Honegger had no qualms about collaborating with other composers and understood the team spirit necessitated by the exigencies of film production, commenting that in popular music

> we very frequently find composers who have no technical knowledge . . .
> Such writers are dependent on collaborators who edit their improvisations,
> harmonize them, orchestrate them. On the one hand is the inventor of
> ideas; on the other, the technician who builds the piece from these ideas.
>   In American film music this practice has taken on the status of a
> tradition. It is perfectly legitimate, because the men who have a knack for
> melody are not necessarily practitioners. When music draws closer to
> business methods, then all talents take on a different colouring. We have
> never required Ford or Citroën to mount their coaches personally on the
> chassis because they perfectly conceived and perfected the motor;
> nevertheless, they put their names on the car.   (Honegger 1966 [1951], 66)

Many films scored by Honegger contain music composed, arranged or orchestrated by others; as Alain Lacombe notes, in these collaborative scores it is often difficult to tell who was responsible for what (Lacombe and Porcile 1995, 46). A frequent collaborator was the Belgian composer Arthur Hoérée, with whom Honegger worked on the Swiss film *Rapt ou la séparation des races* (dir. Dimitri Kirsanov, 1934), a work by a musically sensitive director in which the role of a mountain as a silent 'character' was treated with a visual poetry inherited from the finest silent films of the 1920s. Hoérée conceived an extraordinary sound montage in *Rapt*, for which he manipulated storm-effects improvised by the orchestral musicians in order to create a synthetic soundtrack fashioned from such novelties as reversed recordings and sounds from which the initial attack had been removed (R. James 1986, 79–80). Honegger's use of small string sections and solo winds, ahead of its time, has been obscured by modern recordings of his film music which have utilized full symphony orchestras on the debatable grounds that since his music is 'clearly conceived symphonically, it needs a larger ensemble for modern balance requirements' (Adriano 1993, 6).

Another prominent concert composer who worked with Honegger on film projects was Darius Milhaud. Milhaud's own early entry into the world of the sound film came with his score for Cavalcanti's *La P'tite Lilie* (1929), recorded in Berlin and represented not only at Hindemith's festival at Baden-Baden but also in a concert series organized by Copland and Roger Sessions in New York in 1931 (which also showcased music by Marc Blitzstein and Colin McPhee for short abstract films). Later in his career Milhaud habitually recycled his film scores for the concert hall, highlights including a substantial funeral march extracted from the Spanish Civil War film *Espoir* (dir. André Malraux, 1939) and excerpts from his music to Alain Resnais's short film *Gauguin* (1950), which he fashioned into a Divertissement for wind quintet. Milhaud scored only one film in Hollywood: *The Private Affairs of Bel Ami* (dir. Albert Lewin, 1946), set in the Paris of the 1890s; he was not warmly received, and 'knew he would never be asked again' (Nichols 1996, 37). Other French composers from the classical arena who occasionally undertook film work included Jacques Ibert (a onetime silent-cinema pianist), Jean Françaix (notably for director Sacha Guitry), André Jolivet, Eugène Bozza and Germaine Tailleferre. Like these, many of the country's younger film composers received traditional educations in the classical arena: the Paris Conservatoire was the *alma mater* of Vladimir Cosma, Georges Delerue, Antoine Duhamel, Maurice Jarre, Michel Legrand and Jean-Paul Petit, their teachers including (both at the Conservatoire and privately) Milhaud, Nadia Boulanger, Honegger and Messiaen.

The first high point of the French sound cinema was Clair's exuberant cultivation of a new type of musical film in which music and sound were both treated prominently and imaginatively, and enjoyed an interdependent relationship subservient neither to dialogue nor to visual image (see Chapter 2). Clair's films in the early 1930s, like the best musicals in the USA at this time, were brilliantly successful in their middle-brow balancing of aesthetic experimentation and sheer entertainment: Constant Lambert hailed him as cinema's Offenbach (Lambert 1934, 223), and the memorability of the scores to *Sous les toits de Paris* (1930; music arranged by Armand Bernard, with songs by Raoul Moretti) and *A nous la liberté* (1931; music by Georges Auric) set a standard of melodiousness to which many French films subsequently aspired.

Popular song was to remain an important source of inspiration to French film-makers. The 'realist songs' popular at café-concerts donated to the screen their brand of often cynical commentary on urban low-life as stars from the music halls and *chanteuses réalistes* discovered new careers for themselves as film actors in the 1930s. Songs of this ilk were featured in films by directors as diverse as Clair, Julien Duvivier, Jean Renoir and Anatole Litvak, their (mostly female) performers exuding a 'cultural resonance' that became 'a shorthand for female transgression, for the Parisian underworld and the working class, and for the intense emotions of sexual desire, melancholy, and despair' (Conway 2001, 137). Kelley Conway draws attention to telling moments where such films put their soundtracks to bold use: the wedding scene of *Cœur de Lilas* (dir. Litvak, 1932), where the dark mood of singer Fréhel is captured by a minor-key nondiegetic transformation of her diegetic song; the asynchronous singing of Damia in *Sola* (dir. Henri Diamant-Berger, 1931) and the Inspector Maigret tale *La Tête d'un homme* (dir. Duvivier, 1932), in both of which her disembodied voice seems to induce mental derangement in a male character; and the way in which the voice of the murdered Lucienne (Louise Brooks) in *Prix de beauté* (dir. Augusto Genina, 1930) outlives her violent death in the projection room where her screen tests are being scrutinized. At the moment of her fatal shooting the film 'continues to run through the projector, and, in a breathtaking moment, the reflection of Lucienne's film image flickers across her lifeless face . . . Her mechanically reproduced voice and image sing on, while Lucienne the woman (and female spectator, as it were) dies' (Conway 2001, 153). Renoir included realist songs in various 1930s films, and continued to do so as late as *French Cancan* (1954), featuring Edith Piaf, and *Le Petit théâtre de Jean Renoir* (1969). The prominent use of diegetic songs and their popularization via the media of radio and gramophone (and as stand-alone items in the French cinema, which until the 1950s routinely screened short filmed treatments of popular songs as a prelude to main features) broke the hegemony of romantic orchestral film music inherited from the silent era. Prolific French composers whose careers were furthered by writing songs for films included Vincent Scotto, who penned in excess of 4,000 and was particularly noted for his collaborations with writer-director Marcel Pagnol and performer Tino Rossi.

The 1930s: Maurice Jaubert and Joseph Kosma

In the realm of instrumental scoring, Jaubert became the leading French film composer until his untimely death on active military service in 1940. His film career began in 1929 when he scored Hanns Schwarz's *Le Mensonge de Nina Petrovna* with a characteristic blend of transparent orchestration and preference for variation rather than organic development of material. Jaubert is best remembered for his inventive collaboration with director Jean Vigo, whose equally premature death allowed him to finish only two features. Vigo's successful blend of comedy, surrealism, social comment and high drama is well demonstrated by *Zéro de conduite* (1933), the tale of a schoolboy revolt against authority, sufficiently anarchic in spirit to be banned and not seen publicly until 1944. Jaubert's score begins with a jaunty march-like children's song over the main titles, the music following on from the unseen noises of children playing. The ensuing train journey is scored with mechanistic music featuring saxophone above an ostinato accompaniment, the latter continuing while Jaubert superimposes wonderfully spiky and playful ideas, including circus-style trombone glissandi. (For a detailed analysis of this sequence, including a thematic-pictorial chart, see Gorbman 1987, 118–34.) The *joie-de-vivre* of childhood is throughout the film captured in brittle and energetic music of this kind, presented in economical chamber scoring; in drab contrast, military drum-rolls parody the rituals of the strict school environment. The celebrated pillow-fight scene introduces strong dissonances and fanfare clichés, this music stopping abruptly as the images decelerate into slow motion and the soundtrack introduces an ethereally distorted song-theme, created by recording a retrograde performance of the melody and running this recording backwards so that the apparently prime version on the soundtrack sounds disconcertingly unorthodox in its reversal of the normal order of attack and decay (Gorbman 1987, 138). Before the anarchic climax at Commemoration Day, the randomly dissonant tuning-up of the diegetic band neatly reflects the growing panic of the staff, who are alarmed at the boys' barricading themselves in the attic.

Vigo's and Jaubert's second collaboration, *L'Atalante* (1934), ushered in a golden age of poetic realism. As with the train in *Zéro de conduite*, so the engine on the barge on which the action in *L'Atalante* takes place inspires appropriate music as she casts off to an ostinato pattern which opens into expansive watery music and a love theme on solo saxophone; other musical cues are similarly triggered by diegetic sounds. Quirkily distorted dance music for piano reflects the excitement of the arrival in Paris, where scenes of metropolitan sophistication receive jazzy music reminiscent of Milhaud. Much use is made of diegetic musical trickery, sometimes with Clair-like wit, as when a finger drawn across the grooves of a gramophone record seemingly produces accordion music only later revealed to have emanated from a real-life accordion played by a cabin-boy off screen; the same record, when played properly, issues forth a Jaubert waltz which turns nondiegetic to accompany the remarkable extended sequence of events that follows, before being restored once more to the diegetic phonograph from which it initially emerged (Lack 1997, 99–100). In an act that paralleled the commercially minded intervention of producers in some American films, the distributors heavily re-edited *L'Atalante* to include the popular song 'Le Chaland qui pass' ('The Passing Barge'), which gave the revised version of the film its new title; the integrity of the score by Jaubert, who had already supplied his own popular-style song for the film, was destroyed in the process. (The film was not fully restored until the 1990 Cannes Film Festival.) After Vigo's death in

1934, Jaubert worked for other directors, providing scores for Marcel Carné's bleakly pessimistic *Quai des brumes* (1938) and *Le Jour se lève* (1939), which marked the culmination of his technique of composing music 'enshrined in real sound, provoked by it' (Lacombe and Porcile 1995, 237). Carné, who observed parallels between Jaubert's music and the idiom of Ravel, was impressed by the former's willingness to participate conscientiously in all aspects of film production (Lacombe and Porale 1995, 56).

Visiting London in 1936, Jaubert publicly railed against what he viewed as the impoverished nature of contemporaneous American film music, in particular its heavy reliance on illustrative and synchronized effects as typified by the work of Steiner. Jaubert's views were outlined in several articles published in French and English in 1936–7, in which he dismissed the mickey-mousing in Steiner's score to *The Informer* as 'puerility' and for exhibiting a 'complete misconception of the essence of music', particularly by its lack of attention to rhythmic continuity. Jaubert concluded:

> There has arisen a kind of musico-cinematic language combining the less commendable of Wagnerian influences (let's not forget the formidable predominance of the Germanic element, above all in America, in the guild of film composers) with pseudo-Debussyan sweetness . . . A formidable affectation, courtesy of which numerous musicians wish to prove to us that, if normally required to toss off a popular song destined to travel around the world, they are equally capable of expressing in eight bars, and with great reinforcement from the brass, all human passions. Let us encourage these musicians to adopt a little humility.
>
> (*Esprit*, April 1936; cited in Lacombe and Porcile 1995, 55)

Jaubert's philosophy was that music should 'deepen and prolong in us the screen's visual impressions' by adding to the whole 'the gift of a poetry all its own'; it should 'support the plastic substance of the image with an *impersonal* texture of sound' and 'make physically perceptible to us the inner rhythm of the image, without struggling to provide a translation of its content, whether this be emotional, dramatic, or poetic' (Jaubert 1937, 111–15). Above all, Jaubert argued, the film composer's craft should be marked by economy: 'three notes on the accordion, if they correspond to the demands of a particular image, will always be more effective, in context, than the Good Friday music in *Parsifal*' (quoted in Lacombe and Porcile 1995, 261). The accordion was destined to remain a suggestive timbre in French film soundtracks from the 1930s to the present day, often as a 'marker of utopian community' (Powrie 2006, 150).

The later 1930s proved to be a difficult time for French cinema, with censorship by the Government providing a bitter foretaste of the totalitarian strictures on film distribution later perpetrated by the country's Nazi occupiers. With Vigo's death and Clair's sojourn in the UK, it was left to Renoir and others to keep the flame of poetic realism burning. Hungarian-born composer Joseph Kosma provided scores for several of Renoir's seminal films at this time, including *La Grande illusion* (1937) and *La Bête humaine* (1938). A powerful prisoner-of-war drama passing insightful comment on various social issues, *La Grande illusion* – its very title condemning the futility of warfare – was predictably banned by the Nazis. Renoir and Kosma avoided underscoring the crisp theatrical dialogue, and in the first part of the film used diegetic music to draw attention to class distinctions: a popular First World War song playing on the gramophone in a bar is contrasted with a refined Johann Strauss waltz for the chivalrous German officers. In one nondiegetic cue, Kosma's music appears to emulate Jaubert: dissonant music suggests the train journey to another camp and is combined with a theme suggesting heroic struggle, the music slowing down and speeding up in correspondence with the fluctuating motion of the train. In a moment reminiscent of Clair, a sombre minor-key waltz at Christmastide is revealed to be issuing from a diegetic gramophone only when the music slows down mechanically. For the most part, Kosma's scoring tends more towards the melodramatic than Jaubert's, and this old-fashioned quality clashes with the realism of *La Bête humaine*, based on the vivid railway novel by Zola. Overly lush and emotional both in its main-title and love-making music, and with silent-cinema 'hurry' music and a hammered-out Verdian diminished-seventh chord after the murder takes place on board a train, Kosma's operatic indulgences jar with Renoir's often inventive visuals and sensitive application of sound effects. As François Porcile noted:

> the journey of the locomotive from Paris to Le Havre, without a word of dialogue between the two engineers, has only the sonic jubilation of a mechanical symphony made up of various conflicts of rhythm, intensity and colour (going over a bridge, the interior of a tunnel, brakes, whistles, etc.) – a true operatic overture, of such a dramatic intensity that the instrumental 'music' which closes the sequence seems singularly superfluous to the formidable musicality of the sound montage that precedes it.
>
> (Lacombe and Porcile 1995, 236)

Kosma, who had studied in Berlin and knew both Weill and Eisler well, was more successful as a composer of songs – many written in collaboration with lyricist and screenwriter Jacques Prévert. Antoine Duhamel pointed out that (like Weill, Eisler and Paul Dessau) Kosma felt subversive songs should convince the listener primarily by the corrosive nature of their lyrics, which might be allied either to equally corrosive music or else disturb the listener further by being set to music inappropriately easy-going in style (Lacombe and Porcile 1995, 79). Kosma went on to write music for many of Renoir's post-war films, and also for films by Carné (including a prizewinning score for *Juliette ou la clé des songes* in 1951), who recalled that he could be decidedly prickly on the subject of intellectual rights and attributed authorship of songs.

Georges Auric and others

For all their eccentricities, the films of Jean Cocteau logically bridge the gap between the French cinema of the 1930s and the *nouvelle vague* of the 1960s. Cocteau was keenly sensitive to the power of music, though musically illiterate, and his creative associations in the heady Parisian days of the 1910s and 1920s had included seminal encounters with Satie and Stravinsky. Cocteau played a vital role in the foundation of the group of composers known as Les Six (which included Honegger and Milhaud); the youngest member of this group of *enfants terribles*, which continued Satie's and Stravinsky's stance against what they perceived to be the excesses of impressionism, was Auric, who became Cocteau's favoured film composer. They first worked together on the privately financed surreal film *Le Sang d'un poète* (1930–32), Auric's music for which provides an excellent illustration of the suavely economical style so typical of Les Six. Cocteau strove to break away from using music as mere illustration, detesting as much as Jaubert the inflexibility of mickey-mousing: 'Nothing, it seems to me, can be more vulgar than musical synchronism in films. It is, again, a pleonasm. A kind of glue where everything gets stuck rigid, and where no play (in the sense of "play" in wood) is possible' (quoted in Manvell and Huntley 1957, 75; 1975, 91). In *Le Sang d'un poète*, Cocteau experimented with what he termed *synchronisme accidentel*, choosing to displace some of Auric's cues from the locations for which they had originally been intended in order to create a more random conjunction of music and image. In the more assured *La Belle et la bête* (1946), Cocteau felt that Auric – occasionally annoyed by the director's apparently cavalier attitude towards his music – had as a result attempted to write a certain degree of anempathy into his score in advance, for example by accompanying fast action with slow choral music (though in fact the actress's running which Cocteau had in mind here is rendered in visual slow motion too). Cocteau's sumptuous fairy-tale not surprisingly elicited some standard romantic and impressionistic scoring, including clichés such as infernal trombones heralding the appearance of the Beast and a luminous Debussyan tritone to promote expectancy as Belle mounts her horse to set off for his château.

Cocteau had left Auric's carefully sequenced score for *La Belle et la bête* reasonably intact so as not to disrupt its internal rhythm, but this was not to be the case in *Orphée* (1949). In direct anticipation of techniques later exploited by the *nouvelle vague,* Cocteau had Auric's music for this updated myth recorded apart from the images and deliberately assigned to the 'wrong' scenes in postproduction: Cocteau himself cited the reloca- tion of a 'scherzo [Auric] had composed for the comic home-coming scene into the chase through the deserted house' (Marvell and Huntley 1957, 76). Cocteau included three diegetic hearings of a recording of Eurydice's lament from Gluck's opera based on the same myth, which first issues forth from the radio in her house; he also set incongruously dated ragtime piano music against a riotous brawl in the Café des Poètes sparked off by high-spirited youths who have just been dancing to a more up-to-date boogie-woogie. Among the novel sound events were an eerie humming noise signalling the passage through the dissolving mirrors that serve as portals to the under- world, created by recording a tuning fork and removing the initial attack, and the drumming representing the Bacchantes towards the conclusion, which switches from the energetic swing style of jazz drummer Gene Krupa to the more ritualistic pounding of Katherine Dunham's band. In spite of its claims to originality, however, Cocteau's accidental synchronism in *Orphée* is not especially arresting. Because Auric's compositional idiom is fairly neutral in emotional terms, his cues can be happily situated with almost any imagery without creating a disconcerting effect, and the fact that Cocteau elects to recapitulate the music for the descent through the battle-scarred 'Zone' link- ing the real and supernatural worlds during Orpheus's subsequent return journey shows a conventional desire for structural parallelism.

Auric's talents as a film composer were sufficiently prodigious to allow him to work with ease in several countries, and in genres as diverse as Clair's musical films, horror movies, big-budget epics and English comedies (for the last, see Chapter 6). In 1955 he scored Jules Dassin's influential heist thriller *Du Rififi chez les hommes* (*Rififi*), one of the grittiest examples of a genre that blossomed in post-war France in response to the influence of American *film noir* and the Italian realist cinema that was shortly to have a renewed impact on the *nouvelle vague.* Influenced by jazz and (like many French film scores) featuring prominent saxophone, Auric's music for *Rififi* nevertheless avoids the blues-related clichés of contemporaneous jazz scores in Hollywood while still inevitably associating the instrument with sugges- tions of urban decay. Although the score is at times unnecessarily prominent and over-elaborate, Auric showed commendable restraint in one important instance: the film's half-hour action sequence, performed without a word of dialogue, was initially fully scored, but the composer happily ditched the cue in its entirety when Dassin showed him how effectively the scene played in silence (or near-silence: sporadic notes played by accident on a piano in the apartment where the crooks are cutting through the ceiling create a tension quite incommensurate with the modest means employed). This was precisely the opposite of Herrmann's insistence that he be allowed to provide music for the equally tense and wordless shower scene in *Psycho*, which Hitchcock originally felt should be left unscored.

The war years had inevitably seen a dip in the production of quality films as many directors emigrated to the UK and USA, though an enforced lack of foreign competition had in some ways proved beneficial to the French film industry. Outstanding at this time were the films of Jean Grémillon, whose early work in documentaries (see Chapter 7) paralleled the aspirations of Gance and Clair towards a supposedly 'musical' use of the visual image. In *Le Ciel est à vous* (1943) Grémillon told, with the aid of music by his favoured composer Roland-Manuel, the fictional story of the Gauthier family, torn between their passions for aviation (the parents) and music (their daughter). The drama is initiated by a prominent sound event: the family piano's discordant collapse, which leads to the acquisition of a new instrument. The mother sells this to finance the purchase of an aeroplane but the daughter continues to practise scales at the home of a poet, philosopher and violinist; both his and the family's destiny is symbolized by occurrences of the melody of a popular song. In all his films, Grémillon meticulously planned the relationship between music and other elements of the soundtrack in advance, a favourite device being the transformation of diegetic noise into music at strategic moments. He worked with several leading composers, among them Henri Dutilleux (*L'Amour d'une femme*, 1953). One prolific film composer who remained active in France during the war was Jean Wiener, whose career included collaborations with L'Herbier, Renoir, Duvivier and Epstein. For Epstein's *L'Homme à l'Hispano* (1933), Wiener had composed a novel orchestral cue featuring motor horns sounded in various rhythms. Like Honegger, he was no stranger to working with other composers on a single project, and told an amusing tale of how Duvivier duped him into allowing a supposedly unknown composer to contribute a song to the score of *Sous le ciel de Paris* (1951) – only to discover that the composer in question was in fact highly experienced and his song sufficient of a hit to give the film its title and achieve phenomenal record sales that comfortably eclipsed anything penned by Wiener himself (Lacombe and Porcile 1995, 81–2). Wiener provided an emotionally detached, neo-classical piano score for Clair's silent science-fiction film *Paris qui dort* (*The Crazy Ray*, 1923) when it was re-released in a truncated version in 1950.

After liberation, jazz – which had been banned under the Nazi regime, though this proscription was less strictly enforced in France than in Germany – began to assert itself in French soundtracks, alongside the continuation of the pre-war tradition of infectious dance-band music and popular songs of musicians such as the melodically gifted Georges Van Parys (composer of Clair's 1931 musical, *Le Million*), Paul Misraki (who had composed for Argentinean films during the war) and swing exponent Ray Ventura. The music of both Van Parys and Misraki continued to dominate French soundtracks for decades. Van Parys wrote songs for Renoir and Clair in the 1950s and remained active as a film composer until the mid-1960s, by which time Misraki's prodigious talents had already been exploited by inventive directors such as Buñuel and certain leading lights of the *nouvelle vague*: Roger Vadim (*Et Dieu créa la femme*, 1956), Claude Chabrol (*Les Cousins*, 1958; *A double tour*, 1959; *Les Bonnes femmes* (with Pierre Jansen), 1960) and Jean-Luc Godard (*Alphaville*, 1965). In *Et Dieu créa la femme*, Misraki's Latinesque jazzy dance music is constantly triggered by a range of different diegetic sources, becoming background music with the same sense of flimsy pretext as the film's plot serves to encourage Brigitte Bardot to divest.

Nouvelle vague

The French New Wave arguably did more to revolutionize the techniques and aesthetic perspectives of film music – and all other parameters of film production – than any other movement in the history of cinema. It was born of the sometimes self-conscious theorizing of directors and critics in the journal *Cahiers du cinéma* (founded in 1951 by André Bazin and others), and the austerity of the work of Robert Bresson and the contrasting audio-visual experimentation and bold camerawork of Max Ophüls in the early 1950s. The critic Alexandre Astruc's vision of expressive camerawork (*caméra-stylo*) as a powerful tool that would accord directors the same privileged status granted to literary authors (*auteurs*) and allow them to break from the tyranny of rigid narrative conventions was put into practice by a clutch of talented young directors, including Chabrol, Godard, Jacques Rivette, Eric Rohmer, François Truffaut and Agnès Varda. Traditional montage techniques were largely rejected in favour of long and often static takes that encouraged spectators to immerse themselves fully in the cinematic experience; documentary-style realism came to the fore, sometimes involving the use of amateur actors and improvised dialogue; and individual directors strove to make their mark as *auteurs* by evolving sometimes idiosyncratic personal styles.

In rebelling against classical narrativity, the New Wave sought to eliminate the transparency of filmic discourse in which production methods were constantly geared towards allowing films to appear as seamless and effortless exercises in story-telling. Spectators who previously might have been blissfully unaware of the presence of a camera or a film editor could

now be rudely awoken by jerky camera movements, jump cuts and seemingly illogical sequencing that sharply drew attention to the artificiality of
the film-making process. Several New Wave films, for example Godard's *Le
Mépris* (1963) and Truffaut's *La Nuit Américaine* (*Day for Night*, 1973), both
with music by Delerue, took this further by being set in the context of the
film industry so that the making of a film-within-a-film of necessity kept the
tools of artifice constantly in view. At the same time, composition-in-depth
and the long shot removed the need for manipulative editing and selective camera work, and established what Robert P. Kolker has aptly termed a
'democracy of perception' (Hill and Gibson 1998, 16) by allowing spectators
to contemplate – sometimes at extreme length – any aspects of a scene of
interest to them personally.

The functions of film music similarly came under scrutiny: it might be
used anempathetically or cut off abruptly to draw attention to its intrusive
artificiality, or nondiegetic music might be avoided altogether if a director
felt its presence would detract from low-key realism. In Buñuel's erotic classic *Belle de jour* (1967), for example, there is no music of any kind: a more
conventional director might have underscored the protagonist's bizarre sexual fantasies with atmospheric or disturbing music, but Buñuel's refusal to
do so helps blur the distinction between reality and the imagination. The
New Wave movement brought with it a marked decline in traditional symphonic scoring in general, and of the popular monothematicism that had
come to dominate mainstream French films. Scoring trends at this time
were vividly demonstrated by Alain Lacombe, who analysed 400 film scores
from the period 1955–63, of which no fewer than 263 were monothematic,
with a general-purpose use of a unifying theme; 32 used pre-existing music
such as classical, folk or self-quotations (e.g. of themes associated with a
series of related films); 84 fell into generic typecasting, such as the use of
jazz for crime thrillers; and 21 featured anempathetic music to bring out
the film's hidden 'interior' (Lacombe and Porcile 1995, 116). Lacombe saw
this last minority as the most interesting category, and it was one of several
new approaches to film music espoused by the avant-garde, who might also
encourage a depersonalization of musical style to promote irony and distanciation (a latent feature of French film music since Satie's *Entr'acte*), suggest
an improvisatory feeling, or shock an audience with daring spotting.

None of this came without controversy. Just as unsympathetic critics
might lament the New Wave's apparent equation of visual stasis with pro-
fundity, and suggest that a director's failure to embrace conventional film-
making techniques sprang more from incompetence than imagination, so
Georges Hacquard declared: 'It is clear that for many mediocre composers,
asynchronism can serve as the justification for their inability to adapt music
to the image' (quoted in Lacombe and Porcile 1995, 234). Conversely, some

composers simply floundered when given *carte blanche* to write any music they liked. René Clément related how Angelo Lavagnino was fazed when left to his own devices in scoring *Quelle joie de vivre* (*Che gioia vivere*, 1960), having been told merely that the director did not want to utilize traditional thematic and associative methods:

> The poor guy was terrified; at the very least he wanted to know whether I wanted period music or not . . . [H]e came up with a very pleasant waltz for the lovers' promenade, an excellent boston, a very good shimmy. I accepted his music, but instead of allocating the pretty waltz to the lovers, I used it for the fracas at the grocer's, and the unhappy Lavagnino was very sad, convinced everything had misfired.   (Lacombe and Porcile 1995, 122)

Jean-Luc Godard

Hacquard's scathing remarks were made in a book published in 1959, the year in which several seminal New Wave films were made, and in which *nouvelle vague* became a buzz-phrase associated with the cultural and political optimism of De Gaulle's new regime (Hill and Gibson 2000, 79). Of these films, perhaps the most remarkable was Godard's debut feature *A bout de souffle* (*Breathless*), released in 1960 and steeped in a chic trendiness soon to become typical of the new decade. The film's jazz score by Martial Solal was not in itself unusual: indeed, it seemed squarely to place the film in the mainstream genre of urban crime thriller, albeit somewhat light-heartedly given the up-beat nature of much of the music. But time and again Godard paralleled his unpredictable jump-cut editing with equally startling uses of music, both diegetic and nondiegetic. A lush string-dominated passage from the nondiegetic orchestra serves as an unlikely introduction to unaccompanied and raucous diegetic singing of the protagonist as he drives his car; then the nondiegetic jazz from the start of the film materializes from his car radio; light music from the same source underscores his humorous monologue, but when he retunes the station and rediscovers the jazz, this becomes appropriately frenetic as he is pursued by police motorcyclists. As he cleans his shoes with a newspaper in the street following his murder of one of the cops, mechanical piano exercises are heard – for no apparent reason, and with no apparent diegetic source. (As a similar but more explicit occurrence of this device in Godard's later *Une Femme est une femme* confirms, this is a reference to Truffaut's film *Tirez sur le pianiste*, also released in 1960. Such esoteric allusions to other films were endemic in the work of *nouvelle vague* directors.) Banal dialogue in the street is accompanied with extravagantly scored orchestral music. But the most striking use of

8.1 Anna Karina as the broody Angela in Jean-Luc Godard's *Une Femme est une femme* (1961), in which Michel Legrand's score wittily parodies the conventions of the Hollywood musical.

music occurs in the film's extended bedroom sequence, in which the protagonist's girl stops playing classical music on her gramophone because he dislikes it: a jerky edit at the moment she is assumed to turn on the radio makes the spectator uncertain of whether the ensuing piano jazz is in fact diegetic, and this ambiguity is strengthened when – no fewer than seven times – the music stops abruptly and later restarts (in the majority of cases identically) after appreciable pauses. This disconcerting manipulation of the soundtrack occurs under a long stretch of commonplace dialogue, and ceases when an obviously diegetic spoken radio programme intrudes. At no point up to this moment has the spectator seen either character operate the radio.

Godard's sonic idiosyncrasies were put to brilliantly witty use in the domestic comedy *Une Femme est une femme* (1961), which – at Legrand's suggestion – emerged during postproduction as something of a bizarre tribute to the American musical. Taking as its central proposition the assumption that the fantasy world of the musical and the neo-realist immediacy of quasi-documentary film-making have nothing in common, Godard and Legrand used the soundtrack as the primary means by which the central incongruity of the film's style is highlighted. Godard continues to exploit the abrupt cessation of diegetic music, most obviously when Angela turns on a tape recorder to play a honky-tonk accompaniment to her song (a real pianist is visible in the background, sitting with arms folded), but with each verse she sings the recorded accompaniment is suddenly suppressed to leave her unaccompanied. (This same pianist earlier suffers the indignity of a deliberately mismatched soundtrack when his diegetic playing of an acoustic piano is dubbed with a mixture of acoustic and crude electronic sonorities.) Godard spasmodically cuts off ambient noise altogether so that the images sometimes run in total silence in the middle of an otherwise fully soundtracked scene, even when noisy activity (e.g. traffic) continues to be visible. The film's humour mostly derives from Legrand's eclectic nondiegetic score, which combines the extravagance of the film musical with the harmonic sophistication of Stravinsky and the raw energy of big-band jazz. The commonplace dialogue and uninspiring contemporary settings are accompanied by the full panoply of devices used in musical comedies: stinger chords, melodramatic underscoring, and snippets of music punctuating dialogue in the manner of *recitativo secco*. At times, as often with Godard, the music is allowed to drown out the diegetic dialogue in a telling inversion of conventional Hollywood sound-dubbing practice. One jazzy cue is played back at high speed for comic effect; an orchestral cue steeped in the operatic style of high romanticism accompanies workaday images of smoking in the street and a long shot of an apartment's windows; a circus-style wrong-note waltz underscores the moments where Godard freezes Angela and her partner Emile and the camera pans away from them to allow on-screen text to explain their motivation; when the couple momentarily step outside the diegesis to bow and curtsey direct to camera, they do so to music that delicately parodies ornate classicism; and at several other key moments their movements are seemingly choreographed to the nondiegetic score. In contrast to the often breathtaking rapidity with which the spectator is bombarded by different musical tricks, at the film's heart is a complete performance of a song by Charles Aznavour, played on a diegetic jukebox as Angela sits with her would-be lover and contemplates lyrics directly applicable to her own situation.

Godard's obsessive use of repeated snippets from classical music in numerous contexts has been noted by Royal S. Brown (1994, 188), who provides an extended analysis of the soundtrack to *Vivre sa vie* (1962), a film cited by Gorbman as an example of the director's deliberately drawing attention to the score by abruptly terminating cues (Gorbman 1987, 14). The film's composer, Legrand, himself paid tribute to Godard's decision to jettison most of the theme and eleven variations he had been asked to compose in advance, instead restricting the nondiegetic score to a repeated twelve-bar fragment that is never allowed by Godard to reach Legrand's terminal cadence. Brown concludes that 'the filmic situations cause the nearly identical musical situations to be perceived as variations throughout the film'; furthermore, he links the music's abrupt stops and starts to wider aspects of the film's content: 'it is the music/silence dialectic itself that tends to reflect on some of the film's narrative-based polarities – life/death, art/reality, meaning/nonmeaning, and so forth' (R. S. Brown 1994, 200, 192). Characteristically, supposedly diegetic music is interrupted and restarted for no obvious reason.

Godard's *Le Mépris* (*Contempt*, 1963) featured music specially composed by Delerue and subjected to provocative postproduction spotting by the director. At the outset, the uneasy conjunction of romantic music with a monotonous voice-over and commonplace visuals is followed by the use of a Fauré-like dignified melody to accompany Bardot's long and matter-of-fact recitation of body parts; the removal and introduction of red and blue filters in the visual image coincide with stops and starts in the music, which breaks off seemingly to throw emphasis on her reference to her breasts. Later nondiegetic cues seem to be introduced almost at random, and are often intrusive, the music sometimes continuing impassively (and at considerable volume) in spite of jump-cuts and repetitious content in the script; verging on the drearily repetitive, the music track is nevertheless an element of ongoing stability that throws the fluctuation of the on-screen characters' relationships into stark relief. (When released in Italy, the film was given a replacement jazz score by Piero Piccioni and the outraged Godard refused to allow his name to appear in the credits.) As with Delerue's music for *Le Mépris*, Godard treated Duhamel's for *Pierrot le fou* (1965) as pre-existing raw material. Duhamel composed four substantial instrumental numbers which were again truncated and resequenced by the director, who overrode the niceties of musical syntax in the interests of creating his own audiovisual collage, which also includes typically disconcerting manipulation of pseudo-diegetic cues (R. S. Brown 1994, 200–19).

Such kaleidoscopic soundtracks occur throughout Godard's oeuvre and have been much imitated, though – as with other mannerisms of the *nouvelle vague* – one is at times left wondering whether cultivation of personal directorial style is more important than meaningful content. His output nevertheless embraces an unusually wide range of musical idioms. *Le Petit soldat* (released in 1963 after a three-year ban prompted by its treatment of the Government's handling of the Algerian crisis) featured an anempathetic use of classical music: the film's torture scenes are accompanied by the slow movement of a Beethoven piano sonata apparently issuing from a portable radio, but one on which the visible operation of the dials appears to have no bearing on the sound quality of the music; this keyboard sonority is directly linked to the evocative original score, composed for piano and percussion by Maurice Le Roux (a former pupil of Messiaen's) in an ominous chromatic idiom reminiscent of the darkest Ravel. *Bande à part* (1964) also used music anempathetically, and included a memorable scene in which characters dance to pop music on a jukebox. *Alphaville* (1965) was Godard's homage to *film noir*, its alternately turbulent and sultry orchestral score by Misraki paying clear dues to Rózsa; as in *Le Mépris*, Godard's relentless repetitions of the same cues makes the atmosphere somewhat leaden. *Weekend* (1967), a savage satire on bourgeois consumerism replete with sickeningly graphic imagery and culminating in cannibalism, included original music by Duhamel based partly on simple and sinister drones and partly on a dark and spiky neo-classicism, spotted by Godard with characteristic randomness and often masking dialogue (most blatantly in a monologue of explicit sexual detail rivalling that in Ingmar Bergman's contemporaneous *Persona*). Other prominent features of the film's soundtrack are the veritable symphony of car horns accompanying a ten-minute tracking shot surveying a bizarre traffic jam on a seemingly endless country road, and surreal open-air diegetic performances of a Mozart piano sonata and pop drumming. (Godard's provocative use of classical music in various contexts is further discussed in Chapter 11.)

From the late 1960s onwards Godard increasingly abandoned narrative structure, in *One Plus One* (*Sympathy for the Devil*, 1968), for example, juxtaposing a rehearsal by the Rolling Stones and militant comment from the Black Panthers to show how the former's 'blind love for black music' contrasts with the latter's preference for 'the socially galvanising force of African congas as a mantra to rise up and take over the new oppressors' (Brophy 2004, 229–30). Alan Williams commented of Godard's films that 'if the sensory impact of recorded sounds and images is maintained by their textual differentiation and organization, so are the sociohistoric associations of the objects and events represented', noting that in essence this strategy derived from Brecht's concept of a separation of the elements that together make up a theatrical experience (Weis and Belton 1985, 344). In terms of which Godard would undoubtedly have approved, Brecht commented negatively on the Wagnerian concept of *Gesamtkunstwerk*, that specious ideal under the heavy pretensions of which much film-music criticism has groaned and creaked since the days of silent film:

> so long as the arts are supposed to be 'fused' together, the various elements will all be equally degraded, and each will act as a mere 'feed' to the rest. The process of fusion extends to the spectator, who gets thrown into the

melting pot too and becomes a passive (suffering) part of the total work of art. Witchcraft of this sort must of course be fought against. Whatever is intended to produce hypnosis, is likely to induce sordid intoxication, or creates fog, has got to be given up.

Words, music, and setting must become more independent of one another.

(Willet 1964, 37–8)

In Godard's work, and for the first time in narrative cinema, they did; and, as director Mike Figgis has observed, this process of distanciation can paradoxically and intensely involve the listener-spectator in the cinematic experience, while coincidentally ensuring that Godard's idiosyncratic conjunctions of sound and image have not dated (Figgis 2005).

François Truffaut

Far more conservative in outlook but with an equal respect for the powerful presence of music in film was Truffaut who, like Chabrol, was a great admirer of Hitchcock as an auterial role-model: Truffaut published a book on him in 1967, at the time when the French director was fortunate enough to secure the services of Herrmann to score two of his own films (see Chapter 5). Truffaut's debut feature, *Les 400 coups* (1959), had music by Jean Constantin, who wittily deconstructed his main theme so that it fizzles out as a decelerating violin pizzicato ostinato based on the five notes of the principal motif, this reductive process occurring both at the end of the main title and again at the conclusion of the film where it is neatly timed to coincide with the final freeze-frame (a Truffaut hallmark) of the boy Antoine's face. *Tirez sur le pianiste* (1960) marked the beginning of the director's long association with Delerue, whose score includes honky-tonk diegetic piano music for the pianist of the title, portrayed by Aznavour, which captures the 'wistfulness and surreptitious force' (Cowie 2004, 64) at the heart of this idiosyncratic tribute to the American gangster film.

The strong influence of Renoir on Truffaut's work was shown by *Jules et Jim* (1961), which inspired one of Delerue's finest scores. This 'musical film', in which Truffaut even regarded the alliterative names of the eponymous characters as a sonorous element (see Moreau 2002), relates a tale of free love seen as a distant and objectivized memory of youth. At times Delerue's music emphasizes this effect, either by using carnivalesque comedic underscoring, for example a laughing saxophone with honky-tonk piano and muted trumpet for Catherine's insouciance as she dresses up as a man, or simple devices such as an oscillating semitone on the flute to accompany a bicycle ride, 'the sensation of mechanicalness . . . reinforcing the detachment conveyed in the high-angle shot' (Gorbman 1987, 16).

The helter-skelter circus style of the early cues yields to more atmospheric music scored for harpsichord and warmer romantic material for strings; old-fashioned conventions are alluded to when Delerue provides a stinger for Catherine's unexpected plunge into the River Seine and melodramatic tremolandi when she pulls a gun on Jim. Archival sequences are supplied with brilliantly inventive short cues, first when shots of the Armistice celebrations use the interval of a rising sixth from a brittle allusion to the *Marseillaise* to segue directly into elegiac string music, and then in a tantalizing ten-second snippet of gently dissonant honky-tonk piano music which perfectly evokes silent footage of Paris. As in Godard, who clipped the reverberation off the end of some of the piano cues in *Le Petit soldat*, so Truffaut truncates one of Delerue's expansive ideas before the sound has naturally decayed in order to jump abruptly to a bleak discussion of Catherine's failure to conceive a child. The film revolves around her extended diegetic performance of the folk-style song 'Le Tourbillon' (composed by Bassiak), the only segment of the film in which the sound was recorded on set and not supplied in postproduction. By the time of Truffaut's undistinguished melodrama *La Femme d'à côté* (*The Woman Next Door*, 1981), however, Delerue's musical contribution had become more stereotypical in its string-based romanticism, perhaps in response to directorial powers that had failed to sustain the level of innovation they initially promised. Delerue's string writing occasionally recalls the idiom of Herrmann's *Psycho*, most obviously when an agitated cue comes to rest on an unresolved dissonance.

After his collaborations with Herrmann, Truffaut requested Duhamel to supply a Herrmann-style score for *La Sirène du Mississippi* (1969) and the result proved disappointingly stilted (Lacombe and Porcile 1995, 281). Duhamel also provided music for Truffaut's *Baisers volés* (1968), its style somewhere between the restraint of Copland and the eccentricity of Herrmann's *Fahrenheit 451*, and *Domicile conjugal* (1970), his score for which was at times spikily Stravinskyan. Truffaut thereafter turned towards a more traditional sound, which suited his requirements for period settings and the articulation of a simple narrative across extended time-spans (Lacombe and Porcile 1995, 117); he found a ready-made source in the music of Jaubert, whose 1930s scores he reused in *L'Histoire d'Adèle H.* (1975), *L'Argent de poche* (1976), *L'Homme qui aimait les femmes* (1977) and *La Chambre verte* (1978). His consultant on the music tracks for these projects was Porcile, who was instructed when embarking on the score for *L'Histoire* to feature a prominent solo saxophone, which came to represent Adèle's reflective character; as with many other French films scores, the American jazz sound is avoided and the tradition evoked is rather that of the concert usage of the instrument in France stretching back to Bizet. Jaubert's music is used not to create atmosphere but to underline important moments in the plot, such as dreaming and letter-writing. In a procedure harking back to the days of silent film, Truffaut had certain cues played on set to inspire Isabelle Adjani (Adèle) to act as if in a 'danced film', commenting that 'carried by the music, [actors] will not be afraid of stylized gestures which they would reject if asked to do them cold, such as slowly stretching the arms out in front or leaving a room backwards' (quoted in Lacombe and Porcile 1995, 256). Anachronism is generally avoided on account of Jaubert's emotionally neutral style which at times suggests parallels with the austere repetitiveness of Satie, and when Adèle secretly pursues the object of her unrequited love she does so to a curiously abstract fugato. That Jaubert's music could nevertheless exert powerful extra-musical associations was vividly demonstrated to Porcile when working on *La Chambre verte*. He and Truffaut agreed that Jaubert's *Concert flamand*, a concert work extracted from a score to a documentary by Henri Storck entitled *Regards sur la Belgique ancienne* (1936), perfectly fitted the 'grave lyricism, austerity and restraint' required by Truffaut's two important chapel scenes. Neither had seen the Storck film, and when Porcile eventually came across it he was astonished to discover that Jaubert had originally written the music to go with the candlelit interior of a church (Lacombe and Porcile 1995, 244).

French modernism

Other New Wave directors opted for bolder idioms in their music tracks. Alain Resnais, for example, turned to music by avant-garde composers such as Hans Werner Henze (*Muriel, ou le temps d'un retour*, 1963; *L'Amour à mort*, 1984) and Krzysztof Penderecki (*Je t'aime, je t'aime*, 1968), commenting that Henze's chamber music for *Muriel* had been conceived to conflict with everyday imagery in order to encourage the spectator to remain lucid and refrain from yielding to emotional identification with the film's characters. Music, Resnais said, should be used to create anxiety in order to unlock personal reflection: in many ways it was more important than the images since 'in the cinema one can shut one's eyes, but not one's ears' (Lacombe and Porcile 1995, 124, 242). He liked to draw comparisons between the structures of his films and the formal patterns of modern concert music. Weill provided the inspiration for the documentary *Toute la mémoire du monde* (1956), and Jacques Rivette noted that Resnais's *Hiroshima, mon amour* (1959) featured quasi-rhythmic disruptions in its juxtaposition of static and travelling shots which reminded him of Stravinsky: both the latter's 'perpetual rupture of the rhythm' and Resnais's editorial pacing seemed to Rivette to seek 'simultaneously an effect of opposition and an effect of profound unity' (Hillier 1985, 66). Godard described *Hiroshima* as 'Faulkner plus Stravinsky' (Hillier 1985, 59), while Resnais himself compared the film to a musical quartet, using a theme with variations and recapitulations, and with a finale comprising a slow and disconcerting decrescendo – all of which would be meaningless to anyone who was not prepared to enter what he termed the 'game' of the film. This game begins with a stunning fifteen-minute montage featuring uninterrupted music by Giovanni Fusco, dissonant in places (and appropriately Stravinskyan in some of its details) and emotionally detached, which is combined with ambiguous visual images and an incantatory voiced-over text so hypnotic in effect that it amounts to 'music put into words' (Mitry 1998, 242). Resnais had come to know Fusco's work through the latter's longstanding association with the films of Michelangelo Antonioni, but after Fusco's lean chamber score was completed Resnais felt compelled to commission Delerue to write additional music in the shape of a waltz. 'In order to keep the French mood of the film, we needed a French musician', recalled Resnais: '[Delerue] worked from the records of Japanese music I had collected in order to introduce a Japanese sound into the French music. Besides,' he added wryly, 'I always like to have a waltz in each of my films' (interviewed in Cowie 2004, 45).

Messiaen declined an invitation to score Resnais's *L'Année dernière à Marienbad* (1961), as Dallapiccola had done when invited to compose the score for *Hiroshima*. The final choice of composer for *L'Année dernière*, Francis Seyrig (brother of the film's leading lady), did not quite meet the demands of the script, which was written by Alain Robbe-Grillet, a leading light of the avant-garde *nouveau roman* movement, who had precisely indicated the kind of music he had in mind for the project: a disjointed modernism which, for the uninitiated spectator, should be 'both irritating and somehow continually unresolved' (quoted in R. S. Brown 1994, 187). According to Robbe-Grillet, whose own films (especially those made in collaboration with technologically adept composer Michel Fano) were furnished with striking soundtracks, Seyrig's score for *L'Année* – written for solo organ in a style strongly reminiscent of Messiaen – was a last-minute addition overtly geared towards enhancing the film's popular appeal (Lack 1997, 159). The choice of organ provides at a basic level an aural equivalent to the sumptuous baroque architecture of the palatial hotel in which the film is set, and the music's non-functional dissonances and static nature can promote a sense either of cold distanciation or eerie foreboding according to the individual spectator's personal sensibilities – an ideal sonic ambiguity given the film's designedly open-ended nature, in which narrative ambiguities and contradictions sit oddly alongside a visual and editing style steeped in self-conscious formalism. At times, most obviously in the extended opening cue, the organ music is allowed to blot out diegetic dialogue and even voice-over narration – the latter often revealed to be diegetic monologue once the speaker enters the camera's field of vision.

Throughout his career, Resnais showed considerable flexibility towards the music of his films: it differed wildly in style from one film to the next, was used either entirely autonomously or in accidental synchronism with the images, and sometimes deployed strategically to emphasize a film's inherent structure. Among the wide range of composers he employed was Rózsa (*Providence*, 1976), who paid tribute to the director's intense musicality but confessed not to have even remotely understood the film for which he was engaged.

Modernist musical leanings also informed the films of Chabrol, whose favoured composer Pierre Jansen had studied with Messiaen at the Darmstadt summer school in 1952. Chabrol's passion for Hitchcock at first led Jansen to provide him with music reminiscent of Herrmann, but by the late 1960s Jansen had begun to experiment more liberally with avant-garde techniques. Chamber sonorities and athematic atonality had already artic-ulated the dramas of *La Femme infidèle* (1968), scored for piano trio with occasional discreet splashes of colour from vibraphone and electric organ, and *Le Boucher* (1969). Jansen's music for both is analysed in detail by Brown, who concludes that its modernity 'tends to impose itself on its own terms rather than in the more traditional cine-affective exploitation of the consonance/dissonance dialectic' (R. S. Brown 1994, 223–5). Certainly in *La Femme infidèle* the rarefied atonal music, owing much to both Webern and Messiaen, seems emotionally detached from the sometimes banal domes-tic situations depicted on screen, though at times (and again according to individual viewers' sensibilities) it might be thought to signify foreboding or icy coldness, or simply in its trio texture (also represented by a classical piano trio played diegetically on a bedroom gramophone) to represent the eternal love triangle at the heart of the story. (This last idea was to find a more complex and ambiguous realization in *Un Cœur en hiver* (dir. Claude Sautet, 1992) where Ravel's Piano Trio illuminates various aspects of the drama: see J. Brown 2004.) Yet the most likely explanation for the presence of atonality in a story not far removed from a television soap opera is that, like Resnais, Chabrol wanted his viewers to be subliminally disturbed in order to render them more attentive to the images and their implications.

In *Le Boucher* the same ambivalence between disturbing chilliness and emotional distanciation, promoted again by a fragmentary avant-garde idiom that often accompanies scenes of utter ordinariness for no appar-ent reason, is less effective as a structural articulation of the drama than the recurrent sonic image of diegetic chiming bells (church, school, shop) which lend the narrative a ritualistic quality. (A more sophisticated use of this device occurs in the strategic deployment of clock chimes throughout

Bergman's *Cries and Whispers* (1972), their sound distilled into abstract punctuating strokes timed to coincide with the changing main-title cards of white letters on a red background: what appears to be an entirely abstract title sequence is soon revealed to have epitomized the audio-visual essence of the film when the chimes are attached to diegetic timepieces, the costumes and décor of the *mise-en-scène* are revealed to be respectively white and red, and the subsequent blackouts in the editing of the visual images are idiosyncratic 'redouts' – this colour associated by the director with the inner depths of the human soul.) By the time of *L'Enfer* (1994), superficially a similar tale of infidelity but now made more compelling by the suspicious husband's growing dementia, music by Chabrol's son Matthieu attempted something similar through tonally based harmonic eccentricity and an unpredictable mélange of idioms that included neo-classicism and bits of Dvořák's Cello Concerto and French popular song.

In Chabrol's *La Rupture* (1970), Jansen combined atonality with the timbre of the ondes martenot and associated one of the film's characters with avant-garde music for string quartet that looked ahead to similarly intense but non-representational chamber sonorities in numerous later New Wave films. Two very different examples of this trend from the 1980s are Varda's *Sans toit ni loi* (*Vagabond*, 1985) and Rohmer's *Le Rayon vert* (1986), both of which won the Golden Lion Award at the Venice Film Festival. Varda's composer Joanna Bruzdowicz supplies athematic and atonal string-quartet music, reworked from a pre-existing piece, that suggests the bleakness of the wintry landscape in which the protagonist's corpse is discovered at the start of the film, and accompanies moments of solitude in the succeeding flashbacks that gradually explain how this situation came to pass; as one character comments, 'total freedom means total loneliness'. Here, however, the music might be regarded as much as an agent of distanciation, matching the quasi-reportage of the *mise-en scène*, as the supplier of appropriately bleak atmosphere. Rohmer, who rarely uses nondiegetic music in his films, introduces snippets of music for solo violin by Jean-Louis Valero to punctuate his scenes of improvised dialogue; heard only four times, this material – based on the musical acrostic B-A-C-H – eventually forms the basis for a string-quartet fugato that brings the film to a close.

That a film as drearily banal as *Le Rayon vert* could be greeted with critical accolades is a pertinent reminder that, for better or worse, New Wave experimentation continued to exert a powerful fascination on *cinéastes* long after its initial surge of creativity dwindled. As had always been the case, many important directors working in France towards the end of the twentieth century whose work betrayed this influence were not French by birth, most notably Kieślowski (whose work is discussed below). The French cinema's fascination with jazz and classical music (both of which are also

8.2 Sisters in fact and fiction: Catherine Deneuve (as Delphine Garnier, left) and her real-life sibling Françoise Dorléac (as Solange Garnier, right) rehearse their routine in Jacques Demy's *Les Demoiselles de Rochefort* (1967), filmed shortly before Dorléac's untimely death in a road accident at the age of 25.

considered elsewhere) continued alongside a flexible attitude towards music that could at one extreme see it featured prominently or at the other abandoned altogether.

At home and abroad

Modernism in French film music suffered a setback when leading composers such as Duhamel and Jensen defected – the former to work in musical theatre in the 1970s and the latter to television in the early 1980s. Other talented French composers found themselves seduced by the lure of lucrative work in Hollywood. One such was Legrand who, in addition to his early work for Godard, had also provided scores for Varda's *Cléo de 5 à 7* (1961), in which he also acts, and her husband Jacques Demy's award-winning musical *Les Parapluies de Cherbourg* (1964). The last took the unusual step of rendering all its dialogue in song; in spite of the commercial risks attendant upon such a bold venture (so acute that Legrand personally had to finance the pre-recording of the 90-minute score in the absence of investors), the film was a considerable success internationally and launched the hit song 'I Will Wait for You'. It was after providing music for Demy's follow-up musical *Les Demoiselles de Rochefort* (1967), starring Gene Kelly, that Legrand decided to chance his arm in Hollywood, where he was fortunate enough to become a protégé of Henry Mancini's – the latter securing him the commission for *The Thomas Crown Affair* (dir. Norman Jewison, 1968), his score for which won an Academy Award. In Hollywood Legrand continued to draw on his parallel talents as a master of popular styles and a harmonic innovator, insisting on doing all his own arrangements and orchestrations: to *Thomas Crown*, for example, he contributed both a popular song hit (the Oscar-winning 'The Windmills of Your Mind' for the glider sequence) and telling nondiegetic scoring, notably when the diegetic tolling of a bell at the cemetery climax is harmonized dissonantly in the underscore; the composer recalled that the film achieved its workable structure only when an unwieldy five-hour rough cut was drastically pruned and reorganized around music written away from the images. Legrand won further Academy Awards for his work on *Summer of '42* (dir. Robert Mulligan, 1970) and *Yentl* (dir. Barbra Streisand, 1983), and recalled that his decision to divide his time between US and European cinema came at the urging of Edith Piaf, who warned him that staying permanently in Hollywood would make him 'lose his talent' because of the need to conform to commercial pressures: 'What Americans call safe music bores me. If you're expecting music that has no surprises, then it's no use calling me. That ambition has made me take risks, even if it meant that some filmmakers turned my scores down [e.g. *Robin and Marian* (dir. Richard Lester, 1976), for which his neo-classical score was jettisoned in favour of a replacement by John Barry]. It doesn't bother me: at least it proves you're alive' (Lerouge 2005, 31).

The prolific Delerue, disillusioned with what he termed the lack of respect accorded to music in the French cinema (by which, in effect, he meant the lack of money allocated for it), undertook many Anglophone films from the 1970s onwards and in 1980 relocated to Hollywood: his American films included *The Day of the Jackal* (dir. Fred Zinnemann, 1973), *Silkwood* (dir. Mike Nichols, 1984) and *Platoon* (dir. Oliver Stone, 1986). Maurice Jarre came to international prominence following the success of his Oscar-winning music to David Lean's rambling epics *Lawrence of Arabia* (1962) and *Doctor Zhivago* (1965): for many, Jarre's catchy themes for these movies remain their most memorable element, even though they caused 'irritation to his colleagues and censure from French critics' (Lacombe and Porcile 1995, 128). Introducing the ondes martenot to American cinema with his score for *Lawrence*, Jarre later came to work extensively with electronics – for example, in *Witness* (dir. Peter Weir, 1984) and *Fatal Attraction* (dir. Adrian Lyne, 1987) – and with ethnic music in order to avoid the typecasting likely to arise from his early big-theme scores. In a refreshing reversal of traditional European views, he remained heavily critical of what he saw as intellectually arrogant and professionally sloppy attitudes in French cinema that he felt were no comparison to the discipline and devotion to duty of the Hollywood artisans. It was nevertheless with a European director, Volker Schlöndorff (who graduated from the Institut des Hautes Etudes Cinématographiques in Paris in that crucial year, 1959), that Jarre – like Hans Werner Henze, who scored Schlöndorff's *The Lost Honour of Katharina Blum* (1975) – did some of his most inventive work. Jarre's music to Schlöndorff's *The Tin Drum* (1979) appropriately mixes militaristic, childlike and surreal elements, and makes brilliant use of diegetic tin-drumming when the stunted protagonist Oskar throws a diegetic band off key at a Nazi rally: the child-actor's drumming was coached by the principal percussionist of the Munich Philharmonic and exudes an extraordinary and hypnotic power.

Alongside low-budget experimentation, the French film industry towards the end of the century devoted much of its energy to the production of big-budget costume dramas and literary adaptations that fared well at the global box office at a time when fewer than 2 per cent of films released internationally hailed from Europe (Hill and Gibson 2000, 62). Not surprisingly, the music for these 'heritage' films often harked back to traditional values of film scoring and drew heavily on romantic and other appropriate period styles. Several were scored by Jean-Claude Petit, who combined melodramatic romanticism with restrained references to Verdi's *La forza del destino* in the acclaimed Pagnol diptych, *Jean de Florette* and *Manon des sources* (dir. Claude Berri, 1986). (By contrast, Yves Robert's diptych based on Pagnol's early life, *La Gloire de mon père* and *Le Château de ma mère* (both 1990), received easy-going tunefulness from Vladimir Cosma that typified a melody-dominated naïvety commonly used for rural settings in much mainstream continental cinema in the 1980s and 1990s.) In *Cyrano de Bergerac* (dir. Jean-Paul Rappeneau, 1990), a swashbuckling adventure to rival those of Errol Flynn in the 1930s, Petit avoided overblown romanticism in favour of a straightforward tonal idiom with hints of classical pastiche; in the same director's *Le Hussard sur le toit* (1995) he contrastingly let his romantic passions come to the fore. Seventeenth-century authenticity was the priority in *Tous les matins du monde* (dir. Alain Corneau, 1992), a dramatization of the life of Marin Marais for which Jean-Louis Charbonnier and Jordi Savall drew on music by Marais, Couperin and Lully as the basis for a score largely comprised of diegetic viol performances. For opera director Patrice Chéreau's *La Reine Margot* (1994), set in 1572 and based on the historical drama by

Dumas, Goran Bregovic's eclectic score exploited anempathy (gentle unaccompanied vocal music matched to scrolling titles relating of Paris in the grip of rebellion and internecine religious strife), anachronism (a Gothic *Gloria* with full organ and choral interjections reminiscent of Handel and Monteverdi for the wedding scene) and electronics (atmospheric rhythmic swoops and funky bass riffs for an action sequence, mixed with Renaissance percussion and turning into a hybrid pseudo-archaic pop song). Pastiche neo-classicism and balletic cues reminiscent of Stravinsky and Prokofiev respectively coloured Philippe Sarde's music for the musketeer-style comic romp *Le Bossu* (dir. Philippe de Broca, 1997), which also featured popular classical melodies by Mascagni and Charpentier. A sense of nostalgia informed Jorge Arriagada's orchestral score to expatriate Chilean director Raoul Ruiz's treatment of Proust's *Le Temps retrouvé* (1999), with its elements of impressionism and occasional operatic manner: the diegetic performance of a pastiche romantic violin sonata in the manner of César Franck is enlivened by the director's novel decision to mobilize his sedentary salon audience on surreally gliding rows of seats.

Claude Lelouch's ambitious updating of Hugo's *Les Misérables* (1995) was scored by Francis Lai, an experienced song composer who first worked with Lelouch on *Un Homme et une femme* (1966) and subsequently abroad, his career embracing projects as diverse as Hollywood romance (*Love Story*, dir. Arthur Hiller, 1970), a popular children's movie (*International Velvet*, dir. Bryan Forbes, 1978) and soft porn (*Emmanuelle 2*, dir. Francis Giacobetti, 1975; *Bilitis*, dir. David Hamilton, 1976). The score for *Les Misérables* also involved music by Didier Barbelivien, Erik Berchot, Philippe Servain and Legrand, and serves to illustrate how lessons learned from the New Wave crept effectively into mainstream French cinema aimed at an international audience. After a 'cold' start (industry parlance for main titles run without musical accompaniment), a decadent *fin-de siècle* ball is scored with a waltz, supposedly diegetic – the camera lingers on the orchestra – but enhanced by an unrealistic degree of reverberation and couched in an anachronistically modern harmonic idiom typical of Legrand's style; the music thus doubly draws attention to itself so that when it is transformed seamlessly into minor-key underscoring, the ambiguity between diegetic realism and nondiegetic mood-music is clear. The same ambiguity, deriving from stylistic anachronism, pervades the wedding waltz at the end of the film, and the solo-piano music accompanying Cosette's ballet performance in 1931, which again seems diegetic until it ends with a dissonant stinger as the ballerina collapses in slow motion. Almost all the music in the film is similarly nondiegetic posing as diegetic: during the Nazi occupation, an SS officer visibly plays a darkly romantic piano piece which continues to accompany cross-cutting between scenes of torture and escape from captivity, a trick used elsewhere but always with similar diegetic pretexts for the inclusion of foregrounded melodramatic music. In a later scene, Nazi officers dance with French hostesses to dreamy piano music, even though no pianist is sitting at the piano visible in the shot: exactly as in the ballet sequence, the piano music is cut off abruptly when a woman spits in a German's face. By contrast, when genuinely nondiegetic music is used it is invariably mixed at such an unusually low volume level (even when not competing with dialogue) that it seems like a distant and elusive memory.

As with Godard's, so more commercial French films of the 1980s drew attention to tensions between popular and elitist cultures. In *Diva* (dir. Jean-Jacques Beineix, 1981), a prima donna has publicly declared that she will never preserve her voice on record; secret tape recordings of her voice become a filmic character in their own right, and singing which appears to be nondiegetic is twice revealed to be diegetic in origin when it ceases abruptly as the lad responsible for making the recordings turns off the portable tape player that accompanies him on his bike rides. (The same device has since become commonplace: it is used, for example, in the far cruder context of Virginie Despente's and Coralie Trinh Thi's exploitatively pornographic thriller *Baise-moi* of 2003.) Cosma's score for *Diva* juxtaposes rock beats, electronics, operatic underscoring and mystic Asian music, all of which (including pre-existing piano music by Satie) is at some stage or another rendered diegetically, usually in the form of a recording – a telling irony given the protagonist's refusal to commit her voice to this method of preservation. The diegetic/nondiegetic interplay becomes anempathetic when jaunty accordion music, first heard played incongruously by a supposedly blind busker at a moment of high drama, is later heard emanating from the dislodged earpiece of a murdered hoodlum.

Beineix's enormously successful *37.2° le matin* (*Betty Blue*, 1986) drew wide attention to the work of Lebanese-born composer Gabriel Yared, who had previously provided music for Godard's *Sauve qui peut la vie* (*Slow Motion* (UK) or *Every Man for Himself* (US), 1980). For the Godard project, Yared had been encouraged to write music on the basis of the script not the images, and had been given free rein; for *Betty Blue*, in contrast, the music had to be meaningfully integrated with the narrative. This prime example of what is sometimes termed 'cinéma du look' in reference to a certain slick coolness, a mood that in this case culminates in a tragic but uplifting ending, was simply scored with a moody saxophone theme and, most memorably, ineptly amateurish two-piano music apparently made up on the spot during a scene in a piano showroom but then taken up in the nondiegetic score with an infectiously catchy road-music beat. Heather Laing (2004, 27, 36) sees both the pervasive trans-diegetic migrations of the saxophone theme and the hesitancy of the diegetic two-piano music as directly representative of the by turns fragile and obsessive relationship between the two central characters, Zorg and Betty; indeed, some of Yared's music was composed in advance and played on set to inspire the actors (Laing 2004, 7). Yared was subsequently much in demand, the high point of his career being his elaborate Oscar-winning score to Anthony Minghella's *The English Patient* (1996).

Luc Besson's brand of 'cinéma du look' benefited from the rock-tinged music of Eric Serra, their successes with *Subway* (1985), *Nikita* (1990), *Atlantis* (1991), *Léon* (1994) and *The Fifth Element* (1997) all eclipsed by the multi-million sales of the music track to *Grand Bleu* (*The Big Blue*, 1987) – Serra's score to which was unaccountably replaced with music by Bill Conti for the film's American release. Like British composer David Arnold, Serra's pop orientation helped update the sound of the James Bond series in the 1990s (*GoldenEye*, dir. Martin Campbell, 1995). Pop-oriented marketing, common enough in mainstream French cinema of the 1960s, remained prominent in the 1990s, with youth films such as *La Haine* (dir. Mathieu Kassovitz) spawning two CDs, the second of which featured rap music only tangentially related to the film which supposedly 'inspired' the disc, and became a chart hit. *La Haine* belongs to the contemporary genre known as *cinéma de banlieue*, a French inner-city response to the tough world of the American urban gangland film, aimed at the same market as John Singleton's *Boyz 'n the Hood* (1991) and similarly tapping the commercial success of hip-hop. Other examples include *Bye-Bye* (dir. Karim Dridi, 1995) and *Rai* (dir. Thomas Gilou, 1995), both with music by Jimmy Oihid; *Krim* (dir. Ahmed Bouchaala, 1994), with music by Djamel Benyelles; and *Etat des lieux* (dir. Jean-François Richet, 1995), with music by Assassin.

More mainstream contemporary French films often combine standard atmospheric underscoring with popular styles: a typical example is the bittersweet cross-dressing comedy *Ma Vie en rose* (dir. Alain Berliner, 1997), with music by Dominique Dalcan. Others subscribe to the apparent interchangeability of different national styles typical of many popular European films at the end of the century: Manuel Malou, for example, contributes undistinguished Spanish-sounding music to *Gazon maudit* (*French Twist*; dir. Josiane Balasko, 1995) just as Nicola Piovani donated an incongruously Italian sound to Bigas Luna's utterly Spanish black comedy *Jamón Jamón* (1992; see Chapter 9). Popular styles with prominent accordion parts and naïve waltz melodies remained essential geographical and cultural identifiers in internationally successful films such as the nightmarish black comedy *Delicatessen* (dir. Jean-Pierre Jeunet and Marc Caro, 1990; music by Carlos d'Alessio) – the musical highlight of which is a delicious diegetic duet for solo cello and bowed saw – and the contemporary fairy-tale *Le Fabuleux Destin d'Amélie Poulain* (*Amélie*, dir. Jeunet, 2001; music by Yann Tiersen), both of which included minimalist cues in which the emotional neutrality of Satie is updated via the influence of Michael Nyman and others. More sentimental, yet skilfully realized, was the strategic diegetic and nondiegetic use of the boy trebles' simple theme in *The Chorus* (dir. Christophe Barratier, 2004; music by Bruno Coulais), a period drama in which the power of music effortlessly combats the problems of delinquency.

Poles apart: Krzysztof Kieślowski and Zbigniew Preisner

The widespread international respect accorded to the Polish team of director Krzysztof Kieślowski and composer Zbigniew Preisner would scarcely have been possible had they not achieved their finest work in the Francophone cinema. That they should be singled out for discussion in the present context is testament to an ongoing tradition of innovation brought to French-language films by directors hailing from outside France (of whom the first notable example was Buñuel), and the originality of their own particular synthesis of aural and visual elements, in which restraint and simplicity were the key concepts. In a glowing tribute to his composer's contributions to his films, Kieślowski commented:

> Preisner is an exceptional composer in that he's interested in working on a film right from the beginning and not just seeing the finished version and then thinking about how to illustrate it with music . . . He can think . . . about [the music's] dramatic function, about the way it should say something that's not there in the picture . . . It's interesting – drawing out something which doesn't exist in the picture alone or in the music alone. Combining the two, a certain meaning, a certain value, something which also determines a certain atmosphere, suddenly begins to exist. The Americans shove music in from beginning to end.   (Stok 1993, 179)

Some of Kieślowski's early work had been scored by the distinguished Polish composer Wojciech Kilar, including a short documentary about a night porter in a factory (1977) and *Blind Chance* (*Przypadek*, 1981). Preisner became Kieślowski's sole composer from *No End* (*Bez Końca*, 1984) onwards, though Kilar himself found belated international success as a film composer with his lush music for *Bram Stoker's Dracula* (dir. Coppola, 1992).

Kieślowski's directorial technique was initially sharpened by work on Polish documentaries, which gave his later fictional films an aura of realism typical of general trends in the French New Wave. His taste for economical spotting of music – in both low-budget and artistic-restraint senses – is shown by his first important feature, *Camera Buff* (1979), with its understated chamber-music cues by Krzysztof Knittel. Kieślowski's ten celebrated television shorts, the *Dekalog* (1988–9), by which he first made his name outside Poland, refused to pander to the commercialism associated with the medium, although they grossed $3 million in export sales on a budget of only $100,000 (Kieślowski 1995); he regarded his film and television work with equal seriousness, though he admitted that audiences in the cinema tend to concentrate more because they have invested financially and physically in the experience (Stok 1993, 153–4), and two of the films were remade in extended versions for theatrical release. Filmed by ten different cinematographers with markedly different visual styles, *Dekalog* was given some sense of cogency by Preisner's music. In the second film of the cycle, director and composer experimented with a basic ambiguity between diegetic and nondiegetic music: the character Dorota plays an LP which comes to serve as moody nondiegetic scoring as she gazes out of the window, but the 'record' stops without mechanical intervention when she answers the door to a postman – a trick Kieślowski may have learnt from Godard. Melancholic music for strings provides atmospheric continuity across contrasting scenes before its diegetic source (the orchestra in which Dorota plays) is revealed. Utter economy informed the music for the tenth film, in which stark drum-roll crescendos served as stingers for moments of sudden realization, and other percussive effects well suited the emotionally cold tone of an episode concerned with obsessive cupidity. The film ends with a rock track – the protagonist's son is a rock singer, this previously having been signified by a brief twang of electric guitar in the soundtrack – with lyrics by Kieślowski himself, sung by Zbigniew Zamachowski and 'Rose Europe'.

Music came to the fore in Kieślowski's first film made in France, *La Double vie de Véronique* (1991), a dark fairy-tale about a Doppelgänger based on an idea suggested by the ninth part of *Dekalog*, in which a woman singer mentions the fictional Dutch composer Van den Budenmayer ('He's difficult, but I sing him'), and the surgeon who will operate on her plays a recording of one of his works for soprano and orchestra, of which an instrumental version is then used by Preisner nondiegetically. Van den Budenmayer's (i.e. Preisner's) music features heavily in *Véronique*, a project on which composer was – in spite of meticulously planned musical events stipulated in the initial screenplay – accorded a free rein similar in extent to that habitually entrusted by Kieślowski to his cinematographers. The director was prepared to take a back seat because, as he pointed out, the descriptions of the music in the scenario 'didn't really change anything because a composer has to come along, in the end, and make something of what's been written in a literary language. How can you describe music? That it's beautiful, for example, sublime? That it's memorable? That it's mysterious?' (Stok 1993, 177). Favouring simple melody-plus-bass textures with slowly moving melancholic harmony, the

first part of Preisner's music track climaxes in a diegetic concert at which
the Polish Veronika, a singer, collapses in mid-performance of a cantata
by Van den Budenmayer after executing an extraordinary example of vocal
portamento, and is pronounced dead; at this point the narrative switches
to focus on her double, the French Véronique, another singer and teacher
whose life becomes increasingly haunted by Veronika's aura, this reflected
in subtle reworkings of the music associated with the Polish woman and
some astonishingly beautiful conjunctions of sound and image. A deeply
ambiguous film, its ending had to be made more concrete in the version
released in the USA in order that viewers should not be perplexed by loose
narrative ends left untied (Stok 1993, 7). In France, Preisner's music – which
included such esotericism as a vocal setting of Dante in the original Italian –
sold 50,000 copies on its initial release (Stok 1993, 179), an exceptionally
rare phenomenon in the world of 'art' cinema.

Although not a French speaker, Kieślowski elected to stay in France after
Véronique and his best-known work, the trilogy *Trois couleurs* (1993–4), was
inspired by the ideals of liberty, equality and fraternity as represented by the
colours of the French national flag (blue, white and red respectively). Much
of Preisner's music for this project was composed in advance of shooting,
and the director permitted him to spot it in surprising and unorthodox
locations. In the case of *Bleu* – which relates the tale of a composer's widow
and required diegetic and metadiegetic music purportedly composed by
him, and central to the plot – 90 per cent of the music track was recorded
in advance. Similar in aura to Mozart's Requiem, the unfinished music left
by the dead Patrice had been intended to commemorate the Unification
of Europe and his widow Julie plans its completion and performance by
twelve orchestras in twelve cities, instructing her assistant to add in some
Van den Budenmayer at the end ('You know how much he loved him'). At
the same time, Julie is attempting to free herself from the past and build
a new life, so each time the past returns in the shape of her husband's
music it threatens to restrict her future growth; as Kieślowski put it, 'The
music is cited all through the film and then at the end we hear it in its
entirety, solemn and grand. So we're led to think that she's played a part
in its creation' (Stok 1993, 224), yet the biggest musical outburst in the
film occurs in a near-operatic climax when she makes love with another
man. Again the idiom is fundamentally simple and statuesque, as Preisner
recalled:

> Kieślowski liked simple music, although played by a huge orchestra. That is
> why very often in order to stress the emotions and achieve a strong effect I
> wrote in unison but in widely spaced octaves. It gives the impression that
> this music is very expansive and monumental . . . Kieślowski thought that

> the best expression of the feelings or important experiences of his main
> characters should be through the music. This is metaphysical and nothing
> to do with acting. (Russell and Young 2000, 168)

The most unusual feature of the film is the strategic location of four sudden
fade-outs where image and music both abruptly cease, only to return as
the image fades in again at exactly the point whence it vanished, an effect
designed by the director 'to convey an extremely subjective point of view . . .
Not only does the music come back to her but time stands still for a moment'
(Stok 1993, 215–16).

Blanc, a story centred on a Polish protagonist who ends up in his native
country when symbolically dumped on a garbage heap by a band of thieves,
is the most tongue-in-cheek member of the trilogy, and Kieślowski intended
its black comedy to be enhanced by a score inspired by Polish folk music and
to be 'a bit coarse yet at the same time romantic' (Stok 1993, 225). Imbued
with a sense of nostalgia for the Polish homeland, Preisner's music emulated
the refined style of (the prototypically Franco-Polish) Chopin in order to
create tension in conjunction with the dramatic portrayal of a nation gone
to seed, the music gaining a new dynamism by aping the rustic qualities
of a folk tango as the protagonist's fortunes improve. (The soundtrack to
Polanski's wartime drama *The Pianist* (2002), with original music by Kilar,
used Chopin for the same purpose.) The complex circular nature of the
plot in *Rouge*, in which flashbacks from an old man's life are played out
by another younger actor as if they are happening in the present, and in
which characters from the other two films make fleeting reappearances, was
captured by a repetitive bolero theme, planned in advance by both composer
and director, and designed to represent 'the will to fight, the will to live, the
unexpectedness of events and the willingness to discover more about other
people' (Russell and Young 2000, 173). In a musical joke now wearing rather
thin, the female protagonist listens to music by Van den Budenmayer on
headphones in a record booth, and the spurious Dutch composer receives
his own mention in the end credits. Kieślowski and Preisner had become so
immersed in this ruse that they even assigned Van den Budenmayer's works
catalogue numbers which were allocated to recordings (Stok 1993, 225).

9 Global highlights

EARLY SOUND FILMS IN THE SOVIET UNION
Dmitri Shostakovich

Kozintsev's and Trauberg's *The New Babylon* had allowed Shostakovich the opportunity to compose out substantial and elaborate musical conceptions free from the conflicting demands of dialogue and sound effects. As with all composers who had worked in silent film and progressed to the sound film, the sonic competition presented by other elements of the pre-recorded soundtrack forced him to reconsider his approach. The same directors' *Alone* (1931) saw Shostakovich in less expansive mode, though typically indulging in both grotesque parody and simple leitmotivic techniques; rather bitty music had been added to this initially silent film in preference to speech and sound effects because reproduction of the last two were notoriously deficient in early Soviet sound technology (Egorova 1997, 15–16). Shostakovich was able to provide fuller cues for *The Golden Mountains* (dir. Sergei Yutkevich, 1931), for which he wrote the popular song 'If Only I Had Mountains of Gold'; the score's instrumentation featured a Hawaiian guitar, sitting strangely alongside a neo-classical fugue for organ and orchestra accompanying a scene depicting strikes (Riley 2005, 15–17). Organ music was later to feature prominently in *The Gadfly* (dir. Alexander Faintsimmer, 1955), with its 'Romance' winning popular success.

The *Counterplan* (dir. Yutkevich and Fridrikh Ermler, 1932), the soundtrack for which included an ondes martenot and a creative use of factory noises of which Clair and Vigo might have approved, spawned another Shostakovich hit tune: the banal, diatonic and patriotically uplifting 'Song of the Counterplan'. Fusing traditional folk style with the propulsive march rhythm of a defiant proletariat, the song was recycled by Shostakovich in other contexts, its success initiating a trend towards song-based scores in the USSR which paralleled cinematic developments in France during the same period: the song later appeared in *La Vie est à nous* (dir. Jean Renoir, 1936). Also coinciding with similar trends in French cinema, diegetic singing became a powerful communal element in *The Youth of Maxim* (dir. Kozintsev and Trauberg, 1935) and *Girlfriends* (dir. Lev Arnshtam, 1936). The former was the first member of a trilogy completed by *The Return of Maxim* (1937) and *The Vyborg Side* (1939), which won a Stalin Prize; in the first two films diegetic music, sometimes used dramatically to disguise political activity, is largely based on genuine popular and revolutionary songs. Among the most successful song-based films by other composers were the musicals scored by Isaak Dunayevsky for director Grigori Alexandrov, including *The Merry Fellows* (US title *Moscow is Laughing*, 1934), *Circus* (1936) and *Volga-Volga* (1938), an important body of work which drew on Dunayevsky's considerable experience in vaudeville and the circus, and took as its guiding principles the use of a pervasive theme song and straightforward illustrative cues (Egorova 1997, 35–47).

In contrast to song-based scores, what Egorova terms 'the symphonic type of dramaturgy' (Egorova 1997, 29) found in Shostakovich's more expansive film music was also encountered in film scores by Gavriel Popov (*Chapayev*, dir. Sergei and Georgi Vasiliev, 1934) – who indeed also wrote symphonies. But there were dangers inherent in the tendency towards structurally cohesive musical autonomy in the cinema of a totalitarian state. When *The Golden Mountains* was re-released in 1936, the scene with the fugue was excised, perhaps because of its apparent allegiance to the kind of musical formalism loathed by Stalin and his henchmen (who had already decided that *The New Babylon* was counter-revolutionary), and after Shostakovich's infamous lambasting in the pages of *Pravda* in 1936, his innate musical wit and populism were also to be suppressed – though allusions to popular songs and a lightweight waltz style found a specific application in *Zoya* (dir. Arnshtam, 1944), the true story of a teenage partisan girl executed by the Nazis. As Stalin's grip on cinematic output tightened, relatively few films were produced each year in accordance with the leader's naïve belief that this would guarantee a stream of masterpieces, and work in progress was vetted in his private cinema in the Kremlin (Volkov 1979, 194–5).

An inevitable consequence of such censorship and more drastic state terrorism was the rise in safely bland music, a weakness seen in Shostakovich's score to *Friends* (dir. Arnshtam, 1938), taken to task by John Riley for 'often merely anonymously accompanying the film – the very approach he had explicitly criticised' (Riley 2005, 38). Yet, in an atmosphere in which the film's entire production team 'shook in their shoes' with fear because the film's subject (Betal Kalmykov) had just been proclaimed an enemy of the people, this was hardly surprising (Volkov 1979, 114). The assassination of the politician Sergei Kirov in 1934 saw Raya Vasilyeva, the screenwriter of *Girlfriends*, put on a *Pravda* blacklist as part of the reprisal purges (she was later executed), and amongst the propagandist film assignments assigned to Shostakovich was a two-part misrepresentation of the circumstances of Kirov's death in order to justify the concomitant reign of terror (*The Great Citizen*, dir. Ermler, 1938–9). Other propaganda films on which the composer worked included *The Man With a Gun* (dir. Yutkevich, 1938), one of many tributes to the achievements of the heroic Lenin. It was perhaps inevitable that the composer's inspiration would flag in these dubious projects; later, he also had to provide music for films celebrating the exploits of Stalin, and found a niche for the brittle militaristic music that had always been a central feature of his orchestral style. Examples include *The Young Guard* (dir. Sergei Gerasimov, 1948), *The Fall of Berlin* (dir. Mikhail Chiaureli, 1950) – which reuses the march theme from the Seventh ('Leningrad') Symphony and contains some material he would in turn reuse in the Tenth Symphony – and *The Unforgettable Year 1919* (dir. Chiaureli, 1952), which strangely sought refuge in a nostalgic style reminiscent of Rachmaninov (Riley 2005, 74).

The 'Leningrad' Symphony had been introduced to American audiences at around the time Shostakovich appeared on the front cover of *Time* magazine dressed as a heroic firefighter defending his city from the Nazi siege, and its music had been appropriated by Dimitri Tiomkin in his score to Frank Capra's *The Battle of Russia* in 1943. George Antheil alleged that, in order to secure up-to-date Western sound equipment to improve the lamentable quality of Soviet film sound, an approach was made to Russian-born Paramount magnate – and Soviet spy – Boris Morros with a view to lending Shostakovich to Hollywood in return for the loan of some US sound technicians (Riley 2005, 32); most Soviet cinemas had not received provision for sound until 1938, shortly after the belated cessation of silent-film production. American jazz was banned under Stalin's regime for its decadence, and the jazziness of Shostakovich's early music now had to be carefully controlled; it nevertheless became an appropriate anti-American propaganda vehicle in *Meeting on the Elbe* (dir. Grigori Alexandrov, 1949).

A decree published widely in the Soviet media by Stalin's sidekick Andrei Zhdanov in 1946, arising from official disapprobation of *A Great Life* (dir. Leonid Lukov, music by Nikita Bogoslovsky) but taking in other targets as well, resulted in the suppression of four films, including Part II of Eisenstein's *Ivan the Terrible* (see below) and *Simple People* (dir. Kozintsev and Trauberg), with music by Shostakovich harking back to the orientalisms in which he had specialized during his work as a silent-film accompanist and which had also been evident in the *japonaiserie* for the Japanese assault on Vladivostok in *Volochaev Days* (dir. Georgi and Sergei Vasiliev, 1938). After this stern public warning, film production was severely curtailed. A further and specifically anti-formalist decree aimed at composers in 1948, again promulgated by the detested Zhdanov, cited *Simple People* and Prokofiev's score to *Lieutenant Kizhe* as examples of 'formalistic cinema-music tumours' (quoted in Riley 2005, 60). The decree also criticized works by Aram Khachaturian, whose output of film music, beginning in the embryonic film industry of his native Armenia, later included a score for the first Soviet Shakespeare film. (For this and Shostakovich's renowned Shakespeare films from the 1960s, see Chapter 4.) Khachaturian also scored the kind of Stalin-glorifying pro-paganda films which were one of the few officially sanctioned genres at the time, for example the two-part *Battle of Stalingrad* (dir. Vladimir Petrov, 1949–50). In 1949 *Michurin* (dir. Alexander Dovzhenko) was rejected by Stalin, and simpler 'music for the masses' by Shostakovich replaced its first score, by Popov, which was branded as 'gloomy and hysterical' and allegedly marred by 'formalism and excessively complicated musical language' (Riley 2005, 65). In 1952 only five films were completed in the Soviet Union, in sharp contrast to the 432 made in the USA during the previous year (D. Cook 2004, 691), and it was not until after Stalin's death in 1953 that production began to increase, and not until the late 1960s that experimentation returned to Soviet soundtracks.

Vsevolod Pudovkin and Yuri Shaporin

Eisenstein's famous 'Statement on Sound' (1928) had passionately advo-cated a 'contrapuntal' use of sound and underlined the need for a 'sharp discord with the visual images' if the sound component were not merely to become redundant by duplication or reinforcement of the suggestions of the image track (see Chapter 2). His fellow director and co-author of the 'State-ment', Vsevolod Pudovkin, demonstrated the potency of a conflict between audio and visual components in his 1929 text *Film Technique* (enlarged and revised in 1933), in which he declared that music should never be merely accompanimental to the images, but retain its own discrete line (Pudovkin 1958 [1933], 190). The book included two chapters on film sound and film music: 'Asynchronism as a Principle of Sound Film' and 'Rhythmic Prob-lems in My First Sound Film'. As case-study, Pudovkin discussed his recent film *Deserter* and its composer Yuri Shaporin, who went on to score the same director's *Victory* (1938), *Minin and Pozharsky* (1939) and *Suvorov* (1940). Pudovkin clearly regarded his creative collaboration with Shaporin on *Deserter* as an important breakthrough in sound-film aesthetics, dis-cussing it again in his later text *Film Acting* (1937).

In *Deserter*, Shaporin was asked to respond to a clash between workers and police not graphically but with music that 'expresses from first to last the will to resistance and the ultimate certainty of victory. It reveals implicitly what becomes explicit only at the end of the film' (Irving *et al.* 1954, 105). As the director himself put it:

> The image's progress curves like a sick man's temperature chart; while the music in direct contrast is firm and steady. When the scene opens peacefully the music is militant; when the demonstration appears the music carries the

spectators right into its ranks. With its batoning by the police, the audience feels the rousing of the workers, wrapped in their emotions the audience is itself emotionally receptive to the kicks and blows of the police. As the workers lose ground to the police, the insistent victory of the music grows; yet again, when the workers are defeated and disbanded, the music becomes yet more powerful still in its spirit of victorious exaltation; and when the workers hoist the flag at the end, the music at last reaches its climax, and only now, at its conclusion, does its spirit coincide with that of the image . . .

It will be appreciated that this instance, where the sound plays the subjective part in the film, and the image the objective, is only one of many diverse ways in which the medium of sound film allows us to build a counterpoint, and I maintain that only by such counterpoint can primitive naturalism be surpassed and the rich deeps of meaning potential in sound film creatively handled be discovered and plumbed.

(Pudovkin 1958 [1933], 192–3)

Pudovkin's attitude was admired by British film-maker Paul Rotha, generally sceptical about the validity of nondiegetic film music, who described various anempathies in the audio-visual montage of *Deserter*: 'Gay music accompanies a suicide, busy traffic is cut to the rhythm of a waltz to express the lazy luxury of the capitalist world, with the policeman at point-duty performing the dual tasks of conductor of traffic and music' (Rotha 1958, 133).

Deserter was also significant for its experimental sound-montage techniques, by which Pudovkin cut and spliced elements recorded from real sounds in order to create 'a clear and definite, almost musical, rhythm' (Pudovkin 1958 [1933], 198). In order to capture the bewildering noise of a May Day demonstration, he recorded two marching bands and mixed their playing with a collage of real-life noises in an avant-garde stew poised, like Charles Ives's infamous compositional experiments, halfway between graphic realism and avant-garde expressionism. The comparison with Ives is not fanciful, since Pudovkin himself directly likened his creative sound montage techniques to the process of musical composition and regarded individual sonic fragments as musical notes to be manipulated in the services of a wider audible structure (Pudovkin 1958 [1933], 199–203).

An essential difference between Pudovkin and Eisenstein was that the former favoured 'linkage' montage dictated by narrative logic, whereas the latter valued psychological stimulation above story-telling. It was the narrative strength of Pudovkin's image sequences (using 'relational editing' techniques based on principles of contrast, parallelism, symbolism, simultaneity and topical leitmotifs) that permitted the kind of musical independence that reflected the ideal of audio-visual counterpoint, a concept that Eisenstein

9.1 Sergei Prokofiev (left) and Sergei Eisenstein (right) in the early 1940s.

later found harder to rationalize when his own film scores increasingly paralleled rather than counterpointed his dialectically conceived editing.

Sergei Eisenstein and Sergei Prokofiev

Eisenstein did not find the opportunity to make a sound film himself until some ten years after the provocative 'Statement': his ambitious but abortive attempts to make films in the USA and Mexico in the early 1930s had revealed pro-Western leanings that led him to be berated at the 1935 Congress of Party Film Workers and subsequently attacked in *Pravda*. In 1938 his fortunes revived when he embarked on the prestigious historical epic *Alexander Nevsky*, which served a useful propagandist purpose in its depiction of the defeat of Teutonic knights attempting to invade Russia in the thirteenth century: the knights' costumes and heraldry were designedly close to those associated with the modern Nazi stormtroopers who, in 1941, were also to invade Russia with disastrous consequences. The film, which won its director two awards from Stalin, had to be withdrawn following the Nazi–Soviet Pact in 1939 but was triumphantly re-released after the 1941 invasion.

By the time of *Nevsky* Eisenstein's theories of audio-visual montage had evolved considerably from his early adherence to the 'cinema of attractions', a term that not only harked back to his early love of the circus, but also denoted (as he put it in 1923)

> any aggressive moment in theatre, i.e. any element of it that subjects the audience to emotional or psychological influence, verified by experience and mathematically calculated to produce specific emotional shocks in the spectator in their proper order within the whole. These shocks provide the only opportunity of perceiving the ideological aspect of what is being shown, the final ideological conclusion. (Taylor 1998, 30)

Eisenstein's 'montage of attractions' in his early theatrical work proved to be equally applicable to cinema, and his calculated agitational stimuli had worked in tandem with Meisel's aggressive music to *Battleship Potemkin* (see Chapter 1) – a silent project which the director felt was nevertheless his first 'sound' film. The director's preoccupation with conflict led to a Marxist theory of dialectical montage in which a series of pictorial and/or conceptual collisions (thesis + antithesis) led to a temporary resolution (synthesis), which in turn would provide the basis for a new conflict, the process of conflict and temporary resolution theoretically continuing ad infinitum. An extension of this principle was the 'vertical montage' between sound and image, a concept coined in an article of 1940 and referring to an audio-visual effect greater than the sum of its parts:

> For the musical overtone (a beat) the term 'I hear' is no longer strictly appropriate.
> Nor 'I see' for the visual.
> For both we introduce a new uniform formula: '*I feel*'. (Taylor 1998, 17)

Eisenstein was thus one of the first film theorists seriously to contemplate the possibility of what Michel Chion later termed 'sensory cinema' (1994, 152).

Eisenstein's composer for *Nevsky* was Prokofiev. Like Eisenstein, Prokofiev had (in 1938) gained first-hand experience of the American studio system during a visit to the USA, and had already made a contribution to Russian cinema with his popular score to Faintsimmer's *Lieutenant Kizhe* (US title *The Czar Wants to Sleep*, 1933) which gained a new lease of life in the concert hall after the composer fashioned a suite from it in the following year: the catchy 'Sleigh Ride' has remained a perennially enduring yuletide favourite. *Nevsky*, too, gave Prokofiev the opportunity to fashion a substantial concert work (a dramatic cantata) from the new film score soon after he had finished work on the project, though this naturally lacks the impact of the experimental recording methods used by Prokofiev during studio work on the music track – including deliberate distortion by placing wind and brass instruments too close to the microphone in order to make the Teutonic fanfares sound terrifying, and a pioneering use of multiple microphones to create unorthodox balance between the constituent elements in the orchestra.

During work on the project both men attained a happy balance in terms of input, with the composer modifying musical ideas to suit the director's wishes and the director in turn editing some sequences to pre-composed music and tweaking the music itself where he deemed alterations to be necessary. For example, where peasant militia attack the rear of the German troops Eisenstein extended a four-bar repetition in Prokofiev's music to twelve bars in order to create 'an effect of growing excitement [which] never fails to win the spectators' approval' (Eisenstein 1948, 80). Their working methods were a practical vindication of Eisenstein's firm belief that whether the music or images were established first was entirely immaterial to his audio-visual purposes provided the latter were coherent and laid down in advance (Eisenstein 1948, 124), a good example being the 'Dawn of Anxious Waiting' (images edited first) followed immediately by the 'Battle on the Ice' (music composed first). Foreshadowing Rózsa in Hollywood, Prokofiev toyed with the idea of using genuine thirteenth-century music but decided that the authentic idiom 'had become so alien to us, that it could not have nourished the spectators' imagination' (quoted in Egorova 1997, 62). Prokofiev's most important artistic victory (especially notable given the political climate at the time) came when he held firmly to his belief that a film with a tragic opening scene could not commence with a heroic overture, as Eisenstein had suggested.

Collaborating with a composer of Prokofiev's stature intensified Eisenstein's sense that his audio-visual achievements were somehow 'operatic'; and, like many directors of the 1930s, he used analogics with autonomous musical forms and contrapuntal texture, calling *Nevsky* 'a fugue on the theme of patriotism' (quoted in D. Cook 2004, 300) and noting in a lecture on his later epic *Ivan the Terrible* that an effective montage 'begins to sing out' when 'the combination of sections starts to attain the regularity of a musical construct' (Taylor 1998, 172). Such overly convenient comparisons with autonomous musical structures have been perpetuated in the work of some modern commentators, one of whom likens the audio-visual structure of *Nevsky* to sonata form (Egorova 1997, 61). As David Schroeder points out, Eisenstein's own terminology 'may easily crumble under musical scrutiny, but that sort of analysis misses the point: for Eisenstein the entire process runs parallel to music, and he searched for the musical terms to unlock the complexity of this organicism. In fact, he appears to be going even further with this, into the realm of synesthesia' (Schroeder 2002, 59). Eisenstein's belief in synesthesia extended to relationships between colour and music, a woolly concept with which he was nevertheless clearly fascinated: to him, musical pitches equated to playing with light while a vague concept of 'tonality' corresponded to the phenomenon of colour (Eisenstein 1948, 72–80).

Eisenstein's theoretical rationale for *Nevsky* has been much criticized in film-music literature. (For a useful digest of the dissent, see N. Cook 1998, 57–65 and, for a sympathetic middle ground, see R. S. Brown 1994, 134–45; see also Mitry 1998, 260–3.) Like Schoenberg, who after adopting his serial method wrote an elaborate and unconvincing theoretical reassessment of his early First Chamber Symphony with the benefit of hindsight, so Eisenstein admitted that his theories came long after filming *Nevsky*, but liked to think the later theoretical analysis vindicated the role of his directorial intuition in arriving at the 'correct audio-visual structure' (Eisenstein 1948, 153). At the heart of the controversy this later theorizing engendered lies the director's fluctuation between perpetuating the 'collision' model of dialectical montage, in which images clash with one another and music also collides with the image, and on the other hand delighting in musical cues that apparently parallel the visual image to the extent that individual notes can allegedly correspond to individual photographic details (such as flags on a horizon or a row of soldiers' helmets glinting in the sunlight) – a specious concept sharply criticized by Adorno and Eisler (1994 [1947], 152–7). Parallelism of this kind had been graphically illustrated by the director's now-famous chart offering a neat but contrived audio-visual analysis of the segment at the start of 'The Dawn of Anxious Waiting' (discussed at length in *The Film Sense*, and reproduced in Cooke 2001, 803), which appears fundamentally flawed by assumptions of a direct equivalence between musical and visual rhythm. Eisenstein summarized the process as one of '*vertical correspondences* which, step by step, relate the music to the shots *through an identical motion*' (Eisenstein 1948, 136). His supporting argument makes only a hazy attempt to discuss the mystical 'inner movement' he claimed to be inherent in the combination of music and image, but he recalled that when Prokofiev watched the film's rushes the motion of the composer's fingers on the arms of his chair showed him to be 'measuring out the structural pattern in which the length and rhythm of individual episodes are interwoven' (Limbacher 1974, 160). Of their subsequent collaboration on *Ivan the Terrible*, Eisenstein reported that he had given Prokofiev extremely precise instructions about setting a song text, describing his indications as to how to pace the mood implicit in the words as a 'rhythmical drawing' and claiming that Prokofiev 'always asked that his task be laid down as precisely as possible, and the more complex the task was, the more rigid its parameters and the more enthusiastically did he work' (Taylor 1998, 168).

Ivan the Terrible was planned in three parts, but only the first two were completed: the first (1945), in which Pudovkin appears as The Fool, won a Stalin Prize but the second (1946) was banned for what Stalin perceived as its implied criticisms both of his secret police and of his own character as leader. (Part II was finally released in 1958.) Prokofiev's music is even more 'operatic' than in *Nevsky*, a label which may perhaps be justified on account of the leisurely dramatic pace, sense of spectacle and musical pageantry of certain sequences, and not least because Eisenstein had in the interim gained experience of directing Wagner at the Bolshoi Opera in 1940. The stories of Ivan the Terrible and his son-in-law Boris Godunov had both been presented prominently on the Russian operatic stage, and Mussorgsky's *Boris Godunov* was Stalin's favourite opera: Eisenstein's new film project showcased two spectacular generic dramatic situations beloved of nineteenth-century Russian grand opera, the coronation scene and wedding feast. Prokofiev later reworked a cue from the siege of Kazan as part of his own opera, *War and Peace*. (He had earlier recycled music from the opera *Semyon Kotko* (1939) in his score to Faintsimmer's film *Kotovsky* (1942), so this was a two-way process.) Prokofiev's score for *Ivan* makes full use of the stirring choral-orchestral writing that was so memorable in the earlier film's cantata spin-off. Eisenstein admired Prokofiev's 'archaic' modernism; in contrast to *Nevsky*, however, *Ivan* demonstrated how linear musical consistency formed an effective contrast with the disjointed editing of the visual images. High points of Part I were the stunning diegetic singing by a magisterial cantor whose intense chant rises inexorably through a chromatic scale before the entry of major-key choral jubilation and cascading coins; the strained and quirky use of the E flat clarinet; a trudging march in triple time for the hauling of assault guns to Kazan; acerbic wind writing against a light drumming ostinato for the grotesquely memorable stringing up of exotic prisoners, and some thrilling battle music in rapid triplets – all of which ameliorated the dreadfully melodramatic acting and tendency towards static tableaux. In Part II Prokofiev again contrasted a straightforward ceremonial style with moments of quirkiness, the E flat clarinet making another tense appearance at the decapitation of the treacherous Boyars, and the tension of the funereal march for wordless chorus and orchestra leading up to the botched assassination attempt was superbly realized.

The final section of Part II was shot in colour, an innovation that inspired the director to extend his theories of audio-visual montage to chromatic elements, declaring in a lecture of 1947 (during the course of which pertinent questions from the audience showed them to have been just as baffled about the apparent inconsistencies in his theories as more recent commentators) that there 'is no difference at all between working with colour and with music', and that he aimed for 'polyphonic montage in colour'; fancifully, he

warmly praised the composer's ability 'to translate the rhythm of a shot's yellow tone into [an] accompanying musical tone . . . Prokofiev was amazingly
adept at this' (Taylor 1998, 169–73). Eisenstein again showed inconsistency
in his discussion of *Ivan*, in which Prokofiev's music for a song about the sea
manages to capture specific physical attributes of water at the same time as
re-creating the concepts in a different medium from the visual images: the
music 're-created' rather than 'copied', and it 'brought to life, rather than
imitating life' (Limbacher 1974, 161). For the dance of the *oprichniki* in
the colour sequence, however, Prokofiev's music was composed first and
the images edited to the recording, and more important than any speculative colour-based synesthesia was the composer's resourceful and dynamic
use of his ballet idiom. Praise has rightly been bestowed on the ingenuity
with which Eisenstein creatively manipulated diegetic musical elements in
the soundtrack (notably the chiming of bells), the sources for which are
rarely visible on screen and their presence producing a distanciating effect
that encourages the spectator to appreciate the interaction of music and
image 'vertically', and the novelty of applying the Hollywood technique of
fading out and fading in to the music track rather than the visual images
(R. S. Brown 1994, 140, 144). This flexible attitude towards spotting was
enabled by Eisenstein's asking Prokofiev to provide generic cues for particular dramatic topics (e.g. monarchy and treachery) so that the director
could locate them and manipulate them at will, 'in a way that often seems
crude to Western ears used to a more sophisticated matching or mating of
the musical and the visual' (Palmer 1991, 179). This authorial control of the
soundtrack looked ahead to similar creative experimentation on the part of
New Wave directors in other countries from the 1950s onwards.

For all their visual beauty and fine scores, *Alexander Nevsky* and *Ivan the
Terrible* both laid themselves open to accusations of coldness and dramatic
stasis. Mitry described them as 'the swan song of the pictorial conceptions of early cinema . . . a kind of monstrous ballet. The tediousness of
these films (notwithstanding the suffocating beauty of their images) comes
from the fact that they are neither painting nor choreography (though they
have elements in common with both). *They are, as it were, movements with
nowhere to go, a static ballet*' (Mitry 1998, 190; emphasis in original). Andrei
Tarkovsky, one of the most highly regarded modern Soviet directors, stated:
'I reject the principles of "montage cinema" because they do not allow
the film to continue beyond the edges of the screen; they do not allow
the audience to bring personal experience to bear on what is in front of
them on film' (quoted in Taylor 1998, 1). Tarkovsky's own powerful historical epic *Andrei Rublev* (1966), comparable to the work of Eisenstein
for its lyrical and memorable reconstruction of a remote historical epoch
(and also, for a time, banned in the USSR for its negative portrayal of

Russia's glorious past), provides in its score by Vyacheslav Ovchinnikov a contrasting example of the application of elusive and economical cues in a modernist idiom veering between simplicity and complexity: its wordless choir and funereal idiom for the crucifixion in the snow inevitably suggest parallels with Prokofiev, while austere unaccompanied choral music for the siege of the cathedral at Vladimir in 1408 betrays the strong influence of Orthodox Church music. The film's soundtrack demonstrates both vertical montage and linear continuity when glassy avant-garde instrumental twitterings accompanying images of eerie witchcraft become strongly rhythmicized and transform themselves into pseudo-diegetic music for the naked torch dance in the river, this memorable cue yielding in turn to simple but effective string trills and a moaning choir as a coffin floats inexorably downstream.

INDIA: BOLLYWOOD AND BEYOND

Since the early 1970s, India has boasted the largest and most prolific film industry in the world, its studios currently producing up to 800 new feature films each year. Music has always been a central element of Indian films and the general importance accorded to it in the country's culture as a whole is directly reflected in contemporary audiences who possess a knowledge of, and passion for, film music deeper than that found in any other country on earth. 'Film music' in India effectively means popular song: 'Background music and other musical components of the film, corresponding to the term "film music" in the West, have little market value beyond the production' (Alison Arnold 2001, 253). Because films are often three hours in length, songs are occasionally excised for Western screenings; as Rosie Thomas notes, however, this can work to the detriment of the film's aesthetic effect since 'Hindi film songs are usually tightly integrated, through words and mood, within the *flow* of the film' (quoted in Hill and Gibson 1998, 542). In addition, song and dance in Indian cinema were crucially important romantic expressive agents in a context of strict censorship which for decades demanded the avoidance or excision of any explicit sexual elements – even simple kissing. The predominance of musical over visual elements in a film's design is suggested by the term 'song picturization' used in India to describe the process whereby pre-existing music is imaginatively visualized (Majumdar 2001, 167).

Film songs in India are widely disseminated via radio and television broadcasts, often in advance of a film's release, and the success of a new film can be judged solely on whether its songs are considered to be good or bad. In marked contrast to the subservient position occupied by music in the planning of so many Western movies, in India an appropriate composer must normally be signed up to work on a production even before its funding can be secured (Kabir 2001, 27). Since the 1950s, it has been common for the composer's name to be featured on a film poster alongside that of the film's director, and in the same font size – and, on occasion, famous composers sometimes receive higher fees than their directors. As famous as the composers are the so-called 'playback' singers whose voices are lip-synched by the on-screen characters. In the cover art for many Indian soundtrack CDs, a photograph of the unseen singer will appear, rather than an image of the dubbed actor or actress. The most famous playback singers of the past 50 years are Mohammed Rafi, Manna Dey, Mukesh, Talat Mahmood, Kishore Kumar (a rare example of a playback singer who also acts), the sisters Asha Bhosle and Lata Mangeshkar, Geeta Dutt (wife of director Guru Dutt) and Shamshad Begum. As Neepa Majumdar has shown (2001, 161–81), the superstar status of the legendary Mangeshkar exceeds that of even the most successful screen actors, and her distinctive voice has dominated Indian soundtracks for half a century. In sharp contrast to the Hollywood musical, with its constant attempt to mask the technology permitting playback dubbing in the interests of transparency and suspension of disbelief, the Indian spectator will derive additional pleasure from the act of simultaneously perceiving the 'dual star reference' combining both the actor's bodily presence and the disembodied but utterly familiar sounds of the singing star (Majumdar 2001, 166).

International views on Indian cinema have inevitably been coloured by the proliferation of formulaic musicals created in 'Bollywood' – a popular term conflating the names Bombay (Mumbai) and Hollywood. These Hindi-language productions, formerly dismissed (as much by intellectual Indians as by Westerners) as mindless escapist entertainment for the masses, are now increasingly celebrated for their unique qualities and for promoting music to the forefront of films in a manner only matched by the Golden Age Hollywood musical. (For a persuasively positive assessment of popular Hindi cinema, see R. Thomas 1985.) This recent shift from condemnation to appreciation has also been affected by a general trend towards a more sympathetic understanding of the value of popular musical traditions in film that only began to take hold in film-music studies in the 1990s.

Early Indian cinema

A few Indian films survive from the silent era, and in these mythological subjects predominate. Nasreen Munni Kabir relates how both these and imported films were exhibited with live music:

English language films shown in India's big cities had a violinist and pianist providing the music . . . usually musicians from Goa – a Portuguese colony at that time – who had studied music and could sight-read. The harmonium and the tabla [hand drums] were the main instruments played with Indian silent films . . . Bhaskar Chandavarkar notes that 'The harmonium and tabla players were not only the first music directors, but also dialogue writers and dubbers, as they were expected to stamp their feet, shout and trigger excitement during the action scenes, crying "Maro" ["Hit him"], "Chup, saale" ["Shut up, you bastard"] or "Khamosh" ["Silence!"] while the villain got what was coming to him'.

(Kabir 2001, 114)

Interesting here are the early polarization between Western instruments and traditional Indian instruments according to the provenance of the film being shown, and the beginnings of the strong tradition of vociferous audience participation that continues to the present day and includes such demonstrative actions as shouting, dancing in the aisles and throwing coins at the screen.

The 1920s saw the foundation of a number of powerful studios, which came broadly to parallel Hollywood conveyor-belt practices in both their working methods and relentless promotion of star actors and actresses. The most influential were New Theatres in Calcutta, Prabhat in Pune, and Bombay Talkies. Hindustani productions issued from Bombay, while Calcutta and Madras were the centres for Bengali and Tamil films respectively. Sound came to the Indian cinema in 1931 with the Bombay production *Alam Ara* (dir. Ardeshir M. Irani), with music by Ferozshah Mistri, which owed its phenomenal success to its roots in traditional musico-dramatic genres that already enjoyed a strong popular following. A seminal influence on the development of this and subsequent examples of the song-and-dance romantic film was the vibrant Urdu Parsee Theatre, elements of which were combined with music from the Bhakti and Sufi traditions (Kabir 2001, 121). Songs from these films became hits with a life of their own outside the cinema: recordings issued in the 1930s by HMV helped to establish film songs as the first and most enduring kind of Indian popular music (Kabir 2001, 156). Mythological films also benefited from synchronized scores in the early sound era, a high point being *Gopal Krishna* (dir. V. Damle and S. Fatehlal, 1938), shot in both Hindi and Marathi versions with music by Master Krishnarao.

By the 1940s a distinctive film-specific type of popular song had evolved. As Alison Arnold relates, this was

different from existing [Indian] genres, synthesizing native and foreign musical features. The vocal melody had become simpler and less ornamented than non-film vocal music, the lyrics contained less poetic, more 'everyday' language, the song settings incorporated more prominent

> instrumental interludes, the orchestral arrangements included Western
> harmonies, and advances in recording technology enabled the introduction
> of effects such as reverberation and echo.   (Alison Arnold 2001, 254)

Hindi film songs adapted traditional structures, including the ubiquitous bipartite pattern of verse and refrain common in both northern and southern Indian traditional music. The accompanying ensemble expanded from the quartet of harmonium, violin, *sārangī* (vertical fiddle) and *tablā*, typical of the late silent era and the early 1930s, to include increasing numbers of both Western and traditional Indian instruments, thereby creating a hybrid orchestra appropriate for a style that trod a middle ground both between East and West, and between classical and popular idioms. Originally recorded live on set as in early Hollywood, and with the same practical limitations, film songs were dubbed in postproduction from the mid-1930s onwards and the birth of the 'playback' tradition dates from *Dhoop Chaon* (dir. Nitin Bose; music by Rai Chand Boral and Pankaj Mullick) in 1935. In the same year, the influential *Devdas* (dir. P. C. Barua; remade in 1955, dir. Bimal Roy, and 2002, dir. Sanjay Leela Bhansali), which featured different scores for its simultaneously produced Hindi and Bengali versions, pushed Calcutta's New Theatres to the forefront of song production and popularized orchestral backing. In the 1940s, many stars were proficient as both singers and actors. In *Anmol Ghadi* (1946), for example, by the director–composer team of Mehboob Khan and Naushad Ali, the talents of singing stars Suraiya, Norjeehan and Surendranath were prominently displayed. As playback practices proliferated, such dual accomplishments were no longer necessary as a springboard for a successful acting career. It was not until 1949, however, that the names of the previously anonymous playback singers began to feature in screen credits.

Successes abroad: Ravi Shankar and Satyajit Ray

After independence from Britain in 1947, the Indian government actively fostered production of quality films and aimed 'to discipline the film industry into adhering to new cultural and ideological priorities' (Hill and Gibson 1998, 537). The first blockbuster of the 1950s was Raj Kapoor's *Awaara* (1951), in which the actor-director was dubbed by playback singer Mukesh, with whom he would come to be inextricably associated. The film, which started a trend of locating songs in dream sequences, achieved phenomenal international success and was shown as far afield as Russia and China with its songs translated into the relevant vernacular languages and re-recorded. Kapoor thereafter utilized music for impressively large ensembles, with prominent massed violins in song accompaniments, and pioneered the use of specific instruments to represent specific on-screen characters (Alison Arnold 2001, 256). Bimal Roy, music for many of whose films was supplied by Salil Choudhury, scored a major commercial success with *Madhumati* (1958); an inventive experimenter with soundtracks, Roy tended to keep dialogue to a minimum and 'knew how to use song effectively in the narrative. He created many of his musical moments by holding wide shots and close-ups for a long time, allowing the tune and the lyrics, more than camera movements and fast cutting, to determine the pace and rhythm' (Kabir 2001, 132). Several leading film-makers in the 1950s managed to combine output in unashamedly popular formats with more thoughtful and socially aware work, music remaining central to the impact of all their projects. Two representative examples may be drawn from the work of directors Mehboob Khan and Guru Dutt.

Mehboob's *Mother India* (1957) was the first Indian film to be nominated for an Academy Award. It featured music by Naushad Ali who, like many music directors, drew inspiration from the traditional music of his home region – in his case, Uttar Pradesh (Alison Arnold 2001, 254). Mehboob and Naushad worked together on numerous films and their relationship typifies the strong sense of team-work that distinguishes the best of Indian cinema; similarly, Naushad was a longstanding collaborator with lyricist Shakeel Badayuni, with whom he wrote the songs for *Mother India*. These songs are sometimes lip-synched and sometimes voiced-over, the latter approach well suited to sequences that depict the passage of time, and are concerned with standard topics such as healthy young love, fertility and diligently working the fields. The songs for the heroine Radha, acted by Nargis, are dubbed by the most famous female playback singer of all, Lata Mangeshkar. Instrumental cues are sometimes traditional in scoring and idiom, especially in outdoor bucolic scenes, but often the music is Westernized: comedic mickey-mousing techniques sit alongside melodramatic music loaded with crude dominant-seventh harmonies and basic sequences, and at times the Indian and Western elements come together in an attractive folk-inspired modal style not dissimilar to that of Vaughan Williams. Typical of much Indian film music is the use here of impassioned unison strings to underscore moments of pathos and defiant struggle. The eclecticism of the music is unwittingly emphasized by the crude sound editing with its noisily abrupt splices between instrumental passages and the unconnected songs that follow them.

Dutt's *Kaagaz ke Phool* (*Paper Flowers*, 1959), with music by his longstanding collaborator S. D. Burman (who provided sensitive underscoring and memorable songs for Roy's 1955 remake of *Devdas*), was the first Indian film to be shot in the widescreen format of CinemaScope. A tribute to the

Bengali cinema of the 1930s, it includes songs in a decidedly nostalgic vein, many of which are voiced-over rather than lip-synched to convey the impression of interiorized contemplation. The vast majority of the instrumental cues are thoroughly Westernized, with traditional elements appearing only in an occasional flute flourish; as in many Indian films, a solo violin carries much of the emotional weight in an obvious throwback to the silent era. The comedy of manners at the heart of the film – in which native characters dress like the British, smoke pipes and utter frequent clichés in English – is underlined by the fresh sounds of harmonica and accordion, while other moods are scored orchestrally with heart-on-sleeve sentimentality. Diegetic dance music is jazzy, featuring saxophone and trumpet, and steeped in blue notes that occasionally invade the nondiegetic cues. Jazz elements had been introduced to Indian soundtracks by music director C. Ramchandra in films such as *Shehnai* (1947) and *Shin shinaki boobla boo* (1952), both directed by P. L. Santoshi.

A vital influence in shaping the development of music in the non-commercial Indian cinema was virtuoso sitarist Ravi Shankar. In 1945 he joined the Indian People's Theatre Association (a cultural organization backed by the Communist Party), for which he provided music for two 'highly realistic, down-to-earth movies, dealing with poverty and exploitation of the poor' (Shankar 1999, 106). Shankar noted that these projects, *Dharti Ke Lal* (dir. K. A. Abbas) and *Neecha Nagar* (dir. Chetan Anand), made in 1945–6, broke new ground because

> the subjects of most Indian films were mythological or historical, or even if social were quite artificial and lacking in such realism.
> The trend towards phoneyness in Indian films had already been established by then. Today it has been blown out of all proportion, almost ninety per cent of them now being based on borrowed and concocted stories, with an unwarranted eight to ten songs and dance sequences . . . These [films] were (and are) designed as the only entertainment for the large section of the public that is repressed. (Shankar 1999, 106–7)

The two films backed by IPTA allowed Shankar to experiment with nondiegetic music, using cues as a means of depicting the 'pain and exploitation' of the subject-matter. Although the films included a few folk and semi-classical songs, sung on the soundtrack by his sister-in-law Lakshmi, the principal focus was on instrumental music:

> I tried to use as few instruments as possible and, contrary to the common practice of the time (and today, too), I mostly used Indian rather than Western instruments, with the mere addition of perhaps violin, cello or clarinet. I felt pleased with these scores, because they were so innovative. I

may have been the first in India to use voices instead of instruments as
background or incidental music.   (Shankar 1999, 107)

A major turning point in the international fortunes of Indian cinema
came in the mid-1950s with the emergence of the work of director Satyajit
Ray. With the encouragement of Renoir, Ray quit his advertising job to make
his first Bengali feature, *Pather Panchali* (*The Song of the Little Road*, 1955),
the first member of his celebrated 'Apu Trilogy'. Ray, who was himself an
accomplished musician versed in both Western and Indian styles, invited
Shankar to provide music for the film, as the two men had been friends for
some years. For *Pather Panchali*, another simple and realistic tale of human
resilience in the face of poverty and tragedy (in the making of which Ray
had been strongly influenced by the neo-realism of Italian cinema), Shankar
evolved a new and rather rapid method of providing music cues that proved
not to be to the director's liking. The main problem was Shankar's hectic
professional schedule, which left him with only one session in which to
record the music. He failed to complete all the necessary cues, and some
additional music for a sweet-seller had to be supplied by Ray's cameraman:
this caused Shankar embarrassment on a later concert tour when he was
unable to play the sweet-seller's theme when requested to do so (Ray 1997,
78). Shankar's music for the film proved to be versatile, however, when in
1961 he joined American jazz musicians in improvising on its theme tune
(Shankar 1999, 167).

Shankar recalled that the score was recorded in a single nocturnal session
of nine hours' duration, with a band of seven musicians:

> I would watch a section of the film, roughly time it, then sing the music or
> play it on the sitar, and [flautist] Aloke [Dey] would transcribe it into
> Indian notation for the musicians. We would record it there and then in the
> studio. This is the style of scoring I prefer, and to some extent still use . . . I
> have done all my best work by watching the film in a traditional screening,
> and only writing down a few notes during it, since my purpose is to absorb
> the spirit of the film.   (Shankar 1999, 124)

Shankar's first action was to compose a principal theme evoking the mood
of the film, and the remainder of the music was a mixture of cues suggested
by the director and a collection of short sitar pieces in various styles which
could be used for any sundry purposes felt useful at the time of the final
editing (Ray 1997, 76–8). The most memorable parts of the music track are
those moments, suggested by Ray, where Shankar's contribution becomes an
expressionistic depiction of cruel events on screen – as when Apu's mother
drags her daughter Durga along by the hair, and the use of a wailing high-
pitched fiddle (*tar shehnai*) to depict the mother's unheard cry after her

daughter has died and she clutches a new sari unwittingly bought by the girl's father.

Pather Panchali features neither songs nor love interest, and these were two reasons why Ray experienced considerable difficulties in securing financial backing for the project (Ray 1997, 58). But the film met with critical accolades after its première screening at New York's Museum of Modern Art, and it received an award for Best Human Document at the 1956 Cannes Film Festival. In that year *Aparajito* (*The Unvanquished*), the second part of the Apu Trilogy, was released, Ray commenting that 'the audience . . . had lapses. I justly ascribed this to Ravi Shankar, who had again done a rush job and hadn't provided me with music in a few scenes that called for it. The stretches of silence were oppressive' (Ray 1997, 120). Alongside these longeurs, the film included musical rhetoric seemingly designed to speak to a universal audience: simple bamboo flute melody for bucolic scenes, frisky music for children playing, a screaming flute outburst for the death of Apu's mother, and tense tremolandi for various key dramatic moments (the father's collapse, Apu's face slapped by his mother, and the boy's later discovery that she is dead). The trilogy was completed in 1959 with the release of *Apur Sansar* (*The World of Apu*), in which Shankar finally endeared himself to the director by undertaking no fewer than three recording sessions and providing all the music requested of him (Ray 1997, 144).

Shankar also provided music for Ray's film *Paras Pathar* (1958), for which he utilized Kabuli folk music, and composed playback songs for several Hindi films, including Hrishikesh Mukherji's award-winning *Anuradha* (1960), S. S. Gulzar's *Meera* (1979) and Mrinal Sen's *Genesis* (1985). Outside India he provided music for Norman McLaren's stop-time animation *A Chairy Tale* in Canada (see Chapter 7), Arne Sucksdorff's *The Flute and the Arrow* (1957) in Sweden, and Conrad Rook's *Chappaqua* (1965) – in the last serving as replacement for avant-garde jazz saxophonist Ornette Coleman, the director's first choice of musician. Shankar was justly proud of the fact that he had contributed authentic Indian music to films that did not involve Indian subject-matter, such as Ralph Nelson's *Charly* (1968). He was naturally much in demand for Western films depicting Indian subjects, most notably Richard Attenborough's *Gandhi* (1982); Shankar's music for this project, which was partly based on a raga he had composed shortly after Gandhi's assassination in 1948, was offset by Western orchestral music provided by George Fenton, their combined efforts receiving an Academy Award nomination.

The soundtrack was an important structural element in Ray's film *Jalsaghar* (*The Music Room*, 1958; music by Vilayat Khan), which featured what the director termed a 'legitimate' use of music and dance as part of the plot (Ray 1997, 121). In the West, however, the use of authentic Indian music was not always congenial to unsympathetic critical ears, and the extraordinary verdict of critic Stanley Kauffman serves as a reminder of an unfortunate cultural narrow-mindedness: '[the film's] chief indigenous element, the Indian music, is simply uncongenial and tiresome to our ears. No doubt these are excellent musical performances for those who understand them, but they make us start counting the bulbs in the theater chandelier' (J. Walker 2006, 798). When Ray and his cameraman Subrata Mitra came to provide music for the early Merchant–Ivory production *Shakespeare Wallah* (dir. James Ivory, 1965), which treats the subject of the ascendancy of popular Indian cinema over classical Western stage drama and includes a scene satirizing the filming of a typical Hindi playback routine, their score was designed to appeal to a global audience by fluctuating between a number of contrasting idioms. Using a mixture of Indian and Western instruments, the music ranged from lyrical love music to a surreal and etiolated version of rock'n'roll and simple diatonic Western harmonies couched in an intimate chamber idiom. For most of his own later films, Ray provided music himself: examples include *Mahanagar* (*The Big City*, 1963), *Charulata* (*The Lonely Wife*, 1964), *Aranyer din ratri* (*Days and Nights in the Forest*, 1970), *Ashanti sanket* (*Distant Thunder*, 1973), *Shatranj ke khilari* (*The Chess Players*, 1978; in Urdu), *Ghare baire* (*The Home and the World*, 1984), the Ibsen adaptation *Ganashatru* (*An Enemy of the People*, 1989) and *Agantuk* (*The Visitor*, 1991).

Whereas Ray continued to exploit the manifold creative uses to which film music could be put, other independent directors who emerged after the international decline of the studio system in the 1950s sometimes tried – like the members of the French *nouvelle vague* who inspired them – to do away with music altogether in the interests of their new realism. Termed 'New Cinema' or 'Parallel Cinema', their films not surprisingly dispensed with integrated song routines. As director Girish Karnad recalled: 'The kind of films we attempted to make were the art films. They remained pure, they didn't have songs, and in those days [the 1960s], if you sold your film in London or Berlin, it covered your costs' (quoted in Kabir 2001, 5). Other directors active in this school were Ritwik Ghatak, Mrinal Sen and Shyam Benegal. Ghatak's Marxist-influenced student Mani Kaul made documentaries about Indian classical music and singers (*Dhrupad*, 1982; *Siddheshwari*, 1990), while Gautan Ghosh's *Meeting a Milestone* (1990) was based on the life of the musician Bismillah Khan.

Modern commercial cinema

Mainstream Indian film-making changed little after the 1950s, apart from the introduction of colour photography in the 1960s that almost compelled costumes and choreography to become even more lavish and spectacular at the expense of the dramatic intimacy of many older monochrome productions. James Ivory's and Ismail Merchant's *Bombay Talkie* (1970) provides an entertaining look behind the scenes of indigenous production of commercial musicals at the time, including affectionate jokes at the expense of playback methods of which René Clair might have approved. A culturally ambiguous internationalism is hinted at by the juxtaposition of scenes in which an unhappy Indian couple play over-emotional Western pop music in their bedroom, cross-cut with an Englishwoman seeking solace in a guru's teaching of traditional Indian music. The 1970s were characterized by the development of violent action movies, in which songs still invariably featured, though fewer in number than their counterparts in romantic films. Action songs, which included disco numbers, reflected a change of style in order both to reflect and accommodate the on-screen antics by using agitated vocal lines and rapid rhythms, and incorporating lengthy instrumental passages; prominent composers in this style included the teams of Lakshmikant–Pyarelal and Kalyanji–Anandji (Alison Arnold 2001, 254, 255). The late 1980s saw an unexpected resurgence of romantic musicals, initiated by *Qayamat Se Qayamat Tak* (dir. Mansoor Khan, 1988; music by Anand–Milund) and *Maine Pyar Kiya* (dir. Sooraj Barjatya, 1989; music by Raam–Laxman).

The appearance of song in virtually every successful Indian film, no matter what the subject-matter, has made the appropriateness of the specialized generic label 'musical' in this context somewhat debatable. Today's enduringly popular Bollywood films nonetheless typify a kind of entertaining escapism not dissimilar in essence to that of the Hollywood film musical from which they partly derive their format; and, in an appealing reversal, Corey K. Creekmur has argued that modern Hollywood's pop soundtracks are nowadays aspiring to a self-reflexive song-based aesthetic that has been the defining characteristic of Indian cinema for decades (Creekmur 2001, 393–9). Subject-matter in Indian films typically includes romance, family values, lost-and-found scenarios, love triangles and the kind of binary opposition between good and evil and resolution of other kinds of elemental conflict that helped make another highly stereotyped genre, the American western, so universal in its outlook. At the same time, Bollywood dissolves cultural differences within the subcontinent to create an 'all-India' amalgam that contrasts with lower-profile film production devoted to regional traditions. Especially beloved of producers are so-called *masala* films which, as their culinary name implies, are blends of ingredients that cut across generic boundaries and mix elements as diverse as spectacular action stunts, stereotyped melodrama and broad comedy. The two essential ingredients of any

Bollywood film, no matter what its subject-matter, remain music and dance: on average, a typical specimen will include between six and ten song routines that 'enhance the entertainment value and highlight the film's main characters' (Alison Arnold 2001, 253). So intense is the production line for new film songs that some stereotypical lyrics are today generated by computer software. But fine composers and lyricists still abound, and contemporary lyricist Javed Akhtar has commented revealingly on the nature of his work:

> The music director gives us a tune, the director gives us a situation in which the song will take place, and then we write the words for the tune. I would rather not tell you how easily most of the songs come to me, because my producers will start paying me less! But there are certain songs that do not need any cleverness. Such songs need tremendous simplicity and a surrender of ego; they should be so gentle, and so soft and have an ethereal quality. That kind of song takes time because it's always an effort to shed cleverness and smartness and find innocence within yourself.
>
> (quoted in Kabir 2001, 178–9)

The eclecticism of modern Indian film music may be demonstrated by a brief look at three very different productions from the early twenty-first century. In the English-language *Everybody Says I'm Fine!* (dir. Rahul Bose, 2001; music by Zakir Hussain), a surreal black comedy about a hairdresser who can read his customers' minds, the score draws on a wide range of international styles and includes contemporary pop music, exaggerated orchestral cues for an over-acting thespian, and moody electronics – all combined with heady visuals sometimes suggesting the breathlessness of Australian director Baz Luhrmann. Only a single song-and-dance routine is included, wittily triggered by a TV broadcast in the salon that inspires a visiting group of drop-outs to perform diegetically. The music is generally as up-to-date as possible, and it comes as no surprise when one pompous character says (as she leafs disgustedly through some classical CDs), 'Who the hell listens to Schubert anyway?' The loosely historical epic *Asōka* (dir. Santosh Sivan, 2001) featured an internationalized ethnicity beloved of modern Hollywood in its main-title cue, scored for synthesizers, breathy flutes and ritualistic percussion. The nondiegetic music by Sandeep Chowta reworked other familiar international elements, including neutral underscoring of dialogue and grandiose progressions of minor triads, a suspenseful crescendo at the cliffhanger midway point designed to help lure the audience back into their seats after the intermission, and a general increase in dissonance level as the action grows more intense. Under musical direction by Anu Malik, the film's song-and-dance routines are highly rhythmic and draw on modern

9.2 Aamir Khan (as Bhuvan, left) and Gracy Singh (as Gauri, right) in *Lagaan: Once Upon a Time in India* (2001).

pop styles in both music and montage, the melody of one love song taken up in the nondiegetic score as a love theme in time-honoured fashion. The entertaining *Lagaan: Once Upon a Time in India* (dir. Ashutosh Gowariker, 2001) combines period drama with resolute heroism, comedy, spectacular sporting action and triangular love interest. The music is by A. R. Rahman, who had emerged as one of the most resourceful Indian film composers during the 1990s. Traditional musical styles are reserved for Indian villagers, including conventional gestures such as unison string melodies for pathos; this music is diametrically opposed by a militaristic Hollywood style of orchestral scoring designed to characterize the oppressive British occupiers of the 1890s Raj in which the action is set. The song routines exemplify the best of popular Indian film music in their catchy melodies and expressive dancing, the latter directed by a team of no fewer than five experienced choreographers. But it is in the nail-biting cricket match between oppressed and oppressors, on the outcome of which the future economic security of the villagers rests, that consistently brilliant editing and vivid but economical music-spotting combine to produce a tense climax that outdoes even the finest Hollywood thriller in its sustained dramatic tension and exciting physical action – and in which the audience is kept on the edge of its seats for well over one hour of screen time.

FROM ITALY TO LITTLE ITALY

For all its propagandist intent, Mussolini's foundation of the Centro Sperimentale della Cinematografia in 1936 nevertheless provided Italy with a national film school capable of nurturing such talented student directors as Roberto Rossellini and Michelangelo Antonioni, and the concurrent building of an enormous production facility in the shape of Rome's Cinecittà studios promised to regain for the Italian film industry a success that had eluded it since the extravagant epics of the later silent era. This process was hastened by the banning of imported films from America in 1940, followed by an initial upsurge in the local production of domestic comedies and films based on literary subjects. As a direct consequence of its illegality, American popular culture acquired an almost exotic appeal for Italians during the Second World War ('Do you think Americans really exist?' asks a character in the 1944 setting of Rossellini's *Rome, Open City* as she listens to a jazz broadcast from a proscribed radio station), and at the end of the war came an inevitable demand for imported movies from Hollywood.

A major artistic reaction to the stereotypes of both domestic and foreign films came in the shape of 'neo-realism', a new directorial school (strongly influenced by the French poetic realism of the 1930s) with its theoretical basis argued in the pages of the journals *Cinema* and *Bianco e nero*. Neo-realism was launched in 1943 by Luchino Visconti's *Obsession*, a remake of *The Postman Always Rings Twice* with music by Giuseppe Rosati; the project fell foul of copyright problems and censorship from the ailing Fascist regime, and it was Rossellini's *Rome, Open City* that instead stole the neo-realist limelight in 1945. Hugely successful in France and the USA, Rossellini's grimly realistic account of the fate of Resistance fighters at the hands of Nazi torturers espoused the quasi-documentary hallmarks of using natural light and plausible exterior settings populated by ordinary citizens as extras, some even serving as actors, but allied these novelties to a powerful narrative that continued to appeal to a mainstream audience. Yet the film's music – composed by the director's brother, Renzo Rossellini – failed to live up to the freshness of the images and their persuasive editing, relying on melodramatic clichés and heavily sequential construction, and sometimes intruding gratuitously to sentimentalize intimate dialogue; its contribution to the whole was not improved by poor sound quality that made the orchestra sound as if it were playing miles away. In spite of solid work from composers such as Alessandro Cicognini, Giovanni Fusco, Mario Nascimbene and

Goffredo Petrassi (some of whose work is discussed in Dyer 2006, 34–8), Italian film music only truly escaped from the melodramatic shackles of a stagnantly operatic idiom – one that had continued to feature plentiful diminished sevenths and string tremolos – when the eccentric talents of director Federico Fellini and composer Nino Rota collided headlong in the 1950s.

Federico Fellini, Nino Rota and the circus of life

One of the most celebrated in the history of the cinema, the longstanding working relationship between Fellini and Rota had at its epicentre a profound understanding of the tension between tragedy and comedy which both felt was epitomized in the melancholic burlesque of the circus clown – a subject which towards the end of their collaboration they treated as a television documentary (*The Clowns*, 1970). Unlike Eisenstein's early preoccupation with bombarding spectators with circus-like 'attractions', Fellini saw cinema as a direct extension of the tragicomic life experience of the big top and travelling show, describing film as 'an art form and at the same time a circus, a funfair, a voyage aboard a kind of "ship of fools", an adventure, an illusion, a mirage' (Costantini 1995, 176). He moved away from his initial adherence to the precepts of neo-realism in the early 1950s to achieve more poetic, vivid and disconcerting moods. Fellini, who somewhat disingenuously confessed to disliking music, nevertheless entertained an enormous respect for Rota's artistry. He first hired the composer for the neo-realist *The White Sheik* (1952), and later recalled their instinctive working methods:

> Between us there existed immediately a complete understanding. Nino had no need to see my films. During the screenings, in fact, he would often fall into a deep sleep . . . Then he would have to replay [the images] ten or twenty times to study the tempi and the rhythms – but it was as if he had not seen them . . . When I asked him what were the reasons for the way he scored this or that sequence, I realized clearly that the images didn't concern him: his was an interior world, to which reality had little hope of access . . .
> . . . I would place myself beside the piano to tell him the action of the film, to explain to him what I had intended to convey by this or that image or sequence and to suggest to him how they should be accompanied musically. But he didn't follow what I said . . . You felt his creativity so near at hand that it gave you a feeling of inebriation, the sensation that it was you producing the music. It entered so completely into the characters, the atmosphere, the colours of my films as to permeate them with his music.
>
> (Costantini 1995, 117)

As with other director–composer relationships founded in deep mutual respect, Fellini sometimes asked Rota to compose cues in advance of editing the image track.

The sense of emptiness and longing sometimes engendered by Fellini's tragicomic attitude to the circus was nowhere more forcibly captured by Rota than in his score to *La Strada* (1954), a vivid tale of the maltreatment by a travelling showman of a young girl simpleton whose services he purchases from her mother, which won the Academy Award for Best Foreign Picture in 1956. Working in tandem with Fellini's idiosyncratic blend of realism and symbolism, Rota here found ample opportunity for elaborating circus-style musical cues that on the surface merely set the dramatic scene but at a deeper level hinted at melancholy and despair. The emotional ambivalence in nondiegetic cues was achieved principally through the tempering of sad moods by light-hearted instrumental gestures, creating the bittersweet quality for which Rota is fondly remembered. *La Strada* features inspired diegetic musical clowning, the showman Zampanò teaching his protégée Gelsomina to play both drum and trumpet as part of their comic routine, with her later learning to disrupt the violin playing of one of her circus colleagues with well-timed trombone raspberries; but there are more surreal elements, too, including the jaunty march for three soldier-instrumentalists in the countryside, immediately transformed into a funereal processional for a Catholic ceremony in the town centre, and then heard magically on celeste as Gelsomina watches in wonderment the nocturnal tightrope performance of the Fool (later revealed to be the circus violinist), whose haunting diegetic song-theme is quickly taken up in the score as a leitmotif for their unspoken affection for one another. Years after both their deaths, it is through hearing a washerwoman sing this theme that Zampanò discovers Gelsomina's fate. Throughout the film, it is impossible to separate the extraordinary acting of Giulietta Masina as Gelsomina – with her face making her seem 'more like an artichoke than a woman', as the Fool puts it, and her endearingly Chaplinesque gait – from Rota's memorable music. She also was the star of the surreal domestic fantasy *Giulietta degli Spiriti* (1965), for which Fellini asked Rota to provide music evoking a circus feeling through a young girl's memory, having rejected a pre-existing circus march because he felt its associations were too concrete.

A circus setting provided the bizarre climax of Fellini's *8 ½* (1963), when all the characters from a fictional film director's life and his abandoned movie project dance around the ring to the child-director's shouted instructions. This film is typical of its time in both its (here pessimistic) portrayal of the process of film-making and its tendency towards autobiographical reflection. Stressing subconscious thought and dream-like apparitions militates against linear narrative: the film is a Resnais-like labyrinth of confused

9.3 Giulietta Masina as Gelsomina the Clown in Federico Fellini's *La Strada* (1954), voted Best Foreign Film at the Academy Awards in 1956.

recollections shot with New Wave visual daring. In spite of the complexity of the editing and *mise-en-scène*, the film's 'serious' nondiegetic music is disarmingly basic, utilizing non-functional parallel minor triads and a simple flute melody, and greater impact is achieved when Rota's circus style increasingly obtrudes, sometimes emerging with surreal effect from purportedly diegetic sources (e.g. orchestras on the terrace and in the lobby of a health resort) to accompany montage sequences nondiegetically, and at other times appearing to be nondiegetic until its diegetic source is revealed once a scene is well under way. An example of the latter shift in aural perspective occurs when a recapitulation of a dance-like theme accompanies the film-within-the-film's launch party at its spaceship set, a setting previously accompanied by queasily humming electronics. As Chion points out (1995, 329), the famous Sabre Dance by Khachaturian which this cues resembles was a staple of the musical repertoire of real circuses. Whenever it appears, diegetic music – even the various classical extracts performed for the resort guests – seems decidedly unrealistic. The sabre dance returned in Fellini's filmic memoir of his childhood, *Amarcord* (1974), to accompany the exotic harem of a visiting Emir. The tremendous energy of *Amarcord*'s bawdiness was such that 'action' music would have been gratuitous, so Rota's contribution underlines the film's wit and general craziness with a characteristic mélange of easy-listening dance music and circus-like tunes, the latter typically emerging diegetically (e.g. from a crude small-town band) and prolonged to underscore antics on screen.

For Fellini, the beautiful but chaotic city of Rome was a *circus maximus* that represented 'a victory over the fear of bad taste . . . the vulgarity is an enrichment' (Costantini 1995, 16). This view was celebrated in *La Dolce Vita* (1960) and *Roma* (*Fellini's Roma*, 1972), for both of which Rota's music achieved an appropriately kaleidoscopic quality without sacrificing either modern sophistication or popular melodic appeal. The score to *La Dolce Vita* simultaneously captured both the city's archaic-monumental character and the modern pleasure-seeking at the heart of the plot by recourse to 'primitive' parallel fourths (a type of organum favoured in the Hollywood 'sword and sandal' epics set in ancient Rome) and colourful orchestration reminiscent of the great Italian master of orchestral impressionism, Ottorino Respighi; this music, heard in the main-title sequence, is subjected to a manipulative New Wave device when it is later revealed to have been issuing from a car radio. Popular dance music, as always with Rota, is here suitably hedonistic, deftly subverts its own clichés to prevent predictability or monotony, and often begins on a diegetic pretext but is prolonged as dramatic underscoring. Circus music returns in the cabaret scene as a clowning animal tamer whips three dancing girls dressed as tigers, and a sad clown bursts a balloon which he sucks into his trumpet bell while playing. Both popular and modern idioms are equally disconcerting: the tacky electric organ of Pérez Prado's *Patricia* (later the hit single *Guaglione*) adds a lurid quality to the film's notorious domestic striptease scene, while electronic chords sustained beyond comfortable lengths create a nightmarish atmosphere during the climactic and tempestuous nocturnal argument between Emma and Marcello in the latter's car. In *Roma*, dissonance and archaic organum again co-exist (and are explicitly linked with generic associations of ancient Rome when the material reappears diegetically to accompany a silent historical epic) and the other principal musical elements are thoroughly familiar: circus tunes for a variety-theatre pit band ('vaudeville is a combination of circus and brothel', opines a spectator); modern jazzy dance music serving both period-specific and comedic functions; folksy guitar strumming sitting oddly with electronic wailing, and so on. Another fashionable film about the making of a film, *Roma* takes further inspiration from New Wave influences in the bold *musique concrète* of the deafening symphony of car horns, thunderclaps and police sirens that accompanies the awesome and prolonged road journey into the heart of modern Rome. The quirky organ duet played by two nuns at the savagely parodic ecclesiastical fashion show – later taken up nondiegetically in a bizarre mish-mash of galop, organum, dissonant octatonicism and popular swing that climaxes in a bell-clanging apocalyptic vision of the pope – restores music to the forefront of the witty audio-visual experience.

More conservatively, Rota's music for Fellini was at times still imbued with the spirit of unashamed melodrama that had been such a powerful influence on the early development of film music, and in Italy had also continued to make itself felt on the operatic stage and in early feature-film *verismo*. When Gelsomina leaves her weeping mother to travel with Zampanò in *La Strada*, and when she waves goodbye to the nuns who have been kind to her at the convent where Zampanò abused her, the operatic underscoring seems a natural expression of emotion, if somewhat overdone for modern tastes; the film's main-title cue also begins with romantic music in this vein, initiating a medley overture in which the operatic manner sits disconcertingly alongside the jaunty circus music. Similarly, in *8 ½* an 'operatic' version of the main theme, with soprano vocalise, appears in the film's end credits. More disappointing was Rota's romantic pastiche to Visconti's treatment of *The Leopard* (1963), in which the subtleties of Lampedusa's novel were sacrificed in favour of the visual appeal of extravagant period re-creations and the international cachet of (badly dubbed) foreign stars, to accompany which Rota recycled banal ideas from a concert work written nearly four decades before – and anachronistic in style even then – perhaps so that its hackneyed operatic style might suggest the fading glory of the decaying Sicilian aristocracy. The symphony in question, dating from 1926, had previously been recycled in Rota's popular score to the British film *The Glass Mountain* (dir. Henry Cass, 1949); not specifically Italianate in idiom, the music's reconfiguration in *The Leopard* aped models from German and Russian romanticism. Far more evocative was the diegetic music badly played by a provincial town band, not far removed from the eccentric character of Rota's inveterate circus idiom.

Both Fellini's *Satyricon* (1969) and *Casanova* (1976) delighted in lurid spectacle, the latter inherited not only from ancient Rome, Italian grand opera and the genre of film epic, but also from the same circus of life that had informed so many of his earlier collaborations with Rota. Rota's *Satyricon* score made bold use of percussion and electronics and, like some of his music in *Roma*, 'obsessively evokes the primitive in its atmosphere and the modern in its musical style(s)' (R. S. Brown 1994, 222). The last project on which both men worked was *Orchestra Rehearsal* (1979), a political allegory in which orchestral players revolt against their conductor. Although also celebrated for his tuneful scores for Zeffirelli's Shakespeare films (discussed in Chapter 4), it is the bittersweet circus-dance style for which Rota remains best remembered, an indestructible idiom conjured up by George Fenton in a spirit of affectionate parody to accompany the main-title cloudscape in the surreal Hollywood comedy *Groundhog Day* (dir. Harold Ramis, 1993).

Ennio Morricone and the spaghetti western: eccentricity and populism

Moribund in the USA at the end of the 1950s, the genre of the western came to be significantly revitalized – most unexpectedly – in Europe, at the hands of director Sergio Leone in a series of Italian/Spanish/German co-productions in the 1960s. Popularly trivialized by the label 'spaghetti western', Leone's seminal revision of the genre has remained a potent influence on modern cinema in its unsettling blend of stylization, amoral and brutal violence, heroic action adventure and an aura of modern myth; audiences are at once sucked into uncomfortable modern fairy-tales and ironically distanced from them by cinematic alienation techniques typical of much 1960s European 'art' cinema. The spaghetti western was a team effort, with Leone's tableaux-like and often dialogue-free scenes expressed through vivid production design from Carlo Simi and powerful music from Ennio Morricone – the latter foregrounded as the most prominent element of Leone's obsessive sound design.

The new genre's winning musical formula was established in the proto-typical *A Fistful of Dollars* (1964), its exteriors shot in Spain and interiors in the studio at Rome, and its story based on Kurosawa's *Yojimbo* – the clear link with the Japanese Samurai film suggesting that, as in *The Magnificent Seven*, the mythical content was far more universal than the particularity of the western's geographical setting might imply. Morricone was hired by Leone partly on the strength of his musical eccentricity, since the director considered this attribute might help create a tongue-in-cheek portrayal of the film's iconic Clint Eastwood character, later to be known as the Man with No Name. The film's novel main theme combined Fender Stratocaster guitar, cracking whips, powerful chorus and whistling, all based on an existing pop arrangement that in this reincarnation perfectly encapsulated the rugged and stirring quality of Leone's vision; as in American westerns, this theme is later used to accompany horse-riding in open countryside. Guitar and whistling were both provided by Alessandro Alessandroni, whose input (and choir) remained prominent in later Leone–Morricone projects. After *A Fistful of Dollars*, Morricone no longer bothered to read the scripts in advance since he knew exactly what was required of him for its sequels: a pop-tinged style prone to drawn-out hyperbole at dialogue-free climactic moments, giving a sense of what Chion has termed 'epic immobility' (1994, 82) in much the same way as the temporal extensions in the Eisenstein/Meisel *Battleship Potemkin*. The second film in the Man with No Name trilogy, *For a Few Dollars More* (1965), proved to be the most lucrative Italian film ever made (significantly eclipsing the previous front-runner, *La Dolce Vita*), and this was in no small part due to the success of its music. Morricone's idiosyncratic idiom had been retained even though one of the production team dared to suggest Miles Davis's *Sketches of Spain* as a possible substitute – at which Leone literally threw the offending jazz album out of the window (Frayling 2005, 146). Morricone's main theme for the third film, *The Good, the Bad and the Ugly* (1966), was based on the wail of a coyote and used three different timbres for its three title characters: as with the previous films, the main musical ideas were presented in an animated title sequence. This film includes the most extended of Leone's duel-climaxes, in which the image editing directly follows the mounting tension of Morricone's pre-composed music. Both the title theme and soundtrack album entered the Top Ten in the USA, the album going gold having netted in excess of $1 million (J. Smith 1998, 136).

In testament to Leone's view of his composer's importance, from *The Good, the Bad and the Ugly* onwards the music was composed in advance of shooting so that it could not only serve as a basis for editing the image track, but also be played back on set to inspire the actors. Claudia Cardinale (star of *Once Upon a Time in the West*) singled out the on-set music as the most important feature of Leone's direction, and Eli Wallach regretted he had not been able to hear the music for his scenes in *The Good, the Bad and the Ugly* (he later said exactly the same of Elmer Bernstein's music to *The Magnificent Seven*, declaring of his acting in both films that he would have ridden his horse better if he'd heard the stirring tunes in advance); but Lee Van Cleef did not respond to the on-set music favourably, and Leone's director of photography Tonino Delli Colli found it a downright nuisance because he could not issue instructions to his electricians while it was playing during rehearsals (music was generally not used in the actual takes). According to scriptwriter Sergio Donati, however, when played on set Morricone's music was capable of moving less hardened technicians to tears.

Leone's and Morricone's most sophisticated take on the heritage of American westerns came in *Once Upon a Time in the West* (1968), with its numerous knowing allusions to Hollywood models creating a familiar backdrop against which the defamiliarizing elements stand out in sharp relief. (For a persuasive audio-visual analysis of a crucial scene, see Dyer 2007, 106–13.) Morricone commented on the importance of 'internal' music in this film, comparing its use of a harmonica to the nondiegetic transformation of the chiming-watch motif in *For a Few Dollars More*:

> The first time we hear the harmonica, it is internal to the scene [i.e. diegetic]; when we hear it subsequently, it is no longer internal but it has retained all the dramatic strength, the irony, and the tragedy it originally attracted from its internal setting. The sound of the harmonica was born 'by chance' from the harmonica in the mouth of the brother who supported his elder brother on his shoulders, an elder brother who would die when the younger man collapsed from fatigue. The sound was a symbol in the viewer's memory and also a dramatic representation of the story of the entire film – therefore, it remains present throughout the film. This is something that Sergio really understood. (Frayling 2005, 96)

A similar use of cumulative association was identified by Mitry in the function of the main theme in the seminal John Ford western *Stagecoach* (see Chapter 3).

The epic quality of *Once Upon a Time in the West* exerted a strong influence on emerging young American directors such as George Lucas, Sam Peckinpah and Martin Scorsese, this being the most recent of no fewer than four Leone westerns all released in the USA in 1967–8, by which time their individual budgets had increased from $200,000 to $3 million thanks to major financial input from United Artists and Paramount. The genre blossomed in Italy, too, where up to 100 westerns were made annually in the immediate aftermath of Leone's success, including subgenres such as comedy westerns. The latter were aped in *My Name is Nobody* (dir. Tonino Valerii), produced by Leone, replete with allusions to Peckinpah's *The Wild Bunch* (1969) and to Leone's own previous films, and furnished with a Morricone score including a parodic quotation from 'The Ride of the Valkyries', its musical moods elsewhere veering between melancholy and zany Italianate carnival and sometimes conveying a sense of 'generic form qua form, that is, pastiche' (Dyer 2007, 102). The US–Italian mutual influence came to a head in *Once Upon a Time in America* (1984), in which Leone revitalized the gangster movie in much the same way as he had the western, and with Morricone's music similarly showcased.

The soundtracks of both this film and its spaghetti-western antecedents have frequently been labelled 'operatic', principally because the music takes centre stage at crucial moments and replaces dialogue, freezing the emotion of the moment: Eastwood said Leone had 'opera-cized' westerns, while Christopher Frayling deemed the films to be 'operas in which the arias aren't sung, they are stared' (2005, 101). Laurence Staig and Tony Williams (1975) explored the operatic parallels in detail and Robert C. Cumbow (1997) analysed the films' allegedly Verdi-like structure. As with Fellini's views on grand opera as something emblematically Italian (see below), Bernardo Bertolucci declared that Leone's films were vulgar and sophisticated at the same time (Frayling 2005, 161), a comment that could apply equally to *verismo* operas and to Morricone's musical mentality. In audio-visual and cultural terms, however, what remains most interesting about the Leone–Morricone collaboration is the foregrounding of the music and its clear orientation towards commercial exploitation via the medium of the soundtrack album and pop single. Jeff Smith (1998, 131–53) draws convincing parallels between Morricone's cues and the contemporaneous soundtrack phenomenon of the interpolated pop song, noting that his melodic style at times features pop-like 'hooks' and instrumentation (e.g. electric guitar), that both the quantity and duration of individual cues were clearly geared towards convenient packaging on soundtrack albums, and that some of Leone's audio-visual montage appears to have been influenced by the production techniques of the Scopitone film-jukeboxes which were an antecedent of the modern pop video.

At the time of his international success with Leone's spaghetti westerns, Morricone also gained notoriety for his very different score to Gillo Pontecorvo's political thriller *The Battle of Algiers* (1966), the first serious cinematic treatment of terrorism and one of several hard-hitting Francophone films tackling the French–Algerian crisis; an Italian–Algerian co-production, its torture scenes were part of a neo-realist lineage stretching back to Rossellini's *Rome, Open City*, with which it shares its pseudo-documentary style and explicit violence. Bach's *St Matthew Passion* is heard as a torture victim is released to turn traitor (Bach's organ music later appears to accompany silent scenes of torture), whereupon a jump cut in the soundtrack lurches into Morricone's pounding ostinati for side drum, piano and winds, a grimly stirring and relentless motoric idea used throughout the film for military scenes. Some ethnic music adds local colour (as panpipes were later to do in *The Mission*): for example, a guillotine scene is accompanied by a solo traditional flute. Pontecorvo had originally wanted to become a composer and conductor, and gave himself an on-screen co-credit for his input into Morricone's music track. The director as a result received a music award from Italy's National Union of Film Critics even though he could only whistle themes for others to notate (Cowie 2004, 172), but Japanese director Nagisa Oshima slated the score because 'it doesn't make you think of anything' (1992, 140). The musical collaboration was not without humour. Pontecorvo composed a theme for the terrorist Ali and was amazed when, before he had played his tape recording of it to Morricone, the latter played him his own theme for Ali on the piano and it turned out to be identical: only when the film was screened at the Venice Film Festival did Morricone reveal that he had previously heard the director whistling the theme to himself and had merely reproduced it to dupe him into believing telepathy had been at work (Pontecorvo 2003). A significant element of Morricone's score is the use of a dignified chordal lament based on traditional triadic harmony as an anempathetic backdrop to scenes of destruction following bomb blasts, and for images of their victims, such noble simplicity becoming a prominent feature of many of his later scores for all genres.

Morricone's prolific output of film scores continued to balance eccentricity and heart-on-sleeve melodic appeal. His scores for horror films by Dario Argento (*The Bird with the Crystal Plumage*, 1969; *The Cat o'Nine Tails*, 1970; *Four Flies on Grey Velvet*, 1971) veered between an innocent lyricism anempathetic to the screen images and the dissonant modernism more typically associated with the genre. (Argento, who wrote the plot of *Once Upon a Time in the West*, provided his own music for his later chiller *Suspiria* (1976) with the aid of his rock band, The Goblins, whose music was to be heard in many of his subsequent films.) Morricone's services were later in demand for Hollywood horror films, including John Boorman's *Exorcist II: The Heretic* (1977) and John Carpenter's remake of *The Thing* (1982, based on a film of 1951 scored by Tiomkin): these were not happy experiences for the composer, the former being one of Warner Bros.' greatest commercial disasters and the latter soured by what he regarded as the director's interference in the mixing of the music. More congenial scoring tasks in his native Italy were Bertolucci's sprawling epic *1900* (1976) and the original Franco-Italian *La Cage aux folles* trilogy of gay comedies (dir. Eduard Molinaro and Georges Lautner, 1978–85), of which the first was remade in Hollywood as *The Birdcage* in 1996. Morricone went on to provide Zeffirelli with music for his 1990 version of *Hamlet* (see Chapter 4) and for other English-language films by directors as varied as Roman Polanski (*Frantic*, 1988) and Adrian Lyne (*Lolita*, 1997); after 1986 he was much in demand for Hollywood potboilers (see below).

Morricone's sometimes saccharine tonal harmonizations of rich cantabile themes, often placing a solo wind instrument over simply scored string accompaniments, are exemplified in the Oscar-winning *Cinema Paradiso* (dir. Giuseppe Tornatore, 1989), for which his score was supplemented by a sentimental love theme composed by his son Andrea. One of *Cinema Paradiso*'s wistful themes is intervallically very similar to The Fool's melody in Rota's *La Strada*, and the melodic influence of Rota is even more marked in Morricone's music to *Malena* (dir. Tornatore, 2000), with its Fellini-like Mussolini-era seaside setting featuring children, bawdy energy and sexual awakening: the Rota influence is evident in a minor-key dance theme for the title character's first appearance and a circus-like slow tango for trumpet. As one might expect in another internationally marketed film from the same team, the more lyrical idiom of *Cinema Paradiso* returns in *Malena* in the shape of a rich string melody and naïve diatonic saxophone tune replete with the secondary sevenths and unresolved major-ninth suspensions he habitually used to enliven a basic homophonic texture. For Morricone, instrumental colour and dramatic spotting of themes were far more important than the quality of his themes themselves (Frayling 2005, 97), which may perhaps explain the banality of some of his later work, and his adherence to idiosyncratic sonorities such as whistling, wordless singing (by soprano Edda Dell'Orso), panpipes and untuned percussion. Like Herrmann, he was a rare example of a film composer committed to doing his own orchestrations. At its best, however, and most notably in the Leone westerns, his music could play a major role in the impact of the whole and was indivisible from its filmic context. Not surprisingly, the spaghetti-western scores he initiated have been much imitated, usually (given their partly tongue-in-cheek nature) in a spirit of parody and generic allusion. Notable examples include the gas-station showdown at the start of Luhrmann's film of Shakespeare's *Romeo and Juliet* (see Chapter 4), and the use in Quentin Tarantino's *Kill Bill Vol. 1* (2003) of music from *Il Grande Duello* (UK title *Hell's Fighters*, dir. Giancarlo Santi, 1972), its score by Luis Enríquez Bacalov, an expatriate Argentinean composer working in the Italian film industry who also scored Fellini's *City of Women* (1980) and won an Academy Award for his music to *Il Postino* (dir. Michael Radford, 1994).

Italians abroad

When William Wyler directed the Audrey Hepburn vehicle *Roman Holiday* in 1953, the film's score by Auric eschewed any recognizably Italianate locational flavour in favour of the same general-purpose bustling wit and charm that served the French composer equally well in his Ealing comedies. As Italian cinema and its music became better known internationally during the 1960s and 1970s, a trend towards a recognizably 'Italian' sound came to dominate both domestic films and foreign-language films with Italian settings. Even the spaghetti westerns, with their ostensibly American settings, seemed imbued with a Mediterranean musical spirit: Scorsese commented that when he first saw *Once Upon a Time in the West*, 'as an Italian American, I responded to the music first', and guitarist Alessandroni commented on this influential film's 'Italian folk sound' (Frayling 2005, 202, 93). In some cases it was the specific film-scoring practices of Italian composers working abroad that helped shape the development of an Italianate musical idiom, their presence in America partly fostered by the growing dominance of Italian-born Hollywood producers such as Dino De Laurentiis. Film-industry links between Hollywood and Italy were already strong in the 1950s and 1960s when Hollywood's big-budget 'sword and sandal' epics were shot in and around Rome and at the studios of Cinecittà, and some film music by Italian composers for English-language productions later came to be recorded in Rome – in much the same manner as British film composers today often record their Hollywood scores in London.

Whereas the musical style of late nineteenth-century European opera had helped forge the romantic *lingua franca* of mainstream Hollywood scoring in the Golden Age, a more specific application was later found for the idiom of Italian grand opera, which came to be a rather unsubtle cultural marker for Italian Americans in general and mafia films in particular. Fellini's views on grand opera were disarmingly frank:

> It is a kind of Italian ritual, an emblem of Italian-ness, our most accurate reflection . . . It is the form of spectacle which most resembles us, which most directly expresses our psychology, our mentality, our sense of style. It's as inaccurate, superficial, shoddy, distracting, stupefying – that is to say, Italian – as one can imagine. Furious passions, ferocious vendettas, unimaginably exaggerated affections, unbelievable plots, swashbuckling exploits, insane libretti, costumes hired from funeral outfitters, nonsensical lighting, conductors at odds with the orchestra, singers who start running just when the singing reaches its best point.   (Costantini 1995, 119)

Fellini once intended to direct *Aida* but abandoned the idea: 'What could I add to its circus-like quality, its stature as Verdi's super-spectacular, that *Aida* does not already possess?' (Costantini 1995, 120). His love–hate relationship with the genre was celebrated in the affectionate parody of its theatricality and mannerisms in his final film *E la nave va* (*And the Ship Sails On*, 1983), its score arranged by Gianfranco Plenizio including material from Verdi's *La forza del destino* and *Nabucco*, and other popular classics (Schroeder 2002, 127–39; see also Chapter 4). Its melodramatic sense of fate made the overture from *La forza del destino* a favourite source for period dramas at this time, not just in Italy: in France it appears prominently in the Pagnol diptych *Jean de Florette* and *Manon des sources* (dir. Claude Berri, 1986), while a selection from Verdi's music provided period atmosphere in a British film version of Dickens's *Little Dorrit* (dir. Christine Edzard, 1987).

Verdi's music had already appeared frequently in post-war Italian films (Joe and Theresa 2002, 154–76). Long regarded as emblematic of the Risorgimento, his style was seen by modern composer Luigi Dallapiccola as a medium 'through which the Italian people [in the later nineteenth century] found a key to their dramatic plight and vibrated in unison with it', and in the twentieth century Verdi became a national icon beloved equally by Fascists and their opponents; his music therefore figures prominently in films with settings both period (e.g. Visconti's *Senso* (1954), set in 1866 and revolving around a performance of *Il trovatore*) and modern (e.g. Marco Leto's *La Villeggiatura* (1973), a drama about an imprisoned intellectual in the 1930s).

The melodrama and *bel canto* at the heart of much Italian opera had previously made a significant international impact with the success of Rota's score to Francis Ford Coppola's *The Godfather* (1972), a treatment of Mario Puzo's violent mafia saga that spawned two successors: *The Godfather Part II* (1974), for which Rota's reworking of the same basic melodic material earned him an Academy Award, and *The Godfather Part III* (1990), made after Rota's death and scored in a similar vein by Carmine Coppola (the director's father, who had previously provided additional music for the first two parts of the trilogy). The fame of Rota's first *Godfather* score, its Academy Award nomination having been withdrawn when several Italian composers made an anonymous representation to the chairman of the Academy's Music Branch claiming that one of the themes purportedly written specially for the picture had in fact been reworked from his music to an Italian television movie in 1958, rested squarely on two simple but memorable Italianate melodies, strongly influenced by Verdi (and, in the sometimes lusher idiom of Part II, Puccini): a *lontano* trumpet theme heard with the main titles and a melancholic theme first accompanying the rural Sicilian setting, the generic origin of both as deeply rooted in the country's culture made obvious enough by plentiful Italian dialogue. As Marcia Citron has pointed out, Rota's melodies often emphasize the flattened-second scale degree prominent in Neapolitan music (Citron 2004, 439).

The graphically violent killings for which the *Godfather* films were at the time notorious were left unscored in the interests of matter-of-fact brutality, with the singular and effective exceptions of set-piece climaxes in Parts I and III. In the first, a baptism scene in which Michael Corleone renounces Satan is ironically cross-cut with a series of images of slayings perpetrated by his dynasty's henchmen as insidiously developmental organ music, beginning diegetically at the baptism, both provides continuity to the disjointed images and, as the music darkens significantly, dramatically effective nondiegetic underscoring of them; paradoxically, the organ music is far more prominent when fulfilling this latter function than it is when purportedly 'realistic' in the church setting. Oddly attributed to J. S. Bach in the credits, the sequence was undoubtedly composed by Rota using occasional allusions to Bach's Passacaglia in G minor. (In Part II, a diegetic organ playing at a Mass knowingly quotes a brief snatch of Rota's main-title theme in a telling allusion to this extraordinary scene.) The brilliant baptismal montage of Part I is directly recalled in Part III when a diegetic performance of Mascagni's *Cavalleria rusticana* forms an equally ironic and cohesive backdrop to another climactic series of killings, the irony here stemming from the parallels between Mascagni's melodramatic Sicilian plot and the film's family feud, and musical tension is created by a direct conflict between the opera's music and Rota's familiar themes (Franke 2006, 36–7). Coppola had a deep attachment to *Cavelleria* dating from his childhood, and had instructed Rota to use Mascagni's style as a model for his first *Godfather* score (Citron 2004, 438); the opera's explicit return at the conclusion of the trilogy therefore formed a satisfying and logical climax to the whole.

Apart from their memorable Italianate melodies, Rota's *Godfather* scores are notable for their economical scoring of moments of tension, using his favoured device of simple organum above pedal points, and scenes with diegetic small-town bands playing in the endearingly erratic manner familiar from his work in earlier Italian cinema (such bands themselves having clear antecedents in Italian opera: see Citron 2004, 433–4). But his influence on Hollywood film music derived mostly from the film's 'operatic' sound, and the continuation of the concept of Italian opera as an ethnic marker: indeed, Citron labels one of the *Godfather* melodies as an 'Ethnic Longing Motive' (2004, 443). Italian opera as 'ethnic sonority' (Joe and Theresa 2002, 107) was evident in many subsequent projects, including the mafia comedy *Prizzi's Honor* (dir. John Huston, 1985) which took direct inspiration from Puccini's *Gianni Schicchi* and featured a nondiegetic score by Alex North embodying references to various operas by Puccini and Rossini. In 1980, however, composer John Cacavas had been instructed not to use ethnic musical references in his music to the TV series *The Gangster Chronicles*, in order to avoid 'lashback from Italian organizations' (Karlin and Wright 2004, 88).

Another Italian composer of the older generation who found success in a specific Hollywood genre was Mario Nascimbene, who won respect for his memorable if conventional scores to the historical epics *Alexander the Great* (dir. Robert Rossen, 1956) and *The Vikings* (dir. Richard Fleischer, 1958), and his more adventurous music for *Barabbas* (dir. Fleischer, 1962). Nascimbene also scored such diverse American films as *The Barefoot Contessa* (dir. Joseph L. Mankiewicz, 1954) and *A Farewell to Arms* (dir. Charles Vidor, 1957), his music for the latter receiving an Academy Award nomination in spite of the film's chequered fortunes – which propelled giant producer David O. Selznick out of the industry for good. Passed over in favour of Rózsa as composer for *El Cid*, Nascimbene soon found another specialized niche providing music for the prehistoric series *One Million Years BC* (dir. Don Chaffey, 1966), *When Dinosaurs Ruled the Earth* (dir. Val Guest, 1969) and *Creatures the World Forgot* (dir. Chaffey, 1971), made by the British company Hammer Productions with the music recorded in Rome. In these scores Nascimbene showed a fondness for *musique concrète* (his unorthodox percussion tools including bicycle bells, a typewriter and garden rake), and in *One Million Years BC* he made a Roman-style march for large brass ensemble sound archaic by recording it at double speed and playing it back normally (Larson 1996, 90). He was also employed by MGM for *The Light in the Piazza* (dir. Guy Green, 1962) on account of the film's Italian locations.

The Mission (dir. Roland Joffé, 1986), a big-budget British production, brought Morricone's film music to widespread international attention for the first time since the success of the spaghetti westerns, and he thereafter worked prolifically for English-language films, complaining repeatedly that he felt his contributions to Hollywood productions in particular were under-valued and underpaid. *The Mission*'s famous oboe theme, originating in the protagonist's diegetic oboe playing and its use corresponding to the transfor-mation of 'internal' music identified by Morricone as important in Leone's westerns (see above), co-exists with evocative music for panpipes and Latin choral settings appropriate to the Jesuit subject-matter; Schroeder views the score as a model instance of leitmotifs used to explicate dramatic situ-ations, especially during the battle sequence (Schroeder 2002, 81–3). The score proved to be second only to *The Good, the Bad and the Ugly* in record sales, and served as a stylistic model for John Williams's score to Steven Spielberg's *Empire of the Sun* (1987), at its director's request. Panpipes were to figure again in Morricone's score to Brian De Palma's *Casualties of War* (1989), which was recorded in Italy, the ethnic instrument having previ-ously acquired considerable popularity as a result of Romanian Gheorghe Zamfir's playing on the soundtrack to the internationally successful Aus-tralian film *Picnic at Hanging Rock* (dir. Peter Weir, 1975). Other familiar elements of Morricone's style to recur in *Casualties of War* were the use of a pulsating, tense and economical ostinato pattern for a trudging march in the tropical heat, a dignified theme of almost naïve nobility for the death of a soldier, and a passionately expressive lament for a sick girl; a sombre word-less chorus and orchestra combine to provide a hyperbolic peroration. Two years previously Morricone had scored De Palma's *The Untouchables*, once more relying on simple but effectively propulsive ostinati and drawing on both the eccentric harmonica writing of *Once Upon a Time in the West* and a Sicilian melodic style to capture the film's mafia milieu, which included the almost obligatory opera-house scene (from which Leoncavallo's 'Vesti la giubba', from *Pagliacci*, was used in the film's theatrical trailer).

Morricone's scores for Hollywood productions remained mostly formu-laic. In the thrillers *Wolf* (dir. Mike Nichols) and *Disclosure* (dir. Barry Levin-son), both released in 1994, grating dissonance is strategically deployed both as one-off stingers and insidiously threatening crescendi, with restrained use of electronic sonorities at times and forays into avant-garde complexity for irrational elements, the last contrasting with the persistent use of obsessive regular ostinati and tense pedal points. Both scores include fleeting and sentimental diatonic themes, scored for saxophone and strings towards the close of *Wolf* and for synthesizers in *Disclosure*, and both films offered virtually no opportunity for the kind of musical foregrounding with which Morricone made his reputation. Far better suited to the eccentricity of his earlier scores were offbeat European assignments such as quirky Spanish director Pedro Almodóvar's *Tie Me Up! Tie Me Down!* (1989), in which two stock Morricone techniques – dissonances above a pulsating pedal note and insidiously percussive ostinati – with the simplest of means suggest that ordinary events are not all they might seem. Even in this blackly comedic context, however, the composer cannot resist sentimental circle-of-fifths progressions for moments of tenderness, enlivened by crude chromatic shifts in the bass jerking the music into another key.

As influential on late twentieth-century Hollywood film music as the Italian operatic idiom was Morricone's distinctive brand of sentimental and largely diatonic melody-plus-accompaniment. This idiom is most clearly heard in the work of his compatriots Pino Donaggio and Nicola Piovani, and in Piovani's case the similarity with Morricone's style was so obvious that it was for a time rumoured that Piovani was merely one of Morricone's pseudonyms. Piovani worked with Fellini following Rota's death (*Ginger and Fred*, 1986; *Intervista*, 1987; *The Voice of the Moon*, 1990), and later resorted to the sentimental diatonic style in films as different as Spanish director Bigas Luna's erotic black comedy *Jamón Jamón* (1992), where it seems wildly out of place both culturally and dramatically (though the spaghetti-western-tinged ham-clubbing duel at the climax is a delight), and the Italian production *The Son's Room* (dir. Nanni Moretti, 2001), where the reverbed saxophone solo over a simple accompanying texture does little to raise the film above the level of a tediously manipulative soap opera; here again, other parameters of the film's style (for example the consistently harshly lit visual images) sit oddly with the sentimental music track. Piovani also scored Luna's *The Tit and the Moon* (1994) and received an Academy Award for his score to the concentration-camp comedy *Life is Beautiful* (dir. Roberto Benigni, 1999), not the easiest topic to tackle and one in which the lightweight melody-based style, Rota-inspired diegetic music and simple minor-key material for the Nazi menace proved unexceptional. Donaggio worked more widely outside Italy than Piovani, scoring Nicolas Roeg's *Don't Look Now* (1973) with a strange mixture of banal sentimentality, eeriness and manic baroque pastiche, before coming to wider international attention as De Palma's composer for the Hitchcock-inspired chillers *Carrie* (1976) and *Dressed to Kill* (1980). In *Carrie* Donaggio uses the sentimental idiom to accompany soft-focus imagery and lead spectators up a wickedly manipulative emotional garden path before the sudden and shocking final plot-twist – a notable departure from the usual horror cliché whereby *Angst*-ridden expectant music prefaces terrible events (or bathetic non-events) – and he did precisely the same at the beginning of *Dressed to Kill* before the murder in the shower. In 1993 Donaggio scored *Trauma*, Argento's first foray into the American slasher genre that owed so much to Italian *giallo* roots.

JAPAN

Traditional elements in silent and early sound films

The silent cinema in Japan developed rather differently from that in the West, for two major reasons. First, Japanese silent films from the outset were strongly influenced by the traditional Japanese theatrical arts, most notably the vividly stylized Kabuki theatre, always popular on account of its direct-ness of appeal, excitement and visual splendour. Kabuki elements shaped both the acting style and subject-matter of many early Japanese films and tended to discourage the creative experimentation that might have drawn the Japanese silent cinema closer to Western trends. Second, Japanese silent cinema relied heavily on the use of a *benshi* – a 'narrator–commentator–explainer' (Richie 1972, 6) – to compensate for some of the dramatic and narrative weaknesses in silent presentation that, in the West, could be obvi-ated by appropriately structured musical accompaniment. Because films were expected to be shown with *benshi*, Japanese directors were relieved from the obligation to make their plots and editing clear in themselves since the narrators could be relied upon to interpret any ambiguities and explain elisions for the benefit of the spectators. The *benshi*, many of whom became celebrities, sat to one side of the screen and commentated on the action to the accompaniment of traditional music, drawing the spectators into the drama and preserving a functional link with the side-stage singer–narrators in both Kabuki and its related genre, the puppet theatre Bunraku.

In 1923, the horrific Tokyo earthquake decimated the film industry and the subsequent reconstruction brought a fresh interest in genres and styles inspired by practices in the West. The two principal genres established in the mid-1920s were the *jidai-geki* (period film) and *gendai-geki* (contempo-rary film). Sound was introduced to the Japanese cinema in 1931 but took several years to secure a foothold. The first Japanese sound film to exploit music creatively was *My Neighbour's Wife and Mine* (*Madamu to nyobo*; dir. Heinosuke Gosho, 1931), belonging to the sub-category of *gendai-geki* known as *shomin-geki* (modern middle-class comedies). As befitted the genre, the film's acting style was relatively naturalistic; as in the West in the early years of sound film, the musical provision was predominantly diegetic and used both to create the illusion of space and to mirror dramatic developments, as when the film's protagonist grows increasingly inebriated as his neighbour's wife plays ever more frenetic jazz (Lack 1997, 92–3). By the mid-1930s a studio system had evolved that was similar to the Hollywood model, the three leading production companies being Nikkatsu, Shochiku and Toho. State censorship increased throughout the 1930s as war with China and the West approached; as in all other combatant countries, the Second World War saw the production of numerous propaganda films. Under the post-war US military occupation (1945–52), *jidai-geki* were banned, along with other films that were concerned with feudalism or imperialism. In this period a huge influx of American films resulted in the increasing influence of both Western genres and directorial styles as the Japanese film industry began to broaden its horizons.

Kenji Mizoguchi was one director who had continued to draw on Kabuki for inspiration. His early film *Story of the Last Chrysanthemum* (*Zangiku monogatari*, 1939; music by Shirō Fukai and Senji Ito) was set in a family of Kabuki actors and features diegetic Kabuki performance; the family's theatrical and domestic traditions were contrasted with the individualism seemingly demanded by modern life. Darrell William Davis notes that Kabuki, appropriately for Mizoguchi's purpose, occupies 'a middle ground between [the popular theatre] *shimpa*, on the one hand, with its shifting balance of progressive and conservative associations, and noh, on the other, whose sacramental gravity remains inviolate' (D. Davis 1996, 109). In maintaining a certain degree of aesthetic autonomy between the film's constituent parts, Mizoguchi promoted 'a gap between the expressive functions of acting, camerawork, and music that concentrates and counterpoints these elements, arranging them to interact in a complex spectacle rather than in an organically unified representation' (D. Davis 1996, 117). Eisenstein saw considerable filmic potential in Kabuki, about which he published essays in the late 1920s and further discussed in *Film Form* (1949); it influenced the Burning Fiery Furnace scene in *Ivan the Terrible*, and he admired the genre for its equal balancing of sound, movement, space and voice, with no one element being subservient to another (Taylor 1998, 12). Mizoguchi went on to feature diegetic Nō performance in his *Genroku chushingura* (*The 47 Loyal Ronin*, 1942; music by Fukai). In the 1950s he collaborated with composer Fumio Hayasaka, who had been responsible for founding an Association of Film Music in Japan in 1950 and had earlier studied with Russian composer Alexander Tcherepnin, a great enthusiast for Far Eastern music who had spent much of the 1930s in China and Japan. Mizoguchi's and Hayasaka's treatment of historical feudalism in such *jidai-geki* as *Ugetsu* (*Ugetsu monogatari*, 1953) quickly won international respect. Mizoguchi's *The Crucified*

Lovers (*Chikamatsu monogatari*, 1954) demonstrated an unusually close relationship between Hayasaka's music and the film's sound effects, and confirmed film critic Noël Burch's view that 'Japanese theatrical diction, with its shrieking, panting, rumbling sounds constituting a tonal range similar to that of Schoenbergian *Sprechgesang*, is particularly capable of organically interacting with other forms of sound so as to create a single complex sound texture' (Weis and Belton 1985, 204; Lack 1997, 162). Poulenc, himself no stranger to fusing Eastern and Western musical idioms, saw the film at Cannes in 1955 and praised the unity of its occidental and oriental elements, foreseeing a rich future for Japanese film music if this trend were to continue (Lacombe and Porcile 1995, 121).

The films of Yasujiro Ozu and Akira Kurosawa

Ozu first made his mark as a director of silent films, including the 1932 childhood comedy *I Was Born, But...* (which was furnished with a new score by British composer Edward Dudley Hughes in 2002). He showed himself to be a director sensitive to the power of music from an early stage in his career when he used the American popular song 'Old Black Joe' to disconcerting cultural effect in *The Only Son* (*Hitori musuko*, 1936), with original music by Senji Ito. Ozu specialized in *shomin-geki*, and it has been argued that his constant reuse of the same actors, situations and technical formulae was tantamount to his remaking the same film over and over again throughout his career. David Bordwell has termed this a 'modular' approach to film-making, and noted the importance of music as a consistent element in some of the reworked scenes (which he calls 'detached units'): for example, in 'almost every film there is the "idyll," a scene in natural surroundings during which characters sit quietly and contemplate their lives. In the sound films, these idylls have nondiegetic music playing throughout' (Bordwell 1988, 63). The bitter-sweet flavour of Ozu's minimalist and sometimes visually static family dramas was reflected in their music tracks, for example in *Tokyo Story* (*Tokyo monogatari*, 1953), with music by the director's frequent collaborator, Ichiro (Kojun) Saito. The film starts and ends in silence so that, at the conclusion, 'boats in the nearby harbour sound the only notes, the notes of natural activity' (Tucker 1973, 55).

In his magisterial study of Ozu's films, Bordwell offers many insights into their use of music. Of Ito's score for *The Brothers and Sisters of the Toda Family* (*Todake no kyodai*, 1941), for example, he notes that it serves as

> a model for [Ozu's] postwar efforts, with its surging, melancholy theme, its string runs and harp glissandi, and its use of the vibraphone to pick out the

melody (as at the close of *The Only Son*). Now music will bridge scenes a little more often than in [Ito's earlier score for] *What Did the Lady Forget?* [*Shujo wa nani o wasuretaka*, 1937], and the credits theme reappears at crucial points to underscore motifs associated with Mr Toda.

(Bordwell 1988, 284)

By the time of Saito's score for *Record of a Tenement Gentleman* (*Nagaya shinshiroku*, 1947), the music had become 'in quantity and quality exactly what Ozu would use for the rest of his career . . . at its most soaring, as strings call up a broad hymn-like tune' (Bordwell 1988, 301). Among the more interesting later uses of Ozu's trademark vibraphone is its anempathetic and diegetically ambiguous appearance in Saito's music for *Tokyo Twilight* (*Tokyo boshoku*, 1957), a film unusual for Ozu in its paucity of nondiegetic cues (Bordwell 1988, 341). The unsettling effect of the cheerful vibraphone melody in this film is typical of the director's belief that, as Saito put it, 'if the character is sad, make the music a shower of sunshine' (quoted in Nishijima *et al.* 1984, 259). Nondiegetic music might be used to set up and subsequently defeat audience expectations: in *Equinox Flower* (*Higanbana*, 1958), for instance, Saito provides five nondiegetic cues to serve as links from one scene to the next before this device is abruptly terminated, at which point,

the narration has now questioned the centrality of music as an assured continuity factor, and as the film goes on, it will reinstate the use of music for linkage while challenging it with purely visual transitions or abrupt cuts . . . Of course such manipulation of the music cannot be divorced from its more immediate contextual functions; the point is that tacit expectations about this narrational factor are no less subject to the schema-and-correction process than are any other sort. (Bordwell 1988, 69)

At the other end of the aesthetic spectrum, Ozu called upon music to provide broadly comic effects, from the 'insolent' use of banjo and electric guitar (instruments banned in Japan in 1944 for their American associations) in *What Did the Lady Forget?*, to the rhythmic integration of diegetic outbursts of flatulence in the music for *Ohayo* (*Good Morning*, 1959), composed by Toshiro Mayuzumi (Bordwell 1988, 350, 277).

As with Ray in India at around the same time, it was the work of a single *auteur*-director – Akira Kurosawa, who worked for Toho and whose elder brother had been a *benshi* – that was responsible for bringing the new Japanese cinema of the 1950s to the attention of a global audience. Kurosawa's success in the West inevitably resulted in his being criticized in Japan, where many felt he had betrayed traditional Japanese inscrutability in order for his work to be internationally accessible. Yet his films retained many uniquely Japanese characteristics and demonstrated a flexible attitude towards their musical provision, with emphasis on the music often arising from an avoidance of inessential dialogue (a characteristic he shared with Ozu): Kurosawa's principal working method was to imagine all scenes as playing silently in the first instance, then augment them accordingly. Most notably, and especially when period films began to reappear in the mid-1950s, Kurosawa made economical use of traditional Japanese musical gestures, sometimes in isolation and at other times combined with more Western modes of underscoring. Nō elements appear as early as his Occupation film *The Men Who Tread on the Tiger's Tail* (*Tora no o fumu otokotachi*, 1945), and remained a central feature of many later soundtracks. His early work also demonstrates a keen sense of musical irony: in the propaganda film *The Most Beautiful* (1944), he used Sousa's march *Semper fidelis* for a sequence depicting young Japanese women working heroically in wartime factories and took delight in the fact that this distinctively American music successfully eluded the ignorant censor's scissors.

Kurosawa first won international acclaim with *Rashōmon* (1950), with music by Hayasaka, which received the Golden Lion award at the Venice Film Festival in 1951. The film relates a rape-and-murder mystery from the differing viewpoints of the four characters who witnessed the crime, and the orchestral score is present primarily to create atmosphere in the flashback sequences to the forest location in which the events took place. As a result, the thoroughly Westernized score is indebted to many mannerisms of impressionism; its main theme is uncannily similar to that of Ravel's *Bolero*, for example, and moody material for bass clarinet and double bassoon seems reminiscent of Herrmann. Although the almost continuous music in the flashbacks may appear unduly protracted and over-elaborate, the prominent absence of music from the final flashback (in which events are related by an impartial eye-witness, and all other characters suddenly seem weak and vulnerable) inevitably suggests that we are at last witnessing the true account, and that the fantastic music in the preceding flashbacks was directly attuned to the exaggerated fantasizing of the individual characters relating their own versions of events.

In 1952, Hayasaka scored Kurosawa's *Ikiru* (*To Live*), an example of *shomin-geki* handled with both intensity and sensitivity. The score retains vividly characterized Western instrumentation – a high point is the bubblingly eccentric cue that accompanies a parodic scene of nightmarish civil-service bureaucracy – but marks a new departure in its canny reworking of diegetic music for emotional ends. The popular song 'Life is So Short' first makes an easy-listening instrumental appearance during the main titles, and is later performed diegetically with great pathos when the protagonist, Watanabe, requests it of the piano player in a bar and sings along in a broken voice, poignantly out of synchronization with the pianist; Watanabe again sings the song quietly to himself at the end of the film when he sits alone on a park swing and dies. Telling use is also made of 'Happy Birthday to You', a song often avoided in films because of the high copyright fees charged for its reproduction (in American movies it is often substituted by 'For He's a Jolly Good Fellow'). The famous birthday tune is sung cheerfully by a group of girls and throws Watanabe's self-absorbed melancholy into sharp relief, and when he returns to work in a new mood of quiet determination the tune is worked into the nondiegetic score.

Kurosawa's international reputation was secured with *Seven Samurai* (1954), which was nominated for two Academy Awards. Hayasaka's score makes an interesting comparison with Elmer Bernstein's rousing music for *The Magnificent Seven*, which was directly inspired by Kurosawa's film. In places Hayasaka's music inhabits a jaunty tongue-in-cheek soundworld, with prominent brass scoring, that would not be entirely out of place in an American western – it is worth noting that *Seven Samurai* was Kurosawa's homage to the westerns of director John Ford – and it draws on some of the quirkier gestures of Hayasaka's earlier Kurosawa scores (e.g. a modal march theme for baritone saxophone and percussion). But the use of a shrilly overblown bamboo flute to build tension is a departure looking forward to the more extensive use of traditional instruments in later Kurosawa films, and instead of musical underscoring a creative use of sound effects is sometimes used to articulate action sequences (Weis and Belton 1985, 188). This was Hayasaka's final score for Kurosawa before the composer's death in 1955, and its combination of Western leitmotivic procedures and elements from traditional Japanese music has been viewed as a direct counterpart to the director's characteristic blend of West and East in his dramatic and visual style (Kemp 1999).

A brief look at a more clichéd score from another well-known mid-1950s period film throws Hayasaka's achievements into sharp relief. Ikuma Dan's music for Hiroshi Inagaki's *Musashi Miyamoto* (1954), which received the Academy Award for Best Foreign Film in 1955, accompanies the exploits of the film's eponymous seventeenth-century hero with a succession of banal musical gestures, including sentimental underscoring of dialogue, quiet and homely music for domestic interiors, fussy orchestral atmospherics with over-done harp glissandi, and melodramatic fight music steeped in diminished-seventh chords and not far removed from the soundworld of Steiner's much fresher score for *Gone With the Wind*. Dan's outmoded narrative score may be perfectly attuned to Inagaki's old-fashioned Hollywood-style film-making, but neither composer nor director come close to the symbiosis of action and music often encountered in the work of Kurosawa and his composers.

After his death, Hayasaka's place as Kurosawa's principal composer was taken by his composition pupil Masaru Satō, who completed his teacher's unfinished score for *Ikimono no Kiroku* (*I Live in Fear*, 1955). Satō then provided music for Kurosawa's adventure epic *The Hidden Fortress* (*Kakushi toride no san akunin*, 1958), his first venture into widescreen cinematography. This film, which was later to provide the plot for *Star Wars*, was Kurosawa's most obvious attempt to appeal to a wide popular audience; its music, however, creates tension by means of an atonal and often athematic modernism in which fragmentary woodwind and xylophone twitterings promote edgy black humour and occasionally indulge in mickey-mousing. A contrastingly lyrical folk-inspired and partly pentatonic style is reserved for the character of Princess Yukihime, and it is only when – some 50 minutes into the film – she surveys a panoramic landscape of her lost kingdom that a fully fledged theme emerges. Thereafter the music remains more melody-oriented as the four main characters set out on their picaresque adventures to the accompaniment of suitably heroic brass-dominated orchestrations. Towards the end of the film, Satō mixes Western and traditional Japanese percussion instruments, combining bamboo flute and Nō drumming with timpani for a tense duelling scene, and adding a blaze of snare drum and timpani to Nō percussion when the representatives of the House of Akizuki are finally installed in regal splendour on their private Nō stage.

Kurosawa's *Yojimbo* (*The Bodyguard*, 1961) again featured music by Satō and this film was later remade as *A Fistful of Dollars*, the launch vehicle for Leone's spaghetti-western series. In some ways Satō's score continued Hayasaka's cross-cultural approach (Kemp 2000), but Satō achieved a more contemporary sound by the prominent use of funky electronics and jazz elements closer in style to the work of Mancini and Schifrin in the USA. Satō juxtaposed amplified harpsichord with pounding ritualistic percussion, dark-hued unison melodies reminiscent of Rózsa's *film noir* music, and the nervous interjection of jazzy big-band-style riffs. Most striking of all was the eccentric combination of jazz elements with the traditional sonority of the shamisen during a scene featuring kimono-clad dancing women. Satō's music seems to have directly influenced Morricone's score for Leone's remake in its tense and obsessive response to climactic scenes, particularly when opposing factions menacingly approach each other and prepare for combat, much in the manner of a western show-down.

The influence of the Nō theatre on Kurosawa became apparent in *Throne of Blood* (*Kumonosu jō*, 1957), a reworking of Shakespeare's *Macbeth* in a Samurai setting which, along with *Seven Samurai*, marked the high point of *jidai-geki* in the 1950s. Nō elements include the impassive mask-like face of Asaji (Lady Macbeth) and several moments of highly stylized acting, and are historically appropriate to the period setting: to Westerners, however, these features can appear distant, cold and emotionless. Satō's score utilized appropriately traditional instrumentation, including bamboo-flute shrieks and stark drum strokes as punctuating devices and archaic chanting for the witch; music in Nō style becomes more prominent as Asaji puts Washizu (Macbeth) onto a symbolic platform and demands he steel his murderous resolve. Elsewhere Western and Japanese elements are skilfully mixed, as in the main-title music where a wailing shakuhachi is underpinned by ritualistic percussion and a sombre low instrumental theme that soon merges into Nō-like male monodic chanting setting the scene at Cobweb Castle. Unlike Hayasaka, Satō avoids romantic and impressionistic clichés and works in fragmentary, often atonal instrumental gestures and brooding ostinato patterns; like Hayasaka, however, he is not afraid to create a darkly humorous mood at times, as in the funereal march he supplies for Lord Tsuzuki's approach to the castle where he is destined to die. The overall doom-laden mood of the film is effectively lightened by bright splashes of pentatonic music to accompany daylight exterior footage of agricultural work.

Although he parted company from Kurosawa in the mid-1960s, Satō remained a prolific composer of film scores for other Japanese directors until his death in 1999. The high points of Kurosawa's later career were two Samurai battle epics featuring very different music tracks by other composers. The first of them, *Kagemusha* (*The Shadow Warrior*, 1980), was scored by Shinichiro Ikebe in a tuneful Western manner at times reminiscent of the idiom of Morricone and, in its rousingly heroic moments, with a hint of John Williams's music for *Star Wars* – not coincidentally, perhaps, since George Lucas was one of *Kagemusha*'s American producers. At times the musical sequencing in *Kagemusha* seems ill-considered, for instance when a diegetic Nō performance is interrupted by a cloyingly saccharine orchestral link to a scene featuring a young child dressing. The climactic battle scene plays without music until a solo dignified trumpet supplies nondiegetic commentary on the subsequent images of carnage and devastation: this is a standard piece of Hollywood musical rhetoric, though here the trumpet playing sounds distinctly un-American because of the prominent use of vibrato, which tends to be avoided by session trumpeters in the USA. As Darrell Davis comments of the visual images at this point, 'the horror of battle is suggested precisely through the refusal to dwell upon the moment of killing; we linger in grotesque close-up and slow motion on the aftermath' (D. Davis 1996, 233).

Tōru Takemitsu

A similar directorial approach to scenes of battle received a stunning musical treatment in Kurosawa's *Ran* (*Chaos*, 1985), a Samurai-set interpretation of Shakespeare's *King Lear* for which he secured the services of the internationally respected Japanese composer Tōru Takemitsu, who had previously

9.4 Kyōko Kishida (as The Woman) and Eiji Okada (as The Man) in Hiroshi Teshigahara's *Woman in the Dunes* (1964), with avant-garde music by Tōru Takemitsu linking their erotic adventure with the shifting patterns in the sand.

scored the same director's *Dodes'kaden* in 1970. In *Ran*, Kurosawa suppressed ambient battle noise and sound effects in order to give Takemitsu's searingly intense orchestral music full prominence, a technique later imitated in the heavily scored battle sequences of films such as *Henry V* (1989) and *Gladiator* (2000). In the words of David Raksin: 'Takemitsu did a wonderful thing, which I've wanted to do all my life: a place where there's extreme, dreadful violence, and what is the music talking about? It's talking about the underlying sadness of what will remain on the battlefield after all these great heroes have left. It evokes . . . a kind of intrusion of reality into that world of self-deception' (interviewed in R. S. Brown 1994, 287). It might be felt, however, that the warm humanity of Takemitsu's music sits oddly alongside the bleakness of Kurosawa's vision in *Ran*, which has been described as designedly exposing the 'hollow theatricality' of the so-called 'monumental style' of *jidai-geki*, and perpetuating what David Desser viewed as the studied 'lack of humanity' at the heart of *Throne of Blood* (D. Davis 1996, 244).

Elsewhere in *Ran*, his score for which won the Los Angeles Film Critics Award in 1987, Takemitsu makes economical use of traditional Japanese instruments appropriate to the historical setting. This sat well alongside

Kurosawa's partly Nō-inspired dramatic style, though Davis has pointed out that film critics have a distinct tendency to exaggerate and over-generalize Kurosawa's indebtedness to traditional Japanese drama (1996, 277). Takemitsu's first use of traditional instrumentation was his inclusion of the biwa in his music for director Masaki Kobayashi's violently anti-totalitarian *Seppuku* (*Harakiri*, 1962), a film in which, to give an example of the kind of fanciful comparison between cinema and Japanese traditions alluded to by Davis, '[visual] composition, camera movement, action and sound all combine to make a film equivalent of the highest form of martial art' (Tucker 1973, 100). Takemitsu thereafter frequently used traditional instrumentation to impart an appropriate cultural ambience to his Japanese film scores, although in his more avant-garde concert music he tended to avoid it so that he would not become culturally stereotyped; it was the music of John Cage that inspired him to turn more directly to his own national heritage in the 1960s. Takemitsu, who began film work in the late 1950s under the guidance of Hayasaka and Satō, scored numerous films by Kobayashi, for whose *Karami-ai* (*The Inheritance*, 1962) he turned his hand to pastiche jazz – an avenue also explored in his scores for New Wave director Nagisa Oshima's *The Man Who Left His Will on Film* (*Tokyo senso sengo hiwa*, 1970), *Dear Summer Sister* (*Natsu no imoto*, 1972; see Burt 2001, 21) and *Ai no borei* (*Empire of Passion*, 1978). The last was an erotic ghost story scored with a wide range of avant-garde colouristic devices, Bergian harmony and luminous orchestration, with microtonality for irrational elements – all far more adventurous than Minoru Miki's music to Oshima's earlier erotic tale, the controversial *Ai no corrida* (*The Realm of the Senses*, 1976), which had to be made in France owing to its explicit content and was appropriately furnished with a score juxtaposing Gallic lyricism and traditional Japanese instrumentation. Other directors with whom Takemitsu collaborated included Noboru Nakamura and Hiroshi Teshigahara.

Perhaps Takemitsu's finest film score was composed for Teshigahara's *Suna no onna* (*Woman in the Dunes*), which won the Cannes Special Jury Prize in 1964 and remains the best-known example of Japanese New Wave cinema in the West. This tense and atmospheric tale concerns a woman who imprisons a man in her sand-dune home, and the film uses evocative and economical avant-garde music to equate the natural landscape and obsessive physical love. The shifting patterns of the music for the sand are related to those accompanying extreme close-ups of human skin and body parts, this relationship made crystal clear when the writhing of the main characters' bodies when making love uses the same string glissandi as the music for the sand, the music continuing when the editor cuts away from the lovemaking to a shifting sandscape. The accompaniment is thus perfectly in accord with what Richard Tucker has described as the film's 'meticulous rendering of surface reality in what is a surreal situation' (Tucker 1973, 71). The score was recorded by acoustic instruments, with some pitches raised through electronic processing in order to create disquieting timbres, and its disturbing idiom dominates much of the film to suggest the isolation and tension of the environment in which the action takes place. The unforgettable climax, in which the villagers taunt the lovers at night and force them to make love under the glare of torches shone down into their pit, is accompanied by exciting ritualistic drumming performed diegetically by masked drummers. Only at one poignant moment does real music from the outside world intrude into this unremittingly claustrophobic atmosphere: as the woman suffers a miscarriage, a diegetic radio emits a saccharine waltz. The incongruity of this brilliantly ironic gesture seems, in context, almost physically painful.

Takemitsu recycled material from *Woman in the Dunes* in a concert work for string orchestra (*The Dorian Horizon*, 1966), a practice in which he was frequently to indulge later in his career (Burt 2001, 48). Although the vast majority of his prolific output of nearly 100 film scores was for Japanese movies, he supplied an economical and mostly athematic score for the sharply scripted Hollywood thriller *Rising Sun* (dir. Philip Kaufman, 1993). In this film, as is unsubtly suggested by a television interview in an early scene, it is possible to regard the Japanese and their culture as 'Other' to the American way of life; Takemitsu's music is suitably taiko-flavoured and occasionally includes brief koto twangs for additional ethnic atmosphere, but is otherwise based largely on simple pedal notes and colouristic chords. In the intriguing prologue, what appears to be an American remake of Kurosawa's *Yojimbo*, now featuring Japanese actors in cowboy garb, is accompanied by a wailing flute melody poised somewhere between Nō and Morricone – and then the image metamorphoses into a video clip to which one of the leading Japanese characters is singing karaoke in the present day. The film's often witty references to Kurosawa also include use of the latter's distinctive vertical wipes marking the transition from one scene to the next.

Modern composers, modern genres

At the time of writing, the best-known Japanese film composer in the West is Ryuichi Sakamoto. After working with the early techno-pop group Yellow Magic Orchestra, which produced music directly inspired by the films of Godard, Sakamoto was invited by Oshima to act in his film *Merry Christmas, Mr Lawrence* (1982), starring David Bowie, in which Sakamoto played the part of Captain Yonoi. Sakamoto persuaded Oshima to allow him to compose the music for the film, later commenting: 'When I saw the rough cut I was shocked by my bad acting, so I put my passion into writing the score to compensate'. Oshima recommended that the inexperienced Sakamoto study Herrmann's score to *Citizen Kane* as a working model. Sakamoto elected to portray the personal relationships at the heart of the film through leitmotivic construction, but used electronics to create a sense of 'nostalgia for nowhere', poised in style between East and West (Russell and Young 2000, 176–8). This project immediately brought Sakamoto's work to international attention, and as a direct result of its success he went on to work with Italian director Bernardo Bertolucci, winning the Academy Award for his music to *The Last Emperor* (1987; additional music by David Byrne and Cong Su) – scored, at Bertolucci's request, for full orchestra and embodying careful research into Chinese music. For Bertolucci's *The Sheltering Sky* (1990), Sakamoto drew inspiration from the film's contrast between the cultures of New York and Morocco, relying on Richard Horowitz for research into traditional Arabic music. According to Sakamoto, 'Bertolucci wanted me to bring up my Japanese-ness in a deeper level, some kind of mystical thing about space and time. I'm not sure I have that 100 per cent. I don't think I'm a typical Japanese person' (Russell and Young 2000, 182). In the event, Sakamoto's drearily repetitive string music in *The Sheltering Sky* proved to be no more significant than the pseudo-ethnic music surrounding it, suggesting – as Brown notes in the broader context of postmodern film music in general – that 'the film's musical profile depends not on one particular sound created by one particular composer but on the global presence of various musics as a part of the filmic reality' (R. S. Brown 1994, 365). Sakamoto's later work has shown him refusing to be typecast, his forays into European cinema having included work for Almodóvar and Schlöndorff. For the latter's *The Handmaid's Tale* (1990) he used both electronics with acoustic instruments, including koto, while his music for Almodóvar's *High Heels* (1991) was inspired by the Spanish-influenced jazz of Miles Davis.

Newer exploitation genres became commercially successful inside Japan, notably indigenous gangster films (*yakuza-eiga*), eroticism (*pinku-eiga*) and monster movies (*kaiju-eiga*). The monster craze began with *Gojira* (*Godzilla*, 1954), scored with obsessively descending scales and some genuine aural poetry by the prolific Akira Ifukube, a protégé of Hayasaka's who was still composing *Godzilla* scores in the late 1990s. But it was mostly in the field of animation, which has been a lucrative industry in Japan since the rise of cartoons in the 1960s at a time when (as elsewhere in the world) a decline in the fortunes of mainstream cinema coincided with a boom in television viewing, that Japanese cinema and television began to achieve major international exposure. In this field, Sakamoto's more rock-oriented music has been especially influential.

Modern Japanese 'anime' (animation) is related to comic-book *manga*, and frequently confused with it. Anime covers an extraordinary range of subject-matter and styles, from children's stories (such as *Pokémon*, which exerted a strong influence on American TV animation both visually and musically) to horrifically violent action cartoons and pornography. As a result, it is impossible to generalize about matters of musical accompaniment, though Milo Miles has drawn attention to the disappointing fact that much of the spectacular visual interest of anime is allied to music that is 'surprisingly formulaic, old-fashioned, soppy, and stiff' (Goldmark and Taylor 2002, 219). Sakamoto's vivid electronics and John Zorn's eclectic avant-garde jazz in the late 1980s were two of the prime sources for the more inventive anime music tracks that appeared after the genre took a firm grip on the international market with the success of Katsuhiro Otomo's *Akira* (1988), with music by Shoji Yamashira that creates a futuristic soundworld, appropriate to the Neo-Tokyo in which the film is set, by mixing 'synthesizer washes and pulses with echoes of Javanese gamelan, Tibetan Buddhist chanting, and Japanese taiko drummers' (Goldmark and Taylor 2002, 221). Among the more prominent musicians working in anime at the turn of the twenty-first century were Kenji Kawai and Yoko Kanno.

In addition to anime, modern Samurai epics, thrillers and horror films remained relatively successful in the West. The work of 'Beat' Takeshi (Takeshi Kitano) embraces various musical styles, including Joe Hisaishi's heart-warming score for the children's road movie *Kikujiro* (1999). Hisaishi's unambitious international style, a kind of pop minimalism, was far more effective in this context than in the earlier *Hana-bi* (1997) where it sat uncomfortably alongside the traumatic subject-matter. Keen to be perceived as an *auteur*, Beat Takeshi (best known for violent crime movies) supplied his own music to accompany paintings featured in the film, which were also created by the director – as did James Cameron in *Titanic* at around the same time. A melding of Japanese instrumentation and synthesizers by composer Keiichi Suzuki was a defining characteristic of Takeshi's *Zatoichi* (2004), a film notable in several key scenes for its unexpected and lyrical synchronization of bodily movements with rhythmic pulsations.

The popular *Ring* trilogy of supernatural chillers (which spawned an American remake by Gore Verbinski in 2002, with music by Zimmer) were typical in drawing upon a wide range of horror-film musical formulae useful for an international market. Both *Ringu* (*Ring*, 1998) and *Ringu 2* (*Ring 2*, 1999) were directed by Hideo Nakata with music by Kawai. The second film commenced with an economical use of suggestive electronics, wordless choral moaning and synthesized percussive stingers but confusingly introduced an incongruous rock beat and pop-style synthesizer music in its second half. In *Ringu 0: Bāsudei* (*Ring 0: Birthday*, dir. Norio Tsuruta,

2000), Shinichiro Ogata's music jumps from tense electronics to a kind of nostalgic lyricism reminiscent of Satie, with touches of lush romanticism for the love interest. Both films conclude with gratuitous end-title pop songs bearing no relationship to the music in the rest of the film. This is also true of *Audition* (dir. Mike Takashi, 2001), in which Koji Endo's score is surprisingly sentimental for the most part: the soundtrack is dominated by dreamy piano music, presumably because the protagonist comments at one point that he wishes his future second wife to be a pianist; in fact, the only real pianist in the film turns out to be a wheelchair-bound cripple who plays part of Bizet's *Carmen* in a disused ballet school, and the gruesome conclusion – in which the exquisitely beautiful object of the protagonist's desires tortures him with prolonged acupuncture before dismembering him – is executed entirely without music, and with a clinical precision all the more terrifying in the absence of the earlier saccharine underscoring. Many other Japanese films aimed at the export market, such as the hugely successful and hideously gory *Battle Royale* and *Battle Royale II: Requiem* (dir. Kinji Fukasaku, 2000 and 2003; music by Masamichi Amano), with their hotchpotch scores surveying a wide range of mainstream styles including Western classical music, continue to typify what Philip Brophy describes as the country's tendency towards 'sucking in the infosphere of the West and extruding it into unimaginable forms, constructs and mechanisms' (Brophy 1997).

10 Popular music in the cinema

A large percentage of producers today are so unaware of their pictures they're looking for a musical gimmick to lure the public. Like the hit title tune, a harmonica surrounded by a choral group, the twanging sound of an electric zither, or the wail of a kazoo in an espresso café. Stuff like that. It only takes away from what's happening on the screen. (BERNARD HERRMANN, QUOTED IN *HOLLYWOOD REPORTER*, 14 JULY 1964)

I AM PARTICULARLY CONCERNED WITH THE NEED TO BREAK AWAY FROM THE OLD-FASHIONED CUED-IN TYPE OF MUSIC THAT WE HAVE BEEN USING FOR SO LONG . . . UNFORTUNATELY FOR WE ARTISTS, WE DO NOT HAVE THE FREEDOM THAT WE WOULD LIKE TO HAVE, BECAUSE WE ARE CATERING TO AN AUDIENCE . . . THIS AUDIENCE IS VERY DIFFERENT FROM THE ONE TO WHICH WE USED TO CATER; IT IS YOUNG, VIGOROUS AND DEMANDING . . . THIS IS WHY I AM ASKING YOU TO APPROACH THIS PROBLEM WITH A RECEPTIVE AND IF POSSIBLE ENTHUSIASTIC MIND. (ALFRED HITCHCOCK, CABLE TO BERNARD HERRMANN, 4 NOVEMBER 1965; QUOTED IN S. SMITH 1991, 268–9)

The *Torn Curtain* fiasco, in which Herrmann's score for Hitchcock was rejected partly owing to pressure from the studio to include a hit song which the composer refused to provide (see Chapter 5), drew attention to a fundamental and seemingly irreconcilable tension in the mid-1960s between traditional methods of film scoring – increasingly viewed as outdated and inappropriate as films became more youth-oriented – and a more modern approach in which up-to-date popular idioms prevailed. Prior to *Torn Curtain*, Paramount had already commissioned 'Que Sera, Sera' from Jay Livingstone and Ray Evans for Doris Day to sing in the remake of Hitchcock's *The Man Who Knew Too Much* (1956); the song won an Academy Award, but Herrmann commented 'What do you want a piece of junk like that in the picture for?' (quoted in Pommerance 2001, 56). Herrmann refused to score Kubrick's *Lolita* (1962) when the director insisted he include an easy-listening tune by his brother-in-law, Bob Harris, and the commission went to Nelson Riddle instead. Herrmann's outspokenness against the inclusion of popular music in film soundtracks throughout the 1960s reinforced his reputation as a composer-*auteur*, whose elitist assumptions about the significance of conventional narrative scoring methods were now being seriously challenged.

Tension between the use of popular music and classically influenced scoring begins as far back as the silent film, which had retained popular idioms as an accompanying option as a holdover from one of the medium's immediate audio-visual ancestors, illustrated songs (see Chapter 1). According to Clarence E. Sinn, the accompanists of silent films came to find popular songs useful material, 'especially in sentimental pictures and comedies' (*Moving Picture World*, 26 November 1910), and the song melodies might serve both as musical puns playing on the relevance of a song's title to the film's subject-matter and the more general purpose of tapping the spectators' presumed enthusiasm for recent hits. The use of popular song diminished somewhat in the period *c*.1910–15 when the medium of film was trying strenuously to acquire artistic prestige (Altman 2004, 313), but it soon returned, and by the end of the silent era some film tunes had gained considerable success away from the movie theatre through sheet-music sales. Record companies also became aware of the commercial potential of themes associated with the movies, Columbia Records reminding retail outlets in the 1920s that 'each week the tune studded talking picture leaves customers of yours with impressively presented theme songs echoing in their ears' (Millard 1995, 160).

As studios strove to break away from the punitive synchronization fees for music levied by the American Society of Composers, Authors and Publishers (ASCAP), they acquired their own publishing divisions, and the early boom in sound musicals continued the prototypical synergistic marketing that had existed between West Coast film studios and East Coast music publishers during the silent era. Throughout the 1930s and 1940s, film producers' commercial interests in this genre were also closely linked to the media of radio, theatre and the recording industry. Cartoon shorts provide a good example of the era's systematic exploitation of popular songs of which the rights were owned by film studios: Warner Bros., for example, which had first bought a publishing interest and record company in 1929–30, later invested $8.5 million in the Harms-affiliated music publishers and spent $1 million to purchase the Witmark song catalogue outright (Curtis 1992, 193), thereafter compelling their cartoon composers to use melodies from these resources in each of their scores (see Chapter 7).

In non-musical features, a number of box-office successes included memorable popular songs, both pre-existing and specially composed. Well-known examples include *Casablanca* (dir. Michael Curtiz, 1942) and *High Noon* (dir. Fred Zinnemann, 1952); in the case of *Laura* (dir. Otto Preminger, 1944), Raksin's main-title melody became a hit when subsequently lyricized – as was later to be the case with movie themes composed by Henry Mancini, Johnny Mandel and others. Anton Karas's zither music for *The Third Man* (dir. Carol Reed, 1949) showed that catchy instrumental music could be equally lucrative away from the screen. The monothematic saturation of scores such as these was a major influence on later romantic music tracks based largely on single memorable themes cast in a popular idiom, such as Mancini's *Breakfast at Tiffany's* (dir. Blake Edwards, 1961), Jarre's *Doctor Zhivago* (dir. David Lean, 1965), Legrand's *Summer of '42* (dir. Robert Mulligan, 1971) and Marvin Hamlisch's *The Way We Were* (dir. Sydney Pollack, 1973), all of which won Academy Awards for their music and/or songs. In the case of *Zhivago*, Lean reportedly inserted during postproduction more repetitions of Jarre's 'Lara' theme than had originally been spotted, with a clear eye towards record sales, which were eventually to number in excess of $2 million for the soundtrack album alone (J. Smith 1998, 17). *Casablanca, Laura* and *The Way We Were* all used their principal themes in conjunction with flashbacks, sometimes moving between diegetic and nondiegetic uses to underline the fantastic, nostalgic and utopian suggestions of what Caryl Flinn has termed the 'temporal disphasures' common in narrative film (Flinn 1992, 109). Some composers, notably Mancini, Morricone, Barry and Quincy Jones, combined the strategic repetition of their own saleable melodies with conventional scoring techniques to create what Jeff Smith terms the hybrid 'pop score' (1998, 11), the development and current state of which is considered in Chapter 12.

Music of youth and race

A prominent manifestation of popular musical influences on film scoring during Hollywood's Golden Age was the rise of soundtracks featuring modern jazz, both diegetically and nondiegetically (see Chapter 5). These became significant in the 1950s not only for the stylistic watershed they represented, but for the direct link they often promoted between popular music, social problems and youth culture – a potent conjunction most obviously to be seen in the prototypical 'generation outrage' film, the jukebox-dominated biker movie *The Wild One* (1954). Rock'n'roll became spectacularly successful in film immediately afterwards. *The Blackboard Jungle* (dir. Richard Brooks, 1955) showcased Bill Haley and The Comets' hit 'Rock Around the Clock' in its credit sequences only, but this was more than enough to cause seats to be ripped out in cinemas on both sides of the Atlantic by indomitable youths determined to dance to it: such dancing was typically forbidden in the aisles, so space needed to be cleared for this purpose elsewhere in the venue. The excitement was in part caused by the deliberately high decibel level of the film's soundtrack, a feature to remain essential to the visceral appeal of much later rock, pop and dance music. The film, in which schoolkids symbolically smash a teacher's collection of jazz 78s, paved the way for the hysterical response to the follow-up Haley vehicle, *Rock Around the Clock* (dir. Fred F. Sears, 1956), which starred The Comets and other rock'n'roll musicians and was banned by some local authorities for fear its screening would cause public disorder. The same year produced several other films cashing in on the craze for the new music: *Don't Knock the Rock* (dir. Sears), including performances by The Comets, Little Richard and others; *The Girl Can't Help It* (dir. Frank Tashlin), featuring Little Richard and The Platters; *Rock Pretty Baby* (dir. Richard Bartlett), with its soundtrack overseen by Mancini and Bobby Troup; and *Shake, Rattle and Rock!* (dir. Edward L. Cahn), in the plot of which an attempt to ban rock'n'roll is defiantly contested. These movies laid the foundations for the 'teen-pic' formula of youth-oriented commercial cinema still prevalent in the industry today.

All these rock'n'roll films exploited the popularity of a fashionable musical style rather than an individual star's charisma. A shift of emphasis in favour of the latter came with the wide exposure of Elvis Presley's singing and acting in *Love Me Tender* (dir. Robert D. Webb), *Loving You* (dir. Hal Kanter) and *Jailhouse Rock* (dir. Richard Thorpe), the first also dating from 1956 and the two last both released a year later. The Elvis phenomenon was paralleled in the UK by the meteoric rise to stardom of Tommy Steele, whose autobiopic *The Tommy Steele Story* appeared in 1957 only a matter of months after his music hit the charts (Medhurst 1995, 62), and by a series of films starring Cliff Richard: *Expresso Bongo* (dir. Val Guest, 1959), a topical continuation of the backstage musical genre notable for the censor's retention of its footage of a Soho strip-club on account of the scene's documentary feel (Romney and Wootton 1995, 39); *The Young Ones* (dir. Sidney J. Furie, 1961), in essence another old-fashioned show musical; and the perennial British favourite, *Summer Holiday* (dir. Peter Yates, 1963). Several of these films were rooted in the British coffee-bar culture in which Steele and Richard had first made their marks (Donnelly 2001b, 5–6).

The early 1960s brought the twist craze, which ensured that dance scenes began to proliferate in movies such as *Twist All Night* (UK title *The Young and the Cool*, dir. Allan David and William J. Hole, Jr) and *Twist Around the Clock* (dir. Oscar Rudolph), both released in 1961 and the second starring Chubby Checker. *Twist All Night* was produced by American International Pictures (AIP) which, at around the same time, cornered the market for beach-party films inspired by student antics in Florida and California. The new genre was launched by MGM's *Where the Boys Are* (dir. Henry Levin, 1960, music by George Stoll) and later included Paramount's *The Girls on the Beach* (dir. William Witney, 1965), the only one of many such films made between 1961 and 1967 that featured The Beach Boys themselves, who came to prominence as the craze was beginning to wane and managed to outlive it. Some of AIP's beach and bikini-boom films grossed ten times their production costs, their marketing experts having decided that the most lucrative target audience was nineteen-year-old males. Logic decreed that a younger youth will watch anything an older one will watch (but not vice versa), and a girl will watch anything a boy will watch (but not vice versa); the resulting strategy was dubbed the 'Peter Pan Syndrome' (Denisoff and Romanowski 1991, 118–21).

The early star-persona vehicles were completely eclipsed by the international success attained by the Beatles in *A Hard Day's Night* (dir. Richard Lester, 1964), which absorbed the fresh cinematographic techniques of the

UK's Free Cinema movement. As in the far more outrageous work of Godard in France, which included the politically motivated Rolling Stones documentary *One Plus One* (*Sympathy for the Devil*, 1968), popular culture and avant-garde film-making proved to be potent bedfellows; in the case of the Beatles, the fresh visual style of *A Hard Day's Night* made the group intellectually intriguing and the project therefore seduced both youngsters and intelligentsia (Denisoff and Romanowski 1991, 136–7), while at the same time including social commentary by showing modern youths rebelling against age and class distinctions. Moments of surrealism include a card game in a train's baggage compartment that begins with an asynchronous song on the soundtrack but jump-cuts to the group suddenly playing and singing the same song diegetically in the same location, before cutting back to their card game as the music fades out nondiegetically. Elsewhere they dance to their song 'I Wanna Be Your Man', and give a diegetic performance in a theatre marred by some sloppy miming to playback; the music is more memorable when nondiegetic, as when 'Can't Buy Me Love' accompanies their open-air frolics after they escape from the venue, the photography including swirling aerial shots. The climactic performance of 'I Love Her' in the TV studio is completely lacking in atmosphere: fans are shown in reaction shot screaming and nearly fainting, but the screams are edited out so as not to compete with the singing – until the 'She Loves Me' finale, that is, when the screaming is finally included to help intensify the sense of hysteria, and indeed takes precedence over the music. Vivid crowd and audience reaction shots such as these help foster star-legends, and they would be exploited in later films featuring diegetic pop performances.

Phenomenal ticket sales for *A Hard Day's Night* at the global box office were complemented by sales of the soundtrack album netting over three times the film's production costs. The album, which sold 1.5 million copies within two weeks of its release (J. Smith 1998, 55), was prophetic of later marketing strategies by including songs which did not feature in the film, and also established the concept of a long-playing record made up of multiple singles, each potentially an individual hit; this strategy later had spectacular results for the Bee Gees in *Saturday Night Fever* (see below). Both *A Hard Day's Night* and the Beatles' fantasy follow-up, *Help!* (dir. Lester, 1965), were lastingly influential on the production techniques of later pop films and music videos: indeed, the 'Can't Buy Me Love' sequence described above was later shown on MTV as a plausible videoclip (J. Smith 1998, 160). The music of *Help!* was as phenomenally successful as that of its predecessor: its song 'Yesterday', one of three chart-topping hits from the film, sold more than one million copies in just ten days (Denisoff and Romanowski 1991, 142). Both films and their related recordings fared particularly well in the USA, with United Artists' considerable financial backing helping to cement the success of the British Invasion in American popular culture; at the same time, along with their contemporaneous investment in the James Bond franchise, UA significantly boosted the commercial fortunes of British cinema. One home-grown American group, the Monkees, attempted to follow the Beatles' example in *Head* (dir. Bob Rafelson, 1968), a psychedelic film that proved a commercial failure in spite of the huge popularity of the group's TV series and their high volume of record sales. Their flop on this occasion may be accounted for by the film's boldly non-linear structure and its indulgence in sometimes cynical self-reflexivity; its tie-in album was their worst seller up to this time (Ramaeker 2001, 97).

Popular music as an ethnic marker made an international impact with *Black Orpheus* (dir. Marcel Camus, 1958), shot in Rio de Janeiro and with a lively soundtrack that helped initiate the craze for bossa nova pop-jazz in the early 1960s. Like other types of jazz, and rhythm-and-blues, bossa nova was quickly taken up by white artists and its cultural origins diluted, and it was not until the blaxploitation movies of the early 1970s that black music and culture transferred to the big screen in purer form, though a rhythm-and-blues soundtrack had served cultural and locational purposes in *Nothing But a Man* (dir. Michael Roemer, 1964). In 1963 the National Association for the Advancement of Colored People (NAACP) had threatened sanctions and legal action if more blacks were not employed by the US film industry, with the result that by *c.*1972 around one quarter of the country's film output was black-oriented (Denisoff and Romanowski 1991, 730–1). Soul and funk music dominated the prototypical blaxploitation crime thriller *Shaft* (dir. Gordon Parks, 1971), with its composer Isaac Hayes nominated for Academy Awards for both his score and title song (and winning the latter category with what became a No. 1 hit); his music was retained in the 2000 remake (dir. John Singleton). According to Kodwo Eshun, the use of popular music 'relieves Shaft of his cop status so that he's free to walk through Harlem as a regular guy' (Eshun 1995, 53), though the use of a black musical idiom in an urban crime context also harked back to earlier filmic applications of jazz. Another film influential on the emerging genre was *Sweet Sweetback's Baadasssss Song* (dir. Melvin Van Peebles, 1971), with music by Maurice White's Earth, Wind & Fire.

In the immediate wake of these productions came *Superfly* (dir. Gordon Parks Jr, 1972; music by Curtis Mayfield), of which the soundtrack double-album went platinum, *Trouble Man* (dir. Ivan Dixon, 1972; music by Marvin Gaye) and *Black Caesar* (dir. Larry Cohen, 1973). James Brown's music for the last was recorded without his even bothering to see or discuss the movie during production, his involvement in the project having clearly been intended solely to exploit his fame and popular appeal. The blaxploitation boom was curtailed somewhat by the global disco craze of the late 1970s, but the genre's blend of streetwise cool, comedy, violence and trendy music remained influential on action films and hard-hitting urban movies in general, including the martial arts genre in Hong Kong (Toop 1995, 77). Outside America, the 1970s also saw the birth of reggae-flavoured Jamaican cinema, its launch vehicle *The Harder They Come* (dir. Perry Henzell, 1972) with a plot revolving around a reggae musician whose song becomes a hit just as he turns to drug-related crime.

One of the most enduring musical films made at the end of the 1970s was John Landis's *The Blues Brothers* (1980), which caused controversy because it represented the popularization of a black musical idiom by white performers John Belushi and Dan Aykroyd. They may well have diluted soul in the process, but nevertheless helped widen the international market for rhythm-and-blues (Denisoff and Romanowski 1991, 297). The actors' characters Jake and Elwood Blues had been launched on TV's *Saturday Night Live*, and their action-packed big-screen antics revolved around spirited diegetic performances by the likes of Aretha Franklin, Ray Charles, James Brown and the veteran Cab Calloway. Calloway took the role of an orphanage janitor and had to be dissuaded from the idea of performing 'Minnie the Moocher' in disco style; neither Franklin nor Brown could cope with lip-synching to pre-recorded songs because they were not used to singing a number the same way twice. The soundtrack is eclectic, including the hit tune 'Everybody Needs Somebody', Mancini's *Peter Gunn* theme and even Wagner's 'Ride of the Valkyries' to accompany footage of an Illinois neo-Nazi car crashing to earth amidst Chicago skyscrapers; the spirited diegetic performances by the Brothers brought together a New York front line and a Chicago rhythm section. In 1983 Landis went on to direct Michael Jackson's short film *Thriller*, which broke all previous records for the sale of both soundtrack recording and home-video copies and helped boost the new medium of MTV (see below).

Towards the end of the 1980s, blaxploitation was both parodied and reborn. *I'm Gonna Git You, Sucka* (dir. Keenan Ivory Wayans, 1988) satirized the genre's heavy reliance on nondiegetic funk by having a character walk along the street tailed by the eclectic Los Angeles band Fishbone diegetically performing the theme from *Superfly*. As blaxploitation was replaced by a rapsploitation rooted in inner-city youth culture, so nondiegetic music tended to be replaced by rap issuing from diegetic radios (Eshun 1995, 57). The hip-hop scene was first exploited on film in *Breakin'* (UK title *Breakdance*; dir. Joel Silberg, 1984), and the familiar setting of urban drug-crime recurred in *New Jack City* (dir. Mario Van Peebles, 1991), with music by both its director and Michel Colombier, and a cast including rapper Ice-T (who had sampled 'Pusherman' from *Superfly* in 1988). Another rapper-turned-actor, Ice Cube, starred as Dough Boy in *Boyz 'n the Hood* (dir. Singleton, 1991; music by Stanley Clarke), set in the South Central region of Los Angeles notorious for its rigid law enforcement. For all this film's historical importance as the first mainstream release with such a setting, its narrative, preoccupation with parental responsibility, dialogue and cinematography were all utterly conventional, and most of its music was restricted to ambient diegetic sources apart from a nondiegetic cue that begins diegetically on a car radio, and another that provides continuity throughout a montage of troubled romance – both tried and tested Hollywood formulae. The climactic shooting is accompanied anempathetically by placidly repetitive easy-listening music.

Hip-hop musicians and producers active in film since the 1990s have included Snoop Dogg's producer Dr Dre, who served as music supervisor on the sports/drug-crime hybrid *Above the Rim* (dir. Jeff Pollack, 1994; original music by Marcus Miller), and Wu-Tang Clang's guiding spirit, the RZA. The latter provided music for *Ghost Dog: The Way of the Samurai* (dir. Jim Jarmusch, 1999), the work of a New York underground director who in the 1980s had been well known for his collaboration with Lounge Lizards' saxophonist John Lurie on a variety of films (Reay 2004, 99–100). The RZA commented that working with musicians from different backgrounds on *Ghost Dog* inspired him to become musically literate, and he learnt as much from the instrumental characterizations of Prokofiev's *Peter and the Wolf* as from his blaxploitation idols Hayes, Mayfield and Brown (Allina 2004). The RZA went on to produce music for a number of films, including Tarantino's *Kill Bill* diptych (2003–4) – an appropriate assignment given the kung-fu orientation of his group, which sampled elements from the soundtracks to Asian martial arts films – and the comedy spoof *Soul Plane* (dir. Jessy Terrero, 2004), starring a Wu-Tang Clan member, Method Man.

At the white end of the musical spectrum the later 1960s saw a limited but occasionally creative use of American country music in soundtracks. In *Bonnie and Clyde* (dir. Arthur Penn, 1967), Scruggs-style bluegrass music by Charles Strouse (based in part on 'Foggy Mountain Breakdown') served as tongue-in-cheek getaway music in spite of the plot's violent and anti-social subject-matter, and this was to become a stock application of such music in a wide range of film, TV and cartoon scores. Songs by Tammy Wynette, Hank Williams and others were included in the soundtracks of *Five Easy Pieces* (dir. Rafelson, 1970) and *The Last Picture Show* (dir. Peter Bogdanovich, 1971). In Robert Altman's *Nashville* (1975), with its Oscar-winning song 'I'm Easy' by Keith Carradine, country music is used 'to emphasize the disintegration of America . . . what [the film] has to say about entertainment in America is a devastating commentary on the shortcomings of bicentennial America and the folk musical alike'; it does this most obviously by selling its credits to viewers 'like cheap records on late-night television. Imitating both the soundtrack and the garish visuals of these tasteless ads, *Nashville* identifies its own commercial nature from the start' (Altman 1987, 324). The link between the idiom and venality was perpetuated by the music's more recent appearances in the political satire *Wag the Dog* (dir. Barry Levinson, 1997) and the polemical documentary *Fahrenheit 9/11* (dir. Michael Moore, 2004), both of which linked bluegrass to suggestions of ignorance, corruption and moral decay. As Barbara Ching notes, country music 'sounds the American heart'; it can succeed in 'affirming the purity of the "American way of life"' in mainstream commercial cinema, or in 'condemning a nation hypocritically mired in provincial materialism' in more cynical art films (Ching 2001, 204).

The use of country music in films pales into insignificance alongside the global impact of disco fever initiated by the phenomenal success of *Saturday Night Fever* (dir. John Badham, 1977), a film remarkable not only for the charisma of its star John Travolta and its skilfully photographed dance sequences but also its adult subject-matter. The screenplay's pessimism, bad language, dysfunctional family background and treatment of such uncomfortable topics as abortion and crisis of religious faith made this the pop film's true coming of age: its overriding tone was one of cynicism and survival in the bleak post-Watergate era, and the production's initial demographic appeal was largely to young singles struggling to cope with, and find release from, the drudgery of urban life (Denisoff and Romanowski 1991, 200, 227). Here physical movement and rhythmic pulsation act together as both escapist drug and personal expression. In a rebellious gesture reminiscent of the blatant rejection of outmoded jazz in films such as *The Blackboard Jungle* and *Jailhouse Rock*, Travolta's character Tony regards Latin dance music as old-fashioned when it empties the dance floor ('I can't dance that shit'); but the object of his affections, the ambitious Stephanie, likes it and curtly dismisses Tony as a cliché. Latin music, and the classical ballet which she rehearses to the accompaniment of Chopin, thus become exotic and 'Other' as part of his attraction towards her. The film's main commercial strength was its soundtrack songs by the Bee Gees: there was scarcely any need for the kind of romantic underscoring by David Shire which attempted to underline the sentimental conclusion. A poor sequel eventually followed (*Staying Alive*, 1983), in which director Sylvester Stallone 'just puts the newly muscle-plated Travolta in front of the camera, covers him with what looks like oil slick, and goes for the whambams' (Pauline Kael, quoted in J. Walker 2006, 1102); the basic dramatic formula had already been reworked in another Travolta vehicle, *Urban Cowboy* (dir. James Bridges, 1980), with a soundtrack of progressive country music that modestly revived the commercial fortunes of country-and-western in the record store. *Saturday Night Fever*'s broader influence was considerable, not merely by initiating an immediate rash of disco pictures – including, in Britain, the tawdry Joan Collins vehicles *The Stud* (dir. Quentin Masters, 1978) and *The Bitch* (dir. Gerry O'Hara, 1979), both with music by Biddu, and in the USA by *Thank God It's Friday* (dir. Robert Klane, 1978) and *Can't Stop the Music* (dir. Nancy Walker, 1980), the last with music by Jacques Morali's Village People – but more importantly in its commercially efficacious showcasing of hit tunes and its dance-competition climax, the latter destined to be much imitated.

By contrast, certain films of the late 1970s reflected popular music of far less widespread appeal, notably the British punk movement which was prominent in 1976–9 and commemorated in *The Great Rock'n'Roll Swindle* (dir. Julien Temple, 1980) and *Sid and Nancy* (dir. Alex Cox, 1986), the latter a biopic based on the life of the Sex Pistols' Sid Vicious. Punk's lifestyle and image impacted in particular on the work of independent director Derek Jarman, most obviously in *Jubilee* (1977; music by Brian Eno) and his 1980 film based on Shakespeare's *The Tempest* (see Chapter 4). Fresh trends in youth culture indicating social change were again to affect mainstream cinema with the advent of acid house and the rave scene in *c.*1989. The new dance music coloured films on both sides of the Atlantic, and once again a popular style became associated with a drugs milieu and other urban crime problems, notably in *The Young Americans* (dir. Danny Cannon, 1993), *Shopping* (dir. Paul Anderson, 1994), *Shallow Grave* (dir. Danny Boyle, 1994), *Trainspotting* (dir. Boyle, 1996) and *Human Traffic* (dir. Justin Kerrigan, 1999). While the British productions *Shallow Grave* and *Trainspotting* both received critical acclaim, other less impressive films of their ilk were arguably more powerful by virtue of their dynamic soundtracks than their tired storylines (Romney and Wootton 1995, 6).

Title songs and interpolated songs

The least creative application of popular music common in 1960s soundtracks was the showcasing of main-title songs and interpolated songs performed by commercially viable artists. The inclusion of nondiegetic interpolated songs was often gratuitous, and a ploy to secure consideration for an Academy Award for Best Song; the interpolated performance 'puts the story on hold while the song has a chance to sell itself' (Karlin 1994, 225). Well-known examples are Legrand's 'The Windmills of Your Mind' for the evocative glider sequence in *The Thomas Crown Affair* (dir. Norman Jewison, 1968), which had been accompanied by the Beatles' 'Strawberry Fields' in the temp track (Karlin and Wright 2004, 447); Burt Bacharach's 'Raindrops Keep Fallin' on My Head' for the bicycling sequence in *Butch Cassidy and the Sundance Kid* (dir. George Roy Hill, 1969); Fred Neil's 'Everybody's

Talkin" for the shop-front propositioning scene in *Midnight Cowboy* (dir. John Schlesinger, 1969); and Louis Armstrong's memorable rendition of John Barry's 'We Have All the Time in the World' in the Bond film *On Her Majesty's Secret Service* (dir. Peter Hunt, 1969), this last example perhaps one of the most poignantly effective instances of the strategy.

The indestructible Bond series was responsible for eliciting a fine series of title songs by Barry, each allied to imaginative main-title graphics. The series was launched in 1962 with *Dr No* (dir. Terence Young), with its famous signature tune by Monty Norman (co-writer of the stage show on which *Expresso Bongo* had been based), which became the subject of disputed authorship claims between Norman and Barry that were not to be resolved in Norman's favour until he won a libel case against the UK's *Sunday Times* newspaper in 2001. (For further on the dispute, and on the phenomenon of Bond soundtracks in general, see J. Smith 1998, Chapter 5; see also Leonard *et al.* 1995, 15.) Barry, who had already been successful with his instrumental group The John Barry Seven, assumed full responsibility for the scoring of the series with *From Russia With Love* (dir. Young, 1963), with a title song by Lionel Bart performed by Matt Monro. Three of Barry's own Bond title songs were performed by Shirley Bassey: *Goldfinger* (dir. Guy Hamilton, 1964), *Diamonds Are Forever* (dir. Hamilton, 1971) and *Moonraker* (dir. Lewis Gilbert, 1979). Other artists who sang them were Tom Jones (*Thunderball*; dir. Young, 1965), Nancy Sinatra (*You Only Live Twice*; dir. Gilbert, 1967), Lulu (*The Man With the Golden Gun*; dir. Hamilton, 1974), Rita Coolidge (*Octopussy*; dir. John Glen, 1983), Duran Duran (*A View to a Kill*; dir. Glen, 1985) and a-ha (*The Living Daylights*; dir. Glen, 1987). The choice of the last two bands was clearly aimed squarely at a new generation of young consumers. Many of the earlier songs had achieved modest chart success, but Duran Duran's 'A View To a Kill' outdid them by becoming a No. 1 hit in the USA and reaching No. 2 in the UK.

Barry's occasional absences from the Bond series allowed a number of other composers and performers to adapt their music to the films' winning formula. In 1973, Paul McCartney and Wings recorded a buoyantly sinister title song for *Live and Let Die* (dir. Hamilton, 1973), which did well in the charts, the remainder of the film scored by former Beatles producer George Martin. For *The Spy Who Loved Me* (dir. Gilbert, 1977), Hamlisch's 'Nobody Does It Better' was performed by Carly Simon. The title songs in *For Your Eyes Only* (dir. Glen, 1981; music by Bill Conti) and *Licence to Kill* (dir. Glen, 1989; music by Michael Kamen) were sung by Sheena Easton and Gladys Knight respectively. The only Bond film made outside the powerful franchise of producers Harry Saltzman and Albert R. 'Cubby' Broccoli was *Never Say Never Again* (dir. Irvin Kershner, 1984), with its title song by Legrand performed by Lani Hall. As the Broccoli lineage extended into the

1990s and beyond, *GoldenEye* (dir. Martin Campbell, 1995; music by Eric Serra) received a title song by Tina Turner written by Bono and The Edge, and *Tomorrow Never Dies* (dir. Roger Spottiswoode, 1997) one by Sheryl Crow. British composer David Arnold's title song for the latter, performed by k.d.lang, was relegated to the end credits and renamed 'Surrender'. Arnold then became the series' regular composer, scoring *The World is Not Enough* (dir. Michael Apted, 1999), *Die Another Day* (dir. Lee Tamahori, 2002) and *Casino Royale* (dir. Martin Campbell, 2006), with title songs performed by Garbage, Madonna and Chris Cornell respectively.

Many of the Bond films included end-title songs as well as front-title songs (sometimes simply repeating the opening song at the end of the film), but in other genres it was to remain more common for a title or tie-in song to be reserved until the end credits: an odd move in marketing terms, since audiences tend to quit the cinema as soon as the credits appear on screen and rarely stay to listen to the play-out music that accompanies them. Successful title and tie-in songs since the 1980s have included Bryan Adams's '(Everything I Do) I Do It for You' from *Robin Hood: Prince of Thieves* (dir. Kevin Reynolds, 1991), which remained at No. 1 in the UK for seventeen weeks (Barron 2003, 153), and Celine Dion's 'My Heart Goes On' from *Titanic* (dir. James Cameron, 1997; music by James Horner). Following a well-worn musical format, the Oscar-winning *Titanic* song was used as an instrumental leitmotif during the film and appeared in lyricized form over the end credits. Other end-title songs conceived largely for cross-marketing purposes include Annie Lennox's 'Love Song for a Vampire' in *Bram Stoker's Dracula* (dir. Francis Ford Coppola, 1992); Coco Lee's 'A Love Before Time' in *Crouching Tiger, Hidden Dragon* (dir. Ang Lee, 2000); Faith Hill's 'There You'll Be' in *Pearl Harbor* (dir. Michael Bay, 2001); Enya's 'May It Be' in *The Lord of the Rings: The Fellowship of the Ring* (dir. Peter Jackson, 2001), and Annie Lennox's 'Into the West' for the Tolkien sequel *The Return of the King* (2003), the last winning an Academy Award. Martin Scorsese's *Gangs of New York* (2002), with its end-title song 'The Hands that Built America', performed by U2, is a good example of the stylistic and emotional lurch that results when a modern pop song suddenly intrudes to play out a drama notable for its lavish attention to period detail. Music videos of songs of this general type usually contain images from the films for cross-publicity purposes (see below).

As the list above shows, many film producers in the last half century have set their sights on the Academy's Best Song award as well as on the commercial potential of a song away from the film. The Song award was established in 1934 at the same time as the award for Original Music Scoring, and until the success of Hayes's *Shaft* in 1971 the Song awards without exception went to traditional ballad-style standards or numbers from screen musicals.

Controversy arose in 1954 when Dimitri Tiomkin requested Warner Bros. to include the lyrics to his title song for *The High and the Mighty* in a single copy of the release print screened in Los Angeles specifically so that the song might qualify for the award. (It did not win.) In 1968 the song category was renamed as Song: Original to the Picture, the rider subsequently abolished in 1973; a more cumbersome and politically correct renaming as Achievement in Music in Connection with Motion Pictures: Original Song was briefly in force in 2001. The Bee Gees were not even nominated for *Saturday Night Fever* in 1977 (in spite of protests from producer Robert Stigwood), and the first genuinely modern winner of the award came a year later with Donna Summer's performance of Paul Jabara's disco hit 'Lance Dance' from *Thank God It's Friday*. The smallest number of nominations came in 1988 when fewer than the stipulated minimum of 25 songs were eligible and the short-list was consequently restricted to three entries. In addition to the awards for Original Score and Original Song, the Academy has at various times made awards in a separate Song Score category (see below), primarily designed to cater for musicals; the potential unfairness caused by the suspension of this category in 1985 was shown in 2006 when no fewer than three of the five Original Song nominations (all of them unsuccessful) came from the same screen musical (*Dreamgirls*, dir. Bill Condon).

To be considered for the Original Song award, the song must consist 'of words and music, both of which are original and **written specifically for the film**. There must be a clearly audible, intelligible, substantive rendition (not necessarily visually presented) of both lyric and melody, used in the body of the film or as the first music cue in the end credits' (AMPAS 2006; bold type in original). In 1992, Stevie Wonder's songs from Spike Lee's *Jungle Fever* were deemed ineligible owing to their poor audibility (Karlin 1994, 212). The Academy's rules stress that 'The measure of the work's qualification shall be its effectiveness, craftsmanship, creative substance and relevance to the dramatic whole'; the song must be 'recorded for use in the film prior to any other usage including public performance or exploitation through any media whatsoever', and scores 'diluted by the use of tracked themes or other pre-existing music', or 'diminished in impact by the predominant use of songs', or 'assembled from the music of more than one composer' are all ineligible.

Compilation scores and original song scores

Bolder than attempts to secure airwave advertising and record sales by the inclusion of individual title songs was the compilation score, a music track heavily (but not necessarily exclusively) reliant on a sequence of self-contained pop songs. Such scores generally avoided the accusations of gratuitousness and narrative stasis with which some critics greeted isolated interpolated songs, though (as discussed below) the compilation score raised other controversial aesthetic issues of its own. The prototypical music tracks of this kind were those compiled for *The Graduate* (dir. Mike Nichols, 1967) and *Easy Rider* (dir. Dennis Hopper, 1969); neither film received Academy recognition for its music tracks, with Best Song nominations in those years going instead to up-front interpolations and numbers from conventional musicals. Paul Simon and Art Garfunkel nevertheless won three Grammy awards for their *Graduate* songs, four of which had been extracted from pre-existing albums for use on the film's temp track and were subsequently retained; the only new song required was 'Mrs Robinson', which they reworked as a No. 1 hit. The film, which began the trend of using pop lyrics to suggest a character's otherwise unvoiced preoccupations – most notably in its use of 'Sounds of Silence' in the swimming-pool montage as a 'motif of withdrawal' (Reay 2004, 57) – represented the first attempt to integrate multiple nondiegetic songs with a linear narrative. It proved to be the third highest grossing release to that date, beaten at the box office only by *The Sound of Music* and *Gone With the Wind* (Denisoff and Romanowski 1991, 166–7).

Easy Rider was more provocative in its subject-matter, and received an anthology score compiled from pre-existing songs by various artists. The film tapped into a niche market for biker films (a bandwagon onto which AIP had jumped when the bottom fell out of the beach-party genre), and took the form of a road movie amounting to 'a countercultural reversal of the Hollywood classic western' (Denisoff and Romanowski 1991, 169): drugs replaced the pioneering explorer spirit as a means of seeking out new frontiers of experience. *Easy Rider*'s soundtrack memorably showcased Steppenwolf's 'Born to Be Wild' in its title sequence and elsewhere included music by The Jimi Hendrix Experience, The Byrds and others; influential not only for its music but also its improvisational style and strong violence typical of dramatic trends emerging in cinema at the time, the film grossed $60 million to repay its tiny production budget of only $565,000. Both *The Graduate* and *Easy Rider* had clearly struck a powerful chord with youthful audiences for what R. Barton Palmer describes as a stance 'predictably Oedipal, staging compromised rebellions, in the tradition of J. D. Salinger, against middle-class values and institutions (marriage, settling down, productive employment, "responsibility") in the name of an ever-elusive personal freedom, a quest that could be shaped into either a comic or tragic conclusion' (Kolker 2006, 15).

A compilation score also accompanied Michelangelo Antonioni's *Zabriskie Point* (1969). His earlier *Zeitgeist* film *Blow-Up* (1966; score by

Herbie Hancock) had featured The Yardbirds giving a diegetic performance of 'Stroll On' in a cellar club and typified the decade's swinging London scene. By contrast, *Zabriskie Point* examined the radical politics and hippie love of Californian students and, although the use of music in the film is fairly muted until one of them steals a plane and escapes to the desert, it placed its detailed song credits prominently in the main titles: the artists included Pink Floyd, Youngbloods, Kaleidoscope and The Grateful Dead. The cinematography espoused a quasi-*vérité* handheld-camera style during the opening student debate, with crude swish pans and abrupt zooms mirroring the improvisational acting, and this attempted realism was perhaps partly responsible for the avoidance of prominent nondiegetic music.

More durable and widely appealing was George Lucas's *American Graffiti* (1973), a commercial success story comparable to *Easy Rider* for netting nearly 100 times its meagre budget in box-office takings. Set nostalgically in the car culture of California in the early 1960s, the film's plot was a typical rite-of-passage concerning four high-school boys about to go to college. Its music track of 'golden oldies' initiated a perceptible shift in fashion from the rebellious films of the previous decade to what has been termed the 'complacent 1970s Me Decade' (Denisoff and Romanowski 1991, 176), in which the desire to entertain rather than shock became paramount. The film was also notable for its use of songs as structural units, each scene broadly corresponding to the length of the song featured in it. Lucas's modest budget precluded the use of songs for which the licensing fees were expensive, and this affected the eventual choice of music in the compilation score, much of which (including 'Rock Around the Clock' and 'Smoke Gets in Your Eyes') was unashamedly nostalgic in intent, though occasionally used creatively – as when Booker T and the MGs' 'Green Onions' at first appears to be a nondiegetic prelude to a chicken-run car race but is subsequently heard continuing diegetically as it issues faintly from a wrecked car's radio once the vehicle has gone out of control. Although it has been repeatedly claimed that the songs selected were deliberately chosen for the dramatic ironies inherent in their titles, both Lucas and his sound-montage supervisor Walter Murch claimed that any strong song would have worked equally well for any scene (J. Smith 2001, 410) – an approach that when adopted by other directors would inevitably result in some haphazard conjunctions of music and image, again laying film-makers wide open to claims that pop songs were being included in film soundtracks gratuitously.

Later rites-of-passage movies with compilation scores included *The Big Chill* (dir. Lawrence Kasdan, 1983), with its plot centring on a college reunion at a funeral, featuring music by Marvin Gaye and Procol Harum's 'Whiter Shade of Pale' (Carey and Hannan 2003, 167–9). Kasdan had experienced studio resistance because his golden oldies promised to be insufficiently lucrative, but the soundtrack album sold 750,000 in eight weeks with little use of radio or video plugging (Denisoff and Romanowski 1991, 387, 392). The film's formula was reworked in *St Elmo's Fire* (dir. Joel Schumacher, 1985) which launched a number of 'Brat Pack' acting careers, as did the same year's *The Breakfast Club* (dir. John Hughes). Compilation scores containing pop hits from yesteryear provided both a convenient method of establishing historical periods and a means to promote nostalgic personal identification, and this widespread device was used most systematically in the hugely lucrative *Forrest Gump* (dir. Robert Zemeckis, 1994). Films of the 1990s at times looked back to the 1970s and 1980s for inspiration, *Boogie Nights* (dir. Paul Thomas Anderson, 1997) using lyrics of 1970s songs for a postmodern and occasionally esoteric sexual suggestiveness rather different from their original associations (J. Smith 2001, 423–8), while *The Wedding Singer* (dir. Frank Coraci, 1998) drew on a wide range of hits appropriate to its 1985 setting. In Australia, pop hits from the 1970s made *Muriel's Wedding* (dir. P. J. Hogan, 1994) a good example of a trend towards 'deliberately outdated camp soundtracks' (Wojcik and Knight 2001, 1). Throughout the 1980s and 1990s, both rites-of-passage films and romantic comedies frequently used golden-oldie song titles as their own titles in order to tap nostalgic associations in audiences even before the projector began turning.

The first golden-oldie compilation score in British cinema was *That'll Be the Day* (dir. Claude Whatham, 1973), and scores of this type were to remain successful in the UK where undemanding pop soundtracks for modern romantic comedies such as *Peter's Friends* (dir. Kenneth Branagh, 1992) and *Four Weddings and a Funeral* (dir. Mike Newell, 1994) fared equally well abroad. The *Four Weddings* soundtrack included Wet Wet Wet's 'Love Is All Around', which remained at the No. 1 slot for fifteen weeks in the British charts. The film catapulted British actor Hugh Grant to an international stardom later ruthlessly and unimaginatively exploited by the producers of *Notting Hill* (dir. Roger Michell, 1999) and *About A Boy* (dir. Paul and Chris Weitz, 2002), with songs by Elvis Costello and Badly Drawn Boy respectively, and the so-called 'chick flicks' *Bridget Jones's Diary* (dir. Sharon Maguire, 2001), *Bridget Jones: The Edge of Reason* (dir. Beeban Kidron, 2004) and *Love Actually* (dir. Richard Curtis, 2003), all furnished with easy-going pop scoring. Far more extreme was *9 Songs* (dir. Michael Winterbottom, 2004), a sexually explicit love story intercut with a collection of diegetic concert performances by various artists, of which the hard-core images probably sold far more tickets and DVDs than the film's musical content; the overall result (according to *Times* critic James Christopher) was 'a bad piece of pornography that seems to have got fatally mixed up with [the director's] record collection' (quoted in J. Walker 2006, 832).

Since the end of the 1960s, both individual pop songs and historically res-
onant compilation scores have come to redefine the genre of the war movie
for the post-Vietnam age, helping it move beyond its traditional heroic
and patriotic vein to far darker and disturbing messages of protest laced
with bitter satire. Robert Altman's black comedy *M*A*S*H* (1970) came as
the greatest possible contrast to the well-made but emotionally empty and
expensive Second World War epics *Patton* and *Tora! Tora! Tora!* then in production (and both scored conventionally by Jerry Goldsmith). Set in a US
mobile army surgical hospital during the Korean War of 1950–53 and shot
to a low budget in starkly realist style, *M*A*S*H* deliberately cultivated the
look of the Vietnam war to strike a chord with audiences disaffected by the
ongoing conflict in South East Asia: the implications were so obvious that
the studio forced the director to insert a 'Korea' title card at the beginning of
the film, a stipulation that inspired a nose-thumbing gesture in the soundtrack as the gratuitous piece of locational information is accompanied by a
morphing of the Twentieth Century-Fox fanfare into an inane ceremonial
march. The film's evocative main-title footage of medevac helicopters was
accompanied by Johnny Mandel's song 'Suicide is Painless', originally written (with lyrics by the director's son Michael) to serve a diegetic function
later in the film when it is performed by voice and guitar to accompany the
fake suicide of a dental surgeon nicknamed Painless, a scene consciously
parodying Leonardo Da Vinci's painting of the Last Supper. In spite of its
essentially parodic conception, the song (covered years later by the Manic
Street Preachers, in 1992) was not initially a hit away from the film because
radio stations and record companies refused to entertain lyrics referring to
suicide. It did, however, top the UK pop charts in 1980 on the back of the
successful and long-running TV spin-off series, though as a signature tune it
was adapted as an instrumental version that culminated in a lightweight tag
ending typical of sitcom music on the small screen. The soundtrack of Francis Ford Coppola's *Apocalypse Now* (1979) subsequently linked the Vietnam
War to the rock music of its age by including The Doors' 'The End' and the
Rolling Stones' 'Satisfaction', while music by the Beatles and the Stones featured in the Vietnam movies *Coming Home* (dir. Hal Ashby, 1978) and the
Stones' 'Paint It Black' appeared on the soundtrack of Stanley Kubrick's *Full
Metal Jacket* (1987). Apart from their obvious historical and generational
appropriateness, the Vietnam War being associated with the heyday of rock
just as the Second World War had been inextricably linked with swing bands,
pop songs in war films thereafter continued to provide a sense of irony and
distanciation singularly lacking in old-fashioned heroic orchestral scores
(Romney and Wootton 1995, 16).

As multiple pop songs came to be used on the soundtrack of a single film
to replace conventional instrumental scoring, so the aesthetic functions of

traditional film music came to be undermined, questioned and ultimately reconsidered. The closed form of popular song at first seemed ill-suited to film music's longstanding duty to provide narrative continuity in the short, medium and long terms, and popular styles seemed incapable of monumentalizing banal subject-matter through the classical aggrandizement and emotional hyperbole of the conventional romantic underscore; neither did featured or otherwise isolated songs seem capable of promoting the (admittedly sometimes specious) sense of overall structural coherence suggested by classical thematic developments and long-term harmonic relationships. On the other hand, pop songs were undoubtedly effective in the interests of realism when heard diegetically, and as blatant signifiers of historical period, ethnic group or other culture, as well as political messages both overt and covert (as, for instance, in the black-militancy parameter of Spike Lee's 1989 film, *Do the Right Thing*; see Wright 2003, 17). They were also by far the most convenient (and therefore often lazy) method of ensuring the commercial success of both a film and its soundtrack in the youth and nostalgia sectors of the market. Pop songs could not often undertake the age-old musical function of mickey-mousing physical gestures because they could only be synchronized to movement if pre-recorded and played back on set during shooting, as occurred in the treatment of Marvin Gaye's 'I Heard It Through the Grapevine' in *The Big Chill*, which opens and later punctuates the film. But pacing and momentum could be suggested by a dynamic song in certain situations, notably moving vehicles, as at the start of *Easy Rider* where the (in reality rather slowly moving) motorbikes seem propelled onwards by Steppenwolf's repetitive and hard-driving rhythms, strong bass line and powerful rock sonorities; not surprisingly, music with these ingredients continued to feature heavily in the genre of the road movie.

In contrast to classically derived instrumental scoring, the lyrics of pop songs made them uniquely suited to promoting both audience distanciation or personal involvement, for exploiting emotional and situational anempathy, or for unequivocally underlining unspoken aspects of character and motivation. As with the filmic use of well-known pieces of classical music, however, there remained a danger that once recognized a song might distract a viewer's attention from the intended dramatic function owing to his or her personal feelings about it: after all, 'every viewer comes to the cinema carrying his or her own jukebox ready loaded, waiting only for the film-maker to hit the right buttons' (Romney and Wootton 1995, 2), and even a snatch of a familiar melody can call up a paradigmatic memory of an entire song and its associations. If not causing unplanned distractions, song lyrics – especially when rendered nondiegetically – can nevertheless 'provide a unique opportunity to editorialize and to focus audience attention' (Altman 2001, 26).

Because the use of pre-existing hits is a safer commercial bet than attempting to predict what will be a hit at the time of a film's release, original song-based music tracks (other than conventional musicals) remained relatively rare. This is reflected in the chequered history of the Academy Awards in the Song Score category, which has at times showed a reluctance to regard the creative pop score as something with a unique identity. The category of Original Song Score and/or Adaptation was instituted in 1938 so that dramatic scores and musicals would not compete for the same award, and in 1941 the Song Score award was renamed to refer only to Musical Pictures. In 1957 a single Score category was briefly reinstated but the separate Musical award was resurrected in 1958 (when it was won by *Gigi*). With transfers of existing stage musicals to the big screen now far more common than original screen musicals, in 1962 the Musical award again became one for Adaptation or Treatment, and in 1968 it changed once more to Score of a Musical Picture (Original or Adaptation). In 1970 the Beatles' documentary *Let It Be* (dir. Michael Lindsay-Hogg) won the freshly renamed Original Song Score category, but in the following year a conventional musical (*Fiddler on the Roof*) succeeded in the yet further renamed Adaptation and Original Song Score category. The success of *The Sting* in the 1973 competition for Original Song Score and/or Adaptation, with its music track a compilation of dramatically anachronistic arrangements of Scott Joplin's piano rags, demonstrated that it was unnecessary for catchy tunes to be newly composed in order to succeed.

The Song Score/Adaptation category was dropped in 1980 but reactivated in 1982 before being dropped again three years later. In 1995 musicals were considered under the same heading as original scores for comedies, with a separate award offered for Original Dramatic Score, but these categories were again combined in 1999 when the original 1930s two-award scheme for Music (simply Song and Score) was reinstituted. A third award for Original Musical can still be activated, but 'only by special request of the Music Branch Executive Committee to the Board of Governors in a year when the field of eligible submissions is determined to be of sufficient quantity and quality to justify award competition'. The definition of 'Musical' is now formulated to apply equally to original Song Scores, in that in order to qualify a music track must consist 'of not fewer than five original songs . . . by the same writer or team of writers either used as voice-overs or visually performed. Each of these songs must be substantively rendered, clearly audible, intelligible, and must further the storyline. What is simply an arbitrary group of songs unessential to the storyline of the film will not be considered eligible' (AMPAS 2006). Since 1984, when Prince's *Purple Rain* won the Song Score award, the only song score (apart from those for

Disney's animated musicals) to have received an Academy Award was that accompanying *The Full Monty* (dir. Peter Cattaneo, 1997).

Synergistic marketing

Quite independent from considerations of artistic quality and dramatic appropriateness were the strenuous attempts to sell films on the back of hit songs, and vice versa. An early example of such synergistic marketing was the song 'Ramona', written for the film of the same title and promoted on tour and in radio broadcasts by Dolores Del Rio and Paul Whiteman in 1927–8 in advance of the film's release; it was subsequently recorded by Gene Austin for RCA and sold two million copies (MacDonald 1998, 17). The late silent-film era established the principle of vertical integration in which control of a film's production, distribution and exhibition were directly linked, and in 1929 *Photoplay* remarked: 'Is the motion picture industry a subsidiary of the music publishing business – or have film producers gone into the business of marketing songs?' (quoted in Mundy 1999, 51). Although sheet-music sales flourished during the Second World War, they permanently slumped during the boom in record sales following the introduction of the $33\frac{1}{3}$ rpm LP by Columbia in 1948 and the 45rpm single by RCA in the following year. The success of the recording industry at this time helped accelerate the acquisition of record companies by film studios, and vice versa: Decca bought Universal in 1952, then MCA bought them both in 1959, for example, and United Artists started its own record company from scratch in 1957, with Warner Bros., Twentieth Century-Fox and Columbia following suit a year later so that the West Coast became a significant new rival to New York in the recording business (J. Smith 1998, 33–4). In 1960, UA began to sell its soundtrack albums in the foyers of movie theatres.

A few film soundtrack recordings and spin-off singles had already been bestsellers, notably music from *Spellbound* (1945) and *The Third Man* (1949). Success at the box office would naturally ensure huge sales of recordings of the song or instrumental theme in question, and main-title songs became a simple method for film producers to ensure that their production's title would receive a mention whenever the song was broadcast. Elmer Bernstein lamented that the colossal record sales of his music for *The Man with the Golden Arm* in 1956 were specifically responsible for the development of pop-oriented strategies in film music, through which a film is scored 'in such a way that it will make records that sell, rather than what it does for the film . . . This trend was, I think, absolutely ruinous for the art of film music' (quoted in J. Smith 1998, 45). It was during the 1950s that, to this end, singles started to be released in advance of the movies to which they were attached. Just how lucrative effective cross-promotion could be was shown by *Saturday Night Fever* in 1977, thanks largely to the business instincts of Stigwood (who had already worked on the film versions of the rock operas *Tommy* and *Jesus Christ Superstar*, and in the 1980s would be responsible for constantly swelling Paramount's coffers). *Fever* revitalized the career of the Bee Gees by giving them four consecutive singles at No. 1, thereby breaking the Beatles' previous record of three in 1964: the soundtrack album (which eventually sold a staggering 25 million copies) was released six weeks in advance of the film and the individual singles were gradually released as it took hold at the box office. Because of the adult nature of the originally released R-rated film, a PG-rated version was also made for TV, and so that the production could be further targeted at an under-seventeen audience in a theatrical re-release in 1979 (Denisoff and Romanowski 1991, 231–2). The film resulted in worldwide disco fever, and the Bee Gees' Robin Gibb concluded that it was more important for film songs to be hits in their own right – or sound as if they were – than to be dramatically appropriate to the film to which they were attached, a view with which many producers had concurred since at least the success of *American Graffiti* a few years before.

In the early 1980s, cross-promotion became a sure-hit affair once Music Television (MTV) began to flourish as a cable and satellite service conceived for a new generation of impressionable consumers. Launched in the USA in 1982 and in Europe five years later, the MTV concept replaced old-fashioned radio programming (then aimed largely at those over the age of *c.*25) with slick, modern video presentations of pop songs for a younger audience. MTV's Executive Vice-President, Robert Pittman, stressed the novelty of the audio-visual experience the channel offered, with its emphasis on mood and emotion, and a distinctive style of 'quick-edit communication' deliberately aimed at limited attention spans (Denisoff and Romanowski 1991, 346). The medium of music video broke new ground in its 'breakdown of linear narrativity, of causal logic, and of temporal and spatial coherence' (Björnberg 2000, 348), these characteristics producing a strong sense of fragmentation and eclecticism. Exposure of such videos on MTV boosted sales of recordings significantly, and the videos were also an ideal medium in which to promote new films, functioning both as a trailer seen in the home rather than the theatre, and as an appetite-whetter for a featured song. Videos had already helped promote hits such as Joe Cocker's and Jennifer Warnes's Oscar-winning 'Up Where We Belong' from *An Officer and a Gentleman* (dir. Taylor Hackford, 1982; music by Jack Nitzsche).

In MTV's 'heavy rotation' programming, a video was assured four daily airings, a level of exposure which immediately benefited films such as

Footloose (dir. Herbert Ross, 1984) and *The Breakfast Club*, the former netting two Academy Award song nominations and the latter's 'Don't You (Forget About Me)' by Simple Minds topping the US charts in 1985. Typical of the mixing of pop and film iconography to promote both song and movie simultaneously was the video of Duran Duran's 1985 title song to *A View To a Kill*, which showed the band posing as secret agents in Paris. Nevertheless, *Cocktail* (dir. Roger Donaldson, 1988) demonstrated that more conventional marketing strategies, in which songs and soundtrack albums were launched only after a film's theatrical release, could still pay significant dividends – and even revive flagging musical careers, as happened when the Beach Boys' 'Kokomo' became a US No. 1. After the introduction of the compact disc in the early 1980s, the new medium's practicality and fashionableness further boosted sales of soundtrack albums and film-related songs, one of the first hits to benefit significantly from CD sales being Bill Medley's and Jennifer Warnes's Oscar-winning '(I've Had) The Time of My Life' from *Dirty Dancing* (dir. Emile Ardolino, 1987), which made No. 1 in the USA and No. 6 in the UK in spite of its jarringly anachronistic style for a movie purportedly set in 1963.

MTV's vivid audio-visual style had a significant impact on cinematography and montage on the big screen, and some of its characteristics had already been adumbrated by Alan Parker's film of Pink Floyd's album *The Wall* (1982), which pushed the boundaries of the rock-opera genre by treating its central Freudian subject of a psychological isolation induced by childhood experiences as a combination of startling animations (by Gerald Scarfe) and a rather self-conscious artiness in live-action montage that significantly lacked narrative-furthering dialogue. An early manifestation of the specific MTV influence came soon after in the shape of *Flashdance* (dir. Adrian Lyne, 1983), with its clearly sectionalized structure, ticket sales for which were boosted by Michael Sembello's 'Maniac' videoclip on MTV; Irene Cara's title song 'What a Feeling', composed by Giorgio Moroder, achieved the No. 1 slot in the USA (where it won an Oscar) and was also No. 2 in the UK. The end-credit sequence of the box-office smash hit *Ghostbusters* (dir. Ivan Reitman, 1984) comprised Ray Parker Jr's title song presented in MTV style – a sequence effective enough *in situ*, but with the added advantage of being ideal for wholesale excision for separate exhibition as a promo video. Moroder, who during this period was hired by producer Jerry Bruckheimer specifically to create potential hit songs rather than for compelling dramatic reasons, again netted an Academy Award with his song 'Take My Breath Away' in *Top Gun* (dir. Tony Scott, 1986), an exhilarating glamorization of the work of US Navy fighter pilots slickly edited with a deafening soundtrack; the film grossed $300 million globally, and its album went quadruple platinum. *Top Gun* also benefited (as had Prince's *Purple Rain* two years earlier) from the new market in home-video sales, moving two million units thanks to a low-price cross-promo advertising deal with Pepsi and netting $40 million in its first week on sale (Denisoff and Romanowski 1991, 626; Thompson and Bordwell 2003, 680). In the 1990s, the flamboyant audio-visual style of Australian director Baz Luhrmann directly reflected music-video techniques, even in the hallowed realms of filmed Shakespeare and the period musical (see Chapter 4). In addition to its impact on the big screen, MTV's montage style also affected mainstream TV drama, beginning with *Miami Vice* (1984–9).

Pop (stars) in performance

MTV's ascendancy quickly killed off the more traditional performance-rooted pop films that had continued to be made on the back of the success of *A Hard Day's Night*. As Andy Medhurst notes:

> television always did better pop anyway. Pop TV had no need to try to shoe-horn the music into outdated formats, it had less rules to break and more freedom to move, it was quick, cheap and immediate, just like the music itself. The pop film was quicker than any other genre in poaching personnel and learning tricks from TV . . . but its attempts to keep pace were doomed to failure . . . The truly cinematic option, the arty Pop Art knowingness kickstarted by *Catch Us If You Can* [US title *Having a Wild Weekend*; dir. John Boorman, 1965], led only to a declining spiral of self-referentiality and pretension, a hermetically sealed, gestural cinema that imploded into *Performance* [dir. Nicolas Roeg, 1970] – a key film of its times, to be sure, but scarcely worth five seconds of Mick Jagger singing "Honky Tonk Women" on [BBC TV's] *Top of the Pops*.   (Medhurst 1995, 69)

Performance had undoubtedly reflected 'the self-destructiveness and nihilism at the edges of pop music culture that were becoming evident at the end of the 1960s' (Donnelly 2001b, 23), while demonstrating Jagger's abilities as actor rather than singer.

Since the Golden Age, with the big-screen acting appearances of Frank Sinatra and Bing Crosby, popular singers had – with varying degrees of success – attempted to forge such dual careers for themselves. After the 1950s the heavy emphasis on star persona in marketing individual musical careers meant that singers were not always able or willing to submerge their personalities in acting roles, which for marketing reasons they felt needed to remain both prominent and immediately recognizable. Among the more successful musicians on the big screen since the 1970s have been The Who's Roger Daltrey (*Tommy*, *Lisztomania*), David Essex (*That'll Be The Day*,

Stardust), David Bowie (*The Man Who Fell to Earth, Merry Christmas Mr Lawrence*), Bob Geldof (*Pink Floyd The Wall*), Madonna (*Body of Evidence, Desperately Seeking Susan, Evita*), Prince (*Purple Rain*) and Sting (*Dune, Quadrophenia, Plenty*). Whitney Houston's screen debut in *The Bodyguard* (dir. Mick Jackson, 1992) significantly boosted her singing career via the film's two Oscar-nominated songs, a No. 1 hit in the shape of her cover version of Dolly Parton's 'I Will Always Love You' and sales of the soundtrack album in excess of 27 million (Reay 2004, 101). If Houston clearly represented the commercial bias of pop-influenced films, at the other extreme was Björk's haunting contribution (in both acting and soundtrack) to Lars Von Trier's *Dancer in the Dark* (2000), one of the boldest and least-conventional film projects to have featured a star pop performer. Taking the role of an East European single mother working in 1960s America and striving to save her son from the illness which is making her go blind, and ending her life brutally on the gallows, Björk's character Selma lives vicariously through the utopian escapism of stage musicals; the film appropriately 'combines a documentary home-video style, with its associations of simplicity, domesticity and naturalness, with the intricate, highly stylized ("artificial") choreography of a thirties Hollywood musical using contemporary (post-Madonna) pop-video techniques' (Grimley 2005, 38). Since the 1990s less notable dual careers have been commonplace, with minor pop stars routinely switching between TV soap-opera roles and the recording studio and musical stage, performing artists lending authenticity to rapsploitation films by acting in them, and the now expected crossover between popular cultural activities extending to the involvement of several internationally prominent footballers in minor acting roles on the big screen.

As fictional films featuring pop groups or showcasing the talents of individual singers dwindled, the documentary genre nevertheless produced occasional portraits of real-life musicians that attained creative excellence. In the mid-1960s the Direct Cinema movement, an offshoot of photojournalism, ensured that several of these films achieved a fresh *cinéma-vérité* style (Thompson and Bordwell 2003, 483–5). Early examples were made by the Maysles brothers, who filmed *What's Happening! The Beatles in New York* (1964) and the Rolling Stones documentary *Gimme Shelter* (1970), and by a team lead by directors Don Pennebaker and Richard Leacock, whose *Don't Look Back* (1966) examined Bob Dylan's 1965 tour of the UK, and *Monterey Pop* (made for television but released theatrically) featured Jimi Hendrix and others performing at the Californian venue in 1967. *Woodstock* (dir. Michael Wadleigh, 1970) was a mammoth account of the legendary 1969 festival important not only for its stunningly – and sometimes manipulatively – edited musical performances but also as a powerful

10.1 The eponymous heavy-metal band performs in Rob Reiner's spoof rockumentary *This is Spinal Tap* (1984). Left to right: Harry Shearer (as Derek Smalls), Christopher Guest (as Nigel Tufnel) and Michael McKean (as David St Hubbins).

document of its era that can be read as both a social narrative and even as a carefully structured musical (Altman 1987, 102–3). A more straightforward concert film, distinguished director Jonathan Demme's *Stop Making Sense* (1985) vividly captured Talking Heads' David Byrne on stage at the height of his creative powers. *In Bed with Madonna* (US title *Madonna: Truth or Dare*; dir. Alek Keshishian, 1991) was an account of the eponymous singer's 'Blond Ambition' tour in which colour MTV-style concert performances were intercut with more intimate *vérité*-style monochrome scenes concerned with the singer's private world.

Dramatized films based on pop stars' lives, typically as distorted in their romanticized portrayals of their subjects as were the many biopics set in jazz and classical milieux (discussed elsewhere), achieved a strange blend of verisimilitude and inauthenticity when actors re-recorded the relevant songs themselves: examples include *The Doors* (dir. Olive Stone, 1991), starring Val Kilmer as Jim Morrison; *Backbeat* (dir. Iain Softley, 1994) with its re-creation of the Beatles' singing; and *Walk the Line* (dir. James Mangold, 2005), featuring Joaquin Phoenix as Johnny Cash.

Perhaps the finest rock-milieu film of all was an out-and-out parody, the deliciously silly *This is Spinal Tap* (dir. Rob Reiner, 1984) in which an eminently likeable and inept heavy-metal band are given a spoof documentary profile, the film's success aided by brilliant pastiche song performances, the humour of which functions on several levels (Covach 1995), and a soundtrack marketing campaign that itself parodied the commercial strategies discussed above – down to the last detail of album cover design and tongue-in-cheek video promos. The spoof band became a success in its own right, making live appearances and garnering a significant cult following.

11 Classical music in the cinema

However good our best film composers may be, they are not a Beethoven, a Mozart or a Brahms. Why use music which is less good when there is such a multitude of great orchestral music from the past and from our own time? (STANLEY KUBRICK, QUOTED IN MACLEAN 1994, 6)

Hold it, boys! Beethoven isn't working – try Brahms. (FRED ASTAIRE, IN *FUNNY FACE* (1956))

Classical music, by which is here meant the traditional catch-all definition discussed by Royal S. Brown (1994, 39), was a staple ingredient of silent-film accompaniment, and the stylistic precepts of orchestral romanticism and impressionism subsequently became the solid foundation on which Golden Age film scoring was based. It is therefore not surprising that, thereafter, classical music never had the significant impact on audio-visual style that the fresh perspectives offered by pop music began to achieve from the 1950s onwards. The structural and perceptual implications of pop-based soundtracks revolutionized both practical and aesthetic approaches to the creative combination of sound and image in ways which were to remain dynamic in films of the early twenty-first century. Indeed, it might with good reason be argued that the most significant soundtrack developments of the modern age were initiated by a conscious rejection of the outmoded values of structural cogency, musical logic and pseudo-highbrow art-music styles which the traditional orchestral film score had embodied. As a consequence, uses of pre-existing classical compositions (or, more typically, short extracts from them) in film soundtracks after the 1960s boom in pop scoring tended to draw more obvious attention to themselves than had been the case in earlier films, and only very rarely – as in Robert Altman's *A Perfect Couple* (1979) – did film-makers attempt systematically to reconcile both classical and popular idioms in a single project (R. S. Brown 1994, 247–9).

Brown has argued that this newer sense of showcasing the classics, often presenting the music as a parallel dimension to the filmic image rather than as a direct illustration of it, sprang in part from the accustomed invisibility of a kind of music better known from polished studio recordings rather than live performances and therefore divorced (unless dance-oriented) from any meaningful physical dimension (R. S. Brown 1994, 240). However, cinema history is also littered with examples of live classical performances serving to underpin a climactic event in the narrative: prolonged assassination sequences in such an environment occur, for example, in Hitchcock's *The Man Who Knew Too Much* (1956) and Coppola's *The Godfather Part III* (1990). Somewhere between the two extremes is the diegetic use of Berlioz's *Symphonie fantastique* disembodied on a domestic hi-fi at the climax of

Sleeping with the Enemy (dir. Joseph Ruben, 1990). At the same time as pre-existing classical music made its cinematic comeback, modern large-scale orchestral scoring continued (after a dip in its fortunes during the pop-dominated 1960s and early 1970s) to be heavily derived from classical exemplars and to fulfil the aggrandizing and mythicizing – yet still supposedly invisible – functions of its Golden Age progenitors, the survival of the basic idiom also attributed by Brown partly to audiences' unquestioning acceptance of the conceptual viability of unseen orchestras playing in studios.

Long before these trends were established, the experimental climate of the 1920s and 1930s had elicited a number of bolder filmic uses of classical music. The early surrealist sound film *L'Age d'or* (dir. Buñuel and Dali, 1930) paradoxically used its synchronized classical-music track 'to shock the bourgeoisie [with] the most shocking music possible, which was the most familiar and irreproachably bourgeois music one can imagine' (Barlow 2001, 31). The film demonstrated how well-known music by revered classical composers could, with ironic wit, accompany images of decomposing bodies (Mozart's *Ave verum corpus*) or the sucking of a statue's toe (Wagner's *Liebestod*), gestures thus made more disconcerting than might have been the case had the original plan to commission a modernist score from Stravinsky not foundered (Barlow 2001, 39). (Shock tactics based on such anempathy would later underpin the provocative use of classical music by director Stanley Kubrick, discussed below.) Buñuel synchronized recorded music with his earlier surrealist film *Un Chien andalou* (1929), juxtaposing popular tangos with Wagner's *Liebestod* perhaps to imply that the film 'was as much about the collapse of European culture between the wars as a subterranean voyage through the recesses of the unconscious mind' (D. Cook 2004, 310).

Other film-makers allied to Dada and the avant-garde drew inspiration from the classics. In common with several French directors of the time, *cinéma pur* pioneer Germaine Dulac was fascinated by the ostensible parallels between musical and cinematic rhythm and used music-inspired titles for her films such as *Thème et variations* (1928) and *Arabesque* (1929). She based several of her shorts on classical pieces: for example, *Disque 957* (1928), which includes shots of the music's gramophone record revolving on its turntable, was a visual interpretation of Chopin's Sixth Prelude in the course of which drops of water trickling down a window and a mist-enshrouded alleyway served both atmospheric and structural functions – to the disappointment of Kracauer, who lamented the 'emasculation' of such gestures which 'hold out a promise [of depicting "nature in the raw"] which, by no fault of theirs, is revoked instantly' (Kracauer 1960, 185). Mitry also felt that Dulac, whose experiments were curtailed by the advent of the commercial pressures of the sound cinema, fell into the trap of illustrating the music's programmatic meaning rather than its inherent shapes (Mitry 1998, 257). Another experimental film-maker of the late 1920s, Man Ray, brought classical and popular music into collision in a manner that looked conceptually ahead to the experimental cinema of Godard in the 1960s.

On the filmic interpretation of pre-existing music, Eisenstein declared: 'We must know how to grasp the movement of a given piece of music, locating its path (its line or form) as our foundation for the plastic composition that is to correspond to the music' (Eisenstein 1948, 131; emphasis in original). He noted that ballet had achieved such a conjunction long before the birth of film, and the parallel with ballet was also discussed by Mitry, who drew attention to what he saw as the essential speciousness of experimental animators' attempts to use non-representational images to create a visual 'rhythm' when they were merely accompanying musical patterns (Mitry 1998, 256). Mitry cited the work of Oskar Fischinger, who was active first in Germany and then in America, some examples of which were based on classical pieces: Motion Painting No. 1, for example, was a 1947 Guggenheim Foundation commission inspired by one of J. S. Bach's Brandenburg Concerti (Thompson and Bordwell 2003, 320–1). Fischinger's work had previously left its mark on Disney's Fantasia, a film much admired by Eisenstein. Other early experimenters working with the classics were Alexander Alexeyev and Claire Parker, whose fantasy pinboard animation A Night on Bald Mountain (1934) was based on the eponymous work by Mussorgsky, but their influence on mainstream cinema – as was that of even a globally recognized animator like Norman McLaren – was negligible. (For further on both commercial and experimental animation based on pre-existing music, see Chapter 7.) In the Soviet Union, Mikhail Tzekhanovsky made a film version of Honegger's Pacific 231 (1931) in which shots of a steam train were combined with footage of sections of the orchestra performing the piece; because of its quasi-mechanical and highly rhythmical nature, Honegger's tone poem was a favourite of experimental directors, and was interpreted as a non-illustrative film by Mitry himself in 1949 (Mitry 1998, 265–8). Mitry's Images pour Debussy (1951) was, on his own admission, a more satisfying experiment in classical-music visualization that attempted 'to create a sort of swirling, progressive magic using a dematerialized form of nature perceived through a rhythm appearing to emanate from it' (Mitry 1998, 269); its 'contemplative dream state' was not directly related to extra-musical subject-matter.

For his part, Honegger differed from the clinical tendencies of abstract theorists by opining (in 1931) that 'The sound film is admirably suited to completing and complementing music by giving it an actual meaning... Music has no real, concrete and perceptible representation identical for all listeners. It is possible that sound films will be able to provide it with one' (quoted in Mitry 1998, 259; emphasis in original). However, like many classical musicians, Honegger objected to the 'butchering' of pre-existing music often deemed necessary for its practical cinematic application. This attitude, which has remained relatively widespread (Joe 2006, 58), reflects an elitist view of the classical composer's art that has significantly impeded audio-visual experimentation based on the classics. Also hailing from the same elitism is the condescending notion of using the popular medium of cinema to educate the masses in the riches of classical repertoire, a preoccupation not only of Disney but of Chaplin and other silent-film practitioners before him (see, for example, Boblitz 1920). Endemic elitism notwithstanding, later uses of classical music tended to concern themselves with a few familiar styles, not least because the popular classics have always been marketable in the recording industry. Films featuring classical music in their soundtracks can still significantly boost sales of recordings of the music featured, often aided by the patronage of high-profile musical directors from the classical arena such as Neville Marriner (*Amadeus*, 1984) and Georg Solti (*Leo Tolstoy's Anna Karenina*, 1997), a marketing device harking back to Stokowski's prominent appearance in *Fantasia*: the alluring aura of the maestro became a powerful marketing tool in the record industry after the relentless branding of the charismatic and highly photogenic Herbert von Karajan by Deutsche Grammophon in the 1960s.

Romantic concerto and war film

When is a Concerto not a Concerto?
   The answer is: When a film forms all over it, and when it gets struck by the very dangerous Moonshine of Hollywood, and when the great, tripe-hearted democracy thinks it is going all classical and highbrow as it sits and listens, in the Palmers Green or Peckham Rye Pallas-Athenaeum, to the multitudinous masterpieces of Mr Richard Addinsell, having had, naturally enough till then, not the slightest idea how nice and easy 'nice' music was to listen to.   (Kaikhosru Sorabji 1947, 17)

In 1941, Richard Addinsell composed his *Warsaw Concerto* for the British film *Dangerous Moonlight* (US title *Suicide Squadron*; dir. Brian Desmond Hurst), its romantic plot concerning an amnesiac Polish pilot serving in the Royal Air Force during the Battle of Britain. The *Warsaw Concerto* had been commissioned partly so that the film's audiences would not be distracted by the associations which using a well-known pre-existing classical piece might have elicited (Huntley [1947], 54) – a common concern amongst many observers of the plundering of the classics in the silent era – though it had originally been planned to use a piano concerto by Rachmaninov for which the reproduction rights could not be obtained (Morrison 2004, 178). The *Warsaw Concerto* proved to be hugely popular on both sides of the Atlantic in live performances, broadcasts and on record, the interpretation of the work featured in the film (performed by Louis Kentner and the London Symphony Orchestra) having been issued as one of the earliest examples of a soundtrack recording. Addinsell was a versatile composer, who went on to compose a flamboyantly witty and impressionistic score for David Lean's *Blithe Spirit* (1945), but it was the romantic pastiche of this first example of what soon became dismissed as 'tabloid concertos' that proved to be his most influential achievement. Among its direct imitators was Hubert Bath's *Cornish Rhapsody* in *Love Story* (dir. Leslie Arliss, 1944), a film about a blind serviceman's love for a pianist, and filmic concerti for diegetic use were also composed for cello by Korngold (*Deception*, 1946), and for piano by both Herrmann (*Hangover Square*, 1945) and Webb (*The Enchanted Cottage*, 1945). The lyrical piano solo supported by conventional orchestration was thereafter to remain an indestructible romantic formula in both classically derived and more popular scoring idioms. A more restrained application helped popularize Mozart's Piano Concerto in C major K467 when it was used in the soundtrack of the Swedish film *Elvira Madigan* (dir. Bo Widerberg, 1967) in the unlikely context of a romance between a tightrope walker and an army deserter.

Pre-existing concerti were exploited in the superior Hollywood melodrama *The Great Lie* (dir. Edmund Goulding, 1941; score by Steiner) and the British film *The Common Touch* (dir. John Baxter, 1941), both featuring music from Tchaikovsky's First Concerto. Rachmaninov's Second Piano Concerto made an appearance alongside other classical repertoire in *The Seventh Veil* (1945), in which the LSO performed diegetically while actress Ann Todd mimed to the playing of pianist Eileen Joyce. In 1945, Lean's *Brief Encounter* turned Rachmaninov's Second Concerto into something of a celebrity. The heart-on-sleeve romanticism of Rachmaninov's idiom here served to articulate the protagonists' unconsummated affair. Extracts from the concerto were carefully adapted and spotted to underline dramatic developments, being used both diegetically and nondiegetically – and also, to borrow Claudia Gorbman's term, metadiegetically, for moments of nostalgic reminiscence: the film contrasts ordinary diegetic sound with the 'special realm which is the private province of romantic love' signified by the Rachmaninov (Altman 1987, 63). A structured underscore was thus created by editing a pre-existing work, an initiative in the cinematic application of classical music that proved to be influential. To cite a single later example of the film's influence on soundtrack techniques, witness the treatment of the slow movement from Schubert's String Quintet in C major in *Carrington* (dir. Christopher Hampton, 1995): first heard diegetically in a live performance, the Schubert then plays on a gramophone and is 'interiorized' as Carrington's view passes from a domestic interior to the view outside the window (the sound quality changing from impure diegetic to polished nondiegetic accordingly); the piece ultimately returns as an extended nondiegetic cue to serve as a dignified accompaniment to her suicide.

Hollywood attempted to do for Debussy what *Brief Encounter* had done for Rachmaninov in *Portrait of Jennie* (dir. William Dieterle, 1948). Originally to have been scored by Herrmann (whose song, sung diegetically by Jennie and referred to instrumentally, remains in it), the film was in the event scored by Tiomkin after a fleeting plan to use extracts from Britten's opera *Peter Grimes* as appropriate sea-music was abandoned. Tiomkin's attempt to create a structured underscore from pre-existing music was slated by Lawrence Morton: 'This is the first time Debussy's music has been systematically maimed and then paraded before the world as a cripple . . . This is not the music of Debussy but the music of Debussy-Selznick & Co., which is rather different . . .' Relating the score to the compilations of theatre organists in the silent cinema, he continued: 'It is a pot-pourri, a pasticcio, a hodgepodge, a patchwork, a grab-bag, paste-pot-and-scissors job. All that differentiates it from its ancestors is its slick pretentiousness' (quoted in DeMary 2003, 176).

The continued use of the classical staples of silent cinema in later films occasionally produced impressive results. For example, a striking application of Wagner's 'Ride of the Valkyries', with a clear nod back to its ultra-right-wing associations in Griffith's *The Birth of a Nation*, came in the seminal Vietnam War movie *Apocalypse Now* (dir. Coppola, 1979). Blared diegetically from a tape recorder in a Bell Huey helicopter leading the US airborne attack on a Vietnamese village (the commander shouts 'Put on psy war op. Make it loud . . . Shall we dance?'), the Wagnerian gesture carried uncomfortable overtones of both the Ku Klux Klan and Nazi atrocities: the first shots fired triumphantly in Coppola's film coincide with a glowing major chord in music. The Wagner recording used in the helicopter assault was a Decca release conducted by Solti, but the production team left it until the last moment to request permission from the record company, and – just before the film's release – they declined to grant it. To avoid the expensive contingency plan of making a new recording with the San Francisco Symphony Orchestra under the baton of Carmine Coppola, sound designer Walter Murch launched a manic search for other recordings that would fit the visual sequence:

> I mapped out a chart figuring out what Solti's rhythmic rate was for each
> section of the music . . . He was shifting the regularity to make it breathe as
> any good conductor would. I would listen to these other recordings [*c*.25 in
> number] with a stop watch, counting beats, and I charted out how close

these other ones came to Solti's recording . . . I finally narrowed it down to the L. A. Philharmonic, Zubin Mehta, which was close. But when I transferred it to film and put it in sync with the picture, I just knew instantly that it wasn't going to work . . . What Mehta had done in the music coloristically was not meshing with what I was looking at in the picture coloristically. What Solti had done, for instance, was to emphasize the brass at a certain moment, and the brassiness of that metallic sound went beautifully with the acidic blue of the ocean that you saw underneath the helicopter at that same moment. What Mehta had done was emphasize the strings, and that blue water and the strings didn't go together in an exciting way: they self-canceled.   (LoBrutto 1994, 93–4)

A personal plea to Solti from the film's director resulted in last-minute permission to use the favoured recording, but by this stage the release date was so imminent that the music on the soundtrack remained a primitive 'needle drop', dubbed directly from an LP. Murch won an Academy Award for his influential sound design for the film as a whole, which made creative use of the processed sound of helicopter rotor blades, in some instances mimicked in the throbbing synthesized bass of the original electronic music provided by Carmine Coppola.

In the wake of *Apocalypse Now* came a rash of Vietnam War movies, many (as we saw in the previous chapter) drawing on the rock music appropriate to the period depicted, but also including Oliver Stone's *Platoon* (1986) which did surprisingly well at the box office and made a hit of Samuel Barber's *Adagio for Strings*. As with the competition between music and sound effects in Coppola's film, the Barber is at the opening made to compete with the noise of the propellers on the Hercules aircraft bringing in fresh new US troops as the body bags of the dead replace them for the long journey home. The Barber reappears after the torching of a Vietnamese village, for a trek through the rainy jungle, for aerial shots of a skirmish whilst the troops bug out, and for the final clearing up of corpses and the medevac egress that leads into the end titles with a voice-over intoning 'We fought ourselves and the enemy is in us'. Barber's piece had been used in the film's temp track, and may have been selected in response to the similar use of Albinoni's (spurious) Adagio in Peter Weir's First World War drama *Gallipoli* (1981); Stone eventually retained the Barber cues at the expense of the bulk of the original score by Georges Delerue, which was jettisoned apart from a theme which Delerue had been instructed to model directly on the Barber. Delerue's response to the challenge has the same plain rhythm but is darker in mood, and also recurs in a 'daylight' version founded on solid major triads. Barber's *Adagio* (and its choral version, lyricized with the text of the *Agnus Dei*) became one of the most frequently used twentieth-century classical works in film soundtracks: having already appeared in the context of a freak show (*The Elephant Man*; dir. David Lynch, 1980), after its success in *Platoon* it featured in settings as diverse as New England puritans (*The Scarlet Letter*; dir. Roland Joffé, 1995), crude comedy (*Kevin and Perry Go Large*; dir. Ed Bye, 2000), the creation of a virtual digital actress (*S1m0ne*; dir. Andrew Nicoll, 2002), Oedipal necrophilia (*Ma Mère*; dir. Christophe Honoré, 2004) and documentaries about world peace (*Peace One Day*; dir. Jeremy Gilley, 2004) and the shortcomings of the profit-driven American healthcare system (*Sicko*; dir. Michael Moore, 2007). Barry was called in to score *The Scarlet Letter* at very short notice (see Chapter 12), and had wanted to use the choral version of the Barber owing to pressures of time; he also felt it would give 'a nude scene a touch of class' though, in the event, the producers preferred the nakedness to be accompanied by Barry's own love theme (Schelle 1999, 35–6, 38).

Classical biopics and milieu films

In the genre of the biopic, classical-music subjects generally received a romanticized treatment broadly comparable to the entertainingly distorted filmic portraits of the lives of famous jazz and popular musicians. Early Anglophone examples of various degrees of unintentional hilarity, and all with music tracks arranged by some of the best music directors in the business at the time, included Ealing's *Whom the Gods Love* (US title *Mozart*; dir. Basil Dean, 1936), featuring performances by Sir Thomas Beecham and the London Philharmonic, and *The Great Mr Handel* (dir. Norman Walker, 1942), both with music tracks supervised by Ernest Irving; the much-imitated Chopin saga *A Song to Remember* (dir. Charles Vidor, 1944; mus. dir. Miklós Rózsa and Morris Stoloff), in which the piano playing by Jose Iturbi was not acknowledged so as not to shatter the illusion of the actor's miming to playback (Huntley [1947], 54); the Paganini story *The Magic Bow* (dir. Bernard Knowles, 1946; mus. dir. Louis Levy), in which Stewart Granger mimed to recordings by Yehudi Menuhin; the portrayal of the romance between Robert and Clara Schumann in *Song of Love* (dir. Clarence Brown, 1947; mus. dir. Bronislau Kaper); and the Rimsky-Korsakov romance *Song of Scheherezade* (dir. Walter Reisch, 1947; mus. dir. Rózsa). Many of these pictures concentrated on the composers' love lives, thereby cementing the longstanding association between musical romanticism and diegetic love-interest. The overworking of 'Song' as a generic title continued with the Liszt biopic *Song without End* (dir. Charles Vidor and George Cukor, 1960), for which musical directors Stoloff and Henry Sukman received an Academy Award, and the Grieg drama *Song of Norway* (dir. Andrew Stone, 1970), both of which concentrated on sumptuous production values at the expense of dramatic substance. In the Soviet Union, a series of musical biopics parallel-ing prestigious transfers of Russian operas to the big screen included *Glinka* (dir. Lev Arnshtam, 1946), *Mussorgsky* (dir. Grigori Roshal, 1950; music arranged by Kabalevsky) and *Rimsky-Korsakov* (dir. Gennadi Kazansky and Roshal, 1952). The USSR also saw a vogue for the *kino-kontsert* (film con-cert), which featured classical music and ballet, and included *Concert Waltz* (dir. Ilya Trauberg, 1940), with music by Shostakovich; the general concept provided valuable cultural propaganda during wartime (Riley 2005, 49).

The classical-music biopic was transformed by director Ken Russell in the 1970s into often lurid spectacles that wisely laid no claim to historical authenticity. Experienced from his more sober television 'drama documen-taries' on Delius, Elgar and others, Russell launched himself on the lav-ishly imaginative big-screen biopics *The Music Lovers* (Tchaikovsky, 1970), *Mahler* (1974) and *Lisztomania* (1975). Of these, the last was by far the most poorly received, described by *Sight and Sound* as a 'gaudy compendium of camp, second-hand Freud and third-rate pastiche . . . like a bad song without end' (quoted in J. Walker 2006, 678); the director had cast his *Tommy* star Roger Daltrey in the title role because he regarded Liszt as 'the Elton John of his day', later commenting: 'The fact that the treatment of the subject matter was symbolically and intellectually above the heads of the Daltrey fans was unfortunate, for the film was pure magic' (Russell 2001, 20). The two earlier films were less excessive, but even so the director had difficulty in persuad-ing producers to take the projects on. Harry Saltzman refused to finance the Tchaikovsky film before Russell had completed the far safer commercial bet *Billion Dollar Brain* (1967), telling him 'Get that one under your belt, get yourself a name and then we'll talk Tchaikovsky'. After the Len Deighton thriller proved not to be the hit he had anticipated, Saltzman lost interest and told Russell when he raised the Tchaikovsky subject again: 'Too late . . . Dimitri Tiomkin's gonna make one for the Soviets [*Tchaikovsky*, dir. Igor Talankin, 1969] and he's already writing the music [!]'. Russell eventually sold the idea to United Artists:

> at the mention of the word Tchaikovsky, their faces fell. 'What's it about?' they asked mournfully.
>
> 'It's about a homosexual who falls in love with a nymphomaniac,' I said. Without another word they gave me the money. It was the most successful pitch of my life.   (Russell 2001, 12)

For both his Mahler and Tchaikovsky soundtracks, Russell read explicit biographical meanings into the musical extracts he selected, for instance equating the second subject of the first movement of Mahler's Sixth Sym-phony with 'a musical portrait of [the composer's] wife, which tells us more

11.1 Julian Sands as Franz Liszt (right) and Hugh Grant as Frédéric Chopin (left) in *Impromptu* (1989).

in a few bars than a lifetime's research could ever reveal – not only about the woman but about Mahler himself . . . And so you gradually put the pieces of this symphonic jigsaw together to end up with a colourful portrait, in which the man's life is seen through the mirror of his music' (Russell 2001, 32).

Russell consciously structured his Mahler film in the manner of a rondo, with segments of the composer's long train journey interspersed with episodic flashbacks (Russell 2001, 98). Later biopics continued to explore the creative narrative application of cues culled from pre-existing pieces, a procedure that in essence dated back to the silent era but had become more widespread since the groundbreaking soundtrack for *Brief Encounter*. Like several earlier films in the genre, *Amadeus* (dir. Milos Forman, 1984) was based on a stage play: the narrative flow of Peter Shaffer's vivid fantasia on Mozart's life was somewhat impeded in its filmed version by the gratu-itous insertion of spectacular operatic set-pieces, but disparate chunks of Mozart's music elsewhere were neatly spliced together to serve as effective dramatic underscoring, most noticeably in the direct juxtaposition of seg-ments from two dark works both cast in D minor, the Piano Concerto K466 and the overture to *Don Giovanni* (Joe 2006, 65). *Impromptu* (dir. James Lapine, 1989) retold the liaison between Chopin and George Sand with a modern sassiness and lively spirit all too often lacking in period drama, its wit and energy something of a one-off in the genre. The better-known *Immortal Beloved* (dir. Bernard Rose, 1994), relating a mysterious episode in the life of Beethoven, to some extent marked a return to the romantic clichés of earlier composer biopics, especially in its overdone emphasis on the nature of genius and its retelling of 'the Romantic epic in which the life of a male creative artist is essentially portrayed as the direct result of a hopeless love for a distant beloved, thus showing that through suffering, and only through suffering, the right kind of inspiration could emerge' (Lockwood 1997, 196); but the film again showed how the careful spotting of diegetic and nondiegetic musical extracts from the composer's works could aid both atmosphere and pacing.

Shine (dir. Scott Hicks, 1996) picked up where *Brief Encounter* had left off by showcasing Rachmaninov's Third Concerto as a vital ingredient in the film's portrayal of the mental illness of Australian pianist David Helfgott, whose own performing career was revived as a direct result of the film's success and led both to a global concert tour and an appearance at the Academy Awards ceremony. In the film, the horrendously difficult Rachmaninov work becomes emblematic of a father's overbearing, stifling and unrealistic ambitions for his son, the work's status as a musical White Whale ironically confirmed when, after the son's breakdown (attendant on performing the piece after he has defied his father by moving away from home), he finds creative therapy by playing lightweight classics for the amusement of customers at a bar called Moby's. Slow-motion footage of Helfgott trampolining while listening on his Walkman to a serene aria by Vivaldi suggests the powerfully therapeutic nature of such pre-romantic music, and a still image from this scene was deemed strong enough to feature on the film's poster and other publicity material. Both this film and *Hilary and Jackie* (dir. Anand Tucker, 1998), based on the controversial memoirs of cellist Jacqueline Du Pré's siblings, clearly illustrate the basic scoring techniques commonly encountered in modern classical biopics. In both, the nondiegetic scoring (in *Shine*, composed by David Hirschfelder) highlights the solo instrument played by the protagonist; both soundtracks later focus on a single pre-existing work that acquires various levels of extra-musical meaning, and also include other pre-existing pieces for the relevant instrument as nondiegetic cues; both are about family relationships strained by eccentric geniuses and therefore acquire a universal appeal outside their specific musical milieux; and both use distorted sound effects and slow motion during live-performance sequences to indicate incipient mental breakdown.

The original score for *Hilary and Jackie* by Barrington Pheloung features a nondiegetic solo cello 'protagonist', most strikingly in the film's mysterious prologue where the two young Du Pré sisters encounter a mysterious stranger on the beach: the cello commences in the murky depths as the main titles begin, then ascends in tessitura as the girls are revealed, before ushering in the full orchestra for the blaze of sunset against which the stranger is silhouetted. The pre-existing work chosen to acquire accumulated extra-musical meaning throughout the course of the film is, not surprisingly, Elgar's Cello Concerto, with which Du Pré was inextricably associated. This is first used structurally when Du Pré practises the solo part of the first movement in the middle of the night in order to disturb her sister's lovemaking: as the solo part makes its thrilling ascent to a top E and the full orchestra enters, there is a synchronized jump cut to a shot of the cellist being evicted from the sister's cottage. By the time of Du Pré's mental and physical breakdown and subsequent untimely death, the Elgar has acquired a special poignancy that is fully exploited in the epilogue, a surreal recapitulation of the prologue in which the stranger on the beach is finally revealed to be the adult Du Pré talking to her child-self, this disturbing image now accompanied by the Elgar and not the Pheloung cue from the beginning of the film. Always a popular concert and recorded item, the choice of the Elgar Concerto both helped the film's marketing and boosted sales of the sheet music, which was reissued by Novello with a still from the film on the cover.

Like the biopics, fictional films set in a classical-music milieu or featuring well-known musicians in starring roles also ranged from the ludicrous to the sublime. British examples from the 1930s included the Paderewski vehicle *Moonlight Sonata* (dir. Lothar Mendes, 1937), in which the pianist interacts with survivors of a plane crash. For *Men of Two Worlds* (US title *Witch Doctor*; dir. Thorold Dickinson, 1946), Arthur Bliss supplied a 'Baraza' concerto, supposedly written by an African composer; the film's soundtrack was highly unusual for its time in also utilizing field recordings of traditional African music (Huntley [1947], 86). A superior classical-milieu melodrama from an expatriate director working in Hollywood, Max Ophül's *Letter from an Unknown Woman* (1948) was an acknowledged masterpiece of the 'woman's picture' genre that transformed its ostensibly chocolate-box view of old Vienna into a haunting and sensitive tale of a woman's unrequited love for an objectionable pianist, its music track (arranged by Daniele Amfitheatrof) making structural use of piano music by Liszt in a manner analogous to the scoring of *Brief Encounter*.

A rich use of classical music was always a notable characteristic of French cinema. Jean Renoir's *La Règle du jeu* (1939) includes a memorably choreographed version of Saint-Saëns's *Danse macabre* on player piano, to which a skeleton and ghosts dance as part of the house party's theatricals. Robert

Bresson's early films in the 1940s were scored symphonically by organist Jean-Jacques Grünenwald, but the director's output from 1956 onwards tended to feature pre-existing classical pieces by composers such as Mozart, Lully (e.g. *Pickpocket*, 1959), Schubert and Monteverdi. Bresson's choice of classical tracks was somewhat arbitrary and the music used with a clinical sense of filmic architecture, typical of the New Wave, that arguably dated back to the abstract use of baroque music in Jean-Pierre Melville's Cocteau tale *Les Enfants terribles* (1950). Bresson's *Un condamné à mort s'est échappé* (1956), for example, is punctuated by extracts from Mozart's Mass in C minor K427 in a manner through which the music 'strictly speaking loses its privileged status to become simply raw material' (Lacombe and Porcile 1995, 269). By contrast, the framing use of Monteverdi's Magnificat in *Mouchette* (1966), although not intended to support or reinforce specific visual imagery, had a specific extra-musical purpose in seeking to 'envelop the film in Christianity' (quoted in Lacombe and Porcile 1995, 268); indeed, the music – which at the end accompanies a sustained shot of the river in which Mouchette has suddenly drowned herself – is the only comforting element in a thoroughly bleak story about a young misfit. Bresson's companion piece to *Mouchette*, a Christian parable about a saintly donkey entitled *Au hasard Balthazar* (also 1966), relied on the sharp contrast between popular jazzy songs in a contemporary idiom by Jean Wiener, always functioning diegetically (as had Wiener's pop instrumentals in *Mouchette*), and the nondiegetic use of brief excerpts from an austere piano sonata by Schubert, consistently associated with the animal and the innocent and docile girl to whom it belongs. The Schubert is sometimes used anempathetically, with a major-key passage accompanying melancholic images and minor-key music tracked against scenes of childhood joy, and the only moment of levity comes in the extended main-title cue which is suddenly interrupted by the disembodied braying of the unseen donkey before being resumed.

For François Porcile, one of the few benefits of the explosion of classical-music plundering in post-war French films was an increased public awareness of music then little known in the country; areas of neglect included works by Brahms, whose first String Sextet was featured in Louis Malle's *Les Amants* (1958) as an accompaniment to 'one of the most lyrical love sequences in film history' (Cowie 2004, 35). Malle's later uses of classical music were more restrained, notably the simple deployment of a recurring Schubert theme of dignified simplicity in *Au revoir les enfants* (1987) – a film in which the only other music was a violin-and-piano accompaniment to a diegetic screening of Chaplin's *The Immigrant*, the choice of Saint-Saëns's *Rondo capriccioso* dictated by the need for 'something quite bizarre' (French 1993, 174). In his study of the aesthetics of French film music, Porcile cited as examples of French directors' 'melomania' a string of usages of music by Beethoven and Mozart in the films of Aurel, Demy, Franju, Godard, Kast, Reichenbach, Valère and Varda, and lamented a parallel trend towards demanding straightforward pastiche classical styles from versatile but undervalued film composers such as Delerue and Duhamel (Lacombe and Porcile 1995, 276–8). With Hitchcockian resonances, Truffaut set a scene in *The Bride Wore Black* (1967) at a classical concert, and had his serial-killer heroine play a recording of her favourite Vivaldi Mandolin Concerto at crucial moments in the plot.

Another French director who plundered classical music for his sound-tracks was Bertrand Blier, for example in the romantic comedies *Préparez vos mouchoirs* (1978) and *Trop belle pour toi* (1989). In a riotously hilarious take on Godard-like black humour, Blier's surreal *Buffet froid* (*Cold Cuts*, 1979), based on elements from *film noir* and the *roman policier*, used no music at all for nearly one hour then introduced an unseen diegetic performance of Brahms in a domestic interior; the entering police inspector promptly complains 'Damn it! Music! I hate it! Especially strings! Let's get out! I smell trouble!' Later, the afflicted cop ends up in bed in the same building and is forced to endure the chamber ensemble play Brahms's G major Quintet to him in his bedroom for therapy. He shoots his way out by killing all five off screen, and it is later revealed (when he arrests an innocent string player who moves into his high-rise) that his late wife had been a violinist whose scales got on his nerves – so he had killed her by plugging her violin into the mains. Among the more sober applications of classical music in recent French cinema was *Beau travail* (dir. Claire Denis, 1999), a modern updating of Melville's naval yarn *Billy Budd* now reset in the French Foreign Legion and drawing on music from Britten's opera based on the novella, which was spotted seemingly at random so that energetic Britten climaxes coincided with slowly moving meditative scenes of implied homoeroticism (Laing 2006).

Godard's idiosyncratic soundtracks (considered in Chapter 8) some-times brought classical music into direct collision with popular culture, nowhere more bizarrely than in *Weekend* (1967), which includes a surreal diegetic performance of Mozart's Piano Sonata in D major K576 on a concert grand in a ramshackle village square, during which the pianist interrupts his playing in order to philosophize about the aesthetics of music – in pointed contrast to the spontaneous pop drumming later performed in a forest by a member of a group of hippy cannibals. Fragmentary use of musical snippets from Beethoven's string quartets is a characteristic of Godard's *Le Nouveau monde* (1962), *Une femme mariée* (1965) and – more substantially – in

Prénom: Carmen (1983). In the last, the Beethoven extracts are heard not only nondiegetically (when the director uses his familiar ploy of suddenly truncating and restarting the recording) but also performed diegetically by a string quartet rehearsing for their unwitting participation in the soundtrack of a spurious film project designed as a cover for a kidnapping; typically, Godard's image track and soundtrack appear to be significantly at odds until the connection between the subplots is revealed at a late stage, and the disorientation this creates in the spectator has been identified by Annette Davison as a critique of traditional Hollywood-style film scoring (Davison 2004, 84). At a crucial point in the narrative two entirely different chunks of Beethoven, one diegetic and the other assumed to be nondiegetic, are disconcertingly superimposed. The director claimed that it was his personal experience of listening to Beethoven before working on the film that inspired some of the mechanics of its plot, and confirmed that part of the desire to use profound art music of this kind was to instil a sense of seriousness into a project that might otherwise be considered overly clinical (Schroeder 2002, 257).

French classical-milieu films acquired a new surface glossiness after the release of Claude Sautet's *Un Cœur en hiver* (1991). The intellectual interest of the film's audio-visual structure notwithstanding (see J. Brown 2004), the restrained acting and clinical cinematography of this enterprise would on their own have offered perilously little emotional suggestiveness without the soundtrack's pervasive use of ravishingly beautiful music by Ravel, the film's plot a love triangle between two stringed-instrument manufacturers and a glamorous performer – the triangular relationship loosely reflected in the instrumentation of Ravel's Piano Trio. Designedly disturbing was the conservatory-set *The Piano Teacher* (*La Pianiste*; dir. Michael Haneke, 2001), in which all music cues were diegetic and classical, though some continued into succeeding scenes to serve continuity purposes; the emphasis on melodious Schubert was traditional enough, but the dramatic context of graphically portrayed sexual urges and even self-mutilation reflected a Kubrick-like degree of calculated anempathy. Greater subtlety informed *The Page Turner* (*La Tourneuse de pages*; dir. Denis Dercourt, 2006), an understated psychological revenge thriller with a strong and direct diegetic use of uncomplicated music by Schubert and Shostakovich, specifically selected by the director (himself a professional viola player) so that it could be played accurately and without undue effort by the actors: they all knew how to play the relevant instruments, but in the interests of performative quality mimed to professional playback recordings on set. Similarly, the cello playing in *Hilary and Jackie* (by both young and old protagonists) had been distinguished by considerable accuracy of left-hand fingering and bowing, the turning point in verisimilitude of playback miming having come

with Richard Chamberlain's intensive preparation for his Tchaikovsky performances in Russell's *The Music Lovers* (Russell 2001, 61); all these examples were a marked improvement on the often hilariously inept miming in
Golden Age music films.

Period, nationality, class

One of the most common and least creative uses of classical music in
film is as an agent for establishing appropriate period, national or cultural associations, a device common to all national cinemas in the West
and increasingly widespread since the 1950s when Rózsa's epic assignments
had demonstrated the dramatic usefulness of musico-historical awareness in film soundtracks (see Chapter 5). The eighteenth-century theatricals of Renoir's *Le Carrosse d'or* (*The Golden Coach*, 1953), for example, are allied to the music of Vivaldi, and Visconti used the music of
Bruckner for his *Senso* (1953), its plot concerned with the Austrian invasion of Italy in the 1860s. Years later Visconti famously foregrounded the
'Adagietto' from Mahler's Fifth Symphony in his evocative treatment of
Thomas Mann's *Death in Venice* (1971), a *belle époque* story that takes place
less than a decade after the symphony was completed. Artistic licence or
plain ineptitude sometimes defeated historical accuracy, as in Kubrick's
Barry Lyndon (1975), in which the inclusion of the slow movement from
Schubert's E flat major Piano Trio was an anachronism for action set in
the 1770s, as was the diegetic performance in London of a concerto by
Bach. Straightforward examples of period-establishing classics from late
twentieth-century films include the exclusive use of Verdi for the Dick-
ensian ambience of *Little Dorrit* (dir. Christine Edzard, 1987); of Handel
in *The Madness of King George* (dir. Nicholas Hytner, 1994), alongside
adapted cues subtly recomposed in Handelian style by George Fenton; and
of the Russian romantics in *Leo Tolstoy's Anna Karenina* (dir. Bernard Rose,
1997).

National and artistic cultures are similarly characterized by appropriate classical music. Thus the Mahler usage in *Death in Venice* is entirely
apt to accompany the decline of a protagonist who (in Visconti's idiosyncratic reworking of the novella) is a troubled German romantic composer
who has formerly spent his creative summers surrounded by the beauty of
nature, and the film can be interpreted using either of two quite different
perceptions of Mahler's art: as a weary expression of what Adorno termed
'the truth of the unattainable', or as the last kitsch-laden gasp of a degener-
ate romanticism (Flinn 2004, 70). Even in the often New Age soundtracks
of German director Werner Herzog, the music of Richard Strauss can be

used to conjure up an aura of high Teutonic culture, as when strains from the tone poem *Death and Transfiguration* accompany moody images of the title character's steamship plying the Amazon in *Fitzcarraldo* (1982), other musical elements here including folksy popular electronics from Popol Vuh and a diegetic gramophone recording of Caruso's singing played to compete with native drums, the eclectic soundtrack as a whole serving as an example of what Caryl Flinn has termed a 'profound sense of aesthetic impurity' (Flinn 2004, 3). Flinn has closely analysed the myriad uses to which directors of the New German Cinema from the mid-1960s to the 1980s put the masterworks of the Austro-German tradition in their soundtracks in order to deconstruct traditional perspectives on their country's classical canon – particularly the music of Beethoven and Wagner, which had formerly been associated both with German dominance of the development of high art and the egregious genocide of the ultra-nationalistic fascist impulse. Beethoven's Ninth Symphony thereby becomes an 'acoustic icon of official German culture' (Flinn 2004, 13) and is subjected to various ironic applications in films such as Hans-Jürgen Syberberg's *Our Hitler* (1977), Rainer Werner Fassbinder's *The Marriage of Maria Braun* and Alexander Kluge's *The Patriot* (both 1979). Fassbinder's preferred living composer Peer Raben exemplifies the New German Cinema's tendency to draw attention to the artifice of using pre-existing music as a mechanism for discrediting its extra-musical associations: 'Recordings are smashed or badly performed, pieces altered or damaged, as he wages violence against Europe's canonic repertoire' (Flinn 2004, 85).

Elsewhere we have seen how nineteenth-century Italian opera has consistently been used to characterize both European Italians and Italian Americans (see Chapter 9). In *The Unbearable Lightness of Being* (dir. Philip Kaufman, 1987), the eccentric chamber music of Janáček provides a suitably wistful and enigmatic atmosphere for the story's austere setting in Soviet-controlled Czechoslovakia. Sometimes deliberate anachronism can make a cultural point, as when Elgar's 'Nimrod' (from the *Enigma Variations*) intrudes at the close of the stylish Tudor political thriller *Elizabeth* (dir. Shekhar Kapur, 1998) to suggest the dawn of an Elizabethan patriotism that will shape British culture for centuries to come, or Baz Luhrmann's decision to end his otherwise pop-dominated *William Shakespeare's Romeo + Juliet* (1996) with Wagner's *Liebestod*, not only to highlight the universality of the tragedy but also to harmonize with the visually lush quasi-operatic tableau with which his film concludes. Occasionally an ironic usage demands pre-knowledge for the allusion to work: in *Billion Dollar Brain*, for example, the march from Shostakovich's Seventh ('Leningrad') Symphony accompanies an American megalomaniac's inciting a Baltic state to rebel against the Soviets in a neat inversion of the music's staunchly pro-Soviet origins.

In Luhrmann's *Romeo + Juliet,* bustling Mozart is used to character-ize preparations for a party in the mansion of the well-heeled Capulets. The close identification between elegant classical music and class, refine-ment and wealth is long established in the cinema: in *The Paper Chase* (dir. James Bridges, 1973), baroque music seems appropriate to the Har-vard setting, while even in a low-budget domestic drama such as *Kramer versus Kramer* (dir. Robert Benton, 1979) the snippets of Vivaldi and Pur-cell – the former at one point making a surprise diegetic appearance in the hands of street buskers – seemingly add a dash of middle-class dignity to the divorce proceedings. More interesting have been the anempathetic uses to which classical music has been put (see below) and, in Hollywood at least, its pervasive function as a means to typecast master criminals of non-US descent. Taking its hint from the Bond baddies of the 1960s, the Holly-wood thriller and disaster movie in the period between the fall of the Berlin Wall (when the traditional Soviet enemy became redundant) and the Gulf-dominated 1990s (when Moslem terrorists began to be featured in its stead) often portrayed its evil characters as highly cultured Europeans with thick accents, a phenomenon discussed in detail by Robynn Stilwell in her analy-sis of Michael Kamen's reworking of Beethoven's Ninth to characterize the German terrorist leader in *Die Hard* (dir. John McTiernan, 1988): the ter-rorist's elegant appearance and implied musical refinement provide the strongest possible contrast to the all-American vest-wearing Bruce Willis hero who listens to pop music and ultimately saves the day (Stilwell 1997a). Kamen initially resisted McTiernan's suggestion that he use Beethoven's Ninth for this purpose ('please, if you want me to fuck with some German composer, I'm very happy to take Wagner to pieces . . . This is one of the greatest pieces of music celebrating the nobility of the human spirit of all time and you want me to aim it at a bunch of gangsters in an American com-mercial film'), and only relented when the director explained that he viewed his baddies as direct descendants of the droogs in Kubrick's *A Clockwork Orange* (Shivers 1995, 13; see below).

Ken Russell commented of the protagonist in his *Dogboys* (1998):

> as every filmgoer knows, if a character plays classical music in movieland, he
> is inherently evil and beyond redemption: characters like the wicked
> Captain Nemo in *20,000 Leagues under the Sea* [dir. Richard Fleischer, 1954],
> playing Bach on the organ, and the insane Laird Cregar in *Hangover Square*
> [dir. John Brahm, 1945] playing Bernard Herrmann's manic piano concerto
> as the house burns down. So I supposed the baddie's love of Bach was just a
> cinematic cliché, a sort of last straw at an attempt at characterisation.
>
> (Russell 2001, 50)

Russell's baddie listens to Bach on his Walkman while hunting down escaped convicts as a sport, and in the process demonstrates a fondness for German shepherd dogs. In order to get into his part, the Method actor taking the leading role demanded an explanation for these character traits, so Russell concocted a spurious back story relating how the man's daughter had been a gifted organist who was raped and murdered by an escaped prisoner in spite of her pet Alsatian's martyrdom as it tried to ward off the fatal attack.

Stanley Kubrick

The front-rank director who engaged most thoroughly and influentially with classical music was Kubrick, who in his youth had been deeply impressed by Prokofiev's score to *Alexander Nevsky*. Early in his career Kubrick directed a number of films with music by Gerald Fried, from his first foray into documentary making to the feature film that brought him international recognition (*Paths of Glory*, 1957). Fried's scoring for Kubrick was in places modernistic; percussion featured prominently, perhaps because Kubrick had himself been an amateur percussionist in his schooldays, and this was to remain a prominent aspect of the director's later compilation scores. After Kubrick and Fried parted company, the latter commented of the director's evident dislike of working with composers: 'Either I was so good that he couldn't replace me or I was so bad that he lost faith in contemporary composers' (quoted in LoBrutto 1998, 150). More plausibly, Kubrick's notoriously obsessional attitude towards the craft of film-making and his growing status as a major *auteur* in the 1960s may have influenced his decision henceforth to work largely with pre-composed music rather than collaborate with musicians. The control he exerted over his music tracks in later years was absolute, and even when using music by contemporary composers such as Ligeti and Penderecki he resorted to dismembering pre-existing works rather than commissioning bespoke scores from the composers he admired.

In 1960 Kubrick was given the opportunity to work with a leading Hollywood composer, Alex North, on the Roman epic *Spartacus*, but because the director had been brought in to rescue a troubled project and North had already been contracted to compose the score, the collaboration was (for Kubrick) wholly atypical. The director restlessly experimented with the temporary provision of pre-recorded music during editing, and it was his fondness for such 'temp tracks' that ultimately led to the notorious rejection of North's elaborate score to *2001* some years later (see below). For his darkly comic version of Vladimir Nabukov's notorious novel *Lolita* (1962), Kubrick was evidently still prepared to contemplate collaborating with an established film composer, since he invited Herrmann to compose the music. Herrmann predictably refused when Kubrick stipulated that the score be based on a theme in a popular idiom that had already been composed by Bob Harris. The task of scoring *Lolita* passed to Nelson Riddle who, in addition to supplying conventional underscoring, arranged Harris's theme for piano and strings in a warmly romantic vein with more than a hint of the Rachmaninov used throughout *Brief Encounter*. Ever aware that Nabukov's screenplay dealt with the highly sensitive issue of pederasty and might therefore fall foul of the censors, Kubrick stopped a recording session when he felt one of Riddle's minor-key themes to be too darkly suggestive (LoBrutto 1998, 214). (When *Lolita* was remade by director Adrian Lyne in 1997, Morricone's score also inhabited dreamily romantic territory before the inevitable deterioration of the relationship between Humbert and Lolita.) Kubrick made more overtly satirical use of popular styles in his next black comedy, *Dr Strangelove or: How I Learned to Stop Worrying and Love the Bomb* (1964), with music by Laurie Johnson: especially witty conjunctions were the slushily romantic music accompanying the opening aerial shots of a B52 bomber copulating with the boom of an in-flight refuelling aircraft, and the use of the wartime hit 'We'll Meet Again' for the climactic dropping of the atomic bomb.

It was with his science-fiction classic *2001: A Space Odyssey* (1968) that Kubrick became infamous both for his use of classical music and for his peremptory rejection of the score originally commissioned for the film. With its colossal special-effects budget, the movie was something of a gamble for MGM and the producers were disconcerted when it emerged that Kubrick intended to use pre-existing music in the soundtrack. After the first month of filming they were shown a demonstration reel onto which the director had dubbed music from Mendelssohn's incidental score to *A Midsummer Night's Dream* and Vaughan Williams's *Sinfonia Antartica*; the latter was also played on set to create an appropriately mysterious mood when Kubrick later shot the sequence in which the astronaut Bowman makes his climactic journey through the kaleidoscopic Star Gate (LoBrutto 1998, 304). Neither the Mendelssohn nor Vaughan Williams extracts were used in the film, and a scheme to record segments of Mahler's Third Symphony for this purpose was also abandoned.

The MGM executives made it clear that they preferred Kubrick to commission an original score. The pioneer of inventive science-fiction scoring, Herrmann, was again approached but demanded double his usual fee (R. S. Brown 1994, 291), and Carl Orff was also considered since Kubrick was very much taken with *Carmina Burana* at the time (Chion 2001, 12). The task of scoring *2001* eventually fell to North, who was told by Kubrick that, because of the complexity of the production, the music would need to be composed independently from the visual images. North felt uncomfortable about the director's evident wish to retain some music from the temp track and expressed the desire to compose new music 'that had the ingredients and essence of what Kubrick wanted' and would give the film 'a consistency and homogeneity and contemporary feel' (quoted in Townson 1993). North completed more than 40 minutes of music for *2001*, which was recorded in London in January 1968 and covered the first half of the film up to and including the intermission 'entr'acte' that was then a standard feature of epic scores. At this point, he was told by the director to compose no further cues because the remainder of the film would be accompanied by sound effects, including the noise of breathing. Kubrick, as he had perhaps intended all along, rejected North's music in its entirety after he heard it and duly reinstated his favoured temp cues. North only learnt of this decision when he attended the New York première of the film in April 1968. He later recycled some of the music in his score for the film *Dragonslayer* (dir. Matthew Robbins, 1981), for which he received an Oscar nomination.

The material used by Kubrick for his definitive music track in *2001* embraced a wide variety of styles, and this diversity has been sharply criticized by some commentators who feel that the film demands the kind of musical homogeneity and (arguably inappropriate) narrative momentum that North's score might have provided. The old criticism that the use of familiar classical music can result in a spectator bringing all kinds of extraneous associations to the movie is turned on its head by the argument that, since *2001*, many movie-goers have carried with them indelible associations between the pieces concerned and the images they saw in the film. This is most true of the main-title cue, the opening of Richard Strauss's *Also sprach Zarathustra*, which is now inextricably associated with outer space in the popular imagination – an identification that was quickly strengthened after the film's release when BBC TV used the piece in 1969 as the signature tune for its coverage of the first Apollo moon landing. (Kubrick once said to Leone: 'I've got all Ennio Morricone's albums. Can you explain to me why I only seem to like the music he composed for your films?' Leone replied: 'Don't worry. I didn't think much of Richard Strauss until I saw *2001*' (Frayling 2005, 82).) The phallic symbolism of the music's association with the film's monolith was seemingly tapped when Mike Nichols chose to use it in his otherwise music-less *Catch-22* (1970) to accompany a pretty Italian prostitute sauntering across a Roman piazza and swaying her hips while pursued by the protagonist Yossarian. Nichols's isolated Strauss cue, like Kubrick's, is loud and prominent, reflecting Kubrick's general strategy to foreground the music whenever it is used: as Chion puts it, in *2001* 'the music is *exhibited*, and is rarely mixed with sound effects, more rarely still with dialogue; it refuses to melt in or make common cause with other soundtrack elements' (Chion 2001, 71).

Zarathustra was an apt choice, given the Nietzschean resonances of *2001*'s treatment of human evolution from its origins up to the *Übermensch*, and Kevin Mulhall has observed that the rising three notes of the opening fanfare create an audio-visual correspondence with the alignment of the earth, moon and sun depicted at the beginning of the film. More controversial was the choice of Johann Strauss's *Blue Danube* waltz to accompany the sequence in which a spacecraft travels to, and docks with, a revolving space station. Kubrick felt the waltz would intensify the scene's graceful elegance as an aerial ballet, and cut the images to the rhythm of the recorded music; he had intended to use triple-time music from the outset, trying out the scherzo from Mendelssohn's *A Midsummer Night's Dream* and also request-ing an original waltz from North before settling on the *Blue Danube*. It has been argued that the ultra-familiarity of the Strauss waltz suggests that space travel in the twenty-first century has become commonplace, and that when we continue to hear it during interior shots of the spacecraft it functions as 'muzak'. Given Kubrick's penchant for surreal comedy, however, the musical gesture could simply be an elaborate joke (Kolker 2006, 38). A mournful and meandering melody from Khachaturian's ballet *Gayaneh* is used in the later stages of the film, when the spaceship *Discovery* is on its mission to Jupiter: Kubrick played a Chopin waltz on set to inspire his cast before deciding to use the Khachaturian (Chion 2001, 18–19). Those sceptical, like North, of the use of European romantic music in a futuristic outer-space context will undoubtedly find the film's various applications of the avant-garde music of Ligeti more in keeping with its subject-matter: extracts from *Atmosphères*, *Lux aeterna* and the Requiem provide an eerie accompaniment to the align-ing of the monolith with the sun and the moon, the trip by moon rocket bus, the monolith floating in deep space and the psychedelic trip through the Star Gate. Ligeti's music was also used to replace North's 'entr'acte' during the film's intermission (Chion 2001, 67). As Arved Ashby has pointed out, however, not all listeners will equate Ligeti's music with unsettling emotions and here – as we have elsewhere noted in connection with the soundtracks of the French New Wave – non-representational musical modernism can simply encourage auditors to explore their own subjective responses to the visual images and therefore functions as a 'kind of Rorschach test' (Ashby 2004, 366).

In 1993, Jerry Goldsmith conducted a magisterial recording of North's rejected score to *2001*. A close friend of North's, Goldsmith commented that when he first saw the film he was 'cringing at what I consider to be an abominable misuse of music', and felt that the choice of music was 'idiotic' (LoBrutto 1998, 308). His views were firmly in sympathy with those of North himself, who felt that Kubrick's choice of classical music was inappropriate for Arthur C. Clarke's tale because it indicated a 'Victorian approach with mid-European overtones' (quoted in Townson 1993). North's main-title cue was cunningly modelled directly on the rhetorical gestures of the opening of *Also sprach Zarathustra* in the hope that Kubrick would grow to like it, and the composer provided two alternative types of music for the opening scenes of apes in their prehistoric habitat – a sequence accompanied by no music in the final edit. North's music for the space-station docking sequence is a sparkling scherzo designed to replace the Mendelssohn and Johann Strauss temp tracks, and he provided a haunting vocalise for the moon rocket bus. Electronics are avoided throughout, with a large symphony orchestra used to provide a wide range of timbres (the instrumentation includes organ, harpsichord, celeste, bells, vibraphone and vocalists). Kubrick had at the outset of work on *2001* immersed himself in recordings of electronic music and *musique concrète* before rejecting them in favour of full-blooded romanticism (Chion 2001, 12).

Still more unsettling applications of classical music were to come in Kubrick's *A Clockwork Orange* (1971), based on the book by novelist and composer Anthony Burgess. The principal interests of the film's central character, a schoolboy 'droog' called Alex, are – in the words of its publicity tag – 'rape, ultra-violence, and Beethoven!' The film's graphic portrayal of the first two of these obsessions lent it extraordinary notoriety, with a series of copycat acts of violence in the real world following its release resulting in Kubrick's decision to withdraw the film from circulation in the UK until after his death. (It was duly re-released posthumously in 2000.) Its treatment of classical music was disturbing on account of the unprecedented equation of music traditionally associated with the highest plateau of Western culture with mindless acts of extreme violence. An earlier, unachieved attempt to film *A Clockwork Orange* was to have starred Mick Jagger and the Rolling Stones (Burgess 1990, 142), and the use of rock material as the backdrop would undoubtedly have seemed more logical and consequently less arresting.

After the brightly coloured main-title cards accompanied by Walter Carlos's and Rachel Elkind's electronic transformation of Purcell's *Funeral Music for Queen Mary* (a stark sound recurring throughout the film), provocative use is made of famous works by Rossini, Beethoven, Rimsky-Korsakov and Elgar in a soundtrack that was the first in cinema history to feature Dolby noise reduction throughout. Rossini's overture to *The Thieving Magpie* provides a surreal accompaniment to an early scene of a gang rape carried out by a group of thugs dressed in Wehrmacht uniforms. Carlos created an accelerated version of the *William Tell* Overture as accompaniment to the fast-motion footage of Alex's manic orgy with two compliant young women, while the use of the *Magpie* Overture as Alex beats up his fellow droogs is a further example of simple anempathy. The slow introduction to the *William Tell* Overture is the only classical extract used in genuine empathy with the visual images, accompanying the aerial shots of the prison in which Alex is to be incarcerated and the pathetic scene when he is rejected by his parents after his release.

Alex's obsession with Beethoven – whose music he describes as 'a bit of the old Ludwig van' – is the most notorious element in the film's music track. Kubrick's dark wit is never far below the surface, as when a doorbell chimes the opening 'fate-knocking-at-the-door' motif from Beethoven's Fifth Symphony immediately prior to Alex's bursting into the writer's home, crippling him and raping his wife (as he jauntily sings 'Singin' in the Rain'). Later in the film, the owner of a health farm attacks Alex with a bust of the composer, for which she is bludgeoned to death with an enormous phallic sculpture. The 'Ode to Joy' from the Ninth Symphony is sung diegetically, and with extreme incongruity, by a patron of the milk bar where the droogs hang out. Dressed as a dandy, Alex strolls jauntily through a shopping mall to the accompaniment of an electrified version of the march from the Ninth's finale; he pauses at a record stall which is prominently displaying the soundtrack album from *2001*. Alex's bedroom is a veritable shrine to the great composer: a poster of Beethoven's face dominates the room as Alex fantasizes to the accompaniment of the Ninth's scherzo. Later, his prison cell is seen to contain a bust of Beethoven, though it is to the patriotic strains of Elgar's *Pomp and Circumstance* marches that we are introduced to the Minister of the Interior who selects him for experimental reform. The funky version of the march from Beethoven's Ninth returns as Alex is forced to watch footage of Nazi goose-stepping and associated atrocities ('it's not fair I should feel ill when I hear lovely lovely Ludwig van!' he screams), and the writer subsequently tortures him by playing him the scherzo of the Ninth at considerable volume. Alex is as a direct result compelled to throw himself from the window of his locked room, the Beethoven having been distorted electronically to intensify the sense of nightmarish terror.

Kubrick commented that in *A Clockwork Orange* his intention had been

> to be faithful to the novel and to try to see the violence from Alex's point of view, to show that it was great fun for him, the happiest part of his life, that it was like some great action ballet . . . It was necessary to find a way of stylizing the violence, just as Burgess does by his writing style. The ironic counterpoint of the music was certainly one of the ways of achieving this. All the scenes of violence are very different without the music . . . the violence is turned into dance . . . in cinematic terms, I should say that movement and music must inevitably be related to dance, just as the rotating space station and the docking Orion spaceship in *2001* moved to the 'Blue Danube'.
>
> (quoted in LoBrutto 1998, 338–9)

Burgess was not a great admirer of Kubrick's film, but he singled out the film's music track as conceptually remarkable:

> There was, certainly, an influence that could not be wholly malign, and that was the musical content of *A Clockwork Orange*, which was not just an emotional stimulant but a character in its own right. If the pop-loving young could be persuaded to take Beethoven's Ninth seriously – even in its Moog form – then one could soften the charge of scandal with the excuse of artistic uplift. But the film, and perhaps the book, seemed to deny the Victorian association of great music with lofty morality. There were still musicologists around who alleged that Beethoven opened up a vision of divinity. Alex gets something very much opposed to that out of the scherzo of the Ninth, which sets ikons of Christ marching while making a communist salute.   (Burgess 1990, 246)

When invited to dinner at Kubrick's house, Burgess illustrated at the piano how 'the Ode to Joy and "Singin' in the Rain" . . . go in acceptable counterpoint. I could see the gleam in [Kubrick's] eye of a commercial exploitation, but he let it go' (Burgess 1990, 246). Their meeting spurred Burgess to write his Regency novel *Napoleon Symphony*, to be based on the four-movement pattern of a Mozart symphony; Kubrick made the obvious proposal that Beethoven's 'Eroica' Symphony should be Burgess's model, and had in mind that the resulting novel would provide the basis for a screenplay on the life of Napoleon he had long wished to film but which in the event would remain unachieved.

Kubrick made sustained but much less imaginative use of classical music in the soundtrack to his film version of Thackeray's novel *Barry Lyndon* (1975), although his first and somewhat extraordinary thought had been to buy the rights to Rota's famous *Godfather* theme for this purpose. Distinguished by its beautiful photography and meticulous attention to period detail, *Barry Lyndon* was marred not only by its pedestrian script and sometimes wooden acting, but also by an obsessive overworking of a limited amount of musical material. The director commissioned Leonard Rosenman to adapt and conduct selections from baroque and classical works, including music by Bach, Handel, Mozart and Vivaldi. Rosenman's most important contribution to the film lay in his canny rescoring of a baroque bass-line for ominous percussion: when heard in isolation, as during duel scenes, this idea generated considerable tension. But, as ever, Kubrick had control over the disposition of the music in the final edit, and Rosenman was staggered by the ineptitude of the results: 'When I saw this incredibly boring film with all the music I had picked out going over and over again, I thought, "My God, what a mess!". I was going to refuse the Oscar [which the film subsequently received for best adapted score]' (LoBrutto 1998, 405).

More considered was Kubrick's tracking of *The Shining* (1980) with modernistic music by Bartók, Penderecki and Ligeti. Wendy (formerly Walter) Carlos and Rachel Elkind supplied additional electronics, which Kubrick termed 'low fly-bys', meaning 'sounds that would sneak into you, subconsciously' (LoBrutto 1998, 448), and ominously reworked the *Dies irae* chant for the main-title sequence. By focusing on a suggestive tritone at the first appearance of the two murdered girls at the haunted Overlook Hotel, they created a satisfyingly audible link with the soundworld of Bartók's *Music for Strings, Percussion and Celeste*. The eerie 'night music' of the latter's slow movement was carefully matched to the visual images, notably in the first sequence in the hotel's maze where a *sforzando* coincided with Jack Torrance's bouncing of a ball and the changes of musical texture were synchronized with the shift from an aerial view of an architect's model of the maze to a bird's-eye shot of the real exterior with Jack's wife and child at the centre (Donnelly 2005, 48–50). Elsewhere, the sounds of the East European avant-garde perfectly intensified the various senses of claustrophobia, expectancy, nightmarish terror and fundamental irrationality central to Stephen King's chilling tale, and furthered by Kubrick's vivid use of (then novel) Steadicam techniques. Shooting many scenes without sound, which was dubbed in postproduction, Kubrick took advantage of the silent-film tradition of playing atmospheric music on set to inspire his actors: Stravinsky's *Rite of Spring* was played on a portable cassette machine during the filming of the climactic scene in the maze in which the demented Jack pursues his son with an axe, for example.

The music tracks for Kubrick's last two films were tame by comparison with the landmark efforts of *2001, A Clockwork Orange* and *The Shining*. His contribution to the genre of the Vietnam war movie, *Full Metal Jacket* (1987), made prominent use of pop; there was so little original music by Abigail Mead – the pseudonym of Kubrick's daughter, Vivian – that her score was disqualified from consideration for an Oscar nomination. (The ensuing controversy occurred at a time when there was some consternation at Herbie Hancock's Oscar success with a 'score' largely comprised of on-set performances of jazz standards, and in 1987 the Academy Award rules were amended so as to exclude scores 'diluted by the use of tracked (inserted music not written by the composer) or pre-existing music'.) *Eyes Wide Shut* was released, with excessive hype, in 1999 following the director's death. In addition to original music by Jocelyn Pook and the uninspired use of a banal waltz by Shostakovich, the film's music track is in the latter stages dominated by an obsessive oscillation of two pitches a semitone apart, performed on a solo piano and extracted from Ligeti's *Musica Ricercata II* ('mesto, rigido e ceremoniale'). Whether viewers will find the latter tensely threatening, 'passionate and subjective' (Gorbman 2006, 11), or merely mind-numbingly repetitive will depend on the extent to which they have identified with the thin psychological content of this dreary sex melodrama that quickly collapses under the weight of its own pretensions.

Back to Bach

The diversity of filmic applications to which classical music has been put may be illustrated by a brief examination of contrasting treatments of works by J. S. Bach, whose music is the most inherently abstract in conception of any classical style to have featured prominently in the movies, and thus perhaps the most susceptible to contrasting interpretations. At the time of writing, the Internet Movie Database lists over 300 uses of Bach's music in the movies, in contexts as diverse as Golden Age biblical epics, the Soviet sci-fi film *Solaris* (dir. Andrei Tarkovsky, 1972: see Chion 2001, 157, for a comparison between this film and *2001*), and the modern videogame-inspired fantasy *Lara Croft: Tomb Raider* (dir. Simon West, 2001).

In his native Germany, Bach had in the modern age been transformed into 'an ahistorical myth of German nationality . . . museumized, his music confined to the rarefied realm of concert halls' (Flinn 2004, 2), and as a result the use of his music in the popular medium of cinema sometimes proved to be controversial. This was the case in *Chronicle of Anna Magdalena Bach* (dir. Jean-Marie Straub and Danièle Huillet, 1967), which unusually for its time used period instruments in its soundtrack firmly to anchor the composer's output in a specific historical moment rather than suggest a mythical eternity; the film, in common with others of its time, was identified by critics as an example of musical form apparently influencing cinematic form rather than being subservient to it (Flinn 2004, 2). Outside his native country, Bach's music might be used as emblematic of the powerful irony that the pinnacle of high art it represents hailed from the same culture as the inhuman evils of pernicious fascism. In Steven Spielberg's holocaust film *Schindler's List* (1993), for example, a Wehrmacht soldier plays a rapid movement from one of Bach's English Suites on an upright piano in the Krakow ghetto during its brutal liquidation: the manically aggressive nature of the diegetic performance is well suited to the ongoing massacre, but it is the singular inability of the soldier's comrades to identify the composer (one thinks it might be Mozart) that creates an ironic conjunction of sophistication and brute ignorance.

Fugal techniques, as we saw in Chapter 3, are occasionally used in film music to indicate activity or pursuit, and fugues by Bach have been deployed in such contexts in films of remarkably different natures. When trying to find an apt piano accompaniment to *Battleship Potemkin* in the late silent era, for example, Lev Arnshtam

> struggled for two nights and, finally, having played one of Bach's fugues during the high-powered motion of the ship's engines in the last reel . . . was astounded by the unexpected rhythmic combination that emerged. Then I began to arrange the fugues of the *Well-Tempered Clavier* to sequences of the picture. The combination was grandiose.
>
>   The great mathematician Bach with his iron inevitability of construction seemed to have something in common with the mathematical construction of the picture. I had an almost tangible sense of the growth of architectural form! So the whole picture was tied together with Bach's fugues. Only for the last part did I not remain true and took Bach's 'Chaconne' in Busoni's adaptation.
> (Marshall 1978, 111)

Bach's fugal writing was orchestrated to comparable – if more prosaic – ends to accompany a Harvard student's relentless research work as part of John Williams's score to *The Paper Chase* (Darby and Du Bois 1990, 528). The essentially abstract nature of Bach's counterpoint was visualized with remarkable boldness in the opening section of Disney's *Fantasia* (1940), an interpretation of Stokowski's orchestral version of the Toccata and Fugue in D minor for organ. Used pervasively in the accompaniment to silent films and early sound films based on classical extracts, such as *The Black Cat* (dir. Edgar G. Ulmer, 1934), as title music (for example, in Mamoulian's 1931 *Dr Jekyll and Mr Hyde*), and as conveniently diegetic Gothic underscoring (as in the churchyard assignation scene in *The French Lieutenant's Woman* (dir. Karel Reisz, 1981), a film furnished with a melancholic pastiche score by Carl Davis imbued with the dark colours of Schoenberg's *Transfigured Night*), Bach's famous organ work 'should perhaps be considered as the first major film-music cue ever composed' (R. S. Brown 1994, 182). In *Fantasia*, Bach's music is realized on screen by patterns that gradually shift in the Prelude from live-action shots of sections of the orchestra to stylized instrumental imagery and colour, then – via images of moving bows – to animated graphic effects in the Fugue influenced by the work of Fischinger. Such abstraction is exceptionally rare in commercial cinema, but the quasi-scientific quality of 'pure' music for which Bach's output is often celebrated can make it especially apt for settings involving scientific investigation: an example occurs in the Napoleonic naval adventure *Master and Commander: The Far Side of the World* (dir. Peter Weir, 2003), in which the Cello Suite in G accompanies the ship's surgeon's Darwinesque examination of new species encountered in the Galapagos islands. The nondiegetic usage of Bach is here doubly apposite because, as in the Patrick O'Brian novels on which the film is based, the surgeon (a cellist) and his captain (a violinist) play string duets by Corelli and Boccherini in the captain's cabin for purposes of recreation.

Bach's cello suites, which also feature as nondiegetic scoring in *Hilary and Jackie*, are a recurrent theme in Ingmar Bergman's work. A wry reference to the Swedish director's obsession with Bach's sarabandes for cello appears in his early film *Journey into Autumn* (1954) when a naïve and hedonistic young woman, rifling through a rich older man's record collection after he has invited her to his home for champagne, rejects a recording of a Bach sarabande with some distaste before alighting on some big-band boogie-woogie that delights her. The Sarabande from the Second Cello Suite in D minor was a prominent nondiegetic element in the soundtrack to *Through a Glass Darkly* (1961), a study of schizophrenia to which the Bach brought an additional air of dark introversion well suited to the film's recurrent image of people constructing defensive circles around themselves. The film was the first in a trilogy of what Bergman termed 'chamber plays' in a direct comparison with the intimacy of chamber music, the others being *Winter Light* (1962) and *The Silence* (1963). The latter's soundtrack included a diegetic radio broadcast of Bach's *Goldberg Variations* at a crucial moment of communication in an otherwise dysfunctional personal relationship. Married at the time to a concert pianist, Bergman's musical studies were so important to him that in 1962 he professed the (unachieved) desire to spend an entire year studying Bach's music; he also strongly believed that classical musicians were of a spiritual importance equal to that of prophets and saints.

In a characteristically esoteric gesture, Stephen Sondheim's musical *A Little Night Music* (1973) – based on the plot of Bergman's *Smiles of a Summer Night* (1955) – includes an original sarabande for solo cello played by the character of Henrik. Another Bergman character named Henrik, who appears in the director's final film *Saraband* (made for Swedish television in 2003), is both a cellist and organist, and attempts to teach his talented daughter the cello as she grapples with the difficult decision of whether to embark on a solo career or be an orchestral musician (a professional and social dilemma Bergman had earlier explored through the character of the violinist in *To Joy* (1950), a domestic drama about two married musicians). The suicidal Henrik of *Saraband* is embroiled in an incestuous and utterly dependent relationship on his daughter and finds temporary solace only in Bach's organ works and the ambiguously chromatic Sarabande from the Fifth Cello Suite in C minor – a favourite work of the director's. Again a Bach cello work stands for what Henrik's father terms 'voluntary isolation', but snippets of this and other classical pieces (by Bach, Brahms and Bruckner) also serve a purely structural function in this most tightly organized of all Bergman's films: the ritual is played out in ten segments punctuated by title cards coinciding with asynchronous sound events, each segment involving a 'duet' between two of the four characters and the director regarding the film as a whole as a *concerto grosso* with four soloists. Although a direct sequel to *Scenes from a Marriage* (1973), *Saraband* also serves as a conceptual sequel to the musical and personal preoccupations of another earlier film with a musical metaphor in its title – *Autumn Sonata* (1979) – in which Ingrid Bergman starred as a famous concert pianist who communicates with her disturbed daughter through a focal piano lesson on Chopin's Second Prelude, another ambiguously chromatic work chosen to be emblematic of enigmatic emotional repression. In this film, too, solo cello music by Bach is heard in a flashback of the pianist's dead lover playing the instrument.

In another film with prominent cello playing, *Truly, Madly, Deeply* (dir. Anthony Minghella, 1990), music by Bach performed by the female protagonist's deceased lover has a calming influence on her bereavement, its diegetic and nondiegetic status sometimes subtly blurred according to the progress of their ongoing ghostly relationship (Stilwell 1997b). The monochrome main-title sequence shows him playing a viola da gamba sonata, the image suddenly freezing to become a still portrait in a photo frame as the camera pans away to show her continuing the piece alone by singing the melody to her own piano accompaniment. This eloquently suggests that his performance was merely an interiorized memory. In a gently comic moment later in the film, he reappears with a number of other deceased musicians to serenade her with a supernatural performance of a Brandenburg Concerto. *The English Patient* (1996), another film by Minghella, made similarly creative use of both genuine and imitation Bach. The Aria from the *Goldberg Variations* is played diegetically (and, since the performance is from memory and perfectly in tune, somewhat implausibly) by a nurse in wartime Italy who discovers a decrepit piano in bombed-out ruins; but to facilitate the merging of various musical strands towards the end of the film, composer Gabriel Yared supplied pastiche Bach that would fit neatly with both the lush romantic orchestral theme from his original score (which won an Academy Award) and the Hungarian folksong used evocatively in the main titles. A fondness for Bach's keyboard music typecast one of the most notorious screen villains of the modern era, the cannibal Hannibal Lecter, as a typically refined and cultured monster in *The Silence of the Lambs* (dir. Jonathan Demme, 1990) and *Hannibal* (dir. Ridley Scott, 2001). And pastiche Bach has been a useful resource for other films composers, including Rota (whose use of it in *The Godfather* is discussed in Chapter 9) and Legrand, whose score for Losey's *The Go-Between* (1970) included cues in French overture and fugal idioms, their conscious stylization well suited to the emotional restraints of the period setting but also reflecting a neo-classicism that may have been an attempt to provide the director with something altogether different from the rejected score by Richard Rodney Bennett.

Music by Bach might also be present simply to suggest class and cultural distinctions between privileged admirers of the classics and adherents of pop culture, for example in the opening audio-visual mélange of *Harvard Man* (dir. James Toback, 2001). In another film aimed at a teenage market, *Cruel Intentions* (dir. Roger Kumble, 1999), Bach's Fourth Brandenburg Concerto plays nondiegetically to suggest the affluence of a country mansion, and elsewhere in the film the differing implications of diegetic classical music (Beethoven, viewed as objectionable) and pop (a far preferable choice to accompany seduction) are as sharply contrasted as they are in *Harvard Man*. Other considerations behind filmic uses of Bach range from its usefulness as a cheap source of neutral continuity music, as in the appearance of the first prelude from *The Well-Tempered Clavier* in *Picnic at Hanging Rock* (dir. Weir, 1975), where along with the slow movement from Beethoven's 'Emperor' Concerto it also provides a contrast to the haunting panpipe music by Gheorge Zamfir used for the film's more atmospheric sequences, to the conscious sense of tragic aggrandizement that inspired Scorsese to accompany the sordid demise of a Las Vegas crook in a car bombing with an extract from the *St Matthew Passion* in *Casino* (1995) – the Bach coming into its own as the explosion and the crook's catapulted body turn into typically psychedelic main-title animation by Saul and Elaine Bass.

The sombre idiom of Bach's Passions has more typically been associated with dramatic events directly or obliquely recalling the Passion of Christ. When Raksin scored the Passion film *El Redentor* (*The Redeemer*; dir. Joseph Breen and Fernando Palacios, 1959), a joint US/Spanish production, he found his initially dull response to a mediocre picture was suddenly improved by the realization that

> of all the depictions of Jesus and his trials in the world, the greatest was the music of J. S. Bach. And so the whole score is a homage to Bach, and it quotes him in one place. Right near the end, I quoted two bars from the Chromatic Fantasia and Fugue. What I had hoped to do had there been time, which there wasn't, was to get to a certain point and then quote the 'B.A.C.H.' motif [the German pitch spellings of Bach's musical monogram, B♭–A–C–B♮] . . . When I was working on that film, one of the people in the projection room said to me, 'I don't understand this. Everybody in the film is Catholic except you, and you're Jewish. How do you explain that?' I said, 'Simple. It's insurance. I'm a relative of the deceased.'
>
> (interviewed in R. S. Brown 1994, 286)

Although the use of the *St Matthew Passion* (along with other classical gobbets) in Pier Paolo Pasolini's *The Gospel According to St Matthew* (1964) might have seemed far more logical than Scorsese's application of it, the soundtrack of Pasolini's bleak documentary-style film (for which the music was arranged by Luis Enríquez Bacalov) posed more conundrums than it solved by curtailing several of its (often very brief) musical extracts without letting them cadence, and by crudely splicing other segments of music together to prolong them, thereby suggesting an objective attitude towards the music at odds with the raw expressiveness of the African and blues-style vocal pieces used at focal moments in the drama. Significantly, at the still heart of the film when Christ is alone in the wilderness, it is Webern's idiosyncratically clinical arrangement of the six-part fugue from Bach's *Musical Offering*, twice interrupted before it stops dead in mid-structure, that accompanies him.

For Lumet's film version of Peter Shaffer's dark psychological drama *Equus* (1977), Bennett's music sympathized with the plight of the disturbed stable hand – who blinded six horses in a violent frenzy – by taking up an idea linked to the specific reason for his derangement: a picture of Christ crucified over his bed, favoured by his fervently religious mother, had been torn down by his cynical father and replaced with a picture of a horse, onto which icon the boy transferred his worshipping tendencies by relating the animal's suffering (inflicted by equestrian whips and chains) with the torturing of Christ on the cross. Bennett appositely builds a modernized form of melancholic Bach passion music into his sombre score for violin-less string orchestra, the idiom's dramatic identification only made explicit when the boy's psychiatrist comprehends the significance of the two pictures and the Bachian music comes to the fore in an intense two-minute cue as he ponders the boy's bizarre paraphernalia, which included scribbles on a notepad reading 'surely he hath borne our griefs'.

12 State of the art: film music since the New Hollywood

After the crisis in the Hollywood film industry attendant upon the 1948 rulings by which the studios lost their monopolies of distribution outlets, and fuelled by the stiff competition presented by the enormous boom in television viewing in the 1950s, film-makers had attempted to lure spectators back into theatres with widescreen spectacles (as we saw in Chapter 5). Escalating budgets and poor revenue conspired to make many of these high-profile projects commercial failures, however, and the ailing studios came to realize that making feature films, documentaries and cartoons specifically for televisual broadcast – as well as generating income by selling existing films to television networks – was a more viable way of ensuring a 'stabilized economics of distribution' for its products (Neale and Smith 1998, xv). By the beginning of the 1960s, Hollywood had therefore become responsible for providing around 80 per cent of all American primetime television output, half of its contribution consisting of original material and half broadcasts of old films (Maltby 1998, 29). Shrewd executives tapped the lucrative television market before reinvesting in theatrical releases, a strategy demonstrated by Lew Wasserman, the President of MCA responsible for that company's purchase of Universal in 1962, and Steven J. Ross, whose Kinney Corporation absorbed Warner–Seven Arts to become Warner Communications, Inc. in 1969. Ross's empire, which among its activities included a pioneering belief in cable television, was an early example of the vertically integrated media conglomerate that later came to dominate a globalized entertainment industry (Gomery 1998). As a rising generation of independent directors and producers brought with them a greater sense of experimentation and creative daring than cinema had seen either before or since – and an apparently concomitant lack of commercial potential – so the major production companies still continued to pour money into hugely expensive theatrical features that played to ever-dwindling audiences. In 1968 the television networks suddenly lost interest in buying new theatrical films for broadcast, one of the factors which precipitated another severe financial crisis for the film industry at the beginning of the 1970s. At around the same time, musicians' livelihoods were affected by a thirteen-month strike by the Composers and Lyricists Guild of America in 1971–2, and a subsequent legal action against the Association of Motion Picture and Television Producers (settled out of court) over vexed issues of working conditions and copyright (Prendergast 1992, 156–8).

As these difficulties coincided with a crucial moment in cinema's search for new aesthetic horizons, regarded by some commentators as a period of directionless floundering and the failure of innovation to sustain itself (see, for example, Belton 1994), it was inevitable that the fortunes of Hollywood film-making could only be revived by an initiative that sought to recoup the greatest possible dividends from the safest possible projects. The establishment of a New Hollywood order in the mid-1970s was solidified by the financing – on an individual 'package' basis – of big-budget adventure blockbusters aimed at a largely undifferentiated and increasingly international spectatorship, revenue being generated by exhibition through the saturation booking of projection venues (which became more adaptable to fluctuating needs with the establishment of the multiplex format in the 1980s), relentless television advertising, and synergistic ties with record and merchandizing companies. Wasserman blazed this populist trail with Steven Spielberg's *Jaws* in 1975, devoting $1.8 million to advertising the film prior to its release (McBride 1997, 255) and establishing the modern practice of spending more on a film's advertising than on its production budget. Universal's enormous successes with Spielberg culminated with *E.T. The Extra Terrestrial* (1982) and his work also provided blockbuster hits for Columbia (*Close Encounters of the Third Kind*, 1977) and Paramount (*Raiders of the Lost Ark*, 1981). Meanwhile George Lucas's *Star Wars* (1977) netted spectacular revenue for Twentieth Century-Fox and was the first such film to demonstrate that merchandizing could generate even more income than ticket sales: in just five years following the film's release, tie-in products had garnered some $1.5 billion (McBride 1997, 335).

The new blockbusters drew heavily on the excitement-generating serial construction of old B-movies and reworked elements from formerly specialized genres such as science-fiction and horror, now generally sanitized for a family audience. Elements from diverse genres were ingeniously melded so that, for example, *Star Wars* tapped aspects of the heroic western as much as the monster movie and the sci-fi spectacle, thereby providing a good example of what Rick Altman has identified as the creative interaction of semantic and syntactic generic expectations, the former relating to a genre's broad subject-matter and the latter to its audio-visual language (Altman 1987, 115, 117). The blockbusters' fundamentally conservative bias towards episodic linear narrative was bolstered by a resurgence of the solidly crafted symphonic score that had temporarily been put out of fashion during the pop-dominated 1960s and early 1970s. In the hands of a resourceful composer such as John Williams, the results were impressive and his idiom continued to reinvent itself (within clearly defined stylistic parameters) well into the twenty-first century. But the very success of the Williams model also led to pale imitations that exacerbated the sense that in its over-reliance on formulaic responses to the visual image the modern Hollywood film score – and its imitations in other national cinemas, especially those reliant on US funding – had, like other aspects of commercially oriented film production, sunk firmly into a deep rut of predictability.

John Williams and the new symphonism

Jaws (and *Jaws 2*, 1978), *Close Encounters*, *Star Wars* (and its two sequels and three prequels, 1980–2005), *Raiders of the Lost Ark* (and its two sequels, 1984 and 1989) and *E.T.* were all scored by Williams, who at the time of writing has long been reputed to be cinema's most highly paid composer and whose music has since the mid-1970s consistently dominated both soundtrack and awards charts: his scores currently adorn six of the top twelve highest-earning movies of all time (Movieweb 2007) and in 2005 three made it into the American Film Institute's Top 25 Greatest Film Scores of all time (see Table 12.1, which reveals the pro-Anglophone and anti-pop bias of the selection).

Although Williams is often credited with single-handedly restoring to the modern cinema a robust symphonic style that harked back to Golden Age structural principles, several leading lights of an earlier generation of Hollywood composers had remained active into the 1980s and 1990s and continued to write orchestral scores founded on similar principles but with fewer conscious nods to the past. Alex North, for example, died in 1991, having received an Honorary Academy Award for Lifetime Achievement in 1986 (though none of his fifteen Oscar nominations in previous years had been successful); had Kubrick not rejected North's bold orchestral score for *2001* (see Chapter 11), the credit for restoring orchestral music to the genre of science-fiction would have fallen to him and not to Williams. Elmer Bernstein remained active until his death in 2004, tackling a wide range of genres, including westerns (see Chapter 3), action adventure scored with Schifrin-like symphonic jazz and a Bond-style theme song (*Gold*, dir. Peter Hunt, 1974), horror (*An American Werewolf in London*; dir. John Landis, 1981) and period drama enhanced by pastiche romanticism (*The Age of Innocence*; dir. Scorsese, 1993). He significantly influenced comedic scoring after working with Landis on *National Lampoon's Animal House* (1978), the director suggesting it be scored as a drama not a comedy; the experiment worked and Bernstein's subsequent deadpan parodies of melodramatic styles proved to be ideally suited to the emerging genre of spoof comedy. *Airplane!* (dir. Jim Abrahams, David and Jerry Zucker, 1980), an early

Table 12.1 *The American Film Institute's 25 greatest film scores (source: Sikoryak 2005)*

Position	Film	Date	Director	Composer
1	*Star Wars*	1977	George Lucas	John Williams *
2	*Gone With the Wind*	1939	Victor Fleming *et al.*	Max Steiner +
3	*Lawrence of Arabia*	1962	David Lean	Maurice Jarre *
4	*Psycho*	1960	Alfred Hitchcock	Bernard Herrmann
5	*The Godfather*	1972	Francis Ford Coppola	Nino Rota
6	*Jaws*	1975	Steven Spielberg	John Williams *
7	*Laura*	1944	Otto Preminger	David Raksin
8	*The Magnificent Seven*	1960	John Sturges	Elmer Bernstein +
9	*Chinatown*	1974	Roman Polanski	Jerry Goldsmith +
10	*High Noon*	1952	Fred Zinnemann	Dimitri Tiomkin **
11	*The Adventures of Robin Hood*	1938	Michael Curtiz & William Keighley	Erich Wolfgang Korngold *
12	*Vertigo*	1958	Alfred Hitchcock	Bernard Herrmann
13	*King Kong*	1933	Merian C. Cooper & Ernst B. Schoedsack	Max Steiner
14	*E. T. The Extra-Terrestrial*	1982	Steven Spielberg	John Williams *
15	*Out of Africa*	1985	Sydney Pollack	John Barry *
16	*Sunset Boulevard*	1950	Billy Wilder	Franz Waxman *
17	*To Kill a Mockingbird*	1962	Robert Mulligan	Elmer Bernstein +
18	*Planet of the Apes*	1968	Franklin Schaffner	Jerry Goldsmith +
19	*A Streetcar Named Desire*	1951	Elia Kazan	Alex North +
20	*The Pink Panther*	1964	Blake Edwards	Henry Mancini +
21	*Ben-Hur*	1959	William Wyler & Andrew Marton	Miklós Rózsa *
22	*On the Waterfront*	1954	Elia Kazan	Leonard Bernstein +
23	*The Mission*	1986	Roland Joffé	Ennio Morricone +
24	*On Golden Pond*	1981	Mark Rydell	Dave Grusin +
25	*How the West was Won*	1962	Henry Hathaway, John Ford & George Marshall	Alfred Newman & Ken Darby +

* = Academy Award for score
** = Academy Awards for score and song
+ = Academy Award nomination for score

landmark of the genre, owed its hyperbolic music to Bernstein's consciously putting himself in the role of an inexperienced but ambitious young composer 'who's worked on minor, low-budget films all his life and, finally, this is his big chance to do a big score for a big film!' (Schelle 1999, 56). Later comedies scored by Bernstein included *Stripes* (dir. Ivan Reitman, 1981), *Spies Like Us* (dir. Landis, 1985) and *Ghostbusters* (dir. Reitman, 1984), the last replete with references to old-fashioned scoring styles and primitive 1940s electronics – though, like many films of the time, it was commercially successful partly on the strength of its pop song (see Chapter 10).

The exceptionally prolific Jerry Goldsmith, who also died in 2004, continued to produce finely crafted modernist-tinged orchestral scores, revitalizing neo-*noir* and horror idioms with his music for *Chinatown* (dir. Roman Polanski, 1974) and *The Omen* (dir. Richard Donner, 1976, and two

12.1 Alex North receiving his Oscar awarded 'in recognition of his brilliant artistry in the creation of memorable music for a host of distinguished motion pictures' at the Academy Awards on 24 March 1986.

sequels, 1978 and 1981). His Gothic choral-orchestral idiom for the latter, strongly influenced by the Stravinsky of *Oedipus Rex* and *Symphony of Psalms* and by Orff's reworking of Stravinskyan mannerisms, was widely imitated in later contributions to the genre. In big-budget assignments Goldsmith made refreshingly unclichéd contributions to epic war films (*The Blue Max*, 1966; *Patton* and *Tora! Tora! Tora!*, both 1970), science-fiction (*Capricorn One*, 1978; *Alien*, 1979; and *Star Trek: The Motion Picture*, 1979), action adventures (the first three *Rambo* films, 1982–8; *Executive Decision*, 1996; *Air Force One*, 1997; *The Edge*, 1997) and the glossily nostalgic revival of traditional fantasy-horror subjects typical of the 1990s (*The Mummy*, 1999). Goldsmith's scoring was often economical and he once commented that a feature film should ideally contain no more than 30 minutes of music (Darby and Du Bois 1990, 500). A good example of this restraint is to be found in *Papillon* (dir. Franklin Schaffner, 1973), which is sparsely spotted and has no music at all during the first 20 minutes; a long dialogue cue is then underscored by a solo clarinet, the music only becoming expansive when the convicts escape by sea (the moment of escape having been accompanied by diegetic music from a military band) and later cues drawing on both violent expressionism (for the hunting down of the escapees) and an idyllic folk idiom (for bare-breasted native women). Twenty years later he was still achieving the same balance between variety and economy, scoring *The River Wild* (dir. Curtis Hanson, 1994) with both propulsive additive rhythms and reworkings of the simple folksong 'The Water is Wide' (a melody better known in the UK as 'O Waly, Waly'), also heard diegetically in the film in the hands of a passing violinist.

Goldsmith sometimes turned away from the spirit of experimentation evident in his avant-garde score to *The Planet of the Apes* (see Chapter 5). He had wanted the soundtrack of *Alien* (dir. Ridley Scott, 1979) to have a romantic breadth more akin to the approach in Williams's *Star Wars* but the director insisted the emphasis be on terror and accordingly jettisoned the composer's main-title music. In its place, Goldsmith provided a cue which he described as a 'bunch of effects' (complaining 'it gets boring when you're just writing fear all the time') and which he claimed took him only five minutes to assemble; nevertheless, the score as a whole – which included the exotic sounds of sea shells, didgeridoos and serpents – became highly regarded for its menace, and the franchise was a considerable success (Bond 2004d, 13). Because little happens in the first half of the film, Scott's idea had been to keep up a sense of foreboding so that the spectator would be 'spring-loaded' for the outburst of shocking events in the second half. The expansiveness for which Goldsmith had hoped found fuller expression in his music for another successful sci-fi franchise initiated by *Star Trek: The Motion Picture*, directed by the veteran Robert Wise in the same year.

Both Bernstein and Goldsmith were active as conductors in the concert hall, especially late in their careers when film music began to feature more widely on international concert programmes. As with Williams's conducting appearances, chiefly with the Boston Pops Orchestra, these composers all promoted the 'symphonic' nature of their and others' film music by demonstrating how carefully sequenced extracts could achieve a structural autonomy that defied the more fragmentary techniques of the pop score, and both Bernstein and Goldsmith championed neglected or abandoned orchestral scores as a further addition to the growing canon of 'classic' film music. Like Herrmann, who rearranged and rerecorded some of his film scores for audio release so that the discs might better reflect his structural

12.2 Film music in concert: John Williams at the podium with the Boston Pops Orchestra in 1988.

strategies, Williams acquired a reputation for overseeing soundtrack albums that restored to his music a formal integrity which the original movies had not always respected, and sometimes included on them cues which had not survived into a film's release print (Bond 2000, 32–3). Williams, however, claimed that his film music 'may seem to have more architectural and conscious interrelatedness than I actually intended to put there' (Byrd 1997, 18).

Bernstein's and Goldsmith's many varied achievements notwithstanding, the longstanding collaboration between Spielberg and Williams is universally regarded as emblematic of the perfect marriage of audio-visual creative imagination, technical accomplishment, solid narrative and commercial savvyness that distinguished the finest Hollywood blockbusters of the modern age. Both served apprenticeships in television during the 1960s, Spielberg first coming to wider attention for the technical brilliance of his

nailbiting chase movie *Duel* (made for Universal TV in 1971, with *Psycho-*
influenced music by Billy Goldenberg, and later released theatrically in an
extended version) and Williams making his mark in the genre of epic disaster
movies with his Oscar-nominated scores for the theatrical features *The Posei-*
don Adventure (dir. Ronald Neame, 1972) and *The Towering Inferno* (dir.
John Guillermin and Irving Allen, 1974). A keen clarinettist and connoisseur
of classic soundtrack albums, Spielberg had tracked his student films with
pre-existing film music, recorded his own music for one such project, and
later in his career sat in as clarinettist in the recording of Williams's score for
Jaws (McBride 1997, 33, 86–7, 104). As an amateur musician with an acute
ear, the director naturally had a keen interest in the creative possibilities
of soundtracks and, when directing an episode of the TV series *Columbo*
in 1971, he dared to suppress the sound of a visible scream in favour of
musical accompaniment. Spielberg first hired Williams for his theatrical
feature *Sugarland Express* (1974), commenting that the Americana of the
composer's scores for Mark Rydell's *The Reivers* (1969) and *The Cowboys*
(1972) made him yearn 'to meet this modern relic from a lost era of film
symphonies' (McBride 1997, 222).

Jaws was in certain ways broadly equivalent to *King Kong*, and not merely
because of its special effects, sonic design and box-office success. Spielberg
regarded *Jaws* as 'a primal scream movie' that tapped the base terror instincts
of the traditional monster film, but felt the audience would also sympathize
with the shark's plight as they had with the giant ape in the 1930s: both
creatures are aggressively pursued by mankind to the point of destruction
(McBride 1997, 246). In *Jaws* the shark's point-of-view is a key element
of the cinematography, and Williams's celebrated menacing leitmotif for
the animal serves not only to promote a sense of impending threat to the
pursuers but can also suggest the panic of the pursued. This motif – a simple pulsating semitone figure in lower strings, which Spielberg thought too
simplistic until Williams persuaded him otherwise (McBride 1997, 253) –
frequently indicates the shark's proximity when it is invisible, such off-screen
presences a favoured cohesive device in New Hollywood narratives in general and in Spielberg's films in particular (Buckland 1998, 172). Perhaps
the most important link with *Kong* is the fact that in both films the much-
vaunted special effects failed to create the necessary sense of terror until
the music track was added, the scores in both cases serving as a vital agent
for promoting suspension of disbelief. Unlike Steiner, however, Williams
cultivated a new kind of thrilling dynamism more akin to his self-confessed
idol Korngold, a retrospective collection of whose film scores appeared on
record in the 1970s and did much to stimulate interest in classic soundtracks. (The superficial similarity between Williams's *Star Wars* march and

a melodic shape from Korngold's score to *King's Row* (dir. Sam Wood, 1942) has often been noted.) But Williams is far more eclectic than his Golden Age forebears, juxtaposing in *Jaws* terror-inducing atonality, violent orchestral expressionism, expansive seafaring melodies, exciting heroism and even a fully-blown fugue; his harmonic idiom, though at its most complex still rooted in the polytonal chord-building techniques of composers like Ravel and Stravinsky, could be surprisingly advanced for its context.

The distinctive heroic strain in Williams's musical armoury was further developed not in *Close Encounters*, which presents a benign view of aliens very different from the insidious threats of infiltration and world dominance in the typical Cold War sci-fi movie (and uses a memorably simple five-note motto theme as their diegetic calling card), but in the intergalactic swash-buckling of Lucas's *Star Wars* adventures. Williams, who was responsible for dissuading Lucas from his original plan to track the first movie with classical music, was also sceptical of its substance, commenting in 1988: 'I have no pretensions about that score, which I wrote for what I thought was a children's movie. All of us who worked on it thought it would be a great Saturday-morning show. None of us had any idea that it was going to become a great world success' (quoted in Kendall 2004, 28). He later came to realize that the venture's staggering international success could be attributed to its reaching 'across cultural bounds and beyond language into some kind of mythic, shared remembered past – from the deep past of our collective unconscious' (Byrd 1997, 18). Similar considerations may explain the universal appeal of Peter Jackson's *Lord of the Rings* trilogy nearly 30 years later.

Williams's scores for the first *Star Wars* trilogy – brilliantly recorded by the London Symphony Orchestra, as was the music for the second trilogy of prequels two decades later – not only imbued the films with a spirit of hero-ism in the face of threatened evil and humanized what had formerly been a genre marked by the calculated strangeness of electronics and atonality: they also tended towards the old manner of saturation scoring, a trend often noticeable in genres that require a high degree of suspension of disbelief (e.g. cartoons and fantasy). For the second film in the series, *The Empire Strikes Back* (dir. Irvin Kershner, 1980), Williams composed approximately two hours of music, of which cues totalling 100 minutes were used (Kendall 2004, 27): this enormous score still had to be generated within the max-imum eight-week period typically granted to modern film composers for each project, and not surprisingly a heavy reliance on skilled orchestrators – of whom Williams's favoured collaborator was Herbert Spencer – remained as essential as it had been in the Golden Age. The pattern had not changed in 1999 with the recording of the score to the first prequel, *The Phantom Menace* (which set a new record in the USA for box-office takings on its release date): two hours of music, amounting to nearly a thousand pages of orchestral score, were recorded at Abbey Road in sixteen three-hour sessions (Dyer 1999, 18, 21).

Williams's *Star Wars* scores rely on the tonality and rhetoric of high romanticism, which the composer recalled was a conscious move in order to give them not merely a 'familiar emotional ring' even when accompanying images of aliens (Alan Arnold 1980, 265) but also to tap specific memories of shared nineteenth-century theatrical experiences (Byrd 1997, 18). His adherence to a leitmotivic manner of construction offered considerable practical benefits when recycling music for sequels. So strong is the thematic basis of his work that most analyses of Williams scores concentrate on thematic shapes at the expense of his not inconsiderable subtleties of harmony and timbre. Kalinak, for example, who demonstrates a tonal paradox in the Darth Vader theme from *The Empire Strikes Back* (Kalinak 1992, 194–5), divorces the melody from its crucial harmonic support and thereby gives a misleading impression of its essential communicative qualities. The theme in question, known as the 'Imperial March', inhabits the soundworld of Tchaikovsky's *Swan Lake*, and Williams's film scores often reveal the strong influence of the ballet music of both Tchaikovsky and Prokofiev; the latter's angular melodies and enlivenment of solid tonal harmonies with acerbic added dissonances are two of the most prominent aspects of Williams's style. Pastiche Prokofiev accompanies the parade of the Ewoks in the third film of the trilogy, *Return of the Jedi* (dir. Richard Marquand, 1983), as part of a score that elsewhere suggests the strong influence of the militaristic scherzo of Shostakovich's Tenth Symphony. In *Star Wars*, an even more obvious classical model was the pounding triplet rhythms of 'Mars' from Holst's *The Planets*, which was a conscious borrowing (Karlin 1994, 6). Other recognizable models were the haunting opening of Part II of Stravinsky's *The Rite of Spring*, the oscillating non-functional triads of which are unmistakably heard in Williams's music for the Dune Sea of Tatooine, and Walton's coronation marches, the stirring idiom of which is heard in Williams's end-title music. Benny Goodman's 1930s swing-band style was the unlikely model for the diegetic cantina band, Williams composing a witty distortion of the idiom and scoring it (eschewing electronics) for Caribbean steel drums, out-of-tune kazoos and toy instruments (Byrd 1997, 21). So memorably ahistorical is the result that it has not dated, and these cues – like the weird jazz in Goldenthal's score to *Titus* – still sound today like plausible popular music from an alien world.

In the *Star Wars* series, the melodically expansive American idiom of the traditional trail-blazing western is reserved for the famous main-title march, which includes the distinctive flat-seven to major-dominant chordal progression discussed in Chapter 5 as typical of the cowboy genre's 'big themes'.

Such dynamic march themes became a Williams trademark, also characterizing Spielberg's Indiana Jones trilogy (the second and third members of which were based on stories by Lucas) and *Superman* (dir. Richard Donner, 1978). Williams's handling of his Indiana Jones march in the sequels to *Raiders of the Lost Ark* is subtle, and at the beginning of *Indiana Jones and the Last Crusade* (1989) he delays its appearance most effectively, hinting at the theme's familiar intervallic shapes long before its eventual outburst. Another memorably expansive main theme, in triple time, captured the exhilaration of the youthful bicycle flights in *E.T.*, one of Williams's most cogent and endearing scores, which provides a good example of the skill with which he (like Korngold) composed extended finales to serve as a satisfying culmination to both dramatic and musical developments.

Although he perpetuated his exciting blockbuster idiom for fantasy adventures such as Spielberg's *Hook* (1991), *Jurassic Park* (1993) and the latter's first sequel *The Lost World* (1997), Williams's later work also included more contemplative and economical scores. *Presumed Innocent* (dir. Alan J. Pakula, 1990) showed what he could do for a tense courtroom story requiring minimal music, his score based largely on a simple brooding ostinato pattern, and understated scores were also well suited to the intimate drama *Angela's Ashes* (dir. Alan Parker, 1999) and gentle comedy *The Terminal* (dir. Spielberg, 2004) which, like *Schindler's List* (see below), consciously tapped ethnic folk associations in some of its thematic material and instrumentation. The slave drama *Amistad* (dir. Spielberg, 1997) included a bizarre attempt to link diegetic sound and nondiegetic music: at the climax of the film, an intimate scene (cross-cut with the spectacular naval bombardment of a fort on the West African coast) depicts President Van Buren – clearly in a world of his own – attempting to tune his harp, and as he raises the pitch of a string to match that of his tiny handbell, so the bell and string are neatly harmonized by the invisible orchestra. Unfortunately, Van Buren is plucking the string with one hand and ringing the bell with the other, so he would have needed a third hand to alter the tension of the string in the way suggested on the soundtrack. Spielberg's interpretation of H. G. Wells's *War of the Worlds* (2005), shot in a bleak heightened-reality style, received a Williams score devoid of big themes and including at both its opening and conclusion some avant-garde atonality and electronics merging into more traditional orchestral writing. The music is subservient to visceral sound effects, and heavily reliant on pulsating Stravinskyan ostinati because the movie is predominantly concerned with fleeing from a threat; Williams humanized the picture not with the warm-hearted romanticism of his earlier sci-fi scores but through the use of female vocal shrieks and sub-bass male chanting better suited to the victims of aliens who (unusually for Spielberg) are utterly malign.

Williams's two most notable achievements in his later career were the haunting and widely admired music for Spielberg's 1993 holocaust film *Schindler's List* and his development of a distinctive idiom for the enchantment of childhood. The production of *Schindler's List* overlapped with that of *Jurassic Park*, but the two films proved to be so different they scarcely seemed to be the work of the same team. Both composer and director achieved a new depth and seriousness in *Schindler*, reflected in the sombre monochrome photography and lyrical string-dominated score showcasing the intense violin playing of Itzhak Perlman (and clearly influencing Legrand's solo-violin music for Danièle Thompson's 1999 French film *La Bûche*). At the same time, an experienced understanding of how traditional scoring methods can simultaneously provide continuity, atmosphere and momentum was shown in Williams's unobtrusive handling of the extended montage during which workers are recruited for Schindler's enamel factory: the simple underscoring has a distinctively Jewish flavour (minor mode with flattened fifth, becoming optimistically major only when the workers are safely inside the plant), with a doggedly repetitive nature suggesting both resilience and a strong work ethic; the music is designed to be at its simplest under dialogue; and a satisfying congruence of audio-visual structure is achieved by the bass line's sequential shifts carefully synchronized with new camera shots. Developing aspects of his *E.T.* score, Williams's music of childhood magic was prominent in two commercially successful series directed by Chris Columbus. First came the McCauley Culkin vehicles *Home Alone* (1990) and *Home Alone 2: Lost in New York* (1992), both warm-hearted Christmas comedies for which Williams continued to tap his Russian-ballet interests: these scores are replete with references to Tchaikovsky's *Nutcracker* (e.g. prominent celeste in the main titles, and a reworking of the Cossack *trepak* dance for manic rushing to catch a plane) and Prokofiev remains a palpable influence on many aspects of melody, harmony and instrumentation. Both films include memorable original songs and carols by Williams and lyricist Leslie Bricusse, 'Somewhere in My Memory' in the first and the rousing choral-orchestral 'Merry Christmas' for the end titles of the second. At the turn of the century, the Columbus–Williams pairing achieved an international (and relentlessly merchandized) serial success, second only to that of *Star Wars*, in the films of J. K. Rowling's phenomenally popular children's books *Harry Potter and the Philosopher's Stone* (2001) and *Harry Potter and the Chamber of Secrets* (2002). Williams continued to rework the formula with director Alfonso Cuarón (*Harry Potter and the Prisoner of Azkaban*, 2004), his main theme for the series again carrying strong echoes of Tchaikovsky and Prokofiev. The franchise was one of the few that deliberately eschewed pop songs (including a potential Potter hit penned by Bruce Springsteen), for fear of offending the stories' author (Bond 2004c, 26), but in other respects the success of this enterprise indicates that the marketing strategies and filmic idioms of the New Hollywood have changed very little in the past 30 years.

The fundamentally conservative nature of the symphonic idiom best represented by the Williams model left little room for orchestral experimentation, and consequently few established composers from the classical arena (with the exception of the minimalists discussed below) made an impact in film scoring in the blockbuster age. A singular exception was John Corigliano, who was invited by Ken Russell – precisely because the composer lacked film experience and would be unlikely to resort to cliché – to score the Jekyll-and-Hyde science fantasy *Altered States* (1980). Although the director subsequently jettisoned some of Corigliano's most imaginative ideas and liberally plastered sound effects over several cues, the composer produced a fine example of neo-modernist film scoring – one which, in spite of its Academy Award nomination, was atypical of an age in which modernism would remain a viable aesthetic concept in film music long after it had been superseded by postmodernism everywhere else. Arved Ashby identifies Corigliano as a 'phantasmagoric' modernist whose avant-garde textures and sonorities ideally suited his music to the film's scenes of hallucination (Ashby 2004, 377). The score included the irrational sound of pianos tuned in quarter tones and pushed other acoustic instruments to their limits (only using a smidgeon of electronic effects), Corigliano devising a graphic-notation system for what he termed individual 'motion sonorities' based on simple repetition that, when combined, give 'a tremendous, boiling cluster of sound' (Schelle 1999, 172). The adherence to conventional orchestration permitted the music to be easily recycled for the concert hall under the title *Three Hallucinations*. Corigliano's subsequent film work was limited, but included music for *Revolution* (dir. Hugh Hudson, 1985) that, at the composer's own suggestion, created anempathy by playing a slow lament against images of violent battle, as in Takemitsu's contemporaneous score for Kurosawa's *Ran* (see Chapter 9); this lament later found its way into Corigliano's First Symphony (Schelle 1999, 162, 169). He won an Academy Award for his richly allusive score to *The Red Violin* (dir. François Girard, 1998), largely based on a progression of seven chords devised as a 'musical thread' to give an 'organic quality' to a story that sprawled across several centuries and several different countries (Schelle 1999, 160). This intellectual approach to a perceived need for structural cogency reflects the classically trained composer's traditional preoccupations with autonomous form, though in cues such as the passage-of-time montage during which the red violin is kidnapped by gypsies Corigliano memorably showed himself to be a master of the film-specific techniques of continuity, cultural suggestion and dynamic thematic transformations at a local level.

Electronics, sound technology and recording

Scoring with electronics flourished in spite of the Williams phenomenon, and only a year after the release of *Star Wars* the first music Oscar awarded for an electronic film score went to Giorgio Moroder for *Midnight Express* (dir. Alan Parker, 1978) in the face of competing nominations from Goldsmith, Morricone, Grusin and Williams. Moroder's other synthesized scores at this time included *American Gigolo* (1980) and *Cat People* (1982), both directed by Paul Schrader. Like Greek composer Vangelis, Moroder relied on an unadventurous melodic use of synthesizers, eschewing the more radical timbral possibilities of the developing technology in favour of quasi-orchestral textures that offered the promise of both low budgets and mass-market appeal. Moroder and Vangelis were both potent forces in the pop industry, Moroder in particular scoring a string of film-specific vocal hits through his work for producer Jerry Bruckheimer in the later 1980s (see Chapter 10).

Vangelis's music for the unlikely British box-office success *Chariots of Fire* (dir. Hugh Hudson, 1981), which in the hands of producer David Puttnam seemed to offer new hope for an ailing national film industry, did well in the charts on both sides of the Atlantic (the album went platinum) and typifies Vangelis's easy-going tunefulness within the instantly recognizable sound-world of the Yamaha CS80. As with the minimalism emerging in US film soundtracks at around the same time (see below), Vangelis's idiom proved readily adaptable to a wide range of genres, as varied in subject-matter as the neo-*noir* thriller *Blade Runner* (dir. Ridley Scott, 1982) and the period naval drama *The Bounty* (dir. Roger Donaldson, 1984). According to some reports, the composer liked to work 'without reference to specific timings for scenes and merely delivers finished tracks to the music editor who is then expected to edit them to the appropriate length for a given scene' (Prendergast 1992, 305). David Toop opined that although Vangelis's scoring can 'lift banal sequences into a quasi-mythic realm', the music of *Blade Runner* is 'a schizophrenic mess of inspiration and cliché' (Toop 1995, 77); a sympathetic response to early New Age ambient music of this kind is often a prerequisite for enjoyment, another critic declaring that the *Blade Runner* album is 'an evocative experience, less a soundtrack, more an ambient journey through one of the richest of Vangelis's sound worlds' (M. Walker 1998, 207). The idiom is arguably at its most effective when simplest, as in the characteristic sustained tones and threatening percussion of the *Bounty* music – the kind of simple rhetorical gestures that can be used in many different dramatic contexts. By the 1990s, in common with other film composers at the time, Vangelis had begun to mix electronics with acoustic instruments and voices, for example in *1492: Conquest of Paradise* (dir. Scott, 1992), music from which topped the German pop charts (Donnelly 1998, 144). Elements from early

New Age electronic music dated quickly and for some would forever remain associated with the 1980s; paradoxically, they were referred to by Goldenthal in his music for the futuristic *Demolition Man* (dir. Marco Brambilla, 1993) precisely 'because everybody knew the 1980s were the future' (Kendall 1994, 15).

A landmark film for both special effects and electronic music, *Tron* (dir. Michael Femer, 1982) marked Disney's adoption of computerized animation in the science-fantasy genre. Its hybrid electronic and orchestral score was by Wendy Carlos, who had worked with Kubrick on the electronic elements in *A Clockwork Orange* and *The Shining* (see Chapter 11). Carlos's electronics created the soundworld inside the computer circuits where the virtual action of *Tron* is played out, and the spinoff videogame was one of the earliest examples of musical elements from a film soundtrack being redeployed in this medium (Bond 1999, 22). Although the electronic and orchestral elements in the film had to be recorded separately owing to technological limitations, their equal status in the finished product was a notable advance on earlier attempts to combine electronics and acoustic instruments, such as Goldsmith's score to *Freud* (dir. John Huston, 1962). Goldsmith espoused synthesizers enthusiastically in the 1980s, providing scores with electronic elements for *Runaway* (dir. Michael Crichton, 1984), *Hoosiers* (dir. David Anspaugh, 1986) and *Criminal Law* (dir. Martin Campbell, 1989) using the Yamaha DX7 popular at the time. Elmer Bernstein belatedly adopted the ondes martenot in 1981 after discussing its potential with his British orchestrator Christopher Palmer, and noting its prominent melodic use in film scores by Richard Rodney Bennett (Schelle 1999, 51–2); Bernstein used the instrument as a colouristic effect in the portmanteau animated feature *Heavy Metal* (dir. Gerald Potterton, 1981) and the more conventional Disney adventure *The Black Cauldron* (dir. Ted Berman and Richard Rich, 1985), and deployed it melodically in *My Left Foot* (dir. Jim Sheridan, 1989). John Barry's part-electronic scores included *Jagged Edge* (dir. Richard Marquand, 1985), in which synthesizers were joined by flute and piano, and he also took a quasi-orchestral approach to the electronic sonorities at his disposal (Schelle 1999, 30). Relative newcomer Howard Shore entered the electronic arena with *Scanners* (1980) and *Videodrome* (1982), utilizing experiments with tape and the state-of-the-art Synclavier, later going on to become one of the most inventive users of synthesized sound in his long-standing creative partnership with the films' director, fellow Canadian David Cronenberg. The sound of primitive electronics from a bygone age was later consciously tapped as a nostalgic device: both Shore's music to *Ed Wood* (dir. Tim Burton, 1994) and Danny Elfman's to *Mars Attacks!* (dir. Burton, 1996) resurrected the theremin, and Shore wryly resorted to the ondes martenot in the religious comedy *Dogma* (dir. Kevin Smith, 1999) to suggest the purity of God.

German bands Tangerine Dream and Popol Vuh also made their mark on film soundtracks in the later 1970s, the former influencing the electronic scoring of emerging young US film composers such as Mark Isham (who consciously emulated their sound in his 1986 score to Robert Harmon's *The Hitcher*). Typically, Tangerine Dream's synthesizers created mood music rather than following the dynamics of a sequence of visual images, their output ranging from quiet contemplation to aggressively percussive rock style, and often reliant on direct and prolonged repetition of basic ideas. After their first film assignment, *Sorcerer* (UK title *Wages of Fear*; dir. William Friedkin, 1977), they were chosen by director Michael Mann for *Thief* (1981) specifically because he felt their brand of electronics would suit the film's 'high-tech political metaphor' far better than the more obvious choice of blues-based popular music appropriate to the film's setting in 1960s Chicago (Romney and Wootton 1995, 127). Thereafter their film work seemed squarely aimed at the youth market, not just in the early Tom Cruise vehicle *Risky Business* (dir. Paul Brickman, 1983) but most notoriously in the fantasy *Legend* (dir. Scott, 1985), Goldsmith's score for which was replaced by their music for the film's US release on the grounds that the veteran composer's approach was too sophisticated; the producers also included an end-title song by Bryan Ferry. A similar situation arose with the film of George Orwell's *1984* (dir. Michael Radford, 1984), its score by Dominic Muldowney ditched in favour of what Mark Kermode terms 'some hideous techno groaning by the Eurythmics', a move on the part of the producers that annoyed the director to the extent of his openly criticizing Virgin at the BAFTA awards (Kermode 1995, 19). Muldowney's Soviet-like Oceania music arguably made considerably more sense in the Orwellian 1940s-style setting than Eurythmics' reliance on a 'fast and busy drum machine' (Donnelly 2001b, 103), and again the desire to appeal to a particular market seemed to have overridden aesthetic considerations.

Popol Vuh became closely associated with the work of German director Werner Herzog (Donnelly 2006). Like Vangelis, they exploited a simple but moody style of synthesized music, the timbre often suggesting vocal qualities and their idiom particularly evocative in the context of Herzog's myth-laden and contemplative Amazonian films (Rogers 2004). In *Aguirre, Wrath of God* (1972), visuals and music combine in doggedly slow pacing, the score evoking both the expanse of the Amazon and (with viol-like electronic timbres) an archaic mood; as in many historical films set in South America, panpipes (here played diegetically) make a telling appearance, their jaunty syncopated melody providing anempathy after the expedition's leaders are shot. Herzog's retelling of the German classic of expressionist silent cinema, *Nosferatu the Vampyre* (1979), was even more leisurely paced, the electronic score seemingly divorced from time or place in its repetition of simple diatonic ostinati. In this film the Prelude from Wagner's *Rheingold*, with its exceptionally slow harmonic rhythm and sense of expansiveness, was also used for the specific purpose of emphasizing the protracted nature of the story.

Synthesizers provided John Carpenter with a low-budget means of creating a music track for his seminal shocker *Halloween* (1978), originally to have been without music until the director realized that the film simply wasn't scary enough and decided to add some threatening electronic ostinati himself. Carpenter, whose simple but insidious keyboard doodlings have been much imitated (and sampled effectively by gangsta-rapper Ice-T), remains one of the few directors also to have provided music tracks for his films, later examples including *The Fog* (1979), *Christine* (1983), *Big Trouble in Little China* (1986), *Prince of Darkness* (1987), *They Live* (1988), *In the Mouth of Madness* (1995) and the spaghetti-western-tinged score for the cool New Mexico vampire hunters of *John Carpenter's Vampires* (1998). For some of these projects he collaborated with synthesizer player Alan Howarth and composer Shirley Walker. The cheaply produced *Halloween* music, and other even more meagre electronic scores, led to the myth that music tracks of this kind were favoured by the industry primarily on account of their low cost. Maurice Jarre, whose electronic scores included *The Year of Living Dangerously* (dir. Peter Weir, 1982), *Witness* (dir. Weir, 1985), *Fatal Attraction* (dir. Adrian Lyne, 1987), *No Way Out* (dir. Roger Donaldson, 1987) and *Jacob's Ladder* (dir. Lyne, 1990), praised the possibilities synthesizers offered for understatement, subliminal suggestion and emotional detachment, but preferred to record his electronic scores by using several live players rather than a single operator and noted that (in spite of rumours to the contrary) his music for *Witness* was more expensive to produce than if it had been recorded by a conventional orchestra (MacLean 1993, 36). However, in the case of Jarre, Barry and other composers not themselves experts in synthesizer technology, this was partly a function of the time spent in requesting players to demonstrate the capabilities of the medium.

The work of Tangerine Dream and Popol Vuh had shown how elements of early New Age electronic music and adult-oriented rock could, unlike the overly neat packaging of mainstream pop music in saleable song forms, prove versatile at sustained atmospheric underscoring, and other pop and rock musicians capitalized on this potential. Mike Oldfield's 'Tubular Bells' functioned in the eclectic soundtrack of *The Exorcist* (dir. Friedkin, 1973; original music by Jack Nitzsche) in a similar manner to Carpenter's unsettling *Halloween* riffs, the film also containing music by Penderecki and other avant-garde composers. Oldfield went on to score *The Killing Fields* (dir. Roland Joffé, 1984), which balanced musicless *vérité* narrative with moments where nightmarish electronics were allowed to dominate. Other British rock talents who first became active in film scoring during the 1980s were Cream's Eric Clapton, who collaborated with Michael Kamen and saxophonist David Sanborn on the *Lethal Weapon* franchise (1987–98), contributing blues-guitar music for the Mel Gibson character, and later scoring Gary Oldman's *Nil by Mouth* (1997). Dire Straits' guiding spirit Mark Knopfler scored the diverse genres of comedy drama (*Local Hero* and *Comfort and Joy*; dir. Bill Forsyth, 1983–4), fairy-tale (*The Princess Bride*; dir. Rob Reiner, 1987), gritty social comment (*Last Exit to Brooklyn*; dir. Uli Edel, 1989) and amiable political satire (*Wag the Dog*; dir. Barry Levinson, 1997). The results could be surprisingly soft-centred, however: Knopfler's music for *Last Exit* is at times reminiscent of the sentimental Morricone of *Cinema Paradiso*, with rich dominant thirteenths and impressionistic augmented triads that seem distinctly out of place in the context of novelist Hubert Selby's tough Brooklyn neighbourhood of 1952, and only the electronic timbres lend the music track a thin veneer of contemporaneity. In the USA, slide-guitarist Ry Cooder had collaborated with Nitzsche on the soundtracks of *Performance* (dir. Nicolas Roeg, 1970) and *Blue Collar* (dir. Paul Schrader, 1978) before recording his evocative score to Wim Wenders's *Paris, Texas* (1984), a Franco-German co-production that did much to bridge the gap between art-house European cinema and mainstream Anglophone releases and made creative use of everyday sounds (especially those associated with the restlessness of modern transportation). Cooder later played a key role in Wenders's documentary about ageing Cuban musicians, *Buena Vista Social Club* (1999). In film work Cooder identified two stumbling blocks arising from a lack of imagination on the part of conservative producers and familiar to film composers of both classical and rock orientations: the constant desire to include songs that 'stop the film', and a marked tendency to typecast musicians – in his case rigidly, as solely an exponent of the blues (Romney and Wootton 1995, 121, 134).

Most film composers since the 1980s have needed to be equally proficient in electronic techniques and conventional orchestral scoring, often combining both media to effect in a single project: a representative early example is George Fenton's eclectic score to *The Company of Wolves* (dir. Neil Jordan, 1984), in which lush orchestral impressionism and electronic soundscapes are linked by common motivic material, and offset by a parodic use of a pre-existing work by Beethoven. Towards the end of the decade sequenced electronic tracks began to provide a solid rhythmic underpinning for a conventional orchestral overlay, an approach seen in Barry's score to the Bond film *The Living Daylights* (dir. John Glen, 1987) and remaining prevalent, along with simple devices such as electronic drones of low tessitura, to the present day. Technological improvements enhanced a composer's ability to lay down elaborate electronic tracks prepared in advance with the aid of computers. MIDI technology permitted the rapid and relatively cheap preparation of electronic mock-ups, used not only as demonstrations to a director of work in progress but sometimes as the end product itself. As sampling burgeoned, so electronic film music came under the influence of contemporary dance idioms and the DJs and producers responsible for conditioning public tastes: David Holmes, for example, was involved in shaping the music tracks for the British film *Resurrection Man* (dir. Marc Evans) and Steven Soderbergh's *Out of Sight* (both 1998), the latter using sampling techniques involving dialogue and Latin pop elements (Reay 2004, 78). Some DJs embarked on parallel careers as music supervisors for films, a role that became increasingly powerful after the 1980s as licensing and publishing arrangements became more expensive and complex.

In spite of its commercial appeal, popular electronic music has never succeeded in displacing the old-fashioned orchestra, which some directors specifically request composers to use as a means of what Thomas Newman termed 'a way of bringing class to an environment' (Schelle 1999, 272) – a directive which he consciously resisted (see below). When Christopher Young was asked to score *A Nightmare on Elm Street Part Two: Freddy's Revenge* (dir. Jack Sholder, 1985), he was asked not to provide electronic music like that used in the original film because an orchestra would 'lift the film's production values' (Schelle 1999, 390). The aggrandizing and sometimes extravagant tendencies of conventional orchestral scoring were clearly demonstrated in Kenneth Branagh's Shakespeare films with music by Patrick Doyle (discussed in Chapter 4). For some contemporary film composers such as Daniel Licht, the emotional immediacy and subtlety of live performance in any case remained preferable to the detached and fabricated sounds of the synthesizer and sequencer (Schelle 1999, 223).

Innovations from the 1970s onwards meant that the sound quality of music tracks continued to improve both in the theatre and at home. The multi-track stereo sound of Panavision and other 70mm formats developed in the 1950s had only been reproducible in the best-appointed venues, more modest cinemas using versions with a reduced number of tracks, and cheaper mono sound was still in use in the 1960s. MCA's and RCA's Sensurround (launched in 1974) experimented with additional low-frequency vibrations in order to create a visceral impact on spectators, a strategy also to be found in the tendency of modern scoring of thrillers and action movies to build such physicality into the music rather than the technology. Far more enduring than Sensurround were Dolby's directional Surround Sound and Noise Reduction systems, also launched in the 1970s. In a concerted attempt to ensure consistent standards of sound reproduction, at first in cinemas and later domestic video equipment, George Lucas launched his long-running THX enterprise in 1983: the clarity and dryness of the standardized sonic experience it offered were not to all tastes, Chion dismissing it as 'inflated personal stereo sound' (Chion 1994, 101). Long after the introduction of the compact disc in 1982, cinema-goers continued to listen to optical sound-tracks in theatres – these were retained owing to the expense of re-equipping projection venues with new technology – even though they could listen to the same music digitally at home. The digital revolution only caught up with film sound at the start of the next decade, with Sony and Dolby both launching digital systems in 1992–3, and Universal and Spielberg develop-ing a relatively inexpensive Digital Theater Systems technology for playing back a separately supplied CD-ROM soundtrack in synchronization with the image; a backup conventional soundtrack is nevertheless still included on the celluloid, and the historical irony of this return to sound-on-disc has not gone unremarked (Allen 1998, 113–19; Eyman 1997, 373).

Advancements in the editing of both sound and image have conspired to ensure that today's film composers are under even greater pressures to meet short deadlines and revise their work on the spot than were their hard-working Golden Age counterparts. Composers are still almost always brought into a project at the last moment, unless they enjoy a close and longstanding relationship with a particular director, and expected to work with digital equipment that facilitates instant experimentation and alter-ation. Film editing grew more rapid with developments of postproduction techniques using videotape technology in the early 1970s, followed by the virtually instant editing of sequences on laserdisc in the early 1980s and the introduction of full digital editing on computer in the 1990s that finally made the Moviola and flat-bed editing devices all but extinct (Allen 1998, 121–2). The modern Avid digital editing system allows for huge changes to a film's structure and proportions to be made at the click of a mouse, placing the quick-witted composer in often impossibly demanding major rewrite situations. As ever, composers still work with a music editor who can now perform all the traditional functions of creating temp tracks, and generating timing notes, punches, streamers, click tracks and even preset accelerations and ritardations using various computer systems (for example, Auricle and Streamline), and who also prepares music for dubbing and is present at the final mix. The role of the music copyist has been somewhat diminished by computer notation programmes, although orchestrators remain more vital than ever in a generation of keyboard-reliant composers from non-classical backgrounds, and are paid handsomely at rates still calculated per four-bar page. Synchronization of electronic mock-ups with the first cut (formerly known as the rough cut) is assured via the time-code system of the Society of

Motion Picture and Television Engineers (SMPTE) which indicates timings and precise frame counts and allows digital sound and image to be precisely locked. A far closer creative interaction between music and sound effects is permitted by their both being stored and manipulated digitally – though the traditionally rigid division of postproduction functions in the areas of sound, dialogue and music editing has meant that meaningful interactions between them remain rare in mainstream commercial cinema. At the final mix, the traditional three-person team has generally been replaced by two (one handling sound effects, and the other both dialogue and music), who create three individual master tracks in 5.1 Surround Sound (Karlin and Wright 2004, 362).

During recording sessions electronic tracks prepared in ProTools can have certain components muted and replaced with live instruments, and complex 'stem' files – frequently including as many as 64 individual tracks – can be mixed in advance. Conversely, old-fashioned 'sweetening' (duplicating overdubs) can be achieved by adding electronics to acoustic recordings. Many contemporary composers from a non-classical background work with expert assistants in order to realize ideas from their mock-ups. Former Pop Will Eat Itself member Clint Mansell, for example, relied on David Lang to write out the 'string' music for *Requiem for a Dream* (dir. Darren Aronofsky, 2000) that the composer had prepared on a Roland JV-880 synthesizer. The Logic Audio program readily transcribed simpler material into comprehensible notation, but for his complex and randomly programmed music for the end of the film Mansell confessed to being 'clueless because it was playing these samples and I am not musically trained'; Lang duly prepared parts from the mock-up that were subsequently recorded by the Kronos Quartet, the director chipping in an inspired suggestion that the ambiguous sounds of the Quartet tuning up should infiltrate the film's first scene ('Downbeat' 2000, 18–20). Experienced composers often benefit from working with established teams in the studio, for example James Newton Howard's collaborations with Auricle exponent Richard Grant, electronics producer Jim Hill, mixer Shaun Murphy and conductor Pete Anthony.

Pop scoring, dual tracking and the modern soundtrack album

The revival of symphonic scoring at no point distracted producers' attention from the lucrative opportunities for exploiting pop music in film soundtracks, though it seemed after the 1970s as if bets were forever to be hedged between the two formerly mutually exclusive scoring approaches. This was partly because, by the 1980s, orchestral soundtrack albums could sometimes achieve sales and acclaim to rival those of the most popular vocal artists.

Williams's *Jaws* album won a Grammy in 1975, the *Star Wars* soundtrack reached the *Billboard* Top 20 charts and his *E.T.* album went gold in 1982. Two years later ten very different soundtrack albums all achieved platinum sales: they included pop scores for *Purple Rain, The Big Chill, Footloose* and *Breakin'*, the musical *Yentl* and *Ghostbusters*. All five top-selling pop singles that year had been featured in movie soundtracks. As Claudia Gorbman notes, the period 1986–90 represented a significant boom in the influence of music-video techniques on film production, not just in isolated sequences but more generally as a continuation of 'the bricolage aesthetic of the song score' (Gorbman 1996, 30). The end-credit song in particular was to remain a familiar ploy in the early twenty-first century. At the same time, however, orchestral soundtrack albums were to remain big sellers into the 1990s and beyond, music from blockbusters such as *Gladiator* and *Titanic* rivalling the success of *Star Wars* and their albums plugged in advance of their release in a manner comparable to hit songs. By the 1990s, melody-based orchestral film music had become so successful as audio recordings that it routinely featured in the album charts of more populist classical-music radio stations, such as the UK's Classic FM.

In a characteristic outburst from David Raksin during an interview conducted in 1991, the veteran composer bitterly lamented the modern cinema's

> totally abysmal reliance on hit songs. My students ask me why I have such an antipathy to this, and I said, 'The only way some of these scores can be explained is that everybody in the picture has a transistor radio in his navel tuned to a top-forty station.' They're making pictures which are ostensibly adult stories about people with adult emotions and they're scoring it with music, for Christ's sakes, that was meant for teeny boppers. What sense does that make? (R. S. Brown 1994, 287)

Raksin had seen no reason to change this view at any point during the previous two decades, having commented back in 1974 that the desire 'to appeal to the "demographically defined" audience, which is a symbolic unit conceived as an object of condescension' partly arose because 'so many directors and producers, having acquired their skills and reputations at the price of becoming elderly, suddenly find themselves aliens in the land of the young' (quoted in Prendergast 1992, 166–7). In popular idioms as well as orchestral scoring, conservatism remained endemic, however, as Danny Elfman complained: 'Film people want rock songs, they want pop songs, they want hits. They know nothing about music, and their tastes are generally three or four years behind wherever the music scene is' (quoted in Denisoff and Romanowski 1991, 571). As Kalinak summarized the situation: 'Like the jazz-oriented score and the theme score before it, the pop score initially challenged the classical model as a radical alternative, only to find its most iconoclastic characteristics excised in the process of fitting itself into Hollywood' (Kalinak 1992, 187). Pop-music tracks had initially been more foregrounded than traditional scoring, but by the end of the century they could be as inaudible or as much taken for granted as 'wallpaper' music had been in the Golden Age. Anahid Kassabian (2001), who draws a distinction between the 'assimilating identifications' of a traditional composed score featuring rhetorical signifiers and the more flexible 'affiliating identifications' of a compiled song-score to which the auditor brings personal associations, nevertheless highlights a particular way in which the song score was significant in the 1980s and 1990s by becoming associated with marginalized demographics such as gays, blacks and females while the conventional orchestral score continued to flourish in the old-fashioned context of white heterosexual male heroes.

Since the 1960s there had also been a middle ground of pop-influenced orchestral scoring developed by film composers with backgrounds in the recording industry and jazz, chief among them Morricone, Barry, Mancini and Quincy Jones. The importance of these composers' achievements has been identified by Jeff Smith:

> Though the idiom was contemporary, the pop score itself served many of the traditional score's functions by establishing setting, by representing characters' points of view, and by expressing a scene's overall mood. Significantly, by combining popular styles and song forms with the developmental forms of the orchestral score, composers like Mancini and Barry deftly juggled the pop score's commercial and narrative functions.
>
> (J. Smith 1998, 11)

Smith plausibly argues that Mancini broke significant new ground in systematically designing film scores with a view to packaging them as long-playing albums: his theme-based writing – for example, in *Breakfast at Tiffany's* (dir. Blake Edwards, 1961) and *Charade* (dir. Stanley Donen, 1963), both of which showcased original and highly successful songs – constantly seemed to 'aspire to the condition of the musical'. Mancini habitually re-recorded his film music for soundtrack albums, often including lightweight subsidiary themes that seemed to be present in the film's music track merely so the resulting album would be sufficiently varied (J. Smith 1998, 78–9). These tendencies were continued by Mancini's protégé Dave Grusin in fine jazz-flavoured scores such as *Tootsie* (dir. Sidney Pollack, 1982) and *The Fabulous Baker Boys* (dir. Steve Kloves, 1989), though his solitary Academy Award was achieved for his economical non-jazz score to *The Milagro Beanfield War* (dir. Robert Redford, 1988). For his part, Mancini regretted that the success of his innovative scoring style had kept producers' eyes firmly on the benefits of tie-in record sales, commenting 'It's the kind of thing where the tail is wagging the dog. I don't think the craft of film scoring is being furthered by this particular development' (quoted in Thomas 1997, 268).

The modern dilemma of whether to endow a film with an orchestral score or a pop compilation was predictably solved by a simple method of dual tracking summarized by K. J. Donnelly:

> the norm for film music by the 1990s was that there would be a selection of pop songs as well as an orchestral underscore. There would be a divide in function between the two: the non-diegetic underscore would be designed to elicit emotional effects and mark action much as traditional underscores, while the pop songs would be an attraction, either foregrounded as non-diegetic music, or appearing only momentarily in the film but available fully outside the film as a tied-in product. (Donnelly 2001b, 153)

This procedure made it feasible to issue two separate soundtrack albums for a single film, one aimed at the pop market and the other carrying the orchestral score; furthermore, a new concept of 'songs inspired by the motion picture' allowed revenue to be generated from the reissue of existing songs with often only tenuous connections to the film concerned (Barron 2003). An example of this policy was the British hit *Four Weddings and a Funeral* (dir. Mike Newell, 1994), of which the soundtrack album contained four pop songs not heard in the film. But record labels went even further in issuing multiple albums to tie in with a single movie. Thus the live-action comic-book adventure *Dick Tracy* (dir. Warren Beatty, 1990) spawned no fewer than three discs, one featuring the score by Elfman, another carrying Andy Paley's pastiche 1930s numbers and a third, by Madonna (*I'm Breathless*), including both 'songs inspired by' the film and the three original songs which Stephen Sondheim had composed for her to sing in it – one of which, 'Sooner or Later', won an Academy Award. (Madonna's patronage of songs by the world's most acclaimed composer of intelligent musicals was somewhat tarnished by her reported exclamation 'What is this highbrow shit?' on first seeing them.) Another live-action comic-book project, *Batman* (dir. Tim Burton, 1989), had similarly resulted in two albums, and the trend continued with *Titanic* (dir. James Cameron, 1997), *The Matrix* (dir. Andy and Larry Wachowski, 1999) and *Magnolias* (dir. Paul Thomas Anderson, 1999). The first *Titanic* album to be released did not include the popular diegetic Irish folk music from the soundtrack, thereby compelling consumers to buy the second album (*Return to Titanic*) as well if they wished to hear it. More than twenty other CD releases attempted to cash in on the *Titanic* phenomenon in the immediate aftermath of the film's success (Donnelly 2005, 173).

The oddest example of the 'inspired by' phenomenon arose from the horror film *The Blair Witch Project* (dir. Daniel Myrick and Eduardo Sanchez,

1998), a superb exercise in the heightened reality of amateur documentary style. The film purported to be assembled from raw video footage shot by a group of students who mysteriously disappeared, and music was therefore entirely absent from its soundtrack. A tie-in album, *Josh's Blair Witch Mix*, cunningly continued the illusion by purporting to be based on a tape found in the car of one of the ill-fated protagonists, whose musical tastes revealed a 'prophetic sense of morbidity and doom' (Barron 2003, 160). This, Lee Barron argues, is perhaps the ultimate example of the modern soundtrack album's function as a direct extension of the viewing experience by exploiting modern multi-media to capitalize on consumers' desire to buy into the dramatic experience outside the confines of the film itself, a phenomenon not only encountered in soundtrack albums but also in interactive videogames based on fantasy and action movies.

Minimalism

In the concert hall and opera house, the minimalist music emerging in the USA in the late 1960s and early 1970s owed its success partly to its clear and strong reaction against the excessive complexity and unpredictability of much avant-garde writing of the time. In the hands of Steve Reich and others, minimalism's accessibility allowed it to cross quickly over into jazz and rock markets and secure for itself a firm place in the middle ground between consumers of art music and pop – a fertile soil subsequently cultivated by many modern-jazz, rock and New Age instrumentalists in the 1980s and 1990s, both in the USA and Europe. As a new generation of film composers struggled to negotiate between the fundamentally different demands of the traditional orchestral score, electronics and pop-based music tracks, so minimalist styles were adopted by some as an ideal compromise. A compositional idiom based on the extended repetition of simple motivic patterns proved to be a gift to the modern film composer for reasons both aesthetic and practical. The mechanical nature of such repetition, in which the music sometimes pursues a path quite independent from the suggestions of the visual image, could readily foster emotional neutrality and distanciation; at the same time, the fact that such music was not only speedy to compose (and could even be improvised on the spot) but also readily extensible or truncatable made it ideally suited to the tight deadlines and last-minute alterations endemic in film work. Furthermore, minimalism could in the USA serve as a new kind of understated nationalism in a postmodern age when jazz (having become an international musical language) could no longer fulfil this function, and the style remained commercially viable by continuing to tap crossover markets in the record industry.

In embryonic form, minimalist techniques are to be found in Herrmann's ostinato-based music in the 1950s and in isolated passages such as Alan Hoddinott's ambush cue for Hammer's *Sword of Sherwood Forest* (dir. Terence Fisher, 1960), somewhat prophetic of the style of Philip Glass (Larson 1996, 138), and Benjamin Frankel's hypnotic tuned-percussion writing for the release of the reptile in *The Night of the Iguana* (dir. John Huston, 1964). Surprisingly, perhaps, the first notable examples of extended minimalism in film scoring occurred not in the USA but the UK. Peter Greenaway's films consistently included music by British composer Michael Nyman, who wrote a pioneering study of experimental music (Nyman 1974) and who – like Glass and Reich – worked largely with his own group of musicians, mixing both acoustic and electronic resources. Greenaway's strong visual style dominated the viewer's perceptions and prevented undue attention being paid to music that at its best was electrifying and at its worst drearily monotonous; the director's characteristic avoidance of conventional narrative structures also allowed for flexible and sometimes provocative combinations of music and image. His first feature-length collaboration with Nyman was *The Falls* (1980), for which the director suggested the composer write 92 variations (one for each of the film's characters) on four bars from the slow movement of Mozart's *Sinfonia Concertante*. Nyman's fondness for this piece subsequently led to its use in Greenaway's *Drowning By Numbers* (1988) as a punctuating device after each of the film's watery deaths. The Restoration mystery *The Draughtsman's Contract* (1982) was furnished with one of Nyman's finest scores, in which catchy elements borrowed from the historically apt style of Purcell are transformed into funky bass lines and quirky timbres perfectly attuned to the idiosyncratic and highly stylized scenario and cinematography. This score proved popular and enduring enough for elements from it to resurface in two costume dramas made more than twenty years later: *A Cock and Bull Story* (dir. Michael Winterbottom) and *The Libertine* (dir. Laurence Dunmore), both released in 2005.

In *A Zed and Two Noughts* (1985), Nyman's mannerisms are the same: baroque-style ground-bass forms, simple triadic harmonies, pulsating repeated-note bass lines beneath syncopated melodies, and the repetition of a limited number of basic ideas (often varied solely by a change in instrumentation). Accelerated cues wittily accompany time-lapse photography of images of decaying animals and fruit, Nyman's repetitive idiom in accord with the circularity of life cycles with which the film is concerned (Hubbard 1994, 11); for the final such episode, in which twin brothers commit suicide having set up a time-lapse camera to record their posthumous decomposition, the rapid music is suddenly revealed to be diegetic when their camera and lighting eventually fail and a formerly unseen record player also grinds to a halt. The soundtrack's inclusion at several points of Henry

Hall's ancient BBC Dance Orchestra recording of 'The Teddy Bear's Picnic' sits alongside the funky minimalism remarkably well, both texturally and timbrally. Nyman supplies the simplest possible diegetic music (a repeating four-note pattern played very softly) to accompany television broadcasts and for a restaurant scene, these having a subliminal impact in terms of the film's sonic cogency.

Undoubtedly the principal elements of Greenaway's films – a stylized theatricality with self-conscious attention to pictorial details, a strong vein of black humour and often obtrusive symbolist details – found its ideal match in Nyman's doggedly quirky music. By the time of the grotesque revenge tragedy *The Cook, the Thief, His Wife and Her Lover* (1989), the Nyman formula could be categorized as 'predominantly self-subsistent, anempathetic music' expressed in 'ritualistic, repetitive scores' (Kershaw 1995, 142); the cues gave the impression of being spotted at random, with their static nature encouraging the possibilities for contemplation offered by widescreen composition-in-depth. Greenaway's *Prospero's Books* (1991), based on Shakespeare's *The Tempest,* was a refreshing departure for Nyman in its focus on vocal music, the score including five songs for Ariel (performed by Sarah Leonard in boyish tones) and a fully fledged Masque for the betrothal of Prospero's daughter to Ferdinand. Described by one writer as 'A typically insistent score' which 'adds to the monotony' of the film (Rosenthal 2000, 156), Nyman's music from here on began increasingly to run up against critical malaise. Without the dazzling inventiveness of Greenaway's visual imagination to support it, his music for other directors often seemed ponderous and ill-conceived, most noticeably in the sci-fi film *Gattaca* (dir. Andrew Niccol, 1997) and the wartime drama *The End of the Affair* (dir. Neil Jordan, 1999), a drab remake of a 1955 film originally directed by Edward Dmytryk with music by Frankel. Nevertheless, Nyman's solo-piano music for Jane Campion's *The Piano* (1993), in spite of its dreary and mechanical performance, became something of a hit, resulting not only in concert spin-offs (including *The Piano Concerto*) but a host of imitations. His score for *Carrington* (dir. Christopher Hampton, 1995) was more arresting with its moments of vibrant intensity and a use of strings both suggesting English pastoral overtones and linking with the Schubert Quintet that becomes a focal element in the soundtrack (see Chapter 11). Nyman also composed scores for French director Patrice Leconte (*Monsieur Hire*, 1989; *The Hairdresser's Husband*, 1990), and the influence of his style may be heard in the work of some younger French film composers (see Chapter 8).

French films were also a source of work for veteran minimalist Philip Glass, whose scores for Godfrey Reggio's documentaries were examined in Chapter 7. Glass also wrote music for Anglophone features by directors of markedly different temperaments, including Paul Schrader (*Mishima,*

1985), John Irvin (*Hamburger Hill*, 1987), Errol Morris (*The Thin Blue Line*, 1988), Bernard Rose (*Candyman*, 1992), Christopher Hampton (*The Secret Agent*, 1996) and Richard Eyre (*Notes on a Scandal*, 2006). Some of Glass's feature-film work received critical and popular acclaim, notably his music to Scorsese's *Kundun* (1998), which was honoured by an LA Critics Award and nominations for an Academy Award, Golden Globe and Grammy, and his contribution to *The Truman Show* (dir. Peter Weir, 1999), which received a Golden Globe for Best Score. The *Kundun* score, conceived for a story about the Dalai Lama, mixed minimalist and neo-romantic elements and used both Western and Tibetan instruments, bringing together similar sonorities from each tradition (e.g. bass trombone with ethnic long horns); a large part of the music was composed in advance on the basis of the script, with some of the images edited to pre-existing cues and Scorsese redeploying other cues to parts of the picture for which they were not originally intended. As with Nyman's, however, the composer's sometimes dreary music has not been universally admired, Jeff Bond noting its unrelenting lack of engagement with character and how *Kundun*'s 'two-hour running time seems to stretch out in the mind of the beleaguered viewer to three or four ... By the second half of the film, Glass's use of repetition starts to reinforce in the viewer the realization that nothing is happening onscreen' (Adams 1998a, 27). The bleak melancholy of some of Glass's string writing seemed appropriate for the dark period atmosphere of *The Secret Agent*, but a tendency towards drabness did little to enhance Stephen Daldry's Virginia Woolf film *The Hours* (2002). A comparison with Nyman's limitations is revealing: both composers' repetitive idioms work exceptionally well when they can pursue their own autonomous course set against vivid or contemplative visual images that do not require a linear logic, but the essentially static nature of their music and sometimes impoverished powers of invention can hinder the pacing of more conventional narrative structures.

This objection to filmic minimalism does not hold true for the more flexible work of Alfred Newman's son Thomas, however, whose music first came to prominence in the 1980s and who at the time of writing remains one of Hollywood's most imitated composers. Newman's background in rock and wide experience of electronics based on sampled acoustic rather than synthesized sounds led to a distinctive minimalist idiom emotionally neutral enough to serve as background music to almost any dramatic situation: thus the rustic milieu of *The Horse Whisperer* (dir. Robert Redford, 1998), the gangster setting of *Road to Perdition* (dir. Sam Mendes, 2002) and the jolly animated clown fish of *Finding Nemo* (dir. Andrew Stanton, 2003) all receive remarkably similar treatments. In the opening sequence of *Perdition*, Newman persuaded the director to abandon his idea of using an expansive orchestral cue to give 'a sense of the size of the movie', supplying small-ensemble rustic ostinati that better suited the bike ride (Karlin and Wright 2004, 7). That Newman's reworkings of a basic and instantly recognizable formula work so well is a tribute to the close attention he pays to what he calls

> the nature of how you repeat a phrase, and what repeating a phrase does in terms of the ear's ability to listen to other things. Oftentimes by using sampled instruments the main motoric drive starts to disappear and begins to allow the ear to listen out. Often if it's a real performance, the performance itself demands more from the ear. The ear keeps listening to that performance change, and then is less accommodating to other overdubbed sounds . . . [I]f you're dealing in the realm of color . . . there have to be ways of letting harmony do less so that you listen more sonically. I think that's why drones interest me so much. They allow the ear to go to a different spatial place as opposed to a harmonic place.   (Adams 2004, 15–16)

His style became globally familiar as a result of the widespread exposure of the soundtrack to *American Beauty* (dir. Mendes, 1999), which has been ubiquitously recycled in commercials and in close imitations.

Newman's emphasis on tuned percussion played with mallets and a variety of plucked string timbres, generally recorded with close microphones to stress individual solo lines rather than the homogeneity of the ensemble as a whole, reveals folk, country and jazz influences. Crucial to the development of his trademark sound was the spontaneous creativity of a number of kindred spirits, among them Rick Cox (prepared guitar), George Budd (processed phonograph and other sonic experiments) and Chas Smith (pedal steel guitar, resonators, bowed plates, etc.). Basic ideas are explored and honed in workshop sessions involving a considerable degree of improvisation, during which the musicians 'mess around with colors' using samples – a favourite processed sound is that of the hurdy-gurdy – and trading melodic and rhythmic ideas off one another; Newman admits that the approach is essentially abstract, and as a result the output 'can be anything for any amount of time' (Schelle 1999, 270–1). It is an essentially intuitive process that continues right up to the final mix. Immediately recognizable fingerprints are a fondness (in quieter moments) for parallel major triads voiced with the third scale degree at the top and moving up by a minor third to create a luminous false relation, especially over a soft pedal point, and drone patterns based on folk-like chains of parallel perfect fifths. Both devices may clearly be heard in the opening minutes of *Scent of a Woman* (dir. Martin Brest, 1992). Newman remains unconvinced about the usefulness of traditional orchestral scoring in modern films, describing it as 'a ludicrous ritual' and identifying minimalism and the use of pre-existing music as two important ways in which film music can escape from its historical shackles. But the static nature of his overdubbed music means that when he chooses to write expansive melodic lines for strings and wind – as he does for the bird's eye view of the prison in *The Shawshank Redemption* (dir. Frank Darabont, 1994), for the emerging Chicago skyline in *Road to Perdition* and the open country in *The Horse Whisperer* (the last negated by summary ducking of the music to make way for gratuitous sound effects of horses snorting) – the effect on the spectator is one of a spellbinding broadening of horizons.

Minimalist writing has occasionally been adopted by film composers not primarily associated with it. In a sci-fi context it served Morricone well in his score for *The Humanoid* (dir. Aldo Lado, 1979). John Williams used it in two Spielberg films: in the robotic futuristic context of *A. I. Artificial Intelligence* (2001), and – like the Newman of *American Beauty* – as a US cultural marker in *The Terminal* (2004), where the bubbling diatonic music in additive rhythms offers a deliberate contrast to both the East European folk idiom characterizing the immigrant protagonist and the lushly conventional love theme. Other exponents include Scott Johnson (*Patty Hearst*, 1988), Bill Conti (*The Thomas Crown Affair*, 1999), Murray Gold (*Beautiful Creatures*, 2001), Elliot Goldenthal (*Alien³*, 1992; *Demolition Man*, 1993), Clint Mansell (*Requiem for a Dream*, 2000), Edward Shearmur (*Cruel Intentions*, 1999) and the film work of performance artist Laurie Anderson. For his work on the *Matrix* trilogy (dir. Andy and Larry Wachowski, 1999–2003), Don Davis took as a starting point a minimalist approach suitable for the films' hi-tech milieu but recognized the need for more dynamic composing for action sequences. By contrast, the opening of *Little Miss Sunshine* (dir. Jonathan Dayton and Valerie Faris, 2006) showed how ill-conceived Nymanesque minimalism, here penned by Mychael Danna, could temporarily bog down an otherwise well-paced comedy.

Modern *auteurs*: Martin Scorsese, Quentin Tarantino and David Lynch

After Kubrick, a number of directors with strong personal styles continued to make creative use of pre-existing music, both popular and classical, in preference to freshly composed original scores. Among the boldest were Martin Scorsese and Quentin Tarantino, both of whom were steeped in film history and littered their work with knowing references to audio and visual elements from other films. Overall sound design became crucially important to the impact of their films, a preoccupation also encountered in the often subtler work of David Lynch.

Scorsese's occasional collaborations with composers of the stature of Herrmann and Elmer Bernstein brought particular stylistic resonances to his work, which (as in the case of *Taxi Driver*) he knowingly tapped. More characteristic was a realist aesthetic which, even in his first film *Who's That Knocking at My Door?* (1968), aimed to capture the effect of being bombarded by wildly different types of music in a cosmopolitan neighbourhood, whether opera, rock'n'roll, radio, jukebox or jazz: 'That was just how crazy this world actually was, and it made me think, why don't they do that in films?' (Thompson and Christie 1989, 28). He was intrigued by scores comprised exclusively of source music, such as that to William Wellman's seminal gangster film *Public Enemy* (1931; music by David Mendoza), an interest that later bore fruit in *Mean Streets* (1973). In Scorsese's boxing biopic *Raging Bull* (1980), he 'was able to use the songs that I grew up with and draw on my own collection of 78s. Each scene is set at a certain date and there's not a song in the background of the film that wouldn't have been played on the radio at that time. In the mix, I could also slip lyrics that I liked in between dialogue' (Thompson and Christie 1989, 83). Feeling that merely using music to establish period and location was inherently uninventive, he aimed to give his cues emotional impact too, as is readily evident by the time of his later gangster movie *Goodfellas* (1990). Very different from the Rota-style ethnicity of earlier gangster scores (see Chapter 9), the film's 'golden oldies' music track included 'Italian doo-wop' decadence with Vito and the Salutations' version of 'Unchained Melody', but also featured Cream's 'Sunshine of Your Love' for the year 1967; this seemed bizarre to some, but the record was in the US charts at the time, and it was the only one of no fewer than ten songs tried out against the image sequence that gave 'a real sense of danger and sexuality'. Other songs were selected by Scorsese not just for emotional impact but also for their dramatically appropriate lyrics, and some were played back on set during shooting (Thompson and Christie 1989, 160–1). The same approach conditioned the soundtrack design of *Casino* (1995), where the eclectic mix was extended to include Bach's *St Matthew Passion* alongside the music of Louis Prima and many others. In general, Scorsese 'used pop music as a Greek chorus, an off-screen commentary which gave the audience a clearer sense of passing time than his insulated characters and which indicated some intriguing links between the conservatism of romantic nostalgia and the capacity for violence' (Toop 1995, 75).

Scorsese was also interested in the work of contemporary recording artists, notably Peter Gabriel, but occasionally fell foul of licensing problems (as he had in *Mean Streets*). He had hoped to use Gabriel on the soundtrack for *The Color of Money* (1986) but encountered difficulties in negotiating a deal with his record label, Geffen, which also meant that music in the film by Robbie Robertson could not feature the latter's voice and even the singer's atmospheric moaning had to be cleared for use (Thompson and

Christie 1989, 110). Gabriel eventually contributed music to *The Last Temptation of Christ* (1988), drawing on elements of North African and Middle Eastern ethnic traditions appropriate to the biblical setting, and recording with Egyptian drummers, Pakistani vocalists and Indian string players. Scorsese had wanted him for the project because 'the rhythms he uses reflect the primitive, and his vocals reflect the sublime – it's as if the spirit and the flesh are together right there' (Thompson and Christie 1989, 142). Conventionality intruded when the human side of the dual Jesus character grows old in the company of a guardian angel to synthesized baroque pastiche, but the eruption of a triumphant pop theme for his entry into Jerusalem on Palm Sunday after 90 minutes without memorable melody is effectively timed. Gabriel was also involved in the soundtrack for *Gangs of New York* (2002), in which the opening fight sequence emulated the high degree of stylization of music video and undoubtedly reflected the influence on Scorsese of the vivid styles of younger directors Baz Luhrmann and Tarantino.

Even more than Scorsese, the idiosyncratic Tarantino – like his idol Godard – preferred absolute control over the musical elements in his films, commenting 'I'm a little nervous about the idea of working with a composer because I don't like giving up that much control. Like, what if he goes off and writes a score and I don't like it?' (Romney and Wootton 1995, 127). Ideas for films often came from specific musical stimuli ('I immediately try to find out what would be the right song to be the opening credit sequence even before I write the script') and it mattered not whether the subject-matter or date of the songs were relevant to the story as long as they had 'the right sound, and the right feel' (Romney and Wootton 1995, 130). Unlike commercial producers, Tarantino claimed to have no interest in using pop songs to sell soundtrack albums and felt that using well-known songs to pander to audience tastes is 'lazy film-making – unless you're doing it for a specific reason' (Romney and Wootton 1995, 131, 139). (MCA's album from *Pulp Fiction* nevertheless spent two years in the charts and sold over three million copies: see J. Smith 1998, 195.) One of his most powerful specific reasons is deliberate anempathy, notoriously demonstrated in *Reservoir Dogs* (1991) by the provocative use in a gripping torture scene of Stealers Wheel's 'Stuck in the Middle with You', part of a stream of diegetic bubblegum rock broadcast in 'K Billy's Super Sounds of the 70s' in real time as part of a retro Seventies weekend. The strategy exemplifies what Chion terms the 'cosmic indifference' displayed by such inappropriate music 'progressing in a steady, undaunted and ineluctable manner . . . [its] studied frivolity and naiveté reinforce the individual emotion of the character and of the spectator, even as the music pretends not to notice them' (Chion 1994, 8).

Tarantino's choice of songs in *Pulp Fiction* (1994), which contains no commissioned music in its soundtrack, was in part occasioned by the dramatic suitability of, or irony in, their lyrics. For example, a ceramic kangaroo in Bruce Willis's apartment is linked to the Statler Brothers' 'Flowers on the Wall', with its reference to 'Captain Kangaroo' (a usage ironically referenced in Willis's film *Die Hard with a Vengeance*, released in the following year), and Urge Overkill's cover of Neil Diamond's 'Girl, You'll Be a Woman Soon' plays diegetically before the fragile Mia accidentally overdoses. To this extent, Tarantino indulged in a basic recognition game familiar since the days of silent film, and deducing the appropriateness of his song choices became so familiar a game that aficionados dedicated entire websites to it. Mia's passion for old songs is reflected in her reliance on outmoded audio equipment, a reel-to-reel tape recorder for 'Girl' and a turntable for Dusty Springfield's 'Son of a Preacher Man'. Music is generally foregrounded in the film's more consciously stylized scenes and does not interfere with the *vérité*-style narrative advancement. A potent influence here was the French New Wave. Godard, whose unpredictable and anempathetic use of music Tarantino much admired, provided a specific model in the shape of *Bande à part* (1964), the latter's jukebox-dance the inspiration for the expressive twist performed (to the strains of Chuck Berry) by John Travolta and Uma Thurman with a studied amateurishness. Also reminiscent of Godard is the manner in which the Dusty Springfield song is only revealed to have been diegetic when we see the needle come up from the LP at the end of the scene in question, and further New Wave wit underlies the title sequence in which Dick Dale and the Del-Tones' 'Misirlou' is truncated by a designedly bad sound edit (suggesting the sudden retuning of a radio) to coincide with music supervisor Karyn Rachtman's on-screen credit.

In *Pulp Fiction* Tarantino emphasized surf music because he felt it created something of a spaghetti-western ambience, likening 'Misirlou' (which became a hit again after his film was released) to the soundworld of *The Good, the Bad and the Ugly*. The spaghetti-western influence returned more explicitly in *Kill Bill Vol. 1* (2003) with its strummed guitars, mariachi trumpets, panpipes, whistled melodies and citations of music by Morricone, Bacalov and Armando Tovajoli; the allusions to Japanese music served as a reminder of the American western's debt to the samurai film, with its related obsession with honour and revenge. (The spaghetti-western allusion in Luhrmann's *William Shakespeare's Romeo + Juliet* (1996) seems also to have been motivated by the same dramatic topics.) *Kill Bill Vol. 2* included music by mariachi king Robert Rodriguez, and both soundtracks included the work of hip-hop artist The RZA, who had an intimate knowledge of kung-fu films (see Chapter 10).

The punctilious and sometimes experimental soundtracks of Lynch's films were very much director-led, and reflected his belief that 'The borderline between sound effects and music is the most *beautiful* area' (quoted in Davison 2004, 185). He once commented 'People call me a director, but I really think of myself as a sound-man' (Davison 2004, 170). Like many *auteurs* with strong views on sound design, Lynch deeply distrusted the conventional film-making practice whereby a composer's music is added to a film at the last moment, but found a flexible collaborator in the shape of Angelo Badalamenti, who was unusually accommodating to his wishes; they worked together on the music tracks of *Blue Velvet* (1986), *Wild at Heart* (1990), *Lost Highway* (1997) and *The Straight Story* (1999), and Badalamenti's music appeared in a number of Lynch's projects for television and their feature-length theatrical spin-offs, *Twin Peaks: Fire Walk With Me* (1992) and *Mulholland Drive* (2001). Badalamenti's scoring was at times able to translate Lynch's preoccupation with evil and perversion lurking behind innocent façades into appropriately ambiguous musical moods, and the director's respect for it was demonstrated in the *Twin Peaks* film where the music was allowed to dominate a scene so forcibly that characters' dialogue was rendered virtually inaudible and (in America, at least) had to be subtitled – an exceptionally rare phenomenon. Lynch's work is acclaimed for its imaginative sound design (especially his juxtaposition of conceptually or physically related sound events in linear editing), and Badalamenti recalled that he would sometimes provide raw musical material with which the director could himself experiment:

> On both *Lost Highway* and *Mulholland Drive*, I gave David multiple music tracks, which we call 'firewood.' I'd go into the studio and record these long 10- to 12-minute cues with a full orchestra. Sometimes I'd add synthesizers to them. I'd vary the range of the notes, then layer these musical pieces together. All would be at a slow tempo. Then David would take this stuff like it was firewood, and he'd experiment with it. So that's what a lot of the 'musical' sound design stuff is that you're hearing. David really creates beautiful things with it.
> (Schweiger 2001, 26)

Provocative use is sometimes made of pre-existing music, most famously the anempathetic application of Roy Orbison's 'In Dreams' in *Blue Velvet* (1986) where collisions between easy-going popular music and images of violence and bloodshed seem to look ahead to the Tarantino of *Reservoir Dogs*: a tape of the Orbison played in a car diegetically accompanies a brutal beating, while Ketty Lester's rendition of 'Love Letters' forms a seemingly nondiegetic accompaniment to the discovery of two grisly corpses (though, in a Godardian touch, the music cuts off abruptly as the door is closed on the scene, suggesting a possible diegetic source). Lynch's soundtracks have been closely analysed by Annette Davison, who demonstrates how they can represent a reaction against the traditional postproduction distinctions between music, sound and dialogue. Her case-study of *Wild at Heart* (Davison 2004,

12.3 Isabella Rossellini (as Dorothy Vallens) performs diegetically in David Lynch's *Blue Velvet* (1986). At the piano is the film's composer, Angelo Badalamenti (as Andy Badale).

170–95) shows how a complex web of musical elements, both diegetic and nondiegetic, is seemingly governed by the character of Sailor, who 'functions as a stand-in for Lynch as controller of the soundtrack' (Davison 2004, 72); the sharp contrast between Strauss's *Four Last Songs* and a contemporary speed-metal band sets up a violent stylistic and cultural antithesis which Chion sees as a further instance of the influence of Godard (Chion 1995, 357).

Those who wish to pursue *auteur* theory to its logical limits will be disappointed that exceptionally few film directors have also composed the music to their own films. The case of John Carpenter was examined above, and Mike Figgis wrote his own sometimes jazz-tinged scores to his films *Stormy Monday* (1987), *Internal Affairs* (1990), *Liebestraum* (1991), *Leaving Las Vegas* (1995), *One Night Stand* (1997), *The Loss of Sexual Innocence* (1998), *Miss Julie* (1999), *Timecode* (2000), *Hotel* (2001) and *Cold Creek Manor* (2003). John Ottman worked on *The Usual Suspects* (1995) in the unusual dual roles of composer and film editor, and wrote several scores for other directors before making his own directing debut with *Urban Legends: Final Cut* (2000), for which he also provided parts of the music track and film editing. On that project Ottman tried to keep his three functions separate, however, and subscribed to the old belief that 'the score's job is to make the film better. To me the challenge and the excitement of scoring is to fix as many problems in the movie and come out with people saying, "God that works now"' (Koppl 2000, 33). Alejandro Amenábar composed electronic music for his Spanish films *Luna* (1995), *Thesis* (1996) and *Open My Eyes* (1997), and for several films by other directors. For his first English-language feature, *The Others* (2001), he supplied impressionistic orchestral scoring in a traditional vein, confessing to the influences of Elmer Bernstein, Goldsmith, Williams and Herrmann.

At the other extreme, Danish director Lars Von Trier's Dogme 95 initiative attempted to do away with the concept of authorship once and for all, reclaiming for film a purity that he felt had been sullied by bourgeois romanticism: the movement's ten rules constituted a 'vow of chastity' and included a ban on nondiegetic music and genre films. Dogme 95 lasted from 1995 until 2002, when the proponents realized that it had in fact created its own distinctive genre by default. Trier's controversial *The Idiots* (Dogme 2, 1998), which broke the manifesto's own rules in its inexplicable inclusion of snippets of Saint-Saëns's *The Swan* arranged for solo harmonica, showed that the results could be little better than what might be expected from a second-rate film student let loose with a hand-held video camera, no budget and a desire to shock by breaking an enduring taboo (in this case, mental handicap). In his other work, including the unorthodox musical *Dancer in the Dark* (see Chapter 10), Von Trier demonstrated an imaginative approach to tracking, for example his deployment of glam-rock recordings from the 1970s both structurally and emblematically in *Breaking the Waves* (1996: see J. Smith 1998, 221–3).

The modern mainstream

Film music in today's Hollywood, though more eclectic than ever in its mix of orchestral, electronic, ethnic and popular elements, has seen little essential change in the past three decades. Composers work on a freelance basis, striving either with an agent or (more rarely) independently to achieve commissions. Package deals give composers personal responsibility for making all recording arrangements and meeting necessary expenses, while non-package deals mean the composer receives a lower fee and assistants are paid individually. In 2004, package deals ranged from approximately $15,000 on independent productions to as much as $800,000 on major features; the additional cost of licensing pre-existing music, which increased significantly owing to the boom in soundtrack-album sales in the 1980s and can now be enormous, has to be carefully controlled for total music budgets not to be prohibitive, though pop music remains a somewhat special category as a unique marketing tool and synergistic interests help finance its use (Karlin and Wright 2004, 466). So-called 'back-end' deals provide composers working on low-budget projects with the opportunity to make their money after a film's release if it proves to be successful: an uninspiring growth area in this regard since the 1990s has been formulaic erotic thrillers that can become money-spinners on cable and satellite TV after initial late-night theatrical screenings. Music contractors (fixers) play a crucial role in securing professional performers who, even at their most experienced, generally record only two to four minutes of music for each hour in the studio and work for two three-hour sessions daily. Sustaining a career as a successful freelance film composer is a complex affair in which creative ability is by no means the leading requirement: entrepreneurial skills, efficiency, adaptability and the ability to function effectively as part of a team are more important.

As with other aspects of film-making, studio recordings are an international business, with facilities in Europe and elsewhere often used instead of those in the USA for reasons both of economics and availability. Significant stateside competition to musicians based in Los Angeles also comes from standing symphony orchestras in Seattle and Utah that record film music through deals negotiated directly with production companies. Michael Kamen thought highly of the Seattle orchestra when it recorded his music to *Die Hard With a Vengeance* in 1995, but wondered whether, because the *Die Hard* franchise represented 'a particularly energetic LA kind of movie', he 'should be working with the LA musicians . . . They can turn on a dime, there's nothing they can't play . . . Like many other things the field of play is changing and it's very expensive to record a score in LA . . . In a nutshell it boils down to going to Seattle and knowing that I can have an artistic great time with the orchestra' (Shivers 1995, 15). Many tributes have been paid to the standards of musicians in London, but some Hollywood composers felt a need to be more conservative in style when working in England. Marc Shaiman, for example, was not convinced British musicians could achieve a Stalling-like cartoon style of playing for *George of the Jungle* in 1997 and got his own way by persuading Disney to relocate the recording sessions to LA (Schelle 1999, 298–9). Thomas Newman found he worked more cautiously when away from his regular collaborators and recording the music for *Little Women* in London in 1994 (Schelle 1999, 280). Howard Shore found British percussionists too 'square' and not as hip as LA session musicians, though in the end felt this suited his purposes when the London Philharmonic played his bongo-dominated Beatnik dance music in *Ed Wood*, recorded in the UK because the LA studios were fully booked (Schelle 1999, 353). Significantly, objections of this nature from US composers tend to concern styles of music closely associated with their homeland.

The most active and sought-after freelance composers as the century turned (with the exception of those from the older Williams generation discussed above) all began their careers in the 1980s. Prominent among them were Danny Elfman, Elliot Goldenthal, James Horner, James Newton Howard, the late Michael Kamen, Howard Shore and Hans Zimmer. Less well known internationally but equally proficient and versatile were Marco Beltrami, Bruce Broughton, Carter Burwell, Bill Conti, Mark Isham, Mark Mancina, Basil Poledouris, Marc Shaiman, Alan Silvestri and Christopher Young. With the exception of Shore (Canada) and Zimmer (Germany), the above all hailed from the USA, though a significant number of composers from other countries carved important niches for themselves in Hollywood in both the 1980s and 1990s: these included David Arnold (UK), Mychael Danna (Canada), Patrick Doyle (UK), George Fenton (UK), Trevor Jones (UK), Wojciech Kilar (Poland), John Powell (UK), Zbigniew Preisner (Poland), Graeme Revell (New Zealand), John Scott (UK) and Gabriel Yared (Lebanon/France).

Apart from Gillian Anderson's indefatigable work in the silent-cinema revival (see Chapter 1), scoring opportunities remained indefensibly few for women composers even well into the 1990s. The first major Hollywood commissions for a female composer went to the late Shirley Walker for John Carpenter's *Memoirs of an Invisible Man* (1992) and the animated feature *Batman: Mask of the Phantasm* (dir. Eric Radomski and Bruce W. Timm, 1993). The first Academy Awards for film music written by women went to two British composers, first Rachel Portman for her score to the Jane Austen adaptation *Emma* (dir. Douglas McGrath, 1996), then to Anne Dudley for her music to the hit comedy *The Full Monty* (dir. Peter Cattaneo, 1997), both films significant successes for the British film industry but as ever dependant on US funding. In other capacities, however, women were increasingly active and influential in the film-music business as music supervisors, composers' agents and orchestral contractors.

Most music by the composers named above still continued to fall squarely into the three traditional categories of scoring identified by Broughton: catching the action (mickey-mousing), suggesting the mood, or not referring 'to anything in particular' (Schelle 1999, 91). Calculated anempathy remained rare. The first of Broughton's three approaches was generally restricted to cartoons, fantasy, comedy and some action adventures, being considered too superficial for serious subject-matter. Basic mood music was found in all genres. The third category of neutral music was a particular hallmark of the minimalists, or of those working in other emotionally detached styles. That Broughton does not identify the use of pre-existing music as a valid method of scoring is symptomatic of the lack of control composers often have over such an approach, which nevertheless remains widespread (as we saw in Chapters 10 and 11) and is usually more the province of directors and music editors. Staunch adherents of original scoring still regard the compilation pop score as an 'enemy' of the traditional approach (Bond 2004c, 22), and full orchestral scoring remained a quality signifier in epic productions with huge budgets.

With productions undertaken on an individual package basis and unable to be subsidized by the financial security of the old studio system, today's film composer is even more at the mercy of producers and market forces than in the Golden Age. Many scores are rejected seemingly on a whim, and often at the last moment: a representative selection, including some famous earlier examples, is given in Table 12.2. (For a fuller list, see Bettencourt 2002.) A glance down the composer columns, in which names migrate laterally in both directions, reveals that decisions to reject scores are in no way based on an individual's personal credentials. Sometimes music is rejected when it proves unpopular in pre-screenings held in Los Angeles to gauge audience expectations and responses. These previews, which are also held in the preparation of trailers, are as old as the silent cinema and were used exhaustively by D. W. Griffith, who would screen his films 'not once or twice but dozens of times and . . . would seek out the most unsophisticated audiences that he could find' (Fairservice 2001, 142). As a result, Griffith had continued to rely in part on crowd-pleasing melodramatic elements alongside more innovative techniques. The inevitable conservatism arising from public views expressed at such screenings remains tangible today. By the 1960s, previews were being used to test both the success of conventional underscoring and the commercial viability of a popular song and its artist: Jeff Smith cites by way of example the detailed comments from a preview audience about Quincy Jones's and Ray Charles's contribution to Norman Jewison's 1967 film *In the Heat of the Night* (J. Smith 1998, 53).

By the mid-1990s a Hollywood film would typically be previewed as many as six times, with the audience filling out a questionnaire and further reactions garnered from a smaller focus group of between fifteen and twenty viewers whose opinions might seal the fate of a film's score. Yared's score to *Troy* (2004), for example, was rejected after the film was shown only once, to a group of fewer than twenty people who found it 'old-fashioned', in spite of the director's previous enthusiasm for the music; the devastated composer posted the jettisoned music on his personal website. Yared commented in an interview that previews of his work for Anthony Minghella had previously generated useful constructive criticism, but in the case of *Troy* the rejection was summary and he was not permitted to meet objections that had not been made clear to him; a year's work was wasted (Bond 2004b, 21). Sometimes

Table 12.2 *Selected scores rejected from US and UK features, 1966–2005*

Release date	Film	Director	Rejected score(s)	Release score
1966	*Torn Curtain*	Alfred Hitchcock	Bernard Herrmann	John Addison
1968	*The Lost Continent*	Michael Carreras	Benjamin Frankel	Gerard Schurmann
1968	*2001: A Space Odyssey*	Stanley Kubrick	Alex North	Classical music from temp track
1969	*Battle of Britain*	Guy Hamilton	William Walton	Ron Goodwin
1969	*The Reivers*	Mark Rydell	Lalo Schifrin	John Williams
1970	*The Go-Between*	Joseph Losey	Richard Rodney Bennett	Michel Legrand
1971	*Blind Terror* (US title *See No Evil*)	Richard Fleischer	(1) André Previn (2) David Whitaker	Elmer Bernstein
1972	*The Getaway*	Sam Peckinpah	Jerry Fielding	Quincy Jones
1972	*Frenzy*	Alfred Hitchcock	Henry Mancini	Ron Goodwin
1973	*The Exorcist*	William Friedkin	Lalo Schifrin	Jack Nitzsche
1974	*Chinatown*	Roman Polanski	Philip Lambro	Jerry Goldsmith
1976	*Robin and Marian*	Richard Lester	Michel Legrand	John Barry
1979	*Apocalypse Now*	Francis Ford Coppola	David Shire	Carmine Coppola
1983	*Something Wicked This Way Comes*	Jack Clayton	Georges Delerue	James Horner
1985	*The Journey of Natty Gann*	Jeremy Kagan	Elmer Bernstein	James Horner
1985	*Ordeal by Innocence*	Desmond Davis	Pino Donaggio	Dave Brubeck
1988	*Alien Nation*	Graham Baker	Jerry Goldsmith	Curt Sobel
1991	*The Prince of Tides*	Barbra Streisand	John Barry	James Newton Howard
1991	*White Fang*	Randal Kleiser	Hans Zimmer	Basil Poledouris
1992	*The Bodyguard*	Mick Jackson	John Barry	Alan Silvestri
1992	*The Public Eye*	Howard Franklin	Jerry Goldsmith	Mark Isham
1992	*A River Runs Through It*	Robert Redford	Elmer Bernstein	Mark Isham
1994	*Interview with the Vampire*	Neil Jordan	George Fenton	Elliot Goldenthal
1994	*The River Wild*	Curtis Hanson	Maurice Jarre	Jerry Goldsmith
1995	*The Scarlet Letter*	Roland Joffé	(1) Ennio Morricone (2) Elmer Bernstein	John Barry
1995	*The Perez Family*	Mira Nair	Zbigniew Preisner	Alan Silvestri
1996	*Marvin's Room*	Jerry Zaks	Thomas Newman	Rachel Portman
1996	*Mission: Impossible*	Brian De Palma	Alan Silvestri	Danny Elfman
1996	*Ransom*	Ron Howard	Howard Shore	James Horner
1997	*The Wings of the Dove*	Iain Softley	Gabriel Yared	Edward Shearmur
1998	*Dangerous Beauty*	Marshall Herskovitz	Rachel Portman	George Fenton
1998	*The Horse Whisperer*	Robert Redford	John Barry	Thomas Newman
1998	*Les Misérables*	Bille August	Gabriel Yared	Basil Poledouris
1998	*Practical Magic*	Griffin Dunne	Michael Nyman	Alan Silvestri
2002	*Gangs of New York*	Martin Scorsese	Elmer Bernstein	Howard Shore & Peter Gabriel
2003	*The Hulk*	Ang Lee	Mychael Danna	Danny Elfman
2004	*Troy*	Wolfgang Petersen	Gabriel Yared	James Horner
2005	*King Kong*	Peter Jackson	Howard Shore	James Newton Howard

a score can be rejected for veiled political reasons even after it has been successfully received at a preview, as was the case with Fenton's contribution to *Interview with the Vampire* (1994), and sometimes a film might have two scores by different composers rejected before a third is finally adopted, for example in *The Scarlet Letter* (1995).

Since the 1970s, which saw an increase in market research in the film industry, temp tracks have been an important element in music-track planning. Temp tracks also became important in the preparation of trailers, most of which are initially tracked with proven pre-existing music (often from other films) that needs to be imitated at low cost and considerable speed: some composers, for example John Beal, have specialized in this work. Unless composers stay ahead of the game by succeeding in getting into feature-film temp tracks demos of their own music that may serve as early discussion points with the director (as Elmer Bernstein did with live instruments for Scorsese's *The Age of Innocence*, and most younger composers now do with electronic mock-ups), they will often be put under considerable pressure to provide music close in style to cues already assembled on a temp track, which might include classical works or existing film scores by others. This is the only reason, for example, why a Mozartean idiom is heard in Broughton's music to *Harry and the Hendersons* (dir. William Dear, 1987), the musical style having nothing to do with the film's topic of family campers encountering Big Foot (Schelle 1999, 92), or why the ghost of Enya is present in Horner's score to *Titanic* (dir. James Cameron, 1997). Often cues from the temp track will be retained in the finished product, and the necessary reproduction rights secured. According to music editor Jeff Charbonneau, temp tracks mean that composers are effectively 'castrated before they've even started the job' (Karlin and Wright 2004, 26).

Not surprisingly, in their attempts to emulate pre-existing music on temp tracks some composers have narrowly avoided, and in some cases come close to prosecution for, plagiarism. Many such borrowings have been identified in the work of the prolific Horner, another composer whose career initially blossomed as a result of the boom in sci-fi blockbusters in the wake of *Star Wars* (he came to prominence with scores for *Star Trek II: The Wrath of Khan*, 1982; *Star Trek III: The Search for Spock*, 1984; and *Aliens*, 1986), but dipped after legal action from Rota's estate alleging that *Honey, I Shrunk the Kids* (1989) contained an uncredited reuse of a theme from *Amarcord* and a similar allegation about the soundtrack's unauthorized use of music by Raymond Scott (see Chapter 7). A list of Horner's alleged borrowings, and a sympathetic discussion of them, is given by Doug Adams (1998b), who cites an amusing anecdote about a director who is reputed to have 'held up cards to the orchestra naming each composer as the score was recorded' (Adams 1998b, 38). The most recent accusation at the time of writing concerns the similarity between a music cue in the sword-and-sandals epic *Troy* (2004) and a passage from the Sanctus of Britten's *War Requiem* (which is still in copyright); other works Horner appeared to have plundered in this score include Shostakovich's Fifth Symphony and Prokofiev's *Alexander Nevsky*, and the end-credit song was based on Vaughan Williams's *Tallis Fantasia* – a model also for the string writing in Horner's score to *Glory* in 1989 (Donnelly 2005, 77). The strong Russian influences on his music seemed more apt in his compelling score to the Stalingrad drama *Enemy at the Gates* (dir. Jean-Jacques Annaud, 2001).

Part of the recycling problem may well be the need to produce readily communicable music at high speed: as the table of rejected scores shows, Horner is often in demand to provide replacement scores, and at exceptionally short notice. Six to eight weeks remains the normal turnaround time for writing and recording Hollywood scores, but a replacement score can be accomplished in as little as four to five; Horner's music to replace Yared's rejected score to *Troy* was reportedly assembled in just two. Horner, like many hard-pressed film composers, also recycles his own material relentlessly from film to film, and himself noted that there have been cases of composers running into trouble with directors for reproducing the music from previous projects too closely (Bond 2004a, 18). Ubiquitous Horner fingerprints include sonorous trombone triads an augmented fourth apart – a device occurring in *Braveheart*, *Apollo 13* and *Titanic* – and stereotypical action music with prominent percussion. *New Yorker* critic Alex Ross summarized the situation regarding *Troy* with a witty swipe at both the lack of originality in modern film music and the pretentiousness of some contemporary critical appraisals of it:

> There are two possible interpretative approaches to this challenging opus. One is that Horner is presenting us with a kind of musical meta-narrative of deconstructive requotation – a postmodern tour-de-force on par with the Pierre Menard *Don Quixote*. Notice the emphasis on Shostakovich and Prokofiev, two composers who served unwillingly as mouthpieces for totalitarian terror. We are being told that the hero Achilles has let himself become a figurehead for the tyrannical Agamemnon. The citation of Britten, meanwhile, is a sly acknowledgement of the story's homoerotic subtext, which was evidently omitted for fear of persecution by the Bush regime. Thus, music becomes what Theodor W. Adorno might call a *negative dialectic of original unoriginality*, allowing the seeming banality of impoverished invention to serve as a vessel for the lamentations of the outcast. By reducing other people's masterworks to cheap ditties, Horner shakes his fist at the suffocating weight of bourgeois culture. In the absence of an individual voice, we are given to perceive the destruction of individuality itself.
>
> That's one explanation. The other is that the man is a hack.   (Ross 2004)

In spite of damning criticisms of his recyclings, at the end of the 1990s Horner held joint first place with Williams as the two film composers with the greatest number of Top 10 successes in the *Variety* charts, and in 1998 Horner's first *Titanic* album beat even the Spice Girls in quantity of sales (Sikoryak 2000, 25).

Temp tracks are also a convenient way for recording labels to attempt to persuade film-makers to adopt pop songs from their catalogues. MCA and other record companies routinely send samplers from their back catalogues and new releases in a blanket approach to today's all-powerful music supervisors in the hope that, if something gets its way into the temp track, the director might grow attached to it and keep it in the finished product (J. Smith 2001, 412–13). Since the 1970s music supervisors increasingly served as 'a sort of musical casting director':

> Once the score's concept is agreed upon by the film-maker, distributor, and record company, then the music supervisor will assist in providing suitable composers, songwriters, and recording artists to match that concept. In doing so, the music supervisor operates with an eye toward budget considerations, the promotional value of various musical materials, and the dramatic appropriateness of the score's concept.   (J. Smith 1998, 210)

In seeking 'suitable composers', rigid typecasting is common: a risk is unlikely to be taken on an unproven composer or one who likes to experiment. Typecasting might arise from proven generic specialisms: Broughton was much in demand for westerns, for example, Beltrami for horror, Elfman for fantasies, Isham for jazz scoring and Powell for CGI animation. Alternatively, a composer might be typecast according to specific successes with either traditional orchestral scoring or electronics because, as Thomas Newman bemoans, 'In Hollywood, you are what people think you are' (Schelle 1999, 273).

In other ways working in modern Hollywood productions presents problems identical with those of the earlier age. Sound effects still dominate the final mix and drown out music cues – good examples occur in the action scenes of *Titanic* where Horner's music is almost inaudible – a bane of their existence that leads some composers into often vain attempts to find out the director's or sound department's intentions in advance. Stock instrumental gestures remain commonplace, for example bluesy saxophone for sleaze and the more refined soprano saxophone for gentler romance. Isham has identified the sheer quotidian functionality of such rhetoric: 'you throw a soprano sax in there for the romance and it works fine for a film that's gonna play its five weeks in the theaters and then sit in the video store. Why not?' (Schelle 1999, 208). A basis on recognizable themes is as common as it was with the work of Williams in the 1970s, as is the use of a fundamentally tonal idiom with modernist outbursts reserved for violence or irrationality – especially in that most clichéd of all generic types, the horror film. Some composers, notably James Newton Howard and Thomas Newman, avoid writing specific themes for individual characters, but a leitmotivic basis is otherwise commonplace.

Musical Americana, already prominent in 1950s film scores and especially westerns, was further developed in the 1960s by songwriter Randy Newman (Alfred's nephew), who later embarked on film scoring with nationalistic elements and in recent years has worked extensively in CGI features (P. Winkler 2000, 56). A post-Copland pandiatonic 'presidential' idiom remained indestructible: in the 1990s it continued to reflect the patriotic overtones of certain films scored by Newton Howard (*Dave*; dir. Ivan Reitman, 1993), Horner (*Apollo 13*; dir. Ron Howard, 1995) and Shaiman (*The American President*; dir. Rob Reiner, 1995). It also received darkly hued reworkings in Williams's scores for *JFK* (1991) and *Nixon* (1995), both directed by Oliver Stone. Williams's music for Spielberg's *Saving Private Ryan* (1998) was typical of the style's indelible association with the military when the noble diatonic harmony is coloured by a trumpet solo *da lontano*, another of many such instances being Horner's music for *Courage Under Fire* (dir. Edward Zwick, 1996). *Forrest Gump* (dir. Robert Zemeckis, 1994), a film that excited much attention for its systematic use of pop music from different eras (see Chapter 10), was arguably more significant for its strategic deployment of linking music by Alan Silvestri in a sentimental-presidential vein as a cohesive device, this without any trace of the irony that would be necessary for the film to be viewed as a statement to the effect that 'you have to be an idiot to believe in the American dream' (J. Walker 2006, 418). Shaiman pulled off a tour-de-force mini-anthology of varied Americana in a bravura cue for the animated main-title sequence of the comedy western *City Slickers* (dir. Ron Underwood, 1991), with its brilliantly timed allusions to metropolitan jazz, cartoon gestures and the rousing prairie music of Elmer Bernstein: written with the aid of a MIDI keyboard in just a day and a half and patched together from short recorded segments in the studio (Schelle 1999, 296), this showed how a pressurized working environment and reworking of clichés could still reap impressive creative results.

At the turn of the century, the blockbuster mentality persisted, and composers were far more likely to achieve international recognition from their music for extravagantly expensive epics than for their less predictable work in other genres. Howard Shore, for example, who began his career as musical director for *Saturday Night Live*, achieved fame with his huge scores for Peter Jackson's *Lord of the Rings* trilogy (2001–3) – that for *The Fellowship of the Ring* alone required 170 hours of studio recording sessions, split between New Zealand and London – with music far more direct in appeal than the experimentation he had demonstrated in his earlier collaborations with Cronenberg. The latter had given him the freedom to explore avant-garde leanings that seemed suited to the disturbing psychological undercurrents of many of his unorthodox films, among them *The Fly* (1986), its score based on tonal harmonies overloaded with added dissonances for eeriness, *Dead*

Ringers (1988), *Naked Lunch* (1991) and *Crash* (1996), the last a particularly bold and chilling score involving multiple electric guitars, harps, wind, percussion and electronically processed sound. In the otherwise aesthetically moribund genres of horror and thriller Shore had also excelled, proving something of a specialist in handling the psychologies of serial killers: *The Silence of the Lambs* (dir. Jonathan Demme, 1990) was imbued with a sense of foreboding by the carefully controlled dissonance levels of what the composer termed his 'dread tonality' (Schelle 1999, 347–8) and his contribution to *Se7en* (dir. David Fincher, 1995) helped to make it one of the finest neo-*noir* ventures of the decade; his work in this vein continued impressively in his rejected score for *Ransom* (1996). But for *Lord of the Rings*, Shore forewent such experimentation and produced the kind of sombre music in slow harmonic rhythms, predominantly minor in key and almost wall-to-wall, typically used in modern epics to suggest an awe-inspiring mythology but usually resulting in moments of leaden dramatic pacing. This tendency is particularly noticeable in modern takes on epics set in ancient Mediterranean civilizations, in the 1950s splendid in their pageantry but in the 2000s altogether darker affairs; conservatism is endemic in these scores, whether the recitative-like underscoring of dialogue with low strings in Horner's *Troy* or Vangelis's characteristically slow rate of harmonic change and alternation of basic idioms for struggle and heroism in *Alexander* (dir. Oliver Stone, 2004), a score which contains 1950s clichés such as harp timbres for an intimate interior setting and Rózsa-like diegetic fanfares. A common device in such films is the suppression of ambient battle sound and introduction of dignified music to accompany violence, often in conjunction with slow-motion images; used in Kurosawa's *Ran* (1985) and Branagh's *Henry V* (1989), the technique recurred for the sack of the city in *Troy*, for the elephant attack in *Alexander*, and in *Gladiator* (dir. Ridley Scott, 2000), scored by Zimmer.

Zimmer was propelled into the international limelight by being in the right place at the right time – and working on high-profile money-spinning genres, often those produced by Bruckheimer. Like that of many film composers of his generation, Zimmer's background was in television and rock music, his score for the British production *My Beautiful Laundrette* (dir. Stephen Frears, 1985), financed by Channel 4 and its music co-composed by his mentor Stanley Myers, catching the attention of Hollywood director Barry Levinson. In order to create a deliberately unorthodox ambience designed to reflect the USA as seen through the eyes of an autistic savant, Levinson made *Rain Man* (1988) with the German composer and an Australian cinematographer. That this film and Zimmer's next assignment, Bruce Beresford's *Driving Miss Daisy* (1989), both won Academy Awards for Best Picture, helped rapidly secure the composer work for a clutch of front-rank directors in 1990–91, including Schlesinger (*Pacific Heights*), Weir (*Green Card*), Scott (the seminal feminist road movie *Thelma and Louise*) and Howard (*Backdraft*). Still wider exposure came with his involvement in Disney's *The Lion King*, which won him an Academy Award in 1994. Although Zimmer's music can lay little claim to originality, he exploited a basic electronics-plus-orchestra formula that became omnipresent in the scoring of thrillers, especially those involving seductive technology: as Isham describes the approach, 'You get the rhythmic drive from a synthesizer and overlay an orchestra on top of it to give you that big Hollywood quality', a technique Isham himself emulated in his scores for *The Getaway* (dir. Roger Donaldson, 1994) and *The Net* (dir. Irwin Winkler, 1995). Isham admits that such music 'has a very utilitarian role. It's just there – it's just churning along. You could write decent music, you could write brilliant music. I don't really know if it would make that big a difference in a film where music is used in that way' (Schelle 1999, 215–16). Zimmer also fronted a team of up-and-coming film composers working under the aegis of his Remote Control Productions company (formerly Media Ventures).

A rising star of the 1990s who began in the recording industry was James Newton Howard. Like others from such a background, he thrived on working in an environment where collaboration is the order of the day and likened creating film music to conceiving an album based on rhythmic grooves. He found that his style expanded on the job, gradually moving away from the piano-dominated textures of his early work to more inventive textural and timbral possibilities. He scored a wide range of genres with economy and restraint, including domestic drama (*The Prince of Tides*, 1991), thriller (*The Fugitive*, 1993), costume drama (*Restoration*, 1995) and horror (*The Sixth Sense*, 1999), the last initiating a number of collaborations with director M. Night Shyamalan (*Signs*, 2002; *The Village*, 2004). Howard's typical method of working is to give sequences to a copyist who processes them as MIDI files then prints them out for the composer to edit (Schelle 1999, 190), a procedure also used by Elfman; as with most composers versed in electronics, synthesized mock-ups can be prepared by Howard in his own studio to serve as demos for a director. When brought in to rescore Peter Jackson's remake of *King Kong* at short notice in 2005 (Shore's score having been rejected in spite of his recent successes with the same director's Tolkien epics), the logistics were typically complex. The orchestral music had to be recorded in sessions arranged over thirteen days at four different studios owing to booking pressures on the venues (Sony Studios at Culver City, Todd-AO and Warner Bros. at Burbank, and Fox in Los Angeles), with some cues only completed the night before a session and still being orchestrated at 4am. Howard never met Jackson in person but discussed mock-ups with him via a video link to the director's native New Zealand.

(Similarly, Williams had sent music cues for *Jurassic Park* to Spielberg daily via secure communications links when the latter had already embarked on shooting *Schindler's List* in Poland, and Horner did not deal face-to-face with Cameron when working on *Titanic*.) During mixing, Howard's electronic mock-ups and orchestral material were reworked – the original mock-ups were so complete and convincing that the director could not always tell the difference between prototype and finished product – and both director and composer commented that, far from being a hindrance to creativity, the pressure of time and adrenaline rush were crucial to the intensity of the end-product (P. Jackson 2006). Imaginative use was made of elements from Steiner's 1933 score, its main motif occurring subtly when Cooper is mentioned as a possible director for the film-within-the-film and the original film score accompanying the Broadway stage routine before the climax, the theatricality of the new setting neatly preventing Steiner's idiom from sounding unduly dated.

After Spielberg and Williams, the most distinctive and enduring composer–director partnership in Hollywood has been that between Danny Elfman and Tim Burton, whose Gothic sense of fantasy has been played out in an important and substantial corpus of highly imaginative films. Beginning his career as a member of rock group Oingo Boingo, Elfman was brought into film work by Burton for the low-budget *Pee-wee's Big Adventure* (1985) and their later collaborations were *Beetlejuice* (1988), *Batman* (1989), *Batman Returns* (1992), *Edward Scissorhands* (1990), *The Nightmare Before Christmas* (1993), *Mars Attacks!* (1996), *Sleepy Hollow* (1999), a remake of *Planet of the Apes* (2001), *Charlie and the Chocolate Factory* (2005) and *The Corpse Bride* (2005). Elfman was a great admirer of Herrmann's film scores and these were to exert a tangible influence on his own methods, particularly the quirky Herrmann of Harryhausen's fantasy animations, which influenced Burton's stop-time animation in *Nightmare* and *Corpse Bride* (the piano in a scene from the latter sports the name 'Harryhausen' as its manufacturer, and the plot includes an underworld skeletons' cabaret of which the earlier animator would have been proud). The psychedelic main-title sequence of *Charlie* is a direct throwback to the distinctive combination of Bass's swirling graphics and Herrmann's pulsating ostinati in their Hitchcock collaborations. Like Herrmann, Elfman found his music occasionally criticized for being too dark in mood: Burton recalled that the producers of *Beetlejuice* were unhappy with the atmosphere it created but (in a rare inversion of preview outcomes) retained it when audiences at a pre-screening thought it significantly enhanced the film (Salisbury 2006, 66). Hallmarks of Elfman's style include the fairy-tale sound of wordless children's voices, especially prominent in *Scissorhands*, a solid but often unadventurous tonal idiom with a penchant for minor keys, low-tessitura melodies, and a restless quirkiness universally familiar from his character-istically Lydian-inflected signature tune to the TV animated sitcom *The Simpsons*. Like Zimmer, he often lays down synthesized percussive tracks (based on his own library of samples) prior to overdubbing a live orches-tra, in which scenario a high proportion of the result consists of his own performance: representative examples are his scores to *Dead Presidents* (dir. Allen and Albert Hughes) and *To Die For* (dir. Gus Van Sant), both written in 1995. His sonic experimentation shows an acute ear for timbre, as in the main-title music of *Planet of the Apes* with its memorable combination of sampled pizzicato mixed with an ethnic bamboo percussion instrument.

Critical opinion remains divided on whether Elfman's reworkings of familiar Hollywood gestures constitute a direct continuation of the Golden Age tradition, or a knowingly ironic take on them that equates to a kind of film-scoring neo-classicism, or indeed merely show regressive tendencies as symptomatic of technical limitations. The Gothic fantasy idiom certainly sounded a fresh note in film music, and its specific influence is traceable in Michael Andrews's music for *Donnie Darko* (dir. Richard Kelly, 2001) and a rash of TV commercials, but in other respects (e.g. plentiful thematic rep-etition, occasional recourse to mickey-mousing and a host of conventional instrumental gestures) Elfman's work remained thoroughly conventional. The success of the Batman franchise typecast him as a composer ideally suited to the genre of live-action films based on famous comic-book charac-ters, and for directors other than Burton he accordingly scored *Spider-Man* and its sequel (dir. Sam Raimi, 2002 and 2004) and *Hulk* (dir. Ang Lee, 2003).

Collaboration is an essential feature of modern film scoring, and all the more likely in contexts where composers hail from a rock or recording-industry background or work with their own longstanding groups of musi-cians who are given free creative rein. Arrangers and orchestrators remain crucial to a composer's ability to turn an assignment around by a tight deadline, and it is often far from clear where the line between composition and arrangement should be drawn. Elfman's heavy reliance on assistants made him something of a scapegoat for a persistent and elitist view of the composer's art that insists work achieved by an individual is inher-ently superior to that on which a team has collaborated. This general view was expressed by John Scott, who drew attention to how modern tech-nology allowed untutored composers to work relatively easily in the film business:

> The orchestrator has always been one of the most important elements in
> film scoring but he is even more important for those who compose by
> humming or playing something by ear on a synthesizer and relying on a

computer to print it out. In that sense it's easier to be a composer than it was before. If such a composer is lucky enough to write for a successful picture, then he, too, is a success. But success on those terms is not really what music composition is all about. Also, so much of filmmaking today, every aspect of it, is done by committee decision – and nothing is worse for music than a committee decision.   (quoted in Thomas 1997, 307)

Allegations have been made that Elfman was not responsible for some of the music credited to his name, and his background in pop made him (and others) easy targets in this regard (Halfyard 2004, 10–19). Both Elfman and his principal orchestrator Steve Bartek learnt on the job, Elfman being 'not good at bass clef' and Bartek not having undertaken a large-scale orchestration until he found himself working on *Pee-wee*; they received advice from renowned music editor Bob Badami and conductor Lennie Niehaus, but strenuously denied the allegations of using ghostwriters, while readily admitting that some individual cues had to be written by others owing to pressure of time (Kendall 1995). Uncredited ghostwriting and a farming out of creative tasks have nevertheless long been reputed to be part and parcel of Hollywood film scoring (Schelle 1999, 145). Shirley Walker, who served as Elfman's assistant and conductor on *Batman* and found that the gossip about his reliance on her put a strain on their relationship, commented on the general situation in the business: 'you were paid big money to not talk about the fact that you were doing it and to support the illusion or delusion, whichever you prefer, that composer X was actually doing the work that they were being paid for' (Schelle 1999, 364).

Very different in background to Elfman is Corigliano's pupil Elliot Goldenthal, whose other principal mentor was Copland. With a versatile compositional technique and sharing Corigliano's interest in the East European avant-garde, Goldenthal's film work developed in the 1990s and benefited from his parallel career in the theatre (an experience later reflected in his score for *Titus*, examined in Chapter 4). His filmic working practices, as exemplified by writing the score for *Demolition Man*, drew on the best of both worlds: traditional manuscript composition for 'the general drama of the thing that it's going to be' and computer technology which he believed was useful not only for precise catching of the action but also for enhancing the intimacy and intensity of the creative process: 'when the expression in a person's face is locked into the computer, MIDI-wise, then I can keep going back to that same little glance exactly, and it almost becomes like accompanying an actor in a room' (Kendall 1994, 15). Like most film composers having to produce complex multi-media scores at speed he relies on assistants, including music producer Matthias (Teese) Göhl, who both helps edit the composer's cues to fit changing durations and co-ordinates electronics and live performing forces, and electronic music producer Richard Martinez. The vast majority of a typical Goldenthal score is first prepared as an electronic mock-up, as is now standard practice. Stylistically, many projects reflect his interest in what he terms 'composition as collision' (quoted in M. Walker 1998, 85), a process that draws on idioms ranging from jazz to atonality, often unorthodox instrumentation, imaginative vocal writing, a penchant for explosive passages of violent expressionism, and a strong vein of black humour evident in moments of parody.

The global and the glocal

Although its dominance of international distribution and production funding would suggest that the modern American film industry is the most prolific in the world, only one-tenth of the approximately 4,000 films made each year hail from North America, and the US film industry lags behind India, China and even the Philippines in quantity of output. Two-thirds of all new theatrical films originate from Asian countries, and the combined releases from all European film industries exceeds American productivity by 70 per cent. Within Europe, France is the largest producer, its annual output around half that of the USA, and creating double the quantity of films typically made by the smaller film industries of Italy and the UK (Wilkinson 2007, 52–3). These figures notwithstanding, the powerful American hegemony has seen Hollywood aptly renamed 'Hollyworld' (Thompson and Bordwell 2003, 706). The US film industry continues to capitalize on the massive growth in global media and communications empires since the 1980s, when Warner Communications Inc., Gulf and Western (Paramount), Disney and MCA (Universal) were already leading conglomerates with important recording and publishing interests. Australian newspaper tycoon Rupert Murdoch took over Twentieth Century-Fox in 1985 and established its TV network, founding UK's Sky TV three years later. Japanese electronics manufacturers invested in Hollywood when Sony bought CBS Records and Columbia Pictures in 1986 and 1989 respectively, Matsushita following suit with its purchase of MCA in 1990. These Asian initiatives added hi-tech domestic equipment to the complex dynamics of modern synergy: for example, customers could now play Sony-owned CDs and videos on Sony hi-fis, televisions and VCRs, and by the mid-1990s the company could easily recoup any losses on film investments from its income generated by recorded-music sales (J. Smith 1998, 194). Other multi-billion-dollar mergers included that of Time-Life and Warner in 1989 and Viacom and CBS in 1999. Time-Warner became yet more powerful when it merged with America On Line (AOL) in 2000.

The 1980s also saw a significant growth in sales of the new medium of home video, which sustained a boom in US annual film production from *c.*350 features in 1983 to *c.*600 in 1988; films aimed at the video aftermarket helped the fortunes of new 'mini-major' producers like Cannon and Orion, and independent companies such as New Line (Balio 1998, 58–9). New Line began with adult films in the 1970s, exploiting the allure of the 'X' certificate in the ratings system that had been introduced in 1968, and from 1983 divided its output into commercial films and the art-house tendencies of its Fine Line Features division, which included successes such as Robert Altman's *The Player* (1992), *Shine* (1996: see Chapter 11), and the controversial Cronenberg project *Crash* (also 1996). Another important newcomer, Miramax, also tousled with the ratings system with their Greenaway–Nyman films and Almodóvar's *Tie Me Up! Tie Me Down!* (1989) and did well from films that mixed art-house tendencies with commercial appeal; major successes were *Pulp Fiction* (1994) and *The English Patient* (1996). New Line was acquired by Turner and Miramax by Disney in 1993–4. Also in 1994, the highly successful DreamWorks production company was founded by Spielberg, record magnate David Geffen and former Disney producer Jeffrey Katzenberg, becoming part of the Viacom empire in 2006. Record company Polygram financed independent productions from 1994 onwards and, in Europe, artistically minded television companies did their best to fund relatively low-budget features; in the UK, Channel 4 was particularly important in this regard, co-producing the hit *Trainspotting* (1996) with Polygram and other investors, while in France the cable company Canal Plus poured vital funding into film-making, including the production of highly exportable heritage productions (see Chapter 8). US investment in the European film and television industries increased apace after the relaxation of transatlantic trade restrictions by the European Union in 1992 (Balio 1998, 64), increasing pressure for film-makers to conform to the American industry's norms in order to secure global distribution and financial success. Annette Davison notes that film scholars, though now moving towards a holistic view of world cinema, have still not grappled sufficiently with the extent of the influence of the US film industry's globalizing tendencies, and that in musical specifics the traditional Hollywood score remains a 'dominant ideology in relation to which alternative scoring and soundtrack practices may assert themselves' (Davison 2004, 6) – if they are not to buy wholesale into the Hollywood model.

Paradoxically, as the commercial world shrank, so the global village left its colourful mark on film music in one of the very few fresh scoring trends to emerge since the 1980s: a pervasive use of ethnic instruments and voices, sometimes lending authenticity to a film's cultural or geographical milieu, but at other times perpetuating a generalized timbral exoticism that suggested Hollywood stereotyping was still a guiding spirit. An early pioneer was Mancini, who had used the Japanese mouth organ (*shō*) in *Wait until Dark* (dir. Terence Young, 1967) and a selection of Chinese and Japanese instruments in *The Hawaiians* (dir. Tom Gries, 1970). Next came Jarre, who included Afghan, Persian, Japanese and Indian instruments in his music for the India-set *The Man Who Would Be King* (dir. John Huston, 1975), in contrast to the conventional sounds of the London Symphony Orchestra (MacLean 1993, 36–7). Among those playing ethnic instruments on the soundtrack was George Fenton, who went on to provide acclaimed scores for films set in India (*Gandhi*; dir. Richard Attenborough, 1984) and South Africa (*Cry Freedom*; dir. Attenborough, 1987), for which specialized ethnic musical elements were provided by Ravi Shankar and Jonas Gwangwa respectively. Jarre sampled Indonesian gamelan music in his electronic score to *The Year of Living Dangerously* (dir. Peter Weir, 1982), suggesting that ethnic timbres might provide the same sense of 'otherness' as electronics had formerly done, and used Bulgarian singing in *Jacob's Ladder* (dir. Adrian Lyne 1990). A veritable panpipe craze was initiated by Morricone's music for Joffé's *The Mission* (1986) and De Palma's *Casualties of War* (1989). Bits of Moroccan and Spanish music were sampled and looped by Shore for Cronenberg's Tangiers-set *Naked Lunch* (1991), then combined with the music of Ornette Coleman, who had also recorded with Moroccan musicians (Schelle 1999, 335–6). Moroccan music surfaced again in *8mm* (dir. Joel Schumacher, 1999) where Danna used it to suggest that the underworld of illegal pornography in Los Angeles corresponded to an exotic kasbah.

Goldsmith's score for *The Russia House* (dir. Fred Schepisi, 1990) employed the *duduk*, an Armenian double-reed instrument played by Djivan Gasparyan, whose artistry was also heard in the soundtrack to *Gladiator* along with Eastern-sounding vocals from Zimmer's co-composer Lisa Gerrard. The *duduk* also made its presence felt in Stone's *Alexander* and Scorsese's *The Last Temptation of Christ*; indeed, so widespread did its distinctive sound become, one commentator likened its use to a sonic fetish (Bond 2004d, 16). Ancient epics attracted a good deal of ethnic sonorities, Yared's rejected score to *Troy* replete with Turkish, Macedonian and Bulgarian singers, Celtic harps, crumhorns and medieval instruments. In other quasi-mythical realms, archaic or ethnic elements – both musical and linguistic – lent a timeless and universal quality to sagas such as *Lord of the Rings*, where Shore included a Samoan Maori all-male choir singing Dwarvish and instruments from Africa and India, and *Star Wars: The Phantom Menace*, for which Williams included a choral setting of a Celtic text translated into Sanskrit. Specific ethnic sonorities remained useful as cultural markers, Newton Howard for example pressing Japanese instruments into service for *Snow Falling on Cedars* (dir. Scott Hicks, 1999), but they could also liberate a composer from cultural stereotyping, as when Licht used Indonesian elements not only to characterize Native Americans but also to evade traditional horror music in *Children of the Corn II* (dir. David F. Price, 1992). The thin, nasal sound of authentically played period stringed instruments proved a useful device for simultaneously capturing a historical setting and avoiding romantic musical stereotypes: cold-sounding viols provided a suitably uncomfortable element in Fenton's music to *The Crucible* (dir. Nicholas Hytner, 1996), for example, and folk-like string playing fulfilled a similar function in Yared's music for *Cold Mountain* (dir. Anthony Minghella, 2002).

Celtic music in general, and traditional Irish music in particular, were widely exploited to serve cultural and commercial ends. Period films featuring Irish-Americans routinely received such treatment, well-known examples being *Titanic* (where the Enya of the temp track was replaced by Irish-influenced Norwegian singer Sissel Kyrkjebø) and *Gangs of New York*. The Irish uilleann pipes provided an instant 'Celtic' marker in *Titanic*, and had previously been used by Horner in the Scots saga *Braveheart* (dir. Mel Gibson, 1995); in both cases, as in his music to *Legends of the Fall* (dir. Edward Zwick, 1994), Horner pursued the ethnic suggestiveness through simple folk-inspired orchestral themes. When working on *A River Runs Through It* (1992), director Robert Redford played Mark Isham the unlikely model of Malcolm Arnold's *Scottish Dances* and the music of Jean-Pierre Rampal for inspiration, Isham's eventual policy being to allow folk-like themes to speak for themselves, with interest created primarily by varied orchestrations (Schelle 1999, 208). Goldenthal's score for *Michael Collins* (dir. Neil Jordan, 1996), another soundtrack to feature uilleann pipes, avoided making Irish elements too explicit (Donnelly 2005, 69). In a rare attempt to bypass 'Celtic' clichés altogether, Alan Parker focused instead on 1930s American jazz in his film *Angela's Ashes* (1999), such music being appropriate to the geographical origins of its young protagonist.

On the other side of the world, traditional music and stereotyped Western rhetoric similarly mingled. Chinese cinema, as with the influence of kabuki on early Japanese films (see Chapter 9), had begun as a straightforward extension of Beijing Opera before coming under ideological control from the state. For years Westerners associated the region primarily with the martial-arts genre cultivated by the commercially minded Hong Kong film industry in the 1970s. Attention turned to China in 1985, when the so-called 'Fifth Generation' of Chinese film-makers suddenly came to international prominence with the unveiling of Chen Kaige's *The Yellow Earth* at the Hong Kong Film Festival. As had Indian and Japanese *auteurs* three decades earlier, Chinese directors now found a ready audience in the West and their work (sometimes discredited at home) henceforth negotiated a

cultural middle ground: 'produced by and for Chinese, it also belongs to
an international film history through which China and the West have constructed exotic spectacles for each other' (Reynaud 2000, 161). That this
'otherness' is a two-way process is clearly reflected in modern Chinese film
music. The score for *The Yellow Earth* was by Zhiao Jiping, whose music
became relatively well known in the West following the international success
of *Farewell My Concubine* (dir. Kaige, 1993), a film crucially important for
its melding of elements from Western art film and commercial genres with
the traditional Chinese performing arts (Silvio 2002, 177–9). Jiping's score
likewise brings together East (Chinese fiddle and Beijing Opera percussion)
and West (lush non-functional string chords plus underscoring with drums
and electronics). Jiping also scored *Red Firecracker, Green Firecracker* (dir.
He Ping, 1994), again combining indigenous instruments with modal string
writing; the result, as in some modern Chinese concert music, is remarkably close to how one might imagine Vaughan Williams arranging Asian
folk material. His music for the melodrama *Ju Dou* (dir. Zhang Yimou and
Yang Fengliang, 1990) achieves what has been described as an 'otherworldly
wistfulness' (Mohr 2000), again suggesting a merging of Asian and Western
aesthetics. In 2000, the cross-fertilization between the film traditions of both
hemispheres evident for some years finally struck commercial gold in the
shape of Ang Lee's Oscar-winning *Crouching Tiger, Hidden Dragon* (2000),
a Hong Kong, Taiwanese and US co-production. Its music, by Tan Dun and
recorded by musicians from Shanghai, once more trod a safe cultural middle ground, with renowned cellist Yo Yo Ma playing in portamento Chinese
style, ritual percussion for martial-arts sequences, atmospheric electronics,
a sometimes haphazard juxtaposition of diegetic traditional music (Jen's
wedding procession) and Hollywood-style action music (the attempted
kidnap) – and, inevitably, an end-credit pop song.

European film music remains a neglected area of study, with the first
scholarly book devoted to it appearing as recently as 2006. Its editors,
Miguel Mera and David Burnand, suggest that it is a fallacy to imagine
a pan-European film industry demonstrating consistent characteristics; as
with other aspects of European culture, diversity has always been the watch-
word. It remains relatively rare for non-Anglophone film-makers to make a
significant mark internationally, not only because of film-goers' inveterate
resistance to having to read subtitles but also on account of a fairly rigid distinction between big-budget films (backed by American finance, and often
starring actors with proven international reputations) and the lower-key
art-house cinema which remains the principal forum for innovation but
also inevitably restricts a film's circulation. A case in point is Greek composer Eleni Karaindrou, who since 1982 has been associated with the work
of Theo Angelopoulos – a director, initially much influenced by the French

New Wave, whose laboriously paced and austere films can only appeal to a niche art-house market both in their own country and abroad. Karaindrou's flexible applications of folk elements (sometimes including mandolin and accordion in her instrumentation), classical techniques, jazz and a use of drones is conceptually similar to Preisner's work with Kieślowski in its belief in simplicity, directness and an avoidance of linear narrative flow; her cues often surface 'at moments where metaphorical, political or philosophical issues need to be highlighted, but not necessarily where emotional response is to be elicited' (Mera 2006, 140). Although some of her music is familiar through its appearance on the European modern-jazz record label ECM, her work with Greek directors other than Angelopoulos is not known abroad (Mylonás 2001, 170–3).

European directors who reach wider audiences are likely to do so by tapping contemporary cultural and youth resonances of little interest to an insular figure such as Angelopoulos. Perhaps the best example is Spanish director Pedro Almodóvar, who was a member of Spanish pop subculture before he found fame in film. His early soundtracks were of the 'bricolage' variety (Knights 2006, 92), with pop songs and Hispanic traditional music used for camp coolness and as cultural locators, but grew more conventional from the 1980s onwards. The music track for *What Have I Done to Deserve This?* (1984; music by Bernardo Bonezzi) is partly cast in the typical pop-folk style, with accordion, mandolin and a waltz for the main title, to be found in contemporary films from France and Italy as well as Spain (examples from films by Alain Berliner, Bigas Luna and Jean-Pierre Jeunet are discussed elsewhere). Almodóvar's preferred composer Alberto Iglesias has commented that – as with modern Hollywood composers – his most important attribute is an aptitude for 'polystylistics' (Vernon and Eisen 2006, 51). That European film-makers can achieve an ironic self-referentiality in their use of music to rival that of a Tarantino or the Coen brothers was shown in François Ozon's *8 Women* (2001), a surreal blend of murder mystery, black comedy and the musical embodying plentiful allusions to both US and European filmic traditions. Its score, by Krishna Levy, interrupted the plot with incongruous songs that are recognized as sheer artifice even by the participants themselves: one character curtly asks another as she finishes singing, 'Now you've done your number, when did you last see my husband?' Orchestral underscoring replete with references to the *noir* style of Rózsa and thriller style of Herrmann – and an obvious homage to the main theme of Raksin's *Laura* – sit with calculated oddness alongside the saturated colours of Demy's 1960s French musicals.

Both the film composer's role and the nature of film music continue to change with shifting patterns of production and consumption. Home video sales leapt from around three million in 1980 to 220 million in 1990

(Maltby 1998, 35), and remained buoyant after the turn of the century owing to the popularity of the DVD technology that was launched in 1997 and quickly superseded videotape. Extended directors' cuts released on DVD after a film's theatrical exhibition can now require composers to provide supplementary cues, Shore for example composing as much as half an hour's additional music for each *Lord of the Rings* film solely for the DVD version. This new technology has also affected the way consumers approach a film, which is no longer fixed as an artefact: home viewers can choose between alternative soundtracks, allowing rejected cues and even entire scores to be heard for the first time (e.g. Goldsmith's *Alien* and Walton's *Battle of Britain*), and silent films can be issued with a choice of commissioned scores. By the end of the 1990s distributors (notably Columbia) were including music-only tracks on their DVDs, and some predict that a widespread adoption of this policy may sound the death knell for the traditional soundtrack album. Films can be shortened or resequenced at will according to personal preferences, a *Pulp Fiction* DVD, for example, making provision for a viewer to isolate the chapters in which songs are showcased. The powerful domestic PC encourages an interactive approach to multi-media whereby music and video can be readily downloaded, and both commercial CDs and DVDs provide facilities for accessing material on the internet. Most interactive of all are the products of the videogame industry, which require their own movie-style music (analysis of which is a growth area for academic study). In their interactive and non-linear narratives computer games have come to influence scoring approaches in feature films. Anahid Kassabian sees Shore's score to *The Cell* (dir. Tarsem, 2000) as symptomatic in this regard, being 'neither music nor not music' and caught up in an 'iterative narrativity' (Kassabian 2003, 93, 95). Linear momentum and traditional concepts of tension and release were also avoided in the looped samples of Graeme Revell's music to the console-to-cinema transfer *Lara Croft: Tomb Raider* (dir. Simon West, 2001; Kassabian 2003, 98).

The canonization of classic film music has been aided by a strong collector's market in soundtrack albums, both original and re-recorded, fostered by labels such as Chandos, Intrada, Marco Polo, Naxos, Silva Screen and Varèse Sarabande. The respectability of the film composer's art has been recognized by the international proliferation of pedagogical courses devoted both to its practical techniques and academic study, formerly the exclusive province of respected US seats of learning. Alongside commercial musical styles aimed at youth-oriented multi-media interactivity and the continuing allure of technological innovation allied to popular culture, traditional orchestral film scoring remains seemingly indestructible and occupies a secure and largely middlebrow place in the music industry. The film soundtrack remains a sometimes therapeutic arena where composers frustrated by the esotericism of modern classical music or the commercial pressures of the pop world can simply write the kind of old-fashioned and expressively tuneful tonal music that some might well have been inclined to produce for the concert hall had there been no aesthetic stigma attached to it. Hollywood's constructed utopia thus beckons as strongly as it always did. As John Williams describes his seminal role in the indestructible factory of dreams: 'I'm a very lucky man . . . If it weren't for the movies, no one would be able to write this kind of music anymore' (Dyer 1999, 21).

Bibliography

Abbate, Carolyn, 1991. *Unsung Voices: Opera and Musical Narrative in the Nineteenth Century*, Princeton: Princeton University Press

Abel, Richard, 1996. ed. *Silent Cinema*, London: Athlone Press

Abel, Richard and Rick Altman, 2001. eds. *The Sounds of Early Cinema*, Bloomington and Indianapolis: Indiana University Press

Adams, Doug, 1996. 'David Shire's *The Taking of Pelham One Two Three*', *Film Score Monthly* 68 (April), 18–20

  [with Jeff Bond], 1998a. 'Zen and the Art of Motion Picture Scoring', *Film Score Monthly* 3/2 (February), 24–30

  1998b. 'A Score to Remember? James Horner's Technique Critiqued', *Film Score Monthly* 3/3 (February), 38–43

  2004. 'Finding Newman: An Interview with the Overdubbing Prince of Hollywood Film Scoring', *Film Score Monthly* 9/1 (January), 14–17

Adorno, Theodor and Hanns Eisler, 1994 [1947]. *Composing for the Films*, with a new introduction by Graham McCann, London: Athlone Press

Adriano, 1993. CD liner notes to recordings of Honegger, *Crime et châtiment* and other film scores, Naxos 8.223466

Allen, Michael, 1998. 'From *Bwana Devil* to *Batman Forever*: Technology in Contemporary Hollywood Cinema', in Neale and Smith 1998, 109–29

Allen, Robert C. and Douglas Gomery, 1985. *Film History: Theory and Practice*, Boston: McGraw Hill

Allina, John, 2004. 'The RZA Makes His Own Breaks', *Film Score Monthly* 9/3 (March), 28–9

Altman, Rick, 1987. *The American Film Musical*, Bloomington and Indianapolis: Indiana University Press; London: BFI Publishing

  1992. ed. *Sound Theory/Sound Practice*, New York: Routledge

  1996. 'The Silence of the Silents', *Musical Quarterly* 80/4, 648–718

  2001. 'Cinema and Popular Song: The Lost Tradition', in Wojcik and Knight 2001, 19–30

  2004. *Silent Film Sound*, New York: Columbia University Press

Altman, Rick, with McGraw Jones and Sonia Tatroe, 2000. 'Inventing the Cinema Soundtrack: Hollywood's Multiplane Sound System', in Buhler *et al.* 2000, 339–59

Alwyn, Mary, 1993. CD liner notes to *William Alwyn: Film Music*, Chandos 9243

Alwyn, William, 1959. 'Film Music – Sound or Silence?' [BFI lecture], *Films and Filming* (March), reproduced in Thomas 1997, 31–7

  1967 [1956]. 'Ariel to Miranda', *Adam International Review* 316–18, 4–84

AMPAS, 2006. Academy of Motion Picture Arts and Sciences, 79th Academy Awards Rules, Rule Sixteen: Special Rules for the Music Awards, http://www.oscars.org/79academyawards/rules/rule16.html (accessed 12 April 2007)

Anderson, Gillian B., 1987. 'The Presentation of Silent Films, or Music as Anasthesia', *Journal of Musicology* 5, 257–95

    1988. *Music for Silent Films, 1894–1929: A Guide*, Washington, DC: Library of Congress

Arnold, Alan, 1980. *Once Upon a Galaxy: A Journal of the Making of The Empire Strikes Back*, New York: Ballantine

Arnold, Alison, 2001. 'India, VIII, 1: Film Music' in Sadie and Tyrrell 2001, vol. 12, 253–6

Ashby, Arved, 2004. 'Modernism Goes to the Movies', in Arved Ashby (ed.), *The Pleasure of Modernist Music: Listening, Meaning, Intention, Ideology*, Rochester, NY: University of Rochester Press, 345–86

Aumont, Jacques, Alain Bergala, Michel Marie and Marc Vernet, 1983. *Esthétique du film*, Paris: Editions Nathan; English translation by Richard Neupert published as *Aesthetics of Film*, Austin: University of Texas Press [1992]

Bakshy, Alexander, 1930a. 'Screen Musical Comedy', *The Nation*, 5 February
    1930b. Review of *Happy Days*, *The Nation*, 5 March

Balázs, Béla, 1953. *Theory of the Film: Character and Growth of a New Art*, trans. Edith Bone, New York: Roy

Balio, Tino, 1998. '"A Major Presence in All of the World's Important Markets": The Globalization of Hollywood in the 1990s', in Neale and Smith 1998, 58–73

Ballard, Bambi, 1990. ed. *Napoléon as Seen by Abel Gance*, trans. Moya Hassan with an introduction by Kevin Brownlow, London: Faber and Faber

Banfield, Stephen, 1993. *Sondheim's Broadway Musicals*, Ann Arbor: University of Michigan Press

    1995. ed. *The Blackwell History of Music in Britain, volume 6: The Twentieth Century*, Oxford: Blackwell

    1998. 'Popular Song and Popular Music on Stage and Film', in Nicholls 1998, 309–44

Barlow, Priscilla, 2001. 'Surreal Symphonies: *L'Age d'or* and the Discreet Charms of Classical Music', in Wojcik and Knight 2001, 31–52

Barnouw, Erik, 1993. *Documentary: A History of the Non-Fiction Film*, 2nd rev. edn. New York and Oxford: Oxford University Press

Barrier, Michael, 1999. *Hollywood Cartoons: American Animation in its Golden Age*, New York: Oxford University Press

Barrios, Richard, 1995. *A Song in the Dark: The Birth of the Musical Film*, New York: Oxford University Press

Barron, Lee, 2003. '"Music Inspired By . . .": The Curious Case of the Missing Soundtrack', in Inglis 2003, 148–61

Bazelon, Irwin, 1975. *Knowing the Score: Notes on Film Music*, New York: Van Nostrand Reinhold

Behlmer, Rudy, 1989. *Behind the Scenes*, Hollywood: Samuel French Trade

Belton, John, 1994. *American Cinema / American Culture*, New York: McGraw Hill

Berg, Charles M., 1976. *An Investigation of the Motives for and Realization of Music to Accompany the American Silent Film, 1896–1927*, New York: Arno

Bernstein, Elmer, 2004. *Elmer Bernstein's Film Music Notebook: A Complete Collection of the Quarterly Journal, 1974–1978*, Sherman Oaks, CA: The Film Music Society

Bettencourt, Scott, 2002. 'The Missing: Rejected and Corrected. A Revised Chronology of Rejected Film Scores', http://www.filmscoremonthly.com/articles/2002/09_May-Rejected_Corrected.asp (accessed 4 August 2007)

Beynon, George, 1921. *Musical Presentation of Motion Pictures*, New York: Schirmer

Björnberg, Alf, 2000. 'Structural Relationships of Music and Images in Music Video', in Middleton 2000, 347–78

Blandford, Steve, Barry Keith Grant and Jim Hillier, 2001. *The Film Studies Dictionary*, London: Arnold

Block, Geoffrey, 2002. ed. *The Richard Rodgers Reader*, New York and Oxford: Oxford University Press

Blom, Eric, 1954. ed. *Grove's Dictionary of Music and Musicians*, 5th edn, London: Macmillan

Boblitz, K. Sherwood, 1920. 'Where "Movie Playing" Needs Reform', *Musician* 25 (June), 8, 29

Bond, Jeff, 1999. 'A Clockwork Composer', *Film Score Monthly* 4/3 (March), 18–23
    2000. 'The Head, the Tail, the Whole Damn Thing', *Film Score Monthly* 5/5 (June), 32–5
    2004a. 'Horner Revealed', *Film Score Monthly* 9/2 (February), 16–20
    2004b. 'The Fall of Troy: Gabriel Yared and the Fate that Sank a Thousand Notes', *Film Score Monthly* 9/4 (April–May), 18–22
    2004c. 'Song Sung', *Film Score Monthly* 9/5 (June), 22–6
    2004d. 'The Gold Standard', *Film Score Monthly* 9/7 (August), 12–18

Bordwell, David, 1985. *Narration in the Fiction Film*, Madison: University of Wisconsin Press
    1988. *Ozu and the Poetics of Cinema*, London: British Film Institute; Princeton: Princeton University Press

Bordwell, David, Janet Staiger and Kristin Thompson, 1985. *The Classical Hollywood Cinema: Film Style and Mode of Production to 1960*, New York: Columbia University Press

Bradley, Scott, 1947. 'Personality on the Soundtrack: A Glimpse Behind the Scenes and Sequences in Filmland', *Music Educators Journal* 33/3 (January), 28–9

Brakhage, Stanley, 1960. 'The Silent Sound Sense', *Film Culture* 21, 65–7

Bratton, Jacky, Jim Cook and Christine Gledhill, 1994. eds. *Melodrama: Stage, Picture, Screen*, Bloomington, IN: University of Indiana Press; London: British Film Institute

Braudy, Leo and Marshall Cohen, 1999. eds. *Film Theory and Criticism: Introductory Readings*, 5th edn, New York and Oxford: Oxford University Press

Bridcut, John, 2006. *Britten's Children*, London: Faber and Faber

Brill, Mark, 2006. ed. *Leith Amadeus Stevens: A Festschrift* [*Journal of Film Music*, 1/4]

Brophy, Philip, 1991. 'The Animation of Sound', in Alan Cholodenko (ed.), *The Illusion of Life: Essays on Animation*, Sydney: Power Publications, 67–112

1997. 'Sukiyaki, Chow Mein, Minestrone', *Wire* 162 (August), available at
http://www.philipbrophy.com/projects/scrthst/OnceUponTimeEast.html
(accessed 25 August 2007)

2004. *100 Modern Soundtracks*, London: British Film Institute

Brown, Julie, 2004. 'Listening to Ravel, Watching *Un cœur en hiver*: Cinematic
Subjectivity and the Music-film', *twentieth-century music* 1/2, 253–75

Brown, Royal S., 1994. *Overtones and Undertones: Reading Film Music*, Berkeley and
Los Angeles: University of California Press

Brownlow, Kevin, 1980. 'Silent Films: What *Was* the Right Speed?', *Sight and Sound*
49/3 (Summer), 164–7

Buckland, Warren, 1998. 'A Close Encounter with *Raiders of the Lost Ark*: Notes on
Narrative Aspects of the New Hollywood Blockbuster', in Neale and Smith 1998,
166–77

Buhler, James, 2000. '*Star Wars*, Music, and Myth', in Buhler *et al.* 2000, 33–57

Buhler, James and David Neumeyer, 1994. Review of Flinn, *Strains of Utopia*, and
Kalinak, *Settling the Score*, *Journal of the American Musicological Society* 47,
364–85

Buhler, James, Caryl Flinn and David Neumeyer, 2000. eds. *Music and Cinema*,
Hanover, NH: Wesleyan University Press, University Press of New England

Buhrman, T. Scott, 1920. 'Photoplays DeLuxe', *American Organist* 3/5, 171–3

Burgess, Anthony, 1990. *You've Had Your Time, Being the Second Part of the
Confessions of Anthony Burgess*, London: Heinemann

Burt, Peter, 2001. *The Music of Tōru Takemitsu*, Cambridge: Cambridge University
Press

Burton, Humphrey, 1994. *Leonard Bernstein*, London: Faber and Faber

Burton-Page, Piers, 1994. *Philharmonic Concerto: The Life and Music of Sir Malcolm
Arnold*, London: Methuen

Butler, David, 2002. *Jazz Noir: Listening to Music From* Phantom Lady *to* The Last
Seduction, Westport, CT, and London: Praeger

2009. '"No Brotherly Love": Hollywood Jazz, Racial Prejudice and John Lewis's
Score for *Odds Against Tomorrow*', in Lock and Murray 2009

Byrd, Craig L., 1997. 'The *Star Wars* Interview: John Williams', *Film Score Monthly*
2/1, 18–21

Carey, Melissa and Michael Hannan, 2003. 'Case Study 2: *The Big Chill*', in Inglis
2003, 162–77

Carr, Ian, 1998. *Miles Davis: The Definitive Biography*, rev. edn, London: Harper
Collins

Carroll, Brendan G., 2001. 'Erich Wolfgang Korngold', in Sadie and Tyrrell 2001,
vol. 13, 823–4

Caute, David, 1994. *Joseph Losey: A Revenge on Life*, London: Faber and Faber

Ching, Barbara, 2001. 'Sounding the American Heart: Cultural Politics, Country
Music, and Contemporary American Film', in Wojcik and Knight 2001, 202–25

Chion, Michel, 1994. *Audio-Vision: Sound on Screen*, trans. Claudia Gorbman, New
York: Columbia University Press

1995. *La Musique au cinéma*, Paris: Fayard

1999. *The Voice in Cinema*, trans. Claudia Gorbman, New York: Columbia
University Press

2001. *Kubrick's Cinema Odyssey*, trans. Claudia Gorbman, London: British Film
Institute

Citron, Marcia J., 2000. *Opera on Screen*, New Haven and London: Yale University
Press

2004. 'Operatic Style and Structure in Coppola's *Godfather* Trilogy', *Musical
Quarterly* 87/3, 423–67

Cohan, Steven, 2002. ed. *Hollywood Musicals: The Film Reader*, London and New
York: Routledge

Cohen, Annabel J., 2000. 'Film Music: Perspectives from Cognitive Psychology', in
Buhler *et al.* 2000, 360–77

Conway, Kelley, 2001. 'Flower of the Asphalt: The *Chanteuse Réaliste* in 1930s
French Cinema', in Wojcik and Knight 2001, 134–60

Cook, David A., 2004. *A History of Narrative Film*, 4th edn, New York and London:
W. W. Norton and Co.

Cook, Nicholas, 1998. *Analysing Musical Multimedia*, Oxford: Clarendon Press

Cooke, Mervyn, 1998. *Britten and the Far East: Asian Influences in the Music of
Benjamin Britten*, Woodbridge: The Boydell Press

1999. ed. *The Cambridge Companion to Benjamin Britten*, Cambridge: Cambridge
University Press

2000. 'Bernard Herrmann', in Russell and Young 2000, 18–31

2001. 'Film Music', in Sadie and Tyrrell 2001, vol. 8, 797–810

2005. ed. *The Cambridge Companion to Twentieth-Century Opera*, Cambridge:
Cambridge University Press

2009. 'Anatomy of a Movie: Duke Ellington and 1950s Film Scoring', in Lock and
Murray 2009

Cooke, Mervyn and David Horn, 2002. eds. *The Cambridge Companion to Jazz*,
Cambridge: Cambridge University Press

Cooper, David, 2001. *Bernard Herrmann's* Vertigo: *A Film Score Guide*, Westport,
CT, and London: Greenwood Press

2003. 'Film Form and Musical Form in Bernard Herrmann's Score to *Vertigo*', in
Rosar 2003, 239–48

2005. *Bernard Herrmann's* The Ghost and Mrs. Muir: *A Film Score Guide*,
Lanham, MD: Scarecrow Press

Copland, Aaron and Vivian Perlis, 1984. *Copland: 1900 Through 1942*, London and
Boston: Faber and Faber

1992 [1989]. *Copland: Since 1943*, London: Marion Boyars

Costantini, Costanzo, 1995. ed. *Fellini on Fellini*, trans. Sohrab Sorooshian,
London: Faber and Faber

Covach, John, 1995. 'Stylistic Competencies, Musical Satire, and "This is Spinal
Tap"', in Marvin and Hermann 1995, 399–421

Cowie, Peter, 2004. *Revolution! The Explosion of World Cinema in the 60s*, London:
Faber and Faber

Craik, T. W., 1995. ed. *King Henry V* (Arden Shakespeare), London: Routledge

Creekmur, Corey K., 2001. 'Picturizing American Cinema: Hindi Film Songs and the Last Days of Genre', in Wojcik and Knight 2001, 375–406

Cumbow, Robert C., 1997. *Once Upon a Time: The Films of Sergio Leone*, Metuchen, NJ: Scarecrow Press

Curtis, Scott, 1992. 'The Sound of the Early Warner Bros. Cartoons', in Altman 1992, 191–203

Dahl, Ingolf, 1949. 'Notes on Cartoon Music', *Film Music Notes* 8/5 (May–June), 3–13

Dalton, David, 1975. *James Dean*, London: W. H. Allen

Daniel, Estelle, 2000. *The Art of Gormenghast: The Making of a Television Fantasy*, London: Harper Collins

Darby, William and Jack Du Bois, 1990. *American Film Music: Major Composers, Techniques, Trends, 1915–1990*, Jefferson, NC, and London: McFarland

Darreg, Ivor, 1946. 'Electronic Music and the Films', *Film Music Notes*, available at http://www.sonic-arts.org/darreg/dar1.htm (accessed 28 August 2007)

Daubney, Kate, 2000. *Max Steiner's Now, Voyager: A Film Score Guide*, Westport, CT, and London: Greenwood Press
  2006. 'Music as a Satirical Device in the Ealing Comedies', in Mera and Burnand 2006, 61–72

Davis, Darrell William, 1996. *Picturing Japaneseness: Monumental Style, National Identity, Japanese Film*, New York: Columbia University Press

Davis, Miles and Quincy Troupe, 1989. *Miles: The Autobiography*, New York: Simon and Schuster

Davison, Annette, 2004. *Hollywood Theory, Non-Hollywood Practice: Cinema Soundtracks in the 1980s and 1990s*, Aldershot: Ashgate

Davy, Charles, 1937. ed. *Footnotes to the Film*, New York: Oxford University Press

Deathridge, John, 2005. 'Wagner and Beyond', in Cooke 2005, 14–25

De Mille, Agnes, 1952. *Dance to the Piper*, Boston, MA: Little and Brown

De Palma, Brian, 2002. Interview for DVD release of *Obsession*, Anchor Bay ABD4114

DeMary, Thomas, 2003. 'The Mystery of Herrmann's Music for Selznick's *Portrait of Jennie*', in Rosar 2003, 153–82

Denisoff, R. Serge and William D. Romanowski, 1991. *Risky Business: Rock in Film*, New Brunswick and London: Transaction

Dickinson, Kay, 2003. ed. *Movie Music: The Film Reader*, London and New York: Routledge

Donnelly, Kevin J., 1998. 'The Classical Film Score Forever? *Batman*, *Batman Returns* and Post-classical Film Music', in Neale and Smith 1998, 142–55
  2001a. ed. *Film Music: Critical Approaches*, Edinburgh: Edinburgh University Press
  2001b. *Pop Music in British Cinema: A Chronicle*, London: British Film Institute
  2003. 'Constructing the Future Through Music of the Past: The Software in Hardware', in Inglis 2003, 131–47
  2005. *The Spectre of Sound: Music in Film and Television*, London: British Film Institute

2006. 'Angel of the Air: Popol Vuh's Music and Werner Herzog's Films', in Mera and Burnand 2006, 116–30

Doran, Mark, 2004. CD liner notes to *Love from a Stranger: Four British Film Scores*, NMC D073

'Downbeat', 2000. 'Dark Dream: Behind the Score to *Requiem for a Dream*', *Film Score Monthly* 5/8 (September–October), 17–20

Duchen, Jessica, 1996. *Erich Wolfgang Korngold*, London: Phaidon

Dümling, Albrecht, 1998. ed. *Hanns Eisler and Film Music*, special issue of *Historical Journal of Film, Radio and Television*, 18/4

Dunwell, Wilfrid, 1960. *The Evolution of Twentieth-Century Harmony*, London: Novello and Company Ltd

Dyer, Richard, 1999. 'Making *Star Wars* Sing Again', *Film Score Monthly* 4/5 (June), 18–21

2006. 'Music, People and Reality: The Case of Italian Neo-realism', in Mera and Burnand 2006, 28–40

2007. *Pastiche*, London and New York: Routledge

Dym, Jeffrey A., 2003. *Benshi, Japanese Silent Film Narrators, and their Forgotten Narrative Art of Setsumei: A History of Japanese Silent Film Narration*. Lewiston, NY: Edwin Mellen Press

Egorova, Tatiana, 1997. *Soviet Film Music: An Historical Survey*, trans. Tatiana A. Ganf and Natalia A. Egunova, Amsterdam: Harwood Academic Publishers

Ehrlich, Cyril, 1985. *The Music Profession in Britain since the Eighteenth Century: A Social History*, Oxford: Clarendon Press

Eisenstein, Sergei, 1948 [1943]. *The Film Sense*, trans. and ed. Jay Leyda, 2nd edn, London: Faber and Faber

1960 [1949]. *Film Form: Essays in Film Theory*, trans. and ed. Jay Leyda, London: Dennis Dobson

Eisler, Hanns, 1941. 'Film Music – Work in Progress', reprinted in Dümling 1998, 591–4

Eshun, Kodwo, 1995. 'From Blaxploitation to Rapsploitation', in Romney and Wootton 1995, 52–9

Evans, John, Philip Reed and Paul Wilson, 1987. *A Britten Source Book*, Aldeburgh: Britten Estate

Evidon, Richard, 1992. 'Film', in Sadie 1992, vol. 2, 194–200

Eyman, Scott, 1997. *The Speed of Sound: Hollywood and the Talkie Revolution, 1926–1930*, Baltimore and London: The Johns Hopkins University Press

Fairservice, Don, 2001. *Film Editing: History, Theory and Practice*, Manchester: Manchester University Press

Fawkes, Richard, 2000. *Opera on Film*, London: Duckworth

Fiegel, E. Todd, 2003. 'Bernard Herrmann as Musical Colorist: A Musicodramatic Analysis of His Score for *The Day the Earth Stood Still*', in Rosar 2003, 185–215

Figgis, Mike, 2005. Interview for DVD of Jean-Luc Godard's *Weekend*, Artificial Eye ART 258

Flinn, Caryl, 1992. *Strains of Utopia: Gender, Nostalgia, and Hollywood Film Music*, Princeton: Princeton University Press

1994. 'Music and the Melodramatic Past of the New German Cinema', in Bratton *et al.* 1994, 106–18

2004. *The New German Cinema: Music, History, and the Matter of Style*, Berkeley: University of California Press

Follett, Jonathan, 1997. 'The Men with the Junk Metal Instruments', *Film Score Monthly* 2/8 (October), 15–16

Ford, Fiona, 2003. 'Shostakovich and the Silent Screen', MA dissertation, University of Nottingham

2007. 'The Role of Ophelia's Unaccompanied Songs in Kozintsev's *Hamlet*', *DSCH Journal* 26 (January), 24–32

Fordin, Hugh, 1996 [1975]. *M-G-M's Greatest Musicals: The Arthur Freed Unit*, New York: Da Capo Press

Franke, Lars, 2006. '*The Godfather Part III*: Film, Opera, and the Generation of Meaning', in Powrie and Stilwell 2006, 31–45

Frayling, Christopher, 2005. *Once Upon a Time in Italy: The Westerns of Sergio Leone*, London: Thames and Hudson

French, Philip, 1993. ed. *Malle on Malle*, London: Faber and Faber

Gabbard, Krin, 1996. *Jammin' at the Margins: Jazz and the American Cinema*, Chicago: University of Chicago Press

Gish, Lillian with Ann Pinchot, 1969. *Lillian Gish: The Movies, Mr. Griffith, and Me*, Englewood Cliffs, NJ: Prentice-Hall

Gladstone, Kay, 2001. 'Introductory Text' to DVD of Leni Riefenstahl's *Triumph of the Will*, DD 3878

Glinsky, Albert, 2000. *Theremin: Ether Music and Espionage*, Urbana and Chicago: University of Illinois Press

Goldmark, Daniel, 2005. *Tunes for 'Toons: Music and the Hollywood Cartoon*, Berkeley, Los Angeles and London: University of California Press

Goldmark, Daniel and Yuval Taylor, 2002. eds. *The Cartoon Music Book*, Chicago: A Cappella

Gomery, Douglas, 1998. 'Hollywood Corporate Business Practice and Periodizing Contemporary Film History', in Neale and Smith 1998, 47–57

Gorbman, Claudia, 1987. *Unheard Melodies: Narrative Film Music*, Bloomington: Indiana University Press; London: British Film Institute

1996. 'Aesthetics in the Age of Gump', *Film Score Monthly* 65–7 (Winter), 30–1

1998. 'Film Music', in Hill and Gibson 1998, 43–50

2006. 'Ears Wide Open: Kubrick's Music', in Powrie and Stilwell 2006, 3–18

Gorin, Natalio, 2001. *Astor Piazzolla: A Memoir*, Portland, OR: Amadeus Press

Gottlieb, Robert, 1997. ed. *Reading Jazz*, London: Bloomsbury

Grant, Barry Keith, 1995. ed. *Film Genre Reader II*, Austin, TX: University of Texas Press

Grimley, Daniel M., 2005. 'Hidden Places: Hyper-realism in Björk's *Vespertine* and *Dancer in the Dark*', *twentieth-century music* 2/1, 37–51

Hacquard, Georges, 1959. *La Musique et le cinéma*, Paris: PUF éditeur

Hahl-Koch, Jelena, 1984. ed. *Arnold Schoenberg–Wassily Kandinsky: Letters, Pictures and Documents*, trans. John C. Crawford, London: Faber and Faber

Halfyard, Janet K., 2004. *Danny Elfman's* Batman: *A Film Score Guide*, Lanham, MD: Scarecrow Press

Hammelmann, Hanns and Ewald Osers (trans.), 1961. *The Correspondence Between Richard Strauss and Hugo von Hofmannsthal*, with an introduction by Edward Sackville-West, London: William Collins; repr. Cambridge: Cambridge University Press [1980]

Hammond, Antony, 1981. ed. *King Richard III* (Arden Shakespeare), London: Methuen

Hasan, Mark Richard, 2001. 'The King of Hip: A Quincy Jones Retrospective' [part 2], *Film Score Monthly* 6/8 (September), 16–23

Hayes, Malcolm, 2002. ed. *The Selected Letters of William Walton*, London: Faber and Faber

Heller, Berndt, 1998. 'The Reconstruction of Eisler's Film Music', *Historical Journal of Film, Radio and Television* (October), 556–9

Henderson, Sanya Shoilevska, 2003. *Alex North, Film Composer*, Jefferson, NC, and London: McFarland and Company

Herrmann, Bernard, 1941. 'Score For a Film: Composer Tells of Problems Solved in Music for "Citizen Kane"', *New York Times*, 25 May

   1945. 'Music in Motion Pictures: A Reply to Mr. Leinsdorf', *Music Publishers Journal* 3/5 (September–October), 17, 69

Hill, John and Pamela Church Gibson, 1998. eds. *The Oxford Guide to Film Studies*, Oxford: Oxford University Press

   2000. eds. *World Cinema: Critical Approaches*, Oxford: Oxford University Press

Hillier, Jim, 1985. ed. *Cahiers du cinéma. The 1950s: Neo-Realism, Hollywood, New Wave*, Cambridge, MA: Harvard University Press

Hinton, Stephen, 1990. *Kurt Weill: The Threepenny Opera*, Cambridge: Cambridge University Press

Honegger, Arthur, 1966 [1951]. *I am a Composer*, trans. Wilson O. Clough and Allan Arthur Willman, London: Faber and Faber

Hubbard, Robert, 1994. 'Michael Nyman', *Film Score Monthly* 46–7 (June–July), 10–11

Huckvale, David, 1990. '*Twins of Evil*: An Investigation into the Aesthetics of Film Music', *Popular Music* 9/1, 1–35

Huntley, John, n.d. [1947]. *British Film Music*, London: Skelton Robinson

   2002. Interview with Tommy Pearson, 'Stage and Screen', BBC Radio 3, 18 March

Husted, Christopher, 2003. CD liner notes on Benjamin Frankel's and Franz Waxman's scores to *Night and the City*, Screen Archives CD, SAE-CRS-0008

Inglis, Ian, 2003. ed. *Popular Music and Film*, London: Wallflower Press

Irving, Ernest, 1943. 'Music in Films', *Music and Letters* 24, 223–35

   1959. *Cue for Music*, London: D. Dodson

Irving, Ernest, Hans Keller and Wilfrid Mellers, 1954. 'Film Music', in Blom 1954, vol. 13, 93–110

Jackson, Peter, 2006. 'Post-Production Diaries: Music', DVD of *King Kong*, Universal 8242456

Jackson, Russell, 2000. ed. *The Cambridge Companion to Shakespeare on Film*, Cambridge: Cambridge University Press

James, Eric, 2000. *Making Music with Charlie Chaplin: An Autobiography*, Lanham, MD: Scarecrow Press

James, Richard, 1986. 'Avant-Garde Sound-on-Film Techniques and Their Relationship to Electro-Acoustic Music', *Musical Quarterly* 72/1, 74–89

Jarman, Derek, 1989. *War Requiem: The Film*, London: Faber and Faber

Jaubert, Maurice, 1937. 'Music on the Screen', in Davy 1937, 101–15

Jefferson, Alan, 1985. *Richard Strauss: Der Rosenkavalier*, Cambridge: Cambridge University Press

Joe, Jeongwon, 2006. 'Reconsidering *Amadeus*: Mozart as Film Music', in Powrie and Stilwell 2006, 57–73

Joe, Jeongwon, and Rose Theresa, 2002. eds. *Between Opera and Cinema*, New York and London: Routledge

Johnson, Bruce, 2002. 'The Jazz Diaspora', in Cooke and Horn 2002, 33–54

Johnson, Ian, 2005. *William Alwyn: The Art of Film Music*, Woodbridge: The Boydell Press

Kabir, Nasreen Munni, 2001. *Bollywood: The Indian Cinema Story*, London: Channel 4 Books

Kalinak, Kathryn, 1983. 'Impetuous Rhythm: Edmund Meisel's Score for Eisenstein's *Battleship Potemkin*', *Purdue Film Studies Annual* 7, 33–43

   1992. *Settling the Score: Music and the Classical Hollywood Film*, Madison and London: University of Wisconsin Press

Karlin, Fred, 1994. *Listening to Movies: The Film Lover's Guide to Film Music*, New York: Schirmer

Karlin, Fred and Rayburn Wright, 2004. *On the Track: A Guide to Contemporary Film Scoring*, 2nd edn, New York: Schirmer

Kassabian, Anahid, 2001. *Hearing Film: Tracking Identifications in Contemporary Hollywood Film Music*, New York and London: Routledge

   2003. 'The Sound of a New Film Form', in Inglis 2003, 91–101

Kater, Michael H., 1992. *Different Drummers: Jazz in the Culture of Nazi Germany*, New York and Oxford: Oxford University Press

Keller, Hans, 1950. 'William Alwyn: Bad and Great Work', *Music Review* 11, 145–6, 216–17

Kemp, Philip, 1999. 'Video Essay', DVD of *Seven Samurai* (dir. Akira Kurosawa), BFIVD501

   2000. Commentary to DVD of *Yojimbo* (dir. Akira Kurosawa), BFIVD505

   2001. Sleeve notes to DVD of *The Adventures of Prince Achmed* (dir. Lotte Reiniger), BFIVD523

Kendall, Lukas, 1994. 'Elliot Goldenthal', *Film Score Monthly* 41–3 (January–March), 14–16

   1995. 'Danny Elfman' [part 2], *Film Score Monthly* 64 (December), 11–16

   2004. '*Star Wars*: Anal-retentive Trivia on the Lost Music, the Lost Scenes, and So On', *Film Score Monthly*, 41–3 (January–March), 26–9

Kennaway, E. D., 2000. CD liner notes to *Battle of the Bulge: The Original Score by Benjamin Frankel*, CPO999696–2

   2002. CD liner notes to *Benjamin Frankel: Music for the Movies*, CPO999809–2

Kennedy, Michael, 1980. *The Works of Ralph Vaughan Williams*, 2nd edn, London: Oxford University Press

   1989. *Portrait of Walton*, Oxford: Oxford University Press

Kermode, Mark, 1995. 'Twisting the Knife', in Romney and Wootton 1995, 8–19

Kershaw, David, 1995. 'Film and Television Music', in Banfield 1995, 125–44

Kieślowski, Krzysztof, 1995. 'A Short Film about *Dekalog*', *Dekalog: The Ten Commandments Parts 6 to 10*, Artificial Eye DVD 024B [2002]

Kildea, Paul, 2003. ed. *Britten on Music*, Oxford: Oxford University Press

Kolker, Robert, 2006. ed. *Stanley Kubrick's 2001: A Space Odyssey. New Essays.* Oxford and New York: Oxford University Press

Koppl, Rudy, 2000. 'John Ottman's *Urban Legends*: Final Cut', *Music from the Movies* 28 (August), 31–9

Knights, Vanessa, 2006. 'Queer Pleasures: The Bolero, Camp and Almodóvar', in Powrie and Stilwell 2006, 91–104

Kracauer, Siegfried, 1960. *Theory of Film: The Redemption of Physical Reality*, New York: Oxford University Press; repr. Princeton University Press, 1997

Lack, Russell, 1997. *Twenty Four Frames Under: A Buried History of Film Music*, London: Quartet

Lacombe, Alain and François Porcile, 1995. *Les Musiques du cinéma français*, Paris: Bordas

Laing, Heather, 2004. *Gabriel Yared's* The English Patient: *A Film Score Guide*, Lanham, MD, and Oxford: Scarecrow Press
  2006. '"The Rhythm of the Night": Reframing Silence, Music and Masculinity in *Beau Travail*', in Mera and Burnand 2006, 163–77

Lambert, Constant, 1934. *Music Ho! A Study of Music in Decline*, London: Faber and Faber; repr. Hogarth Press, 1985

Lang, Edith and George West, 1920. *Musical Accompaniment of Moving Pictures: A Practical Manual for Pianists and Organists*, Boston: Boston Music Co.

Larson, Randall D., 1996. *Music from the House of Hammer: Music in the Hammer Horror Films, 1950–1980*, London: Scarecrow Press

Leck, Robert van der, 1994. 'Concert Music as Reused Film Music: E-W Korngold's Self-Arrangements', *Acta Musicologica* 66, 78–112

Leeper, Jill, 2001. 'Crossing Musical Borders: The Soundtrack for *Touch of Evil*', in Wojcik and Knight 2001, 226–43

Leicester, H. Marshall, Jr, 1994. 'Discourse and the Film Text: Four Readings of *Carmen*', *Cambridge Opera Journal* 6/3, 245–82

Leinberger, Charles, 2002. 'Thematic Variation and Key Relationships: Charlotte's Theme in Max Steiner's Score for *Now, Voyager*', *Journal of Film Music* 1/1, 63–77

Leonard, Geoff, Pete Walker and Lukas Kendall, 1995. 'John Barry and James Bond: The Making of the Music', *Film Score Monthly* 63 (November), 15–18

Lerouge, Stéphane, 2005. *Le cinéma de Michel Legrand*, notes to accompany CD recordings, Universal Music SA France, 982 908 1

Leyda, Jay, 1988. ed. *Eisenstein on Disney*, trans. Alan Upchurch, London: Methuen

Limbacher, James L., 1974. *Film Music: From Violins to Video*, Metuchen, NJ: Scarecrow Press

LoBrutto, Vincent, 1994. *Sound-on-Film: Interviews with Creators of Film Sound*, Westport, CT, and London: Praeger
  1998. *Stanley Kubrick: A Biography*, London: Faber and Faber

Lock, Graham and David Murray, 2009. eds. *Thriving on a Riff: Jazz and Blues Influences in (African) American Literature and Film*, New York: Oxford University Press

Lockwood, Lewis, 1997. 'Film Biography as Travesty: *Immortal Beloved* and Beethoven', *Musical Quarterly* 81/2, 190–8

London, Kurt, 1936. *Film Music: A Summary of the Characteristic Features of its History, Aesthetics, Technique; and Possible Developments*, trans. Eric S. Bensinger, foreword by Constant Lambert, London: Faber and Faber

Low, Rachael, 1979. *The History of the British Film 1929–1939: Documentary and Educational Films of the 1930s*, London: Allen and Unwin

McBride, Joseph, 1997. *Steven Spielberg: A Biography*, London: Faber and Faber

McCarty, Clifford, 1989. ed. *Film Music I*, New York and London: Garland
  2000. *Film Composers in America: A Filmography 1911–1970*, 2nd edn, New York and Oxford: Oxford University Press

MacDonald, Laurence E., 1998. *The Invisible Art of Film Music: A Comprehensive History*, New York: Ardsley House

McLaren, Norman, 1953. 'Notes on Animated Sound', *Quarterly of Film, Radio, and Television* 7/3, 223–9

MacLean, Paul Andrew, 1993. 'An Interview with Maurice Jarre', *Film Score Monthly* 30–1 (February–March), 35–8
  1994. 'Does Classical Music Have a Place in Films?', *Film Score Monthly* 48 (August), 6

Majumdar, Neepa, 2001. 'The Embodied Voice: Song Sequences and Stardom in Popular Hindi Cinema', in Wojcik and Knight 2001, 161–81

Maltby, Richard, 1998. '"Nobody Knows Everything": Post-classical Historiographies and Consolidated Entertainment', in Neale and Smith 1998, 21–44

Mancini, Henry with Gene Lees, 1989. *Did They Mention the Music?*, Chicago: Contemporary Books

Manvell, Roger and John Huntley, 1957. *The Technique of Film Music*, London and New York: Focal Press; rev. edn by Richard Arnell and Peter Day, 1975

Marks, Martin Miller, 1997. *Music and the Silent Film: Contexts and Case Studies, 1895–1924*, New York and Oxford: Oxford University Press

Marshall, Bill and Robynn Stilwell, 2000. *Musicals: Hollywood and Beyond*, Exeter and Portland, OR: Intellect

Marshall, Herbert, 1978. ed. *The Battleship Potemkin*, New York: Avon

Marvin, Elizabeth West and Richard Hermann, 1995. eds. *Concert Music, Rock, and Jazz since 1945: Essays and Analytical Studies*, Rochester, NY: University of Rochester Press

Medhurst, Andy, 1995. 'It Sort of Happened Here: The Strange, Brief Life of the British Pop Film', in Romney and Wootton 1995, 60–71

Mera, Miguel, 2006. 'Modernity and a Day: The Functions of Music in the Films of Theo Angelopoulos', in Mera and Burnand 2006, 131–44

Mera, Miguel and David Burnand, 2006. eds. *European Film Music*, Aldershot: Ashgate

Middleton, Richard, 2000. ed. *Reading Pop: Approaches to Textual Analysis in Popular Music*, Oxford: Oxford University Press

Milhaud, Darius, 1952. *Notes Without Music*, trans. Donald Evans, London: Dennis Dobson Ltd

Millard, André, 1995. *America on Record: A History of Recorded Sound*, Cambridge: Cambridge University Press

Mitchell, Donald and Philip Reed, 1991. eds. *Letters from a Life: The Selected Letters and Diaries of Benjamin Britten 1913–1976*, vol. 1 (1923–1939) and vol. 2 (1939–45), London: Faber and Faber

Mitry, Jean, 1998 [1963]. *The Aesthetics and Psychology of the Cinema*, trans. Christopher King, London: Athlone Press

Mohr, Wolfgang, 2000. CD liner notes to *Electric Shadows: Film Music by Zhao Jiping*, Teldec Classics/WEA017114

Moreau, Jeanne, 2002. Interview, DVD of *Jules et Jim* (dir. François Truffaut), Tartan 3362

Morrison, Richard, 2004. *Orchestra. The LSO: A Century of Triumph and Turbulence*, London: Faber and Faber

Movieweb, 2007. Box office charts at http://www.movieweb.com/movies/boxoffice/alltime.php (accessed 13 July 2007)

Mundy, John, 1999. *Popular Music on Screen: From Hollywood Musical to Music Video*, Manchester: Manchester University Press

Murray, Bruce, 1990. *Film and the German Left in the Weimar Republic: From Caligari to Kuhle Wampe*, Austin, TX: University of Texas Press

Mylonás, Kóstas, 2001. *I Mousikí ston Ellinikó Kinimatográfo* [*Music in the Greek Cinema*], Athens: Kedros

Naumberg, Nancy, 1937. ed. *We Make the Movies*, New York: W. W. Norton and Co.

Neale, Steve and Murray Smith, 1998. eds. *Contemporary Hollywood Cinema*, London and New York: Routledge

Newsom, Iris, 1985. ed. *Wonderful Inventions*, Washington, DC: Library of Congress

Nicholls, David, 1998. ed. *The Cambridge History of American Music*, Cambridge: Cambridge University Press

Nichols, Roger, 1996. *Conversations with Madeleine Milhaud*, London: Faber and Faber

Nishijima, Norio, Yasuo Horikiri and Michihiro Maekawa, 1984. eds. *Libro Cinématheque Ozu Yasujiro: Tokyo Monogatari*, Tokyo: Riburopoto

Nyman, Michael, 1974. *Experimental Music: Cage and Beyond*, London: Studio Vista; 2nd edn, Cambridge: Cambridge University Press, 1999

O'Neill, Norman, 1911. 'Music to Stage Plays', *Proceedings of the Royal Musical Association* 37, 85–102

Oshima, Nagisa, 1992. *Cinema, Censorship, and the State: The Writings of Nagisa Oshima, 1956–1978*, ed. Annette Michelson, trans. Dawn Lawson; Cambridge, MA, and London: MIT Press

Palmer, Christopher, 1990. *The Composer in Hollywood*, London and New York: Marion Boyars

1991. 'Prokofiev, Eisenstein and *Ivan*', *Musical Times* 132, 179–81

1992. CD liner notes to *Virgil Thomson: Louisiana Story*, Hyperion CDA 66576

Parlett, Graham, 1999. *A Catalogue of the Works of Sir Arnold Bax*, Oxford: Clarendon Press

Parkinson, David, 1995. *History of Film*, London: Thames and Hudson

Paulin, Scott D., 2000. 'Richard Wagner and the Fantasy of Cinematic Unity: The Idea of the *Gesamtkunstwerk* in the History and Theory of Film Music', in Buhler *et al.* 2000, 58–84

Phillips, James, 2002. 'A Touch of Elegance: The Film Music of Richard Rodney Bennett', *Film Score Monthly* 7/2 (February), 24–8

Piazza, Jim and Gail Kinn, 2006. *The Academy Awards: The Complete Unofficial History*, rev. edn, New York: Black Dog and Leventhal

Pommerance, Murray, 2001. '"The Future's Not Ours to See": Song, Singer, Labyrinth in Hitchcock's *The Man Who Knew Too Much*', in Wojcik and Knight 2001, 53–73

Pontecorvo, Gillo, 2003. Interview for DVD of *The Battle of Algiers*, Argent AGTD001

Potamkin, Harry Alan, 1929. 'Music and the Movies', *Musical Quarterly* 15/2, 281–96.

Powell, Michael, 1986. *A Life in Movies: An Autobiography*, London: William Heinemann

Powrie, Phil, 2006. 'The Fabulous Destiny of the Accordion in French Cinema', in Powrie and Stilwell 2006, 137–51

Powrie, Phil and Robynn Stilwell, 2006. eds. *Changing Tunes: The Use of Pre-existing Music in Film*, Aldershot: Ashgate

Prendergast, Roy M., 1992. *Film Music: A Neglected Art*, 2nd edn, New York and London: W. W. Norton

Previn, André, 1992. *No Minor Chords: My Days in Hollywood*, London: Doubleday

Priestley, Brian, 1982. *Mingus: A Critical Biography*, London: Quartet

Pudovkin, V. I., 1958. *Film Technique* [1929, rev. 1933] *and Film Acting* [1937], trans. and ed. Ivor Montagu, London: Vision Press

Pytel, Marek, 1999. *New Babylon: Trauberg, Kozintsev, Shostakovich*, London: Eccentric Press

Raksin, David, 1985. 'Life with Charlie', in Newsom 1985, 159–71

Ramaeker, Paul B., 2001. '"You Think They Call Us Plastic *Now* . . .": The Monkees and *Head*', in Wojcik and Knight 2001, 74–102

Rapée, Ernö, 1924. *Motion Picture Moods for Pianists and Organists: A Rapid-Reference Collection of Selected Pieces*, New York: Schirmer
    1925. *Encyclopaedia of Music for Pictures*, New York: Belwin

Ray, Satyajit, 1997 [1994]. *My Years with Apu*, London: Faber and Faber

Reay, Pauline, 2004. *Music in Film: Soundtracks and Synergy*, London and New York: Wallflower Press

Reed, Philip, 1999. 'Britten in the Cinema: *Coal Face*', in Cooke 1999, 54–77
    2007. CD liner notes to *Britten on Film*, NMC D112, 8–19

Rees, Brian, 1999. *Camille Saint-Saëns: A Life*, London: Chatto and Windus

Reisz, Karel, 1953. *The Technique of Film Editing*, London: Focal Press

Reynaud, Bérénice, 2000. 'Chinese Cinema', in Hill and Church Gibson 2000, 159–65

Richie, Donald, 1972. *Japanese Cinema: Film Style and National Character*, London: Secker and Warburg

Riley, John, 2005. *Dmitri Shostakovich: A Life in Film*, London and New York: I. B. Tauris

Robinson, David, 1990. 'Music of the Shadows: The Use of Musical Accompaniment with Silent Films, 1896–1936', *Le giornate del cinema muto, Pordenone*, supplement to *Griffithiana* 8/39 (October)

Rogers, Holly, 2004. 'Fitzcarraldo's Search for Aguirre: Music and Text in the Amazonian Films of Werner Herzog', *Journal of the Royal Musical Association* 129/1, 77–99

Roller, Alfred, 1909. 'Bühnenreform? ["Stage Reform?"]', *Das Merker* 1/5 (10 December), 193–7; reproduced, in an English translation by Meredith Oakes, in Sutcliffe 1996, 427–31

Romney, Jonathan and Adrian Wootton, 1995. eds. *Celluloid Jukebox: Popular Music and the Movies Since the 50s*, London: British Film Institute

Rosar, William H., 1983. 'Music of the Monsters: Universal Pictures' Horror Film Scores of the Thirties', *Library of Congress Quarterly* 40, 390–421
   2002. 'Film Music – What's in a Name?', *Journal of Film Music* 1/1, 1–18
   2003. ed. *Herrmann Studies*, special issue of *Journal of Film Music* 1/2–3
   2006. 'Music for Martians: Schillinger's Two Tonics and Harmony of Fourths in Leith Stevens' Score for *War of the Worlds* (1953)', in Brill 2006, 395–48

Rosenthal, Daniel, 2000. *Shakespeare on Screen*, London: Hamlyn

Ross, Alex, 2004. 'Das Lied von der Brad', http://www.therestisnoise.com/2004/05/symphony_of_bra.html (accessed 1 March 2007)

Rotha, Paul, 1958. *Rotha on the Film: A Selection of Writings about the Cinema*, London: Faber and Faber

Rózsa, Miklós, 1982. *Double Life: The Autobiography of Miklós Rózsa*, Tunbridge Wells: Midas Books; New York: Hippocrene Books

Rushton, Julian, 1981. *Wolfgang Amadeus Mozart: Don Giovanni*, Cambridge: Cambridge University Press

Russell, Ken, 2001. *Directing Film: The Director's Art from Script to Cutting Room*, Washington, DC: Brassey's, Inc.

Russell, Mark and James Young, 2000. eds. *Film Music: Screencraft*, Hove and Crans-Près-Céligny: RotoVision SA

Sabaneev, Leonid, 1935. *Music for the Films: A Handbook for Composers and Conductors*, trans. S. W. Pring, London: Pitman

Sadie, Stanley, 1992. ed. *The New Grove Dictionary of Opera*, 4 vols., London: Macmillan

Sadie, Stanley and John Tyrrell, 2001. eds. *The New Grove Dictionary of Music and Musicians*, 2nd edn, London: Macmillan

Sadoul, Georges, 1948. *Les Pionniers du cinéma: de Méliès à Pathé, 1897–1909*, Paris: Denoël

Salisbury, Mark, 2006. ed. *Burton on Burton*, rev. edn, London: Faber and Faber

Sanjek, Russell, 1988. *American Popular Music and its Business: The First Four Hundred Years*, 3 vols, New York: Oxford University Press

Schelle, Michael, 1999. *The Score: Interviews with Film Composers*, Beverly Hills: Silman-James Press

Schroeder, David, 2002. *Cinema's Illusions, Opera's Allure: The Operatic Impulse in Film*, New York and London: Continuum

Schweiger, Daniel, 2001. 'The Madman and His Muse', *Film Score Monthly* 6/8 (September), 24–7, 44

Seredy, Julius S., 1929. ed. *Carl Fischer Analytical Orchestra Guide: A Practical Handbook for the Profession*, New York: Carl Fischer

Shankar, Ravi, 1999. *Raga Mala: An Autobiography*, ed. George Harrison, New York: Welcome Rain

Shapiro, Anne Dhu, 1984. 'Action Music in American Pantomime and Melodrama, 1730–1913', *American Music* 2/4 (Music of the American Theater), 49–72

Shivers, Will, 1995. 'Kamen Hard', *Film Score Monthly* 58 (June), 12–15

Shostakovich, Dmitry, 1981. *Shostakovich: About Himself and His Times*, ed. Lev Grigoryev and Yakov Platek, trans. Angus and Neilian Roxburgh, Moscow: Progress Publishers

Sikoryak, Joe, 2000. 'The Film Score Decade', *Film Score Monthly* 5/5 (June), 24–5
    2005. 'The AFI's Top 25', *Film Score Monthly* 10/6 (November–December), 32–3

Silvester, Christopher, 1998. ed. *The Penguin Book of Hollywood*, London: Viking

Silvio, Teri, 2002. 'Chinese Opera, Global Cinema, and the Ontology of the Person: Chen Kaige's *Farewell My Concubine*', in Joe and Theresa 2002, 177–97

Skelton, Geoffrey, 1975. *Paul Hindemith: The Man behind the Music*, London: Victor Gollancz Ltd

Smith, Jeff, 1998. *The Sounds of Commerce: Marketing Popular Film Music*, New York: Columbia University Press
    2001. 'Popular Songs and Comic Allusion in Contemporary Cinema', in Wojcik and Knight 2001, 407–30

Smith, Steven C., 1991. *A Heart at Fire's Center: The Life and Music of Bernard Herrmann*, Berkeley: University of California Press

Sorabji, Kaikhosru, 1947. *Mi Contra Fa: The Immoralisings of a Machiavellian Musician*, London: Porcupine Press

Staig, Laurence and Tony Williams, 1975. *Italian Western: Opera of Violence*, London: Lorrimer

Stanfield, Peter, 2005. *Body and Soul: Jazz and Blues in American Film, 1927–63*, Urbana and Chicago: University of Illinois Press

Steiner, Fred, 1974a. 'Herrmann's "Black-and-White" Music for Hitchcock's *Psycho*', *Film Music Notebook* [part 1] 1/1, 28–36
    1974b. 'Herrmann's "Black-and-White" Music for Hitchcock's *Psycho*', *Film Music Notebook* [part 2], 1/2, 26–46

Steiner, Max, 1935. Interview quoted in 'Music in the Cinema: Hollywood Has Discovered How the Score Improves the Photoplay', *New York Times*, 29 September
    1937. 'Scoring the Film', in Naumburg 1937, 216–38

Sternfeld, Frederick W., 1947. 'Music and the Feature Films', *Musical Quarterly* 33, 517–32

1951. 'Copland as a Film Composer', *Musical Quarterly* 37, 161–75

Steyn, Mark, 1997. *Broadway Babies Say Goodnight: Musicals Then and Now*, London: Faber and Faber

Stilwell, Robynn, 1997a. '"I just put a drone under him . . .": Collage and Subversion in the Score of *Die Hard*', *Music and Letters* 78, 551–80

1997b. 'Symbol, Narrative and the Musics of *Truly Madly Deeply*', *Screen* 38/1 (Spring), 60–75

2002. 'Music in Films: A Critical Review of Literature, 1980–1996', *Journal of Film Music* 1/1, 19–61

Stok, Danusia, 1993. ed. *Kieślowski on Kieślowski*, London: Faber and Faber

Stravinsky, Igor, 1936. *An Autobiography*, New York: Simon and Schuster

Stravinsky, Igor and Robert Craft, 1962. *Expositions and Developments*, London: Faber and Faber

1968. *Dialogues and a Diary*, London: Faber and Faber

Sudendorf, Werner, 2001. 'The Chronicles' and 'Commentary', *Josef von Sternberg's 'The Blue Angel'*, Eureka DVD, EKA 50009

Sutcliffe, Tom, 1996. *Believing in Opera*, London: Faber and Faber

Swynnoe, Jan G., 2002. *The Best Years of British Film Music, 1936–1958*, Woodbridge: The Boydell Press

Tambling, Jeremy, 1987. *Opera, Ideology and Film*, Manchester: Manchester University Press

Taylor, Richard, 1998. ed. and trans. *The Eisenstein Reader*, London: British Film Institute

Taymor, Julie, 2000. *Titus: The Illustrated Screenplay, Adapted from the Play by William Shakespeare*, New York: Newmarket Press

Thomas, Rosie, 1985. 'Indian Cinema: Pleasures and Popularity', *Screen* 26/3–4 (May–August), 116–31; abridged reprint in Hill and Gibson 1998, 541–2

Thomas, Tony, 1973. *Music for the Movies*, South Brunswick and New York: A. S Barnes; London: Tantivy Press

1979. *Film Score: The View from the Podium*, South Brunswick and New York: A. S. Barnes

1991. *Film Score: The Art and Craft of Movie Music* [rev. edn of Thomas 1979], Burbank, CA: Riverwood Press

1997. *Music for the Movies*, 2nd edn, Los Angeles: Silman-James Press

Thompson, David and Ian Christie, 1989. *Scorsese on Scorsese*, London: Faber and Faber

Thompson, Kristin, 1980. 'Early Sound Counterpoint', *Yale French Studies* 60, 115–40

Thompson, Kristin and David Bordwell, 2003. *Film History: An Introduction*, 2nd edn, New York: McGraw-Hill

Toch, Ernst, 1937. Interview quoted in 'The Cinema Wields the Baton', *New York Times*, 11 April

Toop, David, 1995. 'Rock Musicians and Film Soundtracks', in Romney and Wootton 1995, 72–81

Townson, Robert, 1993. 'The Odyssey of Alex North's *2001*', CD liner notes to *Alex North's 2001: The Legendary Original Score*, Varèse Sarabande VSD 5400

Truffaut, François, 1967. *Hitchcock*, New York: Simon and Schuster

Tsivian, Yuri, 1995. 'Dziga Vertov's Frozen Music: Cue Sheets and a Music Scenario for *The Man with the Movie Camera*', *Griffithiana* 54, 92–121

Tucker, Richard N., 1973. *Japan: Film Image*, London: Studio Vista

Vaughan Williams, Ralph, 1987 [1963]. *National Music and Other Essays*, 2nd edn, Oxford: Clarendon Press

Vernon, Kathleen M. and Cliff Eisen, 2006. 'Contemporary Spanish Film Music: Carlos Saura and Pedro Almodóvar', in Mera and Burnand 2006, 41–59

Volkov, Solomon, 1979. *Testimony: The Memoirs of Dmitri Shostakovich*, trans. Antonina W. Bouis, London: Hamish Hamilton

Waletzky, Joshua, 1994. *Music for the Movies: Bernard Herrmann*, television documentary, Columbia/Sony

Walker, John, 1995. ed. *Halliwell's Filmgoer's Companion*, 11th edn, London: Harper Collins

　2006. *Halliwell's Film, DVD and Video Guide 2007*, 21st edn, London: Harper Collins

Walker, Mark, 1998. ed. *Gramophone Film Music Good CD Guide*, 3rd edn, London: Gramophone Publications

Walsh, Christopher, 1996. 'Beauty and Philip Glass', *Film Score Monthly* 65–7 (Winter), 34–5

Walton, Susana, 1988. *William Walton: Behind the Façade*, Oxford: Oxford University Press

Weis, Elisabeth and John Belton, 1985. eds. *Film Sound: Theory and Practice*, New York and Chichester: Columbia University Press

Weissbrod, Ellen, 1990. *Listen Up: The Musical Lives of Quincy Jones*, television documentary, Warner

White, Eric Walter, 1979. *Stravinsky: The Composer and His Works*, 2nd edn, London: Faber and Faber

Whittle, David, 2007. *Bruce Montgomery/Edmund Crispin: A Life in Music and Books*, Aldershot: Ashgate

Whitworth, Reginald, 1954. 'Cinema Organ', in Blom 1954, vol. 2, 303–9

Wierzbicki, James, 2003. 'Grand Illusion: The "Storm Cloud" Music in Hitchcock's *The Man Who Knew Too Much*', in Rosar 2003, 217–38

　2005. *Louis and Bebe Barron's* Forbidden Planet: *A Film Score Guide*, Lanham, MD: Scarecrow Press

Wilkinson, Carl, 2007. *The Observer Book of Film*, London: Observer Books

Willet, John, 1964. ed. *Brecht on Theatre*, New York: Hill and Wang

Winkler, Martin M., 2001. *Classical Myth and Culture in the Cinema*, New York and Oxford: Oxford University Press

Winkler, Max, 1951. 'The Origin of Film Music', *Films in Review* 2/34 (December), repr. in Limbacher 1974, 16–17

Winkler, Peter, 2000. 'Randy Newman's Americana', in Middleton 2000, 27–57

Winter, Marian Hannah, 1941. 'The Function of Music in Sound Film', *Musical Quarterly* 27/2, 146–64

Winters, Ben, 2007. *Erich Wolfgang Korngold's* The Adventures of Robin Hood: *A Film Score Guide*, Lanham, MD: Scarecrow Press

Wojcik, Pamela Robertson and Arthur Knight, 2001. eds. *Soundtrack Available: Essays on Film and Popular Music*, Durham, NC, and London: Duke University Press

Wright, Robb, 2003. 'Score vs. Song: Art, Commerce, and the H Factor in Film and Television Music', in Inglis 2003, 8–21

Wyatt, Robert and John Andrew Johnson, 2004. eds. *The George Gershwin Reader*, New York and Oxford: Oxford University Press

Young, Jeff, 1999. ed. *Kazan on Kazan*, London: Faber and Faber

Zuckerman, John V., 1950. 'A Selected Bibliography on Music for Motion Pictures', *Hollywood Quarterly* 5/2 (Winter), 195–9

Index of film titles

General index

Academy Awards 68, 72, 99, 102, 104, 157,
    171, 190, 240, 378, 397, 405, 407–8,
    414–15, 428, 447, 456, 491
Academy format 190
Academy of Motion Picture Arts and Sciences
    (AMPAS) 67, 72, 99, 212, 408, 414
actualités 18, 43
Adam, Adolphe 37
Adams, Bryan 407
Adams, John 182
    Death of Klinghoffer, The 145
Addinsell, Richard 232, 238, 425–6
    Warsaw Concerto 425–6
Addison, John 94, 209, 247–8, 258
Adorno, Theodor 6, 17, 35, 81–3, 133–4, 195
a-ha 406
Albinoni, Tomaso (attrib.)
    Adagio 428
Alessandroni, Alessandro 371, 376
Alessio, Carlos d' 337
Alexandrov, Grigori 44–5, 343, 344
Alexeyev, Alexander 424
Alford, Kenneth 253
Ali, Naushad 356, 357
Alix, Victor 38
Allen, Woody 13
Alloy Orchestra 39, 267–8
Almereyda, Michael 181
Almodóvar, Pedro 212, 381, 504, 508
Altman, Robert 214, 403–4, 412, 422, 504
Alwyn, Mary: *see* Carwithen, Doreen Mary
Alwyn, William 226, 228, 240, 281–2, 283
    Symphony No. 3 241
Amano, Masamichi 395
Amenábar, Alejandro 489
American Federation of Musicians (AFM) 46,
    201
American International Pictures (AIP) 399,
    409
American Society of Composers, Authors and
    Publishers (ASCAP) 148, 184, 397
Amfitheatrof, Daniele 102, 114, 433
Amicus Films 255
Anderson, Gillian 27, 38, 491
Anderson, Laurie 483
Anderson, Lindsay 258
Andrews, Julie 162
anempathy 36, 270, 316, 320, 324–5, 336, 385,
    423, 434, 436, 439, 480, 485
Angelopoulos, Theo 507
animated sound 58–9, 205, 278, 306

animation 75, 148, 163, 213, 278, 287–308,
    393, 397, 424
Antheil, George 110, 191–2, 288, 344
anthologies, sheet-music 10, 15–18
Antonioni, Michelangelo 329, 365, 409–10
Argento, Dario 375, 382
Arkhangelsky, Alexander 35
Arlen, Harold 155
Armstrong, Louis 213, 406
Arnaud, Leo 74
Arnheim, Rudolf 42, 45
Arnold, David 337, 407
Arnold, Malcolm 161, 226, 250, 251–3, 283
    Machines 283
    Scottish Dances 506
Arnshtam, Lev 342, 343, 449
Arriagada, Jorge 335
Astaire, Fred 152, 157–8, 159, 160, 162, 422
Astradantsev, Dmitri 35
Astruc, Alexandre 319
asynchronous sound 45, 60, 61, 64, 269, 320,
    345–6, 400
atonality 118, 194–201, 224, 269, 298, 330,
    331, 388, 462
Attenborough, Richard 247–8, 263, 360, 505
attractions: *see* cinema of attractions
Auber, Daniel-François-Esprit 132
    Fra Diavolo 132
Aubrey, James T. 156
Auden, W. H. 275–7
audience participation 1, 164, 355, 398
Auric, Georges 63–4, 232–4, 316–18, 376
auteur theory 27, 202–3, 319, 394, 440, 483
Avraamov, Arseni 58
Axt, William 26, 49, 267
Aykroyd, Dan 402
Aznavour, Charles 323, 326

B-movies 70, 73, 114, 126, 227, 455
Bacalov, Luis Enríquez 376, 453, 486
Bach, Johann Sebastian 102, 437, 448–53
    Brandenburg Concerti 424, 451, 452
    Cello Suites 449, 450–1
    Chromatic Fantasia and Fugue 452
    Goldberg Variations 450, 451
    Musical Offering 453
    Passacaglia in G minor 378
    St Matthew Passion 374, 452, 484
    Toccata and Fugue in D minor 102, 292, 449
    Well-Tempered Clavier, The 452
Bacharach, Burt 405